COLLECTIBLES

MARKET GUIDE & PRICE INDEX

To Limited Edition Plates, Figurines, Bells, Graphics, Steins and Dolls

Fifth Edition

Executive Editor: Diane Carnevale
Researchers and Writers: Susan K. Elliott
Susan K. Jones
Tom L. Jones
Sara Kirtlink

Printed in the United States of America.
ISBN: 0-930785-03-7.

CREDITS

Book Cover Design and Photo Styling: Valerie Janes
Book Design and Graphics: Customhouse Publishers Services,
Dubuque, Iowa
Color Section Layout and Photo Styling: Valerie Janes

About the Executive Editor

Diane Carnevale is the principal of Professional Marketing Services, a Grand Rapids, Michigan based firm which specializes in media relations, market research and promotions for companies in the collectibles, gourmet cookware and manufacturing fields.

As an experienced collector herself, Ms. Carnevale takes a special interest in the limited edition collectibles field. Since September, 1986, she has been Executive Director of the COLLECTORS' INFORMATION BUREAU. Prior to this, Ms. Carnevale provided enthusiastic and innovative service to the BUREAU almost since its inception and was the Managing Editor of the two prior editions of this book.

Ms. Carnevale holds a B.A. degree in English and journalism from the University of Michigan and resides in Grand Rapids.

Acknowledgments

The Collectors' Information Bureau would like to thank the following persons whose help and support have been instrumental in the creation of this book: Marcia Andrus, chairman of the New England Chapter of the American Bell Association, David Armstrong of Armstrong's, Pat Campbell of Aperturean Delights, William Drueke, Douglas Eisele of Old World Restoration, Cherie Hilgenberg of Cherie's Gallery Art & Collectibles, Valerie Janes of The Hamilton Collection, Ray and Lorrie Kiefer of the National Association of Limited Edition Dealers, Fred and Kay Knight of the Canadian Association of Limited Edition Dealers, Victor Mader of Mader's Tower Gallery, Mrs. W.A. McGriff III, Thomas A. Mier of Arthur Mier Agency, Inc., Cliff Moehring of The Hamilton Collection, Ellen Pedersen of Mill Pond Press Inc., *Prints* Magazine, Marge Rosenberg of Carol's Gift Shop, Sebastian Studios, Thomas Suarez, Sharon Usher of The Greenwich Workshop, Ron and Judy Warpole of Upland Galleries, Joyce Zielinski of Watson's and Cathy Zimmerman of CPS.

In addition, the Collectors' Information Bureau would like to thank the more than 30 limited edition dealers whose dedicated work has helped make our 52-page Price Index possible. We wish we could thank them by name, but they have agreed that to be singled out in this manner might hinder their continued ability to obtain an unbiased view of the marketplace.

The executive editor also wishes to express heartfelt appreciation to the following persons whose enthusiasm, dedication, hard work and encouragement have made this book possible: Catherine P. Bloom, Krystin Davies, Ronald G. Gregory, Ron Jedlinski, Susan K. Jones, Sam Knight, Joan Ostroff, Heio W. Reich and James P. Smith, Jr.

About the Researchers and Writers

Susan K. Elliott is a freelance writer specializing in collectibles and business subjects. Editor of *Plate Collector* magazine for 11 years, she has traveled extensively to interview artists, collectors, dealers and manufacturers throughout the world. Ms. Elliott is currently co-authoring a book on business training programs to be published by Doubleday, and is editorial director for *Collectors Mart*, a quarterly magazine.

She began her journalism career in high school, working for a small-town weekly newspaper, then writing about antiques for *Collector's Weekly*, a nationally circulated tabloid newspaper. At the age of 20, Ms. Elliott assumed editorship of three national collector publications and has been covering collectibles since then. She also helped develop and then edited *Figurine Collector* magazine, as well as numerous other books and newsletters for collectors of limited editions.

Ms. Elliott lives in San Marcos, Texas.

Susan K. Jones has spent more than fourteen years as a writer, observer, collector, and investment advisor for the limited edition collectibles field. Since 1980 she has been the owner of Susan K. Jones and Associates, a consulting and copywriting firm for direct marketers and limited edition marketers. Before that she spent more than three years as a Marketing Manager for The Hamilton Collection, and over three years as a copywriter for the advertising agency which handled writing and marketing assignments for The Bradford Exchange from 1973–75.

Today Ms. Jones serves a number of clients in the collectibles field and contributes to several collectibles publications. She also is the co-author of two business books published by Charles Scribner's Sons, and an adjunct lecturer at Northwestern University.

In November, 1982, Ms. Jones became the Executive Director of COLLECTORS' INFORMATION BUREAU, and was a formative influence in the development of the organization. Since September, 1986 she has been a Special Consultant to COLLECTORS' INFORMATION BUREAU. Educated at Northwestern University, she holds a master's degree in advertising. She lives in East Grand Rapids, Michigan.

Tom L. Jones is a Washington, D.C., based writer, specializing in the collectible art field. A graduate of the University of Iowa's Fiction Writers Workshop, he has observed and written about the world of limited edition collectibles for over six years.

Sara Kirtlink owns Kirtlink Associates in partnership with her son, Lee. The company provides copywriting services to New England businesses, and the Kirtlinks are presently engaged in the writing of a book on popular music.

Educated at the University of Rhode Island, Ms. Kirtlink spent a number of years in advertising agencies, and most recently was a Sales Promotion Manager and Public Relations Manager for Gorham. As the original Emily Graham, she established the Gorham Doll Collectors' Guild, and wrote and edited the guild newsletter. Today she is a contributing writer to the "Gorham Gazette."

Contents

History/Trends

Reference Section

By Heio W. Reich

President of COLLECTORS' INFORMATION BUREAU
and
President of RECO INTERNATIONAL CORP.

FOREWORD

Dear Collector:

As President of Collectors' Information Bureau, it's my personal pleasure to introduce this brand-new fifth edition of "The Collectors' Bible," COLLECTIBLES MARKET GUIDE & PRICE INDEX.

In this 288-page treasure-trove of news, facts and features you'll find over 30 original articles highlighting some of the most exciting artists, collectibles, trends and travel opportunities in today's world of limited editions.

Our authoritative Price Index now covers a full 52 pages—an expansion of nearly 50% over our last book issue. That means that you'll be able to track thousands more of your favorite plates, bells, figurines, graphics, steins and dolls on the secondary market.

Whether you're new to collecting or an art connoisseur of long standing, I know that this volume will bring you a great deal of reading pleasure. Our "how-to" articles will help you plan your collecting, trade on the secondary market, decorate your home and protect your precious works of art. Our much-praised reference section will keep you up-to-date about books and periodicals, collectors' shows, where to buy limited editions and much more.

What's more, the GUIDE goes behind the scenes to introduce the personalities behind some of your favorite collectibles: providing you with fascinating insights about the artists and studios that enrich your collecting experience.

More than ever before, the limited edition art market is thriving. We, the members believe that the better informed you are, the more you will enjoy your collection. That's why we devote so much time, effort and loving care to the creation of this annual GUIDE and its Price Index.

Find a comfortable chair, put your feet up, and indulge yourself! The members of COLLECTORS' INFORMATION BUREAU sincerely hope that you will be pleased with this fifth volume of our informative book—devoted to enjoyment by you, the collector.

Cordially,

Heio W. Reich

Heio W. Reich
Port Washington, NY
November, 1987

P.S. If you wish to inquire about any of the products or artists you see in the GUIDE, please feel free to write their manufacturers directly. They'll be delighted to hear from you!

CIB Members
A Warm Welcome from the
Collectors' Information Bureau Members

In 1982, the COLLECTORS' INFORMATION BUREAU was formed to increase the public's awareness of the collectibles industry, an industry which has experienced extraordinary growth and collector enthusiasm in recent years. The membership roster reads like a "Who's Who" of the collectibles world, being comprised of many of today's most respected makers and marketers of limited edition collectibles.

The COLLECTORS' INFORMATION BUREAU provides collectors with the most accurate and up-to-date information on limited edition plates, figurines, bells, graphics, steins and dolls. Since its inception, the BUREAU has gained the recognition and respect of collectibles manufacturers, media and dealers, as well as collectors in the United States, Canada and beyond.

CIB members fit into two categories: **Members**, who market limited edition items of their own under one or more trade names, and **Associate Members**, who provide materials, accessories and/or manufacturing facilities for limited edition marketers or collectors.

The fifth edition of this book offers informative and fascinating information on contemporary limited edition plates, figurines, bells, graphics, steins and dolls.

MEMBERS

During its first year of existence (1983–84) the CIB Membership Roster included fourteen member firms and six associate members. Over the past two years the roster of member firms has increased substantially to twenty-six firms, an all-time record membership! Here is our membership roster for 1987:

ANNALEE MOBILITEE DOLLS,
  INC.
Box 708 Reservoir Road
Meredith, NH 03253

ARMSTRONG'S
150 East Third Street
Pomona, CA 91766

ARTAFFECTS, LTD.
P.O. Box 98
Staten Island, NY 10307

THE BALLIOL CORP.
10502 Product Dr.
Rockford, IL 61111

BRAD BENNETT STUDIO
2512 Oakwood Dr.
Olympia Fields, IL 60461

DUNCAN ROYALE
1141 So. Acacia Avenue
Fullerton, CA 92631

ENESCO IMPORTS CORP.
1 Enesco Plaza
Elk Grove Village, IL 60007

FLAMBRO IMPORTS
1260 Collier Rd., N.W.
Atlanta, GA 30381

FOUNTAINHEAD
P.O. Box 1739
Willmar, MN 56201

GARTLAN USA
8855 Atlanta Avenue
Suite 4192
Huntington Beach, CA 92646

GOEBEL/DIVISION OF GOEBEL
  ART, INC.*
105 White Plains Rd.
Tarrytown, NY 10591

THE GORHAM COMPANY*
P.O. Box 6150
Providence, RI 02940

THE HAMILTON COLLECTION*
9550 Regency Square Blvd.
Jacksonville, FL 32232

JOHN HINE, LTD.
265 25th Street Suite 4
West Vancouver B.C. V7V 4H9

KAISER PORCELAIN USA INC.
2045 Niagara Falls Blvd.
Niagara Falls, NY 14304

EDWIN M. KNOWLES CHINA CO.
P.O. Box 296
Newell, WV 26050

LLADRO
P.O. Box 1122
New York, NY 10101–1122

MARURI U.S.A.
15145 Califa St.
Van Nuys, CA 91411

MILL POND PRESS, INC.
310 Center Ct.
Venice, FL 34292

POLLAND STUDIOS
P.O. Box 1146
Prescott, AZ 86302

RECO INTERNATIONAL CORP.*
150 Haven Ave.
Port Washington, NY 11050

ROMAN, INC.*
555 Lawrence Avenue
Roselle, IL 60172–1599

ROYAL WORCESTER SPODE LTD.
Severn St.
Worcester WR1 2NE England

SWAROVSKI AMERICA LTD.
1 Kenney Dr.
Cranston, RI 02920

TENGRA
c/o PVP INDUSTRIES, INC.
5310 Derry Ave. Suites E & F
Agoura Hills, CA 91301

JOSIAH WEDGWOOD & SONS,
  LTD.
Baralston, Stoke-on-Trent
Staffs ST12 9ES England

*Charter Member

ASSOCIATE MEMBERS

The associate members of COLLECTORS' INFORMATION BUREAU provide essential funds and services for this not-for-profit business league. Here is a list of our associate members with background material on each:

COMMERCIAL DECAL COMPANY*
c/o Charles Seliger, Vice President
650 South Columbus Avenue, P.O. Box 230
Mount Vernon, New York 10551
(914) 664–1610

Commercial Decal has been printing decals to decorate fine china, earthenware, glass products and plastics for over seventy-five years. Although the firm began with service to the tabletop industry, in recent times it has extended its expertise to fine art reproduction for collector plates and other collectibles.

As Commercial spokesman Charles Seliger says, "The fine art of Commercial Decal is reproduction." The emphasis is on craftsmanship. To maintain a high level of performance, the firm employs the finest artists and highly skilled technicians, an able and creative research staff, and the latest, specially designed printing equipment.

Commercial Decal strives to obtain accuracy and fidelity to every nuance of an artist's original painting. What's more, the firm works to provide economical, production-ready decals in keeping with the type of plate blank and decoration style which has been selected. All this is done with a careful eye toward deadlines.

They print both lithograph and silk screen decals that can be printed in the individual picked color system or in the Company's four-color process technique, developed and patented by Commercial. The four-color process system is similar to the printing methods used in the production of fine art books. In addition, Commercial provides an open and understanding relationship with artists and producers to make sure the finished product pleases everyone involved.

CUSTOM CHINA CREATIONS*
c/o Robert Perkins, President
13726 Seminole Drive
Chino, California
(714) 627–8531

Ceramics engineer Robert Perkins founded Custom China several years ago after extensive production experience with Franciscan China and Gorham China Company. Because of his ceramics expertise, Perkins has established his firm both as a maker of fine plate bodies and as a decorator of excellent-quality, limited edition collector plates.

With state-of-the-art technology as his goal, Perkins has developed a completely automated "body prep" department which can produce between 2,000 and 3,000 fine china, 8 ½″ plate blanks per day. Custom China's own china formula boasts excellent translucency. The china is named "Royal Ashley" after the family which formulated its unique, soft glaze effect.

For decorating, Custom China uses a special type of "tunnel kiln" which Perkins redesigned to accommodate the large art transfers, or decals, necessary to produce fine limited edition collectibles. At Custom China each plate undergoes a full eight-hour firing cycle to assure the utmost in vibrancy and beauty. Custom China has one of the largest capacities of any decorator in the limited edition field.

Recent awards earned by limited edition plates decorated at Custom China include a "Silver Chalice" award at the California Plate Convention and the "Plate of the Show" award at that same convention.

MATTHEYPRINT CORPORATION*
c/o Norman D. Cote
Box 825
Valley Forge, PA 19481-0825
(215) 783–5122

Mattheyprint Corporation is a printer of quality ceramic decals for the collectible plate industry, and a part of the Johnson Matthey Group of worldwide companies. The firm features both the vibrant colors of screen printing and the fine, tonal gradations of ceramic lithography. Technicians and reproduction artists boast a total of 240 years' experience.

The heritage of Mattheyprint Corporation began with the Allied war effort in World War II, producing bombsight and hypodermic syringe markings. Through an evolutionary process, the firm became one of the world's best-known decal makers in England and on the Continent.

Since its inception, Mattheyprint Corporation has spared no expense to provide the finest in ceramic decals. Top-quality materials and equipment as well as experienced personnel continue the Matthey tradition of quality. Collectible plates decorated with the firm's decals already have been voted many honors, including NALED "Plate of the Year."

As the collectibles field grows, Mattheyprint Corporation is confident of its own continued growth, making every effort toward improving price, delivery and quality.

WOODMERE CHINA COMPANY*
c/o Gene Tway, President
P.O. Box 5305
New Castle, Pennsylvania 16105

Woodmere China of New Castle, Pennsylvania is a custom decorator of porcelain and fine china. The company is a major manufacturer of collector plates and limited edition collectibles. These collectibles have ranged from simple, edge-to-edge designs to elaborate, 24K gold-etch reproductions. Woodmere also produces complete dinnerware and giftware lines for the retail market.

Woodmere China has the capabilities of in-house screen transfer production. The company's craftsmen also specialize in hand-painted decorations. This particular skill has won them many prestigious awards including an Excellence in Design award. Woodmere kilns are computerized for exact readings—thus tests can be run on new designs under laboratory conditions.

Because of its advantageous location in the Western Pennsylvania/Eastern Ohio ceramics region, Woodmere China Company has access to some of the most experienced and innovative craftsmen in America. The firm encourages these craftsmen to experiment and to develop new techniques and cost-saving methods which reap benefits for Woodmere customers. As an additional service, Woodmere can drop-ship limited edition items to individual collectors.

*Charter Member

The Excitement of Collecting
Who Collects and Why

"Exhilarating" is the best way to describe the atmosphere of a big collector convention. Collectors enthusiastically try to discover what new collectibles will soon be available, visit with old friends and meet famous artists—creating a charge of enthusiasm that some describe as addictive.

Collector Kaye Innes coined the term "plataholic" a few years ago to define the condition of an uncontrolled plate collector—an addict who doesn't want to be cured. This disease is best treated in the company of fellow collectors, she advised, but don't expect a cure in the traditional sense. Chances are that once hooked, a plataholic will be addicted for life. Doll collectors, print collectors and figurine collectors are just a few of the other collector groups who report similar "happy" addictions.

The "lure of the chase"—looking for an elusive item that not everyone can have—creates much of the excitement. The concept of limited editions provides the exclusivity that collectors want, whether the object of their desire is an exquisite plate, doll, figurine, bell, graphic, stein, or more likely, a combination of these. As today's collectibles reach ever higher levels of quality, the difficulty becomes not in finding anything worthwhile to collect, but in narrowing the choices to an affordable few.

Many collectors who "can't buy just one," find themselves attracted to a variety of collectibles. Top artists often create limited editions in more than one medium, enticing confirmed plate collectors into figurines, print collectors into plates, and figurine collectors into dolls. Then too, innovative manufacturers contribute to this appealing diversity by constantly exploring new types of production. Technological advances now make it possible for manufacturers to create beautiful collectibles at reasonable prices that remove them from museum-only status and make them affordable to a wider range of collectors.

Collecting experts estimate that plate collectors now number from four to eight million, with millions more collecting figurines, prints, dolls and other limited editions. They keep up with their hobbies by reading more than a dozen specialized periodicals—*Plate World*, *Collectors Mart*, *Precious Moments Collector*, *Collector Editions*, *Prints*, and *Dolls*, to name just a few.

Local shops devoted to contemporary collectibles exist in cities large and small, supplemented by mail-order firms who cater to the market by offering items in a wide range of prices. Collectors who wish to buy or sell collectibles turn to dealers, formal exchanges, advertisements in national and local publications, and periodic swap-and-sells.

Major national conventions around the country bring collectors together with fellow aficionados while introducing them to new products and the talented artists who create them. In 1987, collectibles shows featuring limited editions were held in Pasadena, California, and South Bend, Indiana; the American Bell Association staged its annual convention; and major graphics shows attracted huge crowds across the country.

A Leisure Pastime

Not too long ago, the only publications for collectors catered to the wealthy because the two were synonymous. The past two decades have changed all that, with the middle class acquiring the means and the leisure to enter collecting in all areas. The wealthy still pay record prices for Sheraton sideboards and Van Gogh originals, but with the advent of limited editions, the art world has widened to include an entirely new audience.

Typical collectors of the 1980s enjoy collecting because it fills their leisure time and offers a friendly haven in a fast-paced, increasingly technological world. Collector Q. David Bowers describes collecting as a "summer home of the mind," a retreat that one can visit without leaving home. Those who want to really get away from home may join local and national clubs to share information and enthusiasm with other collectors, in addition to attending shows, open houses, seminars and world-wide tours.

Red Skelton is surrounded by his limited edition plates "Anyone for Tennis?" by Armstrong's, as Freddy the Freeloader takes to the court. "Plataholics' will be particularly happy to receive one of the first 1,000 personally signed plates—Super Star Edition—in the strictly limited edition of 10,000.

Cherie Hilgenberg, owner of Cherie's Gallery Art & Collectibles, shows a David Winter cottage to one of her customers, Vicki Wotring of Chicago. Located in Hanover Park, Illinois, this store specializes in limited edition collectibles.

Some buyers begin collecting for investment, but find unexpected bonuses such as a new circle of friends and increased art knowledge. Avid collectors often plan their vacations to coincide with the annual conventions, or even develop new plans for retirement that will keep them in touch with collecting.

Art as part of one's life is entirely different than taking an art history class in college, learning to distinguish between Ionic and Doric columns. The decorating possibilities of limited edition collecting are endless, and add a personal touch to any buyer's home. A whole new world opens to the individual who learns to appreciate the styles of contemporary artists.

Building a Collection

Most novice collectors plunge in, happily buying whatever appealing and affordable items cross their path. Gradually they begin to gather knowledge to enhance their collecting. Others prefer to learn everything they can before making that first purchase, advancing cautiously and carefully. Whichever type of collector you are, this book will be an invaluable benefit. The modern collectibles to be discussed will be: the contemporary field of limited edition plates, figurines, bells, graphics, steins and dolls.

As specialization becomes necessary in most fields of collecting, so it is in this book. We will define contemporary collectibles to be those of the past thirty years—from the 1960s, 1970s and 1980s. The oldest items featured in these pages are the 1890 Villeroy & Boch "Snow White" plate, the earliest known dated collector plate, and 1895 Bing & Grondahl "Behind the Frozen Window," first in the world's longest running Christmas plate series. They link contemporary collectibles to the centuries-old tradition of collecting.

By U.S. Customs definition, the term "antique" applies to any item more than a hundred years old, although variations exist in certain areas such as furniture, where experts looks for pieces more than 150 years old. In cars, a "classic" is any vehicle more than twenty-five years old.

In general, items of beauty, significance, value or interest that are "too young" to be considered antiques acquire collectible status, but may not be limited editions, or even of recent production. Popular items in this category include Carnival and Depression glass, Art Deco and Art Nouveau items, advertising memorabilia, etc.

This is the fifth volume in a continuing series which provides new, in-depth information about limited edition collecting, as well as news about more different products, artists and companies with each updated volume. Whatever your experience in collecting, we hope that this guide will add to your storehouse of knowledge. We leave the fun of expanding your collection to you . . .

Susan K. Elliott

How to Decorate
Making the Most of Your Beautiful Collection

Imagine a comfortable, well-coordinated living room with basic furniture and lighting—but no art. If you are a collector, chances are that the room would seem devoid of personality and life to you. Once one discovers the potential of collectibles for decorating, it is difficult to imagine living without them. The temptation to add your own personality to a room becomes irresistible.

A few tips, then, to get you started if you are a novice collector, or new ideas for the more experienced to give your arrangements a fresh look.

Declare Your Colors

There are few areas in a home that cannot be brightened with well-planned displays of collectibles. Keep in mind that groupings that create focal points in a room will be more attractive than mass displays. Think in terms of making an artistic statement of your own when arranging items.

Illinois collector Josephine Macri demonstrates this principle in her family room with a collection of De-Grazia's Indian *Children* plates hung around an attractive three-foot copper tray. The shape and color of the tray complements the plates for an eye-catching display, and also reminds the viewer that the late artist was the son of a copper miner in Arizona.

Florida dealer Lois Felder of The Village Plate Collector says, "There is no reason to have collectibles hidden away under beds and in vaults. They are meant to be enjoyed. China closets are a very traditional approach to display, but you can easily expand beyond that."

Framing Assets

Walls are a logical display area for plates and graphics, and may also be utilized for steins, figurines, bells and dolls when shelves are used. Framing graphics is a learning experience because the first few you order may be difficult to visualize before they are completed. Rely on a professional framer as you develop an eye for what pleases you. If you opt to use something more elaborate for your plates than wire hangers, a plate dealer or framer can guide you to what's available.

Whether you select custom or ready-made frames, framing can add greatly to a plate's beauty and establish it as a fine work of art in your home. Available in a wide range of prices, modern frames offer many innovative design options. Collectors may choose from round wooden or wood-finish styles with open fronts, or square, glass-front shadow boxes with velvet backgrounds in colors that bring out the beauty of the plate. New collage and modular frames offer exciting possibilities.

Look at the special presentation boxes that producers like Royal Doulton and Pickard issue with their plates for additional display ideas. The colors that their designers select to go behind each plate may be ones you would not have considered.

Plate racks and rails also offer interesting design possibilities, as do multi-plate frames that hold two or more plates. Plate rails can be hung around the room near the ceiling, or in short, double rows above a chest to create a hutch effect. The round sameness of plates can be broken up by using a few of these display devices, or by varying the shapes in which sets are hung. Keep in mind that by planning ahead, incomplete series may be hung with room to accommodate the plates yet to come and still be enjoyed as the collection grows year by year.

Some items are safer (and cleaner) in cases or under glass, so if this is your preference, consider coffee tables with special compartments for display, lighted curio cabinets, or glass domes with wood bases for special pieces.

Custom framing enhances Daniel Craig's "Cats on the Mantle" and "In the Pantry" plate set from Fountainhead. A rough weave linen fabric complements the colors of the plates and could be selected to co-ordinate with a room's decor as well. Note the dainty etched flowers in the glass. (Framing courtesy Upland Wings Gallery, Upland, California.)

Plates from the Living with Nature: Jerner's Ducks *series have been grouped with porcelain, copper and wood accessories displayed on the plate rail and the country sideboard to form a harmonious arrangement. Accessories can fill in spaces of plates yet to come while a series is incomplete. (Plate rail courtesy Van Hygan & Smythe.)*

One California collector shows off an unusual antique wood carpenter's tool chest and her collectibles at the same time. The oak chest has been lined with green felt and is tucked into a corner of her hall with the lid open to show a Ferrandiz *Music Maker* plate and matching woodcarvings. The shallow drawers below are pulled out like stairsteps with a few small tools in each to show the chest's original purpose.

Texas collector Chelsea Cordner uses a three-inch deep round basket to form a distinctive frame for her "Oliver's Birthday" plate, a country touch that could be adapted for a variety of series. The plate is nearly identical in size to the basket and is wedged securely into its bottom. With a little ingenuity (and careful anchoring), small baskets could be used as modified shadow box frames for figurines.

Shake, Rattle and Roll Proofing

Dealers and interior designers each have their favorite methods for securing fragile pieces that might be destroyed by a bump or tremor. Try using florist's clay, candle wax (available in card shops), or rolled up electrical tape to keep items in place.

Group different types of collectibles together when possible for the greatest variety and appeal. Using a print as an anchor, plates may be hung on either side to balance it, or asymmetrically to one side. Special frames are available to hold plates with matching figurines or bells, or you can mix the three

Framed plates from the Rockwell's Light Campaign *series blend with the country theme of this family room display. A pine bench holds a crock of potted daisies and antique quilt and pillows. The plates hang next to a treasured framed sampler and print. (Plate frame courtesy Van Hygan & Smythe.)*

Intricate wood molding and a tatted lace lining frame Daniel Craig's "Cats on the Mantle" print from Windemere Studios. A lace liner would be appropriate for many prints with romantic or nostalgic themes. (Framing courtesy Upland Wings Gallery, Upland, California.)

Special plates can be given star treatment when they are presented in unusual frame shapes such as the ones chosen for these Mario Fernandez Four Seasons *plates from Fountainhead. The frames can be hung as shown with the artist's remarque in the center or regrouped with the angled edges to the outside to form another interesting arrangement. (Framing courtesy Upland Wings Gallery, Upland, California)*

types of items in a shelf unit or bookcase. Keep the scale of each piece in mind when you mix collectibles, and experiment with what you own, or as you acquire new pieces, to achieve the most pleasing result. Another interesting decorative touch might be a doll placed on a chest in a foyer with complementary plates on the wall above.

Felder suggests hanging plates in the dead space above a doorway, a real space bonus above a double doorway.

Three Easy Steps

Decorators emphasize the importance of *space, color* and *lighting* in planning displays. *Space* becomes most noticeable when it's missing. Avoid grouping too many items of one type together as it becomes difficult to appreciate individual pieces. A cabinet full of Hummels is impressive, but be sure to pull individual pieces out from time to time to enjoy their individual charm. Consider selecting a single piece to place on an end table with greenery or flowers once a month, or even more often.

Collectors who understand the best use of space will also be aware of the space around groupings (called "negative space" by artists). Before you hang a new grouping on the wall, place the items on the floor, experimenting with adding and subtracting space between pieces. Put butcher paper underneath the objects to mark placement, and then tape to the wall to show where to nail in picture hangers.

Three small plates hung above a couch with two feet between each one will have less appeal than the same three plates grouped in a triangle in a smaller space. In this case, scale is all important.

Color, the second of these components, can be used to unify or separate a collection. Select a color that coordinates with your collection (pale blue for Danish blue-and-white plates), or offsets it, such as a teak wood cabinet for a grouping of cream-colored steins. Cherry yellow walls in a nursery would be a good backdrop for John McClelland's colorful *Children's Circus* series of plates, while lavender walls would enhance the Villeroy & Boch *Flower Fairy* figurines and plates. If you want to find a color that will be a suitable backdrop for the widest number of items, try off-white or pale blue.

Lighting is an element often overlooked by collectors, but can create dramatic effects when used properly. Track lighting or hidden spotlights aimed at important prints or groupings will emphasize their beauty. Try out the effect in advance by aiming a flashlight at the grouping from the angle that the light will hit. Diffused or indirect light is adequate in most cases, but be careful to avoid direct sunlight as it can damage many pieces. If you want to install dis-

In a seminar on decorating, Lois Felder of The Village Plate Collector shows a velvet backing for a frame designed to hold a quartet of mini plates.

A single plate can be the perfect accent in a bathroom. A framed DeGrazia's "Flower Boy" is shown here above a box full of silk flowers.

A bookcase can be enhanced by adding collectibles along side your favorite books. This bookcase grouping combines a variety of collectibles for everyday enjoyment: a Masseria "Panchito" plate, Cybis "Betty Blue" sculpture, scratchboard painting by Sally Miller, Bialoski Bear figurine and an artist's model for a bisque Dutch girl figurine.

plays in or near windows, you might want to follow the example of museums that use Plexiglass panels on their windows to screen out ultraviolet rays.

Recessed lighting will illuminate dark cabinets, but experts recommend keeping collectibles away from the lights to avoid possible heat damage.

Crystal is one collectible that must be properly lighted for best effect. A representative of Swarovski America Limited, full lead crystal producer, recommends using halogen lamps and spotlights to bring out the sparkle rather than neon or florescent tubes that dull its beauty. And of course, crystal must be kept spotlessly clean to reflect light. Lighted paperweight stands or small mirrors also effectively display small crystal pieces.

Decorator Describes Elements of Design

Interior designer Edna O'Brien, ASID, presented a variety of tips to collectors at a recent collectibles convention. She began by emphasizing four elements of design: *harmony, scale, rhythm* and *balance*.

For locations, she suggested placing plates in a kitchen on the wall above a stovetop, or on the soffit that goes around many kitchens. When choosing plates to hang near the ceiling, O'Brien recommended using plates with strong designs rather than those with lots of detail. The same would apply to those that one might use in a high plate rail.

"Don't always arrange plates in a circle," she said. "Stagger them or place with a figurine and plant. Fill in with other accessories such as silk flowers or a family baby cup in a plate rail when you are waiting for a series to be completed.

"Families with seldom-used powder rooms should consider putting plates on stands on the vanity top as well as hanging plates in the bathroom. If you have a fireplace mantel, accent its architectural importance by placing collectibles on it. Another possibility is to use a sofa table behind a couch for a grouping."

When hanging plates in a large series that is still in progress, O'Brien illustrated a pyramid pattern with three plates on the base and two above that can be easily enlarged as new plates arrive.

Taking a fresh approach to seasonal groupings, O'Brien suggested arranging a Mother's Day plate with a photo of your own mother and a bouquet of her favorite flowers. Put Roman candles and sparklers beside a Don Spaulding "Fourth of July" plate or a porcelain bunny beside an Easter plate.

Collectors of movie theme plates could hang them near an upright piano, or around a framed violin. Bird lovers could be assured of always seeing their favorite warblers by hanging bird plates above a bay window looking out to a bird bath in a garden setting.

A framed "Bell of Hope" plate reflects in this bathroom mirror. Plates make ideal decorations in bathrooms because they are not adversely affected by the humid atmosphere as other types of art may be.

Four different subjects by artist P. Buckley Moss form an eye-catching grouping in a collector's dining room. Additional plates can be hung at the top as the series expands. The smaller size of the plate is enlarged by the use of a glass-fronted frame to balance the grouping.

For dinner parties, weddings, or seasonal displays, Hummel figurines may be added to arrangements of fresh flowers. This grouping was one recently entered in a decorating contest sponsored by the Goebel Collectors' Club.

"Use frames in different shapes and materials for the most variety," O'Brien said. "Get different backings for your frames such as velvet and satin to change their appearance. Acrylic plate stands are also inexpensive and sturdy for use on table tops. Create variety by mixing collectibles with plants and your favorite treasures."

Children Benefit Too

O'Brien described a benefit of collecting that might not be readily apparent. She believes that a home decorated with collectibles can be an asset in educating children. "Teach children culture subtly by surrounding them with plates," she suggested. "Children don't have to be collectors themselves to learn to appreciate what they see around them. It's not necessary to preach to them about it. You can be a little bit sneaky. The chances are that when these children grow up they will have a much greater appreciation for art because of this early exposure."

Bev Lawson of Xenium, a manufacturer of display accessories, says, "Find a good dealer and keep going back for ideas on display to make your collection part of your everyday life. You'll get more enjoyment out of collecting that way."

Susan K. Elliott

Gorham presents "Merrie," the fourth in a series of limited edition dolls, beside her own Christmas tree and fireplace to create a stunning holiday scene.

Make your Thanksgiving table special with a dried flower arrangement and pair of Pilgrim dolls from Annalee Dolls.

Bring out your seasonal dolls for special holiday displays such as this Christmas mantle grouping of Annalee Dolls. Elves on the candles add a whimsical touch.

Purchase or construct the manager of your choice, and arrange Lladro figurines to create a memorable creche scene.

An oak cabinet with compartments provides a perfect display home for a collection of Goebel Hummel figurines. Four Hummel plaques hang nearby on the inside of the open door.

Create an Easter centerpiece using Precious Moments figure "I Believe in the Old Rugged Cross" (103632). Using pinks and peach, the figurine is framed with a dried grapevine arbor decorated with flowers and delicate ribbon roses and picot edged ribbons to create an aura of rebirth.

Collector Tom Suarez chose to display his Lowell Davis farm set in an antique wagon which he covered with glass and converted into a striking coffee table.

Collecting Tips
How to Develop a Great Collection

Whether you are an experienced collector of many years or a relative newcomer to collectibles, guidance from the experts can smooth your path. Perhaps you are the type of collector who is as organized and methodical as any business investor—you keep track of everything you buy and where. Or maybe your style is more relaxed—you don't worry about details. Whatever your approach, understanding the possibilities available in today's market can expand your enjoyment of collecting.

Be an Expert in Five Easy Steps

Today's collector may learn more about the field through a variety of means, tailoring the approach to their personality and interests. Experts suggest five main avenues of education, each with its elements of fun.

Reading Is (Fun)damental

Collector magazines and newspapers cover all aspects of today's market, serving the needs of specialist and generalist collectors alike. Collectors who are interested in more than one type of limited editions (or still exploring) should turn to publications like *Collectors Mart* and *Collector Editions*. If you have already narrowed your interests to a single area, magazines such as *Dolls, Precious Moments Collector, Prints*, and *Plate World* will keep you current on the latest products and news. These magazines' features on artists, manufacturers, clubs, collectors and new issues help those at all levels to understand and appreciate the collectibles available.

Collector publications also review new books for collectors, ranging from price guides to deluxe coffee table volumes featuring individual collectibles. Some are one-time releases while others, such as this *Collectibles Market Guide and Price Index*, are updated regularly. (See "Reading/Conventions/Clubs/Special Events" in the back of this book for addresses of publications and titles of valuable references.) National book store chains carry some of these magazines and books, but others are sold exclusively by collectibles dealers or through the mail.

Get Out in the World

Magazines and books keep collectors happy at home, but those who can travel to one of the national conventions have a chance to learn and enjoy in a supercharged atmosphere. Meeting and talking to your favorite artists, presidents of major companies and other avid collectors create memories that last long after the convention. Producers go to great effort and expense to entertain and inform those who attend the annual shows in Pasadena, California (spring), and South Bend, Indiana (July). Special events often include decorating contests, larger-than-life-size costumed characters who pose with collectors for pictures, facsimile factory tours and demonstrations by painters and carvers from all over the world. Seminars on topics such as how artists create, decorating and manufacturing techniques give collectors a chance to learn and ask questions.

For collectors who cannot travel to the major shows, open houses around the country at retail shops feature individual artists or new collections. Check with your dealer or read national publications for schedules.

Birds of a Feather

Many areas of the country have local clubs where collectors gather at monthly meetings, learning from fellow collectors and programs of various types. Swap and sell events at some clubs allow members to sell and buy back issues. Collector magazines run listings of these groups with their locations and meeting times.

National producer-sponsored clubs cater to those who are interested in the works of one artist or company, such as Lladro, Precious Moments, David Winter Cottages, the Goebel Collectors' Club, or artist Edna

Fascinating and informative events are scheduled at collector conventions. Collectors attending the 1987 International Plate & Collectibles Convention in South Bend, Indiana saw the Goebel Facsimile Factory where they observed West German craftsmanship in action, as artists demonstrated the hand-detailed and painstaking process involved in transforming clay into a beautiful and cherished fine ceramic M. I. Hummel figurine.

The Hamilton Collection and The Bradford Exchange are examples of direct mail companies. The above are examples of the finely crafted collectibles offered by such firms. "Ashley" (top) is the first issue in the Treasured Days *series by artist Higgins Bond, available through The Hamilton Collection. The "Shadow Artist" (bottom) is the eleventh issue in the* Rockwell Heritage *series by The Edwin M. Knowles China Co. for the Rockwell Society of America.*

Hibel. Their newsletters often offer information not available elsewhere and notify collectors of special offers and tours for members only. See "Reading/ Conventions/Clubs/Special Events" for listings.

That's Not Junk Mail

Both dealers and direct mail producers take great pains to create informative literature for new product introductions. Companies such as The Hamilton Collection go into comprehensive detail in explaining the history that inspires their collections, whether it be an artist's technique or the significance of cloisonne art. These firms recognize that today's collector is quite knowledgeable and therefore put extra effort into research. Some collectors develop filing systems to keep track of this literature, preserving collectible history and a record of their purchases at the same time.

Order one or two items from a direct mail producer or catalog company and you will be on their lists to receive future materials. They offer a wealth of information.

Many dealers issue their own newsletters to announce seasonal events or open houses, and enclose literature from manufacturers that shows new issues in color.

Getting Started

One question that collectors frequently face when they first realize that they are becoming collectors is whether to specialize. For some collectors, this answer comes naturally, as they find themselves drawn exclusively to a single item. Generally, specializing is a question of finances as much as individual taste. By specializing, you may become more knowledgeable about an artist's style or how an item such as Hummel figurines or lithographs are made. If you decide to create a collection centered around a particular theme, such as clowns, you express your own personality and can satisfy the urge to buy items in many different media—dolls, prints, plates, etc.

Bob Gartlan of Gartlan USA emphasizes this concept, advising collectors to "go with appeal" when buying and "don't be afraid to try new categories."

David Armstrong of Armstrong's, a producer and retailer with nearly three decades of experience in collectibles, gives further advice on limiting a collection. "There is so much to choose from, literally thousands of designs, so that it has become impossible to purchase everything that comes out. No one has the wall space nor is it affordable to collect every single plate being produced today.

"My advice is to collect the types of subjects that one enjoys living with. Today, some of the finest artists in the world have designed art for the permanence of porcelain. Rather than buying from an investment standpoint, purchase from an aesthetic standpoint.

"In the long run, a collector will be much happier with their collection if they collect art that is meaningful to them and their families. But above all, be your own critic.

"Look for quality of art, quality of product, quality of promotion and quality of communication between you and the collectibles you enjoy," Armstrong said.

Dealer Marge Rosenberg of Carol's Gift Shop has started many collectors in the field. She suggests, "If you're a brand new collector, look into lithographs and porcelains like David Winter cottages. Find out who the artists are in the field. Buy only what you want to put into your home. Don't buy what people say will go up because that's hard to rely on.

"If you've been collecting plates for a while, add lithographs. Look at different areas. Let your heart dictate. If you have unframed plates, look at frames and the new approaches for display that are available today. Look into the world of miniatures. Or if

Dealer Marge Rosenberg advises collectors to add lithographs to their collections, checking on the artists in the field and selecting items that they truly like. "Ramrock—Cougar" by famed artist Ron Parker exemplifies the thought and detail which goes into creating this wildlife print, available through Mill Pond Press.

you've been collecting David Winter cottages for a while, look into the new miniature people that are being made by sculptor Gary Stone to complement them."

Collector Bob Myers of the International Plate Collectors Guild in California, the country's oldest plate collector club, says: "Education is the most important asset a collector can have. Learn all you can about the producers of what you buy, the artists who design them, and the production techniques involved. Plate collecting is a wonderful hobby that becomes even more enjoyable when you appreciate all the elements involved."

Your Buying Connection

No matter where a prospective collector lives, there are many possibilities for finding limited editions to buy. Giftware and limited edition dealers, direct mail or magazine ads, swap and sell events, auctions, antique shops—even garage sales may be fertile fields for the collector. In addition, producers and marketers will also add you to their lists to receive new product offerings if you ask to be on their mailing list. Conventions and collector clubs sponsor regular swap and sell events around the country. Local ads will alert you to estate sales and auctions that may include contemporary collectibles as well as older items. Check flea markets and garage sales as well. Early blue and white collector plates might be

mixed in with a stack of unmatched "dishes", yielding a valuable Bing & Grondahl or Royal Copenhagen plate for the knowledgeable collector.

Retail Shops

Some dealers handle only limited editions, while others present them as part of a wider selection of giftware or other items. Whatever the assortment, you will want a dealer whose staff is knowledgeable and friendly, with a full range of collectibles and a reasonable customer service policy.

The National Association of Limited Edition Dealers (NALED) and the Canadian Association of Limited Edition Dealers (CALED) are national groups of retail and wholesale merchants who are in the specialized market of selling, promoting and exchanging limited edition collectibles. If you are having difficulty locating a dealer in your area, either association would be happy to personally refer you to a nearby retail establishment. The National Headquarters for NALED is located at 26 S. LaGrange Road, LaGrange, Illinois 60525 (Phone: 1 800 HINALED and in Illionis (312) 482-3650). The National Headquarters for CALED is located at 14 Gibbons Street, Oshawa, Ontario, Canada L1J 4X7 (Phone: (416) 436-1595).

Bob Gartlan recommends that new collectors "identify an established retail dealer as the best form of information since they're up-to-date on the widest range of collectibles."

Being able to see an item before purchasing as well as discussing its merits with a knowledgeable dealer are two reasons cited by collectors for developing a relationship with a local retailer. Retailers can fill you in on the background of a collectible when you are just getting started, or let you know about special issues soon to be released.

Don't be afraid to ask questions of your dealer. He or she can explain many facets of the hobby and even provide decorating ideas and advice on care of the items you buy.

So-called "bedroom dealers" (who deal from their homes) may not offer all the services of an open shop, such as notification and guarantee of subsequent items in a series. Discounters also may not offer all the service a collector requires.

Mail Order Firms

If there is no limited edition shop in your area, don't despair. Many firms offer mail-order service to accommodate those who want the largest possible selection and greatest ease in ordering.

In addition to the convenience of buying collectibles by mail, there are several other benefits which seasoned mail order buyers recount. Many collectors believe that the opportunity to sit back and consider an item without pressure — and to learn more about a given item and its history by means of well-written sales literature — is a pleasant way to make a buying decision.

What's more, in buying by mail, the collector who wishes to purchase an entire series of plates, figurines or other limited editions will have each item delivered to his or her door — there is no need to make further efforts to visit a shop and secure later series issues.

Even if they do not complete purchases of certain collectibles by mail, some collectors say they make their buying decisions in this way. Sales literature featuring an interview with an award-winning artist, a step-by-step explanation of how an item is crafted, or a historical perspective of a particular item or the studio that made it may encourage such people to visit a local dealer and see the item for themselves, then buy it face-to-face.

Our experts emphasize the importance of checking the reputation of a mail order firm — perhaps by asking other collectors about their experiences or by ordering a small item to see how your order is handled. A fair returns policy is most often mentioned in evaluating a direct mail company.

Advertising

Two main types of ads offer collectibles for sale. The first is called a display ad, placed by a retailer to announce a new product. The second, a classified word ad, is placed by an individual or dealer to list a group of items, old or new. Many secondary market items are sold this way. You can also place your own Wanted to Buy ad for items that are difficult to find through other sources.

Combining Your Resources

Since it is unlikely that any one source will carry every item you might want to collect, most collectors tap a combination of local dealers and direct-mail sellers to build their collection. Part of the fun of collecting is the search, so keep your eyes open for unusual and out-of-the-way suppliers.

Will You Collect or Speculate?

Despite all the excitement that secondary market appreciation of collectibles creates, a constant refrain for the past few years has been "don't buy for investment alone."

David Armstrong puts it this way, "Don't let someone talk you into buying purely for investment. If an item doesn't go up, the disenchantment with collector plates is magnified because the collector didn't listen to his inner desires."

At the same time, every collector wants to know that he or she has bought wisely. Using a buyer's checklist can provide that assurance for a new collector, or a spot check for more experienced buyers. It will soon become second nature to assess any item you are considering purchasing in this way.

Expert Advice

We asked our panel of experts to explain the collector's market of today to an observer, and to tell collectors how they should approach it. Here are their observations:

Ed Purcell, Maruri   "The last few years have seen a developing strength in figurines, although there is not necessarily a single dominant category of figurines. The public will determine the subjects that will have longevity. I have to emphasize, however, that this strength in figurines does not indicate a weakness in other collecting categories.

"Figurines are described as a new trend but this is somewhat misleading. It would be more accurate to say that they have gained strength in the last few years. People ask about trends, but they usually tend to mean 'what's hot?' and I don't see figurines as hot, but stable.

"If people watch they can see for themselves the new areas developing strength that will be tomorrow's trends."

Phyllis Lerner, Goebel Collectors' Club   "People who have been collecting for a while are looking for very limited items. Those who have large collections are looking for very special items. Price is important to new collectors. Younger and newer collectors are also emphasizing decorating in their purchases, looking for groupings of items that go together."

Brigitte Moore, Reco International Corp.   "Children are still very, very strong. We are trying to introduce other subjects such as animals and Bible series. One trend is that we see collectors looking at the art and trying to decide if it's good. That shows growth and I'm pleased to see it."

Lance Klass, Pemberton & Oakes   "People are realizing that the stock market is overvalued and they're putting their money into fine art, gold,

Sandra Kuck's nostalgic child-subject collector plates are among the most sought after works in today's limited edition market. "Night-Time Story," first issue in The Barefoot Children *series, captures the joy of childhood where little toes can wiggle and bare feet can escape the confinement of shoes.*

paintings, and collector plates—tangibles. Sotheby's (auction house) is having a great year. The antiques market is going sky high. Collectors are more conservative and smarter than ever before. They look at the track record and want to buy good quality."

Bill Hagara, B&J Art Designs and Royal Orleans   "Current trends are for smaller collector plates and people are also into dolls. The doll business is very good so we're trying to put out a variety of designs. Figurines are traditional and popular favorites, and ornaments are becoming very popular. Buying what you like is the most important advice a collector can follow. I know people buy for reasons of general popularity or investment and that's okay if you have something that is good quality."

Dale Lindquist, Fountainhead   "Collectibles are on the verge of taking a giant step ahead in terms of quality and bringing fine art to the collector. There has been a vast improvement in products brought to the market. Collectors should look for quality products, the best art, the most beautiful. Try to collect quality and not quantity. Don't collect for investment. That's the last reason to use. The chances of true value increasing are much greater if your selections are based on quality."

Dealer Lois Felder of the Village Plate Collector "In our shop we have pushed the concept for years, but are now seeing more people buying shadow boxes and creating decorative displays with their collectibles. People are not buying so much to fund their children's college education, but placing more emphasis on enjoyment of collectibles in their homes."

Paul Steffensen, Bing & Grondahl and Royal Copenhagen "Obviously, with our background, we're very traditional. I think sincerely that blue plates will endure the ups and downs of the market because there are fewer of them in the market than other types of plates, fewer producers making them, and they have a long uninterrupted history. The trend is positive. I think we proved that with the introduction of the 'Christmas at Williamsburg' plate in 1986."

Brad Bennett, Brad Bennett Graphics "Collectors should purchase only the things they enjoy and not buy with the intent to sell for profitable gain. People today are looking for graphics which have a timeless quality, both in their production and subject matter. That is the reason I have produced *The United States of America* Collection. As Gutzon Borglum who sculpted Mount Rushmore once said, 'Art in America should be drawn from American sources, memorializing American achievement.' "

Richard J. Habeeb, Artaffects, Ltd. "We at Artaffects (Vague Shadows and Curator Collection) have a great deal of respect for the collectors of today and this respect informs our decisions whether it be concerning selection of artists for presentation or the particular subject matter portrayed.

"Besides demanding quality artwork, we find that today's most savvy collectors acquire pieces because they are responding positively to the artwork, they must like what they collect, rather than acquire things solely for the purpose of investment. Today's smart collectors are adding to their collections and proudly displaying their treasures, not hiding them under beds waiting for quick price appreciation.

"This attitude is a most healthy one, and we urge new collectors to be guided by it. If some of the things collected do go up in price, that's the icing on the cake. Our 'Sitting Bull' plate has shown enormous appreciation, currently trading at many times its issue price of $65.00, but not many are willing to part with it even when offered ten times what they've paid. We also find that collectibles are becoming giftables. More and more people are spreading the word and making gifts to friends and relatives of porcelain collector plates and figurines. This is a trend we expect to continue and it goes hand in hand with the trend to collect for fun first and profit second. People like to share with others those things that they value—high quality collectibles offer an opportunity for memorable gifting."

Jack Innes, G.W.S. Galleries "Developing a relationship with a gallery or a specific person within that gallery can be the most important factor in building your collection. Having someone out there with a day-to-day awareness of the art business, someone who can inform the collector about the availability of works he may be searching for, is very important. Never collect sheerly for investment. If it doesn't speak to you in some way, don't purchase it."

John Conley, Enesco "The scarcity of artisans overseas affects all of us. It takes so long to train someone to do the handwork required for figurine production. It may be three years before a painter becomes skilled enough to do eyes on a Precious Moments piece. Despite the scarcity and increased pricing that we are receiving from overseas, the demand for high quality collectibles has never been greater. Additionally, we foresee an increased shortage in 1988 and continued price escalation. You wouldn't think all this would affect us in this country, but it's one-worldism."

As Conley points out, collecting does not exist in a vacuum. Competition for mastery of the porcelain making process as well as for trained artisans has always been fierce. In the 1970s, the fluctuating value of the dollar forced several European producers to curtail production until they could find less expensive manufacturing sources. Producers adapted then by opening more American factories, bringing new vitality into the market. Problems always beget solutions, often leading in innovative, unexpected directions.

Discerning collectors should appreciate the wide world of talent that goes into today's collectibles, enhancing their future value.

What Is the Secondary Market . . . and Where Do You Find It?
Market Stimulation

Buy a new couch and it becomes used as soon as you take possession. Buy a collector plate, graphic or other collectible, and chances are that it will hold its value or increase in the years ahead. With careful buying you can sell a few pieces from your collection if you need cash, or trade as your interests change. New collectors who find themselves intrigued by beautiful issues of the past can locate them in the secondary market.

Whenever dealers sell all of an edition to collectors, the item is said to enter the secondary market (as opposed to the first dealer sale on the primary market). From that point on, the only way to obtain the item will be to buy it from a collector, or later from a dealer who has bought it back from a collector to meet customer demand.

Various resale structures exist for different collectibles. Plates can be sold through several mechanisms, and graphics also have established resale methods. Figurines are developing a stronger base in the secondary, while dolls, bells and contemporary, limited edition steins have less formal sales systems. The existence of services like COLLECTORS' INFORMATION BUREAU and others new to the market are helping to establish more consistent values for all collectibles, simplifying the process of selling or buying back issues.

Having access to listings of back issues and their values ensures that collectors who want to participate in secondary market sales can speak knowledgeably to potential buyers or sellers. During the plate collecting boom of the 1970s, plate exchanges and price guides created a framework for the secondary market. Price guides for figurines such as Hummel, Royal Doulton and Boehm have also been available during the last decade. The other collecting areas were somewhat overshadowed by the frenzied activity of plate collecting, but appear to be solidifying.

As Louise Patterson of *The Greenbook*, a guide to Precious Moments values, says, "Collectors like to know they've made a wise decision in buying. Not everyone is into selling, but the secondary market does make it fun. We find that some areas of the country are very active while others are unaware of secondary market values."

By understanding the workings of the secondary market, you can participate more successfully and enhance the value of your own collection. To aid you, we will discuss three main areas: the importance of the secondary market, how a collector may use it to buy and sell, and recent secondary market trends.

Market Stimulation

Experts agree that the secondary market is vital for several reasons: to allow experienced collectors to upgrade their collections, to stimulate the market and encourage new collectors, and to permit increases of value for scarce, beautiful and popular collectibles.

Capital Gains

After a few years of collecting, most individuals find that they have at least one or two purchases that do not appeal to them as much as they once did. Either the collector has developed a specialty that is quite different from their early purchases, or their tastes in art have changed. In these cases, collectors often consider selling on the secondary to free up their capital for newer, more enticing collectibles. In this way, a collection can be recycled periodically without any major loss of capital. New collectors also tend to buy less expensive items, so a

Collectors' Information Bureau

PRICE INDEX

To Limited-Edition Plates, Figurines, Bells, Graphics, Steins and Dolls

1988

The Collectors' Information Bureau Price Index is an excellent example of a source for secondary values. The Index also provides valuable reference material regarding who manufactured a specific item, the series name, when the item was produced, the artist, the edition limit and issue price.

more experienced collector can sell a number of early purchases to finance a few high quality items that he or she might have passed by early in their collecting days as too expensive. Dealers around the country report that upgrading is one of the major reasons collectors give for wanting to resell items.

Re-Circulating Classics

Any collector who becomes a student of collectibles history is bound to find a series or two from the past that they would like to own. Theme collectors can discover a bounty of high quality early issues to enrich their collection. For example, a collector of cats might decide to track down early Danish blue-and-white plates such as the 1963 Bing & Grondahl "Christmas Elf" (with a cat at his side) or the 1970 Royal Copenhagen "Christmas Rose and Cat," injecting the thrill of the chase into their collecting. Prints would offer several possibilities, including Irene Spencer's "Christmas Mourning," Lowell Davis's "Surprise in the Cellar," or Richard Zolan's "Christi's Kitty." Numerous figurines, bells, dolls and steins could also round out a theme collection.

This aspect of collecting is important because non-collectors are often introduced to limited editions through a subject that already appeals to them. This introduction might come at an auction, garage sale, antique store or flea market.

Making Money—or at Least Paper Profits

Dealer Eloise Parks of Eloise's reports that very few of her customers try to resell their collectibles "because they didn't buy as investments to begin with. But of course, the psychology of collecting is that limited editions do increase and they enjoy knowing that."

It would be quite satisfying to realize that the "Jockey with Lass" Lladro porcelain that one bought in 1979 had increased in value from $950 to $1,375, even if you wouldn't dream of parting with it, or that your Gorham "Elena" doll had tripled in value. As Houston collector Nancy Selensky explains, "It makes me feel a little smug to look around at my collection and know that I've singled out some very valuable items. We all want to think that we have good taste, and in a sense collecting is an expression of that."

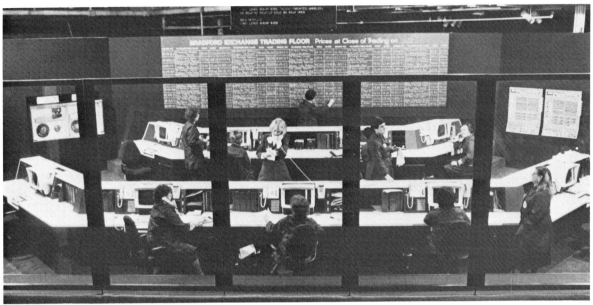

There is a flurry of activity on the Bradford trading floor as The Exchange acts as an agent for buyers and sellers. The phones are ringing, and the computer screens are lit as the transactions are taking place. Bradford also sells new issues created by its affiliated companies and other organizations.

Buying and Selling Basics

Experts recommend several avenues for the collector who wishes to buy or sell a collectible once it is sold out at the retail level. Collector-to-collector sales may be made via ads in collector publications, through The Bradford Exchange (for plates), or at club-sponsored swap meets or auctions. Dealers may also buy from collectors. Here are details on each procedure.

Advertise to Other Collectors—Prime Buyers

By advertising in a collector publication that accepts classified ads, one reaches a wide audience and can normally receive a value closest to an item's market price. The cost of the ad will be deducted from your profit, but because you are selling directly to another collector, it will not be necessary to pay commissions or accept a lower price to allow a dealer mark-up to be added. (See the listing of "Magazines and Newsletters" elsewhere in this book for possibilities.) It is best to state the price you want for your items rather than asking for a "best offer."

Ask a Retailer

When selling to a dealer, a collector should expect less than market value because obviously the dealer will add a mark-up to make the transaction worthwhile for them. Some dealers will work with regular customers to make trades if the dealer needs what

the collector has, permitting them to trade up to a more valuable or newer item. Others may offer to take items on consignment. Each dealer operates differently so expect variable policies. Dealers may also be able to suggest other sales methods.

The Bradford Exchange

Plate collectors can list their plates with The Bradford Exchange or buy back issues from other collectors. The Exchange guarantees that the trader-seller will be paid and that buyers receive plates in mint condition with proper certification. The Exchange acts as broker to ensure trustworthy and fair transactions. There is no fee for listing a plate on the Exchange, but a thirty percent fee will be subtracted from the sale price when a plate is sold. These sales are recorded and maintained on computer to provide information about secondary market sales. For more information, contact The Bradford Exchange and ask for the Trading Floor.

Swap Meets and Auctions

National conventions offer some of the most successful sales events for collectors, permitting all types of collectibles to be entered for a modest table or per item fee. Sales topping $100,000 in as short a period as four hours have been recorded in recent years.

Jim Woodward, show manager for the California Plate and Collectible Show, explains that his show

The 1987 "Buy and Sell" sponsored by the California Plate and Collectible Show proved to be two days full of activity, with some collectors selling their collectibles and others locating that special "hard-to-find" piece. These events have seen sales top $100,000.

has hosted a two-day "buy and sell" in recent years which has proven successful for both the buyer and seller. According to Woodward, the event creates enthusiasm for the collectors who have the opportunity to sell their own collectibles. "The buyers also have the opportunity to fill in their collection or locate a piece they have been searching for." The buy and sells are successful ventures for both parties involved, suggests Woodward.

Local collector clubs may also sponsor buy and sell events at monthly meetings or annual auctions. Bartering or bargaining is also possible since the seller is face-to-face with potential buyers.

A special note: contact members of the COLLECTORS' INFORMATION BUREAU directly if you have questions about selling their products. Some companies maintain list of buyers for scarce items and may be able to assist you. Listings with addresses are shown elsewhere in this book.

Today's Trends

Panelists looking at today's market report that collectors have been turning increasingly to back is-sues, a positive sign for those who have items to sell.

Looking ahead at where the market is going, Heio Reich, president of Reco International and COLLECTORS' INFORMATION BUREAU, says, "I would think that the result of recent collector shows is extremely positive due to the attendance of so many young, new collectors. This group will have an impact on the secondary market. New collectors being exposed to nearly complete series will go back and buy on the secondary."

Donna Polinski of the The Bradford Exchange Brokerage Department reports that movie and wildlife plates are the most active of the plates currently traded on the secondary market. "We are seeing an increase in trading overall because people are becoming more knowledgeable about how to trade and are using the Exchange to locate back issues."

Our panelists agree that there are fewer speculators in the market today, indicating that purchases are being made for collecting enjoyment rather than profit potential—the basis of a healthy primary and secondary market.

Susan K. Elliott

The Production Process
The Art Of Doll Making

A collector's enjoyment is enriched when he or she understands the step-by-step process involved in the creation of a favorite limited edition item. This is the third in a series of articles which will explain how art collectibles are made.

Since the dawn of time, there have been dolls. Although no historical data exists as far back as prehistoric times, it is probable that the first dolls were made from sticks and stones for cave-toddlers jealous of newborn siblings. Archaeological digs have found dolls among the remains of the Pharaohs of Egypt and the aboriginal tribes. So to describe the art of doll making is to describe the creativity of mother and child.

In modern times, dolls have been fashioned of cloth, wood, composition, porcelain, wax, plastic, and even dried fruit. And that just covers the heads and bodies of dolls. Clothing is just as diverse, ranging from the elaborate outfits of the French doll makers of the last century, through the plethora of Barbie costumes, to the simple cotton dress whipped up at home.

Because the field is so broad, and the possibilities nearly unlimited, the focus of this article will be on the most commonly collected dolls: the modern porcelain dolls most familiar to you as you build your own doll collection.

The Steps in Porcelain Doll Making Are Similar to Figurines

Some collectible dolls are all porcelain. Others have porcelain heads, hands and feet and cloth bodies. In both cases, the creation of the porcelain parts is the same. All begin with a model of the piece.

Working from a designer's drawings, a master model maker creates a plasticine or clay model. Once the model is perfect, a waste mold is made by pouring plastic around the model. This mold is used to create a plaster model. In removing this model, the mold is usually destroyed, giving it the designation "waste mold." The solid plaster casting obtained from the waste mold is refined through fine sanding and polishing and it is the model used to make the plaster molds into which the porcelain is poured. Each mold is only used for a few pourings, fifteen to twenty average, before new molds are made from the plaster original. This is to assure the perfection of each casting made from the molds.

Porcelain slip is poured into the mold to form an exact replica of the artist's original. As the plaster mold absorbs the water in the slip, which is clay or a mixture of clays thinned with water to the consistency of heavy cream, a wall of clay builds up on the inside of the mold. It is critical that the doll maker achieves the correct thickness for a durable, perfect part to be made. The delicacy of the sculpture of most faces, hands and heads require an artist's touch in this pouring and setting stage as well.

When the correct wall thickness has been achieved, excess slip is poured out of the mold. Excess that has begun to dry is trimmed from the pouring holes in the mold, and the casting is allowed to dry. Once hard, the casting, now called greenware, is gently released from the mold. In drying, it will have shrunk slightly, allowing an easy release. Extreme care is taken of the greenware, which is still damp and very delicate. At this stage, any holes that will be needed to string the doll (such as arm and leg holes if the doll is all porcelain) and the eyes and mouth of the doll are cut. This is delicate work, with the cutting done very slowly and carefully using sharp instruments. Each surface is cleaned repeatedly with a damp brush to assure there will be no rough edges.

Firing in a Sensitive Kiln Sets the Bisque

After the initial drying, cutting, and cleaning, each doll part is fired for the first time, at a relatively low heat. This is called low bisque firing, and its purpose is to harden the greenware. Once hard, each part can be gently sanded and mold seam lines are removed. After each piece is clean, smooth and perfect, it is fired again,

An artisan begins the delicate task of hand painting the head of a Gorham doll. Notice the tray of heads on the bench waiting attention. All of these heads have been fired twice and cleaned prior to the hand painting step.

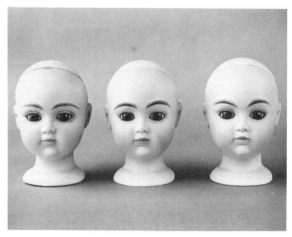

Three heads for Gorham's "Joy" limited edition Christmas doll. Note the differences in these "identical" heads. Even though they are all cast in the same mold, the response of the porcelain to firing, and the hand painting techniques of different craftsmen make each doll an original.

this time at a high temperature. This is a critical step, since flaws in firing will often show up later when the doll is painted. Overfiring can cause warping and blistering, and underfiring can cause a pepper-like effect to appear in the paint. Overfired bisque may be too shiny, and underfired may be chalky and dull. Properly fired bisque will have a finish resembling an eggshell.

The Personality Is in the Painting

Finally the doll is ready for painting, the step in which the artisan really needs an artist's touch. Each piece is sanded again with special rubber and grit sanders, and the individually mixed colors are applied. Besides basic flesh tones, special paints, shaders, and techniques are used for the rosy cheeks, mouth, eyebrows and eyelashes of the doll. If the eyes are painted, that is yet another major step.

The eyes are a critical part of doll making because, just as with a real person, the doll's eyes reflect his or her personality. Some artists prefer painted eyes for just this reason. They feel they can obtain exactly the look and feeling they want for a doll more effectively through their own creativity. Installed eyes can be equally as effective, though, and many collectors prefer the glass "paperweight" eyes usually chosen for fine collectible dolls. Since the eyes are the mirror of the doll's personality it is easy to see why the cutting stage is so important. If you recall, the eye holes are cut when the greenware is

damp and just out of the mold. The craftsman started with a hole drilled in the center of the eye, enlarging it carefully from the center until the whole eye is cut, scoring it many times around the edges to reinforce the desired shape. Obviously this is painstaking work, done slowly and carefully.

The eye to be used is selected with just as much care, and it is fastened behind the eye hole with putty. If eyes that open and close are chosen, the mechanism is put in place in the same way, after the eyes are carefully lined up with the holes.

Stringing Pulls the Doll Together

Next it is time to string the doll. If the doll has an all-porcelain body, all the holes in the various body parts are cut at the greenware stage. If the doll is jointed, body parts include balls to be placed at the hip, knee, elbow, and shoulder, to allow the doll to move. Once all the body parts have been cast, low fired, finished, high fired, and painted, the doll is strung. If the doll is jointed, cotton or paper is stuffed into the lower leg, and the cavity is filled with putty. The hands are also filled with putty, and an "S" hook is embedded in each of these parts. Beginning at the neck, elastic cord is run through the body, upper leg, ball joint, "S" hook on the lower leg, and back up to the neck. This is repeated on the other side, and another cord is run from the shoulder through one arm, elbow joint, and lower arm to

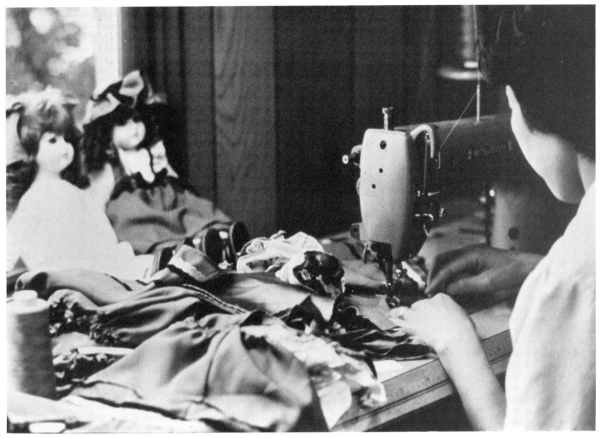

The final step is creating the elegant outfits worn by most porcelain collectible dolls. Here a seamstress sews a dress for Gorham's "Cecile."

the "S" hook in the hand, then back to the shoulder where the process is repeated for the other arm. Both arms are tied off at the shoulder. Usually when a doll is jointed, the head turns as well, and a hook will have been embedded in the neck as it was in the legs and hands. All the elastic cords come together at this hook.

Some porcelain dolls are not jointed. In these cases each one-piece arm and leg is strung with its opposite through the body and are fastened through a hook inserted in the head.

If the doll has a cloth body, the porcelain arms and legs are glued on. Normally, the cloth body is stitched but not stuffed. The sewn arm and leg portions are turned inside out, and glue is applied to the cloth. The cloth is placed over the porcelain piece covering a groove that is at the top of the piece. Strong string is wrapped over the cloth around the groove, and the glue is allowed to dry. After all the pieces are glued and dried, the cloth is turned right side out and the body is stuffed.

Heads and Hair Complete the Doll

Heads are another matter. They can be attached to the body as the arms and legs were, either strung through a hook or glued and wrapped over the groove in the neck. Or a breastplate can be attached to the head, using a fastener of some sort, and then the breastplate sewn to the body. This is usually done to give the doll the appearance of having porcelain shoulders. The head may also be cast with shoulders. In this case there are usually holes in the breastplate of the head. The body is sewn closed and stuffed into the neck for these dolls, and the head is sewn onto the body through the holes in the breastplate. One final method is to gather the cloth of the body at the neck with a strong string, insert the head to the groove, then draw the string tightly and tie. Often glue is also used with this method for additional security.

The last step is the application of the wig. Most heads that are to be wigged are made with a hole in

Doll crafters in the Orient demonstrate the various steps in assembling and clothing the popular, open edition Precious Moments® doll in her embroidered white eyelet christening gown and bonnet with pink accents. This charmer was "born" January 1, 1983, because the information is furnished on the birth certificate in her gift box. The "Katie Lynne" character was inspired by Sam Butcher's real-life grandchild.

the top. A styrofoam ball is measured and cut to fit the hole and is glued in place. The wig is attached to the styrofoam pate. Some dolls have all porcelain heads and painted hair. This is most common in baby dolls and some character dolls.

Just the Beginning of a Very Large Subject

By now it should be clear why we chose to concentrate on just one type of doll in this article. The steps described have just brought us to the completion of the doll production process for dolls made of one material. Even with your beloved porcelain collectible dolls, we have not begun to discuss the steps taken in dressing the doll in her elegant costume. Obviously, beautiful dolls, created with such care, are beautifully dressed. Much of the work in dressing them is done by hand. Just as the porcelain production requires artisans with an artist's touch, the making of costumes requires the dressmaker's art. But we will have to leave it to future articles to detail the creation of cloth dolls and fine fashions . . . the needlework of dollmaking.

Sara Kirtlink

An artisan sews an arm onto the cloth body of Precious Moments Collection doll *"Katie Lynne." Note in the foreground on the workbench the additional arms. The hands are applied to the arm using the glue and wrap method before the arm is stuffed. The completed, stuffed arm with hand is then sewn onto the body.*

Travel for Collectors
Appreciate Your Collection More When You See How It's Made First-Hand

Travel is always fun, but it becomes especially exciting when you combine it with your collecting interests. Add a new level of appreciation to your collection as you travel by searching out the many fine factories, galleries and studios where collectibles are made and displayed.

You will look at your collection in a fresh way after seeing how a Hummel figurine is painstakingly assembled and painted—and your memories of Germany will have extra depth. If a trip to Florida beckons, consider a side trip to the softly lit rooms of the Hibel Museum of Art in Palm Beach. You will see a magnificent collection of colorful and vibrant Edna Hibel originals donated by a couple who were among the artist's most ardent collectors.

One of the true benefits of collecting is to enjoy the special *sympatico* that collectors have for one another, whether they meet on a Lladro porcelain factory tour in Spain, or at the Bradford Museum of Collector's Plates outside Chicago. Use the following list as a reference before planning family vacations or getaway weekend trips. By seeking out others with similar interests, you will broaden your knowledge of collecting and feel at home wherever you go.

United States

Hibel Museum of Art
Tuesday-Saturday 10 a.m.–5 p.m., Sunday 1 p.m.—5 p.m., closed Mondays.
Located next to Royal Poinciana Playhouse in Palm Beach, Florida.
Reservations requested for groups.

Tours tailored to meet the desires of groups. Besides exhibits, the museum will show films on plates, the artist Edna Hibel, or give lectures on various aspects of her art and the collectible industry upon request. The museum exhibits are rotating and include the permanent collection of Hibel paintings, drawings, lithos and porcelain art. The only museum in the U.S. dedicated to the works of a living woman. Gift shop.

The Edna Hibel Society sponsors world tours for its members. In 1987 the group visited the British Isles and Helsinki. For information about upcoming events, write to: Edna Hibel Society, P.O. Box 9721, Coral Springs, FL 33075.

HIBEL MUSEUM OF ART
150 Royal Poinciana Plaza
Palm Beach, FL 33480
305/848-9633

Norman Rockwell Center/
Frances Hook Museum
Monday through Saturday, 10 a.m.–4 p.m., Sunday 1–4 p.m., evenings by appointment.
Located in the Old School in the Village of Mishicot, Wisconsin.
Reservations requested for groups.
(Contact Carol Anderson)

At the Bradford Museum of Collector's Plates outside Chicago, the spectacular collection hangs in special lucite panels to permit viewing of both the front and back of each plate.

Don Polland sculptures are part of the collection of the Favell Museum of Western Art and Indian Artifacts in Klamath Falls, Oregon.

One of the largest Norman Rockwell collections in the world, free slide shows, shop displays of art, limited edition prints and collectibles. The Frances Hook museum/art gallery features her limited edition issues and sponsors an annual Frances Hook Celebration in June, complete with Frances Hook Look-Alike Contest.

THE OLD SCHOOL
315 Elizabeth Street
P.O. Box 91
Mishicot, WI 54228
414/755-4014

The Bradford Museum of Collector's Plates

Weekdays, 9 a.m.–4 p.m., Saturday-Sunday, 10 a.m.–5 p.m., closed Christmas and other major holidays.

Located in the Chicago suburb of Niles, Illinois.

Reservations required for all groups. (Contact Anne Falk)

Admission is $2 per adult, $1 for senior citizens, and children under 12 are admitted free except on Sunday when admission is free; $1 per person for those in groups of 25 or more. Luncheon costs are extra.

The Bradford Museum of Collector's Plates features a collection of more than 1,300 of the most widely traded limited edition collector's plates and a computerized trading floor which handles buy and sell transactions from around the world. Group tours are available which include a special film on plate collecting and a guided tour of the museum and trading floor. Visitors can enjoy lunch in the mu-

seum's tropical indoor-garden cafe during the week. The museum is celebrating its tenth anniversary in 1988. Special events will be planned to promote the museum.

BRADFORD MUSEUM OF COLLECTOR'S PLATES
9333 Milwaukee Avenue
Niles, IL 60648
312/966-2770, extension 424

Annalee Doll Museum

Open seven days a week, February 1 through December 24.

At the end of Reservoir Road and Hemlock Drive in Meredith, New Hampshire.

This quaint barnboard building houses over 600 of doll designer Annalee's earliest creations, including Annalee's first doll created in 1934. Gift shop.

Annalee Doll Society sponsors annual auction and barbecue with factory tour in Meredith.

ANNALEE DOLL MUSEUM
P.O. Box 869
Meredith, NH 03253
603/279-6543

The Official Sebastian Miniatures Museum

Monday through Saturday, 9:30 a.m.–9:30 p.m., Sunday, 12–5 p.m.

Located in the rear of Stacy's Gifts and Collectibles in Walpole Mall in East Walpole, Massachusetts.

Collector-dealers Doris and Sherman Edwards display their personal collection of 700 rare and out-

A Tengra sculptor refines the model for a new porcelain figurine design.

At Lladro's Porcelain City factory in Spain, a view of the sculptors' building.

Member of First Precious Moments™ Collectors' Club Trip to the Orient observes as artisan hand paints a figurine at Design Studio in Nagoya, Japan.

of-production Sebastian Miniatures in their gift shop. Each piece is autographed either by the late Prescott W. Baston or his son Woody Baston. The collection is cataloged and cross-referenced.

THE OFFICIAL SEBASTIAN MINIATURES MUSEUM
Stacy's Gifts and Collectibles
Route One
Walpole Mall
East Walpole, MA 02032
617/668-4212

Favell Museum of Western Art and Indian Artifacts

Monday-Saturday, 9:30–5:30, closed on holidays that fall on Sundays and Mondays.
Admission: $3 adults, $2 seniors, $1 children 6–16.

The museum overlooks the outlet of the largest natural lake in Oregon and its 17,000 square feet of display space is laid out like the spokes of a wagon wheel. Includes works by renowned western artists such as Donald Polland, John Clymer, Joe Beeler, Frank McCarthy, and Mort Kunstler, as well as more than eighty collections of artifacts, including miniature firearms. Gift shop.

FAVELL MUSEUM OF WESTERN ART AND INDIAN ARTIFACTS
125 West Main Street
Klamath Falls, OR 97601
503/882-9996

American Museum of Western Art

Open seven days a week, 10 a.m.–5 p.m., closed Thanksgiving and Christmas.
Winter hours yet to be established.

Dealer-collectors Doris and Sherman Edwards share their collection of Sebastian Miniatures with collectors at their museum in East Walpole, Massachusetts.

Frontenac, Minnesota, is located 65 miles southeast of St. Paul and Minneapolis on U.S. 61 and Old Frontenac is two miles east on County Road 2, off Hwy 61 (one mile past the state park entrance). Admission free, donations requested.

This newly opened museum has previously had its exhibits on display in the Wild Wings Gallery in Lake City, Minnesota. It is a non-profit organization established to further interest in wildlife art—collecting, presenting, honoring and preserving art in this field.

AMERICAN MUSEUM OF WESTERN ART
P.O. Box 10
Frontenac, MN 55026–0010
612/345–5295

Circus World Museum

Museum exhibit buildings and grounds open 9 a.m.–6 p.m. daily except July 18 through August 22 when grounds are open until 9 p.m.

In south central Wisconsin 12 miles from the Wisconsin Dells.
Admission ranges from $7.50 for adults to $25 for a family plan and includes all shows, exhibits, demonstrations and rides (except elephant rides).
Group rates available.

The world's largest facility devoted to the circus, it is located on the site of the Ringling Brothers Circus original winterquarters (1884–1918). The world's largest repository of circus antiques, artifacts and information is recognized by the American Association of Museums and is a National Historic Site. (Collectors of Flambro's Emmett Kelly, Jr. collectibles would find this museum especially interesting.)

CIRCUS WORLD MUSEUM
Baraboo, WI 53913
606/356-8341

Goebel Collectors' Club Gallery

Monday-Friday, 10 a.m.–4:30 p.m., Saturday 11 a.m.–4 p.m., closed some holidays.
Located not far from the Tappan Zee Bridge in Tarrytown, N.Y., overlooks the Hudson River.
Reservations requested for groups as far in advance as possible, especially during the summer months. (Contact Phyllis Lerner)
Admission free.

Two floors of display and exhibits of art by Goebel artists, including Sister Maria Innocentia Hummel, Gerhard Bochmann, Charlot Byj, Gunther Granget, Harry Holt, Laszlo Ispanky, Lore, Janet Robson, Gerhard Skrobek, Irene Spencer, Hanns Welling, and Helen Granger Young. Half-hour film available. Complete tour takes about an hour and a half. Artist appearances are scheduled at various times during the year.

GOEBEL COLLECTORS' CLUB GALLERY
105 White Plains Road
Tarrytown, NY 10951
914/332-0300

Bellingrath Gardens and Home/Boehm Gallery

Open daily, 7 a.m.–dusk. Visitors to home should arrive by 4:15 p.m.
Located west of Mobile on Hwy 90 to Theodore. Exit 15A on Country Rd. 59 and look for billboard and directions.
Reservations recommended for guided tours and for groups of 20 or more.
Admission: Gardens $4 adults, children 6–11 $2; Home $5 (except babes in arms). Boehm Gallery included in gardens.

Boehm Gallery has the largest public display of Boehm porcelains in the world. Over 225 porcelains are exhibited in lighted cases behind glass. The Bellingrath Home has a large collection of porcelains, crystal, silver, paintings and furniture from around the world. Hostesses are on duty to answer questions. The Bellingrath Gardens consist of 65 acres which include a bird sanctuary and chapel. The gardens are planned so as to be in bloom year-round. Gift shop and cafeteria.

BELLINGRATH GARDENS AND HOME
Theodore, AL 36582
205/973-2217

Fenton Art Glass Factory Tour

Monday-Friday, first tour 8:30 a.m., last tour 3:15 p.m., closed national holidays.
Location: Williamstown, W. Virginia, just across the Ohio River from Marietta, Ohio.
Easily reached by Interstate I–77 and from W. Va. State Routes 2, 14, and US Route 50.
No reservations necessary for groups under 20; recommended for more than 20.
Admission free.

Tour of plant allows you to watch highly skilled craftsmen create handmade glass from molten state to finished product.

Fenton Art Glass Museum Tour

Sept-May, Monday-Saturday, 8 a.m.–5 p.m., except Tuesday and Thursday, open till 8 p.m.; Sunday 12 p.m.–5 p.m.
June-August, Monday-Friday, 8 a.m.–8 p.m.; Saturday, 8 a.m.–5 p.m.; Sunday 12 p.m.–5 p.m.
Closed national holidays.
No reservations necessary.
Admission charge: adults $1, children 50¢, 20% discount for groups of 20 or more.

Museum offers examples of Ohio Valley glass with major emphasis on Fenton Glass made 1905–1955. Representative glass of other Ohio Valley companies is displayed along with items of historical interest. Thirty-minute movie on the making of Fenton Glass is shown at regular times throughout the day.

FENTON ART GLASS COMPANY
700 Elizabeth Street
Williamstown, W. VA 26187
304/375-7772

Norman Rockwell Museum (Philadelphia)

Open every day of the year except Christmas, New Year and Thanksgiving, 10 a.m.–4 p.m.

Located 601 Walnut Street, overlooking Independence Hall.

Reservations necessary for groups of 10 or more.

Admission charge: adults $1.50, seniors over 62, $1.25. Group rates available.

Exhibits include one of three complete sets of *Saturday Evening Post* covers (324 pieces), over 700 pieces of additional art including the original art for Rockwell's famous War Bond Poster, a replica of his studio, the Four Freedoms Theater which has a five-minute slide presentation. Extensive gift shop. Tour should take 45 minutes to one hour.

NORMAN ROCKWELL MUSEUM
601 Walnut Street
Philadelphia, PA 19106
215/922-4345

Gallery in the Sun

Open seven days a week, 10 a.m.–4 p.m.

Located 6300 N. Swan Road, Tucson, Ariz.

No admission charge

No reservations needed.

Exhibits in this all-adobe museum include three rooms of the works of Ted Degrazia, one of which is rotated every two months. Exhibits cover all types of DeGrazia sculptures and paintings, including his first painting, which he painted at the age of 16. The museum closes promptly at 4 p.m. in keeping with DeGrazia's policy when he was alive. Gift shop.

GALLERY IN THE SUN
6300 N. Swan Road
Tucson, AZ 85718
602/299-9191

The Norman Rockwell Museum

Wednesday-Monday, 10 a.m.–5 p.m. Arrive no later than 4:15 as doors close promptly at five.

Located on Main Street, Stockbridge, Mass.

Reservations requested for groups.

Admission $3 adults, $1 children 5–18. Preschool free.

This museum contains two floors and shows only original paintings of Norman Rockwell which are rotated once a year in January. It offers the public the opportunity to see original art that is so familiar in print.

THE NORMAN ROCKWELL MUSEUM
Main Street
Stockbridge, MA 01262
413/298-3822

Franklin Mint Museum

Tuesday-Saturday, 9:30 a.m. to 4:30 p.m., Sunday 1 p.m.–4:30 p.m.

Located four miles south of Media on Rt. 1 or 45 miles south of Philadelphia.

Reservations necessary for groups of 35 or more.

No admission fee.

Self-guided tour of museum. All types of Franklin Mint collectibles are showcased in their own section. Exhibited are porcelains, plates, crystal, pewter, books, dolls, lithos, first-day covers, coins and medals, spoons, music boxes, jewelry and tableware with exhibits being constantly updated. Special events are scheduled throughout the year with a Creative People Art Show from June into July. Exhibits the personal works of the artists who create for the Franklin Mint.

This entire area of Pennsylvania has many other museums and points of historical interest. Gallery store and free parking.

FRANKLIN MINT MUSEUM
Franklin Center, PA 19091
215/459-6168

Bell Haven

By appointment only.

Admission $2

Bell collectors will marvel at the 30,000 bells on display.

BELL HAVEN
c/o Iva Mae Long
R.D. #4 Box 54
Tarentum, PA 15084

Foreign

Swarovski Kristall

May-September, Monday-Saturday, 8 a.m.–6 p.m., Sunday 8 a.m.–12 noon.

October-April, Monday-Friday, 8 a.m.–6 p.m., Saturday 8 a.m.–12 noon.

Take the Wattens Autobahn exit on the highway between Innsbruck and Salzburg-Munich in Austria. On Swarovski Strasse.

Wattens is the world-center of the art of glass cutting, home of the Swarovski works. Visitors will see Swarovski's collection of full lead crystal collectibles. Tours show artisans blowing, painting and engraving glass. Gift shop and cafe.

SWAROVSKI KRISTALL, WATTENER GLASHANDWERK
Innstrasse 1
6112 Wattens
Austria
Tel. 05224/3086 (24 hours)

Tengra

Mornings, half-day tours followed by complimentary lunch at nearby restaurant.

At the Goebel Collectors' Club in Tarrytown, N.Y., visitors first see the world's largest M.I. Hummel figurine "The Merry Wanderer" on the front lawn. It is decked out here with balloons for the Club's tenth birthday party, held in 1987.

Make reservations at least 45 days in advance.
Located in small rural village of Benaguacil, 16 miles away from Valencia, Spain, in heartland of country.

Visitors to the Tengra studio see how each figurine is hand-created the way it was done in the eighth century. The locals are proud Spanish, eager to show their art and way of life. Half of the work force are in the orange groves and the other half are artists. Do not expect luxury but be prepared for simplicity in good taste. Company will send information on the best-kept secret places to stay (castles), what to see, and the best local food.

PVP INDUSTRIES, INC.
5310 Derry Avenue, Suite E
Agoura, CA 91301
1–800/642–1818, national
1–800/642–1717, California

Lladro

Open to Lladro Collectors Society members, Tuesdays 4 p.m., appointment only.
Located on the outskirts of Valencia, Spain.

A three-hour tour designed exclusively for members of the Society shows the factory, studios of the three Lladro brothers and step-by-step production of Lladro porcelains. (A Lladro store is nearby in Nuevo Centro Mall.)

The Society sponsors numerous tours to Spain during the year, offering members the opportunity to visit the factory and have dinner with one of the founding Lladro brothers.

Individual visits:

SOCIEDAD DE COLECCIONISTAS LLADRO
Avda. Rey D. Jaime, No. 26B
Tavernes Blanques
46016 Valencia SPAIN
Attn: Javier Royo

To inquire about group tours:

LLADRO COLLECTORS SOCIETY
P.O. Box 1122
43 West 57th Street
New York, NY 10101–1122

W. Goebel Porzellanfabrik

Monday through Thursday, 8–11:30 a.m., 1–3:30 p.m., Friday 8–11:30.
Located in Roedental, West Germany, near town of Coburg.

Tours and talks about M. I. Hummel figurines, Goebel Crystal, dinnerware and giftware, salt-glazed stoneware and other lines at visitor's center. The factory's historical collection spans 3,000 years. Film on figurines and demonstrations of various production techniques. Visitors may purchase limited number of M. I. Hummel figurines. Nearby Coburg, which dates to 1056 and has a much older castle, are "musts" for the visitor. Club members receive a free lunch, with a nominal charge for guests. Only those visiting as part of GCC-sponsored tour group actually go through the factory.

GOEBEL COLLECTORS' CLUB
105 White Plains Road
Tarrytown, NY 10591
914/332–0300

Royal Copenhagen/Bing & Grondahl

Tours on Thursdays, call factory in advance for reservations (phone 01–86–4848).
Located in Copenhagen, Denmark at 45 Smallegade.

With the merger of these two historic factories, the collection of historic porcelain is even more comprehensive than before. Exhibits explain porce-

lain production techniques and visitors see artisans at work throughout the factory crafting and hand-painting Christmas plates, figurines and other items. Retail shops nearby.

ROYAL COPENHAGEN/BING & GRONDAHL
27 Holland Avenue
White Plains, NY 10603
914/428-8222

Precious Moments® Collectors' Club Tour to the Orient

Tour offered annually every spring.
Open to all club members and their spouses.

Precious Moments® Collector Club members can enjoy a memorable 14-day tour to the Orient. The trip includes seven days in Japan, three in Taiwan and four in Hong Kong. Members tour the Design Studio in Nagoya, Japan where they will meet the master sculptor. They will also visit the Precious Moments production facilities in Miaoli, Taiwan.

ENESCO PRECIOUS MOMENTS® COLLECTORS' CLUB
P.O. Box 1466
Elk Grove Village, IL 60007
Shonnie Bilinovich
(312) 640-3998

Club Anri

Open to Club Anri members, Thursdays 2 p.m., appointment only.
Located in St. Christina in Groden, Provence Bozen, Italy.

Club Anri members are given a tour of the Anri workshop to see how the famous woodcarvings are created.

CLUB ANRI
55 Pacella Park Dr.
Randolph, MA 02638
Mary Connolly
(617) 961-3575

Doulton Factories

Monday-Friday, tours 10:15 a.m. and 2 p.m., reservations strongly advised.
Royal Doulton Factory and Sir Henry Doulton Gallery, Minton and John Beswick, Stoke-On-Trent, England
Royal Crown Derby, Derby, England
Royal Doulton Crystal, Stourbridge, England

Arrange your visit through the U.S. offices and receive details on tours of these five factories. These are popular tourist destinations so make your plans well in advance. You will be able to view all types of Doulton products being made: Toby Mugs, lady figurines, dinnerware, and giftware. The Sir Henry Doulton Gallery contains a historical porcelain collection. Leather and Snook on Picadilly Street in London also shows an ongoing historical exhibit of interest to collectors. Gift shops at individual factories.

DOULTON & CO., INC.
700 Cottontail Lane
Somerset, NJ 08873
201/356-7880

Okura Museum

Open 10 a.m.–4 p.m., closed Mondays.
Located in Minato-ku.

Fine exhibits of Japanese sculpture, ceramics, calligraphy, paintings, swords, lacquerware, masks, and books. Similar Chinese objects. Catalog in Japanese and English.

OKURA MUSEUM
3 Aoi-cho
Minato-ku
Japan

Belleek Pottery, Ltd.

Monday-Friday, 10 a.m.–noon, 2–4 p.m., closed holidays and annual vacation period, first two weeks in August, plus local holidays.
Located in County Fermanagh, Northern Ireland.
Free, guided tours.

Demonstrations of Belleek's distinctive porcelain weaving and hand assembly. Call before your visit to verify when the pottery will be open (011 44-36-56-55-01 from the U.S.).

BELLEEK POTTERY
Belleek, County Fermanagh
Northern Ireland
Telephone: Belleek 501

Factories not listed here may also welcome collectors, even if they do not post specific visiting hours. See addresses in "Company Summaries" to contact any firms that you especially want to visit.

Susan K. Elliott

Protecting Your Collection
How to Care and Provide Security for Your Collection

Thieves have become increasingly sophisticated in recent years, striking collectors' homes when the family leaves on vacation or for an afternoon's outing. They know about major collections and have even attended collector gatherings such as the annual Hummel Festivals, no doubt hoping to pick up a few choice pieces from unsuspecting exhibitors.

Collection security involves two areas: protecting your valuables from theft, and the care and handling of fragile collectibles. With a little knowledge, you can preserve the objects you love.

Think About Security

Proper security may prevent most planned thefts from ever occurring. Begin your precautions by viewing your home as a potential thief would, looking for weaknesses that would allow access for an intruder.

Invest in security basics: adequate outside lighting, deadbolt locks, sturdy doors, bars for basement windows, and all-important, smoke detectors throughout your home. Burglar alarms exist in great variety, ranging from buyer-installed pressure sensitive devices placed under a rug to detect intruders, to complicated systems that operate through home computers or cable TV systems.

Some security systems attempt to detect break-ins at windows or doors, silently alerting police or monitoring stations who can send officers to catch the burglars after they enter the home. Other devices concentrate on suspicious movements within the house. Each system has its strengths and weaknesses, so discuss their merits thoroughly with a security expert before buying, or call your police department for an opinion.

Whether you choose to invest in burglar alarms or not, be security conscious in your actions. Don't discuss your collection in public or announce that you will be leaving town while at the gas station, beauty parlor, or dry cleaners, but do notify the neighbors and police of your departure. Consider installing timers to turn on lights in the evenings if you will be away for an extended period. Eliminate the obvious signs of absence—stop mail and newspaper delivery, and have someone tend your yard. Check references on cleaning and repair people who work in your home.

Remember that once stolen, collectibles without individual numbers can be difficult to reclaim (should the police recover the items), unless the owner has marked them in some indelible fashion.

Check with the local police department to see if your town participates in Operation Identification. If so, they will provide tips and marking tools to inscribe your social security number or other personal identification on collectibles. Special pens with "invisible ink" that show up only under black (ultraviolet) light may be used for this purpose.

Care and Handling

Each type of collectible requires different care, as we will discuss, but nothing too difficult.

Plates and Steins: Unless dropped, plates and steins are durable and require minimal maintenance. Dust them frequently to prevent dirt build-up or wipe with a damp cloth. For a more thorough cleaning, put plates or steins in a sink full of lukewarm water with a mild detergent and wash by hand. Dip in clear lukewarm water and dry with a soft cloth. If still dirty, repeat the process. (Do not wash porous, unglazed pieces in this manner. Dust only.)

Never use bleaches or hot water. Do not immerse a plate with a hand-signed artist's autograph in water as it may not be adequately sealed. Be especially gentle with gold bandings as they are the most delicate part of a plate or stein's design.

"Dust and sun are probably the worst enemies of a doll collection,"
warns Sara Kirtlink. Annalee Mobilitee's "Johnny Appleseed" doll is
protected under an attractive glass dome with a wooden base.

The Print Collector, available from Fountainhead, is the patented sys-
tem for housing unframed prints. The system protects prints from
physical damage, soiling, discoloration of the paper and fading of the
image. The Print Collector includes museum-quality conservation
techniques, a complete indexing system, clear print envelopes and fine
furniture cabinetry.

Figurines: Because of their structural differences, figurines require additional precautions.
When handling, lift a piece by its base or a sturdy
part; delicate fingers and branches may snap under
pressure. To clean, dust gently with a feather duster
or man's shaving brush to remove dirt from crevices.
Restorers estimate that up to half of their work is
created by careless dusting and some go as far as to
recommend washing instead of dusting. Be absolutely sure that any cleaning people are instructed in
proper care and that if any damage occurs, they save
the small finger or broken piece for repair. (See restoration tips.)

For more serious cleaning, prepare the sinks or
basins by lining them with towels. Fill the first with
warm water and mild soap, the second with clear
lukewarm water (distilled if your area has hard water), and a third with a vinegar rinse (one-half cup
vinegar to each gallon of water). Move the faucet
out of the way or cover it with towels to avoid
breakage.

Because so many different techniques are used in
figurine production, avoid soaking figurines so that
they will not fade or, even more drastic, lose their
color completely. If the piece has a detachable wood
base, remove it and wipe with furniture oil to highlight the grain if you wish, but be certain not to use
silicone waxes.

Dip the figurine in soapy water, using a brush to
clean nooks and crannies, but do not swish through
the water. Move to the second towel-lined basin,
pouring water over the piece with a styrofoam or paper cup. If you happen to drop the cup, it will cause
no damage. To completely remove soap film, give
the piece a final rinse in a basin of vinegar water. Experts recommend air drying because it reduces handling and the danger of breakage, but you may use
an absorbent cloth. Do not try to speed the process
by using a blow dryer.

Every figurine has at least one air hole so check to
see that the piece drains completely during drying.
Glazed figures do not have glazed bottoms and
should not be allowed to become soaked with water.
Dry thoroughly before returning to a wood shelf or
tabletop to avoid creating a water spot.

Never wash terra cotta pieces such as Hamilton
Collection's hakata figures, or Ceramastone Sebastian Miniatures. If absolutely necessary, Ceramastone pieces may be cleaned with a cotton swap
wrung out of warm water.

Bells: Adapt the above instructions as appropriate to the style and material.

Prints: One of the most important rules in
print preservation is to minimize handling. If you

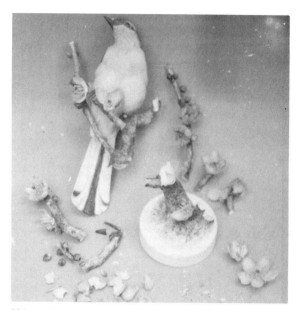 

If the unthinkable happens to one of your collectibles—breakage—companies such as Old World Restorations, Inc. can provide extraordinary assistance. The staff specializes in all forms of restoration and conservation and in most cases where complete restoration is employed, their work cannot be detected by the naked eye. A Royal Worcester Dorothy Doughty Bird (l) is shown as it was received by Old World Restorations, Inc. The same figurine (r) is displayed after restoration.

have unframed prints, store them flat in binders made for this purpose (available at most galleries). A typical binder contains ten acetate sheets with an inside paper cover. When framing, request museum mounting.

Hang prints out of direct sunlight to prevent fading and maintain consistent temperatures in your home. The build-up of moisture between print and glass is a print's biggest enemy.

Dolls: For porcelain faces, hands or legs, follow the guidelines for plate care. Stands that support the doll are effective security and display devices, as are glass domes that will eliminate dulling dust. Keep out of direct sunlight to avoid weakening fabrics and fading colors.

Doll producers such as Gorham recommend that you play hairdresser if your doll's locks are mussed; in most cases dolls' hair is combable. If a costume becomes dirty it may be a simple matter to wash it as you would other clothing. Consult a dry cleaner or fabric expert for elaborate or delicate outfits.

Special Tips: For crystal plates, add a little bit of ammonia to the rinse water for sparkle. Clean metal pieces with gentle polishes created especially for that purpose. (Rub gently or the finish may disappear along with the tarnish.) Items that have been

sealed with a lacquer coating should not be polished, but merely wiped with a dampened cloth.

Do not use oil-based polishes on wooden plates or woodcarvings as it may affect the decoration.

For smoke or sulfur damage on plates, figurines, bells or steins, clean with a soft-scrub type product, applied with a soft cloth. The gloss will be dulled slightly, but the cleaner will restore the piece's beauty.

Most manufacturers will be happy to provide additional guidelines pertaining to their specific products.

Restoration

A skillful restoration may recover 50% to 100% of an item's original issue price. When a damaged piece is scarce or has special sentimental value, collectors often prefer to have it restored rather than accept an insurance company settlement that requires turning over the broken pieces in exchange for its cash value. The Boehm Studios is one producer that maintains a list of restorers qualified to repair their porcelains, available upon request to collectors. Other companies may also provide this service, or assist in finding replacements of broken items.

The Goebel Collectors' Club keeps track of restoration specialists, and provides the following list, based on recommendations of collectors who have used them.

Canada
J&S CHINA REPAIRS
8350 St. George Street
Vancouver, BC

United States
HOUSE OF RENEW
27601 Forbes Road, #15
Laguna Niguel, CA 92677

ATTIC UNLIMITED
1523 West Struck Avenue
Orange, CA 92666

STEWARTS TREASURE HOUSE
Sutter Street
San Francisco, CA

HERBERT KLUG
1001 South Havana, #301
Aurora, CO 80012

WALTER KAHN
Westport, CN

MAISON GINO, INC.
845 Lincoln Road
Miami Beach, FL 33139
Attention: Mr. Irving Sultan

PROFESSIONAL RESTORATION
P.O. Box 16222
Orlando, FL 32861
Attention: R. DiCarlo

MAXINE'S LTD.
7144 University Avenue
Des Moines, IA 50311

JO BE
Sales & Service
Geneva, IL 60134
John & Betty Bazar

WAYNE WARNER
Rural Route 13, Box 557
Bloomington, IL 61701

WIRTENBERG ART RESTORING
581 Boylston Street
Boston, MA 02116

JOHN DELSETTE
68 Linden
Everett, MA 02149

L. MCNAUGHTON
1425 Pontiac S.E.
Grand Rapids, MI 49506

LILO HARRIS
Double L Antiques
1455 W. Fourteen Mile Road
Madison Heights, MI 48071

YOLANDA STUDIO
228 Washington Avenue
Elmwood Park, NJ 07407
Attention: Yolanda DiSalvo

RESTORATION BY DUDLEY, INC.
Box 345B
West Orange, NJ 07052

IMPERIAL CHINA
22 North Park Avenue
Rockville Center, NY 11590

OLD WORLD RESTORATIONS
347 Stanley Avenue
Cincinnati, OH 45226
Attention: Douglas Eisele

BILL EBERHARDT
Harry A. Eberhardt & Sons, Inc.
2010 Walnut Street
Philadelphia, PA 19130

KRAUSES
995 Jefferson Avenue
Washington, PA 15301

MICHAEL'S ART RESTORATION
    STUDIO
8316-8th NW
Seattle, WA 98117
Michael Scheglov, Art Restorator

Expert Advice

GRAPHICS—Betty Oesterling of Lawrence Gallery in Utica, Michigan, tells her customers to treat prints as they would their own hands, "neither too hot nor too cold. Hang graphics out of direct sunlight, especially serigraphs or collotypes, which can suffer burning. Hang sheers over your windows to filter sunlight. Also, it's very important to use museum mounting in framing, (also described as conservation framing)." Until a few years ago when the Professional Picture Framers Association established standards for museum mounting, there was considerable controversy and discrepancy in techniques. That should not be a problem today.

"If you plan to resell a graphic, do not frame it," Oesterling advises. "In framing, a print must be hinged, and that means that it will no longer be mint, no matter how carefully the process is done. A lot of people buy lithographs and treat them terribly. They dent them and crinkle them and that lowers their value. Dents can be pressed out sometimes, but not always." Lawrence Galleries will store prints for up to six months after purchase to avoid damage before a customer is ready to have them framed.

DOLLS—Sara Kirtlink of Kirtlink Associates says, "For porcelain dolls, we recommend that collectors take care of them just as they would their porcelain figurines—dust them or damp wipe them. It's not necessary to put soap and water on them and scrub them.

"Treat the clothing just like you would your own clothes, because the collectible dolls are made with really nice fabrics just like the clothes you would buy yourself. So if you would dry-clean your own dress made of that fabric, you would dry-clean the doll's clothing. The most important tip we offer is to keep fine dolls covered under a glass dome. Dust and sun are probably the worst enemies of a doll collection. Sunlight will definitely fade the fabrics if a doll is placed in direct sunlight."

STEINS—Ken Armke, owner of Opa's Haus in New Braunfels, Texas, says "Steins don't really need a whole lot of care except for dusting. You should obviously try to avoid chipping or accidental damage. It's a product that doesn't require maintenance or require care in the normal sense of the word. There's no preventative maintenance necessary. You treat them like you would a figurine.

"Sterling silver trim and tops are rare, seen on a few antique pieces, but almost never on contemporary pieces. The metal on 99 per cent of today's steins is pewter, which really doesn't require care. It ages naturally and develops a patina that's considered desirable. It definitely shouldn't be polished. Wipe it with a damp rag or follow your normal dusting procedure. If for some reason a Mettlach phanolith stein gets especially dirty, you can scrub it by sponge with a scouring powder. Handle it carefully so you don't drop it. I have even gone so far as to use a scouring pad because the colors are fired in and are permanent so there's not a danger that you will remove the color. You want to do something like that with care; watch what you're doing. If it's a stoneware stein, which most of them are, it's a very hard, durable body and it's difficult to damage it by cleaning it. Dropping it would be the bigger danger."

BELLS—Marcia Andrus, bell collector, says that "bells don't really need any special care. I keep 99.9 percent of my collection behind glass so they're protected from breakage and dust. Being behind glass they're not handled, so there's no problem. They also don't need polishing this way."

PLATES, FIGURINES—Beverly Haddad, Haddad's Gifts, Lansing, Michigan, says, "We suggest to our collectors that if they need to wash anything, say once a year, or every couple of years, they should line their sink with towels so everything is covered and there's no way to bump the plate or figurine. Put about an inch and a half of water in the sink, just as small an amount as they can, and some Ivory soap. Gently wash the pieces, dry them, and let them dry thoroughly.

"In between heavy spring cleaning, when they're on display, plates and figurines just need light cleaning. We recommend Windex and a very soft T-shirt type rag to wipe them off with.

"The reason that we suggest lining the entire sink is because plates and figurines become very, very slippery when wet. We don't recommend soaking them or anything like that. A very soft bottle brush will help get into the cracks of a figurine. Before the plate or figurine is put back wherever it goes, whether it's in a wire holder or a wooden frame, or back in a curio cabinet, it should be totally and completely dry. The pieces should dry for three or four hours.

"Really, as long as a collector uses a very mild cleaner (and that's why I recommend the Ivory soap), there shouldn't be any problem at all, whether the item being cleaned is a plate or a pewter figurine."

Insuring Your Collection
A Guide to Selecting Insurance

If your collection of Hummel figurines were stolen tonight while you were away at a movie, would insurance cover your loss? If fire swept through your home, destroying your P. Buckley Moss prints, Wedgwood Christmas plates and Gorham dolls, would your insurance company recognize the value of your lost collectibles?

No one wants to contemplate the destruction of a collection lovingly assembled, and it need not happen if you take a few precautions.

Insurance Options

Judging from past surveys, a mere third of all collectors have (or think they have) insurance for their collectibles. Only a fraction of that number carry separate policies that list their collectibles individually.

Many collectors believe that their collection is covered as part of their homeowner's policy, but have not discussed this coverage specifically with an insurance agent. They might be unpleasantly surprised to learn that some homeowner's policies specifically exclude collections and collectibles, and replace only items of personal use. If covered, replacement might be at issue price rather than current market value, or even at a depreciated amount.

Even "small" collections have a way of growing like Topsy, quickly adding thousands of dollars worth of value to an inventory of home furnishings, and even more when secondary market value is figured. If you have a homeowner's policy for $50,000, and your collection has grown to a value of $20,000 since you first assessed it, a disaster might leave you with unpleasant choices of what you could afford to replace after settlement. Would you be able to buy new furniture, household items, *and* to replace your collection, or would your collection simply disappear into the past while you rebuilt your home?

Unless provision is made to establish the value of individual items, insurance companies may lump items such as collector's plates or steins in with your everyday dinnerware.

Most companies require detailed listings and documentation with any claims of loss. As not all agents understand limited editions, you may need to explain the basics of price appreciation and why your collection deserves special status among your personal possessions. Chubb Insurance, a major insurer of all types of collections, often relies heavily on collectors' valuations of their treasures, "because they're the specialists."

According to Susan Mahon, a marketing specialist in Chubb's personal insurance division, Chubb does not require appraisals for items valued below $10,000. Other companies may request appraisals for less valuable items.

"Chubb's philosophy on claims is to settle the loss before it occurs because that's when we have the figurine or other item, and that's when we can determine value. After it's gone, it's much more difficult," says Ms. Mahon. "When we take and underwrite your collection, we ask you to tell us what you think it's worth. If we have any questions on it or it's a particularly high value, we might ask you to go get an appraisal, but we don't require appraisals on items unless they're of greater than a $10,000 value."

To establish value, agents will generally accept secondary market values from established price guides such as the *Price Index* in this book, *The Bradex* (compiled by The Bradford Exchange), or *The Greenbook*. Take a copy of the price guide with you when discussing coverage with your agent. If you do need an appraisal, contact your collectibles dealer to see if they make appraisals, or can recommend an expert who will. For example, Precious Moments collectors may receive appraisals for nominal cost by joining The Greenbook Society of Dealers and Collectors, 348 Main Street, East Setauket, New York 11733.

Insurance agent Thomas A. Mier, from Arthur Mier Agency Inc., Grand Rapids, Michigan, explains the types of coverage available to collectors and the importance of adequately insuring valuable possessions.

It is important to keep an accurate record of your collectible purchases. Both record books above provide space for photographs and pertinent information.

Detailed Inventory A Must

If you haven't already done so, begin to compile a listing of all items in your collections. While some companies may not request it, you should have an inventory for your own use to determine your collection's value. And with some policies, it may not be possible to receive reimbursement for the full value of your collection without such a list.

Record the following basic information for each item:

- Manufacturer Name
- Edition Limit/Your Item's Number if Numbered
- Artist Name
- Your Cost
- Series Name
- Added Expenses (Shipping, Framing, Restoration, etc.)
- Item Name
- Special Markings (Artist's Signature, etc.)
- Year of Issue
- Secondary Market History (If Purchased on Secondary Market)
- Size/Dimensions
- Place of Purchase
- Location in Your Home (For Burglary or Loss)
- Date of Purchase
- Insurance Company/Policy or Rider Number

Record each new item you buy at the time of purchase. Make a date with yourself to update this material periodically, possibly after you complete your taxes for the year. The pleasure of seeing how your collection is growing may offset the chore of preparing tax returns.

Large index cards will handle the pertinent information, or you may prefer to invest in one of the published record books that look so official and orderly when placed on your bookshelf. Possibilities to consider include:

The Kovels' Organizer for Collectors by Ralph and Terry Kovel, (Crown Publishers, One Park Avenue, New York, New York 10016);

The Antique Trader Weekly Antiques and Collectibles Record Book, (The Babka Publishing Co., Box 1050, Dubuque, Iowa 52001);

The Official Collector's Journal, (The House of Collectibles Inc., 201 E. 50th Street, New York, New York 10022);

Collectors Inventory File (Collectors News, Grundy Center, Iowa 50638). These books may be available in your local bookstore.

After the material is compiled, make photocopies and keep one set outside the home in case of fire; a safety deposit box is a good location. Photo documentation is also recommended and can be either in the form of still photos or video cassette. Enlist the help of a photographer friend, if necessary, or consult your local photography store for a helpful and inexpensive booklet from Eastman Kodak, "Photos Help You When Disaster Strikes." If not available locally, write to Eastman Kodak, Rochester, New York 14650.

Today's modern technology allows for convenient documentation. Video cameras can be employed to create an inventory of your collectibles as well as other household possessions.

Collectors who own several shelves of stunning and irreplaceable collectibles such as Lladro limited edition figurines should check to see if they are adequately insured.

Video cameras can be rented fairly inexpensively to create an inventory of all your household belongings. Make sure each room is well-lit and pan the camera slowly across the entire scene, turning over pieces such as figurines to expose markings that affect value, or film close-ups of special details, such as a remarque on a print. Replay the film to check that it is not too dark or over-exposed, then store it with your written inventory. Set aside time once a year to repeat the procedure.

Date photos or video film by photographing a card with the collection showing the date.

If In Doubt, Save It

Save all certificates and materials that arrive with your purchases, such as booklets explaining care and cleaning. Controversy exists over whether or not one should keep plate and other product boxes for optimum resale value, but go ahead if you have the space.

Boxes come in handy for moving and buyers prefer to have them if you sell an item later. Top-selling plates have been known to lose up to $35 of their value without the original box, but if the plate is in demand, buyers will usually recognize that the plate is the most important part of the purchase.

Types of Coverage

Once your inventory is complete and you have an idea of your collection's current value, the next step is to shop around for coverage. If your agent is not cooperative, contact the state insurance board for the rates and law in your state. Many states have regulations forbidding arbitrary denial of coverage or cancellation and may even assist in locating acceptable coverage. Independent information services funded by insurance companies can also be helpful.

Types of coverage available include: homeowner's or renter's; a floater or separate endorsement to an existing policy; an endorsement to a business policy; or a completely separate service. Ask what the policy will cover: breakage, burglary, loss, damage, fire, etc.

You might want a personal articles floater with blanket coverage for a specified amount, rather than a policy with scheduled (individually listed) items.

Chubb's Susan Mahon explains how their collectibles coverage works. "In personal articles floaters, jewelry is a category, as is fine arts, and there's even a miscellaneous category. Say you have a collection that's worth $10,000 but it contains a large number of low valued items. Instead of going to the trouble

of listing every single thing and coming up with a dollar amount for each item, you just get the blanket amount of coverage.

"What that provides for you, over and above your homeowner's policy, is 'all risk' coverage. With a few exceptions, we cover your fine arts collection for whatever happens to it, except for breakage. If you have a policy for a lot of breakable items, make sure to ask your insurance agent for breakage coverage and they'll add that on for you.

"There's a per item limit on blanket coverage. Our per-item limit is $2,500, but that would vary from company to company.

"Once the values start getting more significant you would want to list those values on a policy, and we call this policy a schedule. You can have blanket and schedule under the same policy—it's just how you decide to list it. Then under the scheduling you actually write down the description and the value of each item. The item is covered for that amount of money."

Unless your collection is quite large or includes other types of expensive items such as original paintings, most agents will suggest that you insure it as part of a larger policy. Another possibility might be to approach an agent for a collector's club, asking for group rates.

It is difficult to suggest an average rate for comprehensive coverage because so many variables apply. Fire rates vary widely, as do local police protection, crimes rates, weather conditions and the construction of homes—all affecting rates. Ask friends what they are paying for coverage, and shop around for the best rate.

If you already have a homeowner's policy, check the fine print to see if your collection is indeed covered. Fine arts policies are generally best for those who have valuable antiques, sculptures or paintings in addition to limited edition collectibles. Rates are higher because the items covered have no common listing. Make sure that fine arts insurance is the best (not most expensive) coverage if your agent suggests it.

Most important, be sure you understand what your policy covers and what your insurance company will require if a loss occurs. Susan Mahon emphasizes, "The thing collectors should watch out for and be very careful about is that often there's a difference between what is on a person's insurance policy and how it is going to be settled at the time of loss. People should be sure that they question their agent about what they will need to have to prove value.

"It's rather deceiving to have a policy for a $3,000 Hummel and to have it lost, thinking that you're going to get $3,000 for it, then to find out that you have to produce some sort of receipt when you had no idea that would be necessary. Ask your agent what happens at the time of loss." Mahon says collectors should ask the agent, "What do you need of me?"

Check your policy now to find out whether you are actually covered, or take steps to secure this protection for your valuables. Fire destroys a home every 45 seconds in this country, and the incidence of burglary and robbery is even greater.

Susan K. Elliott

The bond between parent and child spreads a special warmth within collectors' hearts. From left to right and top to bottom are: Tengra's "Mother and Child" figurine, Lladro's "Blessed Family" figurine, Artaffects' "Motherhood" plate from the Curator Collection, Lladro's "Good Night" figurine, Artaffects' "Fatherhood" plate from the Curator Collection, Armstrong's "A Pair of Dreams" plate, Kaiser's "Mother and Child" figurine and Artaffects' "Cheyenne Nation" plate from Vague Shadows.

A child's smile, his curiosity or a simple action are among the endearing qualities depicted on numerous limited edition collectibles. Here are some of the finest examples: Armstrong's "Hatching A Secret" plate, Reco International's "Night Time Story" plate, The Hamilton Collection's "Ashley" plate, Roman's "This Little Piggie" plate, Goebel's "Little Goat Herder" plate, Armstrong's "Once Upon A Smile" plate, The Hamilton Collection's "In Disgrace" figurine, Roman's "Sailor Mates" figurine and Enesco's "March" Precious Moments® figurine.

On the right page, from left to right and top to bottom are: The Balliol Corporation's "In Disgrace" and "The Reward" plates, Goebel's "A Gentle Glow" figurine which comes with a removable candle which can be placed in the evergreen bough, Goebel's "In the Meadow," "Kindergartner" and "Sing Along" figurines, The Balliol Corporation's "Sunbeam" plate, Lladro's "Repose" figurine and The Balliol Corporation's "Awakening" plate.

Holidays have inspired many delightful and attractive limited edition collectibles. On the left page, from left to right and top to bottom are several festive issues: Duncan Royale's "The Magi" figurine, Artaffects' "Shining Star" plate from Vague Shadows, Brad Bennett Studio's "Fourth of July" graphic, Annalee Mobilitee's "Santa Trimming Lighted Tree" display, Gorham's "Merry Christmas Grandma" Norman Rockwell bell, Duncan Royale's "The Medieval" figurine, Wedgwood's "The First Meeting" Valentine's Day plate and Gorham's "Kristobear Kringle" bear.

On the right page, from left to right and top to bottom are: Annalee Mobilitee's "Easter Parade Boy Bunny," "Trick Or Treat Mouse" and "Velour Santa," Duncan Royale's "Mongolian Santa" figurine, Gorham's "Merrie" doll, Wedgwood's "Guildhall" Christmas plate and Flambro Imports' "Spirit of Christmas V" figurine.

Birds and animals continue to remain strong in the limited edition market. On the left page, from left to right and top to bottom are: Mill Pond Press's "Cardinal and Wild Apples" and "Blossoms and Berries" graphics and Swarovski America's breathtaking crystal, including duck, hummingbird, "Togetherness" the Lovebirds and a bear. Also pictured are: The Hamilton Collection's "Morning Mist" plate, Wedgwood's 1987 *Calendar Plate* featuring birds and Edwin M. Knowles' "The Wood Duck" plate.

On the right page, from left to right and top to bottom are: Maruri Studio's *Wings of Love* bird figurine, Fountainhead's "Courtship Flight" plate, Maruri Studio's "Eagle in Flight" and *Wings of Love* figurines, Maruri Studio's *American Eagle Gallery* figurine, Royal Worcester's "Birds of Prey" figurine, Fountainhead's "Winter Chickadees" plate and Maruri Studio's *Wings of Love* figurine.

Whether they remind you of your household pet or a stunning species of wildlife, these animal kingdom subjects appeal to millions of collectors. From left to right and top to bottom are: Mill Pond Press's "Out of the Blizzard" graphic, Royal Worcester's "Fishful Thinking" plate, Reco International's "Olepi the Buffalo" plate, The Hamilton Collection's "Double Take" plate, Polland Studio's "Hunting Cougar" figurine, Fountainhead's "The Pantry" plate, Polland Studio's "Hunting Free" figurine, Fountainhead's "The Mantle" plate and Polland Studio's "Federal Stallion" figurine.

Literary and historical themes instill pride in our country and many collectibles are created to honor these people and events. From left to right and top to bottom are: Armstrong's "U.S. Constitution vs Guerriere" plate, The Hamilton Collection's "U.S.S. Constitution" plate, Flambro Imports' "And God Bless America" plate, Artaffects' "Brave and Free" plate from Vague Shadows, Edwin M. Knowles' "The Lincoln-Douglas Debates" plate and Annalee Mobilitee's "Huckleberry Finn" and "Ben Franklin" dolls.

Clowns continue to tickle the funny bones of many collectors, as they are portrayed in many creative manners. From left to right and top to bottom are: "The Harlequin" figurine from Duncan Royale, Flambro Imports' "Wheeler Dealer" and "Over the Barrel" figurines, "Ironing the Waves" plate by Armstrong's, Duncan Royale's "Pantalone" clown figurine and Flambro Imports' "Paul Jung," "Dining Out" and "Abe Goldstein" figurines.

Sports enthusiasts will enjoy many commemorative items featuring their heros who have made major contributions to professional athletics, in addition to favorite sports sites. From left to right and top to bottom are: Brad Bennet Studio's "Wrigley Stadium" graphic, Gartlan USA's "Baseball's All-Star" George Brett plate, ceramic baseball cards featuring Roger Staubach, Mike Schmidt and George Brett, "Power at the Plate" honoring Mike Schmidt and "The Best of Football" honoring Roger Staubach.

Many collectors enjoy owning works of art for their religious and inspirational messages. From left to right and top to bottom are: Roman's "Miracle" figurine, Enesco Imports' "Believe the Impossible Dream" Precious Moments figurine, Edwin M. Knowles' "The Annunciation" plate, Enesco Imports' "Sending You My Love" Precious Moments figurine, Reco International's "Moses in the Bulrushes" plate, Flambro Imports' "Amen" figurine and Roman's "Forgive Our Trespasses" plate.

From the Babylonian age to modern day, romance is still romance, as artists capture the universal feeling in art form. From left to right and top to bottom are: Lladro's "A Flower for My Lady" figurine, "Some Enchanted Evening" plate by the Edwin M. Knowles China Company, the Curator Collection's "Caroline" plate, Tengra's "Babylonian Lady" figurine and "Heaven Bless Your Togetherness" Precious Moments figurine by Enesco Imports.

The dance and instrumentalists portrayed in sophisticated and whimsical limited edition fashion are sought after by music enthusiasts. From left to right and top to bottom are: Tengra's "Ballerina," "Dancing Couple," "Clown with Saxophone" and "Clown with Fiddle" figurines and "The Cornetist" and "The Trombonist" figurines by Roman.

Charming English cottages and attractive collectibles portraying the various seasons represent the variety of limited editions available to collectors. From left to right and top to bottom are: Armstrong's "Katrina" ceramic plaque, Brad Bennet Studio's "Blizzard" graphic, John Hine's David Winter cottages "The Bothy," "Rose Cottage," "The Bakehouse," "Market Street," "Sussex Cottage" and "School House," Kaiser's "A Visit with Santa" plate, Lladro's "Ahoy There" figurine and Kaiser's "Spring Beauty" plate.

The breathtaking items on this page represent the diversity of today's world of collectibles—an industry where the artist captures the imagination of collectors. From left to right and top to bottom are: Mill Pond Press's "Pumpkin and Pines" graphic, Enesco Imports' "Rapunzel" and "Sleeping Beauty" dolls, the Edwin M. Knowles' "The Glamour of the Gibson Girl" doll and "Grandpa's Gift" plate and Swarovski America's stunning crystal chess set.

Annalee Mobilitee Dolls
A Unique Collectible

There is no collectible doll anywhere in the world quite like an Annalee collectible doll. Made of felt over a wire frame to allow the doll to be posed, each doll has a unique personality expressed through a cheery, hand-finished face.

A Family Business For Thirty Years

Annalee and Chip Thorndike began this amazing business after World War II when their chicken farm failed. Annalee is a native of Concord, New Hampshire and Chip, who attended Harvard, is from Boston. They had met when their families summered in Meredith, New Hampshire, and when they married in 1941 they settled in that lovely rural town and started a chicken farm. Business prospered during the war years, but when the post war era brought a serious slump Annalee turned to her hobby, doll making, to make ends meet. Her original dolls were all 10" tall and included skiers, dancers, fishermen, divers, and angels. Chip contributed to the effort by bending the wire forms of the dolls and the pieces of birch used for the skis, and by selling the dolls door to door!

Their first sales were in the display field, to department stores like Jordan Marsh, Macy's and Bambergers. Then in the mid 1950s, a major series was produced for the State of New Hampshire Department of Parks and Recreation. The dolls were all skiers and were used in a display extolling winter fun in the Granite State. They were first shown in New Hampshire state parks and then were displayed at Rockefeller Center in New York. This exposure, and the additional audience who saw the display when it traveled from coast to coast, brought new display customers, and aroused the interest of doll lovers, who recognized something unique in the whimsical, hand-brushed poseable dolls.

A later collection created for the Parks and Recreation Department featured dolls engaged in summer fun activities, and at the first Annalee Doll Auction in 1984 a Photographer Doll from that collection sold for $925, a sure sign that collectors love Annalee dolls.

From Chicken Farm to the Factory in the Woods

The business didn't take long to outgrow the Thorndike home. Gradually sheds, barns and chicken coops became manufacturing, packaging and photographing areas. Today a complex of new buildings including The Factory in the Woods, the Annalee Doll Museum, and a gift shop are all located on the site of the original chicken farm.

As the demand for Annalee dolls grew, so did the variety of characters in the collection. Santas were popular from the beginning, a natural occurrence when you consider that a primary focus was retail display. They are still an important Annalee doll, with Santa, Mrs. Claus, elves and reindeer all in the collection in sizes ranging from 3" to 4'. Skiers are another style that have been popular since early Annalee days, and other "people" designed by Annalee include a monk, leprechauns, Pilgrims and Indians, drummer boys, carollers, angels, and just plain kids.

Animals have always been a major part of any Annalee collection beginning with Santa's reindeer. Today's collection includes bunnies, chicks, ducks, kittens, Christmas geese, frogs and mice.

Whether human or animal, all Annalee characters have one thing in common: a whimsical, hand-finished face featuring round, rosy cheeks, laughing eyes and a smiling mouth.

Annalee's Gift Shop, nestled in the woods, is part of a complex of new buildings, all located on the site of the original chicken farm. A tent full of enthusiastic Annalee doll collectors are gathered together for the annual auction and barbecue.

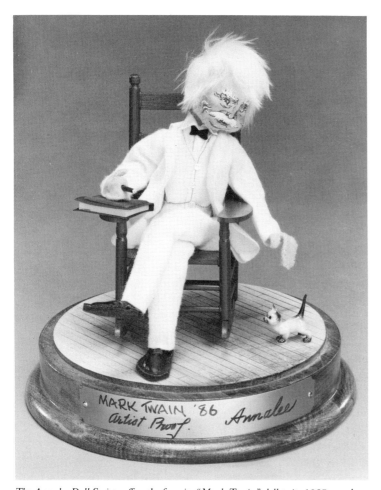

The Annalee Doll Society offers the favorite "Mark Twain" doll to its 1987 members. Similar exclusive dolls are offered to members each year.

Originally Annalee personally hand-painted every face. But as the business grew it became necessary to employ artists to do some of these finishing jobs. Every design, though, is still created by the artist, and her artist's proof is added to the Annalee Doll Museum collection once production has begun. Every phase of production, from the design through the fabricating of wire structures, the cutting and stitching of bodies and clothes, painting of faces, and even the making of accessories such as skis, bows and arrows, sleds and swings is done in The Factory in the Woods, where the Thorndikes now employ 300 people.

Annalee Doll Society Introduced

In 1983 the Annalee Doll Society was introduced, and by June of 1984 there were 2000 members, 450 of whom attended the first annual Society Barbecue. In addition to food, fun, and a tour of The Factory in the Woods and the Annalee Doll Museum, these collectors participated in the first annual auction, where the previously mentioned 1965 doll "The Photographer" sold for $925. Other remarkable prices at that first auction were a Boy Monkey with Banana Trapeze which sold in 1981 for $23.95 and was auctioned at $165, and a 22" Christmas Giraffe which had originally sold for $36.95 and brought $225.00 at auction.

Besides this opportunity to bid on retired Annalee dolls, members are invited to sell their own Annalee dolls at auction. This unusual club benefit not only makes rare dolls available to members; it effectively establishes the secondary market value of these dolls.

Other special opportunities available to members of the Society include a free gift of a Logo Doll, a doll with the adorable face pictured on Annalee letterhead and other printed material, and the chance to purchase limited edition pieces created by Annalee especially for Society members. There are two series being done for members only. The first is called *Folk Heroes* and currently features "Annie Oakley," "Mark Twain" and "Ben Franklin". The first figures, done in 1983 and 1984 and now retired, were "Johnny Appleseed" and "Robin Hood." Members may purchase one of each of these signed pieces, each made exclusively for that member and presented on a wooden base, under a glass dome. The second series is called *Annalee Annimals*™. Available in this series are a mother penguin and chick, a unicorn and a mother kangaroo with joey.

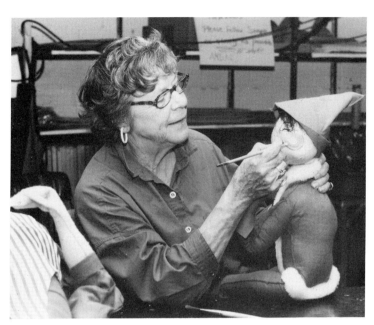

Only good little girls and boys make Santa's gift list, as depicted in the 10-inch "Santa with Toybag and Giftlist." Santa is personalized with a brass plaque, numbered and signed by Annalee.

Doll designer Annalee hand-brushes whimsical faces on one of her creations.

Also specially created, signed and dated, these are available to members in multiple quantities. The base and dome are available for Annalee Annimals™, but are sold separately.

Old Fashioned Values Are at the Heart of Annalee Dolls

Annalee Mobilitee Dolls of Meredith, New Hampshire is a business deeply rooted in family values. Run by Annalee and Chip for most of its thirty years, the company today now sees son Townsend Thorndike as President and Chief Executive Officer. It's a company that has seen its staff grow from 4 to 300, yet still considers itself a family. It's a company that produces thousands of dolls a year and still hears its collectors compare each face to the smiling face of Annalee herself. And it's a company that remembers its roots. As president Townsend Thorndike so well said, "It's a humbling experience as well as a great tribute to my parents to realize that a hobby started over 50 years ago has grown to a national phenomenon."

SARA KIRTLINK

Armstrong's
California Producer Attracts Top Talent

For over four decades, Armstrong's has been a leader in the field of collectibles. Armstrong's spacious gallery in downtown Pomona, California, has long been recognized as one of the nation's foremost repositories for collectible ceramic plates, fine porcelain figurines, crystal and limited edition lithographs.

Over the years, the company has grown in scope and reputation and in 1972, began manufacturing its own line of porcelain collector plates. Today, Armstrong's represents such distinguished American artists as Red Skelton, Walter Lantz, Sue Etem, Miguel Paredes, Alan D'Estrehan, and Lisette DeWinne.

The difficult task of transferring a great artist's work to a porcelain collector plate is under the personal supervision of company president David W. Armstrong. Involved in the fine arts and decor since his childhood, David Armstrong knows what the discriminating buyer looks for in choosing a collectible.

He understands that the best artisans must contribute at each step of production to create the highest quality collectibles. Each piece of art is sent to an atelier in Europe where master craftsmen duplicate the original artwork and create a delicate ceramic transfer. These are then returned to Armstrong's studio in Pomona and carefully baked onto porcelain plates in state-of-the-art kilns. Every plate is inspected for quality and color, then hand-trimmed in 24K gold.

Red Skelton Brings His Humor To Plates

With Armstrong's help, plate collectors have been introduced to a facet of comedian Red Skelton's talent of which his average fan might be unaware--his flair for art. Skelton has been painting in oils since the 1940s, selecting clowns primarily as his subjects. A self-taught artist, he likes to joke, "I had an idiot for a teacher."

Armstrong's suggestion that clowns would be a popular plate subject resulted in the issue of Skelton's "Freddie the Freeloader" in 1976, first in the *Famous Clowns* series.

Some Americans even know Skelton better for his plates than his comedy now. "I'll walk down the street and people will say to their kids, 'do you know who this is?' and the little kid will say 'no'...and the parent will say, 'this is Red Skelton' and the kid will say, 'oh, we have one of your plates,'" says Skelton, breaking into his famous dimpled grin.

"I do a concert or a fair and afterwards people bring their plates for me to sign. They take real pride in their plates. I love that!"

Skelton recognizes that most people cannot afford one of his oil paintings. A Skelton original can fetch anywhere from $35,000 to $75,000. "But almost everyone can afford one of my plates or figurines, " he says.

During a recent collector-plate signing session at his office in Rancho Mirage, California, Red commented on various aspects of modern life.

"It really bothers me," he said, "that a 10-year-old kid can find a drug pusher and the FBI can't." And why, he asks, "do they put handicapped parking stalls in front of liquor stores?" or "when you go to an eye, ear, nose and throat specialist, why do they charge you an arm and a leg?"

Bantering with his friend David Armstrong, the ebullient artist signed his latest collector plate, "Ironing the Waves." The commentary and signing continued simultaneously because Skelton doesn't believe in wasting time.

The 74-year-old performer makes time for painting from 10 p.m. to 2 a.m., when much of the rest of the world is ready to go to sleep. Thus far, he has created sixteen plates and seven figurines with Armstrong's. He delighted fans in 1986 when he personally signed 1,000 plates in gold for a sell-out Super Star edition of "Anyone For Tennis?" With Skelton's prolific output in all areas, collectors can expect to see more of his humorous art designed especially for them, exemplified by his newly released "Ironing the Waves."

Outstanding portrait artist Lisette DeWinne uses beautiful shades of blue and pink to skillfully capture "Katrina," the fourth plate in the Spring Flowers *series.*

The Infinite Love *series calls upon Sue Etem's experiences as a mother to capture the bond between mother and child. "A Pair of Dreams" portrays this precious moment of complete serenity.*

Two-Time Plate Artist of the Year Joins Armstrong's

"Have paint brush, will travel" may well be new Armstrong artist Sue Etem's personal motto. The popular artist has recently returned to the United States from a stimulating, year-long stay in Bahrain, a tiny island nation in the Arabian Gulf. She married Dr. Lawrence Bestmann there in December, 1985, and then stayed on to paint in a rich cross-cultural environment.

While her bridegroom worked with Sheikh Esa bin Mohamed Al-Khalifah as Adviser to Bahrain's General Organization for Youth and Sport, Etem immersed herself in the daily life of this peaceful Arab nation.

"As always, painting children helped me bridge the cultural gap," said the two-time Plate Artist of the Year. "To paraphrase Will Rogers, I never met a child I didn't love. Children in Bahrain were no different from the children of any other country and they became my happy subjects."

For almost a year, Sue Etem led a double life. One day painting Bahraini children...the next, dedicating paint and palette to American children. Under contract to Armstrong's, she had deadlines to meet. The series, appropriately titled *Infinite Love*, depicts the special love between mother and child. "A Pair of Dreams" begins the eight-plate series.

Family History Supports Patriotic Painter

Contributing to the international flavor of Armstrong's artists, French-born Alan D'Estrehan is one of America's most famous nautical artists. His credits include the United States Postal Service First Day Cover for the John Paul Jones commemorative stamp. Born in Nice on the French Riviera, Alan D'Estrehan is now an American citizen, and like the Statue of Liberty, represents a special gift to America from France. D'Estrehan traces his artistic roots to revered American artist John Singer Sargent.

All of D'Estrehan's paintings show the result of extensive research in museums and libraries to establish the accuracy of each detail. His knowledge of ships' structures, sails, and riggings comes from personal experience and study of technical data. His widely acclaimed Statue of Liberty plates and upcoming series on the U.S. Constitution exhibit some of his tremendous talents for the collectible market. All D'Estrehan's paintings exhibit a great love and respect for the period subjects he paints.

Paredes Favors "Spontaneous Realism"

Another Armstrong's find for the collectibles market, Mexican-born artist Miguel Paredes specializes in capturing people--on film, canvas, and in his mind's eye. His scrutiny of the actions of others once led him to think about being an actor rather

Freddie the Freeloader mounts an ironing board and assaults the surf in Red Skelton's "Ironing the Waves." The second issue in the Signature Collection, *it is strictly limited to 10,000 plates, the first 1,000 being signed in gold by Skelton.*

In commemoration of the 200th anniversary of our Constitution, naval artist and historian Alan D'Estrehan has created the "USS Constitution vs. Guerriere" from the U.S. Ship Constitution *series.*

Using bears from Rosemary and Paul Volpp's famous antique toy collection, nationally known photographer Robert Pearcy has created the artwork for "Tiddlywink and Pixie." The Buck Hill Bears *plate series features bears watching the playful antics of their feline and canine friends.*

than an artist, but fortunately for plate collectors, he changed directions.

His first plate series for Armstrong's, *Reflections of Innocence*, depicts toddlers walking hand-in-hand through the woods, romping in the spray of a garden hose, discovering ducklings splashing near an abandoned rowboat, and sharing secrets.

Paredes describes his style as "spontaneous realism," and paints in oil. "The individuality, the behavior and the sense of adventure create a certain unique quality. At the same time, I'm able to apply the techniques of my favorite old masters, Rubens and Rembrandt: direct light, composition and rich coloration."

At the age of sixteen, Paredes had achieved the stature of being a full time artist by working on commissions and selling his drawings by word of mouth. Hotel owners in Mexico City and in coastal towns, amazed by his talent, hired Paredes to design and paint murals for their buildings. In a few years, the young artist's paintings would be found in private collections throughout America, Canada, Alaska, England and Mexico.

The twenty-five-year-old Paredes moved to the United States in 1976 and soon was in demand as a portrait artist and muralist. In 1984 he was introduced to David Armstrong, who was impressed with his realism and subject matter.

In addition to the *Reflections of Innocence* series (with "Me and My Friend," "My Rainbeau," "Rowboat Rendezvous," and "Hatching a Secret"), Paredes has created art for two porcelain plaques issued by Armstrong's. The plaques, "The Stamp Collector" and "Mother's Pride," are made by a process originally developed by Armstrong's, using ceramic porcelain.

"What we're creating now is affordable art," says the Huntington Beach artist, holding an 11x14 inch framed plaque. "Most people can't afford the original canvas, so now they can own a reproduction with lasting quality that won't chip, fade or crack." (The plaques sell for $195, while an original Paredes oil painting sells for $6,000 or more.)

Paredes finds that the plate market offers wider exposure to artists than gallery exhibits, and has recently turned down offers to participate in major art festivals to devote as much time as possible to painting. His new adventure is mastering the art of sculpting. "My work is my world," he says. "If one spends time at anything he enjoys, he will be a success."

This could also describe David Armstrong's involvement (and success) in producing art for collectors. Armstrong's appreciation of quality collectibles continues to attract a team of artists who excite and please collectors.

SUSAN K. ELLIOTT

Artaffects, Ltd.
Gregory Perillo and Rob Sauber Create Original Masterworks for Vague Shadows and Curator Collection

Richard J. Habeeb has a special vision of porcelain art. And for more than a decade he has shared this vision with collectors through his exclusive commissions of some of American's foremost painters and sculptors.

Habeeb's continuing dream for his studio, Artaffects, Ltd., has been to present on porcelain the works of established masters—artists who already have established their credentials and are ranked at the top of their fields—be it in Native American art, romantic paintings, old-fashioned Americana, or murals.

With the commission of Gregory Perillo to create a lithograph called "Madre," Habeeb paved the way for the first-ever original lost wax bronze collector plate, "Buffalo Hunt," by Perillo—and the Artaffects legend began.

Native Americans Inspire Gregory Perillo

Perillo reigned as this generation's most prolific and gifted painter of Native Americans when Habeeb established the Vague Shadows division of Artaffects in 1977 to feature his works. Indeed, this brilliant artist has been fascinated by the American West and its inhabitants since his childhood in Staten Island, New York. There, Perillo's Italian immigrant father would entertain his family with Wild West tales.

As a young sailor in the U.S. Navy, Gregory Perillo had occasion to hitchhike west with a friend from Montana in search of the Old West in his father's stories. When he reached Indian country, Perillo was mistaken for a Native American, something which still happens often to the Italian artist. Somehow this incident solidifed his identification with this land's original settlers, and that first trip West changed Perillo's life. He vowed to develop his talent as an artist and his understanding of Indian history—and to share this view of America with the world.

Working as the only student of his idol and mentor, Western artist William R. Leigh, Perillo developed the active style and "spirit" that characterize his paintings today. Thus he was ready for his "big break" when renowned artist Bill Lawrence sponsored him into the Hudson Valley Art Association. This exposure soon led to national—and then international—fame.

Today, some years later, Gregory Perillo is represented in many of America's finest galleries nationwide. What's more, he has exhibited in successful one-man shows from New York to California, and in Colorado, Texas, and Palm Beach. In addition, the artist's works appear in permanent collections of a number of museums and institutions.

Vague Shadows Presents Perillo Works

The Perillo "Madre" lithograph that inaugurated Vague Shadows represented the first signed and numbered lighograph of the painter's work. It quickly sold out at an original issue price of $125 in an edition of 500.

The initial Vague Shadows/Perillo plate production was "Buffalo Hunt," also a first in that it was the premiere collector plate ever to be cast in bronze by means of the painstaking "lost wax" process. It was cast by the firm of Roman Bronze, which did foundry work for art master Frederic Remington.

This original collector plate was followed by the landmark *Chieftains* series, featuring a first plate called "Sitting Bull" which has appreciated in price from the original issue level of $65.00 to a current value of $550.

"Shining Star" is the first issue in The Perillo Christmas Series *offered by Vague Shadows. Indian youngsters have been a favorite subject for award-winning Gregory Perillo since childhood.*

Rob Sauber's romantic nature is readily apparent in his dramatic "Caroline" plate—premiere of the Portraits of American Brides *collection. This bride of the Old South descends a winding staircase as she prepares to meet her groom for a formal wedding on the lawn of her family's plantation. Sauber created the plate for Curator Collection.*

The Professionals plate series represented a change of pace for Perillo. He painted little children playing their favorite sports, beginning with "Big Leaguer" in 1979. This first plate in the grouping of six has risen in price from $29.95 to $135 today. The matching figurine, "Big Leaguer," was named "Figurine of the Year" by the National Association of Limited Edition Dealers in 1981.

Beyond graphics, plates and figurines, Perillo and Vague Shadows have developed innovative Christmas ornaments, a Nativity set and even a limited edition doll in recent years. The first limited edition annual Christmas ornament and first annual bell ornament were offered in 1985 with issues following in subsequent years. The 15-piece Perillo "Nativity" debuted in 1986, and the first Perillo doll, "Morningstar," sold out its limited edition quite promptly that same year.

Indian Children and Animals Stir Perillo's "Pride"

One of the most prominent recent Vague Shadows productions has been the *Pride of America's Indians* Plate Collection, presented in association with The Hamilton Collection. In this series of eight plates, Perillo portrays the Native Americans' special harmony

with the world around them—especially the animal kingdom. Each plate captures a youngster from a different, prominent North American tribe along with an animal or bird from this child's region.

The series began with "Brave and Free," a portrait of a Blackfoot boy and an eagle. The child wears the fringed natural buckskins of his tribe and a feather on his head—typical attire for these Plains Indians of Canada and Montana. He peers at the horizon with his eagle friend—a bird which symbolizes courage and survival to his people. After more than 30 years as a painter of Native Americans, Perillo has offered this series as a stirring tribute to the American Indian way of life.

"Brave and Free" received the coveted Silver Chalice Award as Plate of the Year in 1987 at the Pasadena Plate and Collectible Show. It was also voted Plate of the Year by the readers of *Plate World* Magazine. "Brave and Free" and Perillo were cited by the National Association of Limited Edition Dealers and given achievement awards in both the Plate of the Year and Artist of the Year categories.

The Romance of Rob Sauber and Curator Collection

Since 1979, another division of Artaffects, Ltd., has showcased the artwork of outstanding American

painters who have achieved recognition in specific fields of art. Prominent among these is Rob Sauber, who has been lauded as this nation's "Master of Romantic Art."

Sauber, who works in sight of the Statue of Liberty from his studio in Brooklyn, New York, invests many hours of research in each of his richly evocative paintings. His study of history, fashion, poetry and music add dimension to his works. Yet the romantic vision of the man shines through, no matter what theme he selects.

Already established as a celebrated illustrator and fine art painter when Richard Habeeb approached him with the concept of porcelain plates, Sauber was intrigued by this new medium of expression. His extraordinary ability to deal with romantic subjects was immediately evident to plate collectors when Sauber debuted the *How Do I Love Thee* series, which drew its inspiration from the romantic poets. Next was *Songs of Stephen Foster*, capturing the romantic essence of the American master's song compositions such as "Oh! Susannah."

But never is Sauber's unabashed romanticism more evident than in the widely acclaimed *Portraits of American Brides*, a series of eight porcelain collector plates featuring American brides of various well-known fashion and historical eras. The series began with "Caroline" the classic Southern belle, who descends the staircase of her family's opulent plantation wearing a hooped skirt and cinched-in waistline in the tradition of Scarlett O'Hara. Other brides from Colonial times to the present day share the universal joy of weddings even as they chronicle the ever-changing fashions of this nation's 200-plus years.

Most recently, Rob Sauber has designed a grouping of ten elegant 10 ¼″ porcelain plates for Curator Collection, featuring artwork appropriate for all of the major gift-giving occasions. These include "The Wedding," "The Anniversary," "Happy Birthday," "Home Sweet Home," "Christening," "Motherhood," "Fatherhood," "Sweethearts," "Sweet Sixteen," and "All Adore Him." Each of these plates comes with a handsome gift box and an indelible pen for personalizing the specially designed backstamp

The Great Train *series represents Jim Duneen's first appearance on fine porcelain plates. "Sante Fe" is a good example of Duneen's careful detailing and complete authenticity.*

so each purchaser can create a "porcelain greeting card" that will last forever.

Artaffects, Ltd. Continues Its Tradition of Excellence

Richard Habeeb searches constantly for art masters whose works will translate well to the porcelain collector plate medium. Among those he has commissioned in recent years are Jim Deneen, painter of trains and other modes of transportation; Alton S. Tobey, a painter, muralist and teacher; George A. Malick, an artist who captures Americana on canvas in the tradition of Norman Rockwell; and Maurizo Goracci, better known as Ma Go, one of the foremost painters of children in the world. With these artists as well as Perillo and Sauber, Artaffects, Ltd. and its Vague Shadows and Curator Collection divisions continue striving to provide collectible art masterworks of lasting appeal and increasing value.

SUSAN K. JONES

Bessie Pease Gutmann
A New Generation Discovers the Warmhearted Charm of "Bessie's Children"

America's children of the 1920s were brought up with Bessie Pease Gutmann. Visit most any nursery, Sunday School room or playroom of that era, and Mrs. Gutmann's endearing pastel prints could be found gracing the walls. Her paintings so captured the imagination of both youngsters and parents that her fame soon spread to England and across Europe as well.

Mrs. Gutmann's paintings are deceptively simple, in that they have endured for generations as timeless depictions of childhood mischief, friendship and adventure. And now that the youngsters of the 1920s are grandparents, these original paintings by Mrs. Gutmann have rekindled strong interest in the gifted painter's works.

The artist's continued popularity stems from the combination of her exceptional talent and her determination to depict happy children exactly as they are: sometimes naughty, sometimes disheveled, but always pink-cheeked, plump and delightful. Her works are like a breath of fresh air to viewers who have grown accustomed to seeing children portrayed as solemn, formally dressed, miniature adults.

Bessie Pease Gutmann Collector Prints and Plates

Seventy years ago, the most prevalent medium for affordable art by beloved artists was that of graphic prints. Indeed, Mrs. Gutmann's own prints of "A Little Bit of Heaven" and "The Awakening" brought her international fame as they were distributed here and abroad.

Today her sunny paintings continue to please collectors all over the world. In fact, Mrs. Gutmann's prints have seen a revival of interest over the past fifteen years. A number of her graphics have multiplied at least ten times in value since 1971, and various reports point to print price increases of as much as 5000% from the 1920s to the present.

But original Bessie Pease Gutmann prints today are quite rare, and difficult to obtain in mint condition. And thus demand for affordable renderings of Mrs. Gutmann's "classics" has inspired two recent series of limited-edition collector plates, with more plates—and hand-painted figurines—to come in the near future.

A Child's Best Friend

One foresighted United States-based firm was fortunate enough to secure rights to all copyrighted Bessie Pease Gutmann artwork, and thus these collector plates may be produced in truly limited editions. That firm is Balliol Corporation, which has selected The Hamilton Collection to create collector plates showcasing some of Mrs. Gutmann's most memorable works on porcelain.

The first of these plates, "In Disgrace," premiered the *A Child's Best Friend* collection. "In Disgrace," is typical of Bessie Pease Gutmann's lively gift: it depicts a little girl and her faithful dog, standing in the corner as punishment for their transgressions in Mother's flower garden. With her chubby arms and legs, brunette curls glinting with gold and droopy socks over blue Mary Jane shoes, this tiny child could melt the heart of any parent or grandparent. And her dog, Rusty, looks so repentant and ashamed that his naughty flower-pulling in the garden must surely be forgiven!

The series of eight plates continues with "The Reward," in which the little girl's punishment is over and she celebrates with an ice cream cone. For his loyalty in time of crisis, the child rewards Rusty with a lick of her cone.

"The Awakening," along with its companion print, "A Little Bit of Heaven," was said to be found in most every home in the United States in the 1920s.

This 1917 print entitled "A Little Bit of Heaven" brought Bessie Pease Gutmann international fame.

A Child's Best Friend Plate Collection features six more Bessie Pease Gutmann originals—each presented for the first time in limited edition collector plate form. Each captures a special moment between a child and a pet—just as it might have occurred under Mrs. Gutmann's watchful eye.

The Gutmann Precious Portraits

In addition to her "action" paintings of youngsters involved in mischief or adventure, Bessie Gutmann prided herself on the ability to capture the personality and joy of youngsters in close-up facial portraits. Some of the most memorable of these inspired a second recent collector plate series entitled *Precious Portraits.*

"Sunbeam" premiered this collection with a rosy-cheeked, blonde-haired youngster brimming with life and happiness. Her eyes gleam as she smiles sweetly toward her viewer, yet her fun-loving nature is readily apparent. She seems ready to toss her golden curls and run off to join her friends at play any moment.

Each of the *Precious Portraits* captures a little girl with a different personality, appearance and style—some dark-haired, some long-haired, some short-haired...some with brown eyes and some with blue. Some appear pensive while others smile broadly. All in all, Mrs. Gutmann has portrayed the charm and individuality which attracted her to childhood subjects throughout her working life as an artist.

Wife, Mother, Aunt and Artist

A bit of research into Bessie Pease Gutmann's personal history reveals the source of her incredible understanding of youngsters, and her ability to capture these little people in true-to-life poses and situations.

As a young woman, Mrs. Gutmann trained at the Philadelphia School of Design for Women, the Chase School of Art and the Art Students' League. She married Helmuth Gutmann, who owned his own art publishing business, and from then on shared both personal and professional life with her husband.

Over the years, the Gutmanns formed a wonderful partnership and a happy home. They raised a family of three children while she painted and he published her works, which included paintings, prints, magazine covers, illustrations, advertisements, calendars and cards.

During Mrs. Gutmann's prime of the 1920s and 1930s she was interviewed and much sought-after by those who admired her works. For today's collectors, rediscovering the art of this wonderful painter, records of these interviews provide a fascinating insight.

"I perfer originating subjects to illustrating incidents already begotten," said the artist in 1927. "I love children and I love to sketch them. Sometimes I have taken to making pictures of children when asleep—the only time when they may really be said to rest, and it is a curious coincidence that one of my most popular pictures shows a child fast asleep hugging a Teddy Bear."

Mrs. Gutmann, a devoted mother and aunt, kept her camera ready at all times to capture special moments of the youngsters around her—whether during waking hours or sleep. Her method of work was very disciplined, beginning in mid-morning and con-

Bessie Pease Gutmann's marvelous understanding of children and their adventures shines through in this collector plate from Balliol and The Hamilton Collection. "In Disgrace" chronicles the aftermath of a little girl's mishap with her dog, in which the pair dug up Mother's flower garden "by mistake."

The saga of "In Disgrace" continues with "The Reward," second issue in the A Child's Best Friend Plate Collection. Here, the little girl shares her ice cream cone with her canine pal, Rusty, in thanks for his loyalty when she was "In Disgrace."

The fresh innocence of childhood is never more apparent than in Bessie Pease Gutmann's "Sunbeam" plate—one of eight paintings of little girls chosen from the Gutmann archives for the Precious Portraits Plate Collection.

tinuing until late afternoon. For each painting she would start with tiny sketches—no larger than a postage stamp—from which she would select the best interpretation. Then this "thumbnail" sketch would inspire a full-size pencil sketch, and ultimately the final painting.

Critical Praise Echos Collectors' Delight

Not long after the publication of "A Little Bit of Heaven" earned Mrs. Gutmann an international reputation, art critics began to recognize her work for its unique qualities. As one English magazine of her day asserted:

"The true delineator of child-life is so rare that little wonder may be expressed at the increasing attention which the work of Mrs. Bessie Pease Gutmann is attracting. Her studies of children are now almost as well known in Europe as across the water. She is an artist whose work has been very little influenced by other masters and whose style is founded upon that of no other painter. Her work is free and unconventional—her children are flesh-and-blood children with nothing of the wingless angel about them. She paints youth full of life, beauty, full of the spirit of infancy and the gaiety of early years."

Seven decades later that spirit and gaiety still attract collectors and critics in equal measure. And with more Bessie Pease Gutmann limited edition plates and figurines on the horizon for Balliol and The Hamilton Collection, it appears that "Bessie's children" will continue to enchant us with their innocence and joy for many years to come.

SUSAN K. JONES

Brad Bennett
Historical Artist Captures the "Color" of Twentieth Century America

The year is 2087. A group of friends has gathered after work for cocktails. They stand in the middle of an ultramodern apartment, with computer-generated Bach flowing from speakers just slightly smaller than the heads of pins.

"I see you have some old books," a young man says to the hostess. He gestures with his hand toward two well-stocked shelves on the far wall. "They look like they must be very valuable."

"Yes, I believe they are," replies the hostess. "But one set is especially valuable." She walks toward the shelves, where she reaches for an attractive, slightly worn boxed volume. "This is part of an historic chronicle of life in the latter half of the Twentieth Century," she says. "There are ten complete volumes—of limited edition prints and accompanying writings. But what makes them very special is that they were done by Brad Bennett—one of the foremost limited-edition historical artists of his day. As a result, they capture a lot more than detail and appearance of their subjects. They capture the 'color' of the times...the 'feel' of each place they portray. As I said, it is a very valuable set, and I'm not just referring to its appraised value. These volumes have been in my family for several generations, and they reflect an important part of our heritage as Americans. I wouldn't part with them for the world."

An Epic Project

We travel back one hundred years, to 1987. Brad Bennett is standing before his easel in a town square in a small southern community. It is one more stop on a ten-year odyssey that will take the artist back and forth across America, many times and in many seasons. When he is finished, his chronicle of our times, "The United States of America," will portray the people, places, and things that make our country special—from a relaxed Hawaiian beach scene to a churning oil refinery in Houston, from an abandoned lighthouse off the coast of Maine to a small-town motorcycle patrolman.

"The personal challenge brought about by a project of this magnitude is obvious," the artist says. "But I view it more for its importance to Americana and American history. It has been more than 100 years since anyone has attempted a chronicle even close to this in scope, and that was John James Audubon's two volumes on the "Birds of America." My challenge is to create something that will endure equally well—to give the world artistic and historical works that will withstand the so-called ravages of time."

The Artist's Midwestern Roots

Already, Brad Bennett is well known for his evocative historical portraits of Middle America—where the artist developed his unique talents. Bennett is a native of Kenosha, Wisconsin, and a graduate of the University of Wisconsin. After working for several years as a graphic designer, Bennett further demonstrated his talent by premiering his first Midwestern scenes in watercolor. Success was quick to follow, as Bennett received honors from state and national shows. In addition, his works came to be shown in museums throughout the country, the Wisconsin Watercolor Society, the New York Art Directors Club, the Society of Illustrators in New York, and a major national exhibition, "American Vision," at the Union League Club of Chicago.

In time, Bennett's unique suites of historic lithographs won him recognition as one of America's "ten best book illustrators." Today, his works are sought by private and corporate collectors, and five completed suites of his prints are registered as historic works by the Library of Congress in Washington, D.C.

"Harvest Time" (top) and "Blizzard" (bottom) are among twelve new titles making up Volume II of Brad Bennett's epic suite, "The United States of America." Ten successive volumes of signed and numbered prints, along with accompanying narratives by the artist, will be issued annually to present a comprehensive pictorial record of late-twentieth century America.

A Major Undertaking

"The United States of America" series already represents some of Brad Bennett's finest work as a painter and writer. (Volume One was published in 1986.) But it will also be remembered as the artist's most ambitious project. Over ten years of research and travel will be required as Bennett works to document "America's cities, rural communities, lifestyles, and cultural events." As a result, collectors are talking of the suite's historic value, because the enormous scope of this project alone ensures its status as a unique historical record—and as a on-of-a-kind collector's item.

Volume I of "The United States of America" suite is seen here in its attractive and durable slipcase. Each of the ten volumes will be issued in this manner, making it easy for collectors to protect and enjoy these valuable acquisitions for years to come.

Each volume of the series will feature an introduction, a title page, twelve prints, and twelve narratives, making a total of 26 pages. The prints will measure 15" x 21" to the edge of the paper and 12" x 18" for the centered image size. In addition, each print will be numbered and signed by the artist, and each will be embossed in the lower left corner with a seal of authenticity.

The paper used for the prints will be "Mirage Plate"—a 100% acid-free rag paper made from cotton fibers. The special qualities of this paper—which are not found in papers made from wood pulp—will guarantee the longevity of each print, ensuring that generations of Americans will enjoy these heirloom-quality works. "Art Print Vellum" sheets will be used for the narrative text pages. This paper—also 100% acid-free—has been specially commissioned by the mill for this production only, adding to the exclusivity of the finished suite.

Of course, great care will also be taken with the color printing of this special limited edition suite. Working from the original watercolors and egg tempera paintings, color separation specialists will create negatives utilizing the latest technology available, including computer operated lasers. Zinc plates will be used in the multi-color lithography printing process, which also involves state-of-the-art computer technology.

Of greatest importance, however, Brad Bennett will oversee the production of these prints at every step, to make sure that the integrity of his original paintings is perfectly preserved. As a result of his careful observation and participation—and his insistence upon using the finest methods and equipment available—the archival quality of this production is assured.

A Once-in-a-Lifetime Opportunity for Collectors

"The United States of America" is a genuine "first" in the field of fine art publishing, because of its historical and social significance. Only recently, the U.S. State Department announced that the volumes of prints will be used as protocol gifts. Furthermore, like much of Bennett's earlier work, the suite will be registered as "a work of history" by the U.S. Library of Congress, certifying it as a valuable historical record as well as a work of fine art.

For these and other reasons, many collectors will consider acquiring the entire suite of prints for its investment potential. But for most collectors, this potential will be only a minor consideration, because these collectors will have no intention of parting with the series, regardless of price appreciation. Rather, these collectors will purchase "The United States of America" suite for their own pleasure—and with the knowledge that this unique historical record will remain in their families for generations to come—even through 2087 and beyond.

TOM L. JONES

"Fourth of July," the first print from Volume I of the series, is already a much-sought-after collectible. Like other prints from the suite-in-progress, the work strives to capture the "feel" of a place and event, as well as the realism and detail.

Duncan Royale
The "Story Telling Company" Creates Its Own
Saga of Success

Horns protrude from beneath his long, dark hair, and he dresses entirely in black. The book in his hand contains the names of children, and it tells him which ones have been good—and which ones have been bad. These naughty children are the ones that bring a malevolent glint to his eyes—for these are the children who will accompany him on his travels through the netherworld.

He is Black Peter—a medieval Dutch portrayal of the Devil. But more surprisingly, he is one of the colorful characters depicted in Duncan Royale's acclaimed *History of Santa Claus* figurine and plate collections. For, as thousands of delighted collectors have learned, the legend of Black Peter is one of several folk stories that helped to inspire our present-day Santa Claus tradition.

A Breakthrough Collection

In the giftware industry for 28 years, Duncan Royale has become known as the "story telling company." In 1983, the California-based company introduced the series for which it is now best known: the landmark *History of Santa Claus*. Years of research and preparation had preceded the series' premiere, as President Max Duncan and his associates visited libraries throughout the country, including the Library of Congress in Washington, DC, and consulted with hundreds of Christmas memorabilia collectors.

Once the research had been compiled, Santa Ana attorney Jim Bates organized the information into book form. *The History of Santa Claus* was published by Duncan Royale in 1983 in an attractive full-color table-top format. The book has since been expanded, to reflect the growth of the series.

The series itself now consists of twenty-four beautifully crafted and handpainted porcelain figurines. Each of these artworks depicts a mythical or historical figure that contributed in some way to our present Santa Claus story. The overall history spans the period from 2,000 B.C. to the twentieth century.

The characters depicted in *The History of Santa Claus* were known for their gift giving, an act that obviously inspired our present Christmas tradition. But as the aforementioned "Black Peter" reminds us, not all of them were known for their goodness. Indeed, Black Peter delivered presents only because St. Nicholas had the power to imprison him for one day each year. And, as we have learned, Peter took greater delight in punishing the naughty and lazy children.

But all of the characters depicted by Duncan Royale's master artisans have one thing common for modern collectors and history buffs: they are fascinating. "Dedt Moroz," or "Father Ice," made his debut in an ancient Russian bedtime story, in which the character took pity on a child abandoned in the forest by an uncaring stepmother. The "Medieval Santa Claus," on the other hand, was a combination of the Christian St. Nicholas and the Norse god Odin, from whom Santa inherited his long white beard and, later, his ability to fly. Santa, to the medieval Europeans, was an eccentric nomad who wandered from village to village, offering gifts—and hope—to the poor and needy.

Fortunately for collectors and folklore enthusiasts, Duncan Royale's figurines are every bit as colorful and endearing as the legends and historical figures that inspired them. The figurines, which vary in height from 8″ to 12″, are also distinguished by their crisp features—the result of Duncan Royale's coldcasting process, which takes about twenty-four hours for each porcelain figurine. In addition, each figurine boasts a special solid brass plate, identifying its historical origins, its individual registration number, and the name of the sculptor. The edition was strictly limited to 10,000 worldwide for each figurine.

The "Medieval Santa Claus" wandered across Europe, bringing gifts to the poor and needy. Although this legendary figure had developed from the Christian tale of St. Nicholas, the now-familiar white beard was borrowed from the Norse legend of Odin.

"Dedt Moroz" was known in Russian fairy tales as the savior of a poor girl left to freeze in the cold by a cruel stepmother. "Father Ice," as he is also called, showered the girl with fine gifts, which led to his association with the Christmas gift-giving tradition.

Renowned Artist Creates "Santa" Plate Series

To accompany the successful figurine collection, Duncan Royale commissioned the well-known plate artist Susie Morton to create a complementary series of 8½" porcelain collector plates. The artwork for these plates depicts each colorful "Santa" character within an accurate historical or mythical setting.

Duncan Royale also introduced a popular Miniature Pewter collection, depicting *The History of Santa Claus.* These figurines, created by specially trained sculptors, measured 2¾" in height and were painted by hand. The figurines sold for $30.00 each, and they were also available in unpainted fine pewter for $20.00 each.

Exciting New "Clown" Series

Continuing the tradition of excellence associated with the "Santa Claus" series, Duncan Royale has announced the introduction of a collection that will acquaint collectors with yet another fascinating history lesson: that of everyone's favorite circus performer, the clown. Twelve hand-painted porcelain figurines will make up the initial offering, with each sculpture depicting an historic clown or entertainer who contributed to our present picture of the clown.

The History of Clowns Collection is a salute to the noble people who give us the gift of laughter. Since the beginning of time, man has found the absurd, the ridiculous and the unexpected a source and a tool for amusement. The masters of these tools have evolved from early Greco-Roman stage performers to the wild "made-up" clowns of today. It has been said "laughter is close to tears" and indeed often the response to our world's pains has been a new form of comedy. As the early court Jester influenced the minds of kings and even changed the course of his-

The Devil may seem out of place in a history of Santa Claus, but in Dutch legends from the middle ages, ol' "Black Peter" was imprisoned at Christmas time by St. Nicholas and forced to deliver presents to the good boys and girls.

tory, we see a joke or a bit of satire is often a reflection of feelings close to heart. Under the makeup or behind the mask there has always been and will be a feeling of the artist capturing our fears, worries, frustrations, absurdities and sorrows and casting them to the wind of laughter.

Behind every smile, every booming laugh is a heritage of comedy, a history of men and places who mirror ourselves and identify with our human condition. This series of fine sculptures — including "Pulcinella" who was the antagonistic, slapstick player in France's Commedia del Arte in the 1400s — is a salute and memorium to the men who have changed the face of the world from a frown to a smile, — our friends, the clowns.

Each of the figurines in this new series will be cold-cast to perfectly preserve the features and details of the artist's original sculpture. Moreover, the skilled artisans of Duncan Royale will hand paint each of the finished pieces, a process that will be supervised by Max Duncan and the original artists. Each figurine will be limited to only 20,000 worldwide, and the edition will be accompanied by the publication of a handsome, full-color *History of Clowns* book.

TOM L. JONES

Enesco
Company With Insight Makes U.S. Collectible History With the Precious Moments® Collection

Collecting interest was at a fever pitch in the late seventies when Enesco introduced the first 21 Precious Moments figurines. Based on a line of inspirational greeting cards designed by Sam Butcher and Bill Biel, the collection debuted in the fall of 1978 and quickly became an enduring hit. Enesco President Eugene Freedman saw something special in the duo's religious art, but it is doubtful that even he anticipated the enormous success that would greet Precious Moments porcelains.

The figurines depict small children with big tear-drop shaped eyes and titles such as "God Understands," "Love is Kind" and "God Loveth A Cheerful Giver". Decorated in delicate pastel shades, the distinctive, hand-painted bisque porcelains with their uplifting messages instantly touched a chord in collectors across the country.

Popularity of Precious Moments Collection Grows

Rather than peaking after a few years and fading away, Precious Moments Collectibles continued to grow in popularity. Enesco developed a club for collectors, various magazines appeared focusing on the subject, and conventions were created just for Precious Moments afficionados.

As new collections of Precious Moments figures were issued each year, collectors began to avidly search for the first issues. Many would go to small towns or out-of-the-way shops to look on the dusty shelves of retailers who might not be fully aware of the collecting craze. Beginning in 1981, the addition of an identifying Christian symbol for each year (dove, anchor, cross, etc.) made it possible to date pieces. The figures produced in 1979 and 1980 carry no marks.

How did this marvel develop? In the beginning, 1970 to be exact, two young artists joined forces, blending their talents for drawing and creative design. This harmony of ability extended to their personal relationship, which paralleled that of the Biblical friends Jonathan and David. Eventually Sam and Bill formed the Jonathan and David greeting card company in Grand Rapids, Michigan, as a way of spreading their message of God's love.

Then, one of their cards found its way to Los Angeles and into the hands of a man from Chicago, the visionary Eugene Freedman, president of Enesco, a leading gift and collectible company based in Illinois.

Known as "The Quiet Giant" of the giftware and collectibles industry, Enesco was founded in 1960. With headquarters in Elk Grove Village, just west of Chicago's O'Hare Airport, Enesco maintains eleven showrooms throughout the country to service thousands of dealers from card shops to department stores.

Enesco Collections Offer Variety

The company's creativity is evidenced in a wide array of predominantly porcelain bisque and ceramic giftware—GARFIELD® by Jim Davis, Lucy & Me™ by Lucy Rigg, Country Cousins®, Treasured Memories®, "Miceville," "'57 Heaven" by Plymouth, Inc., limited editions by noted American doll artist Faith Wick and limited edition wildlife sculptures by Fred Aman, to name a few.

With the keen eye of two decades of experience, Gene Freedman appreciated the promise of Sam Butcher's art. In his mind's eye, Gene added a third dimension to Sam's Precious Moments images and visualized a figurine of irresistible charm.

In 1978, Freedman convinced the reticent Butcher that Enesco could do justice to the artist's Precious Moments images in porcelain bisque sculptures, and that the company's integrity would complement the love Butcher put into his art.

"He Walks with Me," 1987 Easter Seal commemorative figurine, was inspired by a meeting between Sam Butcher and a child benefiting from the local Chicago Easter Seal Society. After speaking with this bright youngster at Enesco International Headquarters, Butcher said, "I was amazed at the inner peace this little one possessed." The Enesco fundraising drive raised over $250,000 to benefit the disabled.

Collector response was immediate and strong. In 1981, Enesco sponsored the formation of the Precious Moments Collectors Club to supply a forum for avid collectors to communicate, exchange information and learn more about the collection. Club membership swelled to 5,000 in just six weeks, and burgeoned to 69,000 by the end of the charter year. Within 18 months of inception, membership was 100,000 strong! Current membership is well over a quarter of a million collectors.

Awards Pour In

Another important milestone in the history of Enesco and the Precious Moments Collection came in July 1984. The National Association of Limited Edition Dealers (NALED) selected Enesco to receive a host of prestigious awards. Presented at the dealers' annual banquet during the International Plate Collectors Convention in South Bend, Indiana, the honors included three First Place awards: Figurine of the Year, Vendor of the Year and Manufacturer of the Year. NALED members also voted the Precious Moments Collection first runner-up for Collectible of the Year.

In 1985, the Precious Moments porcelains walked away with the award NALED Executive Di-

rector Ray Keifer termed, "the highest award in the collectible field"—Collectible of the Year. Enesco also garnered Doll of the Year for "Kristy" and Vendor of the Year. These laurels are an important milestone in the company's history because they have undeniably and officially established the impeccable credentials of the Precious Moments Collection.

In 1986, Enesco and the Precious Moments Collection took NALED awards for Vendor of the Year, first runner-up for Collectible of the Year, first runner-up for the Figurine of the Year, second runner-up for Artist of the Year for Sam Butcher, and second runner-up for Producer of the Year.

Birthday Club for Children

Enesco opened another avenue of collecting with the introduction of the Precious Moments Birthday Club in late 1985. A Precious Moments Birthday Series (a circus parade of animals) for children attracted membership of over 77,000 in the first year.

The company's philosophy is that these works of art are communicators—messengers of love, hope, humor and optimism. In their various forms—figurines, plates, bells and ornaments—these figures of boys and girls with soulful, teardrop eyes evoke a knowing nod of instant recognition in the beholder. They weave themselves into the very fabric of collectors' daily lives, so in touch are they with twentieth century life in all respects.

The Man Behind The Art

Creator of the Precious Moments line, Sam Butcher, is a devoutly religious man who considers himself an "artist in the work of the Lord". In keeping with his philosophies, Butcher draws inspiration for his art from "love—spiritual love—for other people." According to Sam, "I use children as the subject matter because I feel they are an example of the purity and innocence of God's love."

Working in a combination of chalk, watercolor, poster colors and pencils, Sam's artistic gifts are enhanced by his humorous approach to his subjects. "Hello, Lord, It's Me Again," featuring a small boy with a telephone to his ear, is typical of the light touch he uses.

Collectors feel great affection for the artist, and often offer suggestions for future subjects. In 1984, evolving from collectors' desires, Butcher created the first dated Precious Moments Christmas figurine. The subject is an angelic maiden, 1984 dated carol book in hand, singing Christmas carols. Another suggestion resulted in an international nativity set, "For

God So Loved the World," featuring multi-racial figures emphasizing the universality of the spirit of Christmas.

Japanese Sculptor Becomes Co-Partner in Creation Process

To translate Butcher's art into three-dimensional form, Enesco relies on the talents of Japanese master sculptor Yasuhei Fujioka. It required a leap of faith for Butcher to believe that Fujioka could capture his subjects as accurately as the sculptor has been able to do. The two artists have developed what president Freedman describes as "a heart to heart communication" that transcends the barriers of language.

Working from Butcher's original drawing, Fujioka models moist clay into the general form of the subject. Then, striving for perfection, he deftly works the clay—adding and subtracting material—until a fully-dimensional sculpture emerges as the embodiment of not only the shape but also the spirit of Sam's art. Thus begins the process that creates the collectibles so sought by collectors around the world.

Unlikely Background

Part of what makes the Enesco/Precious Moments story so remarkable is Sam Butcher's background. Before he found his devoted audience of figurine collectors, he was struggling to feed an ever-growing family (he and wife Katie have seven children) in the "chalk ministry"—preaching of God's love to children, using illustrations he drew on a blackboard as a teaching aid. The pay was low, so he also worked as a janitor to make ends meet.

He recalls, with a laugh, "I scrubbed so many floors, and I'm glad because the Lord had me down on my knees and I had plenty of time to pray for others."

Today, he and his family live outside Carthage, Missouri. Sam and friend Bill Biel have amicably dissolved their partnership to pursue separate paths. Butcher travels throughout the country for occasional special appearances, and periodically to the Orient to consult with Fujioka and the Enesco artisans who craft the Precious Moments collectibles.

One of his recent projects has been the building of a Precious Moments chapel on his Missouri farm. Inspired by a visit to the Sistine Chapel a few years ago, Butcher says, "It's something I can work on for the rest of my life. This will be my special refuge where I can sort of get away from the business side of things." The forty-foot-high chapel will be open to

Indiana resident Eleanor Strahm watches creator of Precious Moments™ subjects, Sam Butcher, autograph the T-shirt she received from Precious Moments master sculptor Yasuhei Fujioka on her visit to the Precious Moments Design Studio in Japan earlier this year. Ms. Strahm was among 2,500 enthusiasts who heard Butcher tell his special rendering of "The Christmas Story" during the Twelfth International Plate & Collectible Exposition.

"This is The Day Which the Lord Hath Made" is the long awaited complete wedding party figurine on a base which became available in spring of 1987. All members of the wedding party are featured along with their favorite pets. This wonderful bridal commemorative is limited to the year of introduction and crafted only in 1987.

the public and available for weddings. Although he does not intend the chapel to be a tourist attraction, he asks, "If you can bless someone, why not?"

In describing the appeal of Precious Moments subjects, Butcher explains that he was trained as a fine artist, but that he finds special fulfillment in his current art. "The beauty of Precious Moments art is that it cuts across every possible level...both the expert and the person who doesn't understand art. People can see themselves in Precious Moments. They can relate them to their life experience."

Enesco has carried through with its promise to Butcher that the company would capture the spirit of his art, and people who had never given a thought to collecting before have been the beneficiaries—with a whole world of special art to enrich their daily lives.

SUSAN K. ELLIOTT

Emmett Kelly, Jr.
Clowning Around Second Nature
for Performer Emmett Kelly, Jr.

Emmett Kelly, Jr. was many things before he followed in his famous father's footsteps and became a clown.

Emmett's father, Emmett Kelly, Sr. was, of course, a world famous circus performer who developed the "Weary Willie" character. Emmett Sr.'s career spanned over forty years including stints with Ringling Brothers and almost every major circus. Emmett's mother also performed as a high wire aerialist.

As a child, Emmett toured with his circus-performing parents until he was old enough to attend school. He then lived with his grandmother in Hoopeston, Illinois, while going to school in Mulberry Grove. After his parents divorced when he was nine, Emmett began living year-round with relatives throughout the country. Because of his nomadic childhood, Kelly wanted to be a Greyhound bus driver when he grew up. "They were nice to me."

Emmett, Jr. — "The King of the Road"

Just recently Emmett fulfilled a life-long desire of owning his own Classic Greyhound bus. Several years ago, while on tour in Dallas for Flambro Imports, Emmett spotted an ad in the classifieds for a vintage 1947 Greyhound "Silversides." Quickly striking a deal with the owner, Emmett drove the bus home and began a major restoration job.

After he finished restoring the side panels and paint job, Emmett, the inveterate wheeler-dealer saw an ad for a 1951 Greyhound, "Shrimp Boat," nicknamed so because the sides look like the hulls in wooden shrimp boats. This bus had already been totally restored, both inside and out. The interior was finished in comfortable motor home fashion with a kitchen, living room, bedroom, and bathroom. After some very difficult negotiation, Emmett finally was able to conclude the deal by trading his 1947 Greyhound, semi, and tractor trailer rig for the "Shrimp Boat."

So today, Emmett is not only the "Clown Prince of Pantomine," but also the "King of the Road" cruising America in his own Classic Greyhound. In the true fashion of Circus, Emmett and his wife, Nancy, are now traveling to the various personal appearances and Circus dates by bus.

Tracing Emmett, Jr.'s Roots

After school, Kelly went into the Navy for almost three years. He participated in three invasions, including Okinawa and Iwo Jima, during his naval career.

Released from the Navy, Kelly took advantage of the G.I. Bill and learned auto mechanics before joining the Chesapeake and Ohio Railroad as a switchtender. Kelly stayed with C & O for nine years before "boredom set in", and he "decided to go clowning."

By the time Emmett began his new career, his father was winding down his own very successful clown career. In order to keep the tradition alive, father and son both agreed that Emmett, Jr. should continue the character and performances. Thus, "Like Father, Like Son" has been the motto and creed of the second generation, and the quality performances continue for clown lovers everywhere.

After his debut in the late 1950's with the three-day Circus City Festival in Peru, Indiana, Kelly was asked to perform in Austin's Motor Derby. "We averaged 458 miles a day traveling from show to show," Kelly said. Many times, he said, they traveled through the night, arriving just hours before a show would begin.

In 1964, Kelly gave up traveling for a year to work for Kodak at the New York World's Fair Pavilion. After the fair's run, Kodak offered Kelly a year's contract to tour hospitals and special events. His contract was later renewed for three years.

60

"Come One, Come All" to view Emmett Kelly Jr. Collectibles from Flambro's Signature Collection. From left to right, "On the Road Again" (edition of 9,500), "Saturday Night" (edition of 7,500), "The Toothache" (edition of 12,000) and "My Favorite Things" (edition of 9,500).

EKJ Collectibles presents "Hole in the Sole," with an edition of 10,000.

Hospital Visits Make An Impact

Kelly said, "Making sick or lonely people happy is something I enjoy. There isn't anywhere in a hospital I haven't been."

He often was given tours of hospiitals from "top to bottom, front to back and sideways." "Touring hospitals was very rewarding in a lot of ways," Kelly said.

Many years ago, while touring for Kodak, Emmett visited the Burn Ward of the U.S. Naval Hospital in San Diego. Among the patients were thirteen firefighters, who had received second and third degree burns, while fighting a forest fire in which eighteen others were burned to death.

The balance of the story is in Emmett's own words. "I put on a mask and rubber gloves and we went in to see them. If you've never seen it, you cannot imagine what it's like..." "I went around to each one to say hi. I spoke to them, but could not shake hands or touch them. I signed one of my postcards to each and every one of them. About three weeks later, at home in Johnson City, Tennessee, I received a letter from the head Red Cross gal. She thanked me on behalf of all those men, so much in pain, and told me the men wanted me to know they really appreciated my coming to see them. At the bottom of the letter, each and every man had signed his name in pen, pencil, felt marker, whatever he could hold. Now, you know that hurt like hell for them to hold a pen to sign. Those men thought enough of my visiting them to go through all that pain, to thank me for coming."

Kelly, who is sixty-three and proud of it, moved to Tombstone from Indiana because he likes Arizona and can take his Emmett Kelly, Jr. Circus in any direction. The Emmett Kelly, Jr. Circus is the only circus to have played the White House not once, but twice.

"When you're on the West Coast," Kelly said, "all the bookings are in the East and when you're on the East Coast, they're all in the West." Despite all his travels, Kelly said he doesn't plan to retire or ever tire of the traveling.

"It's been a rewarding life. I love it all," said Kelly, who has enough plans in motion to keep him busy for another sixty-three years.

The Kellys—A Great Husband and Wife Act

None of Kelly's five children has pursured circus careers. Since they are "scattered here and there," Kelly said he doesn't see them as often as he would like. The only member of the family who works in Kelly's circus is his wife, Nancy. She helps out as ringmistress, but has done a little of everything including filling in for the star clown.

Emmett Kelly, Jr. is dressed and prepared "to clown around" at one of his numerous personal appearances.

Before becoming ringmistress in 1978, Mrs. Kelly dressed in her husband's makeup for 10 shows while he recovered from multiple cuts on his face and head. After a performance one night in Tarrytown, New York, for a music fair, Kelly walked into the "Wheel of Destiny" counterweight. He needed 100 stitches in his forehead, down the right side of his face to his lip. The back of his head required eighteen stitches.

Emmett and Nancy now make their home in Tombstone, Arizona, site of the famous "Gunfight at the OK Corral." When Emmett is home, he's a member of the Tombstone Vigilantes, a non-profit civic organization that raises money for charity by putting on shows for visiting tourists on the second and fourth Sunday of each month. Emmett plays a U.S. Marshal in the "gunfight," and adds, "the good guys always win."

So, speaking of good guys,...next time you see a vintage Greyhound bus, please honk and wave; it's certainly Emmett and wife, Nancy, on their way to or from making people laugh and smile.

Fountainhead

Famed American Painter Mario Fernandez Soars Free as an Eagle...Sharing the Art He Loves Through Fountainhead

Trapped behind prison bars as a "subversive" in a Cuba newly ruled by Fidel Castro, sixteen-year-old Mario Fernandez fought to retain his strength and his sanity. At any moment a guard might arrive to lead him blindfolded into a courtyard before a firing squad. The soldiers would cock their rifles and young Fernandez would prepare for execution. But this was just a game in Castro's Cuba, designed to break the spirit of a youth who had been active in the resistance underground.

Over and over, the Communist guards threatened Fernandez with death. But between-times, the young man tried valiantly to focus his troubled mind on positive thoughts. His most wonderful dream was that he could turn himself into an eagle and escape the bonds of prison, soaring back to his family on the wings of freedom.

Finally, almost miraculously, after two years Fernandez's father was able to make a deal for his son's release. Mario would be set free if he agreed to leave Cuba immediately, never to return. Fernandez and his parents had only a few tearful moments together before his forced departure. He was never to see his beloved father again.

An Immigrant Entrepreneur

Even at eighteen, Mario Fernandez knew exactly what he would do with his hard-won freedom. He arrived in New York with little more than the clothes on his back, picked up the Sunday *New York Times*, and spied a job offering for a bilingual junior draftsman. On Monday morning, the job was his.

The ambitious Fernandez met and married his wife Gladys in New York, but soon he was on the move again to try the architectural field in California. Then came another move to Minneapolis, where he discovered an opportunity to start his own firm in the microwave industry.

Fernandez's natural entrepreneurial spirit made this venture an enjoyable one for him, but when a major corporation bought the business, the free-flowing days were over. Feeling fettered by corporate bureaucracy, meetings and committees, Fernandez perceived the need to escape.

He turned to art, an interest which he had greatly enjoyed as a youth. Fernandez's father, a hotel magnate in the pre-Castro days, had taken his family to Europe each year on art buying trips. There were numerous art books in the Fernandez home, and the youngster was encouraged to visit museums. Yet other than his architectural drawing classes, Fernandez had never had any formal art training.

A Hobby Leads to a Brilliant Career

Fernandez spent evenings and weekends pursuing his art, and soon decided to specialize in wildlife. He noticed that most wildlife painters were focusing on hunting scenes, so he decided to create portraits of moments in a bird or animal's life rather than pieces which appeared to be viewed from behind a rifle.

In March, 1981, Fernandez entered the National Wildlife Art Show in Kansas City. "Just for the experience," he thought. But to his amazement, the artist earned a Best of Show award for his rendering of a bald eagle entitled "Spirit of Freedom."

Encouraged by his success, Fernandez entered the National Wildlife Art Collectors Show in Minneapolis a few months later. With another "Best of Show" honor under his belt, the artist left the microwave business for good and began to focus full-time on painting.

Now Fernandez could spend long hours in the field, waiting for just the right light effect or unusual movement of a bird or animal to capture on film—and later on canvas. And he could afford the time to exhibit at as many as fifty wildlife shows annually, traveling all over the nation.

Mario Fernandez

The Birth of Fountainhead

Fernandez began to introduce limited edition prints based upon his most popular paintings, and market response was exceptional. Many prints offered through Voyageur Art sold out and began rising in value on the secondary market.

True to his entrepreneurial spirit, the artist had a vision for his own firm that would take special care in the creation and production of Fernandez limited editions. And in 1984, Fountainhead was born.

The mission of Fountainhead was to develop, produce and market Fernandez art products in a variety of media. Soon the firm was offering Print Collector cabinets to house prints, hand-painted sculptures, fine art collector plates, and large, monumental bronze sculptures. From the start, Fountainhead has committed itself to offering only the most unique and finest quality products.

The Fountainhead Art Product Line

The Print Collector, for example, represents the ultimate tool for the serious collector of limited edition prints. It provides ample space for 160 prints or more in a handsome piece of hand-rubbed wood cabinetry, complete with archival-quality print envelopes to protect against acid, moisture, fading, soiling and creasing. The envelopes, however, are clear to allow for easy viewing of the unframed art. The Print Collector is available with a number of options, making it a true custom design for its owner. The Series I unit sells for $1195.

The first offering in the Fountainhead sculpture line is Fernandez's "In God We Trust," a stunning eagle's head available in either a hand-painted, stonecast version at $1250 issue price or solid bronze at $2500. Fernandez decided upon the eagle as his subject for a tribute to the land which received him with open arms from Cuba. As he says, "The obvious choice was the American Bald Eagle, proud and free as we are. I dedicate this sculpture to everyone who has the spirit of freedom and trust in God as the guiding light."

An Immediate Collector Plate Success

Nowhere has Fountainhead's star artist shined brighter than in the limited edition plate field. Just as Fernandez began his career as a wildlife artist with Best of Show awards, his first-ever collector plate, "Courtship Flight," earned multiple Plate of the Year awards.

Few people have witnessed the stunning and natural ceremony in which a mated pair of eagles reaffirm their vows to one another each year. They soar together, performing joyful feats, swooping and diving to celebrate their lives together. Then finally they glide toward one another, meeting in mid-air to lock their talons and cartwheel downward several hundred feet. The eagles part only at the last second, then ascend again in unity.

When Fernandez decided to introduce "Courtship Flight" as an elegant, richly decorated $250 plate, his advisors from the collectibles world shook their heads in disagreement over the steep price. But following his instincts again paid off for the artist/entrepreneur: his generously sized 13" Pickard plate with its five separate ceramic transfers and one-inch pure platinum border sold out immediately in an edition of 2,500. Already there have been reports of "Courtship Flight" bringing well over $1000 on the secondary market.

As a companion piece to "Courtship Flight," Fountainhead soon introduced "Wings of Freedom," a portrait of the eagle pair returning home to their nest after their courtship ritual. It, too sold out in a matter of weeks. Most recently, Fernandez has created a set of bird-subject plates called *The Seasons*, featuring "Fall Cardinals," "Winter Chickadees," "Spring Robins," and "Summer Goldfinches." Each porcelain, gold-rimmed 9-1/4" plate carries an issue price of $85.00 and an edition limit of 5,000.

Mario Fernandez premiered his The Seasons *series of four plates for Fountainhead with "Fall Cardinals." The edition of 5,000 gold-rimmed plates may be acquired for $85.00 each.*

"Wings of Freedom" and its companion plate, "Courtship Flight," established Mario Fernandez as a major force in the world of collector plate art. Lavishly decorated with five separate art transfers and a full one-inch border of pure platinum, this handsome plate sold out immediately in a limited edition of 2,500. The issue price was $250.

Fountainhead Welcomes Robert Olson and Daniel Craig

Mario Fernandez is known in the art community for his open admiration toward other artists of talent and ingenuity. And thus he has invited two such artists to join him at Fountainhead, with initial projects in the collector plate realm.

Robert A. Olson, creator of the award-winning "Piano Moods" print and collector plate, recently was featured as Americana Artist of the Year at the Wildlife Western and Americana Show in Chicago. Soon Fountainhead will reveal the concept behind Olson's first series of plates, a large two-plate series boasting a unique, lavish border treatment.

Another master of Americana is Daniel Craig, creator of two endearing cat portraits for Fountainhead. The plates, entitled "The Mantle" and "The Pantry," capture the cats' individual personalities as they lounge in favorite feline haunts, amidst the atmosphere of a bygone era. Each 8" plate is part of Craig's *Americana Cats* series, offered at an original-issue price of $39.50 each in limited editions of 7,500.

The Eagle Soars in American Style

Little more than twenty years after his arrival on U.S. shores, Mario Fernandez has created a rewarding and successful career for himself as one of America's most respected wildlife artists. As Fountainhead continues to grow, Fernandez soars on the "Wings of Freedom," enjoying the land of opportunity that once seemed only a dream.

SUSAN K. JONES

Gartlan, USA
Collectors Score with Limited Editions
Honoring American Sports Heroes

Millions of "baby boomers" who grew up collecting baseball cards will never forget one thing about their first experience with collecting: it was "fun." Cards were traded, collections compared, and friendships developed, as young sports fans worked together to track down rare issues from Topps, Starr, Kelloggs, and Cracker Jacks.

Today, Gartlan USA is reintroducing collectors to the fun they first associated with collecting. The company has carved a niche by creating limited edition works of art honoring famous sports personalities and events. Many of these items—such as Gartlan's collector plates, figurines, and graphics—are traditional in nature, while others—including the popular *ceramic baseball cards*—are as innovative as they are collectible.

Bob Gartlan, president of the firm, explains how his unusual offerings are bringing new collectors to the hobby. "The special thing about sports collectibles is that they are reaching and educating a much younger consumer," he says. "By the time many of these kids enjoying these fine pieces of art turn 30, there will be a large market that appreciates fine collectibles."

When this happens, Gartlan assures us, these collectors could easily find themselves in possession of some much-coveted—and valuable—collectibles. "One secret to obtaining fine sports collectibles," Gartlan advises, "is to purchase an autographed edition." Underscoring this belief, most of his firm's limited editions are autographed by the heroes they portray, and all of them have been officially authorized by the players.

The "Platinum Edition" Honors Pete Rose

"That's the best I've seen," could well have been a baseball fan's comment upon watching Pete Rose break Ty Cobb's career hit record. But in this case, the remark was made by Pete Rose himself, as he personally approved the artwork for Gartlan USA's tribute to the athlete's historic achievement.
Today, the Pete Rose *Platinum Edition* is regarded as a landmark edition in the field of sports collectibles. The edition is comprised of a ceramic plaque, collector plate, porcelain figurine, a ceramic baseball card—all personally autographed by Pete Rose—a smaller, unsigned version of the ceramic card and an unsigned miniature plate. Gartlan USA produced only 4,192 of each item—to commemorate Rose's recordbreaking number of hits.

An Exclusive Tribute to Roger Staubach

Another Gartlan edition that is highly sought-after by collectors honors one of football's all-time greats, the one-and-only Roger Staubach. This time, the edition was limited to only 1,979 of each item, since 1979 was the year Staubach left professional football.

Even though the Heisman Trophy winner, Super Bowl champion, and Hall of Fame Quarterback is one of the most honored men in football history, Staubach was glad to take an active role in helping to create these exclusive limited editions. The former Dallas Cowboy personally approved the artwork of Charles Soileau, and he autographed each lithograph and plaque, as well as the larger football card and collector plate. Adding to the importance of the collection, Staubach donated his proceeds from sales to charity through the Dallas-based Staubach Foundation.

Collectors and Fans Call for "Reggie!"

To honor Reggie Jackson's historic 500th homerun, Gartlan USA commissioned artist John Boyd Martin to create a suitable tribute, and the result—a limited edition ceramic plaque entitled "The Roundtripper"—was breathtaking. What's more, the edition was personally autographed in gold by Jackson and limited to a

Bob Gartlan, president of Gartlan USA, and Pete Rose proudly display the collector plate honoring Rose's achievement of breaking Ty Cobb's career hit record. The plate was part of a Platinum Edition, *made up of five collectible items, and limited to only 4,192 of each.*

The Roger Staubach Sterling Collection *honors the Heisman Trophy winner, Super Bowl champion, and Hall of Fame Quarterback. As collectors have noted, artist Charles Soileau has achieved a victory of his own, in capturing the intense concentration at the heart of Staubach's personality.*

Reggie Jackson exhibits "The Roundtripper" ceramic plaque, created to commemorate his record-breaking 500th homerun. Acclaimed painter John Boyd Martin created the superb artwork for this now hard-to-find collectible.

The George Brett Gold Crown *Collection includes some very unusual and innovative items, such as the autographed ceramic baseball. The edition, issued in 1986, was limited to only 2,000 of each item.*

worldwide edition of only 500—commemorative of the star's record-shattering homerun. For these and other reasons, the Reggie ceramic plaque is likely to appreciate in value far above its $150 issue price, as have a number of Gartlan's previous sports collectibles.

Collectors Edition Another Big Hit for George Brett

Gartlan USA celebrated George Brett's 2,000th hit—and his overall status as one of baseball's greatest players—with the introduction of the George Brett *Gold Crown* collection in 1986. Appropriately, this edition was limited to distribution of 2,000 worldwide, and many of the pieces were personally autographed by the famed baseball player. For this special collection, artist John Boyd Martin created the original artwork for several very unusual items, including the first regulation-size ceramic baseball. But novelty was only a minor attraction for collectors, who acquired the collection for the appeal of its subject, the superb artistry, and the quality of the production—the winning combination that keeps the *fun* in collecting new offerings from Gartlan USA.

Mike Schmidt: "Power at the Plate"

When Mike Schmidt, third baseman for the Philadelphia Phillies, hit his 500th homerun on April 18, 1987, Gartlan USA released an exclusive limited edition collector plate. The plate is limited to a worldwide edition of 1,987 which represents the year Mike passed his 500th homerun plateau. This handsome plate is banded in 24K gold and is personally autographed by Mike with a special gold pen.

Gartlan Introduces the Gold Rim Collection

For Earvin "Magic" Johnson, 1987 was a banner year. Not only did he contribute to the Los Angeles Lakers NBA championship, but he was named Most Valuable Player for the playoffs. For the first time in his career, Johnson was also awarded the NBA's regular season MVP trophy. To commemorate his superlative performance, Gartlan USA produced a limited edition 10 1/4" collector plate. Limited to distribution of 1,987 pieces worldwide, Robert Winslow created the original artwork for the plate, "The Magic Show," which depicts a portrait of the affable Johnson flanked by poses of his inimitable basketball style. The plate is banded in twenty-four karat gold and is personally autographed by the player.

TOM L. JONES

Goebel Collectors' Club
A Friendly Source of Advice, Guidance and Fun
for Collectors of the Works of Sister M. I. Hummel
and Other Fine Goebel Artists

Visitors to the historic and scenic town of Tarrytown, New York often are startled to spy a child-subject figurine—much larger than life—displayed proudly on the lush, green lawn of a handsome, Georgian-style brick building.

"Who can he be?" they ask, this determined-looking youth with umbrella and satchel in hand, trudging off to who knows where?

But if there is an *M. I. Hummel* collector among them, the mystery will soon be solved. For the figurine represents Sister M. I. Hummel's beloved *Merry Wanderer,* and the building houses the Goebel Collectors' Club Gallery—home of the Goebel Collectors' Club.

Today there are thousands of North American members of this active and constantly growing Club. They collect the charming figurines, plates, bells, dolls and other treasures based on the art of Sister M. I. Hummel, as well as the works of a wide range of other Goebel artists including Gerhard Bochmann, Charlot Byj, Ted DeGrazia, Marion Flahavin, Janet Robson, Georges Selim, and Gerhard Skrobek.

At the Gallery in Tarrytown, visitors are invited to explore a complete collection of all Goebel products distributed in North America. What's more, they may view informative movies in a spacious auditorium demonstrating step-by-step how Goebel collectibles are made, and enjoy historic displays including the only collection of Sister M. I. Hummel's original artwork on permanent exhibition in North America.

But a visit to the National Headquarters is just one of the attractions for Goebel Collectors' Club members. They enjoy Local Chapters and conferences, exciting contests, travel opportunities, and the chance to buy special "members only" Goebel collectibles.

The Goebel Heritage and Sister M. I. Hummel

To fully understand the appeal of the Goebel Collectors' Club, it is important to know a bit of the history of Goebel and its association with the gifted artist, Sister M. I. Hummel.

Born in Bavaria in 1909, young Berta Hummel began sketching and painting as a child, delighting her family with her whimsical renderings of youngsters. When Berta was 18, her father allowed the sheltered young girl to attend the Munich Academy of Applied Arts, where she stayed until age 22. Her teachers agreed that Berta had a brilliant art career ahead of her, but the new graduate surprised them with her decision to enter a convent.

At the Convent of Siessen in the state of Württemberg, Sister Maria Innocentia Hummel was encouraged to continue her art explorations. As she perfected her style of painting adorable, rosy-cheeked children, she attracted the attention of Franz Goebel, fourth-generation owner and head of the company bearing his family name.

Goebel was looking for inspiration for a new line of figurines, and he won the permission of the Mother Superior and Sister Maria Innocentia to translate her two-dimensional art into three dimensions. Although Sister M. I. Hummel died tragically of tuberculosis at the age of 37, in 1946, her many paintings continue to provide the basis for figurines, plates, bells, dolls and other works of art. To this day, a royalty is paid to the Convent of Siessen for each *M. I. Hummel* collectible.

The second in the Celebration Plate Series *from the Goebel Collectors' Club is "Valentine Joy," an endearing glimpse at a little boy offering his Valentine to a loved one. Only Club members may own this special edition at its original-issue price of $98.*

"Morning Concert" represents Exclusive Special Edition No. 11 for Goebel Collectors' Club members only. This charming, three-dimensional portrait of a flute-playing youngster has been based on the work of Sister M. I. Hummel and created by the master craftsmen of W. Goebel Porzellanfabrik.

American Collectors Discover Goebel Masterworks

After World War II, during the American occupation of Germany, many G.I.s and their families fell in love with the pretty *M. I. Hummel* figurines and took them home as special gifts and mementos. *M. I. Hummel* figurines became favorite gifts for the people back home. Soon the figurines were available at exclusive shops throughout the United States and other countries. And beginning in 1971, Goebel added plates to the other collectibles already offered in this country.

As more and more Americans began to collect the works based on the art of Sister M. I. Hummel—as well as of other fine Goebel artists—they became hungry for more information about their beloved collectibles, the artists behind them, and the Goebel company. To fulfill this need, the Goebel Collectors' Club was founded in 1977.

The Benefits of Goebel Collectors' Club Membership

For a current yearly fee of $20.00 ($27.50 Canadian) a Club member receives a wide range of membership benefits, beginning with a membership card and a white bisque membership plaque. The Club's quarterly magazine, INSIGHTS, features articles on Goebel artists and products, how-tos for decorating, travel news and much more. Members also receive a handsome and protective binder to keep their INSIGHTS issues safe for future reference.

Each year, Club members receive a colorful calendar featuring Goebel collectibles which are currently available. In addition to a standing invitation to visit the Tarrytown headquarters, just 30 miles north of New York City, members also are invited to have lunch at the Goebel factory in Bavaria, West Germany, whenever they may be traveling in Europe.

Upon renewal of membership each year, Club members are presented with a special "welcome back" gift from Goebel. And they are enticed in each year to travel with other Club members on exclusive trips, culminating in a glorious visit to the factory.

Special Goebel Products "For Members Only"

From its origins more than 10 years ago, the Goebel Collectors' Club has been renowned for the attractive and finely crafted products offered

regularly for Club members only, and only for a limited time. Indeed, many of the retired pieces have already increased significantly in value, as new Club members compete to own the offerings of prior years.

Upon joining or renewal of each year's membership, Club members receive "redemption cards" for these special pieces, which they may use to acquire the items at the local dealer of their choice. For Year Eleven of the Goebel Collectors' Club, Exclusive Special Edition No. 11 is "Morning Concert"—a charming *M. I. Hummel* figurine featuring a wonderful little boy determined to reach that high note on his flute.

Also available to members during Year Eleven (June 1,1987 through May 31, 1988) is "Valentine Joy," the second in the *Celebration Plate Series*. This bas-relief *M. I. Hummel* plate captures the happy smile of a youngster ready to share his beautifully decorated Valentine with a special loved one. Retail prices for both figurine and plate are $98, and in Canada, prices are $140 for the figurine and $130 for the plate. Redemption cards for each expire on May 31, 1989.

Club Members Share Enjoyment with Local Groups

Many members of the Goebel Collectors' Club also belong to Local Chapters of the Club. These groups meet regularly to share the joy of collecting, decorating tips, guest speakers, and much more. They also organize and attend Regional Inter-Chapter Conferences where they can share ideas with other Chapters, and visit sites of special interest to collectors.

Local Chapters also have had the opportunity to nominate outstanding members for the honor of being named "Local Chapter Member of the Year." The most recent winner (1986) of this coveted award was Carol Moysey of the Greater Cleveland Chapter. Joan N. Ostroff, vice president and executive director of the Goebel Collectors' Club, traveled to Cleveland to surprise Ms. Moysey with a

Joan Ostroff (left) of Goebel Collectors' Club presents Carol Moysey of the Club's Greater Cleveland Chapter with the Sixth Annual "Local Chapter Member of the Year" award, an M. I. Hummel "Adventure Bound" figurine mounted on a specially inscribed base.

special award: The *M. I. Hummel* figurine *Adventure Bound*.

Ms. Moysey's Chapter had nominated her with high praise indeed. Their letter of nomination included these remarks: "(Carol) is the spirit of our Chapter... her energy will charge you up automatically... she is constantly sharing... her horizons are never ending."

New Memberships Invited for Goebel Collectors' Club

Each year, thousands more Goebel collectors—both novices and those of long standing—join and rejoin the Goebel Collectors' Club. For more information on the Club, its activities and membership, contact the Club at 105 White Plains Road, Tarrytown, New York 10591, or call them at (914) 332-0300.

SUSAN K. JONES

Gorham
Dolls by Design

With the introduction of The Gorham Doll Collection in 1981, Gorham became the first major gift and collectibles company to create and market an original line of collectible dolls. Several companies, Gorham among them, had featured antique-look imported dolls in their catalog lines , but this family of ten exquisite dolls with porcelain heads, hands and feet, elaborate outfits, and delicate music, was the first brand-name, original collection offered by a major maker. By 1984, everywhere the collector looked there were dolls. Gift companies all over the country, banking on the interest and loyalty of the doll collector, began producing dolls. But today, among major gift producers, only the Gorham Doll Collection remains. Why? Because only Gorham has the tradition of design originality and production quality needed to continually create dolls that are truly collectible.

A Design Tradition Since 1841

Design has been Gorham's trademark since its founding in 1841. Jabez Gorham began with a line of simple silver spoons, but when his son, John, decided to expand the company, his first move was to travel to Europe in search of fine designers and modern manufacturing methods. One result of his trip was the hiring of William Christmas Codman, who proceeded to design the Chantilly pattern which is still the leading sterling flatware pattern at bridal registries today. Codman also designed exquisite display pieces including a stunning solid silver dressing table and a magnificent silver, ebony and ivory desk, each of which was a gold medal winner at a turn of the century World's Fair. With this heritage, it is no wonder that Gorham dolls are created with the emphasis on design.

Their Faces Are Their Fortune

The very first consideration given a prospective doll line at Gorham is the face. Surveys among members of the Gorham Collectors' Guild have shown this to be the collector's number one concern. Most collectors literally fall in love with a pretty face. In 1980, when the original ten dolls were designed, the decision was made to base the Gorham faces on the famous look of the French doll makers Bru and Jumeau. No thought was ever given to using a copy or reproduction mold. Rather, Gorham designers created their own faces and master models were made. This has been the case as new lines have been introduced. From *Precious as Pearls* to *Petticoats and Lace*, original faces have made Gorham dolls unique.

Susan Stone Aiken Dresses Each Lady

The designer responsible for the elegant outfits, elaborite hats and detailed accessories that have made Gorham dolls the most desired modern collectible doll, is Susan Stone Aiken. A native of Rhode Island who designed her own clothes since childhood, Susan received her formal design training at the University of Maine and the Rhode Island School of Design. Her affection for dolls and for everything antique is a product of her family background, for she is a member of an old New England family that treasured the antique keepsakes handed down through the years. She was chosen in the very beginning to design the outfits for the first ten dolls, and is the designer today, as Gorham passes the 100 mark in its collection.

Susan's method is the same now as it was in the beginning. She sketches the face and her suggested hair style, and from this look and the theme of the collection, she creates an outfit. This is far more extensive than designing a dress. Susan's creations encompass the complete look of the doll. She creates personalities. No

Chantilly, the pattern designed by William Christmas Codman in 1898 is still the leading sterling pattern sold through bridal registries today.

Susan Stone Aiken, designer of the costumes for the Gorham Doll Collection.

detail is too small to consider. Should the buttons be pearls, fabric covered, or crystal? Should the lace trim be identical throughout or should several laces be used? Should the satin ribbon be wide or narrow? Will the hat be more exciting with flowers or feathers, or both?

Once the design is complete, Susan personally selects every fabric, lace and trim, and makes a prototype outfit by hand. Then she puts together a full color sketch on a large board, with a sample of every fabric, lace, ribbon, feather, button, pearl and flower attached and keyed to the design. Both the sample and the board then go to the factory for a production sample to be created. Gorham dolls often make several trips between designer and factory before production can begin, since few substitutions are accepted and no compromises in quality are made.

Precious as Pearls: *A Classic Susan Stone Aiken Design*

The current limited edition series in the Gorham Doll Collection is classic Susan Stone Aiken design.

Called *Precious as Pearls,* the series will have four dolls in total, three of which have already been introduced.

"Colette," the first in the series, sold out in 1986. Her lovely Jumeau-style original face features brown paperweight eyes and is framed with light brown curls. Her exquisite costume of pink chiffon and ivory lace features a tiered skirt with insets of print fabric and an elaborate matching hat with ivory feathers and silk flowers. She also carries a pink and ivory parasol. Her dress is trimmed with pearls, and she wears a Precious as Pearls brooch at her neck. This antiqued oval pin is set with a single pearl, indicating her position as first in the series. Like all Gorham Doll Collection dolls, she is musical, her delicate 18-note musical movement playing "Thank Heaven for Little Girls."

Next came "Charlotte," blue eyed and blonde. For her costume, Susan chose blue taffeta and ivory lace and stayed with the interesting touch of an insert of complimentary print fabric. The mutton sleeves are of lace over taffeta, and the skirt features panels of taffeta trimmed with lace and ivory ro-

Susan Store-Aiken creates "Jacqueline," a stunning bride, limited to 1,500. No details have been left out of this exquisite wedding gown. This musical doll plays "The Wedding March."

"Colette" is the first in the Precious as Pearls *series of limited edition dolls. The single pearl in the brooch at her neck signifies her position in the series.*

settes. Other trims include layers of lace to the tops of blue taffeta shoes, and tiny pearls around the panels of the skirt. Her blue taffeta hat is in an unusual heart shape and is trimmed with feathers, silk flowers, lace and pearls. Charlotte's *Precious as Pearls* brooch is set with two pearls, and she carries a blue parasol. Her music is "My Favorite Things."

Chloe Available for 1988

The current *Precious as Pearls* doll is "Chloe," a charming dark eyed, dark haired beauty in dusky lavender. Her elegant outfit is taffeta with insets of printed fabric and layers of ivory lace. Her hat is trimmed with silk flowers, feathers, lace and pearls, and, like her two predecessors, she carries a parasol and wears a *Precious as Pearls* pin, hers set with three pearls marking her position as third in the series. Chloe's music is "Try to Remember." She is issued,

as all *Precious as Pearls* dolls have been, in an edition of 2500, and is hand numbered near the hallmark on her neck.

Gorham Commitment to Design Continues

Collections like *Precious as Pearls*, and the detail-oriented attitudes of Susan Stone Aiken and the project managers at Gorham don't happen by chance. Gorham has based a business on fine design, exceptional quality, and minute attention to detail for over a century and a half. And there are no plans to change. Collectors all over the world can rest assured that when they select a Gorham doll for their collection, they have chosen a collectible of lasting value. Nearly a decade of continuous excellence has proven that Gorham produces fine dolls, by design.

SARA KIRTLINK

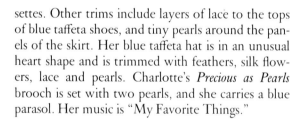

The Hamilton Collection
Beloved Television and Movie Stars Inspire Popular Limited Edition Porcelain Masterworks

Each year, scores of new television series and hundreds of feature films debut in American homes and theaters. Yet only a handful will endure as "classics" to be savored year after year and shared with every new generation of fans.

When a TV show or movie reaches this exhalted, cult-like status, its admirers often seek out ways to share their enthusiasm with others via fan clubs, conventions, and collectibles. Gatherings of enthusiasts for "Star Trek," "The Honeymooners," and other favorite shows attract thousands who enjoy viewing memorable episodes, trading souvenirs, and meeting the series' star actors.

And as The Hamilton Collection has discovered in recent years, an even broader cross section of fans of beloved TV series and movies may have strong interest in owning and displaying works of art commemorating "Star Wars," "Little House on the Prairie," "The Little Rascals," and other time-honored shows and films.

The Fine Art Heritage of Hamilton

Over the past decade, The Hamilton Collection has earned an international reputation for its fine art collectibles from some of the world's most celebrated studios and craftsmen. Working in close cooperation with famed makers including Wedgwood, Royal Worcester, River Shore, Reco International, Roman, Vague Shadows and Maruri, Hamilton develops and produces exquisitely crafted collector plates, figurines, bells and dolls.

Hamilton began producing limited editions based on television and movie characters just a few years ago, and since then, one studio has developed a wide range of these "entertainment-theme" collectibles. Hamilton injects the same high level of quality craftsmanship into each of these collections that brought the studio such a fine name in other areas of the limited edition art world.

The "Star Trek" Adventure on Porcelain

A few years ago, Hamilton's representatives were privileged to preview an original work of art by celebrity painter Susie Morton—the first authorized plate-painting ever created to honor the legend of "Star Trek." Ms. Morton's work captured the cool and rational "Mr. Spock" to perfection—combining the distinctive features of actor Leonard Nimoy and the Vulcan characteristics of this Starship Enterprise Science Officer.

Hamilton formed an alliance with Ms. Morton's home studio of Ernst Enterprises, and soon the *Star Trek®* Plate Collection was unveiled to enthusiastic "Trekkies" and collectors all over America. Before long, "Mr. Spock" and the succeeding issues in this eight-plate series were among the hottest items for sale at "Star Trek" conventions. But the appeal of the "Star Trek" plates ranged far beyond the small audience of loyal fans: people from all walks of life added "Mr. Spock" to their home displays as an enduring reminder of this all-time favorite television show.

The *Star Trek®* Plate Collection thrilled fans with Susie Morton's original paintings of all the series' most beloved characters: "Dr. McCoy," "Mr. Sulu," "Uhura," "Scotty," "Chekov," and of course, their dynamic leader "Captain Kirk." Each offered a remarkable likeness of the popular actor who played this character, as captured by the talented Ms. Morton. These 8-1/2″ fine porcelain plates also bore the memorable motto of the Starship Enterprise crew: "To boldly go where no man has gone before."

The Legend of "Star Trek" Continues

The Hamilton Collection was deluged with requests for more 'Star Trek' collectibles from fans of the Starship Enterprise saga. And thus the "U.S.S. Enterprise" plate, *Star Trek®* Mug Collection, *Star Trek®*—The Commemo-

The calm and rational "Mr. Spock" by Susie Morton premiered The Hamilton Collection's Star Trek™ *Plate Collection – and began Hamilton's impressive stream of porcelain collectibles inspired by classic television shows and movies.*

Favorite "Star Wars" characters like Luke Skywalker and Yoda dominate Hamilton's Star Wars™ *Plate Collection. Also featured in the series honoring this beloved trilogy of films are Han Solo, Princess Leia, Darth Vader, R2-D2, and C-3PO.*

rative Collection, and the *Star Trek*® Doll Collection debuted in prompt succession.

"U.S.S. Enterprise" allowed Susie Morton to utilize a larger porcelain "canvas" of 10-1/4″ to paint a dramatic rendering of the Starship Enterprise, surrounded by stylized portraits of the seven most popular crew members. Many collectors have enjoyed making this larger plate a focal point around which they have displayed the *Star Trek*® Plate Collection in their homes.

Eight richly colored porcelain *Star Trek*® mugs reprise the brilliant art from the original plate collection, with each of the seven characters gracing his or her own mug, plus an eighth group portrait mug. Collectors may use these handsome mugs to enjoy favorite beverages, or strictly as display pieces as they choose.

When the twentieth anniversary of "Star Trek" took place in 1986, a new surge of popularity earned the television show and the four "Star Trek" movies a whole new generation of fans. In fact, "Star Trek IV" became one of the top 1986-87 box office successes. Susie Morton marked this special "Star Trek" birthday with eight more original plate-paintings capturing memorable scenes from favorite "Star Trek" episodes. Beginning with Captain Kirk and "The Trouble with Tribbles," the series won favorable notice—and strong buying pressure—from "Trekkies" and plate collectors alike.

The most recent "Star Trek" collector's item is the "Mr. Spock" doll—a likeness of Nimoy and his alter ego that "Star Trek" Fan Club president Dan Madsen declares "outstanding." Dressed in his original television costume, this hand-painted porcelain doll delights "Trekkies" of all ages. Dolls capturing "Captain Kirk" and other beloved characters follow in the series.

"The Honeymooners" and "Little House on the Prairie"

Fresh from the success of these many handsome "Star Trek" products, Hamilton's art masters proceeded to envision and produce several more well-received collector plate series offering wonderful likenesses of all-time favorite characters from popular television series and movies. And in keeping with its studio policy, Hamilton secured all necessary rights to make each of these presentations completely official and unique.

The Official Honeymooners Plate Collection had gained the blessing and cooperation of Kramden's creator, the late Jackie Gleason, marking the first time this classic comedy series ever has been portrayed on limited-edition porcelain plates. Eight favorite "Honeymooners" scenes are revisited in these heartwarming works of art, showing Ralph, Norton, and their wives, Alice and Trixie, just as they first appeared on television in the mid-1950s.

The *Little House on the Prairie* plates bring back memories of the simple frontier days that Laura Ingalls Wilder wrote about in her charming books. And each painting perfectly portrays the actors who played Mrs. Wilder's family in the long-running television series starring Michael Landon.

Beloved first by moviegoers and then by youngsters watching them on television, *The Little Rascals* now appear in full color as subjects of an eight-plate series bearing their famous name. Spanky, Alfalfa, Buckwheat, Darla and Petey the Dog all come alive on porcelain—always young and mischievous just as we remember them from childhood.

The "Star Wars" Trilogy—Captured on Limited-Edition Plates

When "Star Wars" burst upon the movie scene in 1977, it revolutionized the way films would be produced—and the way audiences would react to special effects. Yet for most fans, the characters of "Star Wars," "The Empire Strikes Back" and "The Return of the Jedi" are the movies' most compelling aspect.

Thus in the Hamilton Collection's *Star Wars®* Plate Collection, "Han Solo," "Luke Skywalker," "Princess Leia," "Darth Vader," "Yoda," "R2-D2 and C-3PO," and many of the other science-fiction creations of George Lucas are the focus of eight remarkable plate-paintings. As the collection unfolds, highlights from all three films in the "Star Wars" trilogy are portrayed in vibrantly colored works of art to be enjoyed forever as porcelain collector plates.

Hamilton Follows Collectors' Wishes

Hamilton Collection officials credit the studio's respect for collectors and their desires as the main reason behind the firm's many successes with entertainment-theme limited editions.

"Staying close to the collector helps us provide our clients with the themes and art they want to own—reflecting contemporary values, interests and lifestyles as well as nostalgic memories," explains Hamilton's Chairman, James P. Smith, Jr.

Susan K. Jones

More than 30 years after its television debut, "The Honeymooners" still attracts daily viewership in the millions. This plate launched The Hamilton Collection's The Honeymooners *collection, paying tribute to the late Jackie Gleason as Ralph Kramden, as well as the other main characters, Ed Norton, Alice Kramden and Trixie Norton.*

This "USS Enterprise" plate captures the drama of Star Trek®, *including portraits of all seven main characters and the crew's starship. The plate served as a popular follow-up to the successful* Star Trek® *Plate Collection.*

David Winter Cottages
British Sculptor Recalls the Lives of His Ancestors to Create Charming Miniature Cottages

David Winter is a man of the countryside. All his life has been spent in British villages and farmlands, and from his earliest years he has been influenced by the craftsman around him. Son of the renowned sculptress Faith Winter, and descendant of a number of prominent architects, David was born with a love for buildings and a talent for three-dimensional artistry. Yet the architecture of full-sized buildings never intrigued the young man. Instead, he aspired to capture—in miniature—the homes in which his ancestors lived and worked in days gone by.

"It's the people—their jobs, their lifestyles, where they lived—which are fundamental to the way their houses were constructed," Winter explains. "I think the charm of them is the way an addition would be made if, for example, a new baby came into the family and a bit might be added, and perhaps, if they became more prosperous, another bit might be added...so it would grow, and eventually you would end up with this higgeldy-piggeldy building with lots of extensions."

John Hine Shares David Winter's Vision

The young artist earned a diploma in sculpture before a major turning point occurred for him in 1978. In that year, Winter met John Hine, and the two men discovered their mutual enthusiasm for exploring the lives of their predecessors. They shared a yearning to find out what life was really like for men and women from a Britain that has changed dramatically.

"Houses accommodate lives, not the other way around," asserts John Hine, and thus the two men became determined to capture something of the essence of life in the past, as seen in the styles and details of peoples' homes and workplaces.

Perseverence Fires the Developing Dream

In addition to their shared vision, David Winter and John Hine discovered a synergy of skills that led to the founding of their joint business in 1979. Winter creates the original for each sculpture, while Hine supervises the mold making, casting, finishing, and hand-painting of each David Winter cottage—a total of 80 different designs to date.

The first cottage took form in the spring of 1979. Winter made the original of wax and matchsticks, with a small piece of lace forming the crest of the thatched roof. The two partners delivered their first two cottages from this original to a shop in Guilford, Surrey, and were delighted to learn that one cottage was sold on that very first day!

Celebration time was short, however. The partners went back to the workbench, made another cottage, and delivered that to Guilford as well. It wasn't long before new shops were requesting the cottages more quickly than Winter and Hine could make them. Enlargment of quarters became a frequent event for the fledgling business, but even today their original 6′x8′ coal shed—where the first two cottages were made—stands as a reminder of their company's humble beginnings.

"We had to push quite hard," Winter recalls with a nostalgia that belies the recency of his studio's origins. "It was extremely tight financially the whole time. There were many, many days when it looked as if we just wouldn't make it. I try to forget how many times it was we thought we were going to go bankrupt."

David Winter Cottages Earn International Praise

In less than a decade, the charming cottages of David Winter and John Hine have become favorites of collectors not only in England, but also in many other countries of the world. United States and Canadian citizens by the thousands now count Winter's finely rendered works among their most treasured possessions.

Yet even as the popularity of their cottages grows, Winter and Hine remain devoted to the time-consuming and painstaking processes that make their works so unique. And when the two men get together for a few moments of leisure, conversation invariably turns to the subject of how our ancestors used to live. For they are observers of human nature as much as they are artists and craftsmen.

The David Winter Creative Process

Each time that he returns to his studio after one of these restful interludes, Winter again becomes completely absorbed in his work. Completing the details on one of his buildings, puffing away at his pipe, he seems to be peering inside the cottage, imagining the movements of the people who might have lived inside it. A finished David Winter cottage has a compelling quality about it—people want to touch it and examine it through a magnifying glass.

In order to achieve detail on such a small scale, Winter is constantly experimenting with different techniques. "It's very difficult to find new methods..." he explains. "But then again that's also part of the satisfaction in doing (the cottages). Every tile is put on individually, as a tiler would put tiles on a real roof of a real house. I think of all these sorts of things in the making of them; if I can do it as much as possible in the way in which they were originally built, I can get a better effect eventually."

Every window frame, every brick, is placed to reflect authentic and accurate building styles; the detail will often take days. Winter even makes his own sculpting tools; creating them as he needs them, from bits of wire, matchsticks and wood. This is where the artist's keen eye and encyclopaedic memory are especially evident. He has a great affinity for the crooked old beams, the warped roofs and the twisted chimneys, and it is this affection for the heritage of his country which gives him the patience necessary to complete the work.

Winter finishes the wax model of a cottage by lettering his name and the date into the base. He does

David Winter

Pilgrim's Rest

this just as patiently as he did the very first shaping of the wax block. Then he leans back and re-lights his pipe, which was forgotten for awhile during a difficult moment of carving.

The Workshops of John Hine Limited

When a David Winter original in wax arrives at The Workshops of John Hine Limited, every effort is immediately centered on recreating the Winter piece in its every exquisite detail. The most difficult and fundamental part of this work is the making of molds from the original wax cottage. This stage requires scrupulous care from the craftsmen involved.

A successful mold is then passed to the casters who use it to produce a perfect cast in the material called Crystacal. Each minute feature inside the

The Village

Castle Gate

mold must be fingered carefully to ensure that none of the fine detail is missed. The same care and concentration are necessary when the mold is removed from the cast piece. Detailed knowledge of the sculpture is vital to avoid damaging the cast as it gradually appears from the mold. If the emerging piece is anything less than perfect, it is destroyed.

Next, pieces of excess material are delicately "fettled" away and the base is made smooth and even. "Resting" in a temperature controlled room is followed by a sealing solution of shellac and white polish—undercoating for the painting to come.

The painters of David Winter Cottages all are naturally talented artists who are thoroughly trained by John Hine and his staff. They are taught the delicate skill of staining the cottages in a manner which highlights the sculptural artistry of Winter's work. The subtle colors and techniques used by these painters emphasize the artist's intention of creating wholly realistic miniatures.

When painting is complete, each cottage receives a final quality inspection before its base covering is applied and its Certificate of Authenticity made ready. As each cottage is settled gently into its box, it is ready for its trip to one of many stores all over the world: a small piece of rural England to enhance a faraway home.

The David Winter Cottages Collectors Guild

Some collectors of David Winter's remarkable works prefer to own his examples of grand buildings like "The Old Distillery," "Castle Gate," "Fairytale Castle," or "Tudor Manor House." Others prefer the compact homes of everyday English people, such as "Spinner's Cottage," "Yeoman's Farm," "Drover's Cottage," or "Cotswold Cottage."

But no matter what their preference in architecture, Winter's collectors are united in their desire for more and more information about the artist, his subjects, and his craft. And thus the David Winter Cottages Collectors Guild has been formed. Each Guild member will receive a special sculpted piece by David Winter, available to members only, and entitled "The Village Scene." Members will also receive an annual gift from the Guild.

In addition to an official Certificate of Membership and Membership Card (for purchasing special Guild pieces at dealers' shops) each member will receive four annual issues of the "Cottage Country" quarterly magazine. Each issue will contain at least 32 pages of authoritative information, news and pictures of great interest to David Winter Cottage enthusiasts. A handsome leather binder will be provided as well to hold and protect these fine magazines.

There will be two exclusive Guild pieces introduced each year, although there is no obligation to purchase them. Further details on the Guild, as well as a membership application and brochure, may be had by writing: David Winter Cottage Collectors Guild, 1830 Peace Portal Drive, Blaine, Washington 98230.

SUSAN K. JONES

Kaiser Porcelain
Continuing a Tradition of Excellence

Even though it is cast in fine porcelain, the stately Bald Eagle almost appears to move as it sweeps down to make a hunter's conquest. The bird's eyes reflect its intensity and power, as it stretches its wings high into the air, casting a long, ominous shadow upon the prairie ground.

"Bald Eagle XI" is one of several major new porcelain works from Germany's famed Kaiser Porcelain, the family-owned firm that has earned international acclaim for the superb quality of its art for the last 115 years. But to tens of thousands of collectors the world over, "Bald Eagle XI" represents something more: the very best of a 280-year-old European art tradition.

The Bavarian Porcelain Legacy

The Bavarian region of Germany has long been known for its exceptional porcelain artistry. Indeed, Europe's first native-made porcelain was created there in 1709. And because it made use of the special kaolin clay so prevalent in the region, Europe's new "White Gold" was exceptionally pure and beautiful.

Just over 150 years later, in 1872, a painter from Thuringia, Germany, decided to establish a porcelain workshop in Coburg, Germany. The painter, August Alboth, had already established a reputation for himself as a superb craftsman and artist, and his new firm quickly became known for the quality of its porcelain creations.

Alboth was later joined by his son, Ernst, who helped him to design and decorate the fine-quality porcelain. Eventually, Ernst moved the business to Kronach, Bavaria, where the company made one of its most important changes. For it was there that the Alboth family merged fortunes with the Kaiser family, when Ernst's daughter, Erna, married Georg Kaiser, who became a partner in the growing porcelain firm.

For decades following, the firm used the trademark "Alka-Kunst," which combined the first two letters of Alboth and Kaiser, and "kunst," the german word for "art." During these years, the business flourished, and in 1953, the partners built a modern, state-of-the-art factory in Staffelstein, West Germany. Seventeen years later, to commemorate the enormous progress that had been initiated by the Kaiser family, and, above all, because of the internationally sounding and effective name "Kaiser" (which is synonymous with "Emperor" in German), the firm made a final name change, from "Alka-Kunst" to "Kaiser".

One of the World's Great Porcelain Studios

Today, Kaiser Porcelain continues to make history, by combining a respect for its tradition with a willingness to take advantage of new production technologies. As a result, the studio's new limited edition sculptures and plates are anxiously sought by collectors around the world—even in the Orient, where the wonders of porcelain artistry were first appreciated. And earlier, successful sculptures, such as Kaiser's elegant 1970 "Cardinal," can now be acquired only at greatly appreciated prices. "Cardinal," incidentally, was the first issue in the acclaimed *Birds of America* Collection, a series of fine limited editions which continues to this day.

The studio's limited edition collector plates are also highly sought by collectors for their superb artistry and flawless craftsmanship. Thus, plates like "Mare and Foal," the first issue in the *Mother's Day* annual series, and "Waiting for Santa Claus" are strong performers on the secondary market.

"We have a very high standard to maintain in the porcelain medium," says Kaiser artist Lee Letts. "This is why I enjoy working with Kaiser, because I share with them this respect for the medium and its tradition." Letts is primarily involved with sculpting and overseeing the final production of Kaiser sculptures depicting bird and animal subjects. The process is an exacting one, consisting of many carefully inspected steps. Letts works hard, he says, to "make sure the integrity of the artist's original expression of the subject is preserved."

The sound of hoofbeats can almost be heard as one admires "Pacer," one of two new elegant equestrian figurines from Kaiser Porcelain. The dramatic sculpture measures approximately 9¼" in height and 14" in length.

"Snowy Owl" continues the Birds of America *figurine tradition begun in 1970. The handsome, hand-painted figurine stands approximately 9½" in height.*

Kaiser Introduces Major New Works

In keeping with its longstanding reputation for extraordinary quality, Kaiser Porcelain has recently introduced several superb limited edition sculptures that are certain to please collectors and other lovers of art. Two new issues honor America's best-loved birds, continuing the tradition begun in 1970 with the first *Birds of America* figurines.

The first is "Snowy Owl," which captures the beauty of this regal but mysterious owl in fine, hand-painted porcelain. The worldwide edition for this new work is limited to only 3,000, and the sculpture is approximately 9½" in height.

The strikingly beautiful "Bald Eagle XI" completes the noteworthy pair of new bird-subject figurines. This superb work depicts the powerful bird as it nears the intense conclusion of a successful hunt. The figurine stands almost 14" in height, as measured from its base to the tip of the outstretched wings.

Like many other figurines in the Kaiser catalog, "Bald Eagle XI" is available both as a hand-painted

"Bald Eagle XI" captures the majesty and power of America's best-known bird of prey. The sculpture, shown here in both hand-painted and bisque (unpainted) form, measures almost 14" in height.

and an unpainted figurine, allowing collectors to choose their favorite form of expression. While it is probably true that most collectors prefer the intricate hand coloration, a sizeable minority appreciate the shimmering beauty of unpainted white bisque porcelain. Both forms, it must be noted, are valued for their fine artistry and investment potential.

Two Outstanding Equestrian Sculptures

With the introduction of two new limited-edition sculptures, Kaiser's talented artists have captured the special beauty and majesty of purebred horses in full gallop. Designed by sculptor Wolfgang Gawantka

who has worked at Kaiser for several years, is the elegant "Traber," or "Standardbred." Admiring this dramatic portrayal, one can almost see the mane and tail flapping in the wind created by the horse's speed. The sculpture is approximately 9″ in height and 15″ in length.

Now taking the lead is "Pacer," another lifelike dramatization of a powerful horse in motion. This sculpture measures approximately 9¼″ in height and 14″ in length. Both "Traber" and "Pacer" are available as either hand-painted or unpainted figurines.

TOM L. JONES

The Edwin M. Knowles China Company
Knowles Enters Doll Market While Remaining A Leader In Collector's Plates

The Edwin M. Knowles China Company, a leading collector's plate maker and winner of numerous collectibles awards, traces its heritage to 19th century Ohio. It was in the late 1860s when Isaac Knowles, father of Edwin, established the family owned pottery, Knowles, Taylor and Knowles, in East Liverpool, Ohio. This was a little town 40 miles south of Pittsburgh, where the Allegheny and Monongahela rivers join to form the mighty Ohio. Isaac Knowles chose the site for its proximity to the river banks and their deposits of high quality kaolin clay.

Knowles, Taylor and Knowles soon became America's largest supplier of delicate china for tearooms and restaurants. Knowles was best known for its exquisite Lotus Ware, a translucent white bone china of unusually high quality that rivaled European soft-paste porcelains of the period. Today, Lotus Ware is prized by aficionados of antique dinnerware and it can be found in collections throughout North America.

Knowles' business boomed during the 1880s, and by 1891, the firm had 29 kilns and was the largest pottery in the country.

Edwin Knowles got his start at the East Liverpool pottery. He served his apprenticeship there after attending Harvard University. He then left the family firm and established his own pottery in Newell, West Virginia, directly across the Ohio River and within sight of the precious kaolin deposits. By the late 1880s, Edwin was pre-eminent among American potters, serving as president of the United States Pottery Association.

After Edwin's death in 1943, the company ceased operations for a period of time until agreeing to an affiliation with The Bradford Exchange to preserve its time-honored name.

Knowles Enters New Era With Dolls

Beginning in 1975, Knowles entered the burgeoning collector's plate market. For the next decade the company was a major producer and innovator in the field, issuing plates with a wide variety of themes that captured collectors' interest. The year 1986 became Knowles' next major turning point.

After years of speculation from experts in the collectibles world that Knowles would turn its talents to other types of collectibles, Knowles produced the company's first doll collection, *Yolanda's Picture-Perfect Babies*, for Ashton-Drake Galleries. The years of experience that made the company a leader in porcelain making were applied to the creation of these life-like porcelain dolls.

Designed by award-winning dollmaker Yolanda Bello, dolls in the series have sculptured porcelain heads, arms and legs, with hand-painted fleshtones and a velvet-smooth bisque finish. Bello, whose name is known to knowledgeable doll collectors, has garnered 59 prizes in major juried doll exhibitions in the past five years, including five Best of Show awards and a 1985 "Doll of the Year" award.

Bello's Ashton-Drake series began with "Jason," a 14-inch smiling infant boy dressed in a powder blue clown costume. He was soon joined by "Heather," who was named 1986 Doll of the Year by the National Association of Limited Edition Dealers (NALED).

Rockwell Legacy Preserved by Knowles

When plate collectors think of Knowles they also recall beloved artist Norman Rockwell. The illustrator's famous depiction of "Angel with a Black Eye" appeared on Knowles' first plate in 1975. The Rockwell Society of America's *Christmas* series was the first of many that Knowles would produce for the Society. Subsequent series have included *Rockwell's Mother's Day*, *Rockwell Heritage*, *Rockwell's Rediscovered Women*, *Rockwell on Tour* and *Rockwell's Light Campaign.*

Knowles' identification with the Rockwell name and artistic legacy became even stronger in 1985 when The Norman Rockwell Family Trust granted the company exclusive rights to produce limited edition collector's plates featuring the artwork of Norman Rockwell. The family had never before sponsored or endorsed the use of the popular painter's work on any collectible product.

The Family Trust sponsorship allows Knowles to make collector's plates featuring any painting from the family's collection of original Rockwells as well as from hundreds of additional Rockwell paintings for which the family holds copyrights. *Rockwell's American Dream* was the first series issued under this agreement.

In 1986 Knowles tapped this veritable treasure trove of art to begin two new Rockwell series: *A Mind of Her Own: Rockwell's Studies of Girlhood* (begun with "Sitting Pretty?"), and *Rockwell's Colonials: The Rarest Rockwells* (begun with "The Unexpected Proposal"). The following year Knowles introduced "Grandpa's Gift" to initiate the *Rockwell's Golden Moments* series.

The Rockwell family assisted in selecting the art for each of these series and provides an intimate knowledge of their father's creation of each painting.

In addition to these special series, Knowles has recently added to other popular Rockwell series such as the *Rockwell Society Mother's Day* ("Pantry Raid," 1986, and "Grandma's Surprise,"1987); the *Rockwell Society Christmas* ("Deer Santy Claus," 1986 and "Santa's Golden Gift, 1987"); and *Rockwell Heritage* ("The Professor," 1986 and "The Shadow Artist,"1987). *Rockwell's American Dream* closed in 1987 with "Love's Reward," the eighth and final plate in the series.

Nature Themes Popular With Collectors

Knowles brought a fresh, modern approach to the subject of wildlife art in 1986, introducing two series by artists new to plate collectors. Well-known conservationist and wildlife artist Bart Jerner painted "The Pintail" to begin a duck series sponsored by the Wildlife Society. The series is titled *Living with Nature: Jerner's Ducks.* Each plate depicts a panoramic view of the particular duck's daily habits within its natural environment so that we are better able to understand how they have survived in man's dominion, and adjusted to the ever-changing world. "The Mallard" was Jerner's second duck subject for the series.

Knowles' second new series, also sponsored by the Wildlife Society, is Wayne Anderson's *Upland Birds of North America.* Begun with "The Pheasant," Anderson strives to share the birds who are our neighbors but that may seldom be seen and fully appreciated because of their protective coloring. Anderson selected "The Grouse" for his second plate subject.

Amy Brackenbury's Cat Tales, a 1987 introduction, is Knowles first series to feature cats. Newcomer artist Amy Brackenbury begins her series with "A Chance Meeting: White American Shorthairs," showing a pair of inquisitive white kittens stalking a turtle on the garden path. Cat Fanciers' Federation, Inc. sponsors this series.

Established Knowles' artist Kevin Daniel directs his talents from birds to *Friends of the Forest*, a series depicting small, furry animals. Released in 1987, "The Rabbit" begins the collection.

Remembering When...

Touching the viewer's emotions without resorting to cliché subjects, *Jessie Willcox Smith's Childhood Holiday Memories* is the first series to feature the work of this famous woman illustrator. Her endearing children capture the holidays "Easter," "Thanksgiving," "Christmas Eve" and "Valentine's Day" in a heartwarming variety of poses.

Capturing the spirit of American naive portraitists, artists Barbara Marsten and Valentin Mandrajji began their 1986 series *American Innocents* with "Abigail in the Rose Garden." Abigail has been joined by "Ann by the Terrace" and "Ellen and John in the Parlor," providing a glimpse into an America long past through these portraits of children in colonial settings.

Moviegoers Love Plates Too

In 1986, Knowles selected *The Sound of Music* for the third Rodgers and Hammerstein movie musical to be captured on collectors plates. Recalling scenes familiar to every fan of the dramatic musical, based on the true story of the Von Trapp family, artist Tony Crnkovich chose as his subjects "The Sound of Music," followed by "Do-Re-Mi," "My Favorite Things," "Laendler Waltz," "Edelweiss," and "I Have Confidence in Me."

In early 1987, The Bradford Exchange released figures that movie plates were among the most active and valued plates on the secondary market. The world's largest trading center for collector's plates re-

"The Gettysburg Address" premieres Knowles' Lincoln, Man of America *series by Mort Kunstler.*

1986 "Jason," first issue in the Yolanda's Picture Perfect Babies *collection from Knowles begins a new era for the American producer.*

Favorite artist William Chambers started a new Mother's Day *series in 1987 with "Mother's Here," showing a mother quieting her little girl's sobs.*

ported that "from December 1985 to December 1986, 48 percent of the top 10 trading plates listed on the Exchange were movie plates."

Of the six movie series listed, the average price of a single plate rose about 14 percent from $55.28 to $62.98. Analyst Diane Therrien said, "In addition, in overall trading, one out of every four plates traded on the Exchange in 1986 was a movie plate."

The Exchange lists six movie plate series: *Wizard of Oz, Gone With The Wind, The King and I, Oklahoma, Annie* and *Gigi.* (*The Sound of Music* was first listed in June 1986, but is not included in the figures quoted here.)

Therrien attributed the growing demand for movie plates to several factors: the highly publicized 50th anniversary of the publication of the book *Gone With The Wind* in 1986, and release of video cassettes featuring many of the movies depicted on collector plates, introducing these movie classics to younger audiences.

With this popularity in mind, Knowles added *South Pacific* to its line-up of movie plates based on Rodgers and Hammerstein musicals. Elaine Gignilliat's "Some Enchanted Evening" initiated the unabashedly romantic series in 1987.

With the completion of his popular *Annie* and *The King and I* series, Knowles asked artist William Chambers to design his first non-movie plate series. The Chicago artist began his interpretation of Mark Twain's classic *Tom Sawyer* novel with "Whitewashing the Fence" in 1987.

The soft, romantic side of Chambers' style will also be seen in a new Mother's Day series for Knowles, begun in 1987. Titled *Portraits of Motherhood,* the first plate was "Mother's Here."

Two other Knowles artists also started new series for the company in 1987. New York sculptor Eve Licea, known to collectors for her technically innovative *Biblical Mothers* series, continues to create biblical subjects for *The Story of Christmas by Eve Licea* series. "The Annunciation" is the first issue in this square plate series.

Respected illustrator Mort Kunstler (who debuted in plates with *Oklahoma*), focuses on the larger-than-life American hero, *Lincoln, Man of America* for his new Knowles series. Kunstler selected "The Gettysburg Address" to begin the collection.

When Knowles announced that it would be producing a series of plates by Edna Hibel in 1984, her fans reacted to the news with applause. It was the internationally famous artist's first plate to be issued under $85 in several years. The resulting plate, "Abby and Lisa," quickly captured Plate of the Year awards from NALED and The Bradford Exchange. Hibel collectors were delighted with her most recent additions to the *Hibel Mother's Day* series, "Emily and Jennifer" in 1986, and "Catherine and Heather" in '87. The *Hibel Christmas* series was expanded with "The Gifts of the Magi" in 1986 and "The Flight Into Egypt" in 1987.

All primary market Knowles plates and dolls are available from gift shops and collectibles dealers in the United States, Canada, Great Britain, Germany, Denmark, Switzerland and Australia. Many plates which were issued before 1987 and are sold out on the primary market, can be obtained from collectibles dealers who are members of The Bradford Exchange. These issues can also be purchased through the Exchange from collectors and dealers.

SUSAN K. ELLIOTT

Lladro
Lladro's Porcelain Flowers—A Blooming Success for Over Thirty Years

When Juan, Jose and Vicente Lladro began in 1951 to create their small ceramic floral decorations, none could have imagined that their homemade kiln and rustic materials would form the foundations for one of the finest and most prestigious porcelain houses in the world. Yet during the past three decades the Lladro brothers have reached a position of global prominence with their porcelain works of art—what other companies have taken centuries to achieve.

The Lladro Quality of Excellence, Attention to Detail

Lladro's distinctive elongated style and palette of pastel tones characterize their elegant creations, be they charming figurines, collectible vases or beautiful miniatures. Raised in the country, the Lladros have never strayed far from their roots, and the beauty and simplicity nurtured by mother nature herself can be found in most all the Lladro renderings. Nowhere is this more evident than in the intricate flowers that often grace a Lladro lady's hair, gentleman's lapel or child's basket. The flowers are so true to life that one is tempted to reach out and touch the petals to make certain they are actually made of porcelain.

From roses to carnations, lilies to violets, each petal, pistil and stamen is closely studied before attempting the painstaking process of duplication in porcelain. Flowers are observed in different stages—from the bud to the full bloom—in order to remain as faithful as possible to the original. Careful testing is carried out to determine the thickness the different flower parts must be to authentically reproduce the blossom, yet fire correctly in the kiln. Both sculptors and technicians join forces in this never-ending union of art and science.

Only after involved preparatory research is completed can the flowers be formed—part by part. Each petal is shaped and modeled to the correct shape and size and then carefully folded over, smoothed and creased as the bloom is meticulously hand assembled by extensively trained artisans.

The end result is breathtaking in its beauty and in its closeness to real life. Whether it be a single boutonniere or a full cart brimming with flowers, the delicacy and attention to detail are obvious at every glance, adding an extra fine touch to an already exquisite figurine.

Lladro Products Offer Diverse Motifs

Many of Lladro's select Limited Editions are adorned with stunning arrangements of flowers. One such issue is "Floral Offering" (LL1490), a member of Lladro's collection of *Elite* figurines. Twin Valencian women, dressed in ornate regional garb, carry a basket overflowing with scores of exotic porcelain flowers. This authentic representation of the colorful procession through Valencia during the spring "Fallas" festival is limited to 3,000 issues.

Brides, glowing with happiness, are even more beautiful when trimmed with garlands of snow white blossoms. "Here Comes the Bride" (L1446) is no exception, with numerous buds, tinged with pink, gracing the hair and the gown of this small bridal entourage. The dainty bouquet is especially attractive with its mixture of flower shapes and sizes.

Children are a favorite motif to artists and collectors alike, with Lladro being no exception. "Courtship" (L5072) is a charming scene of puppy love where pink and violet wild flowers create a tranquil, content mood of shy youth.

The "grand dames" of yesteryear, with their dazzling finery and observant gazes, are ever-fascinating to the modern world. "A Lady of Taste" (L1495) captures the refined elegance of the time period with this regal

88

"Floral Offering," 14-¼" with base.

"Here Comes the Bride"

"Courtship,' 6"

society belle as she prepares for an evening out. The delicate bouquet completes her raiment with a flair, as only flowers can.

Lladro sculptors draw creative inspiration from countries all around the globe. "Tahitian Dancing Girls," style L1498, is just one of the dozens of figurines that bring a taste of the unknown—or a cherished memory—into our homes. Nature is a strong presence everywhere in the islands, and the natives enjoy wearing the offerings of the earth in their hair, on their wrists, and around their necks. Lladro has brought this feeling to life in its many Hawaiian and Tahitian figures, where the intricate flowers are in themselves works of art.

The Lladro Collectors Society, in addition to serving as a central information bureau for Lladro porcelain collectors and admirers, offers exceptional figurines at equally exceptional values to its members. In "Spring Bouquets," the 1987 annual members-only figurine, two armfuls of tiny pink and white blossoms are carried by a darling young-

"A Lady of Taste," 14½"

"Tahitian Dancing Girls," 12" with base

ster, making this third issue of the Society an extremely sought-after collectible.

In addition to serving as beautiful decorations on their porcelain figurines, the Lladro flowers are also made to stand alone, as individual tributes to the mastery of the Lladro craftsmen. Twelve different blooms -- from dahlias, peonies and roses to camelias -- form a beautiful interior porcelian garden, of up to four inches in length. New to the Lladro Studios is the *Caprichos Porcelain Collection* which includes numerous handmade floral arrangements of violets, irises, roses and daisies, stunningly set on delicate porcelain-covered lace. A complimentary Lladro flower catalog, complete with photographs of the intricate hand assembly, is available through the Lladro Collectors Society, P.O. Box 1122, 43 West 57th Street, New York, New York 10101-1122.

Maruri U.S.A.
Oriental Studio Wins Worldwide Fame for Wildlife Art Mastery

Centuries before Marco Polo sailed to the Orient and "discovered" porcelain for the West, the Imperial sculptors of China and Japan used this precious material to create elegant art masterworks. Indeed, Oriental ceramic art from this long-ago era is now considered priceless—and may be found on permanent display in the world's most exclusive museums.

Polo brought back many riches from his extensive travels—but none was more fascinating to Europeans than the milky-white, opalescent "porcellana" which he proudly displayed. The explorer named porcelain for the cowrie, or porcellana, a milk-white sea shell used for money in some parts of Asia.

Thus while Europeans struggled to recreate the formula for porcelain during the 15th and 16th centuries, the art studios of the Orient already had developed their craft to a high level of artistry. Over the years, Oriental art studios flourished through continued family involvement, as techniques were perfected and passed down from grandfather to father to son.

Maruri Thrives in the Japanese Porcelain Capital of Seto

In Japan, many of these ceramics families settled in the town of Seto. The stimulation of constant competition led to higher and higher levels of artistry, and thus Seto is known as the capital of ceramic art for Japan. One of the ancient studios there is known today as Maruri: a family-owned firm established generations ago by the brothers Mizuno.

Today Maruri is one of the world's largest manufacturers of ceramic products, with factories in Mexico, Japan and Taiwan. In the United States, Maruri is marketed under its own brand name, Maruri U.S.A., from the firm's offices in California.

Yet until 1982, American collectors were largely unaware of this outstanding, contemporary porcelain studio. In that year Maruri U.S.A. first introduced its wildlife sculptures by renowned artist W. D. Gaither. Within months Maruri became a respected name in the United States collectibles market.

Maruri's World-Class Wildlife Artist

A survey of today's top limited editon studios shows that the art of porcelain sculpture requires two things above all else: artists and craftsmen of exceptional talent, and total devotion to quality.

Maruri's heritage of superb bird and animal sculptures—and the firm's unparalleled devotion to quality in every aspect of art creation—made this firm a natural for the limited edition market. Selecting the proper artist, however, was a matter of extreme importance.

While many artists and sculptors draw on nature for their inspiration, the number of truly fine wildlife artists—such as Edward Marshall Boehm of the Boehm Studios, Dorothy Doughty of Royal Worcester, and Boleslaw Cybis of Cybis Studios—is quite small. To reach this exhalted level of art mastery, Maruri considered scores of artists before making a final selection.

Eventually, Maruri approached a talented, but relatively unknown, young artist named W. D. "Bill" Gaither about the possibility of producing a number of his pieces in porcelain.

Finding a wildlife artist of this calibre was a rare coup for Maruri, as Gaither represents a new breed of artist. Not satisfied with the stilted sketches of his subjects in the wild, he is a wildlife biologist and environmentalist accustomed to spending a great deal of time in the field.

As a wildlife scientist, Gaither depicts the taut muscle, poised wing or ruffled fur, perfect in every detail. As an artist, he adds that sense of vitality and life that makes his work so breathtaking—a rare blend of realism and art.

His studio is full of mounted specimens and an extensive library in the natural sciences, as well as his countless sketches and partially completed pieces of sculpture. Three of his books and numerous scholarly papers have been published and he is active in a number of environmental associations.

Out of this rich background, Gaither has become a multi-faceted artist. More than 600,000 of his wildlife paintings and prints may be found in galleries and private collections around the country. But it is sculpture that Gaither considers the ultimate medium, where every angle or sublte change of lighting adds new insights. The three-dimensional effect of his work reflects his talent for altering the mood of a piece and giving the viewer endless variety.

The Success of Maruri's Gaither Sculptures

The first W. D. Gaither pieces for Maruri debuted in 1981: "Screech Owl" and "American Bald Eagle I," part of the *Birds of Prey* series. With "American Bald Eagle I," Gaither established himself among today's most gifted sculptor of eagles—and collectors bought out the edition in a matter of weeks. Now this first eagle, which was issued at $165, sells for almost four times that much on the secondary market.

Other Gaither series since 1982 have included a four-piece *North American Waterfowl I* collection, a pair of small mallard ducks for *American Waterfowl II*, and a charming grouping of *North American Songbirds.* Gaither has displayed his remarkable versatility by introducing pieces inspired by baby animals such as lions, wolves and bears, stump animals, shore birds, and African safari animals. His sculpture of an Indian fighting a grizzly bear also reveals the artist's skill with the human figure by capturing the anguish and the terror of man pitted against such a formidable adversary.

The immediate acceptance of Gaither and Maruri as "world class" porcelain craftsmen shows that collectors quickly recognized not only the artist's talent, but also the exceptional quality and craftsmanship of Maruri.

Maruri Debuts American Eagle Gallery and Wings of Love

In 1985, Maruri unveiled an original collection of twelve popularly priced, hand-crafted porcelain eagle sculptures. Each sculpture represents a tribute to this magnificent bird that is also a cherished symbol of American patriotism, and an endangered species.

The "American Eagle Gallery," a series of 12 hand-painted porcelain Bald Eagle sculptures, captures in realistic detail the beauty of our country's proud symbol, the American Bald Eagle. The above sculpture details the proud head.

Ranging in height from 4¾" to 15¼", the Gallery depicts American Bald Eagles in a wide range of poses.

Most recently, Maruri announced a new series of six white porcelain dove figurines entitled *Wings of Love.* Some feature single doves, while others combine two doves with hand-crafted and hand-painted flowers. Each sculpture sits atop a wooden base selected to accommodate the application of an engraved plate, making these works appropriate for gift-giving, especially on romantic occasions.

Maruri Porcelains Require Painstaking Craftsmanship

To achieve its classical porcelain artistry, Maruri invests all necessary time and care in the tradition of Oriental craftsmanship. Often a dozen or more molds must be made to capture all of the individual nuances or details of a figure. Then using the ancient Grand Feu formula for porcelain, a creamy mixture containing feldspar is made into slip. Next each mold is filled with just the right thickness of porcelain. It is then allowed to dry slowly until the exact degree of dryness is achieved and the molds are removed.

Next the pieces are assembled. All seam lines and points of juncture are smoothed and refined by hand

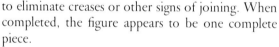

The American Bald Eagle soars proudly in this hand-painted sculpture. Each piece comes with a wooden base and a Certificate of Authenticity.

A Bald Eagle mother caring for her babies stands 15¼" in height and retails for $295.

to eliminate creases or other signs of joining. When completed, the figure appears to be one complete piece.

Support molds are then strategically placed to assure proper drying and the pieces are placed in a temperature-controlled room for several days to continue the drying process. Each piece is then kiln fired for at least 16 hours. The temperature is carefully controlled as it gradually builds to maximum heat and then is slowly reduced. After firing, Maruri artisans carefully inspect each piece for flaws, and as many as 35 to 40 percent may be discarded.

Each piece is then sandblasted to achieve a flawless, smooth surface and again checked for defects. This porcelain is a brilliant white, stronger than granite and more permanent than iron. Once the sandblasting is finished, weeks are required for the artists to hand-paint each piece in color after color.

The number of pieces in each Maruri issue is always published so collectors know the maximum that will be made. Due to the difficulties in production, the actual number produced may be less—but never more than announced.

A "Ground Floor" Collecting Opportunity

Seasoned sculpture collectors have likened Maruri U.S.A. to The Boehm Studio, Cybis or Royal Worcester in their early years of limited edition sculpture production. These legendary firms introduced finely crafted works earlier in this century at most affordable prices. Today, many of these "classics" command thousands or even tens of thousands of dollars at auction. It is difficult to say when the value of Maruri figurines will begin to rise above the price charged at issue, but this much is certain: their potential for growth in the limited edition market has already been established.

SUSAN K. JONES

Mill Pond Press
Quality Comes First for Prominent Publisher
of Limited-Edition Prints

"I agreed to let Mill Pond publish my works because of their insistence upon quality," says watercolorist David Armstrong. Even though his striking portraits of rural America now sell for tens of thousands of dollars and are displayed in galleries throughout the country, the artist considers it a great honor to have his prints published by Mill Pond. "They stand behind the artist," he says. "And they will not publish a print the artist considers inferior, in terms of color, design, or any other criterion. It is that insistence upon quality that makes Mill Pond a great publisher."

Now, David Armstrong will see his works in a 180-page catalog that has been called "the Who's Who of contemporary realist artists." Over fifty of today's best-known painters have their works published by Mill Pond, including Robert Bateman, who is recognized by many as the premier painter of the natural world. Many of Bateman's most distinguished peers are also published by the firm: among them, Maynard Reece, Roger Tory Peterson, Ron Parker, and John Seerey-Lester. Furthermore, the most recent Mill Pond catalog presents a wide variety of artistic styles and subjects. In it, the discerning collector can find dramatic landscapes by Nita Engle, the charming "Primitive" art of Mrs. "B", and the evocative figure paintings of Thornton Utz. Mill Pond's full line also includes original hand-colored etchings.

"I think it is important to have publishers that deal with fine art," David Armstrong says, explaining the need for fine quality prints. "A limited edition print allows people who collect art to display *good art* on their walls, even if they can't afford to spend thousands of dollars on a piece of art. And it helps the artist to reach much more of the public than he could ever hope to reach with the original image."

The World's Busiest Retired Couple

In March 1973, Mill Pond opened the doors to its "world headquarters"—a crowded two-room office in Venice, Florida. The firm had only recently been established as a part-time interest for its retired founders, Bob and Katie Lewin. Mill Pond published its first prints that fall, presenting new limited edition works by Maynard Reece and Roger Tory Peterson. Both artists were long-time business and personal friends of the Lewins. During the following year, the Lewins adopted what seemed at the time a very aggressive plan—Mill Pond would publish one print each month!

The adult children, Dick Lewin and Laurie Lewin Simms, joined the family-owned company and helped to manage its increasingly rapid growth. The roster of artists grew in size as the firm's reputation for quality attracted masters representing many genres of art. New employees worked in improvised office space located throughout the city, wherever Mill Pond could procure it.

Recently, the firm consolidated its sprawling office space, moving into its own new 40,000 square foot office building, in Venice, Florida. "It's a far cry from where we were in 1973," says Production Coordinator Ellen Pedersen, who has been with the firm for fourteen years. "The Lewins must be the world's busiest retired couple, with schedules that keep them on the go twenty-five hours a day, eight days a week! Their 'part-time' interest now employs fifty very full-time people."

A Demanding Process

Although Mill Pond has become one of the largest and most successful publishers of limited-edition prints, releasing 10–12 new pieces each month, the firm continues to give each new print the same attention

Morton E. Solberg brings a touch of surrealism to his limited-edition prints, to accent the wildlife subjects and give the works a sense of movement. The subject of "Edge of Night—Barn Owl," for example, seems to glide across Solberg's churning twilight sky.

The charming folk art of "The Spelling Bee" by Mrs. "B" illustrates the wide variety of artistic genres that can be found in the most recent Mill Pond catalog. Gaiety and warmth abound in the colorful primitives created by California artist Ann Baker.

and care bestowed upon those first limited editions offered in 1973. Because Mill Pond is a publisher rather than a printer, the actual printing is assigned to experienced craftsmen at special firms around the country. This allows Mill Pond to give each print the special treatment it requires, by entrusting the printing to the firm most capable of meeting an individual project's requirements. The printers, in turn, are challenged to meet Mill Pond's extremely demanding specifications.

At every stage of the complicated printing process for each print, "proofs" are shown to the artist. Representatives from Mill Pond also view these proofs, comparing them to the original and consulting with the artist. Corrections are made until the proofs faithfully match the original painting. These adjustments are made by etching the films and producing new printing plates, and by altering the colors and densities of the ink on the press.

Each printing requires several "press runs"—because the proofs, and later the final print, are most often created one or two colors at a time. Sometimes, sixteen or more runs are required to faithfully match the colors of the original painting.

This painstaking process of proofing, consulting, correcting, and reproofing takes several months. But

"High Kingdom—Snow Leopard" from 1987 has become one of Robert Bateman's most popular prints. The limited edition was created to help raise contributions to protect the work's endangered subject. Other Bateman prints have been sold to benefit important conservation programs—most notably, "Giant Panda," which raised money for the World Wildlife Fund, and "Northern Reflections" (The Royal Print), which was authorized by Their Royal Highnesses Prince Charles and Princess Diana, owners of the original painting. Bateman also created the first conservation stamps for Wildlife Habitat Canada, in 1985, and the National Fish and Wildlife Foundation, 1987.

Mill Pond believes every step is necessary if the finished art print is to meet the firm's high standard of quality. "I'm sure we drive our printers crazy at times," Ellen Pedersen says. "But we refuse to accept any finished print that doesn't meet our high standards. Or, as Bob Lewin has said from the beginning, "The final prints must represent the integrity of the original artwork, the artist, and the publisher."

The Mill Pond Difference

"The difference is the quality," Katie Lewin says. And it is this 100% insistence upon quality that continues to attract artists of Robert Bateman's and David Armstrong's stature to the firm—and creates great demand among art lovers for new limited edition prints from the firm. Indeed, many of Mill Pond's issues have completely sold out their editions during the past years, and tens of thousands of art lovers anxiously await new works from artists they admire. Mill Pond's limited edition prints are available from select art dealers throughout the United States.

TOM L. JONES

"Winter Vigil-Great Horned Owl" is a new limited edition print from John Seerey-Lester, one of today's most renowned painters of the natural world. The work is published in an edition of 950, with each print signed and numbered by the artist.

The Polland Collectors Society
Featuring Western Art by One of
America's Greatest Sculptors

Ever since childhood, gifted American sculptor Don Polland has been inspired by the glory of the Old West. With single-minded devotion, Polland creates fine works of art that capture the spirit and substance of life on the plains as it was generations ago.

His passion for telling a story with a single dramatic scene once led him to say that if an artist has something personal to say, "it becomes an obligation to communicate it. If you have to put a paragraph under it, you should have been a writer."

Polland's career has gone through several major evolutions in the past two decades, but has always concentrated on his love of the West and sculpting. After eleven years as a professional artist, he launched his own studio in 1970, crafting finely detailed bronzes in a tiny workshop in Laguna Beach, California.

He first created large bronzes, then chose to focus on the creation of miniature sculptures. Polland realized that many of today's would-be collectors have smaller homes and budgets, yet a high level of art appreciation. His instincts were obviously good because collectors world-wide now await his latest issues.

Polland began scaling down his work after seeing a small European bronze in 1966. Although not as detailed as his later works would be, the European bronze appealed to him because it was possible to hold "the whole thing in one hand, and turn it gently, caressing it as one would a precious jewel."

It took him three years and a sequence of about thirty bronzes before he made the transition to miniatures. Everything he had become accustomed to in his art—the media, tools and process of casting—had to be modified and tested to accommodate his new style.

Because so few artists work in miniature, the art world has no ready niche for this genre, and has at times downgraded its significance. "Gallery" or "museum" size art is considered important, so miniatures must not be, goes the reasoning of some critics. Obviously this view is not held by all, Polland collectors in particular. Polland feels stongly that size "has no place in the judgment of art, or its validity."

His work is not only in numerous private collections and major galleries, but has been exhibited in major museums such as the Whitney Gallery of Western Art and the C.M. Russell Museum. Polland sculptures are included in a permanent collection at the Favell Museum of Western Art in Klamath Falls, Oregon, where in 1980 he was awarded the museum's Western Heritage Award for his art.

More than a studio artist who has little association with the marketing of his art, Polland involves himself in every phase of production and delivery. In the early seventies Polland developed his own manufacturing and distribution network to maintain fair prices for his bronzes. By 1975, Polland's works were being shown in galleries located in virtually every major art center nationally, and also featured in seven prominent museums.

New Media for New Markets

With his bronze works firmly entrenched in the mainstream of the gallery market, Polland decided to further broaden his horizons by entering the gift and collectible market with pewter figurines. The Lance Corporation issued Polland's works in pewter through their Chilmark Collection beginning in the early 1970s.

Always eager to experiment with different materials (even crystal), the artist has most recently embraced cast porcelain as a design medium. Polland began designing for this new "material of the '80s" in 1980, creating a Western Frontier Collection made for Schmid by Border Fine Arts of Scotland. A medium that offers color as well as detail, cast porcelain introduced Polland's art to a new group of collectors.

"Federal Stallion," by Polland, 1987 pewter miniature, limited edition of 1,500, issue price $145.

"Running Free," 1987 pewter miniature by Polland, limited edition of 1,500, issue price $250.

Polland's career in limited editions has resulted in the creation of fifty or more gallery and museum bronzes, many of which have sold out and are doing well on the secondary market, and a series of special Franklin Mint issues based on a research trip to Africa.

Values Go Up

His 1967 "Bull Session," introduced at an issue price of $200, now sells for six times that amount, or approximately $1,200. Polland's masterpiece, a stagecoach-Indian scene with more than two dozen figures, "Ambush at Rock Canyon," debuted at $20,000 in 1971. A limited edition of five, it has more than doubled in auction price to a current value of $45,000 as art connoisseurs compete to own it.

One realizes the impact of Polland's art on collectors after learning that these purchases at issue and at auction have resulted in a full $12 million in sales.

Collectors Society Formed

This sustained demand led to the founding of The Polland Collectors Society in September 1986, and the creation of two pewter figurine limited editions especially for members: "I Come in Peace" and "Silent Trail." The sculptures will be produced expressly for collectors who become members and commission them through December 1987.

In accepting the challenge to create his first two works for The Polland Collectors Society, the artist assigned them his highest priority. He vowed to make these the most profound pieces he could visualize. Part of his goal was to allow the viewer to sense the spirit, the excitement, the vitality of adven-

ture that characterizes life on the American frontier. Polland wants the viewer to "be there," feeling the crispness of a Western winter, traveling on silent snow, being awed by the majesty of America's native Indians.

During the Charter Membership period, members will receive a number of benefits. Membership and a matched, numbered set of "I Come In Peace" and "Silent Trail" figurines may be acquired for $335. Membership alone is $35, and includes the "I Come In Peace" figurine, which represents a retail value of $112. Benefits include a membership card, Polland Society newsletters, advance introduction and closing notices, members-only offers, member discounts on many Polland figurines, and a yearly redemption card to be taken to the dealer.

A Varied Career

Born in California in 1932, Polland has also lived in Utah, Arizona, Colorado and Nevada, developing an intense interest in the golden days of the American West. In early childhood, he carved his own toy soldiers, cowboys and Indians. Summers were spent on his uncles' ranches in Utah, contributing to his love and knowledge of horses.

As a teenager he landed the job of stable boy at the Val Steve Thoroughbred Farm in California's San Fernando Valley, working his way up to exercise boy and finally, apprentice jockey. The intimate understanding of horses that he gained by being around these racing thoroughbreds is evident in his sculptures.

It is a family joke that Polland eventually had to give up jockeying because, as wife Charolette ex-

"Hunting Cougar," 1987 pewter miniature by Polland, limited edition of 1,500, issue price $145.

plains, "He had a terrible fondness for eating, which jockeys weren't allowed to do much of."

From the days of his first toy soldier carvings his talents were recognized by others. In high school he was singled out to attend live model classes reserved for the most talented art students. He continued his art while in the Navy, then began a series of jobs, never losing sight of his goal to preserve the Old West and Civil War era in sculpture. In his twenties he worked as an underground electrician, farmer, commercial artist, tool designer, art director, artist and modeler, lecturer and teacher in his own art school. He became a professional artist in 1969.

Along the way, he was learning all he could about metals, mold making, casting and sculpting. Today, he can handle every step in the intricate creation of a sculpture, from modeling to casting.

Although it would appear that Polland's decision to pursue sculpting was made instinctively almost from the beginning of his career, he explains that he does have a special motivation for creating this form of art. He says the third dimension allows him to "become completely involved, placing myself in the middle of things, to see and feel all that is taking place."

His art becomes nearly like a time machine, as he says, "I can move into my work, almost physically. I can dream of experiences past or wished for. I can transport myself to each happening or area of history."

For more information about The Polland Collectors Society, write to P.O. Box 2468, Prescott, AZ 86302.

SUSAN K. ELLIOT

Reco International
Firm Wins Recognition for New Works by Top Artists

The 1986 National Association of Limited Edition Dealers (NALED) banquet, held in conjunction with the International Plate & Collectible Exposition, was a memorable event for Heio Reich and the artists of Reco International. The president of Reco had received the 1986 Producer of the Year on behalf of his company, and he had joined in the thunderous applause as Sandra Kuck accepted her third consecutive Artist of the Year award, along with the award for Plate of the Year.

Now it was time for the announcement of the recipient of the prestigious Lee Benson Award. Created in 1980 by the National Association of Limited Edition Dealers (NALED) to honor the late and much-missed industry innovator, the award had only been presented five times in six years. The Lee Benson Award winner was determined by the board, and presented only during years when an individual distinguished him or herself by providing exceptional leadership, direction, and support to the collectibles industry.

Thus, it was with great pride that a beaming Heio Reich stepped forward to accept the coveted Lee Benson Award. Marge Rosenberg, the California dealer who had been similarly honored in 1985, presented the award, after reacquainting the South Bend, Indiana, audience with Heio's many contributions to artists, collectors, and the entire limited edition industry.

Following the ceremony, Heio Reich promised collectors that Reco "would not be resting on its laurels." "There are exciting new limited editions by Sandra Kuck, John McClelland, and other fine artists in the works," he assured collectors. "And we fondly hope to be among NALED's top award winners for many years to come."

A True Pioneer

If one word could possibly be used to describe Heio Reich and explain his contributions to the collectibles industry, it might be "pioneer." After coming to the United States from his native Germany, Reich became one of the very first American art plate producers—in 1969. A second breakthrough followed almost immediately afterward, when Heio Reich introduced the first-ever china plate edition to be sequentially numbered—an idea that caught on very quickly among collectors and producers.

In 1976, Heio Reich first saw John McClelland's potential as a plate artist. Again, Reich's "pioneer instincts" proved correct. John McClelland quickly earned a reputation as a major plate artist, and today, two of the artist's creations, "Mary, Mary" and "Little Boy Blue," are among the most coveted plates on the secondary market.

During the years that have followed, the President of Reco International has introduced American collectors to many other talented artists, including Aldo Fazio and, of course, Sandra Kuck—surely one of the most honored plate artists of all time. A number of plates and figurines by these artists, such as Sandra Kuck's almost-legendary "Sunday's Best" collector plate, have sold out their editions and are now available only on the secondary market at greatly appreciated prices. Thus, there continues to be great demand for new limited edition works from these talented artists.

Reco Introduces Major New Issues from Sandra Kuck

Her first-ever Mother's Day plate, "Once Upon a Time," reigns as NALED's Plate of the Year. Her "Sunday's Best" collector plate earned her Plate of the Year, Plate of the Show, and Silver Chalice awards. And she has been voted Artist of the Year by the dealers of NALED an unprecedented *four times*.

Without doubt, Sandra Kuck is one of today's "hottest" plate artists. And accordingly, there is great excitement surrounding the introduction of "A Cherished Time," Sandra Kuck's new *Mother's Day* plate for 1987. Like the famous first issue, "Once Upon a Time," the new plate presents a charming Mother-and-Daughter scene, invoking all the warmth and nostalgia that surrounds this special day.

"A Cherished Time," Sandra Kuck's Mother's Day issue for 1987, presents a charming, nostalgic mother-and-daughter scene. The lovely plate carries forward the impressive tradition started by the first issue, "Once Upon a Time," voted NALED's Plate of the Year for 1986.

"Rama the Tiger" premieres Reco's important new Vanishing Animal Kingdoms Plate Collection. Featuring the artworks of Sy and Dorothea Barlowe, each new issue will draw attention to one of earth's most endangered animals.

Acclaimed international artist Garri Katz has created the beautiful artwork for "Moses in the Bulrushes," first issue in Reco's Great Stories from the Bible Plate Collection. The plate is limited to a 14-day firing period.

Reco President Heio Reich and artist Sandra Kuck are honored by the National Association of Limited Edition Dealers (NALED) at its 1986 Achievement Awards Banquet in South Bend, Indiana. Heio Reich displays the prestigious "Lee Benson Award" along with Reco's fourth "Producer of the Year" award, while Sandra Kuck displays her "Plate of the Year" award and her third consecutive "Artist of the Year" award. Ms. Kuck also earned the "Artist of the Year" award in 1987.

Collectors have also expressed their delight with the recent issue of "Winds of March," the latest addition to Sandra Kuck's popular *Childhood Almanac* Plate Collection. The new plate depicts a charming young girl braving the March cold, as she visits friends more suited to the weather—three adorable, little lambs modelling their "natural" wool coats.

Heavenly New Works from John McClelland

As a previous recipient of NALED's Artist of the Year and Plate of the Year awards, John McClelland is best known for having broken new ground in the collector plate field. But his talents as an artist are far-reaching. And now, with the introduction of his first-ever angel-subject figurines, collectors are invited to see yet another side of the versatile John McClelland. Indeed, *The Reco Angel Collection* is the work of a true master. The twelve porcelain figures have been finely sculpted—to preserve the delicate flow of the gowns and the serenity of the angels' expressions—and glazed to achieve a pristine glow befitting the subjects.

Reco has also recently introduced John McClelland's *Becky's Day* Plate Collection, which, according to the artist, "offers a visual diary of the events in the life of a little girl from sunup to sundown." The first issue, "Awakening," depicts Becky blinking her eyes and stretching her arms, as she is caught off guard by the first rays of morning sunshine. A later issue,

"Muffin Making," presents the charming young girl hard at work, preparing a surprise breakfast treat for her family.

"Sophisticated" New Sculptures from Aldo Fazio

Introduced in 1985, *The Sophisticated Ladies* Plate Collection marked yet another first for Reco—by presenting the first-ever collector plates created by renowned sculptor Aldo Fazio. Now, the artist has taken the subjects of these acclaimed plates and rendered them in his favorite medium, that of sculpture. As a result, collectors can now enjoy the artist's eight tributes to the world's most elegant breeds of cats in beautiful three-dimensional form: *The Sophisticated Ladies Figurines.*

A Tribute to Endangered Species

A sense of urgency surrounds the introduction of Reco's new *Vanishing Animal Kingdoms* Plate Collection, for its subjects are endangered species, and the series is being issued to bring attention to the plight of these unfortunate animals. "Rama the Tiger" is the first issue, and it features a strikingly handsome Indian Tiger, placed in a border composed of classical Indian motifs. "Rama," like the stunning plates that will follow in the series, is the work of celebrated American artists Sy and Dorothea Barlowe. Each plate is limited to an edition of 21,500.

A Monumental New Series by Garri Katz

Reco is also proud to introduce a tribute to one of the greatest and most poignant Bible stories, "Moses in the Bulrushes." Internationally acclaimed art master Garri Katz has created the artwork for the collector plate, which introduces Reco's *Great Stories from the Bible* Plate Collection. The colorful, highly realistic work is strictly limited to a fourteen-day firing period.

The Secret of Reco's Success

In a field where "firsts" do not go unnoticed, Heio Reich's Reco International has consistently distinguished itself by combining innovation with a reputation for quality. As Reich explains his strategy, "I am on a constant search for new and better media and new ways of creating plates that will be attractive not only from a sales point of view. Our plates must have more than salability; they must give me the satisfaction of having produced something I can be proud of."

John McClelland's breathtakingly beautiful new figurine series, The Reco Angel Collection, *is represented by these three superb pieces. Each of the figurines—there are twelve in all—are presented in flawless, white porcelain.*

These "Sophisticated Ladies" are purring with delight, because sculptor Aldo Fazio has honored them with the introduction of these superb hand-painted figurines. The subjects first appeared in Fazio's successful 1985 collector plate series of the same name.

But of greatest importance, Heio adds, "It is *fun* to create new plates and ideas." And this is the secret for the success of Heio Reich and Reco International—the firm that will undoubtably continue to add new awards to its very crowded trophy display. Heio Reich shares something special with collectors the world over: the "fun" of discovering new artists and their works.

TOM L. JONES

Roman, Inc.
Delighting Collectors with Superb New Works from Italy's Fontanini Family

1988 marks the 25th anniversary of Roman, Inc., a firm known for its superb figurines, plates, and lithographs. Here, one finds artwork representing some of our finest contemporary artists, including Frances Hook, Irene Spencer, and Abbie Williams. For the firm prides itself on bringing new and exclusive artistic creations to an appreciative audience of collectors.

Recently, Roman, Inc. continued this impressive tradition when the firm introduced several important works from Italy's famed House of Fontanini, creators of Christmas decorations and nativities for four generations. The Fontanini tradition began in 1908, the year the family created its first Christmas articles. Working with the finest sculptors and painters of Bagni di Lucca in Northern Italy—near Michelangelo's and Leonardo's beloved Florence—the Fontaninis produced figures and decorations of heirloom quality. These works earned acclaim as they were highly detailed, hand painted, and finished with the look of wood.

The Collectible Creche Continues A Centuries-Old Tradition

Inspired by a time-honored tradition, the Fontaninis created their own unique nativity figures. Europeans had been crafting nativity scenes for centuries, ever since the Middle Ages, when St. Francis of Assisi is credited with inventing the concept. As time went by, displays grew more and more elaborate, with the introduction of additional characters. People from all walks of life were depicted coming to honor the Christ Child—a way of showing how God's presence touched everyone.

In crafting such subjects as a woman with spinning wheel, boy at campfire and sleeping shepherd, the Fontaninis laid the foundation for a creche scene that could be expanded through the years and passed on as an heirloom. They called this idea "The Collectible Creche." Imported exclusively by Roman, Inc. to the United States, it has since become America's most successful brand-name nativity program.

Part of Fontanini's wide acceptance is due to its open stock availability. Collectors may add new figures to their scenes each Christmas—there are over sixty to choose from! Many people acquire additional subjects throughout the year, for birthdays, weddings and anniversaries. The figures are available in several sizes, allowing collectors to create creches that will best enhance their homes.

Of course, the durability and superb quality of Fontanini figures also help to account for the enormous popularity of The Collectible Creche. Each figure begins as a highly detailed wax sculpture, which is used to create plaster molds of each part. These molds, in turn, are used as prototypes for the metal master molds, into which a special poly vinyl material is injected. This material captures every line and detail, as it hardens into a detailed reproduction that is virtually impossible to break, chip or nick.

Next, Fontanini's skilled artisans hand-paint the figures to achieve the wood tone or ceramic appearance. Often, these artisans are mothers and daughters, working in teams—representing new generations of families that have worked with the Fontaninis for decades.

Finally, after careful inspection, the figures are bathed in a special patina stain, to achieve an extra dimension of depth. Only then, after one final, careful inspection, are the figures made available to collectors in North America, exclusively through Roman, Inc.

The Holy Family

Another exceptional Fontanini work is the new, nearly life-size Holy Family, which premiered with four-foot cast poly resin sculptures of Joseph and Mary, along with the accompanying sculpture of Baby Jesus. A shepherd, cow, donkey, kings and sheep are also available with additional figures planned for the future. These stunning

The figures of Fontanini's "Collectible Creche" combine to create this spectacular Christmas display. The sculptures are available in a variety of sizes, enabling collectors to create displays that best enhance the beauty of their homes.

creations are the work of Fontanini's master sculptor, Elio Simonetti, who considers them the crowning achievements of his distinguished career. True to the Fontanini tradition, the "Holy Family" sculptures display amazing detail and realism, due in part to the intricate hand-painting process. Again, this set, which is particularly appropriate for display in lobbies, schools or churches, is available in North America exclusively through Roman, Inc.

A Landmark Collector Plate Series

In 1986, Roman was honored to introduce the very first Fontanini collector plate, "A King Is Born". It was a first in one other sense as well, having been the very first bas-relief plate molded from a special, unbreakable material. As such, it was hailed by collectors as one of the landmark introductions in plate collecting history.

The second issue in the series, "O Come, Let Us Adore Him," carries on with this new tradition. Once again, the depth of detail is extraordinary, capturing the wonder on the faces of three shepherds as they admire the newborn Jesus. Indeed the work appears to be carved from a single block of wood—so intricate is the detail. Like the first issue, "O Come" is hand-painted by the skilled artisans of Fontanini's

"O Come, Let Us Adore Him" is the most recent issue in the very first collector plate series from Fontanini—and the first collection ever to feature bas relief plates molded in a special, unbreakable material.

The beautiful Madonna is part of a nearly life-size nativity of cast poly resin, created by Fontanini's master sculptor Elio Simonetti.

Northern Italy, to perfectly achieve the wood-like finish. The third plate, issued in 1988, will feature the Three Kings and the fourth and final issue, scheduled for 1989, will depict the Flight Into Egypt.

Combining Two Great Traditions— Fontanini and Roman

Now, the fine works of Fontanini find themselves in a new family—that of Roman, Inc. They are, quite deservedly, in very good company, taking their place alongside figurines, plates, and lithographs that are cherished by collectors throughout North America.

The sculptures of Frances Hook, for example, have earned her the title of "the Berta Hummel of America" for her ability to capture the expressions and emotions of children. The steadily escalating value of her closed issues is testimony to her fine reputation. Irene Spencer is another widely collected Roman artist. Her variations on the beloved theme of mother and child have won her a broad and loyal following. The plate series and sculptured musicals of Abbie Williams continue to meet with a favorable reception. With outstanding artists like these, Roman, Inc. will continue to delight collectors for many years to come.

TOM L. JONES

Pam Cooper
Animal Artist Thrives on Country Life in the Mountains of North Wales

It is said that an artist should paint what she knows, and thus it comes as no surprise that Pam Cooper paints animals! Raised in rural Lancashire and Cheshire, England, little Pam considered family pets and farm animals her best friends—for she was an only child, and there were very few other children nearby for her to play with.

As Ms. Cooper recalls, "It seems as far back as I can remember I would draw or model the animals in our house and barnyard. And no matter what other commissions I may take, my personal choice always involves painting animals!"

Teachers and family members recognized the young girl's special talent for art, and encouraged her to leave her childhood home to study art at the Royal College in Manchester, England. This formal training was helpful to the fledgling artist, but she credits the influence of Hugh Mc.Neill as the source of her craftsmanship. Mc.Neill was a very successful artist and cartoonist with the International Publishing Corporation in London.

"I worked with him for ten years," Ms. Cooper recalls, "creating characters for children's magazines and the like. My 'bunny couples' were especially amusing. I enjoyed doing these 'just for fun' jobs, but actually my heart always remained with the serious painting of animals.

Marriage and Family Inspire a Solo Career

Like many mothers, Pam Cooper took some time off from her work after the birth of her two daughters, now teenagers. "But my love for animals and painting made me want to return to work," she asserts. The artist began accepting commissions for illustrations, greeting cards and graphics—free-lance works featuring animals and wildlife.

Working from her picturesque, seaside cottage in Conway Valley, North Wales, Ms. Cooper surrounded herself with family, a small circle of friends, and as always—a menagerie of animals. Indeed, the family's animal population continues to grow regularly. Ms. Cooper recently adopted a dog which had been mistreated in its former home. Or, as she explains it, the dog adopted her! And when she is asked to paint puppies, kittens or any other young animal species, the commission provides the perfect occasion for the addition of another animal baby to the fold!

Royal Worcester Commissions Kitten Classics

Several years ago, Ms. Cooper's delightful animal paintings drew the enthusiastic notice of Royal Worcester, one of Great Britain's most honored porcelain studios and creator of finely crafted collector plates, figurines and dinnerware.

The studio decided that this artist's devotion to animal art—and her success in portraying creatures with life-like fidelity to nature—merited the addition of her name to the small and highly respected Royal Worcester "stable" of artists.

With her first Royal Worcester commission, Pam Cooper became a part of a tradition extending back to 1751, when Dr. John Wall and William Davis opened their studio on the strength of a unique discovery: a superb soft-paste porcelain.

Over the past two centuries, Royal Worcester has continued its innovative tradition with the development of true English bone china and the introduction of the first-ever, limited edition porcelain figurines. In this

Pam Cooper

this century, the studio's artists have included Dorothy Doughty, Doris Lindner, Ronald Van Ruyckevelt and other respected names in porcelain art.

Royal Worcester's first animal art commission for Ms. Cooper introduced her to a new field of endeavor: that of limited edition collector plates. The concept was intriguing to a woman with a great love for animals: to portray adorable kittens in typical, mischievous situations.

The Creation of "Cat Nap"

As the owner of many felines over the years, Pam Cooper was ideally equipped to depict sweet little kittens in their most natural and endearing poses. True to her character, of course, she immediately selected and brought home a tiny kitten for daily inspiration.

For her first *Kitten Classics* plate-painting, Ms. Cooper drew upon her knowledge of the typical kitten's day. After hours spent running about, playing with toys and exploring the indoor and outdoor world, most every little feline is ready for a 'Cat

Nap.' And since she believes in pampering her furry friends, Ms. Cooper could easily imagine a kitten lounging in a comfortable bed with her tawny, tiger-striped head upon a flower-strewn pillowcase.

Others of the eight *Kitten Classics* plates show lovable kittens enjoying adventures both indoors and out. Each little feline has her own appealing personality, and each situation and pose developed out of Ms. Cooper's own long hours observing and playing with kittens over the years.

The Next Step: Kitten Encounters

Collectors and cat lovers responded so favorably to the *Kitten Classics* plates that Royal Worcester soon asked Pam Cooper to create still more original paintings inspired by cats and their frolics. She decided to explore kittens' relationships with other animals, birds and even tropical fish in a series entitled *Kitten Encounters*. Each plate shows how a kitten might react upon meeting another creature—in the woods, the barnyard, or at home.

First of these plates is "Fishful Thinking"—a fascinating composition in that the subject, a wide-eyed

What would a kitten most like to do after a long and arduous day of play? Take a "Cat Nap," of course. Pam Cooper has envisioned the kitten's ideal napping place: a people-style bed with a lavish, flower-strewn pillowcase. This charming work of art premiered Ms. Cooper's Kitten Classics *Plate Collection for Crown Ware, a division of Royal Worcester.*

A kitten can't help but indulge in a little "Fishful Thinking" when she encounters a bowl of goldfish, swimming freely and gracefully in their tranquil pool of water. Pam Cooper observed this scenario, and then captured it in a plate-painting as the premiere of her Kitten Encounters *Plate Collection.*

kitten, is seen through a round fishbowl. The viewer spies this little cat as she gazes longingly at the gold-fish swimming freely in their bowl. Other *Kitten Encounters* allowed Ms. Cooper to record the events between kittens and a duck, a rabbit, a horse, and a butterfly.

All the while, Ms. Cooper relied upon her own kittens for daily inspiration and fun. As she recalls, "I always have animals around me so that I can see what they get up to. Watching their antics, poses and expressions keeps an endless flow of ideas coming to me.

"I bought a cream-colored Persian kitten to inspire me for the *Kitten Classics* series, and now that "Muffin" is grown up, we also have a blue Persian called "Sapphire" for me to enjoy while creating the *Kitten Encounters* plates. Having animals around is nothing new for our family, though. We now have three dogs and some rabbits, and we have had everything from goats and ponies to ducks."

Trips Abroad and Quiet Times at Home

Another inspiration for Ms. Cooper is provided by her frequent trips to renowned art capitals such as Florence, Italy. There she draws inspiration from the great masters and renews her energy for her work. As she asserts, "If one loves art, a trip to Italy from time to time is a must!"

But she always returns to the animals and gardens in the Welsh countryside, for they provide an ideal setting for concentrated work.

With more kitten paintings on the drawing board and plans for still another Royal Worcester plate series adding children to the animal mix, Pam Cooper stands at the forefront of today's limited edition world. But her heart remains with the animals, and they are always close at hand. As she describes, "I just keep the kittens in the room with me and observe to my heart's content!"

SUSAN K. JONES

Swarovski America
Introducing the Swarovski Collectors Society

With the introduction in the mid 1970s of Swarovski Silver Crystal collectibles, a whole new experience was made available to the collector. Many theme collectors were able to add dazzling cystal pieces to their families of animals, owls, dogs, pineapples, or nearly any theme imaginable. Collectors of miniatures could expand the range of their collections to include brilliant, exquisitely cut, tiny creatures and objects. And crystal collectors found a whole new dimension to add to their treasury.

Regardless of the collector's area of interest, all of these new Swarovski collectors had one thing in common—they hoped that there would be a collectors' club to give them more product information in addition to availability of exclusive club pieces. Swarovski is proud to announce that the request was heard, and a new, international Swarovski Collectors Society has been formed, with the emphasis (as reflected in the elegant logo of initials and Edelweiss) on the collector.

"Guarantees You The Original Plus"

International in scope, the new Swarovski Collectors Society offers many unique features.

Each member will receive a Certificate of Membership in the form of an exclusive Swarovski full lead crystal paperweight, with the Society insignia beautifully imprinted and reflected in its many facets. The paperweight is mounted for display on a specially designed stand. Members also receive a personalized membership card.

New members receive *Milestones,* an elegant, full color book telling the story of Swarovski crystal and the Swarovski companies. Twice annually, members will receive the *Swarovski Collector,* a full color magazine devoted to crystal collectors and their interests. This fine publication will include a calendar of collectors' meetings which may feature seminars on the crystal production process, and information on periodic tours to Wattens, the Tyrolean home of Swarovski crystal.

"Togetherness", The First Members-Only Limited Edition

The most important benefit the Swarovski Collectors Society offers to collectors is the opportunity to purchase an exclusive, original collectible. The first of these annual editions is "Togetherness—the Lovebirds" which begins a series dedicated to the theme of partnership. Swarovski and its loyal collectors have such a partnership, and so it is fitting that the first series of exclusive pieces should represent the sharing and caring, taking-the-rough-with-the-smooth togetherness that partnership is all about.

The Lovebird is a small African parrot belonging to the Agapornis group. The origin of the name comes from the Greek "agapein", meaning love, and "ornis", meaning bird. In English, of course, this translates directly to Lovebird, which is an apt name, since this species is said to remain faithful for life.

In "Togetherness", a couple is depicted about to touch bills, which is a frequent act of reassurance, greeting, or simply the pure expression of love.

In this remarkable 4" work, the crystal designer has not only captured the natural attitude of the lovebirds but also the very essence of their relationship. Their warmth and affection is exquisitely portrayed in the superbly cut and polished full lead crystal.

The birds themselves are delicately faceted, with bills as smooth as satin, while an amazingly naturalistic effect has been achieved in the frosted crystal branch.

"Togetherness" will make an enchanting addition to any collection. It will be admired for its incomparable artistry and wealth of feeling. And for years to come, the love will shine through like a sparkling rainbow, providing a constant source of happiness in every collector's home.

The new 2" Falcon Head will add fiery brilliance to any collection of bird or eagle figurines, or it can be used as a dramatic desk ornament.

Discerning collectors love the Swarovski chess set, with full lead crystal chess pieces and a shimmering glass board.

Each piece bears the Swarovski Collectors Society logo, which is a mark of distinction for highest quality full lead crystal. The crystal designer's initials and the year of issue enhance the value of this collectible.

Swarovski Silver Crystal Offers Something For All Collectors

The continually increasing popularity of Swarovski Silver Crystal as a collectible is not accidental. Exquisite craftsmanship, and quality of design and detail are the characteristics all true collectors look for in anything they add to a collection, and these are the words that describe every Swarovski piece. In addition, Swarovski Silver Crystal adds a fiery brilliance to a collection, a feature exclusive to crystal, and unmatched in any other crystal collectibles. As if this were not enough, the range of Swarovski design provides something for every collector.

Bell collectors, animal lovers, paperweight collectors—all can find elegant pieces to add to their collections. In the realm of nature is the dramatic "Falcon Head," unique as an addition to a collection of bird or eagle figurines, utilitarian when used as a paperweight. Handmade of 32% full lead Swarovski Austrian crystal, the Falcon Head measures 2" in height and features inset eyes of colored glass, the actual color of a falcon's eyes.

A marvelous Polar Bear will delight animal figurine collectors. Standing 4" tall, this classic example of Swarovski design captures the spirit of this bear of the ice.

"Togetherness," the Lovebirds is the first Members Only limited edition piece offered to members of the Swarovski Collectors Society. This exquisite 4" figure of two lovebirds on a frosted branch is the first in a series of pieces with a Partnership theme.

For collectors of paperweights, Swarovski offers both clear and vitrail crystal. The paperweights vary in size and are in egg, cone, barrel, pyramid and round shapes, with each shape individually cut to best enhance the color and size.

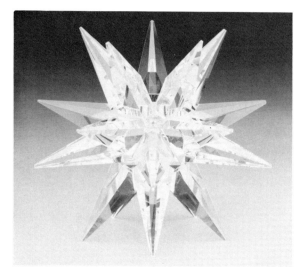

This magnificent star in more than 30% full lead Austrian crystal is actually a candleholder.

Truly discriminating collectors are attracted to the exquisite chess set Swarovski has created in full lead crystal and shimmering glass. Each crystal chess piece has been designed to combine the long traditions of the game with the newer, more sophisticated tastes of today's players and collectors. The elegant board is made of glass, with each etched square reflecting the brilliance of the chess pieces as the moves are made. The set is contained in two cases, one velour-lined to protect the delicate board, and the other fitted with a vacuformed, velour-covered lining to house each chess piece individually.

New or established Swarovski collectors can now learn more about Swarovski Silver Crystal collectibles through membership into the Swarovski Collectors Society. Membership forms are available through authorized Society retailers, who will have the current "Members Only" limited edition piece on display. For further information, and the name of the Authorized Swarovski Collectors Society retailer nearest you, contact Alice Clair, U.S. Society Secretary, Swarovski Collectors Society, One Kenney Drive, Cranston, R.I. 02920-8381.

SARA KIRTLINK

Tengra
Building Upon an Age-Old Tradition
of Fine Spanish Porcelain

They have been called the "fastest-growing collectible in North America," and the figurines created by Spain's TENGRA Studios continue to attract new admirers because of their beauty and faithfulness to classical Spanish styles. These superb porcelain works not only represent almost three centuries of experience in Spain's porcelain industry by the family of TENGRA'S founder. But the firm's most recent works also continue and honor a tradition that is over 1200 years old.

Spains's Great Ceramic Heritage

For centuries, the production of superb ceramic artworks has been part of the Spanish tradition. In fact, according to ancient documents, the first ceramic pottery appeared in Spain around 500 B.C.—during the same time period in which the Chinese and Japanese were perfecting the process of creating porcelain.

But it was during the Moorish invasion of Spain in the early eighth century that the first, distinctive Spanish styles emerged. During this period, the Spanish potters coupled the then-revolutionary techniques of Chin's T'ang Dynasty with glazing techniques borrowed from the ancient Babylonians. The innovative style that resulted involved the application of a white-tin oxide to ceramic works, immediately preceding their second firing. The additional firing produced an elegant glaze, "Reflejo Metalico" (metallic reflection), defining a style that influenced the rest of Europe for hundreds of years.

In the fifteenth century, the ceramics masters of Manises, in the province of Valencia, improved on these methods, by developing the famed "Mudejar Style". New works in this style combined Gothic motifs with Moorish designs, and employed touches of brilliant gold and bright blues, reds, and greens. Immediately popular throughout Europe, the style came to be known in Italy as "Maiolica" and in France as "Faience".

Unfortunately, the "Mudejar Style" lessened in popularity during the following decades, as the French and Italians competed to create designs of their own. But the technique was eventually revived—near the end of the 17th century—at the request of King Carlos III. Artists were brought from France to Alcora in Valencia in order to learn contemporary popular styles. Among these artists was a Mr. Ten, an ancestor of Joaquin Ten, Founder of TENGRA.

In time, Alcora came to be known as a European art center, and it employed more than 300 artisans. It was a reputation that would continue into the present century.

The TENGRA Tradition Begins

From the time of his birth, in 1921, it was apparent that Joaquin Ten Paus would grow up surrounded by ceramics. His grandfather and father had continued the tradition begun in the seventeenth century, and thus, no one was surprised when the boy began creating his first ceramic designs at the age of eleven. But this was only the beginning, for Joaquin's passion for fine porcelain artistry continued to grow, and by 1954, he was honored for successfully combining porcelain with bronze to create innovative designs.

Several years later, the artist's brother-in-law, Jose Luis Grafia, recognized the enormous market potential of Joaquin's art. A partnership was formed—merging Joaquin's artistic talents with Jose's knowledge of economics and administration. Respectfully bowing to tradition, the new partners located their studio in the province of Valencia, and they created the TENGRA name, combining the letters "TEN" and "GRA" of their two names.

Joaquin Ten Paus represents a long line of noted porcelain artists. He works with his brother-in-law and son, continuing the family tradition of the great studios of old Valencia.

Jose Luis Grafia founded TENGRA with brother-in-law Joaquin Ten Paus. Jose brought his expertise in management and economics to the firm, having recognized the market potential of Joaquin's unique porcelain works.

Innovation Tempered by Experience

Today, the TENGRA studio is equipped with modern, state-of-the-art machinery, but the assemblage and painting are done much as they were in the eighth century. Even though more than 200 unique designs have carried the TENGRA logo, each figurine requires three months of labor. The figurines are hand-assembled and hand-painted by experienced artisans working in the studio, and everyone involved in the process wears a spotless white blouse, to ensure that no dust comes in contact with the clay. The work is supervised by Joaquin Ten Paus.

Collectors in the United States and forty other countries anxiously await the issue of new porcelain figurines from the studio, in the knowledge that TENGRA combines a legacy of twelve centuries with the creativity of its artisans and the superiority of its production techniques. And though the editions are not limited to a specific number, each production is "retired" after a certain number of years, turning many of the figurines into coveted collectors' items.

In the United States, the studio's contemporary designs have earned TENGRA the "International Gold Star for Design" and the "American Recognition of Efficiency", both awarded by Business Initiative Directions of San Antonio, Texas. TENGRA was also awarded the "1986 America Award" by the Trade Leader's Club and Editorial Office. The award, given in New York, honored "the most prestigious and fastest-growing collectible in North America". But for Joaquin Ten Paus, the greatest reward continued to come from satisfied collectors, whom he describes as "Friends, sharing a common love for art".

Elegant New Figurines Carry Forward the "Valencia Style"

Recently, TENGRA announced the introduction of three special figurines, created to honor the historic roots of the studio's—and Spain's—ceramic tradition. The three figurines comprise *The Babylonian Collection,* in recognition of that empire's great contributions to the Valencia ceramic process.

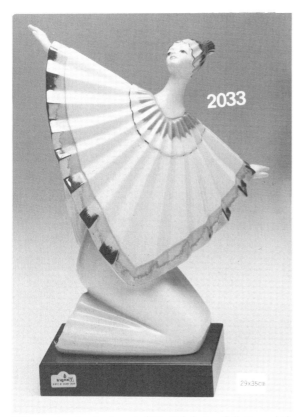

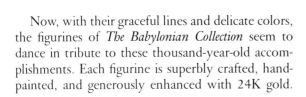

This stunning figurine is part of The Babylonian Collection, which honors the ancient empire's contributions to contemporary ceramics. The Babylonians' tin-glazing technique, discovered over 1,000 years ago, was a major factor in the development and popularity of Spanish ceramic ware.

The creation of a figurine starts with an idea, which is translated into a basic design. After accurate and detailed research, an original TEN-GRA sculpture will be created such as "Girl with Hat" from The Country Collection.

Now, with their graceful lines and delicate colors, the figurines of *The Babylonian Collection* seem to dance in tribute to these thousand-year-old accomplishments. Each figurine is superbly crafted, hand-painted, and generously enhanced with 24K gold.

As a result, the elegant, ancient styles of clothing and adornment are perfectly captured for all time. The three figurines range in height from $13\frac{2}{3}''$ to $21\frac{2}{3}''$.

TOM L. JONES

Josiah Wedgwood & Sons Limited
The Story of England's Most Legendary Master of Ceramic Art and the Company that Bears His Name

A near-fatal bout with a deadly disease may well have changed the course of Josiah Wedgwood's life—and the history of English ceramic arts.

When young Josiah contracted small-pox during his adolescence, he had already begun his apprenticeship as a potter at the studios of his oldest brother, Thomas Wedgwood. Josiah recovered almost completely, but his right knee was affected with the complaint known as Brodie's Abcess, which prevented him from keeping his place at the thrower's bench.

Thus, following his formal apprenticeship to his brother Thomas in November, 1744, the fourteen-year-old Josiah was forced to restrict his work to the less energetic pursuits of designing, modeling and molding.

These activities were later to serve young Wedgwood well, for his daring—and highly successful—experiments in ceramics would earn him Royal acclaim and everlasting renown.

A Family of Potters

Josiah Wedgwood was born the twelfth and last child of Thomas and Mary Wedgwood of the Church-yard Pottery, Burslem, Staffordshire, in July, 1930. His family took its name from a hamlet first settled in the 14th century, named Weggewode—an Anglo-Saxon term for a wayward wood. Considering the number of potters in Wedgwood's ancestry, and their admirable success, the 19th-century historian Eliza Meteyard wrote: "the craft he was destined to pursue had been followed with skill...and inheriting the result of this in an increased degree, in him it culminated in genius. He was as much born a potter as Reynolds a painter..."

At the time of Josiah's birth, several social factors had combined to develop a fast-growing market for ceramic wares. For one thing, more people were drinking tea and coffee, requiring large numbers of cups, saucers and tea pots. By the early 1700s, lifestyles were advancing considerably, with more people entertaining lavishly, requiring large suites of dinnerware and specialized bowls and plates for exotic fruits and vegetables.

Although he worked first for his brother and then with Thomas Whieldon of Fenton, the greatest English potter of that era, Josiah Wedgwood felt a strong desire to establish his own business. This desire was fueled by his passion for experimentation in the hopes of improving ceramic wares, production techniques and methods of decoration.

Arts of Josiah Wedgwood

In 1759, Josiah Wedgwood established his own enterprise, beginning to produce goods then in great demand in Birmingham and London. In her 1873 history entitled *Wedgwood and His Works*, Eliza Meteyard name these as: "...pickle-leaves, knife-hafts in imitation of agate and other crystalline stones, plates resembling tortoise shell and marble, and sugar and honey cups opening in the middle, and so veined and richly coloured as to perfectly represent a fine melon." So charmed was the first-time American visitor Benjamin Franklin with these wares that he sent a pair of these melon-shaped cups to his wife in Philadelphia.

Wedgwood gained early fame for his exceptionally fine works in cream ware, especially pieces glazed in brilliant green and shaped to resemble fruits and vegetables. Then he responded to the public's growing demand for dinnerware with wonderful cream ware services including special containers for fruits, jellies, syrups and creams.

When Queen Charlotte ordered a tea service from Wedgwood in 1765, the young potter worked with his usual skill and care to produce a superior product. Soon the Royal family ordered cream ware table services from Wedgwood. Wedgwood earned the title of Potter to Her Majesty and was permitted to call his new cream ware "Queen's Ware."

This portrait of the Master Potter by George Stubbs is painted in enamels on an oval Queen's Ware (fine earthenware) plaque. It is one of a matching pair—the other being of Josiah's wife, Sarah. Both were painted in 1780 and fired in the kilns at the Wedgwood factory of Etruria.

Each raised (bas-relief) ornament or selection of border motif is hand applied to Wedgwood Jasper Ware by a method that has not altered since the days of the first Josiah Wedgwood—not for the sake of tradition—but because it is the best way to preserve the clarity of fine detail.

The oldest and most skillful of all pottery crafts is called throwing. Thousands of visitors to the Wedgwood factory at Barlaston, Stoke-on-Trent, are fascinated by the creative skill of the "throwers", whose exceptional hand-craft calls for a fine sense of touch and superb dexterity.

A few years earlier, in 1762, Josiah Wedgwood met his partner-to-be, Thomas Bentley, a Liverpool merchant with whom he formed an intimate and lasting friendship. After several years of negotiation, the two signed a partnership in August, 1769, which ended only on Bentley's death in November, 1780. Bentley's taste, knowledge of the arts, and social contacts were of inestimable value to Josiah Wedgwood and his influence was paramount in the international success of the firm.

By 1766, Josiah Wedgwood has prospered sufficiently to buy the Ridge House Estate between Hanley and Newcastle-under-Lyme. There he built a splendid new factory which he named Etruria. It was formally opened on June 13, 1769, and six "First Day's" vases were made by Wedgwood and Bentley to commemorate the event.

The Invention of Black Basalt and Jasper

In the early years of his business, Wedgwood concentrated successfully upon the manufacture of what he called "useful wares." But always he allowed time for exploration: searching for ways to push the boundaries of ceramic craftsmanship based upon his extensive studies of chemistry, mineralogy and classic art.

Once again, the tragedy of his youthful illness had provided Wedgwood with a golden opportunity.

From time to time his injured leg and related illnesses would force him to bed and then to lengthy convalescence, during which the young potter supplemented his meager formal education with voracious reading. Thus he was well prepared to embark upon long and ultimately successful courses of experimentation.

His work initially led to the development of Black Basalt. A crude product called "Egyptian black" was already in use by a number of Staffordshire potters. But this new Black Basalt created by Wedgwood was fine-grained, smooth, and richer in hue. He used it for relief plaques, busts, medallions and cameos, as well as "useful wares" for the table and fine vases. In 1773 he forecast correctly: "The Black is Sterling, and will last forever." It is still one of Josiah Wedgwood & Sons' best-known products.

Further experimentation led to the most famous of all Josiah Wedgwood's inventions. The triumphant outcome of several thousand recorded experiments, Jasper was prized by Wedgwood above all his productions and provides today the most valued and sought-after range of ornamental ware in the world. Never equaled to the present, Jasper is an unglazed vitreous fine stoneware which may be stained in a wide variety of colors, the best known of these being pale blue. The stoneware provides a suitable background for white classic reliefs or portraits in the same material.

A view of the Wedgwood factory at Barlaston, Stoke-on-Trent. In the foreground is a statue of the founder Josiah Wedgwood (1730-1795).

Wedgwood After "The Father of English Potters"

Josiah died in 1795 and is remembered as "The Father of English Potters." But it was not only as a pottery manufacturer that he was renowned and respected in his time. His invention of a thermometer, or pyrometer, had led to his election as a Fellow of the Royal Society.

In the nineteenth century, Wedgwood survived periods of economic difficulty and important progress was made in the use of new machinery, and also in the manufacture of bone china.

In the 1930s, the fifth Josiah Wedgwood decided to build a new factory. A country estate now numbering over 500 acres near the village of Barlaston was selected, and a new expansive, modern, all-electric Wedgwood factory rose on this handsome site. Nearby a garden village was built with houses for key workers. Since 1940, when production began at Barlaston, the factory has been expanded to four times its original size and has become a showplace of British industry.

Wedgwood's Contribution to Limited Edition Collectibles

Josiah Wedgwood & Sons Limited first entered the limited edition plate realm in 1969, with a blue and white Jasper ware Christmas plate entitled "Windsor Castle." Since then, Wedgwood has introduced a new plate to mark Christmas each year. These bas-relief works are inspired by various well-known English landmarks, including "Trafalgar Square," "Buckingham Palace," and "Tower of London." In 1971, Wedgwood introduced its Mother's Day plate series—another Jasper ware collection presented in various color combinations.

Wedgwood also creates collector plates of bone china and other ceramic media, inspired by the artwork of Beatrix Potter, Mary Vickers and many other gifted artists from Great Britain and around the world.

The Visitor Centre at Barlaston

Each year, more and more visitors wish to see for themselves the highly skilled processes of Wedgwood craftsmanship. They are able to observe these traditional crafts—and to visit an exceptionally fine Wedgwood Museum Collection—by traveling to the Wedgwood Visitor Centre, 160 miles from London at Barlaston. There the Wedgwood formula for continued success is applied day by day, just as Josiah himself would wish: skilled craftsmanship allied to advanced technology and imaginative design for the finest in ceramic art mastery.

SUSAN K. JONES

The History and Trends of Plate Collecting
The Market Matures

The world of plate collecting involves much more than brightly colored pieces of inanimate porcelain. Entering its circle inevitably leads to an exploration of art, social customs, holidays, wars and even economics.

An 1890 German plate from Villeroy & Boch claims to be the earliest collector plate, but historians generally agree that the most significant event in early plate collecting history occurred in Denmark in 1895.

That year, the Bing & Grondahl porcelain factory in Copenhagen transformed a custom of the day into the world's longest running plate series. Wealthy Danes traditionally gave food to their servants on simple plates during the holidays. Harald Bing's factory capitalized on that custom by creating a dated Christmas plate. Entitled "Behind the Frozen Window," it was intended for gift-givers to pile high with holiday goodies, giving two gifts in one. The cobalt blue and white bas-relief plate sold for fifty cents.

A Window to History

Bing & Grondahl's panoramic series continued unbroken through both World Wars and appeals to modern-day collectors around the world today. A survey of past designs provides a glimpse into the state of the world that year, or the artist's attempt to divert the audience's attention from it. For example, plates issued during the years of World War II show tranquil scenes such as the "Horses Enjoying Christmas Meal in Stable" for 1941. A poignant snow-covered commemoration cross appeared on the 1946 plate to honor Denmark's fallen soldiers at the war's end.

After Bing & Grondahl's introduction, other factories eventually developed their own annual series, also in blue-and-white motifs.

Royal Copenhagen of Denmark claimed the honors for second-oldest Christmas plate, "Madonna and Child" (issued in 1908), until a 1907 Rosenthal Christmas plate turned up in a German couple's home in the mid-1970s. Before then, 1910 was the date of Rosenthal's earliest known Christmas plate. A former Rosenthal president discovered the 1907 plate when he was invited to view a collection of old plates.

These three series—Bing & Grondahl, Royal Copenhagen and Rosenthal—formed the basis of a quiet hobby for many years, and established certain criteria for plate collecting that endured for seventy years.

Standards Set by Competition

Early Christmas plates were expected to feature historic subjects in winter (Kronberg Castle in Denmark, a street scene in Munich) as well as Christmas themes (angels, wise men, the family going to church, children around the Christmas tree). Royal Copenhagen's 1945 Christmas plate, "A Peaceful Motif," depicted a young angel praying over a snow-covered grave, silent testimony to the war's ravages. These early plates were all bas-relief porcelain in blue and white, dated, and produced only for the year of issue.

The Rosenthal *Traditional Christmas* series (closed in 1974), followed a slightly different pattern. The blue-and-white plates in this series occasionally featured small touches of yellow or brown in their designs. Also, from 1969 to 1971 some of the earlier plates were reissued in small quantities (500 or less), no doubt to satisfy demand that was beginning to emerge from new collectors.

These reissued plates, regardless of the year depicted, have a post-1957 backstamp and their foot rims are not pierced. Rosenthal began a *Classic Rose Christmas* series in 1974 to replace the *Traditional Christmas* series, and no longer reissues plates after the year of issue.

A New Era Changes the Rules

Agreement about what a collector plate should be was the result of coincidence more than conscious planning by early plate makers. In the mid-1960s, the respected French crystal maker Lalique turned all the ba-

sics of plate upside down by issuing a collector plate that was not porcelain, not for Christmas, and not blue and white.

Twice as expensive as any of the other plates on the market at that time ($25 versus $11-12), Lalique's 1965 "Deux Oiseaux" plate featured two entwined birds etched in lead crystal and immediately sold out. "Deux Oiseaux" quickly rose in value to $1,000, focusing the attention of press, collectors and manufacturers on the hobby and its possibilities.

Plates in the Lalique *Annual* series were produced in limited editions of 2,000-8,000 through 1976. Lalique announced how many plates were made each year, adding a new element to the concept of a collector plate.

In 1969, Bing & Grondahl again stepped forward in plate collecting history, creating the first annual Mother's Day plate. The landmark blue and white "Dog and Puppies" captured the public's fancy and led a parade of new series from European and American makers. Plate collecting would never be the same again.

The Explosion Begins

Since part of the advertised attraction of plate collecting at that point was investment potential, American mints sprang up to issue plates in precious metals such as sterling silver and gold. Others selected pewter. Wooden plates from Anri in Italy and Pfaff in Germany began to appear, along with stoneware (Goebel's Hummel plates and Wedgwood's distinctive Jasper ware), and Belleek's parian china from Ireland. Veneto Flair of Italy produced terra cotta plates with an unusual crackled surface in majolica style.

Easter and Father's Day emerged as important holidays on the plate collecting calendar, quickly followed by Valentine's Day.

A crash in the plate market occurred in 1972-73 as the over-emphasis on the investment aspect of plate collecting cooled buyer interest.

The most important and enduring innovations of the early seventies were the introduction of full-color ceramic transfers, the introduction of the first magazine devoted exclusively to coverage of limited edition plates (*Plate Collector*), and the recruitment of accomplished artists to design plates.

New Talent Introduced

These artists used the freedom of a full-color palette to push collector plates to a new level. Series would now tap the finest artistic talent in the world

The American Bicentennial coincided with increased interest in collecting throughout the country. "The Secret Contract," first plate in the Lafayette Legacy *series, was introduced in 1973 through an extensive direct mail campaign. The plates were imported by collectors directly from France.*

with artists such as Bjorn Wiinblad, LeRoy Neiman, Edna Hibel, Irene Spencer and Norman Rockwell. This established a more secure base for the hobby, appealing to an ever-larger group of collectors. These new collectors were attracted to plates primarily for their art, not re-sale value.

The Bicentennial Bonus

The United States celebration of its Bicentennial in 1976 provided further impetus for collecting in the seventies, with some series beginning four years before the event. Amid the hype and hoopla, many fine issues were created by contemporary artists to commemorate the occasion, and significant art of the past was dusted off and reproduced in new forms.

The Bradford Exchange entered the plate market during this period with the D'Arceau Limoges *Lafayette Legacy* series, introducing thousands of would-be collectors to the hobby with massive direct mail campaigns.

During the ensuing years, Bradford would be affiliated with producers such as Knowles (a major influence with its many Rockwell series), Studio Dante di Volteradici, Konigszelt Bavaria, Limoges-Turgot, and the Newell and Davenport Potteries. The company also developed the *Bradex*, a price guide for collectors that tracks the plates in the same manner as the stock market, and offers brokering of

collector plates so that individuals could participate in the secondary market easily. The annual *Bradford Book of Collector's Plates* traces the hobby's past and recent issues.

Not only did the Bicentennial provide fertile subject matter for American collectors, it coincided with increased interest in collecting of all kinds throughout the country. Prosperity gave collectors the means to indulge their wants, and the plate collecting hobby matured to fill this demand.

New Subjects Expand Market

Once the Bicentennial had passed, producers continued to expand the scope of the hobby, introducing more and more series completely unrelated to holidays. Artists of the World, an American producer devoted to collector's plates, turned to a quintessentially American subject with Arizona artist Don Ruffin's *Indians* in 1976.

Royal Doulton was an early leader in non-holiday plates, often in impressionistic style art. The English factory's American division introduced the art of Edna Hibel for a *Mother and Child* series in 1973. Le-Roy Neiman's arty *Commedia Dell'Arte* series in 1974, and marine artist John Stobart's *Log of the Dashing Wave* in 1976, elevating the level of art available in the field.

The Hamilton Collection pleased ballet fans with its 1978 introduction of *The Nutcracker Ballet* plate collection. Building on the success of this series, Hamilton has grown over the past decade to become one of America's leading direct marketers of collector plates. Hamilton's unique strategy is to combine its resources with those of top porcelain firms such as Reco International, Roman Inc., The Boehm Studios, Royal Worcester, Armstrong's, Ernst and Wedgwood.

A Sign of the Times

In 1978, the touring collection of King Tut artifacts on loan to the United States from Egypt offered new inspiration for porcelain collectibles. Boehm Studios of Trenton, New Jersey, received permission to duplicate many of the finest relics of the boy king's reign, writing another chapter in plate collecting history as a reflection of its times. Other plate companies developed their own commemoratives to honor the traveling exhibit.

Artists Benefit from Plate Collecting

Plate collecting provided a new audience for artists, allowing them to share their paintings with thousands of collectors who might never be able to afford their art otherwise. Artists became personally known to collectors by appearing at open houses held by retail shops across the country and at various collector conventions.

Conventions Create Excitement

The first such convention, sponsored by dealer Winnie Watson in South Bend, Indiana, drew a handful of manufacturers and about 500 collectors

The first plate collector convention was sponsored by dealer Winnie Watson in 1975. Dave Armstrong's booths are good examples of the growth and creativity that have transpired over the years. Armstrong's first booth consisted of a skirted table as did all booths. Artist Irene Spencer was in attendance to meet collectors. Armstrong's Pasadena Show booth won the 1987 award for the Best Original Design. The elaborate booth was constructed of giant building blocks spelling the firm's name, giant tinker toys and an erector set.

Prominent artist John McClelland entered the plate market in the 1970s and continues to please collectors today. "Little Bo Peep" is the fifth issue in McClelland's award winning Mother Goose *series by Reco International.*

Mario Fernandez took plate collectors by storm in the 1980s when he created the Wings of Freedom *series. A recent series,* The Seasons, *includes "Spring Robins" produced by Fountainhead. "Through the passing of time, all is changing as the seasons change. With that change memories live on and life itself becomes the only constant," reflects Fernandez.*

to that midwest city in July 1975. Artists Irene Spencer and Lorraine Trester were honored guests at the first convention. Attendance has since grown to a peak of about 14,000, with nearly every major living plate artist visiting the South Bend show at least once.

Collectors return each year to see the newest collectibles, meet their favorite artists and fellow collectors, and learn more about the hobby through seminars conducted by experts in the field.

By bringing together all those involved, the annual South Bend convention (and others held around the country in subsequent years) created a unifying force for the hobby. The interaction among producers, dealers, artists and collectors established a forum of accountability and offered producers face-to-face discussions with buyers about which plates they liked.

Producers, collector clubs and other dealers have also staged conventions around the country, with locales including Los Angeles, New York City, Chicago, Denver, Orlando, Florida, Columbus, Ohio, and Washington, D.C., and numerous Canadian cities. Collectors of Precious Moments, Norman Rockwell art and Hummels attend specialized conventions of their own. General-interest conventions incorporate the full range of plates, figurines, prints, dolls, bells and other limited edition collectibles. These events

have been an important factor in generating ongoing excitement in the hobby.

Investment Frenzy

As the late 1970s approached, plate collecting heated up. The 1971 Goebel Hummel plate was one of many catapulted to investment heaven as speculators jumped into the field with both feet, generating a buying and selling frenzy.

Publications devoted to plate collecting had increased to three by then—*Plate Collector* (begun in 1972), *Plate Market Insider* (1978) and *Plate World* (1979)—with others such as *Collectors Mart, Collector Editions, Antique Trader* and *Collectors News* including plates as a major part of their antiques and collectibles coverage. To keep up with market activity, *Plate Collector* magazine continued to expand its "Plate Price Trends" guide to market values, offering current information to collectors.

At one point the 1971 Hummel plate "Heavenly Angel" sold for $1,800 at a midwest auction, a phenomenal increase from its original $25 selling price. Rapid price increases were seen throughout the hobby.

Because so many of the price increases were artificially created by a sudden influx of speculators,

1987 South Bend N.A.L.E.D. Plate of the Show awards: First runner-up (l) "Brave and Free" by Gregory Perillo offered through Vague Shadows and winner "Christmas Eve in Williamsburg" (r) created by Jack Woodson for Bing & Grondahl.

prices fell when the speculators began selling *en masse*. Shifts in the national economy and record high interest rates contributed to the sudden sale of plates. Sales involved both speculators and collector-speculators (collectors who began dabbling in speculation, stockpiling two or more plates of a single issue instead of their usual one).

Production had been geared up to supply this new group of buyers, but their primary interest was in converting plates to cash in the short-term rather than acquiring plates for long-term art and collectible value. The speculators' unexpected exodus left an imbalance in the market, dropping values and forcing a number of small producers out of business.

New Artist Favorites

During the early 1980s, producers continued their search for high quality art, introducing new stars to the industry such as P. Buckley Moss, Sue Etem, Mario Fernandez, Sandra Kuck, Susie Morton, Fred Stone and Robert Olson. Favorites of the seventies—Donald Zolan, Juan Ferrandiz, John McClelland, Irene Spencer, Gregory Perillo, Ted DeGrazia, M.I. Hummel, Sam Butcher, Lowell Davis, Norman Rockwell, Edna Hibel and Red Skelton—retained their popularity and the loyalty of collectors.

New companies such as Fountainhead, Christian Fantasy, Duncan Royale, Blue River Mill Publishing, Gartlan USA, Hadley House and Sports Impressions presented original subjects to the market.

The Market of the Eighties

Dealers report today that their customers are buying more back issues than a few years ago and again placing emphasis on traditional series such as the Danish blues. They recognize quality and expect producers to adhere to high standards in design, limitation, production and marketing.

A survey of the entire range of plates issued in the past (almost) hundred years of collecting reveals an astonishing array of subject matter and a continual progression of quality. From the relatively simple hand-crafted Danish blues to Bjorn Wiinblad's sophisticated crystal designs of the mid-seventies, to today's popular full-color plates by artists such as Norman Rockwell, collectors may choose a wide variety of art.

In this stable plate market, collectors have an opportunity to acquire some of the finest plates ever issued, while seeing first-hand the latest offerings of the eighties' blending of art and technology. Much as the computer field is undergoing as explosion of products and possibilities, plate collecting has seen similar growing pains and progress in recent years. Collectors can expect many more innovations in the years to come.

Susan K. Elliott

Figurine Collecting
Today's Evolving Limited Edition Figurine Market

Because of the diversity of figurine types, figurine collectors can point to no one event as the hobby's beginning. Most experts give a symbolic nod to Ching te Chen (China), the birthplace of porcelain, although bone carvings date back to cavemen. Porcelain figures were produced in China at least 2,000 years before Europeans began their feverish efforts to duplicate the Oriental masterpieces. Once started on their quest, the European porcelain houses of Meissen and later Sevres poured all their energies into perfecting this difficult art.

Because early subjects were often of human figures, the term "figurine" came into usage although subjects from nature were also popular, then as now. "Sculptures" and "porcelains" also refer to figurines, sometimes designating more expensive pieces.

In addition to porcelain, today's figurine market encompasses a wide range of materials, such as wood, pewter, crystal and modern blends. Each has its devotees from the standpoint of artistic and collecting attraction. And yet, for all the modern appeal of figurine collecting, today's sculptors use much the same techniques as the Chinese did 2,000 years ago.

World Tour

One must tour the world to understand the scope of figurine history. As we have already seen, the story begins in China, then jumps to Europe. Most of the porcelain factories that sprang up throughout Europe from the 1700s onward received royal patronage. A country's honor was at stake in the quality of its porcelain output. Contemporary artists still pay homage to the high level achieved by these early porcelain craftsmen by studying and occasionally recreating their subjects.

Tableware was the primary interest of factories whose names collectors recognize today: Bing & Grondahl (founded in 1853), Royal Copenhagen (1775), Kaiser (1872), Royal Worcester (1751) and Royal Doulton (1815). Setting an attractive table meant more than plates, however, so producers let their imaginations soar with sculptures, continually testing the limits of porcelain and glazing techniques.

This period of growth and creativity laid the foundation for contemporary figurine collecting. The second major period of innovation would occur in the 1930s.

German Contributions

Goebel of Germany made a far-reaching marketing choice when it introduced the first figurines inspired by the work of Sister Maria Innocentia Hummel, a Roman Catholic nun, in 1935. American importers spotted them shortly after the first figures were released, and brought Hummels to the U.S. World War II stopped exports, but after the war, collectors again had access to the charming hand-painted figures of chubby children. U.S. soldiers stationed in Germany started collections and sent pieces home as presents, spreading their popularity.

A favorite for Americans traveling to Europe, the Hummel figurines developed a strong following during the 1950s and 1960s and began showing up on the shelves of gift shops in the United States. In 1971, Goebel enhanced the collectibility of the figurines by introducing the first plate based on Hummel art, "Heavenly Angel," followed by a series of bells in 1978. Collector response was enthusiastic with plate collectors paying new attention to the figurines and vice-versa. Dealer and collector experts emerged in the mid-seventies to answer questions about different trademarks and variations, giving added impetus to the grass roots interest in Hummels. The development of a Goebel Collectors' Club was a milestone for both limited editions and Hummel collecting. Books, conventions, newsletters and columns devoted to Hummels offer proof of their vast popularity.

Max Duncan inspires collectors to enjoy one of his Santa figurines. Duncan Royale presents "Wassail," an English favorite, often referred to as "Father Christmas" due to his appearance at holiday time and always with the Wassail bowl to give good cheer.

Award winning artist John McClelland introduces The Reco Clown Collection. *"Mr. One Note" plays his single-tone flute with all the aplomb of a concert virtuoso.*

At about the same time that Hummels were developed, another German producer appealed to collectors with an entirely different type of figurine subject. Founded by August Alboth at Coburg, Bavaria, the studios known today as Kaiser at first concentrated on tableware and decorator items. In the 1930s the company began to establish its reputation for wildlife art. Kaiser's bird, dog and horse figurines were intended to please German tastes, but Americans also bought them. After World War II, Kaiser re-established operations at Staffelstein, and continued its production of some of the world's most beautiful wildlife sculptures. World attention was recently focused on the studio when Hubert Kaiser presented the late Bepi Tay's eagle sculpture to Ronald Reagan at the White House.

And England Too

An innovator from the first, Royal Worcester began operations in 1751 after Dr. John Wall perfected the formula for soft-paste porcelain. A pioneer in the use of bone china, this British factory developed a rich palette of colors including lavender, yellow, turquoise, apple green, mazarine blue and claret. Con-

tinuing its tradition of pioneering, Royal Worcester commissioned talented sculptor Dorothy Doughty to create a series of sculptures based on the Birds of America in the 1930s.

The factory then decided to offer them in "limited edition": explained to be a small controlled number of figurines cast from an original work and then hand-painted to the specifications of the designer. Despite their high price of several hundred dollars each, collectors competed to own the intricately beautiful Doughty birds perched on flowering porcelain branches. Each sculpture required between twenty to forty molds to execute. The 1936 "Goldfinches and Thistle" from the Doughty collection has increased in value many times, selling at auction for as much as $7,000, up from an issue price of $350.

Because innovation spawns imitation, competitors such as Spode, Minton and Royal Doulton adapted the limited edition concept for their own production.

One English factory to enjoy success with figurine subjects has been Royal Doulton, founded in 1815. It was nearly a hundred years before figurines

German company Kaiser Porcelain has established a reputation for its fine porcelain sculptures and plates. Wolfgang Gawantka has created the delicate ballerina "Julia," available in both color and white.

A favorite among collectors, Irene Spencer depicts the unchanging love of mother and child in "Storytime" (l) and "Miracle" (r), produced by Roman, Inc.

became important in its product line, but there are few subjects that have not been explored by the factory. Over the years Royal Doulton has issued everything from animals and beautiful ladies in Victorian costume to its immensely popular Toby Jugs (small jugs with distinctive character faces). Both Americans and Europeans liked the decorative pieces, but not until the early 1970s did individuals begin to put together collections devoted entirely to Royal Doulton. Connoisseurs then recognized the value of both the company's modern limited editions and the earlier pieces that captured the interests of their day.

The Vision of an Artist

The success of a porcelain studio has always depended on the vision of its founder. This has been especially true in recent years when figurines have been closely identified with the creative genius behind a studio. Many of these new studios have been started exclusively to produce porcelain sculptures.

In the United States, several relatively young studios have played major roles in figurine history. This country's oldest existing art porcelain studio was founded after Polish artist Boleslaw Cybis came to the United States in 1939. The outbreak of World War II prevented him from returning to his homeland. Located in Trenton, New Jersey, the Cybis Studio produces nature, fantasy and historical figure subjects with a reputation for superb quality and beauty.

In 1950, artist Edward Marshall Boehm and his wife Helen (his resident sales force) opened the Boehm Studios in Trenton with the dream of creating fine American porcelain. Within a few years Boehm had secured a spot in the prestigious permanent collection of the Metropolitan Museum of Art with "Hereford Bull." Today the studio's name has been associated with many significant projects, such as President Nixon's presentation of the "Mute Swans" sculptures to China in 1972. (One of the three pairs of swans was later sold at auction for $150,000.)

Each of these studios appeals to collectors of limited editions with affordable issues ranging in price from $100–250.

Sculptor Don Polland is another American artist to bring his vision to collectors through three-dimensional art. His pewter, wood and bronze artworks of Western subjects have been available to a national audience since the late 1960s. Recognizing that today's collector has limited display space, Polland chose to focus his talents on miniature sculptures and

developed an appreciative audience for his work. Polland has been honored in sculpture exhibits at the National Cowboy Hall of Fame and Favell Museum of Western Art, among others.

The Hamilton Collection has become one of the most prominent direct marketing limited edition firms through its association with renowned porcelain firms around the world. Over the past decade, these alliances have included Hamilton's joint ventures with The Boehm Studios, Royal Worcester, Hutschenreuther, Maruri, Kaiser and Roman Inc.

Flambro is another U.S. company to take note of collector tastes. In 1981, Atlanta-based Flambro commissioned a set of figurines featuring the antics of clown Emmett Kelly, Jr. "Sweeping Up" and "Looking Out To See" were two of the sculptures that caught collectors' fancy.

European Artisans

A number of other European studios also cater to contemporary collectors. Among them are Border Fine Arts in Scotland, producer of cold-cast porcelain issues for U.S. producers such as Schmid and American Artists. Newcomer John Hine Limited of England has introduced a best-seller subject that other companies have hurried to copy—the detailed miniature David Winter Cottages, subject of a new collectors' club.

In Spain, collectors recognize two companies for their distinctive contemporary styles: Tengra and Lladro. Nearby in Italy, the House of Anri employs woodcarvers to capture the designs by its studio artists, and others such as Juan Ferrandiz of Barcelona and Australian artist Sarah Kay.

In the Orient, the Maruri Studio applies its backstamp to its own porcelain creations and produces sculptures for companies from around the world that do not have their own manufacturing facilities. Artist Bill Gaither has sculpted many of the Maruri wildlife subjects familiar to American collectors.

Sculptor Robert Olszewski heads one of America's newest studios, Goebel Miniatures in Camarillo, California, backed by the German manufacturer, Goebel Porzellanfabrik. Olszewski is one of the artists who acknowledges his debt to early porcelain masters. He combines his view of himself as a traditionalist and innovator in world art history to educate collectors about miniatures as an art form.

Spain's contribution to the figurine market is exemplified by Lladro's distinctive elongated style and palette of pastel tones. "The Landau Carriage" displays Lladro's quality of excellence and attention to detail.

Related Collectibles

One cannot study figurines without also mentioning plate collecting, since the two have frequently touched and intertwined. Classic examples of this close relationship include Goebel's decision to enter the plate market with a subject that had been successful in its figurine collection for many years. The 1971 "Heavenly Angel" plate launched Goebel's *Hummel Annual* series and firmly established plates as possible figurine companions.

Taking the opposite approach, The Gorham Company looked at its popular Rockwell *Four Seasons* plate series and decided that creating three-dimensional art would be a logical step. Gorham issued the plate subjects one year and matching figurines the next. In today's market, companion plates and figurines are often released together.

The field continues to expand with three-dimensional subjects from artists who had created only paintings before. Notable in this group are John McClelland, award-winning Reco International artist with a knack for capturing children; Gregory Perillo's Indian children for Vague Shadows; the innocent children of the late Frances Hook from Roman; rural humorist Lowell Davis's full line of farm scenes for Schmid; and Ted DeGrazia's brightly colored Indian children (also in miniature form).

Artist Jan Hagara's wide-eyed Victorian children from Royal Orleans are consistent favorites, as are the many inspirational subjects of Sam Butcher for Enesco's *Precious Moments*. It would be impossible to mention modern figurine collecting without referring to this collection, as Precious Moments collectors now rival the number devoted to Hummels. The wood gnomes of Dr. Tom Clark for Cairn Studios stand out as another rising star of recent years.

Looking Ahead

Figurine collectors tend to specialize in one or two areas rather than collecting multiple artists' works. This specialization allows them to fully understand the history of a particular factory, such as Goebel for Hummel collectors, and to better understand trends in the market.

For those who wish to sell, conventions that hold Swap and Sell events offer regular sales arenas for a wide number of figurines, along with national auction houses and collector publications with classified ads. Dealers contribute to secondary market activity by facilitating sales of figurines between collectors or buying issues back from individuals.

The market for figurines looks bright these days, as brisk sales in new limited edition issues ensures that new collectors will be created to support secondary market activity.

Susan K. Elliott

Bell Collecting
How to Select the Bells That Will Become the Treasured Antiques and Heirlooms of Tomorrow

Today's antique bell collectors travel far and wide in search of interesting and valuable old bells to add to their home displays. You may come across these "bell sleuths" at auctions, antique shows, flea·markets, swap meets, rummage and tag sales, and consignment and thrift shops.

The "lure of the chase" keeps these intrepid collectors going, even though most old bells remain a puzzle and a mystery to them. You see, antique bells often bear almost no identification! You might spy a pretty bell and fall in love with it, but keep in mind that there are many things about it that you may never know. When and where was this bell made? By whom? What or whom does it represent?

The handful of older bells which are appropriately marked have become the "stars" of today's bell auction market. For instance, a well documented bell from the Columbian Exposition—dated and signed by its artist—originally sold generations ago for $1.00. It now brings $100 or more! Yet bells from the past with such a clear-cut history, sadly, are few and far between.

The frustration of trying to trace my favorite old bells—and finding nary a clue as to their history—has inspired me to fix my sights upon the present. For in today's world of bell collecting, there are some bells which are truly out of the ordinary. So special, in fact, that I believe these bells stand a good chance of becoming the Antiques of Tomorrow.

What Makes a Contemporary Bell Collectible?

These excellent new bells have several things in common. First and foremost, of course, they are beautifully crafted. Whether they are made of Wedgwood jasper, crystal from Swarovski, fine porcelain from any number of studios, or the traditional bell material of bronze, *they are the finest examples of their type*. Keep in mind that excellent bells need not be expensive. Indeed, most all contemporary, limited edition pieces carry original price tags of less than $100—in an era when antique bell prices are soaring.

Oftentimes these bells are *signed by the artist* or at least marked with his name. My collection includes bells by such well-known contemporary artists as the late Ted DeGrazia, Juan Ferrandiz Castells, and Yin Rei Hicks. Imagine how the collectors of tomorrow will enjoy reading about these 20th-century artists in books such as this one!

Another mark of enduring quality is the *hallmark or name of the manufacturer*. Collectors of antique porcelain and other art materials have made a science out of unscrambling the meaning of tiny manufacturers' marks on their treasures—for these obscure marks hold the key to when and where certain pieces were made. Today's smart bell manufacturers have planned better for the future: on most of my newly acquired bells the name of the maker is clearly indicated inside the bell, and often on an accompanying Certificate of Authenticity as well.

Yet as valuable as a Certificate may be in the short term, I believe that tomorrow's antiques should be fully marked on the body of the bell itself—not just on a tag or paper label that may be discarded or lost over the years. Such documentation should also include *dating or commemorative marking*, to help establish when the bell was introduced, and what—if anything—it commemorated.

The Basics of Bell Collecting

It is easy to check off criteria such as artist name, manufacturer, and dating when evaluating a bell, yet these are only the bare essentials one must consider in bell selection. Based upon my twenty-year experience as a bell collector, here are a few more "pointers."

Lladro Collectors Society introduced its first ever bell/Christmas orna-ment. The bell will be of the same size and shape with a different de-sign every year. The upper and lower bands are lavender, and even the clapper has snow flakes on it.

These adorable "Sunbonnet Babies" bells are a modern reproduction of some of the first-ever limited edition bells from Royal Bayreuth. From the collection of Mr. & Mrs. Alvin W. Bargerstock, Sarver, Pennsyl-vania.

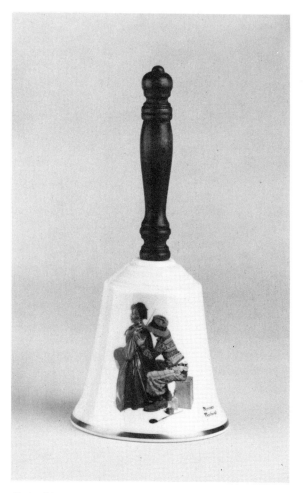

Rockwell items continue to be favorites among collectors. "Love's Har-mony Bell" is produced by Gorham, a company which has issued many Rockwell collectibles.

I would suggest that in choosing any bell, *fine workmanship should be your first criterion.* It is difficult to evaluate quality on the basis of price alone, since a fine-quality porcelain bell with an art transfer design and a gold-rimmed handle might cost considerably less than an ornate yet poorly crafted lost-wax-cast bronze bell—yet the porcelain piece might well be a much better investment.

Each of you can spend only what you can afford, and that is a personal decision. Sometimes it is possi-ble to obtain bargains on holiday bells immediately after the date which they commemorate—mostly in department stores which are not "keyed in" to the lasting value of such commemoratives.

Look for bells that will grow in historical value. These might be pieces inspired by centennials, bicen-tennials, national holidays, events or famous people. *Learn to identify a bell with a fine tone.* It may seem sometimes that bell collectors are more concerned with the appearance of their treasures, but a great deal of the lasting appeal of any bell depends upon the quality of its sound when rung. *Keep an inventory of your bells*, beginning with the very first purchase. Procrastination is the thief of time, and memory.

Above all, take time to *expose yourself to a broad range of bells*—antique and contemporary. I also sug-gest that you *cultivate friendships with other bell collec-tors*—sharing information adds to your growth as a knowledgeable bell owner, and it's a great deal of fun as well.

The Andrus Collection Grows and Develops

My first bell was a charming work of art from Royal Bayreuth. In my efforts to find out more

about the history of bells, I discovered the American Bell Association (ABA) and joined its New England Chapter. My own travels and those of my brother, an Air Force pilot, have helped grow the Andrus collection to include bells from 22 states and 30 countries. Reliving our trips, while looking at the bells, is most enjoyable to us—and to our friends and relatives.

Affiliation with the American Bell Association has also been very rewarding. Over the years, my husband and I have met many interesting people who share our enthusiasm for bells. To find out more about ABA and the local chapter nearest you, write the American Bell Association in care of Louise Collins, Alter Road, Box 386, Natrona Heights, PA 15065.

Marcia T. Andrus is the Chairman of the New England Chapter, American Bell Association. She lives in South Windsor, Connecticut.

Marcia Andrus and her husband, Dr. Larry Andrus, travel the world in search of unusual bells to add to their collection. Mrs. Andrus' brother, an Air Force pilot, also has made many contributions of bells brought back from far-off lands. Mrs. Andrus is Chairman of the New England Chapter, American Bell Association International, Incorporated.

A Brief History of Bells

Bells may well be the oldest collectible item—as old as recorded time. There is no way to tell when the first bell was made, but historians report that bells were part of the culture of most every ancient civilization.

In Persia, bronze bells were used as horse bells and harness ornaments. In ancient Egypt, a bell-rattle was part of the religious ceremony. Israel, Greece, Rome, and cultures in Central America, the Orient, India, Asia and Africa all used bells for worship, to warn of arrivals, as playthings or as decorative objects.

Once porcelain studios opened in Europe, bells of fine china became a part of the art scene. Meissen and Dresden were sites of the creation of many a collectible bell in the 18th century. Wedgwood in England and the various Deftware makers in Holland also made lovely bells using their traditional techniques.

Although the collecting of series of limited edition bells is a rather recent phenomenon, some of the collectible bells of past eras foretold the popularity of this hobby. For instance, Royal Bayreuth of Germany introduced a set of "Sunbonnet Babies" bells at the turn of the century, as well as some charming nursery rhyme bells in a related grouping. Other makers offered flint glass bells—each with a different figure on the handle. Although as recently as 1960 these pieces commanded just a few dollars apiece in antique shops, today they may bring hundreds of dollars each, if they are in fine condition.

American commemorative bells have been collector's items for more than a century, with one early example being the reproduction of the Liberty Bell which was sold at the Centennial Exposition, 1876, in Philadelphia. Then in 1893, two different commemorative bells were available at the Chicago World's Columbian Exposition (as mentioned by Marcia Andrus in the accompanying article). After this, there was at least one special bell offered at most every world's fair and major exposition in the United States.

In recent years, a number of limited edition firms have offered series of bells—often inspired by traditional forms and subject matter. These include Gorham's figural, or portrait bells, Gorham-Norman Rockwell "school" bells, and works in porcelain or metal from studios including Bing & Grondahl, Curator Collection, Danbury Mint, Goebel, The Hamilton Collection, Hutschenreuther, Lladro, Pickard, Reco International, River Shore, Schmid and Wedgwood.

Collecting Graphics
Obtaining Fine Art at Affordable Prices

"I'd love to own that painting" was an oft-heard comment during a recent major exhibition of Robert Bateman's wildlife art in Washington, D.C., as hundreds of thousands of admirers passed by the artist's best-known works.

Few of these art lovers, however, could afford to pay the phenomenal prices these original paintings command. As two visitors from the Midwest remarked, "We paid $60,000 for our home, and that makes it hard to imagine buying a $70,000 painting to hang in the den—as much as we'd love to have one."

Fortunately for admirers of these fine art works, there is a second alternative—and it is considerably less expensive than the first. Authorized and signed limited edition prints are regularly produced from the works of Robert Bateman and other outstanding contemporary artists. The works are still rare, however—as most editions consist of several hundred prints. But an attentive, discerning collector can acquire a beautiful, signed work of art for a very reasonable price.

Collectors Choose from a Variety of Subjects and Styles

Today, collectors can choose from a wide range of limited edition graphics—with variety offered in art styles and artists. Indeed, the selection is as broad as that offered by contemporary art itself, giving collectors a great number of options in selecting the works that best enhance their homes and places of work.

Collectors may also choose between "original prints," which are produced from artwork made directly onto the actual printing surface, and "reproductions," which are approved editions made by a printer using "photomechanical" means to produce the printing surface. At one time, original prints, such as woodcuts and lithographs, were considered to be of greater value than reproductions. This was because collectors perceived a more direct involvement by the artists in their production. During the last fifteen years, however, signed and numbered reproductions have gained greater acceptance from collectors, due mainly to technological improvements in printing techniques. In fact, many enthusiasts claim that new reproductions offer quality far superior to original prints, and almost matching that of the original paintings.

Thus, today's popular "Collector Prints" are generally reproductions. These works have been carefully produced in very small print runs, using one photosensitive printing plate for each of the colors. (Some reproductions require as many as eleven separate color plates.) Editions are usually limited in sizes of 500 to 5,000, and they are approved by the artist at completion.

Established Studios Offer Works by Renowned Artists

The Mill Pond Press offers exclusive limited edition works by some of today's finest contemporary realist artists, including Robert Bateman, David Armstrong, Maynard Reece, John Seerey-Lester, Thornton Utz, and many others. These artists represent the best of several, varied styles, ranging from Bateman's masterful depictions of the natural world to Armstrong's acclaimed portraits of rural America.

Collectors of historical editions find great appeal in prints produced by Brad Bennett, a Midwestern artist whose "limited edition suites" are registered with the Library of Congress in Washington, D.C. Other collectors seek to acquire new works from well-known collectibles studios, such as Roman, Inc., Reco International, and Vague Shadows, which offer limited edition prints by many of their finest artists, including Frances Hook, John McClelland, and Gregory Perillo.

Collectors Learn to Recognize Quality

As print collecting has increased in popularity, collectors have grown increasingly sophisticated in understanding what to look for when purchasing a print. There are several important indicators of quality, many of which can be found simply by seeking a print from an established producer. But it is still important to know and recognize these key indicators:

The *artist's reputation* and *style* must be considered. Look at the artist's background and level of acceptance. And see if the style is currently fashionable, or simply the "last gasp" from a passing fad.

Examine the *paper and print quality.* Is the paper 100% rag? If so, this paper is acid-free and will rarely yellow. Also, is the individual print in good condition, free from stains, tears, fingerprints, and other imperfections?

The *exclusivity* of an edition is determined by its size. Thus, you should ask if excess demand will make the print a coveted rarity? The *subject* will help to determine this—is it a theme that will remain popular, and of greatest importance, and will *you* still enjoy it in five years' time?

Two major factors, of course, are *price* and *documentation.* Does the price reflect fair market value? And does the print documentation include information about the artist, type of print, its status in the edition, method of printing, and verification that the edition is closed?

Caring for Limited Edition Prints

Print collectors have also come to understand the importance of treating their acquisitions with the care they deserve. Unframed prints, for example, must be stored flat. In addition, sheets of acid-free mat board should be used to "sandwich" each print, to protect it from light, heat, and humidity.

Ultimately, however, *framing* is the best way to protect a print. But again, care must be taken to ensure the longevity of the work—much the same as with an original painting. A few basic rules should therefore be followed:

A print should never be permanently mounted on any surface.

A print should only be backed with a 100% acid-free board, and it should be framed under glass or acrylic. The print should not, however, actually touch the glass.

A dust cover should be placed over the back of the frame, to prevent damage from pollution.

Robert Bateman's "Northern Reflections—Loon Family" is one of the most famous limited edition prints of all time. The original painting was presented as a gift from Canada to England's Royal Family, to commemorate the wedding of Prince Charles and Lady Diana. In 1986, the Royal Family authorized Mill Pond Press to create the print, which was sold to help raise funds for important conservation programs in the United States, Canada, and England.

"Michigan Avenue" is one of the limited edition prints from Brad Bennett's ambitious United States of America *suite. This program will offer an historical document of life in the latter half of the twentieth century.*

It should be noted that most prints from established dealers are accompanied by instructions for their care, as part of the documentation. And, fortunately for collectors, these steps can be easily followed, ensuring that a print will remain in mint condition for many years following its purchase, creating in many cases a genuine heirloom for future generations.

Tom L. Jones

Stein Collecting
New Issues Broaden Appeal of Popular Collecting Hobby

When the first steins appeared in Cologne, Germany in the 1500's, these new drinking vessels gained immediate popularity with beer drinkers throughout the region. The steins' hinged lids and stoneware bodies kept beer fresh and cool—and the vessels were inexpensive, because stoneware was much less costly to produce than porcelain. And with their protective coatings of colored glazes, the steins were fairly durable. But they were *not* considered works of art.

The status of these drinking containers would change dramatically during the following 300 years, however. Artisans throughout the southwest region of Germany, and later the United States, created increasingly elaborate designs for the steins' glazed, outer coating. Eventually, these designs were enhanced with the introduction of a bas-relief process, which gave the artwork a three-dimensional quality.

Now, the appeal of the steins was no longer purely functional in nature. Indeed, lovers of beer *and* art joined together to collect the steins for their beauty and uniqueness—a hobby that thrives to this day in Germany, the United States, and many other countries.

A "Golden Age" of Stein Production

Not surprisingly, the greatest demand exists for these later, classic steins, which are treasured for their historic merit as well as their artistic beauty. Collectors are especially impressed with steins created in the town of Mettlach, located in Germany's rustic Saar Valley. Produced by firms like Villeroy & Boch, Simon Peter Gerz, Albert Jac Theralt, Reinhold Merkelbach, and Wick Werke, these steins are today considered relics of a "golden age" that existed during the nineteenth century. The fact that this era came to an abrupt halt—with changes wrought by World War I—helps to make these steins even more valuable, because of their rarity.

Thus, a one-hundred-year-old German stein—which may have sold for no more than $2.00 when it was new—may now bring up to $2,500.00 at auction. In fact, even plain, somewhat ordinary pieces from the eighteenth and nineteenth centuries sell for as much as $500.00 in America.

The demand for these classic steins has increased somewhat during recent years, as exhibited by the growing availability of informational books and price guides on stein collecting. Furthermore, a club called Stein Collectors International has grown to include more than 1500 members and twenty chapters. (The address of Stein Collectors International may be found in the section of this book on Clubs, Conventions, and Travel.)

A Renaissance Takes Form

Along with the growth in collectors' interest comes the exciting news that Villeroy & Boch, Thewalt, and Gerz have recently reentered the field of stein production. Additionally, these famed German studios have been joined by a number of well-known art studios that are new to the stein medium. Thus far, many of the new works from these studios exhibit the beautiful attributes associated with traditional stein design and workmanship.

Villeroy & Boch's recent offerings have given collectors the opportunity to acquire steins similar to the studio's classic, older pieces—without spending thousands of dollars. According to collectors, Villeroy & Boch's turn-of-the-century "cameo" and "chromolith" steins, featuring elaborate artistic depictions of folklore and other subjects, are traditionally among the most difficult steins to locate and acquire. Thus, new issues in these classic styles represent a very important development for contemporary collectors.

A number of superb German steins are offered by Opa's Haus, M. Cornell Importers and Mader's Tower Gallery, three American firms which contract with Germany's best-known stein manufacturers to introduce original limited editions to American collectors. Museum Collections, meanwhile, offers cast steins with hand-painted relief motifs taken from the paintings of Norman Rockwell.

Made in Bavaria, the 1985 King Works Christ-mas Stein, above, is limited to 7,500. This series, begun in 1976, is also available in a musical edition. A concealed music box plays "Silent Night."

This stunning commemorative 1984 Winter Olympic stein, center, is limited and available with a solid German pewter or gold plated lid.

Intricacy of artwork is appreciated by stein enthusiasts. This 1982 limited edition Regimental stein, right, made from century old Germany molds, features an elaborate pewter lid with a German eagle thumblift. The detailed train motif continues throughout the stein.

Acquiring Fine-Quality New Issues

"I think collectors look for one of two things in a newly produced stein," Ken Armké, President of Opa's Haus, explains. "It can be an outstanding work of art or it can offer an interesting background or theme, like the famed story-telling steins. One or both of these two factors gives a stein appeal on the first and secondary markets."

Henry Cornell, President of Cornell Importers, adds that "authenticity" is important. He also believes that the country of origin helps to determine the value of a stein. Germany, he says, continues to offer the best in steins.

Other factors to look for are the intricacy of the artwork ("The more handwork the merrier," says Cornell), the size of the edition limit, and the presence of a hinged lid. Pewter is the traditional material used for lids, but some fine modern steins boast lids made of silver and other metals.

In addition, a quality stein will be distinguished by its weight, for steins are traditionally made of a heavy, clay stoneware. Also, the surface of the stein's interior should be finished with a glaze which prevents absorption. After all, steins have never lost

Peter Duemler steins continue to attract collectors' interest. From left to right: Peter Duemler Bible Stein by Thewalt, Peter Duemler Card Player Stein by Thewalt and Peter Duemler Cheruskan Stein by Thewalt, all limited to 10,000 pieces each.

their original 500-year-old function: they were and are created for drinking. And thus, one measure for determining the quality of a fine stein—apart from its attractiveness as a collectible work of art—continues to be its ability to keep beer cool and fresh.

Tom L. Jones

Doll Collecting—The State of the Art
Dolls Continue to Be One of the Nation's Most Popular Collectibles

What is meant by a "truly collectible doll?" Usually the answer would be one that is original, limited in production, of excellent quality, signed or hallmarked, dated, and packaged in a box in which it can be stored or repacked. Of course, there are always exceptions; there is always that one wonderful doll that just turns up, or a very old doll in new clothes. But basically, those are the characteristics a collector looks for in a collectible doll.

Two years ago, the doll collecting scene was a sea of confusion, with dozens of companies mass producing porcelain dolls marketed as "true" collectibles and having some, or even all, of the important characteristics. But most of these dolls lacked the real critical elements—originality and quality—and a large number of the manufacturers abandoned the market when the collector did not respond to this inferior product.

What remains is a very strong group of collectible dolls, all sharing the critical qualities, and all contributing to a veritable feast for the dedicated doll collector.

Artists' Dolls Are Number One

The artists' doll continues to be the most highly desired doll among collectors. There are still a large number of doll makers who produce one of a kind dolls for collectors who are willing to endure waiting lists of several years' time. Good news for the collector who doesn't want to wait, or can't afford the finished product, is the number of artists who have affiliated with major companies to produce their original designs at a more affordable price.

Gorham is one company that has been the choice of a number of well-known doll artists. Renowned for fine merchandise for over a century, the company was a logical choice for artists seeking to have their work reproduced at the highest quality level. West coast artists Kezi Matthews and Pamella Valentine both selected Gorham. Kezi designed two collections, *Golden Gifts* and *Four Seasons*, which have both been retired. Currently, Gorham is offering a baby doll and two toddlers featuring lovely Kezi faces.

Pamella and Noel Valentine produce one of a kind *Valentine Ladies* in a doll house workshop in San Francisco. They created a collection of nine ladies to be produced in a 14″ size exclusively for collectors who expect the quality apparent in the Gorham Doll Collection. Each of the nine dolls has an original Valentine face, cast in porcelain, and an original Valentine outfit, made of the finest of fabrics and laces. A one-of-a-kind Valentine Lady could be mannequin size, but these delicate miniatures bring the collector the same grace and style they recognize as a Valentine original.

Old Favorites Create Another Popular Category

Second to artists' dolls in popularity among collectors are dolls recreating old favorites from story books, other collectible areas, or even real life. Celebrity dolls have traditionally been a favorite. In this category the dolls range from Elvis and Marilyn to Queen Elizabeth I and Princess Di. In these cases, the collector may forego quality to a certain degree in favor of getting the personality desired. However, here are some firms which can offer both selection and quality to the collector.

When it comes to creating a doll that continues a collectible tradition, one immediately thinks of Enesco and the famous Precious Moments figurines. Precious Moments dolls were introduced in 1983 and were a resounding success with both Precious Moments collectors and doll collectors. The famous large eyed, pastel look has been preserved in 14″ and 16″ dolls of fine porcelain. Each doll is hallmarked and dated, and the originality of the design goes without saying. The current limited edition doll in the Enesco collection is an adorable nurse, truly an "Angel of Mercy," issued in an edition of just 12,500 hand-numbered dolls.

Elegant Tea Cozy Dolls *are a new collectible limited edition series introduced by Goebel. Cast in antique molds from the Goebel archives, what were once everyday household tea pot covers are now lovely, delicate collectible dolls.*

Valentine's Ladies *are an example of coveted artist's dolls being produced by a major manufacturer. Pamella and Noel Valentine had final approval of the production of* "Patrice" *(l) and* "Elizabeth" *(r), two of the 10″ dolls in the Valentine's Ladies Collection from Gorham.*

Modern Antiques Have Collectible Appeal

Another company which has experienced success with dolls based on the same figurine artwork is Goebel. Hummel figurines may be the collectible most significantly responsible for the large market collectible makers enjoy today. The charming children drawn by Sister Marie Innocentia Hummel and translated into three-dimensional figurines by the Goebel company, became the foundation pieces for innumerable collections. Dolls have been produced for several years from the same artwork. But Goebel's most recent success as a doll maker came from a completely different source: their own archives, where molds for porcelains made as far back as the company's beginning in 1871 are stored.

To create the first series of *Archive Collection* dolls, Goebel artists selected molds originally used to produce tea cozies. A tea cozy, as we all know, is a cloth cover to go over a steeping tea pot. In the elegant past, some tea cozies were quite elaborate, and Goebel had once produced a collection in which the tea cozy was the dress of a famous lady of history, represented in porcelain from the waist up. Choosing six ladies, the *Tea Cozy Figurine Dolls* were created, using the original molds for the porcelain doll figurines, and the original patterns for the dresses. Instead of resting on a collector's tea pot, now each lady rests on a wooden base. Lady Emma Hamilton, Marie Antoinette, Madame De Pont, Empress Mary Elizabeth of Austria/Hungary, Madame DuBarry

A current favorite in the Precious Moments Doll series is "Angel of Mercy," who is perfect for curing all ills. She will minister to serious collectors or to someone who just needs to have a good hug.

"Huck Finn," is the 1988 Folk Hero *doll available to Annalee Doll Society members. This 10" doll is mounted on a wooden base and placed under a glass dome with a brass plaque, numbered and signed.*

"Heather," the second issue in Yolanda's Picture-Perfect Babies, *is created by Yolanda Bello and bears the hallmark of the Edwin M. Knowles China Company. Knowles, known as a major producer of fine porcelain collectibles, has just recently entered the limited edition doll market.*

and Jenny Lind are represented in the collection. The dolls are handcrafted using the original mold. The heads and bodices are hand painted and the billowing gowns are hand sewn. Each doll is issued in a limited edition of 500 and individually hand-numbered on a porcelain plaque. Every tea cozy doll is issued with a Certificate of Authenticity signed by Wilhelm Goebel.

All That's Collectible is not Porcelain

Of course there are other collectible dolls that are not made of porcelain but are as popular and valuable. One reason that a number of artists are allowing mass production of their dolls is that there have been significant improvements in the quality of vinyl and composition materials used to make dolls. A number of lovely dolls, including the famous Madame Alexander line and many of the afore mentioned celebrity dolls are made of vinyl. And cloth has been a primary material for doll-making for centuries. Didn't every reader have a Raggedy Ann and Andy as a child? Among the most popular collectible dolls in this category in the 1988 market place are the felt creations of Annalee Thorndike. Annalee's dolls are unique in that they are fabricated over a wire frame making them poseable. Her creations, made in her Factory in the Woods in Meredith, New Hampshire, include Santas, skiers, children, animals, and annual limited edition dolls in both the *Folk Hero* and *Annalee Annimals* series. The Folk

Hero doll for 1988 is "Huck Finn," a darling 10" representation of everybody's favorite teenager. Huck is posed, fishing pole in hand, on a wooden base with a glass dome for protection. Each Huck Finn doll is made in response to an order from a member of the Annalee Doll Society, to whom the right to own one of these dolls is given exclusively. The current Annalee Annimal, also made only for members of the Society, is a unicorn.

Doll Collecting Still a Very Popular Hobby

No one seems to know the source of the often quoted statistic that dolls are the world's second most popular collectible. It is very hard to get any kind of verification of a claim like that, given the fact that anything is a collectible if someone collects it. But one thing that is beyond dispute is the fact that doll collectors are among the most loyal and dedicated of all collectors. The proliferation of doll clubs, the popularity of individual doll artists who feel the need to make their creations more available, and the concrete way in which the collectible doll market weeded itself out after the innundation of gift dolls in the early 1980s, all attest to the dedication and integrity of the doll collector. With their primary concerns being originality and quality, there is no question that the doll collectors are alive and well and here to stay, with more choices than ever from a smaller group of high quality doll makers.

Sara Kirtlink

COMPANY SUMMARIES
About the Marketers and Manufacturers of Limited Edition Collectibles

There are several hundred firms actively involved in today's world of limited edition collectibles, with bases of operation in the United States, Canada, and in many other countries. Here you'll find some basic background information about some of the more prominent firms in the field. With each there is an address, and in many cases a contact person, which you may use to inquire about a firm's products and services. There is also a listing of the types of limited edition products each firm makes or markets.

AMERICAN ARTISTS
GRAPHICS BUYING SERVICE
c/o Peter Canzone
225 W. Hubbard Street
Chicago, Illinois 60610

Plates, Figurines, Graphics

Graphics Buying Service (GBS) originated eight years ago as a firm devoted to the commissioning and marketing of limited edition graphic art. The company was the first of its kind—offering quality, limited edition prints by top plate artists, at affordable prices.

GBS artists have included James Auckland, Irene Spencer, Frank Russell and Gertrude Barrer, Donald Zolan, Richard Zolan, Fred Stone, Dave Chapple and Mary Vickers. Currently American Artists handles only Fred Stone lithographs. Each original edition is signed and sequentially numbered by the artist. These editions are very limited—especially compared to the plate market—and thus they have made for some impressive secondary market gains in a short period of time.

In 1981, GBS began a new division called American Artists, dedicated to the creation of the finest in limited edition collector plates. Today, American Artists/-GBS continues in both the graphics field and the realm of limited edition plates. The firm is currently producing plates by the award winning equine artist Fred Stone, cat plates by Zoe Stokes and Susan Leigh, and works by Donald Zolan.

ANNALEE MOBILITEE DOLLS,
INC.
Reservoir Road, Box 708
Meredith, New Hampshire 03253

Dolls

Had it not been for the collapse of the chicken market after World War II, Annalee Mobilitee Dolls, Inc. may have remained just a dream for founders Annalee Davis and "Chip" Thorndike!

Annalee Mobilitee Dolls, Inc. presents the Collector Santas *series, including* "Santa in Rocking Chair with Child."

Annalee was born and raised in Concord, New Hampshire. In 1941, she married Boston native Charles "Chip" Thorndike. As children, both had spent their summers in Meredith, New Hampshire, and it was there they chose to live and found the Thorndike Chicken Farm.

The chicken market may have slumped after the war, but the doll market thrived. The Thorndike home became the home for skiers, fishermen, dancers, divers and angels, and all figures were christened "Annalee Dolls."

The first Annalee dolls were strapped to the Thorndikes' VW Bug for deliveries, but the situation is much different today. Annalee dolls are now created at the original site of the chicken farm where the "Factory in the Woods" employs 300 people. From Santas to reindeer to whimsical ducks, Annalee allows her imagination to delight collectors around the country.

In 1983, the Annalee Doll Society was introduced. Every year, the Society hosts a barbecue and auction, in addition to providing a tour of The Factory in the Woods and Doll Museum for its members.

The Thorndikes' son, Townsend, President and Chief Executive Officer, sums up the firm's history: "It's a humbling experience as well as a great tribute to my parents to realize that a hobby started over fifty years ago has grown to a national phenomenon."

ANNA-PERENNA PORCELAIN,
INC.
c/o Gesa Thomsen
32 Relyea Place
New Rochelle, New York 10801

Plates, Figurines, Graphics

ANNA-PERENNA Porcelain, Inc. is an international firm specializing in fine

138

art on limited edition collector plates. Offerings of this firm are made of the finest hard-paste porcelain, created in a tradition dating back many generations.

The firm was founded in 1977 by Klaus D. Vogt, former President of Rosenthal, U.S.A. Vogt was fascinated by the possibilities of fine art on fine porcelain, and left Rosenthal to pursue this new art medium with his own firm.

The name ANNA-PERENNA is derived from the Roman goddess of spring. From her name the English words for "annual" and "perennial" are rooted as well. This international firm required a name which could be pronounced easily in English, German or French, and ANNA-PERENNA filled the bill. Even more appropriately, this goddess was also the protectorate of the arts.

ANNA-PERENNA Porcelain has commissioned some of the world's most celebrated and unique artists to create original artwork for collector plates. Each ANNA-PERENNA artist submits paintings "in the round", and as near to the actual size of the plate as possible, as Vogt stresses that this is the only way to achieve fidelity in the creation of multicolored art on porcelain plates.

ANNA-PERENNA artists include: Count Lennart Bernadotte, creator of a collection inspired by his Island of Mainau; Ken Danby, *Canadian Reflections of Youth* series; artist Thaddeus "Uncle Tad" Krumeich, creator of numerous cat-subject plates; Frank Russell and Gertrude Barrer, who introduced the triptych concept to the plate world; actress-turned-artist Elke Sommer; Mary Ellen Wehrli, artist for whimsical studies of bunnies; Margaret Kane, creator of the unique *Masquerade Fantasy* plates; Pat Buckley Moss, artist for American Silhouttes who also has been painting an annual Christmas plate series since 1985. Also included in the roster are Canadian-Indian master artist Norval Morrisseau, cartoonist-turned-plate artist Al Hirschfeld, and Nori Peter, famous for her eskimo subjects.

Pat Buckley Moss's plate "Wedding Joy" is the first and only plate ever to have been voted Plate of the Show by the attendees at both the California Plate and Collectible Show and the South Bend, Indiana International Plate and Collectible

Exposition during the same year, 1986. The second plate in the *Celebration* series, "The Christening," was likewise voted Plate of the Show in Pasadena and South Bend in 1987.

ANRI WOODCARVINGS
c/o April Bargout
55 Pacella Park Drive
Randolph, Massachusetts 02368

Plates, Figurines, Bells
The House of ANRI, located in the South Tyrol, Italy, was founded in 1912 by Anton Riffeser. Since that time, woodcarving as practiced at ANRI has come to be considered one of the most sought-after collectible art forms. The woodcarved and hand-painted limited editions include relief plates and figurines by such renowned artists as Juan Ferrandiz, Walt Disney and Sarah Kay. Club ANRI, a society for collectors of all ANRI Woodcarvings, was formed in 1983.

ARMSTRONG'S
150 East Third Street
Pomona, California 91766

Plates, Figurines, Graphics
For over four decades, Armstrong's has been a leader in the field of collectibles. Armstrong's spacious gallery in downtown Pomona, California, has long been recognized as one of the nation's foremost repositories for collectible ceramic plates, fine porcelain figurines, crystal and limited edition lithographs.

"Rowboat Rendezvous" is the third in the Reflections of Innocence *series created by the famous Mexican artist, sculptor and muralist Miguel Paredes, exclusively for Armstrong's.*

Over the years, the company grew in scope and reputation and, in 1972, began manufacturing its own line of porcelain collector plates. Today, Armstrong's represents such distinguished American artists as Red Skelton, Walter Lantz, Sue Etem, Miguel Paredes, Alan D'Estrehan and Lisette DeWinne.

The difficult task of transferring a great artist's work to a porcelain collector plate is under the personal supervision of company president David W. Armstrong. Involved in the fine arts and decor since his childhood, David Armstrong knows what the discriminating buyer looks for in choosing a collectible.

No phase of the creative process is overlooked. Each piece of art is sent to an atelier in Europe where master craftsmen duplicate the original artwork and create a delicate ceramic transfer. These are then returned to Armstrong's studio in Pomona and carefully baked onto porcelain plates in state-of-the-art kilns. Every plate is inspected for quality and color, and hand-trimmed in 24K gold.

Armstrong's, specializing in the creation of porcelain collector plates, has throughout its history brought to collectors a number of unique designs. Armstrong's has been responsible for many new innovations created especially for the collector market such as porcelain baseball cards, ceramic plaques, and elaborate gold borders on collector plates to enhance the artist's design.

At Armstrong's, perfection rules. "Quality collectibles at affordable prices" is Armstrong's standard. As a result, discerning collectors know that Armstrong's creates unique collector treasures that will be cherished for a lifetime.

ARTAFFECTS, LTD.
P.O. Box 98
Staten Island, New York 10307

Plates, Figurines, Graphics, Bells, Dolls
In 1971 Richard J. Habeeb read an article in the *Wall Street Journal* describing how newly issued silver collector plates featuring artwork by Norman Rockwell were quickly oversubscribed and were racing ahead in price. His interest piqued, Richard began searching for sources that would enable him to begin plate collect-

ing. It was a difficult task in 1971, but he persisted and soon acquired a complete collection of three silver Picasso plates. Over the next several years, the collection grew until no additional wall space remained in the Habeeb household.

It was 1975 when Richard decided to sell several plates so that he and his wife Geraldine could purchase other issues. A small classified ad was placed, and, unexpectedly, a business was born. "Richard's Limited Editions" sold collector plates and figurines via the U.S. mail. A family of 20,000 collectors was developed. It was this exposure to collectors and a developing sensitivity to their needs that spurred Habeeb to begin developing collectibles under his own hallmark, Artaffects Ltd.

Rob Sauber created "Sweet Sixteen" for the Curator Collection, a division of Artaffects, Ltd.

In 1977, a long term relationship with Gregory Perillo was begun, a relationship that continues today and from which Vague Shadows was formed. In fact, the Vague Shadows division of Artaffects Ltd. is the exclusive producer of all Perillo collectibles whether they be plates, figurines, dolls or lithographs.

Throughout the years of his association with Vague Shadows, Perillo has garnered first place awards in all major categories: Figurine of the Year (NALED, 1982), Lithograph of the Year (Silver Chalice Award, 1985) "Out of the Forest", and Plate of the Year (Silver Chalice Award, Plate World Reader Survey, both in 1987) "Brave and Free".

In 1979, Habeeb started the Curator Collection division of Artaffects Ltd. to feature the work of outstanding artists

whose paintings set standards of excellence in their fields.

Habeeb introduced the romantic works of Rob Sauber to a responsive audience and has, since 1982, been working with him to develop a complete line of collectible-gift plates, figurines and bells for every occasion.

Curator Collection proudly represents the inspirational work of internationally acclaimed scholar and artist, Alton Tobey; famed maritime painter, Kipp Soldwedel; Jim Deneen who has been called America's foremost painter of classic modes of transportation; George Malick, the painter who can make us smile as only Rockwell has been able; Narda Caton, a master of the difficult and delicate art of china painting who portrays adorable babies; Lou Marchetti, the creator of magical, romantic citiscapes from both near and far; Donna Diamond, a painter of wonderfully soft and yet detailed wildlife and floral scenes, and, finally, the enormously talented, MaGo whose portraits of children are unsurpassed.

Besides the outstanding roster of contemporary artists, Curator Collection has presented works by Norman Rockwell, Frederick Remington, Mary Cassatt, Jessie Willcox Smith, Charlotte Becker and Bessie Pease Gutmann. In fact, Curator Collection's presentations of Gutmann pieces sparked a revival of interest in her artwork.

What began as a passion and hobby for Richard Habeeb has evolved into Artaffects Ltd., a company that has the highest regard and greatest faith in the discriminating taste of collectors and gift givers.

THE B&J COMPANY
(formerly B&J Art Designs)
P.O. Box 67
Georgetown, Texas 78627

Plates, Dolls, Graphics

The B&J Company was established in 1975 to produce and market reproductions of Jan Hagara's work. It is an independent business owned solely by Bill and Jan Hagara.

Their business began in Tempe, Arizona. At first they produced only cards and fine art prints which featured children with an old-fashioned look that became Jan's trademark.

In 1978 the first series of porcelain plates was introduced. It featured a series entitled *"Yesterday's Children"*. "Lisa and the Jumeau Doll" was the first in the series of four. Jan's work was featured in the *"America Has Heart"* and *"Old-Fashioned Mother's Day"* series for The Carson Mint. In the Fall of 1983, B&J issued two new series featuring Jan's work: a *Christmas* and a *Country* series. Jan's work is also produced by Johnson Creative Arts, a Johnson Wax division that manufactures stitchery designs, and the United States Historical Society which direct markets Jan's designs on glass. The largest part of the Hagara line is marketed by Royal Orleans, also owned by the Hagaras.

The B&J Company is located outside Austin, Texas. It manufactures and distributes Jan's work through both a wholesale and a retail division as well as several exclusive retail store outlets. The Hagaras take great pride in their designs and devote a special interest to their marketing.

THE BALLIOL CORPORATION
10502 Product Drive
Rockford, Illinois 61111

Plates, Figurines

The Balliol Corporation is a licensing company that is extremely active in the collectible field. The company owns and licenses the copyrighted works of many prominent artists, such as Bessie Pease Gutmann, the famed illustrator of children. Among the major licensees of Balliol are: The Hamilton Group (Jackson-

"A Call to Arms" is available exclusively to charter members of the Gutmann Collectors Club.

ville, Florida): ceramic collector plates; The Heirloom Tradition (Long Beach, California): ceramic figurines, Christmas ornaments, mugs, tins, music boxes and other collectible items; Portal Publications, Ltd. (Corte Madera, California): notecards, posters, greeting cards, calendars and diaries; Johnson Creative Arts, Inc. (West Townsend, Massachusetts): needlework kits and booklets; Crown Publications, Inc. (New York, New York): illustrated books; Other licenses for clothing, giftware, papergoods and miscellaneous items are in place in the U.S., Canada and many foreign countries.

The Hamilton Collection's plate series, *A Child's Best Friend,* featuring the art of Bessie Pease Gutmann, was among the most popular plate series ever produced for collectors. The first edition, "In Disgrace," is much sought after in the secondary market just months since the edition closed.

The latest additions to the Balliol Collection are the works of Gre' Girardi, a self-taught master with an extraordinary range of skills. Girardi, the mother of five, resides quietly in the hills of northern New Jersey, where she has delighted local residents for years with her charming pictures. Pleasantly shy and a very reluctant traveler, Gre' has remained a protected local treasure until recently. Fran and Marv Mitchell of Balliol were introduced to this wonderful art by viewing some original works in the Frogmore Country Store in Cranberry Lake, New Jersey. The store owners, George Haddad and David Thompson, avid Girardi collectors, eagerly arranged a meeting between Gre' and the Mitchells. An agreement was soon reached and the works of this talented artist will be widespread in the near future. Girardi's animals, children and country scenes will become the treasured possessions of thousands of collectors.

BAREUTHER
c/o Wara Intercontinental Co.
20101 West Eight Mile Road
Detroit, Michigan 48219

Plates, Bells
The Bareuther & Company porcelain factory of Germany began producing giftware, vases and dinnerware in 1867. Established by Johann Matthaeus Reis, the shop contained a porcelain kiln and an annular brick kiln.

The business later was sold to Oskar Bareuther, who continued to produce quality tableware.

To celebrate the 100th anniversary of Bareuther, the company began to issue limited edition Christmas plates, which are Cobalt blue. Their *Father's Day* series, which features many of the great German castles, was initiated in 1969. The *Mother's Day* series was also initiated in 1969, and the first issue of the *Christmas Bell* series was produced in 1973.

BING & GRONDAHL
225 Fifth Avenue
New York, New York 10010

Plates, Figurines, Bells, Dolls
This Danish firm is known as the "founder of plate collecting" for its 1895 Christmas plate, "Behind the Frozen Window." This first issue began a tradition which continues today with a new, annual, blue-and-white plate to mark each holiday season. Bing & Grondahl also offered the world's first porcelain Mother's Day plate, "Dog and Puppies," in 1969, and the world's first Children's Day plate in 1985.

Bing & Grondahl was founded in 1853 by Frederik Vilhelm Grondahl and M. H. and J. H. Bing. The artist and sculptor was Grondahl, while the Bings provided business expertise. The firm's quality is internationally known, and Bing & Grondahl items are a part of the collections of many museums worldwide. The firm has won appointment to the courts of Denmark, Sweden and Great Britain.

In addition to collector plates and tableware, Bing & Grondahl makes a wide variety of figurines and other porcelain articles. In 1982 the firm introduced its first collectible doll, "Mary," which was inspired by a favorite Bing & Grondahl figurine by the same name. This series has continued each year with another charming doll.

Recent plate introductions include the limited edition *Christmas in America* series designed by American artist Jack Woodson. "Christmas Eve in Williams-burg" marked the first edition in this ten plate series which was created in honor of the celebration of Christmas in America.

BLACK & PATERNO
2948-20th Street
San Francisco, California 94110

Figurines
Black & Paterno, Inc., San Francisco-based manufacturers of fine crystal figurines and limited edition designs, has carried forth the tradition of faceting 32% leaded crystal into handsome decorative objects and sought after collectibles since 1977. With over 150 designs, Black & Paterno's Crystal Caravan Collection offers a wide range of stylized figurines to more than 5,000 fine gift and specialty retailers nationwide.

The Crystal Caravan Collection has received national recognition and public acclaim due to the perceived value of its quality crystal components. What distinguishes Crystal Caravan from that of the competition is a design concept coined, "Crystal in Motion." It refers to the fluid form and painstaking degree of detail that renders each Black & Paterno design amazingly lifelike. It is this meticulous handcrafting and particular attention to detail that sets Crystal Caravan apart from the others.

The Crystal Caravan Collection, which is merchandised according to theme includes: *The Classics, Fantasy, American Wildlife, Toyland, Miniatures and Playful Memories.* The larger, limited edition designs which include the elegant crystal train set and classic car remain the signature pieces of the collection.

THE BOEHM STUDIOS
c/o Virginia Perry
25 Fairfacts
Trenton, New Jersey 08638

Plates, Figurines
From their inception in 1950 The Boehm Studios have specialized in the art of birds, flowers and animals; and Boehm masterworks portraying these have been among the most treasured, highly valued and sought-after works of porcelain art in the world. Edward Marshall Boehm, who died in 1969, and Helen, his wife

and studio partner, started a basement studio in Trenton, New Jersey, ceramic center of the United States since the middle of the last century. The studio was relocated in 1955 to its present location.

When the Boehms opened their studio, Edward Boehm, the naturalist-farmer, had only an innate talent as a sculptor and craftsman which was joined with an intense desire to excel in any endeavor he attempted. Helen Boehm was the perfect complement, a dynamic, energetic, brilliant tactician whose inexperience often proved to be an asset; for she forged courageous new promotional and marketing concepts.

When Edward Boehm passed away it was assumed by many that the studio would not continue. What they did not know were the enormous skills of the art team Mr. Boehm had assembled and trained. One of his unique talents was an uncommon practice of sharing his knowledge and expertise with respected artists and craftsmen who joined him. Perhaps his greatest legacy was his unselfish desire to perpetuate what he had begun.

Leading the team now was his most dedicated student, Helen Boehm. Through the prior two decades of working together they had shared each new art concept. Helen had brought back ideas and needs from the vast market before them. Edward utilized the information when formulating and executing his designs. It was natural in 1969 for Helen Boehm to assume the design responsibility as well—not directly creating the porcelains, but energizing, motivating and orchestrating the "new" designs of the team her late husband had formed.

Today, Boehm porcelains are in more than 117 museums and institutions throughout the world, including the White House, the Metropolitan Museum of Art, the Smithsonian Institution, Buckingham Palace and the Vatican.

Traditionally Boehm artworks were marketed in selected art galleries, fine jewelers and noted retailers. The year 1970 saw the first entry of Boehm into the direct mail market in an association with the Lenox China Company, also headquartered in Trenton. Series of animal and bird plates were introduced and marketed broadly. In recent years Boehm has increased its direct mail activity for the

marketing of fine plates, bisque sculpture, and recently introduced a unique combination of porcelain and bronze. Current activities also include programs with American Express, The Audubon Society and Boehm's own direct mail projects.

ART WORLD OF BOURGEAULT
20538 Therese St.
Mt. Clemens, Michigan 48043

Plates

Canadian born Robert Bourgeault entered the limited edition plate field in 1982, offering collectors the opportunity to own charming English countryside cottage plates. However Bourgeault was no stranger to the art world before this time.

As a young man, Bourgeault was a natural at sketching before the age of seven. Over the years, he pursued his interest in art—not to mention his career as a flying instructor and an aviation/space writer for several newspapers.

After a massive heart attack in 1976, Bourgeault went back to his easel and palette, painting several Canadian scenes and the English countryside. His wife Monica is English and her heritage deeply influenced his canvases.

Bourgeault's work has been widely exhibited for a number of years, winning numerous awards. His works are included in collections throughout the United States, Canada and Europe.

Bourgeault's entry into the limited edition plate field was met by enthusiastic collectors who eagerly acquired his *English Countryside* series and hand-painted exclusive issues such as "Anne Hathaway Cottage" and "Lilac Cottage." Recently, he produced the "John Bunyan Cottage" and the "Thomas Hardy Cottage"—the first two plates in *The Royal Literary Series*, a decal series with a 4,500 edition limit.

"It is my strong desire to reflect upon the simplicity of yesterday, where sunlit skies danced the faces of sleepy country cottages and winding lanes quietly meandered," explains Bourgeault. "Yes, I'm both a dreamer and a romanticist. I enjoy stepping back into an age when time stood still for the master thatcher as he plied his craft. It is my desire for people to

share in the warmth and peacefulness that I enjoy putting into my paintings."

Bourgeault, creator of a cottage industry, now resides in Michigan.

BRAD BENNETT STUDIO
c/o Brad Bennett
2512 Oakwood Drive
Olympia Fields, Illinois 60461

Graphics

Brad Bennett Studio creates and offers the works of Brad Bennett, who paints historical and contemporary depictions of cities, towns, landmarks and events in America and abroad.

Bennett originally created paintings only, and these works still command impressive prices in galleries all over the United States. In recent years, however, he has turned a good deal of his attention to the making of limited edition prints, to share his creations with a wider audience.

Works available from Brad Bennett Studio include: a historical series inspired by the past in Kenosha, Wisconsin; pieces capturing Chicago in all its majestic splendor; and a series of twelve paintings of Houston. Bennett has also captured the festivities of Renaissance amusement parks with his suite, "King Richard's Faire."

"The Grand Canyon" is part of The United States of America, *a limited edition collection of lithographs and narratives by Brad Bennett.*

"The United States of America," a collection of lithographs and narratives, represents Bennett's most recent project. From Maine to California, from the Grand Canyon to the snowy Midwest, Bennett documents America's cities, rural communities, lifestyles and cultural events.

THE BRADFORD EXCHANGE
9333 Milwaukee Avenue
Niles, Illinois 60648

Plates

The Bradford Exchange, the world's largest trading center for collector's plates, puts producers, dealers and collectors from all corners of the world in touch with each other, provides information on the thousands of plates on the market and guarantees the mint condition of plates it trades.

The firm was founded by the late J. Roderick MacArthur, who saw the potential for a collector's plate market in the early 1970s and started importing collector's plates from France and selling them to distributors, dealers and individual collectors.

Today, the Exchange handles approximately 14,000 buy and sell transactions each business day. To help inform collectors about the thousands of different collector's plates on the market, the Exchange publishes *The Bradford Book of Collector's Plates*, an annual reference guide to the international hobby of plate collecting. Six times a year, the Exchange publishes *The Bradford Exchange Current Quotations*, a list of the issue, high bid, low ask, close and market quotation prices for the 1,300 collector's plates listed on the Exchange.

The Bradford Museum of Collector's Plates, Niles, Illinois, maintains the world's only permanent collection of the 1,300 Exchange-listed plates. The collection includes plates produced by more than 60 makers from 15 different countries.

BROWN & BIGELOW
c/o Paul R. Charron
345 Plato Blvd. E.
St. Paul, Minnesota 55107

Plates, Figurines

Brown & Bigelow, the world's largest calendar manufacturer and distributor of Advertising Specialties, was founded in 1896 and soon became a respected leader in calendar advertising promotion. Brown & Bigelow calendars are distributed worldwide. Every year new, original and exclusive artwork and photography are purchased or commissioned for Brown &

Bigelow calendars. Their archives include calendar art from the early 1900s until today.

Heading the list of human interest artists is Norman Rockwell. The center of the entire Brown & Bigelow calendar line is always his incomparable "Four Seasons" art. Rockwell's continuing popularity is based on his ability to arouse sympathy for his characters. His subjects are average people who display common emotions, set in familiar situations.

America's wildfowl are painted by Brown & Bigelow's franchise artist, David Maass, an expert naturalist/artist and twice the winner of the Federal Duck Stamp competition. Other well-known Brown & Bigelow wildlife artists include Richard Bishop and Fred Sweney.

The popularity of Cassius Coolidge's poker-playing dogs is ageless. The first series was issued in 1906 and the canines with human characteristics have remained in print and popular to the present time. One of the most famous illustrators to have a long association with Brown & Bigelow was Maxfield Parrish. He was commissioned by the company in 1936 at the age of sixty-six and went on to produce three decades of calendar art. The beautiful Parrish landscapes are among the best calendar art ever created.

Also included in Brown & Bigelow's outstanding collection of artists are the Western artists Charles M. Russell, Frank Hoffman and Tom Ryan and famous etchers like Al Mettel, R. H. Palenske and Lionel Barrymore.

The names mentioned represent just a handful of the widely recognized artists who are enrolled in the Brown & Bigelow roster.

Brown & Bigelow exclusive artwork also appears on limited edition collectibles such as fine china plates, Christmas ornaments and figurines.

BURGUES PORCELAIN STUDIO
1433 Oakwood
Lakewood, New Jersey 08701

Plates, Figurines

The Burgues Porcelain Studio was established in 1964. Dr. Irving Carl Burgues and his wife, Carol Werner Burgues, are the principal artists for this firm, which

produces porcelain sculptures and hand-painted designer vases.

The Burgues' work was distributed by Spode for four years before Burgues became an independent marketer thirteen years ago.

Works from the artists have been used extensively by United States Presidents and the State Department for Gifts of State to foreign dignitaries and European governments.

Irving Carl Burgues' sculptures are on display in museums including The Smithsonian Institution, and he has been commissioned to sculpt both public and private works. Burgues porcelains are on display throughout the country at prestigious jewelers and porcelain galleries.

In 1978 and 1979, both Burgues artists created limited edition and collector plates which were offered through ANNA-PERENNA.

CHINESE FINE ARTS CO. INC.
c/o LaMont M. Clay
Rt. 2—Box 70
Holdrege, Nebraska 68949

Plates, Figurines

Chinese Fine Arts Co. Inc. was founded by LaMont M. Clay in 1979. Clay is a collector of stone carvings from Mainland China, and was one of the first 600 Americans to visit China after normalization of relations. The firm's objectives are to bring fine-quality sculpture to the American public, to allow the master carvers recognition by signing their work, and to introduce totally hand-produced, limited edition collector plates to the American market. These pieces are carved from stone or hand-painted on fine china.

CHRISTIAN BELL PORCELAIN LTD.
P.O. Box 940
Mount Forest, Ontario NOG 2LO

Christian Bell
P.O. Box 930
Tustin, California 92680

Plates, Graphics

Christian Bell was founded by Horst Muller in 1979. Muller apprenticed as a china painter in Germany and also sold china for various companies before launching

his own firm. Peter Etril Synder was Christian Bell's first artist, and he has completed three collections for the firm: *Preserving a Way of Life Chapter 1*, *Preserving a Way of Life Chapter 2* and *Preserving a Way of Life Chapter 3*. These series are about the Mennonite lifestyle.

Other artists who have created plates for Christian Bell include: Douglas A. Manning, creator of *The Wild North* and *Vanishing Africa* wildlife plate series; Ted Xaras, creator of *The Age of Steam* and *American Steam* railroad plate series, the *Men of the Rails* collection of railroad employees, and the *Memories* series depicting home delivery of the 1930s and 1940s; and James Hill, creator of *The Men of the Sea* plate collection.

Christian Bell also produces an *Annual Canada* series featuring the works of various artists. In July, 1984 the firm introduced a commemorative plate by Ted Xaras called "First Lady of Steam."

CHRISTIAN FANTASY COLLECTIBLES
125 Woodland Avenue
Rutherford, New Jersey 07070

Plates

Christian Fantasy Collectibles was founded in 1984, and the company's formation actually reads like a fantasy.

Enter Priscilla Dailey, a spiritually moved woman, who suddenly heard the phrase "prayer bear" in her mind while riding in her car and regarded this as a message from God.

Three weeks later, Ms. Dailey awoke at 3 a.m. with a poem in her mind. With the help of her husband Bob, the poem was rewritten and revised, and the search began in earnest for just the right illustrator.

Where else would you locate the perfect illustrator for the poem but from a recommendation from a direct sales person selling encyclopedias! Tim Hildebrandt was that referral—a man who has illustrated fantasy for 20 years, including a commission from Twentieth Century Fox to do the original *Star Wars* movie poster, illustrating JRR Tolkien calendars, as well as "Dungeons and Dragons" calendars.

With Hildebrandt's superb illustrations, Priscilla and Bob Dailey created

The Legend of the Prayer Bear plate series including the original heartwarming lyrical poem as part of the backstamp. It is the story of Christ's first night on Earth and the tender love of a poor orphaned bear cub.

Christian Fantasy Collectibles has also introduced the Rita and Tim Hildebrandt *Fantasy Cookbook* plate series, featuring nine recipes selected by Rita from her natural food cookbook and backstamped on each plate. The nine plate series represents a nine-course meal. Also available is *The Realms of Wonder* series by artist Hildebrandt and poetry on the backstamp written by Rita.

The company has also introduced a new plate series featuring the first "matrix" collectibles system.

M. CORNELL IMPORTERS, INC.
c/o Henry Cornell
1462 18th Street N.W.
St. Paul, Minnesota 55112

Steins

M. Cornell Importers Inc. was established in 1959 by Morris and Maria Cornell, two immigrants who came to the United States in 1956. The firm originally imported classic, traditional German giftware such as cuckoo clocks, nutcrackers, music boxes and German beer steins.

Cornell recently celebrated its 28th Anniversary, honoring a period which has shown a rapid evolution in the German beer stein market. A quarter of a century ago, the steins sold in the United States were mainly of a "souvenir" nature. But in the mid and late 1970s, German factories such as Thewalt and Gerz began putting greater emphasis on the American market, and thus the limited edition stein market began to develop.

All along, Cornell has worked particularly closely with the Thewalt factory. In conjunction with Cornell, Thewalt has developed new styles, new colors such as gray-rustica and red-rustica, new lids, and new combinations of the three.

Figurine inlay lids come in a variety of different designs including: knight, hunter, herald, dwarf, barmaid, and wildlife.

Cornell has also taken the initiative to market its own, limited edition steins at affordable prices. For example, the

"Olympic Stein" was the official beer stein of the Los Angeles 1984 Summer Olympics. The "Jousting Stein" is an elegant, 2-1/2 liter piece with a stoneware knight on the lid, inset in pewter.

Other Cornell creations include the Silver Anniversary stein for Coors Brewery and one marking the eightieth Anniversary of the Harley-Davidson Company. Cornell also created the "Tuborg-Glass Horn & Stand" adorned with the official crown of the Royal Danish and Swedish courts.

Over 800 authentic German beer steins are presently distributed by M. Cornell Importers, making their collection the largest in the nation. All 800 items are featured in their four-part, 80 page full color catalog.

CYBIS STUDIO
65 Norman Avenue
Trenton, New Jersey 08618

Figurines

Cybis is America's oldest existing art porcelain studio. It was founded by Boleslaw Cybis, a professor at the Academy of Fine Art in Warsaw, Poland, and an internationally renowned artist.

Boleslaw Cybis and his wife, Marja, came to the United States in 1939 to paint murals commissioned by his government in the Hall of Honor at the New York World's Fair. Unable to return to their homeland after the outbreak of World War II, they chose to remain in this country, founding an artists' studio to create porcelain sculpture in the tradition of the ancient European studios.

The original Cybis Studio was in New York. It later was moved to Trenton, New Jersey, where it continues to flourish today. The Cybis artists create sculptures portraying a variety of themes ranging from the world of nature, to elegant historical figures, to the realm of fantasy.

Cybis sculptures are in major collections throughout the world, including The Vatican, Buckingham Palace, the Moscow Museum and The Smithsonian Institution. During Queen Elizabeth's visit to the United States a few years ago, she was presented with the "Mother Bear with Three Cubs," a Cybis porcelain.

In the belief that imagination is an important attribute to be treasured in to-

day's world, Cybis instituted an award program in 1982. The Cybis Award, to be presented annually, honors individuals for their creativity and imagination.

Joseph W. Chorlton, Chairman of the Board and Chief Executive Officer of Cybis, is determined to carry on the firm's tradition for fine quality porcelains.

DMP-Hackett American
6700 Griffin Road
Fort Lauderdale, FL 33314

Plates, Figurines, Graphics

DMP-Hackett American Collectors Company is a producer and distributor of limited edition collector plates, lithographs, figurines and plate frame accessories. The company was founded in 1984 by Mike Porter. His concept was to fill a void in the United States collectibles market due to the lack of American firms in the industry at that time.

Manager Jim Hackett attributes the growth of the firm to its slogan, "Innovations in Collectors Designs". The company has had many firsts in the industry—from the first baseball collector plate to be issued in the United States to the first biannual series which sold out and increased in price.

New products are developed by some twenty artists with the direction of Hackett American. Hackett American has exclusive contracts with the artists involved in creating new designs. The company additionally has exclusive licensee contracts with the following sports personalities: Arnold Palmer, Gary Player, Tom Seaver, Nolan Ryan, Steve Garvey, Reggie Jackson, Steve Carlton, Sandy Koufax and Whitey Ford.

Hackett has offered over 300 different collector plates featuring artists including Cassidy Alexander, Ivan Anderson, Bob Banks, Lenore Beran, Dave Chapple, Gina Conche, Corita Kent, Rudy Escaiera, Ozz Franca, Joan Horton, Kelly, Sadako Mano, Jo Anne Mix, Irish McCalla, Chris Paluso, Violet Parkhurst, Kevin Platt, Carl Pope, R. E. Russel, William Selden, Louise Sigle, David Smith, and Vincent. Promising new artists for Hackett American are Mr. Greensmith, Charlotte Gutshall, Linda Kish, William F. Powell, Hans Skalagard and Kathleen Smith.

D'ARCEAU-LIMOGES
53 Rue la Fontaine
87000 Limoges,
France

Plates

The name of Henri D'Arceau L. & Fils is one of the most respected in Limoges, the famous French porcelain center. The firm adheres to the original "Grellet Standard" of 1768 for hand-craftsmanship of porcelainware.

D'Arceau-Limoges was commissioned by L'Association L'Esprit de Lafayette to produce a series of plates honoring the Marquis de Lafayette, and to commemorate the United States' Bicentennial in 1976. The series, Le Patrimoine de Lafayette (The Lafayette Legacy) was introduced in 1973.

Some of the firm's newer series include the *Cambier Mother's Day* series, designed by French classicist Guy Cambier, and the *Josephine et Napoleon* series by Claude Boulme. Boulme is the chief designer at Sevres, a world-renowned French company which has been producing fine porcelain since the 18th century.

Other D'Arceau-Limoges series include the firm's Christmas series, *Noel Vitrail; Les Femmes du Siecle* (Women of the Century); *Les Jeunes Filles des Saison* (Girls of the Season); *Les Tres Riches Heures* (The Book of Hours); and *Les Douze Sites Parisiens de Louis Dali* (The Twelve Parisian Places of Louis Dali).

Another recent plate series by D'Arceau-Limoges is entitled *Gigi*. The series is based on the MGM film classic "Gigi," which starred Leslie Caron and Louis Jordan. The plate series features various characters from the movie.

DAUM
41 rue de Paradis
75010 PARIS, FRANCE

Figurines

Since 1875 when Jean Daum acquired the glassworks at Nancy, five generations of Daums have left their mark on every artistic period with their sparkling crystals as works of art.

Daum crystal in the Art Nouveau, Art Deco, free forms and contemporary styles set the stage for their introduction in 1965 of the *Pate de Verre*, an ancient

glass technique discovered in Egypt 3,500 years ago.

Both transparent and opaque, it reflects light with a soft, diffused glow and has attracted artists like Dali and César.

Each year new limited editions in *Pate de Verre* and many Daum creations in crystal are available to collectors. Five years ago, Daum introduced clear crystal with *Pate de Verre* together in collectibles like paperweights, perfume bottles, animals and figurines.

DUNCAN ROYALE
1141 So. Acacia Avenue
Fullerton, California 92631

Figurines, Graphics, Plates

Duncan Royale was founded almost 30 years ago by its president, Max E. Duncan. The company's first years were involved in importing plastic flowers, fruits and a variety of alabasterite and porcelain items. During the last five years, the company has taken a different direction and started designing and creating its own products.

The History of Santa Claus *collection from Duncan Royale includes this Russian "Dedt Moroz" figurine.*

In 1983, Duncan Royale introduced the *History of Santa Claus*, which in 1986 expanded to a 24 piece collection. The *History of Santa Claus* is a collection of 24 porcelain figurines approximately 11" to 12" in height in a limited edition of

10,000. This collection portrays Santa Claus from 2000 B.C. through the 20th century. Related items that have been developed from this collection include miniature pewter figurines, collector plates, lithographs, greeting cards, miniature plates and gift books.

Following the success of the History of Santa Claus Collection, Duncan Royale introduced in June 1987 a *History of Clowns Collection*, tracing the evolution of the clown from the Greek-Roman times through the 19th century. This collection of 12 porcelain figurines should prove to be a tremendous success.

Duncan Royale will continue to introduce collections that relate a story. They allow the collector the chance to enjoy beautiful art as well as experience history and legend that can be shared with others.

Duncan Royale is represented in the United States by Ebeling & Reuss. In Canada the Duncan Royale line is distributed by D. H. Ussher Ltd.

EBELING & REUSS
1041 West Valley Road
Devon, Pennsylvania 19333

Plates, Figurines, Bells

Since its inception over a hundred years ago, Ebeling & Reuss has maintained its heritage and reputation for fine quality European crystal and prestige porcelains such as Irish Dresden figurines. Crystal Signatures™, a new generation of 32% lead-crystal miniatures, were introduced in 1987. Recent additions also include Duncan Royale's *History of Santa Claus* and the *History of Clowns*. Other collectibles represented are the works of Artaffects artists, Gregory Perillo and Rob Sauber, and stained-glass angels from the Glass House Collection.

In recent years E&R has expanded its lines to include Christmas, seasonal and speciality items from the Orient.

EFFANBEE DOLL COMPANY
200 Fifth Avenue
New York, New York 10010

Dolls

Effanbee is one of the oldest and most respected American doll makers. The company was organized in 1910 and known as Fleischaker and Baum, jobbers and retailers of toys. In 1913 they formed Effanbee and began producing rag dolls and dolls of a crude, hard composition.

When the First World War cut off the supply of dolls from Europe, Effanbee accelerated production to fill the need.

Their first major success was "Patsy," introduced in 1928 and long regarded as a classic. It was followed in 1934 by the "DyDee" doll—the first doll to drink and wet. Dydee has celebrated her fiftieth birthday, and Effanbee produced a "Commemorative Edition Dydee Doll" produced through 1984 only.

In 1976, recognizing the need for collectible dolls, Effanbee began to develop the first such collectible series. These include the *International Series* and the *Grande Dames Collection*. Effanbee's famous *Storybook Collection* began in 1977.

In 1980, Effanbee introduced the *Legend* series with a W. C. Fields character doll. It was followed by character dolls of John Wayne, Mae West, Groucho Marx and in 1984 with Judy Garland as Dorothy in "The Wizard of Oz." In addition to the *Legend* series, Effanbee also produces the *Presidents, Great Moments in Literature, Great Moments in Music* (1984 only) and *Great Moments in History* (1985 only) collections.

Effanbee also sponsors a Limited Edition Doll Club, with special, limited edition production issues for members only.

ENESCO IMPORTS CORP.
The Precious Moments® Collection
c/o John Conley, Vice President
Director Collectible Gifts
One Enesco Plaza
Elk Grove Village, Illinois 60007

Plates, Figurines, Bells and Dolls

Nine years ago, the debut of the first 21 Enesco Precious Moments® porcelains capturing the inspirational artwork of Sam Butcher in three-dimensional sculptures marked the beginning of a collectible phenomenon.

Since 1978, the teardrop-shaped eyes and soulful expressions of these exquisite handcrafted and handpainted figurines charmed the hearts of the nation to such a degree that the Enesco Precious Moments Collectors' Club℠ was formed in response to popular demand in 1981.

Within months, the membership swelled to over 100,000 enthusiasts. Today, the Club numbers over a quarter million collectors.

Precious Moments pieces are among the most popular of the collectibles offered by Enesco, 28-year-old giftware and collectible leader, from the firm's international headquarters in Illinois and 12 showrooms throughout the country.

The plates, bells, figurines, dolls and musicals in the collection are communicators . . . messengers of love, hope, humor and optimism. They are mirrors of everyday people in everyday life situations.

In 1985, the Precious Moments sculptures earned the National Association of Limited Edition Dealers (N.A.L.E.D.) Collectible of the Year Award considered

"God Loveth a Cheerful Giver" is one of the first 21 porcelain bisque figurines introduced in the Precious Moments® Collection in 1978. The piece was inspired by artist Sam Butcher's daughter, Debbie, and her affinity for rescuing strays.

the highest honor in the collectible field. Enesco also garnered Doll of the Year for a member of the Precious Moments family of dolls, "Kristy," and Figurine of the Year for "Put on a Happy Face," 1983 Club Members Only offering. Enesco has also received N.A.L.E.D. Vendor of the Year and Manufacturer of the Year awards.

The Enesco Precious Moments Birthday Club℠ for youngsters of all ages was formed in late 1985 and enjoys a growing roster of children collecting Precious Moments porcelains.

Enesco also carries other successful collectibles including Garfield® by Jim Davis; Lucy & Me™ teddy bears by Lucy Rigg; Country Cousins®; Treasured Memories®; limited edition wildlife

sculptures by Fred Aman; limited edition plates, figurines and musical jack-in-the-boxes by noted American doll artist, Faith Wick; and Long Ago & Far Away™ dolls.

R. J. ERNST ENTERPRISES
148 So. Vinewood Street
Escondido, California 92025

Plates

R. J. Ernst Enterprises was founded in 1977. Starting with a small office in the back of Ernst Limited Editions Gallery, two moves and expansions have taken place since then, and the company now has its own warehouses in Escondido, California.

Being an award winning company, R. J. Ernst is dedicated to making fine art affordable. The best art, a good decal transfer, and quality plate materials all go into the very best, which is R. J. Ernst.

Today, Ernst Enterprises is looking back on 10 years of quality service and looking forward to many years of the finest art at the most affordable price.

THE FENTON ART GLASS COMPANY
c/o Don Fenton
700 Elizabeth Street
Williamstown, West Virginia 26187

Plates, Figurines, Bells

The Fenton Art Glass Company was founded in 1905 by Frank L. Fenton and his two brothers, John and Charles. The company started first as a decorating company in Martins Ferry, Ohio; but by January of 1907 it began to manufacture its own glass at a new factory in Williamstown, West Virginia. For over seventy-five years Fenton has made a varied line of colored glass, tableware and giftware. In the early years of the company, it was best known for having originated iridescent glass which is now called Carnival glass. In its second twenty-five years, opalescent glass and milk glass were the best known products. In more recent years, Fenton has recreated Burmese glass, Cranberry and overlay glass and a fine line of hand-decorated, opaque glasses.

The second and third generations of the Fenton family now lead the company, with Wilmer C. Fenton as Chairman of the Board, George W. Fenton as President, Thomas K. Fenton as Vice President of Manufacturing and Don A. Fenton as Vice President of Sales.

In 1970, Fenton entered the limited edition field with its *Craftsman* series of Carnival glass plates designed by Tony Rosena. The first of these plates depicted the glassmaker, with each of the other plates representing some craft. Fenton's line is marketed through department stores and gift shops throughout the United States and in many other countries.

There is a collectors club which is not sponsored by the manufacturer. It is the Fenton Art Glass Collectors of America, P.O. Box 384, Williamstown, WV 26187.

FIREHOUSE
c/o Janet Tuck
1900 W. Garvey Avenue, Suite 200
West Covina, California 91790

Plates, Figurines

Firehouse was founded in late 1982 by Janet Tuck, who had made her reputation earlier as a fine artist. Her oils had won many awards in shows on both coasts of the United States.

She began designing collector plates in 1981 with the *Great Grandma's Dolls* series, featuring dolls from the 1890's in sepia. Her next series, *This Ole Bear*, began with "Chauncey James."

When the producer of "Chauncey James" was unable to continue in business, Mrs. Tuck regained the rights to her plate designs and founded Firehouse in late 1982. Firehouse produced the next two plates in the *This Ole Bear* series, "Emma Louise" and "Buster and Sam." The last plate in the series, "Matilda Jane," was issued in mid-1984.

The *This Ole Bear* series features old teddy bears; some of them over fifty years old. The bears are dressed, and each has a unique personality and charm.

FLAMBRO IMPORTS, INC.
1260 Collier Rd. N.W.
Atlanta, GA 30318

Figurines

Recognized internationally as the leading source for collectible clowns and circus related items, Flambro Imports has es-

tablished itself as a respected vendor to many well-known retailers for its high quality lines of everyday porcelain and ceramic gift items and seasonal decorations for Easter, Halloween, and Christmas as well.

Based in Atlanta for over a quarter century, the company can trace its international business connections back to the Mid-1950s.

Still family owned and operated, the company has based its success on a commitment to quality merchandise at a fair price.

Beginning with the first Emmett Kelly, Jr. product which was released in late 1980, Flambro has continued not only to produce the best-known clown collectibles, but has added additional well-known porcelain categories that appeal to lovers of Americana and nostalgia.

"And God Bless America" completes the Emmett Kelly Jr. *plate series from Flambro Imports.*

With the 1985 appearance of beautifully detailed clowns authenticated by the Circus World Museum of Baraboo, Wisconsin, Flambro has financially aided the Museum. The Circus World Museum, owned and operated by the state of Wisconsin, is the world's largest repository of circus artifacts, memorabilia, and information. It is recognized by the American Association of Museums and is a National Historic Landmark.

Making its debut in 1988 and commemorating their seventieth birthday are the all new Raggedy Ann and Andy Collections. While they are certainly two of America's most widely known characters, most people are unaware they were

created in story-book form by Johnny Gruelle to keep his ailing daughter Marcella amused.

Flambro also manufactures a series of Antique Santa Bells, Musicals, and illuminated porcelains in conjunction with the Christmas Memorabilia & Reproduction Shops. These designs have been verified authentic by renowned Christmas historian Phillip Snyder and the Museum of the City of New York.

FOUNTAINHEAD
1025 S.W. 19th Avenue
Willmar, Minnesota 56201

Plates, Figurines, Graphics

The Fountainhead Corporation was officially founded in 1984 for the purpose of developing, producing, and marketing three-dimensional art products by nationally known wildlife artist, Mario Fernandez. These products to date have included a full line of Print Collector cabinets (for housing collections of limited edition prints), limited edition hand-painted sculptures, fine art collector plates, and large monumental bronze sculptures. From the start, Fountainhead has committed itself to association with only the finest quality products. Collector plates offer a good example of this. The firm's first collector plate, "Courtship Flight," was much larger, much more elaborate, a much smaller edition size, and a much higher price tag than the rest of the plates in the industry. It was Mario's intention to create a work of art on porcelain that could be proudly displayed in the finest gallery. By year end, "Courtship Flight" had been awarded "Best of Show" everywhere it was displayed. It also received Collectible of the Year honors from the National Association of Limited Edition Dealers.

After having spent the first three years solidifying the Fountainhead name in the industry, in 1987 the company introduced the art of Robert A. Olson and Daniel Craig on Fountainhead products in addition to the art of Mario Fernandez. "We are extremely excited about the addition of these two 'fine art' artists to the Fountainhead team," states Mark Quale, Director of Marketing for Fountainhead. "Fountainhead is very different from most companies in that most choose to specialize in an art

"Winter, where even though little of the early signs of splendor remain, a new beauty seems to appear," says artist Mario Fernandez of his "Winter Chickadees" plate from The Seasons *series by Fountainhead.*

form, whether it be plates, sculpture, or prints. Contrary to that, Fountainhead has chosen to specialize in the artist. Promoting the maximum life-time potential of Mario Fernandez, for instance, certainly means doing limited edition plates; but it may also mean doing prints, sculptures, or larger corporate projects. We felt this provides us with flexibility of pursuing the extraordinary project regardless of what direction that might take us."

FRAME HOUSE GALLERY, INC.
110 East Market Street
Louisville, Kentucky 40202-1306

Graphics

Frame House Gallery was founded in 1963 in Louisville, Kentucky, with a dual purpose. It was established to publish fine, limited edition prints of the work of America's leading artists. These prints are sold through a national network of authorized galleries. The second-fold purpose of the Gallery at its founding was to become an active and successful force for conservation in the country. With the expansion of the Gallery's offerings, came the widening of its fund-raising efforts into areas beyond conservation so that now, more than twenty years after its founding, Frame House Gallery has contributed to the endeavors of hundreds of various groups and organizations throughout the Western Hemisphere.

Frame House Gallery artists are experts in their respective fields. Frequently,

they entertain as speakers and authoritative writers. Often they demonstrate their artistic techniques in the classroom or lecture hall. Their knowledge of their subject matter is always thorough and their enthusiasm for their audience apparent as they travel the country visiting galleries and meeting the public.

The Gallery itself has always been a leader in the publishing industry. Through continuing research, Frame House has been able to set and maintain the highest standards of quality. Printing is on acid-free custom made paper, and only the finest lithographic houses are employed to produce the images. As many as 13 plates may be necessary to produce the most faithful reproduction of the artist's original painting. The packaging for all prints is designed to protect the print from damage during handling and to store it properly for years should that be the desire of the purchaser.

The number of prints in each edition is announced prior to printing; there will never be more than the announced number in any edition. All plates, negatives and films are destroyed upon completion of the printing process. All prints are signed by the artist as his endorsement of the quality of the print and the size of the edition. His reputation and that of Frame House Gallery rest with the integrity of that endorsement. They are your guarantee—a guarantee of excellence.

THE FRANKLIN MINT
Franklin Center, Pennsylvania 19091

Plates, Figurines, Bells, Graphics, Dolls

The Franklin Mint is a leading creator of fine, heirloom-quality collectibles and objets d'art. The company offers originally designed, luxury products, including high-fashion jewelry; upscale home decor and table accessories (from fine porcelain sculpture to exquisite crystal); precision-crafted die-cast automobile replicas and porcelain collector dolls; re-creations of famous works housed in world's most prestigious museums, and classic collector books in fine bindings. The company also publishes *ALMANAC*, the world's largest collectors' magazine, with an active circulation of more than one million readers.

148

FRANKOMA POTTERY, INC.
c/o Joniece Frank
Box 789
Sapulpa, Oklahoma 74066

Plates

Frankoma Pottery first opened in Norman, Oklahoma in 1933. John Frank moved his business to Sapulpa in 1938, where he continued to create ceramics from the Oklahoma clay found there on "Sugar Loaf Hill."

Frankoma's *American Bicentennial Commemorative* plates are a series of five, with the first produced in 1972 and the last plate made in 1976. These were created to celebrate 200 years of American independence. The series was significant because it was made of American clay. Each plate portrays a significant event in the American Revolution. On the back of the plates are signatures of the signers of the Declaration of Independence. John Frank created the plate art for 1972 and 1973, and his daughter, Joniece, created the remaining three plates.

The firm also created a *Teen-Agers of the Bible* annual plate collection which debuted in 1973 and ran for ten years, ending in 1982.

Perhaps most significant among Frankoma limited editions is the firm's 1965 Christmas plate—the first annual Christmas plate made in America, and a series that continues today. The plates are inspired by the Christmas story and the life of Christ. They are done in a semi-translucent "Della Robbia" white glaze.

In September, 1983, Frankoma Pottery was destroyed by fire. The firm was rebuilt and reopened on July 1, 1984.

In 1985, a "Phoenix Plate" was introduced in remembrance of the 1983 fire. This flame-colored plate depicts the mythological bird coming out of the ashes, just as Frankoma Pottery came out of the ashes to rebuild and reopen in 1984.

GARTLAN USA
8855 Atlanta Avenue Suite 4192
Huntington Beach, California 92646

Plates, Figurines, Graphics

To a sports fan, nothing is more exciting than attending "the game that made

Artist John Boyd Martin designed the George Brett Gold Crown collection for Gartlan USA including the limited edition plate held by Brett in honor of his 2,000th hit.

history." In 1985 Bob Gartlan founded Gartlan USA to make certain that such games and their respective heroes would be commemorated in suitable fashion.

Headquartered in Huntington Beach, California, the firm creates limited edition works of art honoring famous sports personalities and events.

When Pete Rose hit his 4,192nd career hit to break Ty Cobb's old record, Gartlan introduced the Pete Rose *Platinum Edition*, including ceramic plaque, collector plate, porcelain figurine and ceramic baseball card—all 4,192 of each item autographed personally by Pete Rose. A small unsigned baseball card completed the set.

When Reggie Jackson hit his historic 500th homerun, "The Roundtripper" ceramic plaque, 500 to be exact, were issued by Gartlan USA.

George Brett, Roger Staubach and Mike Schmidt are also suitably honored in Gartlan USA fashion—limited edition collectibles that are personally autographed by the respective heroes.

One of Gartlan's biggest challenges in the business is to obtain licensing permission from the players themselves. Above all, Gartlan must convince the athletes of the product's quality. To add more suspense to this process, Gartlan must negotiate and begin production on his collectibles—well in advance of the record-breaking events!

The market for sports collectibles remains strong, and Gartlan USA will

continue producing high-quality memorabilia to fit the occasion.

THE GHENT COLLECTION
Riverparke Building
Suite No. 103
1653 Merriman Road
Akron, Ohio 44313

Plates, Figurines, Graphics

The Ghent Collection, the limited edition collectibles division of NUMA, Ltd., has offered a variety of fine artwork to collectors over the past thirteen years. The direct mail firm began with a line of heraldic products displaying family crests, and has gone on to offer custom greeting cards, sculptures, medallics, limited edition lithographs and serigraphs, as well as an exclusive line of collector plates.

Master artists including Harry Moeller, Guy Tudor, Edward Bierly, Jay Matternes, Charles Frace, Dean Fausett and Alton Tobey have worked for Ghent Collection. This firm has produced pieces of historical interest such as the *Treasures of Tutankhamun* plate series, and the *American Bicentennial Wildlife Collection*.

A pioneer in new techniques in porcelain, Ghent works with manufacturers including Kaiser, Fairmont, Viletta, Lenox, Gorham, Woodmere, Caverswall, and Porcelaine Etienne.

Other notable issues include the Ghent Christmas and Mother's Day series, a collection called *From Sea to Shining Sea*, the official 1980 Olympic Summer Games plate, and Norman Rockwell's *April Fools Day* plates. Ghent's most recent contributions have been the *American Classics* series, *Lands of Fable, Hans Brinker Delft* plate collection and Official XXIII Olympiad Plate, *Lands of Enchantment, Man's Dream of Flight*, and the annual *Memory* plates.

The president of Ghent Collection is Dennis B. Haslinger, and the vice president of operations is Garrett W. Curtis.

GNOMES UNITED
c/o Edith McLennan Choma
3210 Dunlap Drive
Brandywine Springs Manor
Wilmington, Delaware 19808

Plates, Figurines, Bells, Graphics

Gnomes United was founded by Edith McLennan Choma in 1977. Ms. Choma

is the foremost painter of gnomes, and creates limited edition prints and porcelain collectibles featuring gnomes. Today the firm also creates collectibles inspired by birds, animals, flowers and various scenes.

For the first time in 1984, Ms. Choma's one-of-a-kind porcelains were available to collectors through art shows and Longwood Gardens, Kennett Square, Pennsylvania.

Gnomes United also produces several lovely limited edition Christmas ornaments which are entirely produced on site. Artists pour, clean, fire and hand-paint each ornament.

Ms. Choma has taught ceramics and porcelain art for many years. Her porcelains are included in various important collections all over the world. She has been commissioned by the DuPont family to create special works.

GOEBEL COLLECTORS' CLUB
Division of Goebel Art (GmbH) Inc.
c/o Joan N. Ostroff
105 White Plains Road
Tarrytown, NY 10591
Goebel Canada
100 Carnforth Road
Toronto Ontario M4A 2K7
Canada

Plates, Figurines, Bells, Dolls
The Goebel Collectors' Club is an organization designed to serve and inform those who enjoy and collect works produced by the Goebel Company. In addition, the Club offers items exclusively for its members.

Goebel is known all over the world as a producer of fine collectibles and dinnerware. The firm's name is synonymous with the art of Sister Maria Innocentia Hummel, the talented Roman Catholic sister whose two-dimensional artworks have been produced in three-dimensional form by Goebel since 1935.

Franz Detleff Goebel and his son William founded the F. & W. Goebel Company in 1871 in the Coburg area of Bavaria. Originally the firm made slates, pencils, and marbles. Then eight years later the Duke of Saxe-Coburg granted permission for a kiln for porcelain-making to be built on the factory grounds.

The first porcelain pieces produced were those for everyday table use, but by the turn of the century figurines became part of the line. The beginning of a new era for Goebel came in 1926, when Max-Louis Goebel, the son of William, added earthenware to the line which had been exclusively porcelain. His daring during a time of economic crisis proved wise, for without his foresight, *M. I. Hummel* figurines—with their unique appearance and coloring—would not have been possible.

M. I. Hummel *figurine "A Gentle Glow," by Goebel of West Germany, comes complete with its own removable candle.*

Max-Louis's son, Franz, took up the family banner of innovation in 1934, when he discovered the two-dimensional works of Sister M. I. Hummel and introduced them the next year in three-dimensional form. Today, in addition to the famed *M. I. Hummel* figurines, the Goebel firm offers M. I. Hummel plates, bells, dolls, and a number of other beautifully made collectible items.

THE GORHAM COMPANY
c/o Halena Wolf
P.O. Box 6150
Providence, Rhode Island, 02940

Plates, Figurines, Bells, Dolls
Gorham was founded in 1831 by Jabez Gorham, a silversmith and entrepreneur.

By the turn of the century, the firm was one of the most prestigious silver manufacturers in the world, winning first prize awards at international fairs and expositions. Silver pieces including Martelé, a type of design produced only by Gorham, elegant tea ware, and souvenir spoons, are still treasured by antique collectors and silver collectors today.

Sterling silver flatware and holloware are still primary products at Gorham, but in the mid twentieth century, the firm expanded into the gift market, and soon produced a fine-quality collection of porcelain figurines based on the work of Norman Rockwell. Collectible plates featuring that popular artist's work, and paintings by Irene Spencer, Ted DeGrazia and Lionel Barrymore followed. Today the Gorham figurine and plate lines still include Rockwell, as well as notable artists in the doll and teddy bear fields.

This emphasis is natural because, since 1981, Gorham's major collectible has been the *Gorham Doll Collection*. Since its beginning, the collection of completely original dolls with porcelain heads, hands and feet, and elaborate turn-of-the-century outfits created by artist Susan Stone Aiken, has been a desired collectible of recognized quality and value. The dolls are also enhanced by delicate 18-note musical movements.

New to the Gorham line are dolls created by Pamella and Noel Valentine. The *Valentine Ladies* series are made of bisque porcelain with finely detailed fabric and trim outfits, which portray fashion

"Miss Emily, Bearing Up" is the first plate in the Beverly Port *Time Machine Teddies series by Gorham.*

throughout the late 18th and early 19th centuries.

The latest expansion in Gorham's ever growing collectible family is a group of original, limited edition mohair bears by artist Beverly Port.

THE GREENWICH WORKSHOP, INC.
30 Lindeman Drive
Trumbull, Connecticut 06611

Graphics

In the early 1970s, printing techniques and the public interest in quality art matured together. Into this environment was founded The Greenwich Workshop with a clearly expressed dedication and commitment to provide a quality product to the collector.

Quality and innovation are the words that bind together the world of The Greenwich Workshop and set it apart from other publishers. Quality of artists, of subject matter, of production processes, and service. Innovation of new products and subjects. The firm pioneered Western, Aviation and Fantasy art in limited edition print form. They are continually researching new art forms, products and artists to satisfy the ever changing and demanding market place, and to meet the needs of the collector.

The Greenwich Workshop looks at the world through the eyes of some of the finest artists at work today. Each is a distinguished painter, photographer or sculptor. They are diverse. Their techniques vary. They span all ages. They live throughout the United States, Canada and Europe. Each sees the world a little differently, yet each holds a reverence for life and nature, and an artist's passion that enables them to express it visually.

THE HAMILTON COLLECTION
c/o Karen Stevens
9550 Regency Square Blvd.
P.O. Box 2567
Jacksonville, Florida 32232

Plates, Figurines, Bells, Steins, Dolls

The Hamilton Collection is an international purveyor of fine limited editions, including plates, figurines, bells, boxes, dolls and vases. The firm originated in the Chicago area, but moved corporate headquarters to Jacksonville, Florida, in the late 1970s. The firm is privately held by a group of investors headed by Chairman and Chief Executive Officer James P. Smith, Jr.

In the early 1970s, the firm's Hamilton Mint division created a wide range of precious metal ingots, medallions, plates and jewelry. Then in 1978, the company moved into the collector plate realm with a series of plates honoring *The Nutcracker Ballet*, premiering with "Clara and Nutcracker." A series by Thornton Utz soon followed, beginning with the first-issue "A Friend in the Sky."

Over the past decade, Hamilton has offered a number of extremely successful collections of plates and figurines. Many

John Seerey-Lester, one of today's leading wildlife artists, captures the majestic elegance of North America's Snowy Owl in "Morning Mist," first issue in the Noble Owls of America *series for The Hamilton Collection.*

of these were produced in conjunction with some of the world's most renowned names in collectibles—including Wedgwood, Royal Worcester, Boehm Studios, Pickard, Maruri Studios, Hutschenreuther, Spode, Kaiser, Roman, Villeroy & Boch, and Reco International.

Many other products were researched and developed entirely by Hamilton's own staff artists, including several types of collectibles from the Orient never seen in limited edition plates previously. These include the first cloisonne plate, the first Chokin and porcelain plate, the first Japanese cloisonne and porcelain plate, and the first translucent cloisonne plate.

Another area of note for Hamilton has been works featuring entertainment themes, including the theater, ballet, opera, television, and the movies. The latest successes have included plates featuring *Star Wars*® and *Star Trek*® characters, as well as *Little House on the Prairie, The Little Rascals,* and the *Honeymooners Official Plate Collection.*

Bird and animal subjects have been major areas of interest, also, including bird figurines from Royal Worcester and Maruri, as well as Venetian glass birds, plates featuring cats from artist Pam Cooper by Royal Worcester, dog-subject plates by artist Jim Lamb, and owl and other bird-subject plates from several well-known artists and studios.

But perhaps the best-known category of collectibles offered by Hamilton Collection has been that of child-subject plates. In this area, Hamilton has had a large role to play in making available to collectors several important, recent series from award-winning artists. These include three series of plates featuring works by the great American artist Bessie Pease Gutmann, produced by Balliol; the *Pride of America's Indians* plates by Gregory Perillo from Vague Shadows; many top issues from Reco International by the famed plate artist Sandra Kuck; the *Treasured Days* plates from the popular new plate artist Higgins Bond; and two favorite Rockwell-like series from western artist Don Crook.

HAVILAND & COMPANY
21 Spielman Rd.
Fairfield, N.J. 07006

Plates

In 1839, a young American named David Haviland was in his china shop when a customer brought a cup in to be replaced. Haviland had no replacement, but the piece was so extraordinary that he immediately began to seek out its maker.

His search led him to Limoges, France, where he found the makers of this exceptional china. He immediately began to export it to America. But French and American tastes were different, and the French were unwilling to change their patterns and styles for export. So Haviland decided to move to France and build his own factory in Limoges. There was some resistance, but by 1842, Haviland

was exporting his own products from France.

Haviland always has maintained the highest standards, but the company has also been willing to try new methods. Haviland was the first to engage famous artists to design decorations, and the first to introduce chromo-lithographic decoration.

Haviland's Christmas series include *The Twelve Days of Christmas*, and the series, *'Twas the Night Before Christmas*. In 1986 the company began a new series entitled *Traditional Christmas Carols*. To make each Christmas more joyous and memorable, Haviland presents its annual Christmas Angel. The firm also has offered an American Bicentennial series and a French collection, among other limited editions.

EDNA HIBEL STUDIO
c/o Andy Plotkin, Ph.D.,V.P.
P.O. Box 9967
Riviera Beach, Florida 33404

Plates, Figurines, Graphics

Edna Hibel is among America's foremost artists of international renown. Edna Hibel Studio offers her limited edition graphics, sculptures, plates and other collectible art.

In 1984, Hibel Studio was awarded the "Best Producer of Collectible Art" by the Academy of Collectible Art. In 1986, the Hibel plate, "Angel's Message" was awarded "Best Plate of the Year" by The Bradford Exchange.

Since 1940, museums, galleries and private collectors worldwide have recognized Ms. Hibel's talents. Many of her collectibles are displayed alongside her original oil paintings and drawings in the Hibel Museum of Art in Palm Beach, Florida. This is the only public museum dedicated to the work of a living American woman artist. Included in the museum's collection is Hibel's original "Mother Earth" painting which was recently reproduced as a United Nations commemorative stamp.

JOHN HINE, LTD.
265 25th Street Suite 4
West Vancouver B.C. V7V 4H9

Figurines

It all began in 1978 when young artist David Winter met John Hine, and the

two British gentlemen discovered their mutual enthusiasm for exploring the lives of their predecessors—and capturing the essence of life in the past in the form of miniature sculptured cottages!

John Hine, Ltd. was founded in 1979. Winter creates the original for each sculpture, while Hine supervises the mold making, casting, finishing and hand-painting of each cottage.

Made of wax, matchsticks and a small piece of lace, the first David Winter cottage was created in the spring of 1979 in a 6' x 8' coal shed. Although there were times the partners felt they would go bankrupt, they continued to apply themselves to the task at hand and the charming cottages eventually became so popular that enlargement of quarters became necessary. In less than a decade, the sculptures have become favorites of collectors in countries all over the world.

David Winter created "Squires Hall," one of more than 50 charming and authentic pieces produced at the workshop of John Hine Ltd.

To date, 80 cottages have been designed, and more are being carefully planned. The recent arrival of the David Winter Cottages Collectors Guild was met with great enthusiasm, and collectors now receive information about David Winter, the John Hine Studios and the intricacies behind the cottages and life in bygone Britain.

HUTSCHENREUTHER
PORCELAIN
41 Madison Ave.
New York, New York 10010

Hutschenreuther (Canada) Ltd.
42 Carnforth Rd.
Toronto, Ontario M4A 2K7

Plates, Figurines

Hutschenreuther is a famed German maker of fine porcelain items, located in the Selb region of Bavaria. A long-time leader in superb-quality figurines and other collector's items, as well as fine dinnerware, Hutschenreuther entered the limited edition plate market in 1922.

Since then, the firm has introduced several series of plates by the husband-and-wife team of Charlotte and William Hallett. In 1982, The Hamilton Collection offered Hutschenreuther's *The Roses of Redoute* collection of eight plates. Other artists whose works have graced the plates of Hutschenreuther include Ole Winther, Gunther Granget, Edna Hibel, Hans Achtziger and Dolores Valenza.

INCOLAY STUDIOS, INC.
445 North Fox Street
P.O. Box 711
San Fernando, California 91340

Plates

One of the most ancient forms of art was the detailed carving of cameos from multi-layered gemstones. The white layers were used for the heads, figures and scenes, while the multi-colored layers formed the background.

The artisans of Incolay Studios, Incorporated have revived this lost art by using a totally different medium, handcrafted Incolay Stone.

The Incolay Stone process is a closely guarded secret in which various colored minerals and coupling agents are combined in the stratified background to reproduce the same variegated formations and beauty of natural stone. The minerals include Carnelian, Sardonyx, Onyx, Smokey Topaz, Banded Agate, Sapphire Blue and Rhodochrosite.

In 1977 Incolay Studios entered the limited edition collector plate market with the first issue in the *Romantic Poets* series. This plate, "She Walks in Beauty",

became an immediate success and was named the "favorite collector plate" by the readers of *Plate Collector* Magazine.

In addition to the *Romantic Poets* series in Incolay Carnelian by Gayle Bright Appleby and Roger Akers, Incolay Studios released *The Great Romances of History* series in Incolay Smokey Topaz by Carl Romanelli.

A series entitled *Life's Interludes* has been sculpted by J. W. Roberts and produced in French Bronze and Incolay Ivory.

The *Four Elements* Micro plate series features reproductions of restored museum chalk impressions incorporated in a 2¾-inch Incolay Banded Agate plate with a 24K gold-plated Grecian border.

New series from Incolay include the *Voyages of Ulysses* by Alan Brunettin and *The Enchanted Moments* by Rosemary Calder.

IRIS ARC CRYSTAL
114 East Haley Street
Santa Barbara, California 93101

Figurines
Exquisitely designed faceted figurines of 32% full lead crystal have become the hallmarks of Iris Arc Crystal. Founded by Jonathan Wygant and Francesca Patruno in 1976, Iris Arc Crystal originally marketed faceted crystal in the form of prisms and jewelry. In 1979, Iris Arc Crystal became the first American manufacturer of faceted crystal collectible figurines.

The success of the new company was noticed by *INC.* magazine in 1983 when it was recognized as one of the 500 fastest growing private companies in America.

Iris Arc Crystal's award-winning designers dedicate their talent and vision to creating pieces of incomparable elegance and beauty. Every piece is individually handcrafted from 32% full lead crystal through an exacting process of precision cutting, polishing and expert hand-finishing. Up to 131 individual crystal prisms are carefully shaped and assembled by skilled artisans to create a figurine. Iris Arc Crystal introduces a large selection of outstanding new pieces twice a year. The etched Iris Arc Crystal name and copyright symbol assure collectors of the quality and authenticity of their selections.

SVEND JENSEN OF DENMARK
c/o Per Jensen
1010 Boston Post Road
Rye, New York 10580

Plates
Svend Jensen's creations are the culmination of the art heritage he learned from his father. This talent is evident in his works in glass, porcelain and metal. However, his greatest success was in his favorite art form—plates—where he collaborated with H. C. Torbol, a porcelain expert skilled in producing the "Old Copenhagen Blue."

The crowning moment for Jensen came after the introduction of his first limited edition plates in 1970. King Frederick IX of Denmark honored Jensen's work by presenting him with Denmark's coveted "Symbol of Growth" for his achievements.

That year Svend Jensen issued two limited edition plates which were the premiere offerings in two annual collections. The Christmas collection is based on Hans Christian Andersen's tales. There is a Mother's Day collection as well.

Two artists are primarily associated with these works. Svend Otto is known for his spare, but vigorous, illustrations of the beloved Hans Christian Andersen stories. Copenhagen-born Mads Stage was trained at the Royal Danish Academy of Arts and has won numerous awards for his illustrations of Danish literary works. His simple, almost child-like style has brought him a wide following in both Denmark and the United States.

KAISER PORCELAIN
c/o Viking Import House-Plates
412 S.E. 6th St.
Fort Lauderdale, Florida 33301

Kaiser Porcelain (US) Inc.
2045 Niagara Falls Blvd. Units 11 & 12
Niagara Falls, New York 14304

Kaiser Porcelain Co. Ltd.
5572 Ambler Dr.
Mississauga Ontario L4W 2K9

Plates, Figurines, Bells
In 1872, August Alboth, chief painter at the famous porcelain factory in Thuringia, Germany, decided to establish his own business. Alboth moved to Coburg, where he began to design and decorate

"Mother and Baby" is an example of the fine porcelain figurines created by Kaiser Porcelain Co. Ltd.

porcelain in his workshop. Later, his son Ernest joined his father and the two moved the business to Kronach, Bavaria.

In 1922, Ernest's daughter Erna married Georg Kaiser, who became a partner of the firm. The company's trademark "Alka-Kunst" was created in 1925, combining the first two letters of "Alboth" and "Kaiser," and "Kunst," the German word for art.

The business was a success, and in 1938 the studio bought a well-known Bavarian firm, which had been cited by Ludwig II of Bavaria in 1882 for "magnificent application of Cobalt blue underglaze."

The company is famous for its elegant dinnerware, very fine gift porcelain, graceful figurines, and an exquisite line of collectors' limited editions. Hubert Kaiser is chief executive officer of this international firm, which is still a family-owned concern.

KALEIDOSCOPE, INC.
c/o Leonard E. Padgett, President
PO Box 415
Clinton, Maryland 20735

Plates
Kaleidoscope, Inc. offers affordable, limited edition gift items with a wide range of wares including miniature glass plates, cups and saucers, mugs, steins, thimbles, bells and presentation pieces.

The firm offers choice items in small quantity and can produce personalized

pieces decorated with company logos, historical sites, and other themes which the customer wishes to provide.

The company offers a unique line of miniature glass cup plates featuring a wide variety of designs pressed into high quality glass plates. Decaled designs are also available, and Kaleidoscope debuted "Christmas Secrets" for the 1987 Christmas market as well as a colorful theme on "Puss in Boots."

All pieces are done on high quality glass, china, porcelain, and ceramics. The firm recently won a special award from the Society of Glass and Ceramic Decorators and from the State of Maryland for a special line commemorating the 350th Anniversary celebration of the founding of Maryland.

EDWIN M. KNOWLES CHINA
　　COMPANY
P.O. Box 296
Newell, West Virginia 26050

Plates, Dolls

The firm of Edwin M. Knowles traces its history back to the early 19th century when Isaac Knowles, father of Edwin, established the family business—Knowles, Taylor and Knowles—in East Liverpool, Ohio. After apprenticing with his father, Edwin established his own company in Newell, West Virginia.

After Edwin Knowles' death, the firm ceased operations until entering into an affiliation with The Bradford Exchange to preserve its time-honored name.

The *Wizard of Oz* series by James Auckland was the first proprietary collector's plate series from Knowles. It was followed by the *American Holidays* series by Don Spaulding and the *Gone With the Wind* series by Ray Kursar.

Since 1975, the Knowles name has appeared on issues certified by The Rockwell Society of America. Series sponsored by the society include *Christmas, Mother's Day, Heritage, Rockwell's Rediscovered Women, Rockwell on Tour,* and *Rockwell's Light Campaign.*

In 1985, Knowles was granted an official endorsement from the children of Norman Rockwell to produce collector's plates featuring their father's artwork. The first plate series to be endorsed by the Norman Rockwell Family Trust was

"The Gettysburg Address" is the first issue in the Lincoln, Man of America *series by The Edwin M. Knowles China Co.*

Rockwell's American Dream. Subsequent series bearing this exclusive "seal of approval" include *Rockwell's Colonials: The Rarest Rockwells, A Mind of Her Own: Rockwell's Studies of Girlhood* and *Rockwell's Golden Moments.*

Another popular Knowles plate theme is movies. Artists Mort Kunstler, William Chambers, Tony Crnkovich and Elaine Gignilliat have preserved favorite scenes from classic movie musicals such as *Oklahoma, Annie, The King and I, Sound of Music* and *South Pacific* on Knowles plates.

Birds and animals represent a third category of Knowles plates. Among the growing number of Knowles series featuring these subjects are *Living with Nature: Jerner's Ducks* by Bart Jerner, *Upland Birds of North America* by Wayne Anderson, *Amy Brackenbury's Cat Tales* and *Friends in the Forest* by Kevin Daniel.

New holiday series include *Jessie Willcox Smith Childhood Holiday Memories, Portraits of Motherhood* by William Chambers and *The Story of Christmas* by Eve Licea. Other recent Knowles series are *Tom Sawyer,* also by Chambers, *Lincoln, Man of America* by Mort Kunstler and *American Innocents* by Marsten and Mandrajji.

Knowles entered the limited edition doll market in 1986 with the introduction of *Yolanda's Picture-Perfect Babies* collection. Designed by celebrated doll artist Yolanda Bello, the dolls are produced by Knowles and marketed by The Ashton-Drake Galleries.

KONIGSZELT BAYERN
c/o Johann Seltmannstrasse
8483 Vohenstrauss
West Germany

Plates

The first porcelain bearing the hallmark of Konigszelt of Silesia of Prussia was issued more than a century ago. The likeness of Wilhelm I, King of Prussia and first sovereign of a united Germany, is incorporated into the hallmark of Konigszelt Bayern. The hallmark is a tribute to the King's early patronage under which Bavarian porcelain became recognized as one of the finest porcelains in the world.

Konigszelt Bayern entered the limited edition market in 1979 with the first plate in its Christmas-themes series. The series features artwork by well-known German artist Hedi Keller.

Other Konigszelt plate series are *Grimm's Fairy Tales,* which commemorates the 200th anniversary of the Grimm brothers birthday; *Sulamith's Love Song* series by the famous German artist Sulamith Wulfing and *Deutsches Fachwerk,* which features historically significant German half-timbered houses. Ms. Wulfing's Christmas series debuted in 1985 and her Mother's Day series began in 1987.

LALIQUE
11, Rue Royale
8e Paris, France

Plates

Lalique is a family-owned maker of exceptionally fine crystal products, including one of the most famous plates in the limited edition market: the first-issue, 1965 "Deux Oiseaux." This plate opened the way for a new variety in collectible issues: it was the first non-blue-and-white, non-Christmas, non-porcelain collector plate ever introduced.

The founder of the firm was Rene Lalique, a goldsmith and jeweler. He began his business late in the nineteenth century, and then purchased a small glassworks in 1902. Lalique built a reputation for fine, Art Deco-style items including perfume bottles, vases and figurines. After the death of Rene Lalique, his son Marc took over the presidency until his death in 1977. Then Marie-Claude Lali-

que, Marc's daughter, stepped in to head the firm. She is also its chief designer, and she was the creator of the famous "Deux Oiseaux" and the other plates in the twelve-year annual series.

LENOX
Old Princeton Pike
Lawrenceville, New Jersey 08648

Plates, Figurines, Dolls

Walter Scott Lenox and his partner, Jonathan Coxon Sr., established the Ceramic Art Company in Trenton, New Jersey in 1889. In 1895 Lenox assumed full control of the company that was later to be known as Lenox, Incorporated.

Lenox was determined to make American china the finest in the world. The company produced vases, bowls, and later tableware made of "American Belleek." It was similar to the creamy, ivory-colored china produced in Ireland. However, Lenox slowly developed his own formula and, after the turn of the century, he was making tableware comparable to the best in the world.

During World War I, Lenox was commissioned to supply President Wilson with a complete set of dinner service for the White House. Later, Presidents Franklin D. Roosevelt, Harry Truman and Ronald Reagan commissioned Lenox to make sets of dinnerware.

Lenox China, Incorporated continues to grow, while steadfastly maintaining a reputation for "old world quality" and value. In recent years, the firm has entered the limited edition collectibles market with plates, figurines and dolls on a variety of subjects.

LLADRO
225 Fifth Avenue
New York, New York 10010

Figurines, Bells

In 1951, three brothers named Juan, Jose and Vicente Lladro pooled their talents and finances to start a ceramic-making operation in Valencia, Spain. After building a kiln on the family patio, the brothers began to produce ceramics that made the name Lladro synonymous with superb quality and craftsmanship.

From the very beginning, they concentrated almost exclusively on the produc-

tion of figurines at the expense of the utilitarian wares that commonly provided the backbone of such a company's prosperity. This emphasis, however, reflected the sculptural sympathies of the brothers, and continues even today in the wide range of Lladro figurines.

Many of their first offerings were decorated with delicate, miniature, sculpted porcelain flowers. Their vases were modeled after Dresden and Sevres porcelains. But it wasn't long before the Lladro brothers developed their own highly stylized "signature" figures with their own sense of grace and movement.

In order to create these highly specialized works of art, teams of talented workers of unparalled experience in porcelain manufacture were assembled. They were to become the cornerstone of the present-day company.

Lladro has captured the magical wedding day with "The Bride."

Today, the company sells a wide range of both limited and open-ended edition figurines. The subjects range from flowers and animals to nativity sets and sports activities. In addition, Lladro manufactures vases, lamp bases and miniatures. In a recent effort to expand its scope, the firm founded the Lladro Collectors Society, which is open to those who decorate with or collect Lladro.

Members of the Collectors Society receive a host of benefits, including a free porcelain plaque with the signatures of the three Lladro brothers, a complimentary leatherette binder to store copies of the Society magazine, and a subscription to the award winning publication, *Expressions*, full of everything a collector might want to know about Lladro and its products. The personalized Society card shows associate membership in the Lladro Museum (opening soon in New York) and enables members to purchase the specially designed annual members-only figurine. Collectors catalogs are available to active members for a 50 percent savings on the normal suggested retail price. Society memberships are $25 for one year and $45 for two years.

M & T IMPORTS
P.O. Box 956219
Duluth, Georgia 30136

Figurines, Dolls

M & T Imports was formed in August of 1985 with the purpose of importing high end giftware from Europe. The principles, Marc Petrequin and Ted Daywalt, have extensive backgrounds and knowledge in the business from having lived in Europe. Marc Petrequin is French and Ted Daywalt is American, and both have run successful businesses in the past.

M & T Imports has imported figurines, wood carvings, pewter, stoneware and jewelry. The current major lines are santon figurines of Maryse DiLandro (French) and pottery pigs of Saltford Pottery (English). Both lines are classified "collectibles" and "high end gifts".

Following a test market of the santons in the fall of 1985, the figurines were placed in over 30 national trade shows in 1986. The first year on the market, the figurines were selected to be highlighted by *Doll Reader Magazine* for the 1986 Toy Fair and selected by *Giftware News* in the fall of 1986 for the prestigious *Who's Who In Collectible Dolls*. Santons are dressed figurines and thus are collected in both the doll and figurine markets.

M & T Imports has established Santons d'Art de Provence Collectors Centers throughout the United States of which there are now over 200 locations. There

are over 350 stores carrying the santons of Maryse DiLandro nationally.

During the fall of 1985, the standing santon figurines sold for $60.00. These same pieces today sell for $85.00, a significant increase in value for their collectors!

Maryse DiLandro has introduced a limited edition santon to the United States called "Young Peasant Woman with Wheat." Only 1,000 of these pieces are being made for the U.S. market. The retail price of these signed and numbered pieces is $200.00. An active secondary market is expected to grow in her pieces.

M & T Imports is headquartered in Duluth, Georgia, a suburb of Atlanta, and distributes from a warehouse located in Macon, Georgia. The facilities are being expanded to accommodate new lines.

MARURI U.S.A.
c/o Ed Purcell
15145 Califa Street
Van Nuys, California 91411

Figurines

Until 1982, American collectors were largely unaware of a superb porcelain studio in Japan—a firm with roots in the age-old ceramic capital of Seto. In that year Maruri introduced its wildlife sculptures by renowned artist W. D. Gaither. Within months Maruri became a respected

The "Eagle V" figurine is from the Maruri Studio Birds of Prey collection.

name in the United States collectibles market.

Less than two years after its introduction, the Maruri-Gaither "American Bald Eagle I" brought $600 on the secondary market—up from its modest issue price of $165. The exceptional quality of Maruri which attracted such attention is the result of high standards set generations ago, and observed just as strictly today.

Maruri was founded generations ago in Seto, the fabled Ceramic Capital of Japan. At that time, porcelain craftsmanship flourished among family-oriented workshops, one of which was the family business of Mizuno. The Mizuno brothers named their business Maruri, and soon this studio earned a wide reputation for excellent bone china and porcelain figurines, and true-to-nature bird and animals sculptures.

Maruri prides itself on its studied approach to the creation of limited edition figurines. Each piece takes 30 days or more to complete, using a multi-step process that has been followed faithfully over the years. The studio's premier master sculptor is Ito, who oversees the Seto operation. Ito's understanding of classic porcelain artistry is evident in every Maruri piece. In addition to Ito's many works, Maruri carries on its association with many great artists, creating a wide variety of superb sculptures.

Most recently, Maruri introduced a series of six white porcelain dove figurines entitled *Wings of Love*. Single and double doves are featured with hand-crafted and hand-painted flowers. Each sculpture sits atop a wooden base.

MUSEUM COLLECTIONS, INC.
c/o Donna Benson
2840 Maria Avenue
Northbrook, Illinois 60062

Canadian Distributor:
Ronart Inc.
100 West Drive
Brampton, Ontario
L6T 2J6

Plates, Figurines

Established as The Norman Rockwell Museum in 1978, the museum began manufacturing fine porcelain collectibles inspired by the immortal Norman Rock-

well's works. Today, plates, steins, figurines, bells, mugs and other museum porcelains are sought-after by collectors worldwide. The creative work and marketing of museum products takes place at the firm's marketing headquarters in Northbrook, Illinois. Ralph Gadiel, Chairman of the Board, and Robert Cady, Vice President, direct the firm's sales and marketing operations. Donna Benson, Vice President, is responsible for New Product Development.

In 1986, as the variety of collectibles and giftware created by the Museum increased and diversified, a name change seemed necessary. Consequently, the name Museum Collections, Inc. was chosen to characterize the fine quality of its giftware.

Museum Collections produces a wide ranging selection of products. These include the Rockwell inspired *Saturday Evening Post Collection* of limited edition figurines, Merie Coachman Tankards, ornaments and snowballs. In 1978, the *Robin's Cove Collection* of historic English country cottages and castles was introduced. Also new for 1987 are the Mike Roche *Our American Heritage Collection* western figurines and the whimsical Caren Miller *MVP Collection* of professional and sports figurines.

MILL POND PRESS
310 Center Ct.
Venice, Florida 34292

Graphics, Figurines

Mill Pond Press, Venice, Florida, is a family-owned art print publishing company, and they are proud of their reputation for creating some of the finest limited edition prints in the country. Quality is the foundation on which the firm has built its reputation over the last 13 years.

As the publisher, Mill Pond Press closely supervises the reproduction process of each edition. The artists are consulted at each stage, and their input is vital. As many colors as necessary are used to match the original artwork. Advances in offset lithography printing have made it possible to do this with surprising accuracy. The printing is done by fine craftsmen at firms who find it a particular challenge

156

to meet Mill Pond's high standards. The prints are published on luxurious all-rag, neutral pH paper made to Mill Pond specifications. With proper care, the paper will last for generations.

Mill Pond publishes a color catalog ($5.00) and a monthly newsletter which announces the 10–12 new prints that are released each month. The prints are distributed through a network of dealers across North America.

Mill Pond's full line of limited edition prints includes over 300 images by more than 50 artists of national and international acclaim. Subjects range from nature and sporting prints to Western art— from landscapes and primitives to nudes.

In 1982, Mill Pond added a new dimension to its line—limited edition sculpture. In 1986, the company further expanded its offerings to collectors by adding original hand-colored etchings.

Artists represented by Mill Pond Press include: David Armstrong, Robert Bateman, Mrs. "B", Terance James Bond, Amy Brackenbury, Carl Brenders, Al Buell, Paul Calle, Ken Carlson, Richard Casey, Jim Daly, Yvonne Davis, Nita Engle, Wilhelm J. Goebel, Paul Grant, Philip Jamison, Lars Jonsson, Paul Krapf, Rod Lawrence, Bruno Liljefors, Maggie Linn, Fred Machetanz, Jorge Mayol, R. Brownell McGrew, Burton E. Moore, Jr., Ron Parker, Roger Tory Peterson, John C. Pitcher, Thomas Quinn, Maynard Reece, James E. Reynolds, Sueellen Ross, Harrison Rucker, Steve Russell, Tom Ryan, Sam Savitt, John Schoenherr, Peter Scott, John Seerey-Lester, Keith

Shackleton, Morten E. Solberg, Ray Swanson, Kent Ullberg, Thornton Utz, Melvin C. Warren, William Whitaker and Jessica Zemsky.

PEMBERTON & OAKES

c/o Mary Hugunin
133 E. Carrillo
Santa Barbara, California 93101

Plates, Figurines, Graphics
Pemberton & Oakes is most widely known in the limited edition field for its Donald Zolan collector plates on child subjects.

Beginning with Zolan's 1978 "Erik and Dandelion," the firm issued five Zolan series—*Zolan's Children*, the *Children at Christmas* collection, the *Wonder of Childhood* Collection, the *Children and Pets* Collection and the *Childhood Friendship Collection*. It also has produced figurines and limited edition prints by Zolan.

In addition, the firm issues the *Nutcracker Ballet II* Plate Collection and the Robert Anderson's *Little Girls Collection*.

The Pemberton & Oakes Gallery in Santa Barbara, California offers original works, and displays all the original paintings for the plates in the series named above.

The president of Pemberton & Oakes is John Hugunin, former president of The Bradford Exchange.

PICKARD CHINA COMPANY

c/o Larry Smith
782 Corona
Antioch, Illinois 60002

Plates
Pickard, Incorporated was founded in 1894 by Wilder A. Pickard. For some forty years the Pickard China Studios, as the firm was then known, was a decorating company specializing in hand-painted art pieces and dessert and tea sets.

In 1937 the Studio moved from Chicago to Antioch, Illinois where Pickard's fine china formula was perfected.

The company produces dinnerware, giftware, fine china for the commercial field, and limited edition collector plates.

Pickard has been the recipient of various limited edition awards including

"Best Manufacturer of Limited Editions" from several groups and publications.

The firm produces a wide spectrum of collector plates including a Christmas series which began with the famous "Alba Madonna," the *Wildlife* series by James Lockhart, *Children of Renoir, Mother's Love, Children of Mexico,* and *Symphony of Roses.*

The president of Pickard is Henry A. "Pete" Pickard. He is the third generation to enter the business, which is the only American china company still managed by its founding family.

PoLLAND STUDIOS

c/o Donald J. Polland
P.O. Box 1146
Prescott, Arizona 86302

Figurines
Polland Studios originated twenty years ago as an artist studio devoted to the design and creation of miniature art objects. The studio was unique in that its object and desire was to offer limited edition art objects at affordable prices.

The studio creates figurines both for its in-house manufacturing and marketing, and also creates and prototypes art objects and figurines for other manufacturing and marketing firms in the collectible markets. Polland Studios has, and continues to function in this area for such firms as the Franklin Mint, American Express, the Lance Corporation and Border Fine Arts of Scotland.

Paul Calle portrays the ritual of pipe smoking and the spirit of communication in "The Breath of Friendship" by Mill Pond Press.

Don Polland created "Hot Pursuit," one of the Great Hunt Collection which was presented to the Denver Museum.

Polland Studios began operations in Laguna Beach, California, and today is headquartered in Prescott, Arizona. Principal products include lost-wax bronze figurines, pewter figurines and bonded porcelain, and Polland also provides design and prototype services.

PORSGRUND OF NORWAY
N 3901 Porsgrunn, Box 100
Norway

Plates, Figurines

A happy accident led to the establishment of Porsgrund, Norway's first and leading porcelain factory. Johan Jeremiassen of Telemark in southern Norway was convalescing in Germany after an illness. He noticed that German porcelain manufacturers imported large quantities of quartz and feldspar from Norway, and wondered why porcelain was not produced in his native land. Upon returning home, he looked into the situation and discovered that not only raw materials but also manpower and even a building site with shipping facilities were right at hand.

He soon convinced his wife's family that a porcelain factory would be an excellent investment for them. This family, the Knudsens, were prominent in the shipping business, and to this day their contribution to the company is acknowledged by the anchor in the Porsgrund trademark.

Porsgrund makes fine porcelain of outstanding design, and has received numerous national and international awards and prizes for the past forty years. In 1985 Porsgrund celebrated its 100th anniversary. The firm created its first Christmas plate in 1909, and resumed a series in 1968 which continues today. Porsgrund also has offered Castle, Traditional Christmas, Deluxe Christmas, Easter, Father's Day, Jubilee and Mother's Day plates over the past two decades.

RECO INTERNATIONAL CORP.

c/o Brigitte Moore
150 Haven Avenue, P.O. Box 951
Port Washington, New York 11050

Plates, Figurines, Bells, Graphics

Reco International Corp. was founded in 1967 by Heio Reich, a native of Berlin,

Reco International honors Mother's Day with a charming limited edition plate—"A Cherished Time"—by award winning artist Sandra Kuck.

Germany. From its very inception, Reco has been dedicated to the world of limited editions, and particularly collector plates.

In its early years, Reco introduced innovative plates created in association with renowned European names including Fuerstenberg, Royale, Dresden, Royal Germania Crystal, King's and Moser. All of these series have been completed and now may be found only on the secondary market.

Then in 1977 Reco discovered John McClelland, a well-known illustrator and fine artist with a special flair for child-subject art. McClelland's first series, *The World of Children*, premiered in 1977 with "Rainy Day Fun," and concluded in 1980. McClelland also is the creator of a *Mother Goose* plate collection, and *The McClelland Children's Circus* series. Reco introduced a line of hand-painted figurines, *Porcelains in Miniature* by John McClelland, and a series of clown figurines. McClelland's popular *Becky's Day* series of seven plates was completed in 1987. A new series, *The Treasured Songs of Childhood*, debuted that same year.

Another noted Reco artist is Sandra Kuck, creator of several plate series including *Games Children Play*, *The Grandparent Collector's Plates*, *Little Professionals*, *A Childhood Almanac* and the multi award-winning *Days Gone By* series of nostalgic, child-subject plates. Ms. Kuck's recent offerings include a Mother's Day plate series to be completed in 1988 and the introduction of *The Barefoot Children*.

In 1985, Reco introduced Aldo Fazio's first plate series, *The Sophisticated Ladies Plate Collection*, which depicts elegant cats in a colorful and sophisticated manner. A series of eight cat figurines has been introduced to match the eight plate series.

In 1986, Reco added several new artists whose works will be published on collector plates and giftware. Dot and Sy Barlowe are nature artists, and *The Vanishing Animal Kingdoms* and *Garden of Beauty* series are beautiful additions to the variety of plate offerings from Reco. *Great Stories from the Bible* by artist Garri Katz was introduced in 1987.

In addition to collector plates and the McClelland figurines, Reco has introduced bells, lithographs and various giftware items in recent years.

RIVER SHORE
c/o Karen Stevens
9550 Regency Square Blvd.
P.O. Box 2567
Jacksonville, Florida 32232

Plates, Figurines, Bells

River Shore was founded in 1975, and in 1976 introduced its *Famous Americans* series—the first-ever copper collector plates. The plates were based on artwork by Norman Rockwell and sculpted by Roger Brown to create a bas-relief effect.

Other popular issues from River Shore and Brown have included several series of *Baby Animal* figurines. His most recent collections were the *Babies of Endangered Species*, premiering with an adorable, blue-eyed, Eastern cougar named "Sydney;" and the *Wilderness Babies*, beginning with "Penelope" the fawn.

River Shore has focused its attention on Americana themes in the area of collector plates. A favorite has been the *America at Work* series, featuring Americans in interesting occupations, as portrayed by the legendary Norman Rockwell on the covers of *The Saturday Evening Post*.

Renowned western artist Don Crook has been featured in two of River Shore's more recent plate series—one featuring mischievous *Children of the American Frontier;* and the other honoring the U.S. Constitution's 200th Anniversary, called *We the Children*, and featuring playful scenes of the Bill of Rights in action.

ROHN SCULPTURED PORCELAIN, INC.
c/o Ed Rohn
273 N. West Avenue
Elmhurst, Illinois 60126

Sculpture

The first sculpture edition from Rohn Sculptured Porcelain, Inc. was "The Captain," issued in 1970. Since then, "The Captain" has been joined by over one hundred other sculptures including portraits of Harry Truman, Norman Rockwell and Ronald Reagan. Rohn's clown series, which started with "The White Face," is much sought-after by collectors.

Rohn is assisted by a staff of artisans who help him to achieve the color and delicate details of his porcelain sculpture limited editions. These pieces are available at select art and fine porcelain galleries.

In addition to producing his own collection, Rohn and his staff offer an extensive professional service to other giftware producers ranging from design and sculpturing through prototype and overseas fulfillment.

ROMAN, INC.
c/o Mary Ann Wellander, Dept. 816
555 Lawrence Avenue
Roselle, Illinois 60172-1599

Canadian Distributor:
Kaiser Porcelain
R. R. #3
Shelburne, Ontario
Canada, LON ISO

Plates, Figurines, Bells, Graphics

Roman, Inc. was created in 1963 by Ronald T. Jedlinski. The company began as a wholesaler of religious goods. Jedlinski worked with domestic and overseas suppliers to develop products, and by 1973 was importing regularly from Italy. He purchased many items from the famous Fontanini artisans of Tuscany, eventually becoming their exclusive North American importer. Roman's best-known Fontanini line is The Collectible Creche nativity figures, famous for their open stock availability.

In the mid-1970s, the company established the Ceramica Excelsis line of limited edition porcelains, concentrating on

Artist Frances Hook inspired this "Little Children, Come To Me" bust by Roman, Inc.

Biblical and inspirational subjects. These serially numbered sculptures are crafted in Mexico under the direction of Japanese master sculptors. It was through this arrangement that Roman became associated with House of Maruri in Japan and other porcelain manufacturers, enabling it to expand its presence in the limited edition and giftware markets.

Frances Hook was the first artist to design an entire collection for Roman. Her collector plates, prints and figurines reflect the same sensitivity that endeared her to millions as creator of the original Northern Tissue children. All releases since her death in 1983 have been issued under the close supervision of her daughter Barbara. Recent approvals have included busts made from her acclaimed portraits of Jesus ("The Carpenter" and "Little Children, Come To Me") and collectible bells inspired by some of the most popular figurines.

Mrs. Hook's close friend, Abbie Williams, has produced two limited edition plate series for Roman. *The Magic of Childhood* depicts the friendships between children and animals, while *The Lord's Prayer* illustrates key phrases of Christ's words with heartwarming scenes of youngsters. Ms. Williams has recently created four sculptured music boxes, in addition to a christening plate and medal-

lion that may be personalized with details of a child's baptism on the back.

One of the best-known names in the collectibles field, Irene Spencer, has been associated with Roman since 1985. Her oriental figurines "Moon Goddess" and "Flower Princess" debuted that year, the latter winning "Figurine of the Year" honors. Ms. Spencer's other works for Roman include *Catnippers* figurines and ornaments; *The Sweetest Songs* plate series, based on songs her mother sang to her as a child; the *Heartbeats* collection of mother and child sculptures; and the *Hug Me* collection of lacquered music boxes.

A number of other artists have been associated with Roman. Ed Rohn created busts of clowns and jazz musicians for the company, while Flavia designed figurines, music boxes and ornaments.

In giftware, Roman has produced a number of licensed lines, including The Campbell Kids and The Dance Studio Collection of bone china figurines, endorsed by The Joffrey Ballet.

RORSTRAND PORCELAIN
c/o Ahlstrom-Iittala Inc.
175 Clearbrook Rd.
Elmsford, New York 10523

Plates

Rorstrand Porcelain, founded in 1726, is the oldest porcelain factory in Sweden. Originally founded in Stockholm, it was moved inland to Lidkoping for safety during World War II.

The founding of Rorstrand is tied closely to the European search for the secret of porcelain, which was being imported from China in the early eighteenth century.

An "alchemist" named Bottger was employed by the king of Saxony to make gold—or another material that could bring profit—from the nation's national resources. In his prison cell in 1709, Bottger stumbled on a way to make porcelain from the clay of Saxony. The next year, the first porcelain factory was opened.

In 1726 Rorstrand was founded under governmental patronage. It has earned an international reputation for its original shapes and colors of dinnerware and decorative art in feldspar, porcelain, and high-fired earthenware.

Rorstrand issued a Christmas plate series between 1904 and 1925. In 1968 the firm resumed the Christmas series with a square plate featuring "Nils," a boy from a Swedish literary classic. This was the first square plate ever produced. Gunnar Nylund, the artist responsible for this series, is widely known for his monumental ceramic reliefs and has exhibited at the Swedish National Museum.

ROSENTHAL U.S.A.
66-26 Metropolitan Avenue
Middle Village, New York 11379

ROSENTHAL CANADA LTD.
55 G East Beaver Creek Rd.
Richmond Hills, Ontario L4B 1E5

Plates

Rosenthal was founded by Philip Rosenthal in 1879, in Selb, Bavaria. At first, Rosenthal bought white ware from other porcelain manufacturers and painted it with his own designs. Then in 1895, he established his own factory at Kronach, where he produced fine porcelain with his signature on the back.

The Rosenthal Christmas plate series began in 1910, and ended in 1974. These Cobalt blue plates were reissued in small quantities. The plates all bear a post-1957 backstamp. However, this practice was discontinued after 1971.

A second traditional Christmas series was introduced in the 1970s. This blue-and-white plate series depicts churches and public buildings, and bears the Rosenthal Classic Rose backstamp.

In 1971, Rosenthal issued the first of its Studio-Line Collections with the *Wiinblad Christmas* series. These plates feature intricate modern designs, partially hand-painted in as many as eighteen colors, and embellished with platinum and 18K gold. The series was completed in 1980. A second series by Bjorn Wiinblad entitled *Fantasies and Fables* began in 1976 and contains two plates. In 1976, Wiinblad began a series of crystal Christmas plates for Rosenthal. Based on scenes from the traditional Christmas story, Wiinblad used the traditional Danish colors of blue and white in a unique manner.

Two series featuring the work of Edna Hibel, *The Nobility of Children*, and *Oriental Gold*, were introduced by Rosenthal in 1976.

In 1981, Rosenthal introduced a new series entitled *Christmas Carols on Porcelain*. The plates feature famous carols, which are created with the same coloration as the other series and shaped somewhat like a Japanese square.

Philip Rosenthal, son of the founder, is currently the president and chief executive officer of Rosenthal A.G. He holds citizenship in both England and Germany and is a member of the Bundestag, the German Congress.

ROYAL COPENHAGEN
225 Fifth Avenue
New York, New York 10010

Plates, Figurines

The Royal Copenhagen Porcelain Manufactory Ltd. is Denmark's oldest porcelain maker. It was established in 1775 by Franz Henrich Muller, a pharmacist and chemist who was the first to duplicate porcelain in Denmark. He was supported by Denmark's dowager queen, Juliane Marie.

In 1779 "The Danish Porcelain Factory" came under royal control where it remained until 1867, when it was sold to a private owner. However, the firm still is a supplier to the royal court. The royal control is symbolized by a crown in the firm's trademark. The three wavy lines under the crown part of the trademark represent Denmark's three ancient waterways: the Sound, the Great Belt, and the Little Belt.

The first Royal Copenhagen commemorative plate was produced in 1888, but it was not until 1908 that Royal Copenhagen introduced its Christmas series, which annually depicts a religious motif or a winter scene. The first three plates were six inches in diameter, but after 1911 the size was changed to seven inches.

The Christmas plates were issued with the text in English, German, French, and Czechoslovakian until 1931 when Dutch was added. However, in 1933 the Dutch was dropped. The various foreign texts were available until 1945, when they were dropped.

The Royal Copenhagen Mother's Day series was added in 1971, and ended in 1982. In 1975 the *Historical* series was issued to celebrate the firm's 200th anniversary. A new *Motherhood* series by Svend Vestergaard premiered in 1982.

The famous Danish underglazing technique, introduced by Arnold Krog in 1888, is Royal Copenhagen's most popular finish. The firm's top artists in this porcelain medium have included Kai Lange, whose designs enriched the *Christmas* plate series for many years and Ib Spang Olsen, who was the artist for the original *Mother's Day* series. Today, Royal Copenhagen's famous Christmas plates are designed by Svend Vestergaard.

ROYAL DOULTON USA, INC.
Hattie Purnell-Burson
700 Cottontail Lane
Somerset, New Jersey 08873

ROYAL DOULTON CANADA INC.
850 Progress Ave.
Scarborough, Ontario M1H 3C4

Plates, Figurines

Royal Doulton, a firm with a fine reputation worldwide for quality and excellence in dinnerware, figurines, and other collectibles, also has established itself as a creator of a wide range of limited edition collector plates.

Doulton & Company was founded in England in 1815. In 1901 the firm won its Royal Warrant, and the right to call itself "Royal Doulton."

The company's limited edition plate offerings began in 1972 with a Christmas series inspired by holiday traditions in many lands. The hand-cast plates were hand-painted on a bas-relief surface. In 1973 Royal Doulton introduced a *Mother and Child* series by Edna Hibel, and in 1974 the firm commissioned Leroy Neiman to create the *Commedia Dell'Arte* series. Other artists among the many renowned names Royal Doulton attracts include Hahn Vidal, Dong Kingman, Chen Chi, Lisette DeWinne, Eric Sloane, John Stobart, and Francisco Masseria.

In addition to its collector plates, Royal Doulton attracts collectors by means of its wide range of figurines, and its famous Character and Toby Jugs which depict fully sculpted, amusing characters.

ROYAL ORLEANS
40114 Industrial Park N
Georgetown, Texas 78628

Figurines, Plates, Bells

Royal Orleans first introduced its popular line of collectibles and quality giftware in 1981, emphasizing creative licensed products and fine craftsmanship. The company is known for its quality image of fine licensed products headed by the *Jan Hagara Collectible* line introduced in 1983. One of her first offerings, the "Jenny" figurine, promptly was named top figurine of 1983.

In 1984, Royal Orleans introduced the *Elvis Presley* licensed products line sanctioned by Elvis Presley Enterprises. A figurine, ornament and plate set of his "Aloha from Hawaii" opening act in the *Elvis in Concert* series depicts "the king" performing in 1976. Other concert series followed.

Royal Orleans also produces *Marilyn Monroe* collectibles inspired from six of her movies.

The Coca Cola Company selected Royal Orleans to produce its official *Coke Annual Santa* figurines. Each of the six planned releases is based on Coke advertisements by illustrator Haddon Sundbloom who created the bewhiskered, apple-cheeked, rotund old gent who became America's ideal of "the real thing".

A line of figurines featuring *Charley Chaplin* will be introduced early next year.

Royal Orleans produces all *Jan Hagara* figurines, ornaments, tins, mugs and bells which makes up the largest percentage of the company's business which is owned by Bill and Jan Hagara.

ROYAL WORCESTER SPODE
Severn Street
Worcester, England WR1 2NE

Plates, Figurines

Royal Worcester Spode as a separate organization is of very recent existence, having been born only in 1976. However, as individual companies both Royal Worcester and Spode have been famous in the world of fine china for well over 200 years. Indeed, the Worcester factory, founded in 1751, is the oldest china and porcelain manufacturer in England, and

Spode is a little younger, having started production in 1770.

From the beginning, both companies produced superb table and decorative ware and today old Worcester and Spode are much sought after by porcelain collectors throughout the world. Both companies soon achieved royal recognition and attained coveted warrants from the British royal family of the day—an honor they have both proudly retained ever since.

In the 20th Century, the Royal Worcester and Spode factories have continued to manufacture superb tableware and cookware but have also enhanced

The "Ocean Racing Egg" by Royal Worcester is the fourth in the series produced annually since 1984 and is in the style of the great Russian jeweller Carl Fabergé.

their reputation with the production of magnificent china and porcelain collectibles. Royal Worcester claims the honor of making the first porcelain limited edition in 1935 and this was followed by superb bone china figurines and sculptures by Dorothy Doughty, Doris Linder, Bernard Winskill, Ronald van Ruyckevelt and others. Birds, horses, cattle, kings and queens and historical figures are a few of the subjects which have been created in breathtaking beauty by these wonderful artists.

Today the tradition continues, and both companies are currently producing figurines, plates and other commemorative items for such well known houses as Hamilton, Franklin and Schmid. In 1987, Royal Worcester produced the Ocean Racing Egg—a superb creation in the style of Carl Fabergé and of particular import following the U.S. victory in the Americas Cup races. Spode is also following a maritime theme with a collection commemorating the 4th Centenary of the Spanish Armada in 1588.

SCHMID
c/o Susan Peterson
55 Pacella Park Drive
Randolph, Massachusetts 02368

Plates, Figurines, Bells, Dolls

Since 1931, the name Schmid has been synonymous with the finest gifts and collectibles. Founded by Paul A. Schmid, the company is still family-owned and remains dedicated to the same uncompromising standards of design and workmanship that have made it a leader in the industry for over fifty years.

The Schmid line of gifts and collectibles has expanded considerably over the years. Today, the company boasts a number of sought-after licenses and represents some of the most talented artists in the world, whose collectibles are the finest expressions of the creative mind. Schmid also creates an extensive array of exquisite gifts to be cherished for a lifetime.

SEBASTIAN MINIATURES
c/o Lance International
321 Central Street
Hudson, Massachusetts 01749

Plates, Figurines

Sebastian Miniatures are the creation of Prescott Baston. He designed a pair of Shaker figurines for a friend's restaurant during the 1930s, and she was so pleased that she ordered more. Thus began his prolific career as a sculptor.

Baston began selling his figurines through a gift distributor in 1938, and devoted himself completely to the creation of "Baston figurines." The company was run by his wife during World War II. After the war, the firm moved to Marblehead, Massachusetts. Still working with

the distributor, Carbone, Baston also signed with Schmid to create *Folks in Little* and the *Dickens Collection*. In the period between 1946 and 1950, Baston designed an astonishing 100 pieces for Carbone and Schmid collectors.

In 1951, Baston began to handle more commercial accounts. He designed figurines which were meant to be given away by companies to help identify and promote a product or service. He did work for Puritan Candy, Necco, Jello, Johnson & Johnson, and *The Saturday Evening Post*.

In 1968, Lance Corporation approached Baston's firm, called "Sebastian," with a proposal to produce high-quality pewter figurines based on his designs. These colonial sculptures, along with Baston's series of pewter Currier & Ives plates and a pewter Bicentennial plate series for Royal Worcester, were extremely successful.

With the renewed interest in collectibles and figurines in 1975–76, Lance took over the production and distribution of Sebastian Miniatures and successfully returned the company to the production of collectible figurines. In cooperation with Baston, the first Sebastian limited edition figurines were issued in 1976. Lance and Baston also established the Sebastian Collectors Society to assist collectors interested in their figurines.

In 1981, Mr. Baston's son began to design figurines along with his father. The two of them continued to work together until Mr. Baston passed away in the spring of 1984. Ever since then, his son has been designing figurines for the line. At present, his son has designed approximately 100 different figurines for the Sebastian line.

SILVER DEER LTD.
c/o Page West
4824 Sterling Drive
Boulder, Colorado 80301
1-800-525-7541
1-303-449-6771

Figurines

Silver Deer is an eleven-year-old company which offers a variety of crystal gift and decorative accessory items, crystal prisms, and jewelry. It is best known for its collection of crystal figurines sold under the Crystal Zoo name.

Silver Deer was one of the first North American companies to design crystal figurines using 32% full-lead crystal imported from Austria. The Crystal Zoo Collection has become a standard of excellence, combining the brilliance of imported full-lead crystal with contemporary design and solid American craftsmanship. The Crystal Zoo Collection includes over 140 designs created by master designers.

The Crystal Zoo Collection features limited edition figurines for collectors. Silver Deer's first limited edition figurine "Pinocchio" was introduced in 1984 and fully sold out in one year. The company has since introduced two new Pinocchio's, most recently the 1987 limited edition "Pinocchio And Friend." Several thousand collectors have registered their purchases of limited and special editions from Silver Deer through their official registration cards.

Crystal Zoo figurines are designed by Olga Plam and Gina Truex. Ms. Plam received her MFA degree from the Moscow School of Applied Art. After emigrating to the U.S. she gained national recognition for her original jewelry designs, which have been exhibited in galleries nationwide. Ms. Truex received her degree from Tyler School of Fine Arts and later completed her MFA, specializing in sculpture and drawing. Her works in other media, notably papier-maché, have been exhibited in art galleries and featured in the Nieman-Marcus catalog.

SOUTHERN LIVING GALLERY
500 Office Park Drive
Birmingham, Alabama 35223

Plates, Bells, Figurines; Graphics

Since the 1960s, Southern Living Gallery, the collectibles division of *Southern Living* magazine, has offered art in various media to its audience, primarily through direct mail presentations. The firm's offerings have included art books and limited edition art prints, leather-bound classic books, plates and figurines.

The Gallery's first collector plate series, *Wildflowers of the South*, featured the art of *Southern Living* illustrator Ralph Mark, and was an immediate success. Its subse-

quent offerings, *Game Birds of the South* and *Southern Forest Families*, feature the works of English porcelain artist Antony John Heritage and accomplished nature illustrators Sy and Dorothea Barlowe respectively. Both series are sold out. The *Southern Forest Families* figurine series, based upon the Barlowes' art, presents their expert treatment of forest animals in hand-painted bisque porcelain.

Songbirds of the South, presenting the delicate marriage of fine art from the brush of A. E. Ruffing with fine porcelain, is the Gallery's most recent collector plate series.

Gallery management promises that future issues will add to the breadth of porcelain art offered to the collector world and will include works on such popular themes as nature and various other Southern subjects.

STARSHINE
103 Fairfield Road
Fairfield, New Jersey 07006

Plates, Figurines, Dolls

Starshine Inc. is a New Jersey based collectibles company that was formed in 1986 to market innovative products at very attractive prices.

The Mary Engelbreit Society brings to the collector the wonderful designs of Mary Engelbreit, a St. Louis-based artist whose work has been captured on such products as ornaments, photo frames, shopping bags, stamps, bookmarks, calendars, and greeting cards.

Collectible products available from the Mary Engelbreit Society include: figurines, dolls, plates and stuffed animals. All of the society's products are limited editions, and are individually numbered.

Also available from Starshine is a series of porcelain dolls featuring The Beatles costumed in Sgt. Pepper Band outfits. The dolls are 18" high, and individually numbered, and come complete with autographed doll stand and certificate of registration and authenticity. Importantly, the dolls have been approved by Apple Corps. Ltd. and licensed to Starshine by Determined Inc. The year 1987 marks the 20th anniversary of the recording of Sgt. Pepper which according to many is the best album ever recorded.

SWAROVSKI AMERICA LTD.
1 Kenney Drive
Cranston, Rhode Island 02920

Bells, Figurines

For almost a century, the artisans of D. Swarovski and Co. have explored the mysterious and challenging world of fine crystal with superb results. Since the mid-1970s, American collectors have been privileged to share in the wealth of Silver Crystal with a wide range of crystal collectibles from Swarovski America.

D. Swarovski and Co. was founded in 1895 by Daniel Swarovski of Georgenthal/Bohemia. Young Swarovski began his career as an apprentice in his father's crystal cutting operation, but soon realized that more ambitious means of creating crystal artworks would be necessary to meet growing demand.

He came up with automatic crystal cutting methods and harnessed the energy of "white coal," or water power, in the Tyrol region of Austria for his own crystal factory. There he established the exacting standards which characterize Swarovski works even today: over thirty percent full lead crystal would be used to create artworks of exceptional beauty.

Over the years, Swarovski's children, grandchildren and even great-grandchildren have carried on his work. Today the firm markets under the trademark of Swarovski Silver Crystal, and produces a line of original collectibles and giftware. These range from the elegant to the whimsical and include figurines, table ac-

"Togetherness"—the Lovebirds is the exclusive Swarovski America collectors club figurine.

cessories and collectibles. Subjects are animals, birds, butterflies, fruits, flowers, chess sets, and paperweights. Today, Swarovski employs some 6,000 people on four continents.

The international Swarovski Collectors Society was formed in 1987 to provide members with current product information and the opportunity to purchase exclusive club pieces. Among the many benefits, collectors will receive the *Swarovski Collector*, a full color magazine devoted to crystal collectors and their interests.

TENGRA
c/o PVP Industries
5310 Derry Ave. Suites E & F
Agoura Hills, CA 91391

Figurines

A common passion for porcelain art and family ties brought Joaquin Ten Paus and Jose Grafia Asensio together to found TENGRA in 1961.

The two brothers-in-law began producing TENGRA figurines in Benaguacel, Spain, a small village nestled among orange groves, about 17 miles from Valencia. The firm initially employed 11 individuals, whose innovative and detailed designs drew immediate success. Within five years, TENGRA products were being marketed in most European countries.

Today, TENGRA employs 100 skillful artisans with the marketplace expanding to Canada and the United States.

TENGRA makes true Valencia-style figurines, characterized by the glaze, light colors and smooth finishes. Romantic composition in soft pastel colors, innovative designs in more modern figurines and the use of 24K gold trim all add to the beauty of the handmade pieces.

The firm offers about 200 different designs. Approximately 30 to 40 are retired every year and replaced with new designs.

In 1986, TENGRA received the "1986 America Award" given in New York by the Editorial Office and the Trader's Club for the most prestigious and fastest growing collectible in North America.

Recently, the company introduced the *Babylonian Collection*, consisting of three

"Sitting Girl" by Tengra represents the company's dedication to the handcraft of porcelain art.

figurines in recognition of that empire's great contributions to the Valencia ceramic process—a process requiring delicacy and precision.

UNITED STATES HISTORICAL
   SOCIETY
c/o Emily Preston
25 East Main Street
Richmond, Virginia 23219

Plates, Graphics, Dolls

The United States Historical Society is a private, non-governmental organization dedicated to historical research and the sponsorship of projects and issuance of objects which are artistically and historically significant. The Society works with museums, historic homes and other organizations to create objects for collection that have historic significance, artistic value and a high level of craftsmanship.

Virginius Dabney, the Pulitzer-prize winning historian, is chairman of the Society.

Organizations with which the Society has worked include the National Gallery of Art, the Smithsonian Institution, the National Park Service, the West Point Museum, the Morristown Museum, the Chase Manhattan Bank Collection, Monticello, Winterthur Museum, Eli Whitney Museum, the Buffalo Bill Historical Center, the Confederate Museum, the Wadsworth Atheneum, the Metropolitan Museum of Art, the University of

Virginia, Canterbury Cathedral, Cathedral of St. John the Divine, the Washington Cathedral, St. Paul's of San Francisco and the Los Angeles Cathedral.

Trustees of the Society have included Samuel Eliot Morison, Buckminster Fuller, Alistair Cooke, Henry Steele Commager, Lester Cooke and others.

Among the projects of the Society are the reproduction of George Washington's Flintlock Pistols and his Inaugural Sword, reproductions of Thomas Jefferson's Queen Anne Pistols and his telescope, reproductions of the Alexander Hamilton-Aaron Burr Dueling Pistols, and the issuance of the *Young America of Winslow Homer* Plates, the George Patton Sword, the Robert E. Lee Commemorative Pistol, and the Paul Revere Silver Tankards. The Society is also issuing a continuing series of to-scale *Living Image* portrait dolls of Great Americans and the annual Stained Glass and Pewter Christmas Plate.

Books the Society has sponsored include *The Patriots American Revolution, Generation of Genius, Morristown the War Years 1775–83* and the *Great American Quilts.*

With the New York Council on the Arts, the Society sponsored the composing and presentation at the Kennedy Center of the American Symphony by Morton Gould.

D. H. USSHER LTD
1130 West 15th Street
North Vancouver, B.C.
Canada V7P 1M9

Plates

D. H. Ussher Ltd was incorporated in 1979 as a distributor of limited edition collectibles. Its main office, showroom, and warehouse are located in Vancouver. The firm has representatives covering every province in Canada.

D. H. Ussher represents a wide range of U.S.-based collectible firms in Canada. These include Armstrong's, Hollywood, American Legacy, Artists of the World, American Artists, Ernst Inc., Wildlife Internationale, Fairmont China, American Heritage Art Products, and Artaffects. The firm also distributes brass hangers and plate stands for Briant & Sons and

frames for Lynette Decor Products. In 1985, D. H. Ussher Ltd. began producing for the limited edition market and is currently active with products under the labels Reefton Meadows and Western Authentics.

V. F. FINE ARTS
P.O. Box 246
Lisbon, Ohio 44432

Graphics

V. F. Fine Arts was founded to promote Sandra Kuck's limited edition prints and original artworks. The company is named in honor of Sandra's father, Vermont Franklin, or V. F.

Sandra Kuck has been chosen for virtually every major award including the Silver Chalice, Print of the Year, and NALED's Artist of the Year for four consecutive years. Her distinctive Victorian style has made her a creative force in the collectible market for over 12 years.

V. F. Fine Arts is under the direction of Sandra's husband, John, in New York and is operated by Sandra's brother and his wife in Ohio.

In 1987, V. F. Fine Arts offered through its dealership, some of Sandra's most memorable original oil paintings and also received inquiries for her personal commissioned portraits.

As always, Sandra Kuck's signature means her collectors are receiving only the best in quality and a real investment for tomorrow.

VAILLANCOURT FOLK ART
P.O. Box 582
Millbury, Massachusetts 01527

Figurines

Vaillancourt Folk Art was founded in 1984 by Judi and Gary Vaillancourt. It is located in Sutton, Massachusetts, a small New England town located outside of Worcester. The company employs 20 people.

Vaillancourt Folk Art's main product line is chalkware cast from antique moulds that were originally used to make chocolate or ice cream forms. The moulds date from the mid-1800s to the early 1900s. A plaster-like substance,

chalkware first appeared in the mid-1800s and was referred to as "poor man's Staffordshire." It since has developed into a popular collectible.

Each piece of Vaillancourt chalkware is an original; individually hand-painted, signed and numbered.

Additional Vaillancourt products include hand-painted clocks and special production pieces such as the Vaillancourt Chess Set and Noah's Ark.

Beginning this year, Vaillancourt is offering two limited edition series: *The Vaillancourt Collection*, consisting of 30 finely-detailed, high quality chalkware pieces with a limited production of 500 copies; and *The Vaillancourt Mould Collection*, which consists of four to five moulds limited to five to 25 pieces each. Of special interest to collectors is the fact that the first copy of each piece in The Vaillancourt Mould Collection is being sold in special packaging with its antique mold.

Vaillancourt Folk Art is distributed through folk art dealers, specialty gift stores, art galleries, museum gift shops, leading department stores and fine furniture stores throughout the U.S.

In 1986, Queen Elizabeth II of England was presented with a collection of Vaillancourt Folk Art during her visit to the United States.

VENETO FLAIR
Via Tiberina 3BIS
06053 Deruta-Perugia
Italy

Plates

In Ambria, Italy, skilled artisans use centuries-old techniques to produce the majolica-style limited edition plates which bear the hallmark of Veneto Flair. First produced in the thirteenth century and famous for its vivid painted decorations, Italian majolica greatly influenced the development of European ceramics.

In 1984, Veneto Flair introduced the *St. Mark's of Venice* collector's plate series based on the mosaics of St. Mark's Basilica in Venice, Italy. The series, designed by Italian artist Franco Lamincia, continues the seven-century tradition of the majolica style. Under the direction of Lamincia, each of the plates is hand-painted.

UNITED STATES

VILETTA CHINA COMPANY
8000 Harwin Drive, #150
Houston, Texas 77036

Plates

Viletta China Company was started in 1959 in Roseberg, Oregon, by Viletta West, who hand painted china and sold it through stores in the Pacific Northwest. In 1978, Viletta China relocated to Houston, Texas and expanded its distribution throughout the U.S. and Canada.

The firm is involved in many areas of fine china including commemorative pieces, fine giftware, dinnerware and limited edition collector plates. Recently the firm has enhanced its offerings with crystal and 24% lead crystal products.

VILLEROY & BOCH
c/o Ingrid Vetterl
41 Madison Avenue
New York, New York 10010

Villeroy & Boch
45 Railside Road
Don Mills, Ontario M3A 1B2

Plates, Steins

Villeroy & Boch is a German firm with a long heritage of quality in tableware and art items. The firm was founded in 1748, when Francois Boch opened his first pottery studio at Auden-le-Tiche. The Villeroy family joined with the Bochs in 1836. Together the families became renowned for their innovations and artistic flair—and today an eighth-generation descendant of the Boch family sits as Managing Director of the firm.

Today Villeroy & Boch is an internationally-known maker of dinnerware and accessories in addition to collector plates, plaques, and steins. The firm has as many as 16,000 employees in its eighteen locations across France, Luxembourg, Italy and Germany. Headquarters are at Mettlach, West Germany.

Villeroy & Boch has a well-deserved reputation as the world's finest maker of steins. The firm developed both the Chromolith (etched or incised) process and the Phanolith (cameo) process. Although stein production stopped at Mettlach in 1927, the firm has offered several

contemporary limited editions in recent years.

The Heinrich Studios in the Bavarian town of Selb create most of Villeroy & Boch's collector plates, including three "Flower Fairies" series, the elegant *Russian Fairy Tales*, a current collection sponsored by the World Wildlife Fund and a six-plate series entitled *The Magical Fairy Tales from Old Russia* by Gero Trauth.

STUDIO DANTE DI VOLTERADICI
Via Terra dei Ceci
57023 Cecilla
Italy

Plates

The Studio Dante di Volteradici is located near Volterra in Tuscany, Italy. In this center for the mining and carving of alabaster, Studio Dante di Volteradici continues the Italian tradition of sculptured alabaster.

Studio Dante's first collector plate series, the *Grand Opera*, commemorates the 200th anniversary of La Scala Opera House.

Studio Dante has also introduced the *Living Madonnas* and *Ghiberti Doors* series, and most recently, the *Benvenuti's Muses* series. The *Muses* series, by Italian sculptor Sergio Benvenuti, is the first collector plate series ever to feature sculpture contained within the plate rim.

The first hand-painted ivory alabaster series—*Renaissance Madonnas: Gift of Maternal Love*—began with "The Gift of Wisdom" plate in 1986. That year, Studio Dante also introduced the first plate in its annual *Christmas Creche* series. Created by artist Ennio Furiesi, the plate is entitled "Joy to the World."

WEDGWOOD

41 Madison Avenue
New York, New York 10010

Josiah Wedgwood & Sons (Canada) Ltd.
271 Yorklands Blvd.
Willowdale, Ontario M2J 1S6

Plates, Bells

Josiah Wedgwood, born in 1730, was a fourth-generation potter. He was apprenticed at the age of nine to his brother, and

Second in a series of Wedgwood Mother's Day plates featuring springtime flowers, the 1988 plate features a white bas-relief ornament of tiger lilies on a pale blue Jasper plate.

later became the partner of Thomas Whieldon, England's finest potter of the day.

In 1759 young Josiah founded Wedgwood. A partner, Thomas Bentley, joined the firm in 1769. Bentley provided a knowledge of the arts and many social contacts for the fledgling firm. Josiah Wedgwood's greatest personal achievement was the development of a new and affordable dinnerware. This cream-colored earthenware with a rich glaze was admired by Queen Charlotte. By her command it was named "Queen's Ware." In 1774, Wedgwood received his most prestigious commission—a 952-piece set of "Queen's Ware" dinnerware for Empress Catherine II.

In addition to his "useful wares," Wedgwood experimented with a new Black Basalt which became one of the company's most popular products. His most famous invention was Jasper, an unglazed, vitreous, fine stoneware which can be stained various colors such as blue, green, lilac, yellow or black. It provides a suitable background for white relief work on classic subjects, or portraits.

Wedgwood's policy was to hire leading artists of his time, including John Flaxman and George Stubbs. That tradition continues today, and in recent years artists including Rex Whistler, Eric Ravilious, Edward Bawden, Arnold Machin, Richard Guyatt, Eduardo Paolozzi and David Gentleman have designed for Wedgwood.

Wedgwood has been extremely active in the collectibles field, producing Christmas plates, thimbles, bells and mugs, in their famous Jasper. The firm also produces several plate series in fine bone china and earthenware, including *Calendar Plates, Peter Rabbit's Christmas, Christmas Traditions,* and *The Street Sellers of London.* Wedgwood's most recent release is the 1987 *Mother's Day Plate,* first in a new series featuring "Spring Hedgerow Flowers."

WILDLIFE INTERNATIONALE
INC.
6290 Old U.S. 68
Georgetown, Ohio 45121

Graphics, Plates

Wildlife artist John A. Ruthven founded Wildlife Internationale Inc. in 1971 to reproduce lithographs from his original paintings. His 1960 entry "Redhead Ducks" won the coveted Federal Duck Stamp contest which eventually led to the business of publishing and marketing his own prints in his studio in Georgetown, Ohio.

Ruthven achieves remarkable detail and life-like appearance in his wildlife paintings through careful study of his animal, whether it be the "Indigo Bunting" or the "Black Maned Lion." He may travel to another continent to collect "study specimens" to study and paint his subject. Once the painting is finished, Ruthven donates the mounted subject to the Cincinnati Museum of Natural History.

"I believe that art is as necessary to our heritage as the history book. Both record past and present in the effort to educate and enrich the lives of people today and in the future. It is my endeavor through my paintings, to record for later generations, some of the beauty of nature that exists in my lifetime," states John A. Ruthven.

Meet the Artists
Biographies of Some of Today's Most Popular and Talented Limited Edition Artists

Limited edition artists are the objects of a great deal of interest and admiration on the part of collectors. Some collectors will travel hundreds of miles to attend an open house or convention featuring that special artist or craftsman. Here is some brief biographical information about some of the best-known artists in today's world of limited editions. This listing is not comprehensive, but it will provide an introduction to a good number of the talented men and women whose works bring pleasure to collectors all over the world.

SUSAN STONE AIKEN

From "Rosamond" and "Christopher" in 1981 to this year's limited edition delight, every doll in the *Gorham Doll Collection* has been dressed by Susan Stone Aiken.

A native Rhode Islander with a diverse design background, Susan began creating these elegant outfits as a labor of love. And it still is that for her today.

She begins with a sketch, then personally selects fabrics, laces and trims to create an original sample. Once this is perfect in every detail, she adorns her sketch with samples of every fabric, button, flower, feather and lace, and this board goes to the Gorham factory in Japan for production samples to be made. Susan gets her inspiration from books and photos of turn of the century fashions. In addition she has an instinctive feeling for the era, and for the combinations of materials that are authentic and correct.

"I'm from an old New England family," she says, "and I grew up surrounded by antiques. When I create a costume for a doll, it is like discovering an old friend."

Susan's formal art training was achieved at the University of Maine and Rhode Island School of Design. Her talent as a seamstress is a natural gift.

The culmination of her talents can be seen in the *Gorham Doll Collection.*

FRED AMAN

A mid-life career change has led Fred Aman into the world of fine art sculpture. This Enesco artist spent the first 25 years of his working life as a taxidermist in the north woods of Wisconsin. And today— after more than 15 years as a sculptor in bronze and porcelain—he has earned the respect of noted art critics for his naturalist works. As one observer said, "Fred's owl's eyes blink and you can hear his piglets squeal."

The field of taxidermy allowed Aman to develop an intimate knowledge of wildlife subjects. This combined with his natural art talent has led to a rewarding career in sculpture recognized with accolades, awards and a national reputation for fidelity to nature in his sculptures.

Aman has always lived close to nature to draw upon its inspiration. As a taxidermist, he was sought out by sportsmen from far and wide, including Dwight and Milton Eisenhower, who used to mail their favorite fish specimens to Aman from Washington, D.C. Today, as a sculptor, Aman enjoys working from a Wisconsin studio overlooking the north woods.

When he does bronzes, Aman completes the process from original sculpture to casting to finishing. Without any art instruction, he mastered all phases of the

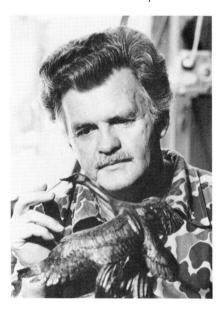

166

lost wax process. Wishing to share his work with a wider array of collectors, Aman has branched into porcelain sculpture in recent years. Using this medium, Aman can present the birds and animals he loves without sacrificing the fidelity to nature he insists upon.

WAYNE ANDERSON

As a native of Wisconsin, Wayne Anderson grew up with a love of nature that is readily apparent in his artwork. He graduated from the University of Wisconsin (Stevens Point) with a degree in fine art. There he studied painting and portraiture in preparation for a thriving career which includes extensive commissions and numerous prominent art shows.

Anderson is well-known in wildlife art circles because of his active participation in exhibitions nationwide. He recently showed his work at the prestigious National Exhibition of Alaskan Wildlife Art at Anchorage, which was presented in conjunction with the Anchorage Audubon Society. Anderson's oil paintings may be found in private collections throughout the United States and Canada.

The artist enjoys using a wide variety of media to showcase his versatility. Among these are colored-pencil renderings and traditional oils. Anderson cites Realist painter Richard Estes and wildlife artists John James Audubon and J. Fenwick Lansdowne as his most important influences. Like these distinguished predecessors, Anderson's work is characterized by technical brilliance. What's more, this young artist offers special insights

into elusive, little-known aspects of nature.

The *Upland Birds of North America* plate collection from Edwin M. Knowles marks Anderson's debut in the medium of limited edition collector plates.

DAVID ARMSTRONG

David Armstrong has painted his world since his boyhood on a rock-ribbed Connecticut farm overlooking the Housatonic River. In the woods and fields of his family's sheep farm, he developed a reverence for the earth and a desire to capture its essence in his painting.

"Over the years, I have developed an overwhelming concern for the beauty the earth has lost and all that still can and must be preserved. I have tried to show through my work the peaceful bounty and beauty of the earth that is timeless, while also expressing my concern for its fragileness. . ."

Eric Sloane, who lived in the next town, recognized David's talent first when he judged one of his early watercolors Best in Show. A relationship of mutual respect developed that led Eric to ask Dave's assistance with the enormous mural project at the National Air and Space Museum in Washington, D.C.

In the rural countryside of central Pennsylvania around Bucknell University, where he attended college, David found the plain and simple landscape he longed to paint. There was also the timeless beauty of nature and people working close to the land who appreciated that beauty.

His farm in the rolling hills and farms of that world put him in touch with the harmony of nature and man, a harmony he has sought to render in his paintings.

Painting outdoors in fields, farms and woods to be at one with nature, his watercolors capture the simplicity of life's most profound lesson—that what is good is lasting, both in nature and man. The dignity and beauty of his subjects attest to his respect for the earth and people close to it.

"I always work in the landscape to be part of the world I am painting. I want people to appreciate the beauty of people and places I find fascinating. My feelings for my subjects can be seen in my works."

In recent years, David has traveled around the country to explore and paint new landscapes and peoples. Two summer trips have taken him to the bayous of Louisiana, the Hopi and Navajo reservations of the southwest, the Puget Sound area of the northwest and the Colorado Rockies. Over the past four years, he has also lived among lobstermen of northern Maine to capture the primordial relationship of man and sea.

Armstrong's watercolors have attracted a sizable following of collectors. He has sold out five one-man shows at Hammer Galleries in New York, where he is scheduled for a show in November, 1987. His works have been exhibited in museums across the land and in major corporate and private collections.

"My paintings represent my continuing appreciation of all that is good and glorious in this great earth. When my watercolors illuminate the timeless respect for nature's and man's works that help others to appreciate those works, then I feel I have created something lasting."

David Armstrong is represented by Mill Pond Press Inc.

DOT AND SY BARLOWE

When Dot and Sy Barlowe first collaborated as fellow artists at New York's Museum of Natural History in the 1940s, they began a harmonious personal and working relationship that has been preserved to this day. Four years after their marriage in 1946, they began working as free-lance illustrators. Since then—together and separately—they have earned national recognition for their historic and naturalist art.

Together, the Barlowes have illustrated nature books for some of the largest publishing houses in America, including Knopf, Random House, Morrow, Follett, American Heritage Press, Putnam, Harper & Row, McGraw-Hill, and Grosset and Dunlap. For the Golden Press alone they have illustrated 15 books, including such well-known nature identification volumes as *Seashores*, *Trees of America*, and *Amphibians of North America.*.

In addition, the Barlowes have contributed illustrations to several Audubon Society guides and to *The Audubon Society Encyclopedia of North American Birds*. They also share their knowledge of nature illustration and botany by teaching at the Parsons School of Design in New York. The artists have done features for publications including *The New York Times* and *Newsday*, and their works have been honored with numerous awards and exhibitions at the Society of Illustrators in New York, and Expo '67 in Montreal.

For the past 30 years, the Barlowes have lived on Long Island. Their two children are Amy, a concert violinist and music professor; and Wayne, an award-winning illustrator in his own right.

Reco International has presented an eight-plate *Vanishing Animal Kingdoms* collection from Sy Barlowe, and a *Gardens of Beauty* Plate Collection from Dorothea Barlowe. The artists also plan to introduce a series of animal figurines through Reco.

ROBERT BATEMAN

Combining two accomplished avocations—the first, always regarding himself

as an artist, and second as a well-trained naturalist—Bateman has in just a few years become one of Canada's, indeed one of the world's, greatest artists depicting the natural world.

A vivid imagination, combined with world travel and exposure along with intensive study in the two fields, culminates in paintings that satisfy his inner quests for truths in both worlds of art and nature.

Bateman's work is refreshing and his concepts unpredictable. With imagination influenced by any one of the multitude of art periods and styles, plus a deep understanding of the natural world, his artistic statements are strong and stunning.

No soul searching for Bateman. He has always known he was an artist—just as the natural world piqued his curiosity, formal training followed as a matter of course.

For example, exploring modern art in his 20s and 30s, Bateman painted contemporary styles from Post Impressionism to Abstract Expressionism. The Andrew Wyeth show in 1962 at the Albright Knox Museum awakened the possibility of rendering the actual surface of the planet as opposed to the mere manipulation of paint.

Wyeth painted the natural world with a real world texture—not with the superficial flat paint surface of the Abstract Expressionists or Op art.

Adopting Realism again permitted Bateman to express his deep knowledge and concern for the particularity of nature. Always an active ecologist, he found it insufficiently fulfilling to portray this in a bold abstract style.

All true artists in history have portrayed subject matter that excites them: Gauguin's Tahitian life, Degas's backstage at the ballet and Warhol's pop culture.

Bateman depicts what moves him most—the natural world. Bateman has always painted with zeal and joy all the great and multitude of images that come to mind.

Bateman has his own unique style. It cannot be imitated. His compositions are unique, and his concepts are always fresh—never repeated.

This artist is a great painter. There are many who imitate the natural world, but if Bateman had a passion to paint the ballet or nudes, his work would still have the breathtaking beauty of the Bateman style.

Robert Bateman is represented by Mill Pond Press Inc.

BRAD BENNETT

Brad Bennett's paintings can succinctly be described as "historic." They are beautiful representational illustrations of our life in the 20th century. Working mostly in watercolor, Bennett's paintings capture moments of time chronicling the day-to-day rigors of everyday life.

Born and raised in Kenosha, Wisconsin, Bennett went on to graduate from the University of Wisconsin-Madison with a Bachelor of Science Degree in Art Education. Shunning the classroom he went straight into commercial art while opening his own graphic design studio.

After several years as a graphic designer he felt less than fulfilled and immersed

himself in painting Midwestern genre in watercolor. His success was immediate with state and national shows and honors. His work has been shown at the Meadows Museum of Art in Shreveport, The Wisconsin Watercolor Society, Society of Illustrators and the New York Art Directors Club. He has produced nationally award-winning book illustrations.

These are books Bennett both illustrates and writes featuring narration and prose. He has, to date, published four "books" which are suites of prints and narratives bound in handmade portfolios and published strictly as limited editions. Each suite of prints is registered with the Library of Congress of the United States as a work of history. Bennett is the only living American artist with this distinction.

These fine limited editions produced from his masterful watercolor paintings are considered collectible by print collectors around the world. Since his first title "Kenosha" was released in 1981 his works have been listed with every print collector guide published in this country.

He now has over 80 limited edition prints published which include the suites: "King Richard's Faire," "Houston," and "Chicago." More prints are planned for release by year's end.

Bennett not only publishes, but fulfills many commissions throughout the year. He currently maintains his studio in Olympia Fields, Illinois with his wife where he continues to create new works of art for the very demanding marketplace. Bennett's works are currently in permanent collections all over the globe and in private collections in the thousands through his prints.

HIGGINS BOND

Although she has been commissioned to paint pictures of buildings, animals, cars and even some of the world's greatest kings, American artist Higgins Bond enjoys painting children best of all. And when she portrays children, Ms. Bond likes to show them in natural settings, for this allows her to combine her love of youngsters with her appreciation of the world around her.

Higgins Bond's artwork is the result of a lifetime spent drawing, painting, study-

ing and practicing her craft. Born Barbara Higgins, the artist began signing her paintings with her last name only while studying at Memphis College of Arts, where she earned a Bachelor of Fine Arts degree. Upon her marriage, she modified her professional signature to "Higgins Bond," although friends still know her as Barbara.

Ms. Bond has earned the commissions of major corporations and book publishers for her original paintings. She has created illustrations for books, magazines and calendars as well as personal portraits for firms including Houghton-Mifflin, Anheuser-Busch, RCA, NBC, McGraw-Hill, Crown Publishers, The Bell System, and Random House. Her works have been exhibited at the Metropolitan Museum of Art in New York, and numerous other museums in New York, Chicago, Indiana and New Jersey.

The artist is an award winner from the Society of Illustrators, and was presented the "Key to the City" of Indianapolis for her artworks. She has been a guest lecturer at numerous colleges, universities and schools, and now resides and works in Teaneck, New Jersey.

The first limited edition collector plate by Higgins Bond, "Ashley," portrays a little girl discovering a butterfly in a field of flowers. It is the premiere of an eight-plate collection offered exclusively by The Hamilton Collection: *Treasured Days*.

AMY BRACKENBURY

Life on a ranch agrees with Amy Brackenbury, creator of the *Amy Brackenbury's Cat Tales* series for Edwin M. Knowles. In her first plate, "A Chance Meeting: White American Shorthairs," she portrays two adorable kittens who happen upon a turtle while exploring the wilderness. Scenes such as this provide daily inspiration for Ms. Brackenbury, who lives today with her husband and two children on part of the old family spread where she was raised in the northern Colorado foothills.

Being in tune with the out-of-doors helps the artist to keep her creative juices flowing, and the surrounding wildlife and domestic animals keep her richly supplied with live subjects. Because she prefers to depict the animals she portrays as close to

life-size as possible, her canvases range in size from 14"x16" to 20"x90".

Ms. Brackenbury studied art and painting at Colorado State University. In 1986 she won the distinction of having her portrait of a blue heron included in a world tour that included California, Hawaii, and China. Her works have been exhibited in group shows, but most of her paintings are distributed through galleries. Signed and numbered limited edition prints are published by Mill Pond Press Inc.

BETSEY BRADLEY

"Having artistic talent shapes my whole life," says American realist painter Betsey Bradley. "It's a creative outlet that always provides me with something fun and relaxing to do. However, having this talent also means that I have an obligation. Since there is a lot I am capable of doing, I feel I should use my talents fully."

Bradley first realized she had artistic ability in the fifth grade when she drew profiles of the students around her and her pictures looked exactly like the children.

She has continued to do portraits ever since—in pastels, pencil, acrylic and oils. She has also branched out into landscapes, still lifes, and most recently the collector's plate series *A Father's Love* produced by the Edwin M. Knowles China Company.

Bradley was born in the suburbs of Chicago in 1949 and grew up in a close, happy family of five. Graduating as vale-

dictorian of her high school class, she went on to major in art at Smith College for Women in Massachusetts, and also studied at the Minneapolis School of Art and the Rocky Mountain School of Art.

Bradley's paintings have been shown in three New York exhibitions, the Catherine Lorrilard Wolfe Show, the National Acrylic and Casein Show, and the Real Show, an exhibition of realistic artwork.

Today Bradley lives in the suburbs of Denver and is the mother of three daughters.

Bradley is best known for the striking realism of her artwork. "My paintings almost look like photographs," she says. "I like the challenge of painting so realistically that people ask me how I do it."

However, for her first collector's plate series, she altered her style somewhat. *A Father's Love* celebrates the father-child relationship, so "instead of being as photo-realistic as I usually am, I softened the lines," she said. "I think it conveys a softer, warmer mood."

Bradley says the inspiration for the new series was her own attentive father. She also supports the recent trend of fathers taking a more active role in parenting, and it is this trend that she has portrayed in her limited edition plates.

CARL BRENDERS

The artistic visions of Carl Brenders reflect his respect for nature. His precise and lively paintings capture the extreme realism of the bird life and mammals he renders.

Brenders was born near Antwerp, Belgium, and has been drawing since childhood. He studied at the Fine Arts Acade-

my in Antwerp and Berchem. Over the last decade, he has produced wildlife illustrations for more than twenty books in a series titled *The Secret Life of Animals.* Because of his love for wildlife, animals and nature have become the chosen theme of Brenders' art. The images he creates are first done as small pencil sketches, and his paintings are then drawn in watercolor and painted in gouache.

His art has been exhibited in the United States, France, Spain, Holland and Belgium.

Carl Brenders is represented by Mill Pond Press Inc.

CAROL WERNER BURGUES

Carol Werner Burgues, renowned sculptor of the Burgues Studios, remembers drawing and painting from earliest youth. She studied art in her native Germany, but today she asserts that she has learned more from experience than from

any classroom or teacher. In addition, as the wife of famed naturalist artist Dr. Irving Carl Burgues, Mrs. Burgues believes she has benefited greatly from her husband's influence and guidance.

Mrs. Burgues always has gravitated toward natural art subjects. She both paints and sculpts flowers, animals and birds with great enjoyment, although in recent years she has concentrated on three-dimensional art. Mrs. Burgues prefers porcelain as the medium for her sculptures, because she enjoys bringing her creations to life by means of intricate hand-painting.

Before beginning a sculpture, the artist spends time in the field, observing her

subject in person. She also does research in zoos, museums and taxidermy studios. In addition, she surrounds herself with reference books and photographs to supplement her own observations.

Each Burgues sculpture emerges after many different sketches, a clay model, and then a plastic one from which molds are crafted. Mrs. Burgues personally observes each step of the crafting process to ensure that her specifications are followed. She hand-paints the final master model, as well.

One of Mrs. Burgues' most recent three-dimensional offerings is the "Common Mallard" sculpture, first of eight in her *North American Ducks* Sculpture Collection presented in association with The Hamilton Collection.

SAM BUTCHER

The artist behind the *Precious Moments®* figurines is Sam Butcher, a man who combines his love of God and his talent for art in his teardrop-eyed porcelains for Enesco. Born in Jackson, Michigan and raised in Big Bend, California, Butcher exhibited art talent from early childhood and attended the College of Arts & Crafts in Berkeley, California.

Becoming a Christian encouraged Butcher to return to his native Michigan where he served the Child Evangelism Fellowship in Grand Rapids as an illustrator. Because he had a wife and a growing family — eventually seven children — to support, Butcher supplemented his income doing janitorial work. Ultimately the demands of these two jobs became overwhelming, and Butcher felt he had to resign from the Fellowship to

find one well-paying job. When Bill Biel came on staff at the Child Evangelism Fellowship, he stood up for Butcher and helped the young artist to obtain a reasonable workload and fair compensation.

In this way, Butcher and Biel began a friendship that led to their partnership in Jonathan & David Inc., a Grand Rapids-based firm that began in 1970. The men chose this name because they felt their personal relationship paralleled that of the Biblical friends, Jonathan and David.

After five years of work in determining the best products for their market, Butcher and Biel introduced the Precious Moments greeting card line in 1975. By 1978, the Precious Moments characters had become porcelain figurines with the help of Enesco Imports Corp.

Today, Sam Butcher lives in Missouri near the site of his new Precious Moments Chapel, a 40-foot-high building created to depict the word of God in the Precious Moments motif. He continues to create the appealing Precious Moments characters, as well. Their purpose, Butcher says, is to help people to understand that someone is there to help—that someone cares. The bisque figurines mirror life's happiest and saddest moments with love, gentle humor and optimism.

PAUL CALLE

Paul Calle is equally skilled at oil paintings and pencil drawings. His drawings, some of them very large, are notable for the incredible control and sensitivity they show, giving them the quality of fine etchings. Here is an artist whose career strongly reflects the dramatic era in which he lives and works.

His selection as an official artist of the National Aeronautics and Space Administration's Fine Art Program gave him the unique opportunity to paint Neil Armstrong's first step on the moon. He was commissioned by The United States Postal Service to design the stamp capturing that historic moment. He has designed several other stamps including the recently released "International Year of the Child" commemorative.

To Paul Calle, the portrayal of Western Art is not a romantic adventure but a realistic challenge—a personal commitment to portray America's past with the

same sense of history that guided his hand in depicting our nation's space explorations. As chairman of the Department of Interior's "Artist in the Parks" program, Calle traveled widely throughout the West. His imagination was stimulated by the majesty of the Western scene and this experience reawakened his early admiration for the panoramic art of landscapists Albert Bierdstadt and Thomas Moran. He knows that space exploration and the Western experience—time and worlds apart—are both part of our heritage, a heritage to be set down in paint.

In addition to major corporate and private collections, his work is in the permanent collections of the Phoenix Museum of Fine Arts, Phoenix, Arizona; Pacific Northwest Indian Center, Spokane, Washington; George Phippen Museum, Prescott, Arizona; The National Aeronautics and Space Administration Collection, Washington, D.C.; The National Portrait Gallery, Washington, D.C.; The National Air and Space Museum, Washington, D.C.; National Park Service, U.S. Department of Interior, Washington, D.C.; and in the U.S. Air Force Historical Art Collection, Washington, D.C.

Paintings and drawings have been exhibited at The Museum of the Southwest, Midland, Texas; The National Gallery of Art, Washington, D.C.; The Stamford Museum, Stamford, Connecticut; The Hudson River Museum, Yonkers, New York; The Phoenix Museum of Art, Phoenix, Arizona; Pacific North-

west Indian Center, Spokane, Washington; The National Air and Space Museum, Washington, D.C.; and at the U.S. Embassy, Stockholm, Sweden. Under the auspices of the United States Information Office his work has been shown at museums in Krakow, Poland; Moscow, U.S.S.R.; Tbilisi, U.S.S.R.; and in Leningrad, U.S.S.R. He is the recipient of the Franklin Mint Gold Medal for Distinguished Western Art.

Paul Calle is the author of *The Pencil* published by Watson-Guptill, now in its fifth printing. The book records his odyssey as "an artist with a pencil."

Paul Calle is represented by Mill Pond Press Inc.

WILLIAM CHAMBERS

"The integrity of the work—that's the thing that's important," says artist Bill Chambers.

This emphasis on artistic accuracy is a fitting philosophy for a man who almost went into the priesthood instead of painting.

Chambers always paints from live models or photographs to ensure that the details are right. The result is an eye-catching realism executed with appealing soft brush strokes.

A native and current resident of the Chicago area, Chambers has been drawing since he was a boy. Not until 1979, however, did he discover his niche as a portrait artist. Previous art experiences had included stints as an industrial designer, illustrator for several Chicago art stu-

dios and freelance artist. Today he is able to paint commissioned portraits full time.

Chambers has won awards at the American Society of Illustrators New York Annual Show and the John Howard Sanden Portrait Seminar in New York. His work is included in the book *200 Years of American Illustration*. He is represented by the largest portrait gallery in the world, Portraits, Inc. of New York City.

Chambers entered the collector's plate market with a bang in 1983 when his first plate, "Annie and Sandy" from the *Annie* series, earned both Plate of the Year and New Edition of the Year honors.

He followed his initial success with another movie series the next year: *The King and I*. The first plate in that series— "A Puzzlement"—was named 1984 New Issue of the Year.

In the wake of these triumphs, Chambers has turned his talents to other subjects. His two latest series for Knowles are *Portraits of Motherhood*, a celebration of Mother's Day, and *Tom Sawyer*, based on the classic Mark Twain novel.

"People are really responding to my art since I started designing collector's plates," he said. "For an illustrator who works alone all the time, this response from people is wonderful."

PAM COOPER

From her early childhood, animals played an important part in Pam Cooper's life. Born in rural Lancashire, England, she spent most of her early life in Cheshire. Almost as soon as she could hold a brush, young Pam painted likenesses of the animals around her, and also modeled them in clay.

Her natural art skill led her to the Royal College of Art in Manchester. After graduation, Pam Cooper set out for London, where she earned a position as illustrator of children's magazines and also studied under noted cartoonist, Hugh McNeill. Later she began to specialize in her first love, animals and wildlife, illustrating and painting for a wide variety of publications. She also created cards and lithographic prints.

Miss Cooper's work has been exhibited at the Assembly Room, Norwich, and also at the Fermoy Gallery, Kings Lynn,

Norfolk. She now lives in a cottage in the beautiful Conway Valley, North Wales, with her family and various animals. There she continues to paint her favorite subjects—animals, flowers and the countryside.

In recent years, she has created three plate collections for Royal Worcester in association with The Hamilton Collection: *Kitten Classics*, *Kitten Encounters*, and *A Child's Blessing*.

PETER N. COZZOLINO

Peter Cozzolino is a sculptor of considerable fame and achievement. He is the executive director of the Old Church Cultural Center and School of Art, in Demarest, New Jersey, which he founded in 1974. Cozzolino is a master of sculpture in a wide variety of media, including bronze, clay, plaster, cement, wood and marble.

His schooling included a Bachelor of Fine Arts degree from the School of Fine and Applied Arts, Boston University, followed by a two-year course of study at the School of Medical Illustration, Massachusetts General Hospital, and then two years of independent study in Italy. From 1965–1968, he attended the National Academy School of Fine Arts, where he studied with noted masters Carl Schmitz, Michael Lantz, Mitchell Fields, and Granville Carter.

With more than thirty exhibitions and shows to his credit, Cozzolino has had occasion to earn a number of awards for his work. He was the recipient of a National Academy of Design Merit Award in 1977, and the coveted John Gregory Memorial Prize in 1979 from the National Sculpture Society. This latter award indicated work which most displayed originality, imagination, and expert craftsmanship.

For The Hamilton Collection, Cozzolino has created three collections of fine, hand-painted figurines: *The Art of the Carousel*, *The Classic Carousel*, and *The Ringling Bros. and Barnum & Bailey Circus Animal Figurine Collection*.

DANIEL CRAIG

Categorizing Dan Craig's colorful paintings eludes most art critics. Although some call his works "Americana," "country," or "sophisticated country," the artist himself prefers the term "stylized realism." By that he means a simplification of form, where everything is slightly idealized.

As a child, Craig considered drawing a prime form of entertainment. He remembers Walt Disney animations as a source of great inspiration for their drama, color and lighting. He continued to develop his skills and broaden his art interests, entering the Minneapolis College of Art and Design after high school. There he joined the Oasis Art Studio and gained a national reputation for his commercial illustrations. Oasis commissions included those of firms such as 3M Company, Honeywell, Northwestern National Life Insurance, Northwestern Bell, First Bank Systems and Zycad Corporation. In addition, some of these works earned the artist a range of prestigious awards.

An accomplished guitarist and bluegrass fiddle player, Craig enjoys the musi-

cal aspect of the arts and has performed professionally. But he says that other than enjoying time with his young son, he prefers painting to most any other endeavor. Craig lives and works in a completely restored, older home, where he listens to a mixture of classical and bluegrass music as he paints.

Today Craig has focused his attention upon fine art painting, with pieces often featured in national publications and galleries coast-to-coast. His recent works include a series of collector plates for Fountainhead, titled *Americana Cats.*

TONY CRNKOVICH

When Tony Crnkovich was a child, he loved to watch old films on television, and then go off to his room to recreate what he had enjoyed on screen. These detailed portraits of famous movie characters foreshadowed Crnkovich's successful

career as an painter specializing in celebrity art, including *The Sound of Music* plate collection for Edwin M. Knowles.

Born on the south side of Chicago, Crnkovich received no formal art training for many years. Then in his late teens he began to study through a correspondence course, and ultimately at the American Academy of Art. There his life drawing classes were especially worthwhile, for he began to see how he could combine his loves for art and for classic movies into a body of work capturing all the appeal and excitement of the great era of cinema.

More than accuracy, Crnkovich works to capture the mood of the film he is painting. An acknowledged rule-breaker, he will do most anything possible on canvas to achieve this goal. He may study a certain film for days and read everything about the characters before he begins to paint. In this way, he is not portraying a stranger, but rather a character who seems like an old friend. His initial *Sound of Music* painting of Julie Andrews offers a case in point in which he has captured the joy and even the musical quality of the character Maria.

DON CROOK

Western artist and illustrator Don Crook is one of today's most prominent painters of Americana. While growing up on a ranch in Oregon, Crook began drawing and painting. He continued to develop his craft as an art major at Yakima Valley College. Crook minored in history, and because of his passion for this subject, he has devoted his career to the creation of historical paintings inspired by his western heritage.

After a time spent as a commercial artist and illustrator, Crook began his practice as a gallery artist and portraitist. His commissions include: four paintings for the Modoc War Series at the Favell Museum in Oregon; an Indian-subject painting entitled "Trail of Tears" commissioned by the Bowles Agency in Tennessee; and portraits of actor Denver Pyle and country and western singer Charlie Pride.

Don Crook has earned more honors from the Western Artists of America than any other artist of the Pacific Northwest. These include ten Best of Show awards

and seventeen medals of excellence, including nine gold medals. His works are shown regularly in galleries all over the western United States, and his paintings appear in a number of museums including the Favell Museum, Museum of Native American Cultures, and the C.M. Russell Museum. Crook originals regularly command $4,000 to $6,000, and exceptional paintings may bring as much as $20,000.

The artist earned the title, "Norman Rockwell of Western Art" for his ability to capture everyday situations with lifelike detail, charm and humor. To set the scene for his nostalgic paintings, Crook engages in extensive historical research to develop scenes of realism and universal appeal. His child-subject paintings now have inspired two plate collections offered exclusively by The Hamilton Collection and River Shore: *Children of the American Frontier,* and *We the Children.*

KEVIN DANIEL

Minnesota wildlife artist Kevin T. Daniel feels strongly about two things—nature and accuracy. The two come together in Daniel's artwork. He is a master at accurately painting birds and animals in their natural settings.

Daniel developed his artistic techniques largely on his own. Outside of some pointers given by an older brother who is an artist, Daniel has never had formal painting lessons. He observed other artists' works, borrowed their techniques, practiced tirelessly, and then went on to develop his own style.

Today he is the frequent recipient of art awards. Most recently, he was one of two artists named Artist of the Year by

the National Association of Limited Edition Dealers (NALED). In 1984, Daniel won two Best of Show awards in the National Wildlife Art Show in Kansas City, took second place in the Minnesota duck stamp art competition, and was named Artist of the Year by the Indiana branch of Ducks Unlimited, a waterfowl conservation group. He also has won Best of Show in three different subject categories at the Oklahoma Wildlife Arts Festival.

To achieve the realism for which he is known, Daniel photographs his subjects in the wild whenever possible. He also visits game farms, taxidermists, other wildlife artists and photographers, and the University of Minnesota wildlife museum to learn all he can about a creature's anatomy and habits.

His attention to authenticity is one of the reasons Daniel was chosen as the artist to created the first series of limited edition plates to earn the sponsorship of Encyclopaedia Brittanica. Entitled *Birds of Your Garden*, the series is produced by the Edwin M. Knowles China Co.

Daniel, who enjoys watching birds at his own bird houses and feeders, says he always has been fascinated by the garden birds he painted for the plates. "Being an artist, I think their color is what I love most," he said. "Also, I think people tend to develop a special love for birds that they see frequently."

In his second series for Knowles, Daniel has turned his attention from feathers to fur. *Friends of the Forest* features small, furry animals such as the rabbit, the squirrel and the raccoon.

Daniel was born in Minneapolis in 1951. He is the third youngest in a family of nine children. Today he paints in quiet solitude in a house surrounded by woods near Chanhassen, Minnesota.

EUGENE DAUB

After an early career in advertising and graphic design, Eugene Daub — husband and father of four — made a daring midlife switch to full-time sculptor. He resigned his position in an advertising agency and attended the Pennsylvania Academy of Fine Art and Princeton's Johnson Atelier Technical Institute of Sculpture. Then, little by little, he began to develop a clientele of his own.

Over the past decade, Daub has earned a number of major awards and coveted commissions for his sculptures in porcelain, pewter and crystal. The famed Artists' Guild has honored him with three separate awards, and he is also the recipient of recognition from the National Academy of Design, FAO International Sculpture Competition, American Numismatic Society, and others.

Daub is the sculptor of "Something Like a Star," a magnificent bronze sculpture, created under the commission of the Philadelphia Center for Older People, developed for the Klein Foundation; and more than 200 figurative sculptures and bas-relief portraits for Franklin Mint, Lance, and The Hamilton Mint.

A ballet aficionado of long standing, Daub recently turned his attention to ballet sculpture for the first time. He lives just six blocks from the Pennsylvania Ballet in Philadelphia, and thus was able to attend numerous performances — and to

have top ballerinas pose for the various subjects in his *The Splendor of the Ballet* Figurine Collection. Created under the commission of The Hamilton Collection, this series includes eight masterworks inspired by some of the most beloved ballet heroines of all time.

NORMAN N. AND HERMAN DEATON

Norman N. (Neal) Deaton and his brother Herman are two of the most talented sculptors of animals living in the world today. Even as youngsters, they were fascinated by the opportunity to observe, study—and model in clay—the small wild creatures of their native Iowa.

Herman Deaton

The Deatons are especially noted for their famous hand-painted animal sculptures for The National Wildlife Federation. Their works are exhibited at such prominent museums as The Smithsonian Institution in Washington, D.C., and The National Museum of Canada in Ottawa. And Deaton works are held in many important private collections—including those of such notables as United States Senators Morris Udall and Frank Church.

In all of their works, the Deatons combine an eye for natural beauty with a passion for authenticity—qualities that distinguish the two groups of hand-painted, cold-cast bronze figurines they have created for The Hamilton Collection—*The Audubon Bronzes* and *An American Wildlife Bronze Collection.*

In 1983, Herman Deaton introduced an eight-piece sculpture collection through

Hamilton, entitled *Great Animals of the American Wilderness.* Then recently he premiered a second eight-issue collection, the *Majestic Wildlife of North America* figurines.

DOROTHY DOUGHTY

Dorothy Doughty was born at San Remo, in Italy, in 1892. Her father was Charles Doughty, traveler and poet, whose major work, "Arabia Deserta," was the inspiration of Lawrence of Arabia and a whole generation of English travelers in the Middle East. As a girl she studied at the Eastbourne School of Art.

Dorothy Doughty's association with Royal Worcester began in 1933 when the Company was anxious to produce a series of limited edition sculptures in bone china based on the illustrations of American ornithologist John James Audubon. Her love of nature, particularly the birds and flowers she was to portray, made her a natural choice for this enterprise. The particular problems of working in bone china did not deter her. In fact by her determination she was often able to devise new techniques which made her work quite outstanding.

Her aim was always to achieve the greatest possible likeness to nature, both in form and coloring. She made two journeys through the United States during which she produced many colored sketch models to capture the image of a moment, the attitudes of a bird or the arrangement of a flower. Her sculptures were completed in her studio at Falmouth where she kept an aviary of specimens from which she worked.

Dorothy Doughty had completed the *American Birds* in 1960 and then moved on to the modeling of the *British Bird* series. This she had wanted to do for many years. At this time she was worried that her eyesight might fail but by unremitting effort she was able to complete the twenty-one models in two years. The completion of this great work came just before her death, following an accident in October, 1962. Her sculptures are avidly collected, for no other artist ever has interpreted in bone china the tenderness and timidity of song birds as well as she.

TED DeGRAZIA

Ettore "Ted" DeGrazia. Born June 14, 1909. Died September 17, 1982. In the span of those 73 years, he became not only a beloved artist of the southwest, but a legend among the people with whom he lived.

He was a man of the southwest who captured the essence of his beloved region in 33 successful books which he both authored and illustrated. His art was showcased in the magazine *Arizona Highways*, where it was seen in 1958 by the Hallmark greeting card company which signed him to a contract. Two short years later, his painting "Los Ninos" was selected by UNICEF to grace the cover of its annual fundraising Christmas card, over 100 million of which have been sold.

It was in DeGrazia's later years that collectors of plates were afforded the opportunity to bring some of his vision into their homes. In 1976 he approved the first limited edition plate bearing the motif of his now familiar "Los Ninos." The plate sold out immediately and DeGrazia, at age 67, was "an overnight success."

Early in 1983, Goebel was approached to develop a figurine series based on his works. Now they are before the public — an exciting, innovative line which Goebel is proud to bring to collectors. It represents a harmonious liaison between the more than a century-old tradition of fine German craftsmanship and the distinctly American cut of one of our outstanding individualists.

In 1985 Goebel Miniatures introduced a new dimension to his artwork with the *DeGrazia* miniature figurines. Each

stands less than an inch and a half tall, yet every piece accurately captures the very essence of DeGrazia's artwork.

Ted DeGrazia. With each new interpretation of his artwork his genius is further revealed. He has become a symbol for the land he loved so well and to which he paid such high tribute.

JIM DENEEN

Jim Deneen is widely recognized as the foremost North American painter of the various modes of transportation. His paintings are characterized by careful detailing and complete authenticity, yet Deneen displays a special talent for capturing the romantic and nostalgic aspects of his subjects.

Deneen's technique is unique due to the dramatic sweep of his paintings and his unerring perspective. He has a special gift for capturing spatial relationships

which give his work a remarkable three-dimensional quality. Vast numbers of Americans enjoy Deneen's collectible prints: it is estimated that there are currently a total of 10,000,000 of his graphics in circulation.

The artist's first series of limited edition collector plates, *The Great Trains*, was created under the commission of Curator Collection. This three-plate grouping features a trio of famous railroad trains: "Santa Fe," "Twentieth Century Limited," and "Empire Builder."

A new series of paintings for Curator Collection offers a pictorial history of North American trains. When presented on collector plates, this grouping by Jim Deneen will present a nostalgic, visual chronicle of railroading in America.

NITA ENGLE

A member of the American Watercolor Society since 1969, Engle lives and paints landscapes on the beautiful upper peninsula of northern Michigan, an unspoiled wilderness. She says Lake Superior has all the advantages of the sea without the tide running out, but that it is a constant challenge to paint with changing lights and different moods.

Although she makes pencil sketches for composition and value in the field and supplements these with black and white photos, Engle is essentially a studio painter. She feels that the artist can be overwhelmed by the subject in on-the-spot painting. In the studio she can arrive at a controlled design through the objective elimination of non-essentials.

She says, "Color is rarely factual but subordinate to the central theme of the

watercolor." Therefore black and white reference and her own mental palette in the studio work best for her. She believes that good decisions exercised by an accomplished painter preserve the original theme and the individuality of the objects of nature.

Nita Engle attended Northern Michigan and Roosevelt Universities, the Art Institute of Chicago and studied in England. She worked nine years as an art director for a national advertising agency. She exhibits extensively and is represented in collections here and in England.

Commissions for illustrations have come from *Reader's Digest, Playboy* and other prestigious periodicals. She is also in demand as a book illustrator. Her philosophy of art and studio painting preference was carried as a feature of the "Watercolor Page" in *American Artist*.

Nita Engle is represented by Mill Pond Press Inc.

ALAN D'ESTREHAN

Although he was born in Nice, France, Alan D'Estrehan's family history includes the Revolutionary War general Nathanael Greene, American artist John Singer Sargent, and Rear Admiral Samuel Eliot Morrison, a famous U.S. naval historian. This background explains D'Estrehan's natural interests in history and art, and his passion for the sea.

D'Estrehan has made numerous voyages across the oceans. His knowledge of ship structure, sails and riggings comes from personal experience and study of technical documents. D'Estrehan served with the French Air Force during World War II and worked as an engineer until his retirement in 1972. He has since devoted all of his time to painting, and has established an international reputation as a naval artist and historian.

In France, D'Estrehan has shown his art at the Salon Nautique in Paris and the Compostel Gallery in Lille. In America, his art is on display at the U.S. Naval Academy, Eagle Gallery in LaJolla, California, Lighthouse Museum in Dana Point, California, and the U.S.S. Constitution Museum Foundation in Boston.

The artist has designed 40 stamps and cachets for nations participating in the official International Commemorative Pro-

gram, "Operation Sail: Salute to Liberty." His collector plates, created under the commission of Armstrong's, include his latest series entitled *The U.S. Constitution* as well as a four-plate *Statue of Liberty* collection.

LISETTE DE WINNE

Belgian-born Lisette DeWinne travels extensively throughout the world, seeking out expressive faces that reflect the varied cultures she encounters as well as universal human feelings. Her favorite subjects are children, portrayed in a loose, impressionistic style.

Ms. DeWinne was raised during a time of turmoil in Europe. Her family was poor, and her artistic ambitions had to be submerged in favor of the day-to-day struggle. When she was a young wife, her husband Werner bought her a set of paints that the couple truly could not afford. Although she tried to convince her husband to return them, he refused. This

gesture on his part encouraged her to become serious about her art ambitions.

In 1957, the DeWinnes moved to America, a dream which had sustained Lisette since childhood. She became a United States citizen in 1963, and before long was able to establish herself as a respected gallery artist. She and her husband take four trips each year, to places around the world. The artist returns from her travels with impressions and ideas stored up for use in her paintings.

Ms. DeWinne's first limited edition collector plates were created for Royal Doulton. She is currently at work on a series of plates for Armstrong's.

JEANNE DOWN

Jeanne Down is a storyteller artist.

"I like for people to be able to look at one of my paintings and see it as a story instead of just saying, 'That's a pretty painting,'" Down says.

Many of her "painting stories" are recollections of her childhood days in Altoona, Pennsylvania. Although she grew up during the Great Depression, she says she has only happy memories.

"Nobody had much of anything, but it wasn't really a bad thing at all, at least not to us kids," she says. "We didn't know anything different. It was a good time, a time of imagination, when children worked with what they had. We had fun."

Down first showed artistic talent as a child and was given valuable lessons in the basics of drawing by her grandfather E. E. Wilt, a Pennsylvania realist painter. After graduating from high school, she married, moved to California and devoted her time to raising two sons.

Sixteen years later she resumed her artwork. She studied oil painting, watercolor and etching under private teachers. Finally she went out on her own, teaching art classes herself in studios throughout California's San Fernando Valley. In 1975 she opened her own studio, where she still teaches and paints every day.

Down describes herself as an "impressionistic realist." Her subjects are easily discerned, but she does not use the photographic realism of her grandfather. Instead she uses impressionistic brush strokes, saying, "I like the colors, the freedom, the feeling achieved with impressionism. Rather than have to say everything in the painting, I can impart a feeling as well as an image."

The feeling she likes to impart most is childhood happiness, which is the subject of her collector's plate series *Jeanne Down's Friends I Remember.* Drawing on her memories and transferring the childhood scenes to the collector's plates, Down says, "I think most Americans share many common experiences, and I hope that my art speaks to that child within each of us that never really grows up."

SUE ETEM

From a very young age, Sue Etem enjoyed all aspects of art. Over the years she tried her hand at traditional graphics, advertising, and fashion design before discovering the satisfaction of painting children.

Traveling the world, Ms. Etem spent hundred of hours "drinking in" the art she found in the greatest galleries of France, Germany, Spain and Greece. Meanwhile, she drew upon this exposure to improve her technique and learn more about her craft, year by year. Although she studied art at Arlington State College in Texas, and with teachers on two continents, Ms. Etem believes that her current success in oils, pastels and acrylics is a direct result of her exposure to the world's finest museums.

Recently Ms. Etem continued her world travel by spending a year in Manama, Bahrain, where her husband worked as an adviser to the president of Bahrain's General Organization for Sport. There she gained additional inspiration for her child-subject works, paint-

ing the dark-eyed Bahraini children. Her ability to communicate warmth and love to youngsters of all nations lets her capture the innocence and joy of childhood on canvas with a special tenderness and understanding.

Sue Etem introduced her first collector plate in the early 1980s with the *Playful Memories* series produced by Hackett-American.

Her *Children to Love* collection by American Legacy brought her the Plate Artist of the Year award in 1983. This led to a commission to paint two plates for the Heart Research Institute at Cedars Sinai Hospital in Los Angeles. Her latest collection of plates is the *Infinite Love* series for Armstrong's and The Hamilton Collection. Beginning with the mother-and-child relationship, this series explores the close ties between babies and their loved ones.

ALDO FAZIO

The work of Aldo Fazio has earned this Larchmont, New York artist international fame. As the winner of the coveted Hall of Fame Award for Equestrian Sculpture, Fazio established his status as a sculptor of animals. His designs have won him prestigious commissions from Abercrombie & Fitch, FAO Schwarz and the Audubon Society, among others.

Fazio began his career with private study under noted sculptors James Earl Fraser and Bethold Nevel, and muralist Barry Faulkner. Under their tutelage, he became fascinated with the animal world

and began to create his award-winning masterworks. Four of his horse paintings appear today in the Museum of Sports, New Haven, Connecticut.

Now Aldo Fazio has added a new dimension to his artistry with the creation of two limited edition collector plate series: *The Sophisticated Ladies Plate Collection*, introduced by Reco International in 1985, and a series of plates capturing favorite American puppy breeds, which was launched by Reco in 1987. In addition, Fazio and Reco have created a grouping of figurines to match his *Sophisticated Ladies* plates.

MARIO FERNANDEZ

Most 16-year-olds enjoy a fairly simple existence of school, friends and perhaps a part-time job. Yet when Mario Fernandez was just 16, he found himself trapped behind prison bars as a "subversive" in Castro's Cuba. After two life-threatening years, Fernandez's family was able to obtain a release for him with the understanding that the 18-year-old would leave Cuba, never to return.

The resourceful Fernandez headed for New York, where he soon obtained a job as a bilingual junior draftsman. His early art studies remained dormant for some years as he built a new life for himself in his adopted country. Fernandez married and developed a successful business career in the microwave industry.

Becoming increasingly frustrated by the bureaucracy of corporate life, Mario eventually sold his microwave business. He turned to his love of art as a respite from business, and in March, 1981, he

entered the National Wildlife Art Show to display a few of his works. Most revolved around the concept of freedom: not surprising for an artist who had spent two of his formative years in Castro's bondage.

To his surprise, Fernandez earned a "Best of Show" award at that first event for his bald eagle painting, "Spirit of Freedom." Before long, the artist left business completely and devoted his full-time efforts to his art. In this way, he could spend long hours in the field observing his wildlife subjects, painting them, and attending wildlife exhibits around the country.

In 1984, Fernandez established Fountainhead as a company that would present his own works, and those of other fine artists who now include Robert A. Olson and Daniel Craig. Since then, Fountainhead has presented scores of

award-winning, sell-out graphics, collector plates and sculptures. Fernandez's first limited edition collector plate, "Courtship Flight," earned multiple "Plate of the Year" awards. Along with its companion plate, "Wings of Freedom," this issue and Fernandez's *The Seasons* collection of bird-subject plates have established him solidly in the collectibles realm.

In addition, Fernandez is pursuing fine art sculpture including both tabletop-sized pieces in various media and a monumental work which serves as the focal point for Freedom Square in Independence, Ohio.

HELMUT FISCHER

A mind soaring with imagination and a careful attention to detail are two quali-

ties that Helmut Fischer blends together in every piece of sculpture. Since entering the W. Goebel Porzellanfabrik apprentice program over twenty years ago, Fischer has demonstrated this skilled creativity in the more than six hundred varied models he has created for Goebel.

As a schoolboy he showed a marked creative aptitude. His father, who was a craftsman in Bavaria, recognized his son's talent while Helmut was still quite young, and encouraged his development.

In 1964, at the age of 14, Fischer followed his father's suggestion and enrolled in the Goebel apprentice program. Since that time, he has created models for a fascinating variety of popular series including *Serengheti*, *Donald and His Friends* (from the *Walt Disney* series), *Glanimals*, glass miniatures, and butterflies from the *Wild Life Collection*.

A striking example of Fischer's artistic expertise and creative versatility is the DeGrazia figurine collection. Though he has not yet been to the American Southwest, he captures the essence of the area with an amazing feel. Using Ted DeGrazia's colorful and vibrant paintings, Fischer creates in each figurine the same love DeGrazia put on canvas. It is this artistry that makes Fischer a leading sculptor.

Through Goebel figurines, Helmut Fischer shares with the world his special talent for capturing a moment in time and immortalizing it for all eternity.

TOM FREEMAN

When he was a teenager in Pontiac, Michigan, Tom Freeman gained national

attention for a painting he contributed to an exhibition held for the International Red Cross. But several years would pass before Tom Freeman began to "chart his course" as a marine artist. During a sailing trip aboard a schooner in the North Atlantic, the young man first answered the "call of the sea"—in its beauty and mystery he discovered the theme that would shape his career as an artist.

Though only in his mid-30s, Tom Freeman now enjoys the respect of his peers, as well as great popularity. His limited edition prints are widely sought by collectors, as are his original paintings, which command prices as high as $15,000.

A member of the exclusive American Society of Marine Artists, Freeman has been honored with exhibitions at prominent galleries throughout the country, including the Smithsonian Institution, the Mystic Seaport Gallery, and Grand Central Galleries. His works may be found in numerous private collections, and four of his original paintings are currently on display at the Executive Mansion of the White House.

Recently, Freeman turned his talents to the collector plate medium for the first time. His dramatic portrayals of this nations's most historic sailing vessels appear in The Hamilton Collection's eight-plate series, *America's Greatest Sailing Ships*.

W. D. GAITHER

W. D. "Bill" Gaither is a multi-faceted artist with hundreds of thousands of paintings and prints on display in galleries and private collections all over America. In addition to his work in the limited edi-

tion art realm, Gaither is actively involved in dozens of environmental and wildlife conservation organizations, reflecting his consuming interest in animals and birds.

As a sculptor and painter, Gaither's special gift stems from his immersion in the world of wildlife. His workshops hold books on myriad subjects, mounted specimens, dozens of sketches, and partially completed sculptures.

The artist prides himself on creating works which are always active, fluid and alive—never static or frozen. His wildlife studies reflect a living moment in time in the animal's life in the wild—feeding, running, attacking, playing, leaping, soaring or charging.

Gaither's first sculpture in association with the Maruri Studio premiered in 1982. In just two years' time his "Ameri-

can Bald Eagle II" rose in value from $165 to $600. Since then, wildlife art connoisseurs eagerly await each Maruri-Gaither introduction—many of which sell out immediately and begin rising in value.

WOLFGANG GAWANTKA

Artist and sculptor Wolfgang Gawantka was born in Dresden in 1930. At the age of sixteen, he began six years of intensive study at the Meissen School of Art, where his teachers included A. Struck, Heinrich Thein, Munch-Khe, and E. Oehme.

An additional year of study at the School of Ceramics at Hermsdorf, Thuringia, netted him a diploma, and readied

him for an immediate position as professional sculptor at the world-renowned Meissen Porzellan Manufaktur.

Gawantka later immigrated to West Germany where he joined the Kaiser Porcelain design staff as a full-time sculptor.

He currently holds the position of master sculptor at the Kaiser Porcelain Factory in Staffelstein, West Germany.

ELAINE GIGNILLIAT

When she was only sixteen, Elaine Gignilliat won her first portrait commission. Her professional career soon took off, as she earned first prize in the Southeastern States Painting Competition at age seventeen. This award brought her a three-year scholarship to the High Museum & School of Art in Atlanta, Georgia.

Ms. Gignilliat embarked upon a successful career as a fashion illustrator for Rich's in Atlanta, Stern Brothers in New York, and *Vogue* Magazine. During these years she received the prestigious National Seklemian Award.

The artist then expanded her work into the field of book illustration. She has created more than 250 book covers for major publishers including: Bantam Books; Hearst Publications; CBS; Harcourt, Brace, Jovanovich; Ballantine; Berkeley; Ace; New American Library; and Doubleday. In 1983 she was named Illustrator of the Year by the Romantic Times National Conference.

Her original interest in portrait commission encouraged Ms. Gignilliat to de-

velop this aspect of her art as well. Today she concentrates on portrait painting, drawing upon her studies with such well-known teachers as Howard Sanden and David Leffel of the Art Students League in New York. The artist's objective in portraiture is not only to achieve a likeness, but also to show the person at his or her best and to create a painting of intrinsic value. Gignilliat originals now sell for as much as $12,500.

Ms. Gignilliat currently is working with Edwin M. Knowles China Company to develop her first collection of limited edition plates based on the Academy Award-winning musical: "South Pacific."

BESSIE PEASE GUTMANN

Born on April 8, 1876, young Bessie Pease was influenced by the "Brandywine school" of illustration that was prevalent in her native Philadelphia, practiced by such master artists as Howard Pyle, Maxfield Parrish, and Jessie Willcox Smith. Early in life she developed her natural art talent at the Philadelphia School of Design for Women.

The young artist continued her studies at the Chase School for Art and the Art Student's League in New York. She was privileged to learn from prominent artists including Robert Henri, William Merritt Chase, Kenyon Cox, Frederick Dielman, Arther W. Dow and Mobray DeCamp.

Her dual career of art and family began in 1906, when Bessie Pease fell in love with and married Hellmuth Gutmann. Mrs. Guttman's three children often were subjects for her paintings. She also drew inspiration from her many nieces and nephews, and later from her grandchildren. Her illustrations in children's books and her prints were quite popular in the early 1900s — both in the United States and in Canada, England, Europe, Australia, Japan and South Africa.

This famous artist did not do simple portraits; rather she used her subjects to envision expressions, positions and attitudes in her completed works. She would often take a photograph of children for reference, or do a quick sketch in pencil, charcoal or pastel. These sketches show great detail and expression and clearly demonstrate her ability to capture the spirit and life of her subjects.

Mrs. Gutmann's successful career spanned nearly five decades. It was not until the 1940s, when she began to suffer from poor vision, that she ceased painting. She died in Centerport, New York, on September 29, 1960, at the age of 84.

Today, the works of Bessie Pease Gutmann have seen a remarkable resurgence of popularity, notably in the form of limited edition collector plates and figurines. Recent collector plate series from Balliol and The Hamilton Collection include: *A Child's Best Friend; Precious Portraits;* and *Bundles of Joy.*

FRANCES HOOK

From the moment she could put pencil to paper, the late Frances Hook knew that she liked drawing more than anything else. Born in Ambler, Pennsylvania, she took art lessons while in high school. This led to a scholarship at the Pennsylvania Museum School of Art, where she studied under illustrator Harry Pitz. She developed a pastel style and a unique way of capturing children.

While in school, Frances met her husband-to-be. After graduation, they married, and each began a career in commercial art. Her first ad was a two-page spread in *The Saturday Evening Post.*

It became increasingly clear over the years that Mrs. Hook's talent lay in her sensitive portrayals of children. She had the ability to capture youngsters in their natural settings. The now-famous Northern Tissue children of the mid-1960's were drawn by Frances Hook. When television reduced the demand for commercial art, Mrs. Hook turned to illus-

trating children's books. In collaboration with her husband, she illustrated *The Living Bible,* by Tyndale Publishing.

In 1979, Roman, Inc., approached Frances Hook and asked her to design a collection of porcelain figurines. These were later grouped around such themes as "Profiles of Childhood" and "School Days."

She also designed several limited edition plate series and prints. Her most famous print, a portrait of Christ entitled "The Carpenter," closed in 1981 and has since commanded up to 20 times issue price on the secondary market. After Mrs. Hook's death in July, 1983, Pickard produced a "Carpenter" plate in tribute to her. It has achieved similar success after closing. The subject's popularity continues with a limited edition porcelain bust, produced by Roman between Easter of 1986 and Easter of 1987.

All releases since the artist's death have been issued at the direction and supervision of her daughter Barbara, who works closely with Roman to ensure the faithful translation of her mother's art into a new medium. New releases include a bust based on Frances' "Little Children, Come To Me" print and plate; giftware featuring her Northern Tissue children; an ongoing series of collectible bells; and a "Madonna and Child" bust.

SISTER MARIA INNOCENTIA HUMMEL

Sister Maria Innocentia Hummel was the creator of hundreds of colorful and charming sketches, drawings and paintings of children. Her work is the basis for scores of appealing, hand-painted fine earthenware figurines, as well as limited edition plates and bells, created and offered exclusively by W. Goebel Porzellanfabrik of West Germany.

She was born Berta Hummel in Bavaria in 1909. Her father had inclinations toward art, and so did Berta, from earliest youth. She was graduated from the Munich Academy of Applied Art, meanwhile devoting much of her energies toward her religion as well.

Much to the dismay of her art teachers, Berta Hummel entered a convent upon her graduation, taking the name Sister

Maria Innocentia. Because the convent of Siessen, a teaching order, was quite poor, she gained permission to raise money by selling some of her artwork for postcards. In 1934 Franz Goebel, the fourth-generation head of the porcelain-producing firm bearing the family name, discovered her art at a time when he was searching for ideas for a new line of figurines.

The first M. I. Hummel figurines debuted at the Leipzig Fair in 1935, and since then have been popular with collectors around the world. Sadly, Sister M. I. Hummel died much too soon, not yet aware of her full triumph as an artist. She succumbed to tuberculosis in 1946 at the age of thirty-seven.

BART JERNER

An outdoorsman. . .a conservationist. . .an artist. These are the three words which best describe Bart Jerner, an accomplished fisherman and sportsman who has spent most every summer for the past forty years hiking across northern Michigan, central Canada, or the Canadian Yukon.

During these extensive tours, Jerner camps in the wilderness and lives off the land. This time in the wild affords the famed naturalist artist a unique opportunity to understand his subjects and to observe and photograph them. In addition, he photographs the natural habitats of his subjects so that he can convey the true sense of the outdoors. Jerner also studies the flight, feeding and breeding patterns of the species to ensure that his portraits are factually correct.

Trained in the fine arts at the Chicago Academy of Art, the Art Institute of Chi-

cago, and the American Academy of Art, Jerner brings the eye of a naturalist and the trained hand of an artist to the creation of his vibrant wildlife art. Jerner's talents have won him a growing following in naturalist art circles, and his work has been exhibited by the National Wildlife Art Collector's Society.

Even as his art reputation grows, however, Jerner considers himself first and foremost a conservationist. His extensive time spent in the wild allows him to learn first hand where breeding grounds have disappeared and wetlands have dried up, and thus he can work to improve conservation measures nationwide.

Jerner's first series of collector plates, *Living With Nature: Jerner's Ducks* has been crafted by Edwin M. Knowles.

GARRI KATZ

Garri Katz was born in the Soviet Union when the dark cloud of war spread over all the nations of Europe. As a child he found comfort in drawing and painting on scraps of paper—an activity which helped calm his fears during the difficult days of World War II. After the war, young Katz completed his schooling at the Odessa Institute of Fine Arts, where he studied for four years before launching his career as a painter and illustrator.

In 1973, Katz and his family immigrated to Israel. His paintings of religious and historic subjects and his celebrations of everyday life in Israel soon earned Katz many invitations to display his works in one-man shows in that land. Then in 1984, Katz began a series of shows in the United States sponsored by patrons who

had discovered his genius during trips to Israel. Today, art connoisseurs from many different nations purchase Katz paintings and watercolors at prices of up to $12,000 each. His works are on display in Israel, Belgium, Germany, Canada and the United States.

Garri Katz's first limited edition collector plate series for Reco represents a commission from Reco International. Entitled *Great Stories from the Bible*, each of eight plates portrays a memorable moment in one of the world's most beloved Bible stories.

CHARLOTTE KELLEY

Charlotte Kelley received a Bachelor of Fine Arts Degree from the University of Georgia. She is an Atlanta native and taught in Atlanta public schools for five years.

Many of Charlotte's early artistic efforts were of circus clowns, especially Emmett Kelly, "America's favorite clown." Her father adds, "The walls of Charlotte's bedroom were covered with drawings of clowns."

She studied portrait painting with Roman and Constantine Chatov in Atlanta.

In 1977, she moved to Florida and studied Commercial Art at Pensacola Junior College. She discovered her genuine love of watercolor in class taught by Jenny Davenport.

Further studies have been with Ed Whitney, Robert Wood, Miles Batt, Tony Van Hasselt and Robert Long.

She belongs to the Florida Watercolor Society, the Southern Society and shows

her work at Quayside Gallery in Pensacola.

Charlotte, her husband and three children live in Pensacola where she paints local history and the beautiful Gulf Coast.

"My desire is . . .to capture someone's attention, to make them smile by recognition of the subject matter or entertainment of the eye; in essence . . .to bring joy to the viewer."

Charlotte's artwork, offered by Flambro Imports, brings joy into the life of thousands of Emmett Kelly clown fans.

SANDRA KUCK

In Sandra Kuck's paintings of children, she displays a rare gift for capturing the true spirit of childhood. The creator of four series of plates and an ongoing collection of lithographs for Reco International, Ms. Kuck lives in Long Island, New York.

She was educated at U.C.L.A., where she discovered that she loved to paint and draw. She moved to New York and entered the Art Students League where she learned to do portraiture and figure drawing. She disliked drawing and painting inanimate objects and soon discovered that people, and in particular children, interested her most. Within a year, she began to win commissions from galleries for portraits and paintings.

Ms. Kuck's fascination with children as subjects began when she was pregnant with her first child. She began sketching children at play in the park, and eventually her own daughter became her best model.

Before long Ms. Kuck's children's paintings were on display in many New

York-area galleries: she has sold more than 1200 original paintings. In a Long Island gallery, Reco International president Heio Reich spotted her work and approached her to create a series of plates, *Games Children Play*. Soon she added *The Grandparent Collector's Plates* series and one entitled *Little Professionals*.

Ms. Kuck's latest collections, *Days Gone By*, *A Childhood Almanac*, annual Christmas and Mother's Day series, and *Barefoot Children*, are being offered by Reco and through The Hamilton Collection. One of the most celebrated plates of the 1980s, the *Days Gone By* first issue, "Sunday Best," won Plate of the Show, Silver Chalice, and Plate of the Year awards among others. In addition, Ms. Kuck has earned the NALED Artist of the Year award four years running—an unprecedented honor. She is also the recipient of numerous Print and Plate of the Year, Plate of the Show, Silver Chalice and other awards.

MORT KÜNSTLER

"I try to paint pictures of American history in a realistic way, and in a way that can't be done by a photographer," says artist Mort Künstler. "My paintings involve complex compositions with actions and situations that require a lot of research and a lot of drawing and imagination."

In his paintings, Künstler chronicles American history from the time of the Indians through the space program.

Künstler's passion for realism and accuracy in his artwork began when he was a child. Drawings he did at the ages of five and six showed his keen power of observation and understanding of perspective.

Künstler received professional art training at New York City's Pratt Institute before he set out on a career as an illustrator. Today he includes in his list of credits more than 2,000 illustrations for books, advertisements and magazines, including *Newsweek*, *National Geographic*, *The Saturday Evening Post*, *True*, *Sports Afield* and *Outdoor Life*.

Painstaking research is a hallmark of Künstler's work. He devotes a great deal of time traveling to the location of a work, talking to people, and piecing together information before picking up his paintbrush.

His passion for detail is showcased in both his collector's plate series, produced by the Edwin M. Knowles China Co. His first series, *Oklahoma*, features scenes from the classic Rodgers and Hammerstein musical that tells the story of the last frontier land rush.

With his second series *Lincoln, Man of America*, Künstler fulfills a lifelong ambition to create historical paintings of his personal hero: Abraham Lincoln.

Künstler's paintings for his plate series were created in his customized studio at his home in Long Island, New York, where the floor is an eight-foot "lazy susan" that can be turned with the changing light.

JIM LAMB

When Jim Lamb was a boy, his artist-father developed a unique way to keep his active son quiet during Sunday church services. The elder Lamb would give young Jim a pencil and pad to doodle with during sermons. Then after church, the father would go over the drawings with his son, helping him to improve his art technique. His father's influence shaped Lamb in another important way as well, for they made frequent trips into the country to observe the nature of the Great Northwest. And regular trips to art galleries allowed Jim Lamb to develop his great appreciation for the Old Masters.

After a time spent in college, young Lamb joined the Navy, and spent those four years devoting all his spare time to art. During that period he put together a portfolio that he used to make his mark in

Los Angeles, soon developing a clientele for book illustrations, sports paintings, advertising, and movie posters.

Yet for all his success as an illustrator, Lamb longed for the freedom to create art on his own terms. What's more, Lamb's family wanted to return to the artist's northwestern "roots." Today the Lambs live in Issaquah, Washington, where the artist works on a variety of assignments including fine art collector prints and limited edition plates.

Many of Lamb's animal and bird prints have sold out within days of their issuance. In addition, his works have been selected for a U.S. postage stamp, the Smithsonian Institution, U.S. Air Force, and the U.S. Forestry Service. Jim Lamb's first venture in the field of limited-edition plates came about as the result of a commission from River Shore and The Hamilton Collection. The series, entitled *Puppy Playtime*, includes eight lively puppy portraits honoring America's favorite pure-bred dogs.

HEIKE LANDHERR

Born in Marne/Dithmarschen, West Germany, Heike Landherr's artistic feeling and creative ambitions were recognized at an early age. From childhood on, her favorite pastime has been painting, and she experimented with all kinds of techniques, particularly with oil colors.

Having finished school, Ms. Landherr attended the Academy of Graphic Arts and Design in Hamburg, where she improved her skill in clay modelling. After graduation, she passed an apprenticeship in a goldsmith's studio, where she gained a specific insight into industrial art.

Most recently, Ms. Landherr has been working for the Kaiser Porcelain Studio as a full-time sculptress where she is the youngest member of their creative staff. In this considerably short period of activity for the Kaiser studios, she has excelled with a series of art figurines. Though her main interest is wildlife, she has also created some beautiful human subjects, such as her striking "Mother and Baby" figurines.

A passionate motorcyclist and cat-fancier, Heike Landherr still devotes time to oil painting and is inventing her very personal style of air brush painting,

apart from her work at the Kaiser studios.

CAROL LAWSON

For as long as she can remember, Carol Lawson has pursued two main interests: drawing and reading. As a child, Ms. Lawson read colorful fairy tales of kings and queens, princes and princesses, enchanted frogs and talking animals. Before long she began to sketch and draw her own interpretations of the stories she had read, and thus began her life's work as an artist and illustrator.

Ms. Lawson lists a number of turn-of-the-century English illustrators among her prime influences. These include John Hassall, Arthur Rackham and Edmund Dulac. She also draws upon her admiration for American painters including Howard Pyle, Maxfield Parrish, Jessie Willcox Smith, and Maud Humphrey.

Youthful art studies led Carol Lawson to college first at Yorkshire and then at Brighton, where she earned a first class honors degree in art and design. When her artist husband began studies at London's Royal College, Ms. Lawson embarked upon her successful career as an illustrator.

All the while, Carol Lawson chose from a growing array of commissions to create book illustrations and designs for limited edition plates, dolls, and bells. Many of her works center upon her favorite theme of fairy tales—as does her recent collection of gold-decorated plates for The Hamilton Collection: *The Golden Classics* Plate Collection.

LEE HAROLD LETTS

Sculptor Lee Harold Letts' studies and work have provided him with rich experiences both here and abroad.

Letts studied with sculptor/architect Truman E. Moore for two years. He continued his training at the School of the Museum of Fine Arts in Boston, where he studied drawing and sculpture and took an apprenticeship with John Franchot Story Street Goldsmiths in Cambridge. Letts also took the opportunity to work in goldsmithing and bronze in The Hague, Holland.

In 1982, Letts' "Bronze Bald Eagle" figurine was accepted by the White House for exhibit through 1988 to commemorate the 200th Anniversary of the National Emblem. The sculpture will be permanently placed in the Reagan Memorial Library and Museum.

Letts is presently involved with sculpting and overseeing the final production of Kaiser Porcelain sculptures depicting bird and animal subjects.

"We have a very high standard to maintain in the porcelain medium," explains Letts. "This is why I enjoy working with Kaiser, because I share with them this respect for the medium and its tradition."

EVE LICEA

Eve Licea's life and art are a study in contrasts.

Licea was born to a poor working class family in New York's Bronx area, a family that had no money to pay for art lessons. Yet today Licea works in a fashion-

able loft in Greenwich Village and has artworks exhibited in such prestigious galleries as Lever House, Pindar Gallery and Les Mouches in New York City. She has received critical acclaim for her embossed lithographs, large cast paper sculptures and contemporary paintings.

Licea's talent, her burning desire to be an artist and her diligence in practicing her self-taught techniques landed her a three-year scholarship at the Parson School of Design in New York City. For the next 25 years she used her artistic talents in a variety of jobs, from doing anatomical sketches for medical films to creating prints in widely varied styles for an art publishing company. Today she is able to devote all her time to creating fine art in her own distinctive style.

The "Licea style" is a unique blend of contrasts: geometric patterns and natural forms, matte and gloss surfaces, raised and flat areas, colors and gold along with expanses of white.

All of these elements are featured in her collector's plate series produced by The Edwin M. Knowles China Co. Her first series, *Biblical Mothers*, was an innovative contemporary treatment of favorite Old Testament Bible stories. In her second series, she applies her unique talents to another beloved Biblical story: the birth of Christ. Licea's unusual square-shaped Christmas series debuted in 1987.

LORE

Multi-talented German artist Lore has never been content only to draw and paint. From the time she was a child, involved in her fantasies and dreams, it was easy for her to make up stories. It was only a matter of time before the adult Lore had convinced her editors that she should not only illustrate books for other writers, but that she should write her own as well—with illustrations by Lore! Since 1946, Lore has been a freelance artist and author, with four of her 40 charming children's books translated into English. It is understandable that she is well-known beyond the borders of her native country.

In the early 1960's, picture greeting cards with the Lore signature were seen by members of Goebel management. These cards bore the unmistakable im-

print of the artist with a loving approach to children and nature, an attitude warmly appreciated by Goebel. Out of the discussions which followed, the concept of the "Blumenkinder" was developed. These flower children are the epitome of romantic grace, white porcelain hand-painted in soft pastel tones, with tender care given to charming details. Some of the children have pets, and all have tiny flowers. Each petal is delicately handcrafted, then painstakingly formed into complete flowers and placed on the figurine.

It was a teamwork of great magnitude that produced each of these gentle reminders of childhood. First came the inspired drawing by Lore, which was brought to the Goebel master sculptor Gerhard Bochmann for his translation into three-dimensional form. Working closely together, this talented team, along with chief master sample painter Günther Neubauer, brought forth these limited editions of which there are only 2,000 each. Each is numbered, and there is a certificate of ownership on record at the Goebel factory for the discriminating collector. Seven *Blumenkinder* editions have been issued.

FRED MACHETANZ

Fred Machetanz, dean of Alaskan painters and one of the world's great wild-life artists, never dreamed while earning his B.A. and Master's degree in art at Ohio State University, that his future lay in the frozen North. A graduation gift of a six-week sojourn in the territory of his uncle's trading post at Unalakleet stretched into a two-year residence during which Machetanz sketched, drew and painted a treasury of scenes and people from a vanishing way of life.

In New York, Fred found books to illustrate, but none about Alaska until he wrote his own. *Panuck, Eskimo Sled Dog* prompted Vilhjalmur Stefansson to recommend the artist for membership in the prestigious Explorers Club, and *On Artic Ice*, a second book, brought an invitation to sail on the Coast Guard's famous Bering Sea and Arctic Patrol.

During World War II, Machetanz returned to Alaska as a lieutenant commander in charge of the Intelligence Center for the North Pacific Command. He

wrote the history of the Alaskan campaign for the Navy.

After many years of struggle—building a log cabin home, photographing on the ice, lecturing in the lower '48 and always painting, Machetanz had his first one-man show in 1962. An "overnight success," he became recognized internationally. His luminous paintings—Renaissance glazes—and a series of 50 stone lithographs, have put him in the Alaska Hall of Fame, won him an honorary Doctor of Fine Arts from the University of Alaska and endeared him to the people of the 49th state as "Alaskan of the Year—1977."

Fred Machetanz is represented by Mill Pond Press Inc.

GEORGE A. MALICK

Many artists have been compared to the late Norman Rockwell, but few capture the classic Rockwell spirit—and the emotions of small town America—as well as George A. Malick. This Pennsylvania artist draws upon the same homey subject matter that Rockwell found so compelling: families togehter, scenes in the general store, and children at play.

Malick's ambition in each painting is to make each viewer feel good, and to recognize himself—or a loved one—in its true-to-life subject. His first collector plate for Curator Collection exemplifies this ambition: "Hometown Hero" shows a Little League slugger making that all-important hit, just in time to save the big game. Just as Rockwell did, Malick carries out a number of "mini-dramas" in each painting as well. The slugger's happiness and the despair of the opposing team's catcher are skillfully juxtaposed. In the back-

ground, the hometown crowd expresses joy in their young hero's triumph.

JOHN BOYD MARTIN

John Boyd Martin is fast becoming one of the country's most respected and popular portrait artists, especially in the sports field. Commissioned by major universities, professional sports franchises and associations, Mr. Martin brings an emotional realism to his art that communicates in dramatic fashion.

Mr. Martin began his career as an advertising art director/illustrator winning more than 150 awards for his work across the country. He then turned his full attention to his first love: portraiture.

Some of his best-known portrait commissions are: baseball greats Joe DiMaggio, Ted Williams and Stan Musial; former Baseball Commissioners Happy Chandler, Ford Frick and Bowie Kuhn; Dallas businessman Lamar Hunt; and golfer Lee Trevino.

Mr. Martin also has done portrait commissions for such institutions as The University of Michigan, The University of South Carolina, Louisiana State University, The Kansas City Chiefs, The Kansas City Royals, The Atlanta Braves, The Detroit Tigers, Major League Baseball Promotions Corporation and NFL Properties.

Recently, Mr. Martin was commissioned by Gartlan USA, Inc. to create *The Gold Crown Collection* to commemorate George Brett's 2000th hit. The collection includes a custom oak-framed ceramic plaque which portrays Brett superimposed against three action shots which illustrate the sports hero in action,

at bat and in the field. "Royalty in Motion" is personally autographed by Brett and Martin.

Artist Martin still keeps his hand in as an illustrator having done program covers for the World Series, the All-Star Game, the NBA All-Star Game and Game Day.

Although Mr. Martin's work has been oriented to sports, he has received noted recognition for his work for business institutions and private collections, as well.

JOHN McCLELLAND

The life-sized portrait of his daughter, Susan, which John McClelland created some years back may well have been the major turning point of his career. An art director used the portrait for an ad in a trade magazine, and Miles Kimball, the

mail order company, spotted it and asked John McClelland to do a Christmas cover for their catalog. That was the beginning of an association which continues today.

Brigitte Moore of Reco International saw McClelland's Miles Kimball art in the mid-1970s, and Reco arranged for the artist to create limited edition plates. McClelland today is one of the field's most celebrated artists, with numerous "Plate of the Year" and "Artist of the Year" awards to his credit.

He also has designed several figurine series, including subjects such as children, clown heads and angels, and is the creator of a number of limited edition lithographs pulled from eight to fourteen individual plates.

A native of Georgia, McClelland pursued his art career in New York after a hitch in the service. He met and married

Alice Stephenson, a fashion artist, and they moved to Connecticut, where they resided for 30 years. In early 1986 the McClellands returned to their native Georgia where they have built a lovely home.

In addition to his many limited edition offerings and his Miles Kimball work, McClelland is a portraitist with a large following. He also has created scores of illustrations for publications including *The Saturday Evening Post, Redbook, American*, and *Readers Digest.*

McClelland has written two "how-to" books for artists: one on painting flowers and the other on portrait painting. He also has taught both intermediate and advanced classes in portrait painting.

SUSIE MORTON

Susie Morton has been creating original art for Ernst Enterprises' limited edition plates since 1978. She specializes in personality plates along with a children's series, *So Young, So Sweet* and a series of women called *A Beautiful World.* Her most recent creations are the *Star Trek* Plate Collection and *Star Trek: The Commemorative Collection.*

A resident of Orange County, California, Ms. Morton had early schooling at the Ringling School of Art in Sarasota, Florida. She worked in pen and ink and in watercolor, and later studied painting and sculpture in California.

For more than a decade she has specialized in professional-quality pastels, with which she is able to capture very realistic likenesses of people. In addition to her portraiture, Ms. Morton is a proficient

sculptress and an expert painter of animals and wildlife.

GERDA NEUBACHER

Gerda Neubacher is a Canadian realist artist who was born in Austria. Artistically inclined since childhood, she studied art at the Grace Kelly School of Art in Zurich, Switzerland. In Zurich she met and married Fred Neubacher, another Canadian realist painter. In 1968 they took up residence in Toronto.

Ms. Neubacher's love for rural scenery and studies of people are reflected in her highly realistic and detailed works of art, such as the popular *Classic Fairy Tales*

Plate Collection she created for Kaiser Porcelain. In her delightful *Christmas Plate* series for Kaiser Porcelain, the children seem to come alive as Ms. Neubacher focuses on the various aspects of the holiday season.

The artist has had major exhibitions in Toronto with Juliane Galleries and Christel Galleries as well as The National Art Center in Ottawa, The Galleria in Houston, the OMNI in Miami, the O'Keefe Centre in Toronto, and many more.

GÜNTHER NEUBAUER

A better indication of the quality of talent attracted to the Goebel company, both past and present, would be hard to find than Günther Neubauer. With Goebel for the last thirty years, Herr Neubauer has attained the highest distinctions.

In 1948, one month following his sixteenth birthday, he entered W. Goebel Porzellanfabrik as an apprentice in the painting department. He was taken under the wing of one of the masters, Arthur Möller, who trained him in all phases from designing to painting, even some sculpting. It soon became clear, however, that his strengths lay in designing and painting, and it was in those areas where his burgeoning career concentrated.

Just three years later, he distinguished himself by passing with highest honors a demanding professional test given in Coburg. In appreciation of this, and in an unusual move, Goebel promoted him quickly. He was now responsible for the decoration of particularly difficult models. It is rare, even today, to find an artist equally at home in both onglaze and underglaze decoration, but Günther Neubauer is a specialist in both areas.

By 1953, he had become head of a large section of the painting department. And he was yet only 21! From this time on, his progression through the artistic ranks of the company was secure. By 1955, he was entrusted with the development of totally new designs. Needless to say, this is the most important and responsible position in a porcelain factory.

From the early 1960s through the present, Herr Neubauer has been directly concerned with the education of the apprentices in the decorating department. He is a recognized teacher, and has as his pupils all apprentices in all production departments of W. Goebel Porzellanfabrik. At the vocational school in Coburg, he has the rank of master.

Günther Neubauer was born in the Sudetenland, the northern part of Bo-

hemia (now Czechoslovakia), an area famed not only for the Bohemian glass so treasured, but also for porcelain. Swimming and skiing are important to him, but for a busman's holiday he prefers to paint! He is also an experienced photographer.

ROBERT A. OLSON

As a founding member of the Minneapolis-based Oasis Art Studio, Robert Olson saw his artworks produced by major corporations while he was still an undergraduate student at the College of Art and Design in Minneapolis. Commissions included those of AT&T, 3M Company, Control Data, and McGraw Hill.

Yet Olson wished to further his artistic expression into the fine art realm, and he continued his education at exclusive New York and Paris workshops. In 1982, with the support of investors familiar with his work for Oasis Art Studio, Olson began Windemere Galleries as a vehicle to market his fine art paintings in the form of limited-edition lithographs and posters.

Olson's lithograph of "Piano Moods," a serene portrait of his wife, Nancy, led to the issuance of his first limited edition collector plate, based upon the same original painting. Meanwhile, Olson continued to earn accolades and awards for his work, including several Society of Illustrators Awards, a New York Desi Award, New York Art Directors Awards, the Publication and Design Award, and the Anaheim Collectors Society Best of Show and Print Design awards.

Now working with Fountainhead, Robert Olson has plans in development for more limited edition plates featuring his romantic and imaginative art visions.

ROBERT OLSZEWSKI

Robert Olszewski was born in a small rural town near Pittsburgh in 1945. As a child he displayed remarkable artistic ability, leading him to an early decision to devote his life to the world of art.

Olszewski was initially attracted to drawing and painting. After receiving a Bachelor of Education in Art degree, Olszewski and his wife moved to California where he taught during the day and painted at night.

It was while scaling down projects for his students that Olszewski became fascinated with the idea of miniaturization. This led to the creation of his first one-twelfth-scale figurines, originally sculpted in 1977.

The popularity of Olszewski's work spread rapidly; collectors and institutions from five continents have acquired his pieces since they first appeared. In 1979, Olszewski signed an exclusive contract with Goebel Miniatures for worldwide distribution of his work.

MIGUEL PAREDES

Adventure and mischief characterize the child-subject paintings of Mexican-born artist Miguel Paredes, and the artist's own life reflects these qualities as well. Paredes' father raised animals for the bullfight rings in Mexico City. Because the young boy was curious and ac-

tive, his mother would often take him to the Parque de Chapultepec in the heart of the city to observe the various characters who gathered there: children, lovers, elderly gentlemen and other parkgoers.

At the age of seven, Paredes began sketching the scenes he found in the park, and before long he was able to sell some of these impromptu artworks to his "models." As he grew, the fearless youngster would run away from home in search of new experiences and scenes which he could draw. He always returned, however, and began entering art contests at the encouragement of his junior high school teachers.

Although he also tried his hand at acting, singing and bullfighting, Paredes eventually realized that he was destined to be an artist. By the age of 16 he worked full-time in this field, receiving commissions and selling drawings by word of mouth. In 1976, he moved to the United States and soon was in demand as a portrait artist and muralist.

When David Armstrong of Armstrong's met Paredes, he commissioned a series of child-subject collector plates, *Reflections of Innocence*. Recently, Armstrong's introduced a new porcelain plaque process using two of Paredes' paintings. In addition, the artist continues to create his fine art paintings which are shown widely at gallery exhibits, commanding $6,000 or more for a single canvas. Paredes also is working to perfect his abilities for three-dimensional sculpture.

RON PARKER

Ron Parker, one of the most exciting talents in the field of wildlife art, is a native of British Columbia.

Parker showed above-normal talent in art as a child, which was not surprising since both parents had artistic abilities. However, as a six-footer in eighth grade, his future seemed to be in basketball. High school was followed by four years of apprenticeship in commercial art.

He attended the University as an architectural student and worked in commercial art. Then came another stint at school and a degree in education. For a time he worked in track and field administration. Appropriate for the 1966 Canadian Decathlon Champion!

When he turned to fine art as a profession, collectors began to buy. Parker now hikes, photographs and paints in a studio not far removed from his subjects.

Ron Parker is represented by Mill Pond Press Inc.

BOB PEARCY

His gentleness and understanding of animals have helped Bob Pearcy to develop his outstanding reputation for the photography of cats and dogs. Raised in San Antonio, Texas, Pearcy grew up without a pet. As a teenager he recognized his knack for photography, which helped him supplement his income as a serviceman after he joined the Air Force at age seventeen.

About three years before he planned to retire from the military, Pearcy picked up a book on how to photograph pets. He tried a few sessions and discovered that he had a natural flair for this facet of his craft, even though he was not an experienced pet owner. Indeed, he is now the author of two books of his own: *How to*

Photograph Cats and *How to Photograph Dogs.*

Today. Pearcy does more than 500 photo sessions per year from his studio in Carmichael, California. He says that female pets are easier to work with than males, because of their even temperaments and smaller size. Although he prefers dogs and cats for subjects, he has photographed everything from panthers to TV's Fred the Cockatoo, the bird that was a regular on the show "Baretta." Most of Pearcy's work is for advertising agencies, animal show entrants, and private clients who wish to capture their pets on film.

Armstrong's has created four series of limited edition plates utilizing Pearcy's charming animal portraits. Now available on porcelain are the *Lovable Kittens* and *Huggable Puppies* series, the first two plates in the *Buck Hill Bears*, and one plate in the *Companion* series.

GREGORY PERILLO

When Gregory Perillo was a child in Staten Island, New York, his Italian immigrant father would tell the youngster colorful stories about the Old West. Young Greg would sketch what he envisioned from those grand tales—always choosing to portray the Indians rather than the cowboys. And he dreamed of the day that he would visit the American Indians for himself.

As a sailor in the U.S. Navy, Perillo shared some of his western sketches with a friend from Montana. Before long, the pair were on their way west, and Perillo had the opporunity to come face-to-face with the American Indians he had read and dreamed so much about. To his surprise, they asked him what tribe he was from. Except for his curly hair, they took

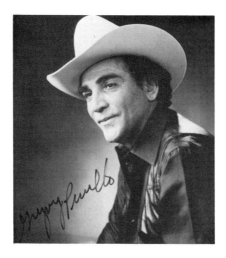

the Italian Perillo for a full-blooded Indian! And somehow, being mistaken for a Native American solidified his identification with the people he was to paint for the rest of his life.

Perillo dedicated himself to portraying the American Indian culture with fidelity and respect. He studied under the western art master William R. Leigh, and later met another great artist, Bill Lawrence, who sponsored Perillo into the Hudson Valley Art Association. With the association's magazine and exposure as a starting point, Perillo soon earned national, and then international attention.

The artist began a series of one-man shows and gallery exhibitions that continues even today. In addition, his works were chosen for the permanent collections of museums and institutions including: the Pettigrew Museum, Sioux Falls, South Dakota; the Denver Museum of Natural History; and the University of Mexico.

In the late 1970s, Perillo began creating limited edition plates, figurines and graphics under the commission of Vague Shadows. Since then he has won numerous awards—both personally, and for his two and three-dimensional portrayals of American Indian life. Perillo's many plate series include: *The Chieftains, The Plainsmen, The Professionals,* and the recent *Pride of America's Indians,* featuring the award-winning first issue, "Brave and Free."

ROGER TORY PETERSON

The author and illustrator of the book which introduced to the world a new and

easy way to identify birds in the field and thus created an army of bird watchers was born in Jamestown, New York. Here the woods, the fields, and the river edges were filled with birds which the boy observed and sketched. And always he read about the giants in nature painting, Durer, Lear, Audubon and Louis Agassiz Fuertes from nearby Ithaca.

After high school Peterson attended the Art Students League in New York and later the National Academy of Design. He then became an instructor of art and science at the Rivers School in Brookline, Massachusetts.

During this time he developed his unique system for identifying birds in the field. In 1934, after rejection by five publishers, his first *Field Guide to the Birds* was published by Houghton Mifflin. With that publicaton his life became a whirlwind of activity. He has continued to paint, to write, to lecture and to travel to

remote corners of the world to record rare and exotic species of birds. Since then he has written fourteen books with a total sale of over 9,000,000.

Honors and responsibilities have been heaped upon him. He has been awarded eleven honorary doctorates and numerous awards and medals including the Presidential Medal of Freedom, the nation's highest civilian honor. Peterson has made a series of motion pictures, lectured, and is a special consultant to the Audubon Society. Only recently has he enjoyed the luxury of painting for its own sake.

A lifetime of artistic discipline, observation and intellectual curiosity has prepared the way for his mature works. They are poems in paint about nature.

Roger Tory Peterson is represented by Mill Pond Press Inc.

DON POLLAND

In early childhood, Don Polland carved his own toy cowboys and Indians. Living in Utah, Arizona, Colorado and Nevada, he developed an intense interest in the golden days of the American West, which he has continued to express in three-dimensional art throughout each phase of his life.

Polland's first career was that of an illustrator for space age industries. He became a professional artist in 1959. His goal as an artist is to express his personal thoughts and beliefs as a storyteller. He strives to communicate his ideas visually, without the need for words of explanation.

A self-taught and highly motivated artist, Don Polland considers creativity his

way of life. His subject matter ranges from working cowboys to wild animals to Indians of the past and present. Because of their great challenge and long history in the world of art, Polland especially enjoys creating miniature sculptures. For commissions by such firms as The Franklin Mint and American Express, Polland has traveled widely, including a voyage to Africa on a research trip.

Polland's extensive list of museum showings includes the Whitney Gallery of Western Art, Buffalo Bill Historical Center, C.M. Russell Gallery and Museum, The Favell Museum of Western Arts and Artifacts, and the Montana Historical Society. His awards and honors include numerous Best of Show and First

Place awards at art shows nationwide. He was awarded the 1980 Favell Museum Western Heritage Award for excellence in portraying America's west and wildlife in sculpture. In addition, Polland is listed in *Who's Who in American Art*, *Who's Who in the West*, and *American Artists of Renown*.

Today, Polland continues to work on his beloved miniature figurines. From the studio which bears his name he also has introduced more than 50 gallery and museum bronzes as well as works for Franklin Mint, Chilmark, and other fine art firms.

BEVERLY PORT

Beverly Port is probably the artist most responsible for the current increase in the popularity of collectible teddy bears.

This Washington State native began creating hand made bears in the 1960s, and in 1976 began to exhibit her creations in west coast doll shows. By the end of the 1970s, she had back orders from collectors for her "Time Machine Teddies", a collection of bears begun in response to a request from her son, who wanted a bear like they had in the "old days". Some of Beverly's earliest bears, "Tedward" and "Tedwina Bearkin," for example, which were copyrighted in 1976, are being reproduced by Gorham

for a larger collecting audience. And her *Time Machine Teddies* are appearing on a series of Gorham collectible plates.

Beverly has influenced a whole generation of artists and collectors through her participation in such organizations as the United Federation of Doll Clubs, and her columns and articles in collectible publications. She writes regularly for *Doll Reader* and *Teddy Bear and Friends*, and her bear Theodore B. Bear (who co-authors her "Teddy Bear and Friends" column) "wrote" for years in *Doll Revue* and *Bambini*.

Beverly Port *Time Machine Teddies* plates for Gorham now include "Miss Emily" and "Big Bear", with "Hunny Munny" and "Beary Mab" soon to be released.

KENNETH POTTS

Kenneth Potts lived and was educated in the County of Cheshire, England. Throughout his early years, he developed an interest in making models, and from the age of four remembers modelling and creating a fantasy world of monsters, men, cars and ships.

After school in 1964, he took a place on a Foundation Art Course at the College of Art, Stockport in Cheshire. He then completed a Diploma Course at Stafford College of Art followed by a second Diploma in Art and Design at Stoke-on-Trent College of Art. Potts spent three additional years studying three dimensional art, modelling animals, portraiture and working from the nude.

After college Potts was offered the position of company modeller with the Design Team of Royal Worcester. He settled in the city of Worcester attending night classes to maintain his interest in life drawing and teaching sculpture in the evenings.

In 1979, he married his wife Anne and moved to a house in the city where he undertook commissions and sculptures of his own. That same year he was commissioned to sculpt the National Monument to the composer Sir Edward Elgar (1859-1936) to be placed in Worcester City. It was a fascinating project which led to meetings with the great composer's contemporaries, Sir Adrian Boult, Dr. Herbert Howells, Yehudi Menuhin, Dr. Her-

bert Sumsion and others. The 15-foot Elgar statue was completed in 1981 and unveiled by HRH The Prince of Wales following a concert in Worcester Cathedral on June 2nd, the anniversary of the Composer's birth.

Numerous commissions and portraits followed including the 15-foot statue of the poet A.E. Housman ('A Shropshire Lad' is his most famous work) for Bromsgrove, unveiled by The Duke of Westminster in March 1985; and a public memorial portrait of John Cassidy for Tameside Metropolitan Borough which was unveiled the same year.

Many of the portraits have a musical theme including 'David' the French Horn Player. A meeting with Stephanne Grappelli led to a portrait of the great jazz player.

His works have been exhibited at the Royal Academy of Arts, London; The Royal Festival Hall, London; The Sladmore Gallery, London; Art Expo, New York; Solihull Annual Exhibition; United Kingdom Touring Exhibitions with the Brotherhood of Ruralists; and Framed Gallery, Worcester.

He has created over 60 models for Royal Worcester and is currently working on several projects for the company including equestrian portraits and models. He is also working on further designs for eggs to be introduced in 1987 and 1988.

THOMAS QUINN

Since a youth in California, Thomas Quinn's intimacy with wild things and their environs has nurtured him and become a wellspring from which his talent flows.

After graduating with distinction from the prestigious Art Center College of De-

sign in California in 1962, Quinn pursued a career as an illustrator in New York.

However, a few years later, Quinn began painting wildlife with intensity and moved to California.

In Thomas Quinn's paintings one can sense the dignity he affords creatures of the wild and the intimacy he holds with his subjects. The elegance and simplicity of Quinn's artistry have won him numerous awards.

Thomas Quinn is represented by Mill Pond Press Inc.

MAYNARD REECE

Maynard Reece was born in Iowa, where he gained first-hand knowledge of the beauty of America's heartland. In 1940 Reece was hired as artist for the Iowa Department of History and Archives in the museum at Des Moines. One of his mentors was Ding Darling, a famous political cartoonist and graphic artist.

In 1948 he won the Federal Duck Stamp Competition for the first of an unprecedented five times. In 1950 Reece became a full-time free lance artist. Since then he has become one of the leading wildlife artists in America with an international reputation.

His work has appeared in prestigious magazines. Artist of the Year for Ducks Unlimited and an Honorary Trustee of that organization, he has received many awards and honors among which are two from the New York Art Directors' Club.

Reece is a dynamic artist who is never satisfied. He continues to grow, to experiment, to search for better ways to capture the elusive nuances of nature.

Maynard Reece is represented by Mill Pond Press Inc.

LUCY RIGG

The porcelain bisque figurines, music boxes, bells, plates and other collectibles of Lucy Rigg showcase her favorite art subject: teddy bears. This Switzerland-based Enesco artist is known as today's most prolific creator of teddy bears — a fascination which has sustained her for nearly 20 years.

Ms. Rigg began making baker's clay figures in 1969 while awaiting the birth of her daughter, Noelle. These "Rigglets," as they were called, won the artist an enthusiastic audience which encouraged her to enter the greeting card field in 1977. A teddy bear collector since 1968, Ms. Rigg fills her home with toys and collectors' items which project the same warmth and joy as her artwork. Another

Rigg collector's item is hats: the artist often wears one and boasts a large and diverse assortment to choose from.

Each teddy bear by Lucy Rigg projects his or her own happy personality. The artist's highly detailed work focuses on the bears' costuming and surroundings as well. Ms. Rigg has expanded her creative horizons in the development of a children's book called *A Special Gift*, in which teddy bears are the star characters.

NORMAN ROCKWELL

"I paint life as I would like it to be," Norman Rockwell once said. "If there was a sadness in this creative world of mine, it was a pleasant sadness. If there were problems, they were humorous problems."

In his thousands of works, Norman Rockwell created a pictorial history of his times and illuminated the lives of his fellow Americans with gifted warmth and insight. Rockwell gained national prominence as an illustrator for *The Saturday Evening Post, Life, Look, Boy's Life*, Boy Scout calendars and major advertisers, all of which brought him close to the hearts of people the world over.

The man who was to become the twentieth century's most popular American artist and illustrator was born in a brownstone in New York on February 3, 1894. He began drawing at five, and at-

tended the Chase School of Fine and Applied Arts and the National Academy of Design. He sold his first *Post* cover in 1916, and by 1920 he was the *Post's* top cover illustrator.

One of his most distinguished projects was a series of more than seventy sketches depicting the American Family for the Massachusetts Mutual Life Insurance Company, a collection which is now on display at The Norman Rockwell Museum. During World War II, Rockwell's "Four Freedoms" art helped raise more than $130 million in war bond money. Beginning in the early 1970's, Rockwell's works became some of the most frequently sought-out subjects for limited edition collectibles. Today Rockwell limited editions are marketed by firms including The Gorham Company, The Hamilton Collection, and Edwin M. Knowles.

Norman Rockwell continued his productive life as an artist and illustrator in his Stockbridge, Massachusetts studio until his death on November 9, 1978.

ED ROHN

Ed Rohn abandoned his career as a sales manager to pursue his true ambition: sculpting. In the years since he moved his family to a Chicago suburb and established his own porcelain studio, he has grown from an amateur to a skilled professional whose works command five figure prices.

His busts have become prized collectibles, ranging from "The Tramp" and various clowns, to Norman Rockwell and Harry Truman. They are exhibited in prestigious galleries and museums nationwide, testimony to the authenticity and detailing he achieves in the demanding medium of porcelain.

Rohn's first works to be within reach of the ordinary collector were busts of the three basic clown personalities for Roman, Inc., entitled *Three-Ring Portraits*. Also available from Roman is the *Jam Session* series which features busts of jazz musicians.

D.L. "RUSTY" RUST

D.L. Rust (Rusty) was born in Erie, PA in 1932. He worked in various fields of art, from grocery store signs as a high school student in the 1950s to book jacket illustrations. He moved to Florida in 1954 and still resides with his family in Sarasota. In his studio are several looseleaf notebooks filled with photos of his portrait work. The portraits range from smiling cherubic little girls to serious business executives and plump 50th anniversary couples. Active both nationally and internationally in fine arts, he has to his credit more than 400 commissioned portaits, mostly of prominent persons.

Rust met Emmett Kelly in 1962 and has painted his clowns in limited paintings of 250 each. He immortalized his good friend, America's most famous clown, and his unforgettable sad-faced clown character "Weary Willie." This portrait is so accurate that it has been purchased by the Smithsonian Institute in Washington, D.C. and will be on display at the National Portrait Gallery.

ROB SAUBER

Because he often portrays lovely ladies in period attire, it comes as no surprise that Rob Sauber mainains a romantic view of life. His own story reads like a tale from a novel: filled with turns of fortune and lucky coincidences.

Out on his own at age 18, Sauber caught on as a fashion designer for a department store in Raleigh, North Carolina. Then he embarked upon a whirlwind of other occupations including food service, free-lance photography, and illustration. Saving money along the way, Sauber eventually accumulated enough to attend the prestigious Art Center in Los Angeles.

Stints as a studio artist and freelancer followed his schooling before Sauber left California for New York at age 30. Soon,

a famous artists' agent signed Sauber and since then he has advanced steadily as an illustrator, watercolor painter and limited edition plate artist.

Sauber's first plate collection was a four-issue series for Curator Collection entitled *How Do I Love Thee*, inspired by the Elizabeth Barrett Browning poem. More recently, Sauber and Curator collaborated on a romantic collection of eight plates entitled *Portraits of American Brides*. Each painting portrays a young bride from a different American fashion period, surrounded by a typical scene from her generation.

JOHN SEEREY-LESTER

One of Britian's leading artists, John Seerey-Lester crossed the Atlantic recently to live and paint in the United States. Working mainly in oils on canvas, his paintings depict East African and North American wildlife. Over the years, his popularity has spread to many private collectors and dealers alike.

Born in England, John Seerey-Lester trained in art at Salford Technical College and undertook his first professional commission at the age of 13 after taking first prize in a United Kingdom national art competition. A free-lance artist for many years, he turned to easel art full time after several successful one-man shows. Earlier, his subject matter varied considerably, ranging from aviation, landscapes and portraits of nobility to international sports.

Nature now dominates John Seerey-Lester's canvases and his recent work on plates. His interest in wildlife began after visits to the more remote parts of southern Europe and Africa. He continues to travel extensively studying wildlife in its natural habitat. It is the essential research that gives his work the atmosphere and authenticity which makes his paintings so popular with knowledgeable wildlife art collectors.

Seerey-Lester's art has aided many charities, in particular the World Wildlife Fund. His last exhibition in Great Britian in November, 1982, was officially opened by renowned ornithologist and artist, Sir Peter Scott, and was held on behalf of the Fund. The exhibition sold out on the second day, raising thousands of dollars for the preservation of endangered species.

John Seerey-Lester is represented by Mill Pond Press Inc.

TED SIZEMORE

Illustator Ted Sizemore was selected by Gartlan USA, Inc. to create the *Pete Rose Platinum Edition*, a series of sports collectibles designed to honor "Mr. Enthusiasm" for collecting 4,192 hits, breaking Ty Cobb's old record.

Sizemore is no stranger to the sports world. Gartlan USA, Inc. selected Sizemore from among 22 artists, because of his exceptional portrayal of Joe Montana. Sizemore has also been commissioned by other athletes for illustrations to add to their personal collections.

Artist Sizemore produced the artwork for the limited edition plate, plaque and ceramic baseball cards. The ceramic plaque entitled "Desire to Win" pictures both Rose and Cobb, along with remark-

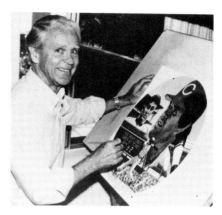

able shots of Cobb about to steal a base, which turns into Rose as he is about ready to dive into the base.

Sizemore worked virtually night and day to produce the artwork for the series, but considers the effort worthwhile. "It was certainly different from anything I had ever done before, but is was exciting, when you consider the historical value," explains Sizemore.

A former resident of southern California, Sizemore now resides in New Hampshire where he continues to do illustrations, including covers for popular romance novels—truly a versatile artist.

RED SKELTON

The fact that he requires no more than three to four hours of sleep per night helps account for Red Skelton's "Renaissance man"-level achievements. Lauded as a "national treasure" for his 40 films and 20 years on television as a comic and mime, Skelton has earned the Governor's Award from the Academy of Television Arts and Sciences. Less well known but equally impressive is his career in music: Skelton has written more than 18,000 musical selections, including 64 symphonies. He also authors books, plays and short stories whenever the mood strikes him.

Skelton always reserves four hours a day, however, for his favorite artistic pursuit: painting. He began "dabbling" in the 1940s and has created hundreds of oils of his favorite subject: clowns. A self-taught artist, Skelton picks up his palette each evening at 10 p.m. and continues painting until 2 a.m.

Red Skelton oil paintings sell for $35,000 to $75,000, and few of the be-

loved comedian's fans can afford them. But since 1976, Skelton has made his art available in a more accessible form: limited edition collector plates. His *Famous Clowns* series began with "Freddie the Freeloader," a self-portrait of the artist playing his beloved clown role. More recently—although Skelton himself does not enjoy active sports—Freddie the Freeloader hit the courts on a porcelain plate entitled "Anyone for Tennis?", and is currently surfing in his latest release, "Ironing the Waves."

Although he is past 70 years of age, Red Skelton regularly schedules himself for 70 to 75 shows and appearances per year. He especially enjoys autographing his fans' collector plates after performances.

GERHARD SKROBEK

Gerhard Skrobek, a master sculptor of the Goebel company, was born in Silesia, the northernmost part of Germany, subsequently moving with his family to Berlin. There, surrounded by museum art treasures and encouraged by his artist mother, young Skrobek became immersed in the heady climate of artistic tradition. From early childhood, he was fascinated with sculpture and its many artistic forms. He studied at the Reimannschule in Berlin, a renowned private academy of the arts, continuing his studies in Coburg. Through one of his professors, he was introduced to porcelain sculpture at the Goebel studios.

Skrobek joined Goebel in 1951, soon becoming one of its leading sculptors and eventually the predominant interpreter of Sister Maria Innocentia Hummel's drawings. It is only he who could have created the nearly eight-foot replica of the "Merry Wanderer", the famous landmark on the front lawn of the Goebel Collectors' Club gallery and museum in Tarrytown, New York. "I am accustomed to creating-normal size figurines from a lump of modelling clay," says Skrobek, "but here I had to work with a very brittle material, and had to bring many forces into play—I became an architect, mason and sculptor all in one!"

In addition to his world-renowned ability at capturing the quality of the two-dimensional artwork of Sister Maria Innocentia Hummel into three-dimensional joyous presentations, Skrobek has contributed his talents to the delightful "In the Spotlight" for members of the Goebel Collectors' Club, with its companion

piece soon to follow. His series, *Today's Children*, the *Co-Boy* and *Charlot Byj* figurines, *Wildlife* Collection, *Childhood Love*, *Childhood Memories*, and many others, are sought after by collectors. Always delighted to meet with collectors, Gerhard looks forward to his visits to North America, and to opportunites to meet friends, both old and new.

JESSIE WILLCOX SMITH

As a contemporary of Howard Pyle, originator of the famed Brandywine school of illustration, Jessie Willcox Smith developed her exceptional gift for art and utilized it as a prolific book illustrator, portraitist and creator of magazine covers. Born in

1863 in Philadelphia, Miss Smith originally planned to become a kindergarten teacher. When one of her instructors encouraged her to pursue more art training, young Jessie vowed to express her love for children in her paintings.

The woman who was to become one of the most acclaimed children's illustrators of all time studied first under Thomas Eakins at the Pennsylvania Academy of Fine Arts. Then she became Pyle's pupil at the Drexel Institute of Arts and Sciences, where she learned from this great master to get to know her subjects and imagine what they thought, felt and did. By following his advice, the children that sprang from Smith's brush came to life.

For Smith, the rewards of her chosen career were many. She became the most highly paid woman illustrator of her day, and the most admired. She illustrated many classic children's books, including *A Child's Garden of Verses*, *The Water Babies*, *Heidi*, and *Little Women*. She also painted portraits of youngsters from wealthy Philadelphia families, but she was most widely known for the *Good Housekeeping* magazine covers which she supplied exclusively from 1918 to 1932.

Today, some of Miss Smith's most charming paintings are available in the form of limited edition collector plates in a series sponsored by The Pennsylvania Academy of the Fine Arts and crafted by Edwin M. Knowles. The series is called *Jessie Willcox Smith Childhood Holiday Memories*.

CHARLES R. SOILEAU

Charles Soileau was born in 1949 in Eunice, Louisiana where he lived and

graduated from Eunice High School. Charles' artistic talent was self-taught; and although he was offered a partial scholarship in fine arts at Tulane University, Charles married and moved to Houston, Texas to pursue a career in commercial art.

Charles was employed by Boone Advertising as its Senior Art Director in 1972. In 1980, Charles formed Soileau Studio, an illustration and graphic design firm. He has since grown from a one man operation to a six-person advertising agency now called Soileau & Associates.

During his career, Charles has received 32 different awards for his illustration and design achievements.

Charles serves on the Board of Directors as Membership Chairman for the Houston Society of Illustrators. He is an active member, past officer on the Board of Directors, and the 1986 Member of the Year recipient for the Business Professional Advertising Association—Houston Chapter.

In 1987, Soileau created *The Roger Staubach Sterling Collection* for Gartlan USA, Inc. to honor Staubach's lifetime of achievement. The line includes ceramic plates, miniature plates, plaques, football cards and lithographs. Soileau painstakingly researched and studied photographs and films of Staubach's playing years from the Cowboys' archives, which enabled him to portray the winning intensity in Staubach's face and penetrating blue eyes.

MORTEN E. SOLBERG

Morten Solberg spent his lifetime developing his unique style of painting. There was never a time when he can remember wanting to be anything other than an artist.

Years of pursuing his craft via design studios and commercial art brought Mort to California where he firmly established himself in the art world with memberships in the American Watercolor Society and the National Watercolor Society. Mort shed his commercial ties and concentrated on fine art. Awards and inclusions in prestigious collections followed.

Mort's interests are many and varied, and they are often reflected in his art. Wildlife, romantic women with parasols, flowers, fishermen, cowboys and American history have provided him with endless colors and shapes with which to design.

His paintings range from tight realism to totally abstract, and he is continually stretching the boundaries of these directions. The combination of these extremes has made his work both unique and popular.

Morton E. Solberg is represented by Mill Pond Press Inc.

IRENE SPENCER

Irene Spencer has long enjoyed recognition as one of America's preeminent artists. Since age nine when she first visited Chicago's Art Institute, Irene sensed her future career as an artist. She was so moved by the paintings there that it became her goal to express herself to others through her painting. Irene began nine years of intensive formal instruction at the Institute, developing the philosophy

that the purpose of art is to improve the quality of life.

Early in her career, Irene had the opportunity to do something many people only dream about: she ran away with the circus. For two years she found vivid and colorful inspiration in the form of clowns, animals and other performers that were captured on her earliest canvases.

After her association with the circus, Irene returned to her home town of Chicago to pursue her career with formal study at the American Academy of Art. Upon graduation, Irene became a commercial artist and gained experience by branching out in several directions. Working for several agencies and doing everything from comic strips to children's books sent Irene on her way to receiving recognition and awards for her outstanding work.

By 1964 Irene had moved to California and developed her own clientele. She was also painting commissioned works for a Beverly Hills gallery. In 1972 she added collector plates to her repertoire and is now one of the industry's most popular artists. Her awards include: Litho of the Year for 1980 and 1981, Plate of the Year for 1981, and the Silver Chalice Awards at the California Plate Collectors Convention in 1982 and 1983. In 1986 she was voted Artist of the Year. One of her first creations for Roman, Inc., the oriental figurine "Flower Princess," was named Figurine of the Year at the same awards ceremony.

Irene's versatility ranges from Western characters to kittens. Roman produces her "Catnippers" figurines and ornaments, as well as plates, figurines and music boxes that celebrate her renowned theme of mother and child.

Ms. Spencer's creativity and commitment to excellence are visible in each of

her works of art. She is a perfectionist in critiquing her issues. Irene spends many hours approving every detail so her collector editions portray the freshness and originality of her art, providing a lasting and valued emotional experience for the admirer. As Ms. Spencer herself says, "My intention in creating is to express, with my best technical ability, a depth of feeling that defies verbal description."

PAUL J. SWEANY

For more than 40 years, Paul J. Sweany has combined his interests in science and art in the creation of exceptionally beautiful naturalist masterworks. Today he reigns as one of America's most honored painters of butterflies, birds and flowers, earning accolades like "a man for all media"..."a vibrant and distinguished artist-teacher"...and "his masterful paintings make the best use of watercolor and composition."

A native of Indiana, Sweany served in the United States Naval Reserve during World War II before completing a Bachelor of Fine Arts degree at the Herron School of Art in Indianapolis. He taught at the Herron School from 1946 to 1976 in many capacities, beginning while still a student. Over the years, Sweany has combined teaching duties with his own naturalist artwork.

Sweany believes that his style of painting has developed through his love of nature. For him, light and atmosphere are tools as important as brush and pigment. He draws heavily upon the traditions of the Old Masters while composing in dramatic and contemporary ways. Sweany

believes that a true artist paints what is as natural to him as eating and breathing.

Paul Sweany has exhibited in more than 125 one-man shows throughout the United States and Europe. He is the recipient of more than 250 awards and has been keynote speaker for several national and state teachers' conventions. Sweany's works may be found in many private and public collections all over the world.

Sweany's first limited edition collector plate series centers upon beautiful butterflies and flowers. Entitled the *Butterfly Garden* Plate Collection, it is a presentation of The Hamilton Collection.

JOAQUIN TEN

Born in 1921 in Valencia, Spain, Joaquin Ten started creating ceramic art

when he was 11 years old. He was influenced by his family who were master ceramists as far back as the seventeenth century.

As a young man, Ten studied art at the College of San Carlos, Center of Ceramic Decoration and Ceramic College of Manises, all located in Valencia, Spain.

After the Spanish Civil War, Ten worked for several ceramic companies. In 1954, he successfully combined porcelain with bronze, which resulted in several innovative designs.

It was in 1961 that Ten achieved his dream by co-founding his own art studio with his brother-in-law Jose Grafia, which they named TENGRA. The company has grown to 100 skilled artisans with the products distributed around the world.

Continuing the family tradition are Ten's daughter who heads the chemical laboratory and his son who heads the export department.

Ten places the emphasis on "art, beauty and quality" as his company continues to create innovative ceramic designs.

ANNALEE THORNDIKE

As the oldest of three daughters, Annalee Davis Thorndike was infatuated with dolls from early childhood. Raised in a large white house in a residential section of Concord, New Hampshire, she grew up in a world of enchantment, her mother an artist and her father a candy maker.

Annalee fondly remembers her childhood activities, particularly her winters spent sledding, skiing and skating. Her dolls are reminiscent of these pastimes, complete with whimsical faces, which display the utter delight experienced by each and every creation.

As a youngster, Annalee loved to make paper dolls and costume them. Her first doll was created at the age of 19 and can be seen today at the Annalee Doll Museum.

Annalee married Chip Thorndike in 1941, and it was after World War II when their chicken farm failed that Annalee turned her doll hobby into a business—with Chip's assistance and eventually that of her family.

The first dolls created were used in displays at department stores like Jordan Marsh, Macy's and Bambergers. Ski dolls were also sold to the New Hampshire State Park and Recreation Department. As the demand for Annalee dolls grew, so did the variety and the facilities. Today, those early dolls, made in 1951-54 during the founding years of Annalee Mobilitee Dolls and originally selling for less than $10 in most instances, have soared over

3000% in resale value. In the last two years, 200 early and more recent dolls have been sold each year at the annual Annalee Doll auction, commanding an astonishing total of approximately $70,000, averaging out to $350 per doll. The actual range of resale value is from $50 to $1,200 depending upon the doll. These auctions, now in their fourth year, and the nationwide interest and membership in the Annalee Doll Society, now over 8,000 strong, have established the Annalee doll as a viable collectible medium.

Today, Annalee creates her dolls at the "Factory in the Woods," nestled among mountains and lakes at the site of the original chicken farm. There are more than 200 dolls in the line, including Santas, ducks, mice, bears, frogs, historical figures and many more, and they are all involved in delightful activites — skiing, playing instruments, sledding, carolling.

What makes Annalee dolls so unique are their faces. As mentioned in an *Annalee* magazine, "She perfected the art of drawing faces by drawing her own face in the mirror in every possible expression-...possibly the reason she is said to resemble her dolls. The smile, the grin, the impishness of childhood, the spontaneous response of boys and girls are all reflected in the faces and poses of Annalee Dolls."

ALTON S. TOBEY

A range of extraordinary portrait commissions has earned Alton S. Tobey an international reputation for art mastery. Educated at Yale, this New York artist has painted General Douglas MacArthur, Arturo Toscanini, Golda Meir and John L. Lewis among many others.

Tobey's murals hang in the Smithsonian Institution, the MacArthur Memorial in Norfolk, Virginia, and in the Hall of Honor at the U.S.S. Intrepid Sea-Air-Space Museum in New York City.

The artist's rich background in anthropology, archeology and history as well as his many years as a fine art painter make him uniquely qualified for a recent commission by the Curator Collection. Tobey's collector plate renderings of Jesus Christ in "Bring to Me the Children," "The Wedding Feast at Cana," and "The Healer" offer sensitive and historically accurate accounts of memorable Biblical events.

For his next Curator Collection plate series, Tobey plans a *Tribute to the 1940s* that will touch the emotions as it recreates the most dramatic moments of the World War II decade.

THORNTON UTZ

The limited edition field has added an exciting new dimension to the many-faceted career of portraitist, fine art painter, illustrator and sculptor Thornton Utz.

Along with Norman Rockwell, Utz provided scores of cover paintings for *The Saturday Evening Post*. His career as an illustrator spanned several decades and included work for nearly every major magazine in the United States.

And during the past ten years or so, Thornton Utz has become known for his portraits and fine art paintings. Utz's appealing style that combines an impressionistic, free-flowing background and a very realistic facial expression has won him international praise.

His list of famous portrait subjects includes the late Princess Grace of Monaco, Astronaut Alan Shepherd, Rosalyn and Amy Carter and other members of the Carter family.

In 1979, Utz and The Hamilton Collection introduced the first issue in his first series of limited edition plates—a piece called "A Friend in the Sky." The plate won the title of "Top First Issue of 1979" in a poll of dealers and collectors.

Later Utz and Hamilton plate offerings include an annual child-subject series which began in 1981, the *Carefree Days* series of boy subjects which premiered in 1982, the *Summer Days of Childhood* series of boy-girl subjects which debuted in 1983, a commemorative plate titled "Princess Grace," and Mother's Day issues for 1983, 1984 and 1985.

Utz's current plate collection is entitled *Springtime of Life*. It is the creation of Reco International, in cooperation with The Hamilton Collection.

Signed and numbered limited edition prints by Utz are published by Mill Pond Press Inc.

PAMELLA AND NOEL VALENTINE

Pamella and Noel Valentine create exquisite dolls called *Valentine Ladies* in their doll house workshop in San Francisco.

Pamella, a native of Australia, was the daughter of a skilled dressmaker who taught her to sew when she was five years old. As a child, any time Pamella wanted something new to wear, she designed and created outfits herself. Later, Pamella was employed to sew "after five" outfits and wedding gowns.

In 1969, she met her husband Noel, and together they moved to San Francisco where their hobby of dressing antique dolls soon became a full-time occupation. Their first major accomplishment was designing a Marie Antoinette gown for a life-size mannequin. This created great interest, and soon Pam and Noel began making gowns for antique dolls.

"Doll collectors would always remark that our gowns were so beautifully and meticulously finished that we should put them on porcelain dolls," said Pamella. "We were determined to produce the best doll possible in terms of looks, proportion and body style, so it took us almost three

years to finally put our first porcelain 'Lady' on the market," she added.

Pamella designs all the costumes and works on the dolls' skirts, frills, trims, hats and parasols. She also creates every mohair wig, making each piece look as natural as possible. Noel handles most of the hand and machine sewing, working on the bodices, sleeves, crinolines, wiring of hat brims and other intricate details.

In 1986 the Valentines decided to bring their collectible dolls to a larger audience. The resulting partnership with Gorham has launched a collection of nine *Valentine Ladies* true in every detail of design and quality to the originals created by Pam and Noel.

Because the Valentines are so detailed in their work, Gorham has been sure to reproduce their designs with just as much care and attention. Each doll is porcelain from head to toe, and every gown is made with the finest materials.

In summing up the relationship between themselves and Gorham Noel says, "We have been fortunate to win every competition we have entered in New England and Los Angeles. Now, a prestigious firm like Gorham will give us the opportunity to share our pride and joy with all its collectors."

ABBIE WILLIAMS

Late in the 1900s, Abbie Williams' great-grandparents honeymooned in East Boothbay, Maine. This established a family tradition, and each summer for generations the artist's family returned to the small coast town.

Ms. Williams settled permanently in the Boothbay area in the early 1970s. Born in New Jersey, she had studied illustration at Moore College of Fine Arts in

Philadelphia. In her new home she met Frances Hook, who was to have a profound influence on her art. The kinship between the two artists was so strong that Ms. Williams studied with Mrs. Hook. Under Mrs. Hook's direction, her technique was refined and matured. Through Mrs. Hook, she also obtained valuable illustration and portrait commissions which enabled her to exhibit her work.

Mrs. Hook also introduced Abbie to Roman, Inc. Her first collector plate series, *The Magic of Childhood*, depicted the warm friendships between children and animals. Her second series uses youngsters to illustrate eight phrases of *The Lord's Prayer*. Both plate series are also

available through The Hamilton Collection.

Ms. Williams' most recent work for Roman is a unique christening plate and medallion which may be personalized with details of a child's baptism. She has just created her first sculptured music boxes for the company.

DAVID WINTER

The son of internationally famous sculptress Faith Winter and an army colonel, David Winter was born in Catterick, Yorkshire, England. Winter's mother is renowned for her Falklands War Memorial and a critically acclaimed bust of Princess Anne. Originally from Ireland, Mrs. Winter's family includes numerous architects, which may help explain the life work of her son: combining three-dimensional art with miniature architecture in the creation of his David Winter Cottages.

Winter studied sculpture in school, where he developed a keen appreciation of the lives of his ancestors. When he met

John Hine in 1978, he found a friend and partner who shared his enthusiasm for the buildings and way of life of the past. Together, Winter and Hine developed their idea for the first David Winter cottage. Called "The Millhouse," it was crafted in 1979.

Before long, many English shops were requesting the miniature cottages of the fledgling firm. Operating from an old coal shed, Winter did the artwork while Hine concentrated on selling the cottages inspired by beloved old buildings of the English countryside.

In the studio, Winter becomes completely absorbed in his work. He seems to imagine the movements of the people who might be inside a cottage he is preparing—whether they be royalty, lords of the manor, or simply peasants. He insists that every window frame, brick and roof tile be completely authentic to the period. Thus since many of the buildings are old, Winter includes crooked, old beams, warped roofs and twisted chimneys, just as they might be found in a tour of historic Great Britain.

Winter often makes his own tools for sculpting, to ensure that he can achieve the effects that he seeks. Some tools are crafted from bits of wire, while others might involve matchsticks or bits of wood. Once his wax models are complete, the studios of John Hine cast, trim and paint each cottage by hand according to Winter's own careful instructions. Since the first cottage was introduced less than a decade ago, David Winter has created an impressive range including castles, manor houses, shops, mills, and cottages and hamlets of many sizes and styles.

Reading/Conventions/Clubs/Special Events
Enrich Your Collecting Experience by Reading About Your Hobby and Participating in Various Organizations and Events

Books

Whether your special area of interest is plates, figurines, bells, graphics, steins or dolls—or some combination of these collecting media—you'll find a great deal of material available to you in collectibles books and periodicals. The books listed here are some of the most prominent in the limited edition collectibles field—there are many more available. To find more books in your area of interest, check "Books in Print" by subject at your local library, or contact a book seller that specializes in limited editions such as the Collector Books, P.O. Box 3009, Paducah, KY 42001.

The Blue Book of Dolls and Values by Jan Foulke. Hobby House Press Inc., Cumberland, Maryland.

The Bradford Book of Collector's Plates, edited by the staff of The Bradford Exchange, Ltd., Niles, Illinois 60648.

Collectibles: A Compendium by Marian Klamkin. Published by Dolphin Books, Doubleday & Company Inc., Garden City, New York.

The Collectors Encyclopedia of Dolls by Dorothy S. Coleman. Published by Crown Publishers, One Park Avenue, New York, New York 10016.

The Collector's History of Dolls by Constance Aileen King. Published by Bonanza Books, New York.

The Collector's Wedgwood by Robin Reilly. Published by Portfolio Press, Huntington, New York.

Contemporary Western Artists. Published by Southwest Art Publishing.

Developing Your Doll Collection by Loretta Holz. Published by Crown Publishers, One Park Avenue, New York, New York 10016.

The Dictionary of Wedgwood by Robin Reilly and George Savage. Published by the Antique Collectors' Club Ltd., Baron Publishing, Woodbridge, Suffolk, England.

The Encyclopedia of Collectibles. Published by Time-Life Books, Time & Life Building, Chicago, Illinois 60611.

The Golden Anniversary Album: M.I. Hummel. Published by Portfolio Press, R.D.1, Huntington, New York 11743.

Greenbook Guide to the Enesco Precious Moments™ Collection. Published by Greenbook, Old Coach at Main, Box 515, East Setauket, New York 11733.

Kovel's Antiques and Collectibles Price List by Ralph and Terry Kovel. Published by Crown Publishers, One Park Avenue, New York, New York 10016.

The Kovels' Illustrated Price Guide to Royal Doulton by Ralph and Terry Kovel. Published by Crown

Publishers, One Park Avenue, New York, New York 10016.

Norman Rockwell Art and Collectibles by Carl F. Lucky. Published by Books Americana Inc., Florence, Alabama 35630.

Norman Rockwell Collectibles Value Guide by Mary Moline. Published by Rumbleseat Press, Inc., San Francisco, California 94123.

The No. 1 Price Guide to M.I. Hummel® by Robert L. Miller. Published by Portfolio Press, Huntington, New York 11743.

The Official Price Guide to Collector Plates. Published by The House of Collectibles, Inc., New York, New York 10022.

The Official Guide to Collector Prints. Published by The House of Collectibles, Inc., New York, New York 10022.

Painting A Brighter World. Published by Plate World Magazine, Niles, Illinois 60648.

Plate Collecting by Eleanor Clark. Published by Citadel Press, Secaucus, New York 07094.

Price Guide to Twentieth Century Dolls by Carol Gast Glassmire. Published by Wallace-Homestead Book Company, 1912 Grand Avenue, Des Moines, Iowa 50305.

Wildlife and Wilderness: An Artist's World by Keith Chackleton. Published by Watson-Guptill Publications, New York, New York 10036.

Wildlife Artists at Work. Published by Watson-Guptill, New York, New York 10036.

Wildlife Painting: Techniques of Modern Masters. Published by Watson-Guptill, New York, New York 10036.

With a Little Luck... by Helen Boehm. Published by Rawson Associates, New York, New York.

Wonderful World of Plates by Louise Schaub Witt. Published by K&L Publications, Box 38, Shawnee Mission, Kansas 66201.

Magazines and Newsletters

The following are independent periodicals about the limited editions field. Many firms also publish newsletters and magazines which they provide free or at nominal cost to their collectors or preferred customers. For subscription information on the publications listed here, write them directly.

AMERICAN ARTIST
1 Color Court
Marion, Ohio 43305

ANTIQUE & COLLECTING
   HOBBIES
1006 S. Michigan
Chicago, Illinois 60605
(312) 939-4767

THE ANTIQUE TRADER
P.O. Box 1050
Dubuque, Iowa 52001
(319) 588-2073

ART TODAY
P.O. Box 1468
Alton, Illinois 62002

THE ARTIST'S MAGAZINE
P.O. Box 1999
Marion, Ohio 43305

COLLECTOR EDITIONS
170 Fifth Avenue
New York, New York 10010
(212) 989-8700

COLLECTORS MART
15100 West Kellogg
Wichita, Kansas 67235
(316) 722-9650

COLLECTORS NEWS
P.O. Box 156
Grundy Center, Iowa 50638
(319) 824-5456

COLLECTORS' SHOWCASE
P.O. Box 6929
San Diego, California 92106
(619) 222-0386

DOLLS MAGAZINE
170 Fifth Avenue
New York, New York 10010
(212) 989-8700

THE DOLL READER
c/o Hobby House Press
900 Frederick Street
Cumberland, Maryland 21502

DOLL NEWS
P.O. Box 14146
Parkville, Missouri 64152
(816) 741-1002

FINE ART & AUCTION REVIEW
2227 Grandville Street
Vancouver, B.C.
V6H 3G1

GOEBEL MINIATURES NEWSLETTER
Country Cousin
P.O. Box 522
Occoquan, VA 22125-0522

INSIGHT ON COLLECTIBLES
R.R. 1, P.O. Box 130
Durham, Ontario
N0G 10R

KOVELS ON ANTIQUES AND
   COLLECTIBLES
P.O. Box 22200
Beachwood, Ohio 44122

MIDWEST ART
7831 East Bush Lake Road
Minneapolis, Minnesota 55435-3875

PLATE WORLD
9200 N. Maryland Avenue
Niles, Illinois 60648
(312) 763-7773

PRINTS
P.O. Box 1468
Alton, Illinois 62002
(618) 462-1468

ROCKWELL SOCIETY NEWS
597 Saw Mill River Road
Ardsley, New York 10502
(914) 693-8800

SOUTHWEST ART
P.O. Box 13037
Houston, Texas 77219

SPORTING CLASSICS
Subscriber Service Center
P.O. Box 2200
Patterson, New York 12563

WILDLIFE ART NEWS
Suite 2, 1245 Carlson Lake Lane
Eagan, Minnesota 55123

Clubs and Conventions

For many collectors, the enjoyment of their hobbies grows even richer when they can share it with others. Getting in touch with fellow collectors to learn...to socialize...and to admire each others' "finds" adds an extra dimension of pleasure to the collecting field.

In recent years, scores of local clubs for limited edition collectors have become active. Some are sponsored by a dealer, while others are completely collector-run and sponsored. In addition, a number of manufacturers sponsor clubs for people who enjoy collecting their products.

Local clubs meet once a month or perhaps every-other month, in most cases. Most charge modest dues in the area of $5 - $10 per person or $10 - $15 per couple annually. Programs may range from members' own presentations to celebrity appearances by top artists. Many manufacturers are producing films about their artists and creative processes, which are available to clubs at no charge or nominal charge for loan. Many clubs also serve refreshments, offer door prizes, monthly swap and sell programs, and other activities.

Manufacturers' clubs may or may not have local organizations with meetings. They usually offer exclusive products to members, as well as newsletters, "insider information," travel tours and other benefits. Some charge a yearly dues fee of $10 to $50, while others have purchase requirements which lead to membership.

Collectors clubs offer the opportunity to learn about the various companies and artists that produce and create limited edition collectibles. Many clubs offer welcome gifts, as well as newsletters and magazines to maintain regular contact with their club members.

Local collector clubs are located throughout the country, much to the delight of collectors. The International Plate Collectors Guild meets the first Sunday of each month at the Artesia Community Center in Artesia, California. The left photograph shows Irish McCalla, popular artist and guest speaker at the local club meeintg. She is talking to club members as she signs pictures for the collectors as a memento of the event. The annual Fourth of July meeting (right) show members dressed in red, white and blue to honor this special day.

Several times a year, conventions in the U.S. and Canada attract collectors from all over the country to view the latest limited editions, meet favorite artists, swap and sell collectibles and enjoy each others' company.

For specific information about dues, benefits, or how to join, please contact the club or clubs which interest you. And if you know of a club which has not been mentioned here, please contact COLLECTORS' INFORMATION BUREAU so that we may list it in our next update.

American Bell Association Convention

AMERICAN BELL ASSOCIATION
c/o Louise Collins
Alter Road, Box 386
Natrona Heights, Pennsylvania 15065

THE ANNALEE DOLL SOCIETY
P.O. Box 1137
Meredith, New Hampshire 03253

THE BELLEEK COLLECTORS'
  SOCIETY
1 Chapin Road
P.O. Box 675
Pine Brook, New Jersey 07058
    or
Villeroy & Boch Ltd.
55A East Beaver Creek Road
Richmond Hill Ontario
L4B 1E8

THE BOEHM PORCELAIN
  SOCIETY
Edward Marshall Boehm, Inc.
P.O. Box 5051
Trenton, New Jersey 08638

P. BUCKLEY MOSS SOCIETY
P.O. Box 486
Wayne, Michigan 48184

CLUB ANRI
55 Pacella Park Drive
Randolph, Massachusetts 02368

THE COLLECTORS GUILD
(David Winter Cottages)
P.O. Box 8048
Blaine, Washington 98230

DOWNS' COLLECTORS CLUB
2778 35th Street
Milwaukee, Wisconsin 53215

EKJ COLLECTORS SOCIETY
(Emmett Kelly, Jr)
P.O. Box 93507
Atlanta, Georgia 30318

FOXFIRE FARM CLUB
(Lowell Davis)
c/o Schmid
55 Pacella Park Drive
Randolph, Massachusetts 02368

THE FRANKLIN MINT
  COLLECTORS SOCIETY
The Franklin Mint
Franklin Center, Pennsylvania 19091

GOEBEL COLLECTORS' CLUB
Division of Goebel Art (GmbH) Inc.
105 White Plains Road
Tarrytown, New York 10591
    or
Goebel Canada
100 Carnforth Road
Toronto, Ontario M4A 2K7

THE GORHAM COLLECTOR'S
  GUILD
P.O. Box 6150
Providence, Rhode Island 02940

GUTMANN COLLECTORS CLUB
  INC.
P.O. Box 486
Neptune, New Jersey 07754

JAN HAGARA COLLECTORS'
  CLUB
40114 Industrial Park North
Georgetown, Texas 78626

INTERNATIONAL PLATE
  COLLECTORS GUILD
c/o Marge Rosenberg
P.O. Box 487
Artesia, California 90701

JERRI COLLECTOR'S SOCIETY
P.O. Box 14087
3238 Robinson Circle
Charlotte, North Carolina 28206

LLADRO COLLECTORS SOCIETY
P.O. Box 1122, 43 West 57th Street
New York, New York 10101-1122

MADAME ALEXANDER (DOLL)
  FAN CLUB
P.O. Box 146
New Lenox, Illinois 60451

ORIGINAL PRINT COLLECTORS
GROUP, LTD.
19 E. 70th Street
New York, New York 10021

THE POLLAND COLLECTORS
SOCIETY
P.O. Box 2468
Prescott, Arizona 86302

PRECIOUS MOMENTS
COLLECTORS CLUB
One Enesco Plaza P.O. Box 1466
Elk Grove Village, Illinois 60007

ROCKWELL SOCIETY OF
AMERICA
597 Saw Mill River Road
Ardsley, New York 10502

ROYAL DOULTON USA
700 Cottontail Lane
Somerset, New Jersey 08873
or

DOULTON CANADA
850 Progress Avenue
Scarborough, Ontario
M1H 3C4

SEBASTIAN MINIATURE
COLLECTORS SOCIETY
321 Central Street
Hudson, Massachusetts 01749

STEIN-A-MONTH CLUB
House of Tyrol, Beer Stein Collector's
Catalog
P.O. Box 909
Gateway Plaza
Cleveland, Georgia 30528

STEIN COLLECTORS
INTERNATIONAL
P.O. Box 11782
Ft. Lauderdale, Florida 33339

SWAROVSKI COLLECTORS
SOCIETY
One Kenney Drive
Cranston, Rhode Island 02920-8381

THE WEDGWOOD COLLECTORS
SOCIETY
41 Madison Avenue
New York, New York 10010

UNITED FEDERATION OF DOLL
CLUBS
P.O. Box 14146
Parkville, Missouri 64152

UNITED STATES HISTORICAL
SOCIETY
First and Main Streets
Richmond, Virginia 23219

DONALD ZOLAN COLLECTOR'S
SOCIETY
133 East Carrillo Street
Santa Barbara, California 93101

Collectors' Conventions

The last few years have seen a boom in full-scale conventions for limited edition collectors. In addition to these large, annual gatherings—which draw anywhere from 3,000 to 30,000 collectors or more over a period of two to three days—a number of regional and local shows are held either annually or on a periodic basis. From time to time a manufacturer or dealer will sponsor an Artists' Fair or Festival as well. Dealers often schedule open houses with specific artists, too.

AMERICAN BELL ASSOCIATION
CONVENTION
Annually in the summer
1988 Hartford, Connecticut: hosted by The New
England Chapter of the American Bell
Association.
1989 Torrance, California: hosted by The
Southern California Campanology Club
Write: Louise Collins
Box 286
R.D. 1
Natrona Heights, Pennsylvania 15065
(412) 295-9623

ART EXPO NEW YORK
Sponsored by International Art Exposition, Inc.
Annually in April: Jacob Javitz Convention Center
Annually in fall: Los Angeles Convention Center
Late fall: Sydney Convention and Exhibition
Center
Write: Art International Exposition, Inc.
747 3rd Avenue 36th floor
New York, New York 10017
(212) 418-4288

CALIFORNIA PLATE & COLLECTIBLES
SHOW
Sponsored by Verity Enteprises
Pasadena, California

Annually in early spring
Write: C.P.C.S.
3089 Clairemont Dr., Sutie 327
San Diego, California 92117
(619) 571-3359 (ask for Jim Woodward)

CANADIAN COLLECTIBLE SHOW AND
SALE
Durham, Ontario
Annually in summer
Write: Lynn Enright
P.O. Box 130
Durham, Ontario N0G 1R0
(519) 369-5157

COLLECTIBLE SHOWCASE EAST
Kingston, Ontario
Annually in early summer
Write: Erin Hess
P.O. Box 2278
Kingston, Ontario K7L 5J9
(613) 549-4066

INTERNATIONAL PLATE
& COLLECTIBLE EXPOSITION
Sponsored by Watson's Collectors Club and the
National Association of Limited
Edition Dealers
Century Center, South Bend, Indiana

Annually in July
Write: Joyce Zielinski
Watson's
135 E. Michigan
New Carlisle, Indiana 46552
(219) 654-3695

STEIN COLLECTORS INTERNATIONAL
CONVENTION
Sponsored by Stein Collectors International
Annually in July
1988: St. Louis, Missouri
1989: Dearborn, Michigan
1990: West Germany
Mid-winter mini-conventions in January
Write: Stein Collectors International
P.O. Box 11782
Ft. Lauderdale, Florida 33339
(305) 772-4490

UNITED FEDERATION OF DOLL CLUBS
NATIONAL DOLL CLUB CONVENTION
Sponsored by United Federation of Doll Clubs
Annually in August
1988: Anaheim, California
1989: St. Louis, Missouri
Write: P.O. Box 14146
Parkville, Missouri 64152
(816) 741-1002

Special Events

Special Events within the collectibles industry come in many different forms — an award, a special gathering, friends. All events help to shape the industry, perhaps tell the "story behind the story," and share with the collectors that special feeling that comes with owning a treasured piece of limited edition artwork.

Precious Moments kids Debbie and Mickey join 1987 Easter Seal Child, Susie Wilcox of Connecticut, for a special encounter. Susie meets with Pat Boone, right, national campaign chairman and telethon host, and Eugene Freedman, president of Enesco Imports Corporation, producer of the first Precious Moments Easter Seal figurine. Freedman holds a poster depicting the poignant sculpture, "He Walks with Me." (left) A new company, Kaiser Porcelain (US) has been formed in Niagara Falls, New York. "For some time, it has been my ambition that Kaiser should have its own operation in the United States, says Mr. Kaiser. Mr. Michael C. O'Laughlin (left), Chief Burgomaster of Niagara Falls, congratulates Mr. Hubert Kaiser (right), President of Kaiser Porcelain, to the formation of his new company in the United States. As a symbolic gesture, the Burgomaster presents the golden key of the town to Mr. Kaiser in front of the famous Niagara Falls. (center) Artist Edna Hibel of Edna Hibel Corporation, was selected by the Special Olympics International to create the only commemorative for its Seventh International Summer Special Olympics Games. The commemorative, a 9 1/2" porcelain collector plate featuring three winners proudly displaying their gold medals, boasts twenty colors plus Hibel's renowned 22 karat gold overlay and a 24 karat gold rim. Entitled "Triumph!-Everyone A Winner," this exclusive commemorative plate is limited to an edition of 19,500 worldwide. (right)

Annalee doll collectors are in attendance at the annual barbecue and auction. Wayne Mock, auctioneer, holds Annalee Doll Soceity members' attention, as several pieces are auctioned during this very popular event.

Joan Ostroff, vice president and executive director of the Goebel Collectors' Club receives New York State Resolution proclaiming May 21, 1987 as Maria Innocentia Hummel Day. The presentation was made by Delores Kenneth, chairperson of the Resolution planning committee and member of the Goebel Collectors' Club Great South Bay and Long Island Chapters.

Carthage, Missouri was the setting for the 10th annual Midwest Gathering of the Artists, which is held every September. Show coordinator Dallie Miessner said approximately 7,500 people attended the three-day event. A highlight of the show was a Saturday night barbecue at Lowell Davis' Foxfire Farm. About 1,300 collectors from every state in the union were on hand to eat beans cooked in old iron kettles, roasted pig and dance to country music. Visitors also attended the art show and auction during the event. On the left, Don Polland (l) and a collector view Polland's artwork and right, Lowell Davis (r) converses with one of the visitors.

Paul A. Schmid III, president of Schmid, congratulates Christopher Gorecki of Blaine, Minnesota, first place winner of a 1987 Frances Hook art scholarship. Paul A. Schmid III was master of ceremonies for the annual dinner dance and auction, held during the International Plate and Collectibles Exposition in South Bend, Indiana. "The young artists we are honoring at tonight's dinner are tomorrow's stars, commented Schmid. "This evening's efforts will go a long way towards helping these young people further their art studies. We are privileged to honor Frances Hook again, as we acknowledge fresh artistic works that have surely been touched by her spirit."

The Sebastian line of figurines has for the past five years introduced into production of the time period of one year a special item to raise proceeds for the Jimmy Fund. The Jimmy Fund benefits the Dana Farber Cancer Institute in Boston. The series was started by Mr. Baston five years ago and the first two pieces were sculpted by him. After his death, his son Woody continued the series, and this year introduced a football player as the fifth and final piece. Over the course of the period, more than $25,000 has been raised to help combat cancer in young children. The 1986 check presentation pictures from left to right, Margery Baston, Scott Baston, Woody Baston (the sculptor), Jim Rice (left fielder for the Boston Red Sox), Doris Edwards, Sherman Edwards and Craig Edwards (owners of Stacy's Gifts and Collectables in Walpole, Massachusetts.)

Glossary

You can better appreciate your hobby by acquainting yourself with commonly used terms referred to by collectors and dealers to describe limited edition collectibles. This list is not all-inclusive, but it will provide a good starting point for approaching the collectibles field. When a term that you don't understand is used, chances are you can find it here. If not, write the COLLECTORS' INFORMATION BUREAU and we'll do our best to define the term for you—and add it to next year's list.

COMMON ABBREVIATIONS

FE—First edition
FI—First issue
LE—Limited edition
M.I.B.—
   In mint condition,
   and in original box

MIN—Miniature
NR—Norman Rockwell
VAL—Valentine's Day
X—Xmas, or Christmas

ALABASTER. A compact, fine-textured gypsum which is usually white and translucent. Some collector plates are made of a material called *ivory* alabaster, which is not translucent, but has the look and patina of old ivory.

ALLOTMENT. The number within a limited edition which a manufacturer allows to a given dealer, direct marketer or collector.

ANNUAL. The term commonly used to describe a plate or other limited edition which is issued yearly, i.e. the Goebel Hummel *annual* plate. Many annual plates commemorate holidays or anniversaries, but they are commonly named by that special date, i.e. the Bing & Grondahl *Christmas* plate, issued annually to commemorate Christmas.

ARTIST PROOF. Originally, the first few in an edition of lithographs or prints created for the artist's approval. Now, many editions contain a small number of prints which are marked A/P instead of numbering—basically as a means of increasing the number in the edition.

BABY DOLL. A doll with the proportions of a baby, with lips parted to take a nipple, and chubby, short-limbed body.

BACKSTAMP. The information on the back of a plate or other limited edition, which serves to document it as part of its limited edition. This information may be hand-painted onto the plate, or it may be incised, or applied by means of a transfer (decal). Typical information which may appear on the backstamp includes the name of the series, name of the item, year of issue, some information about the subject, the artist's name and/or signature, the edition limit, the item's number within that edition, initials of firing master or other production supervisor, etc.

A typical plate backstamp.

BAND. Also known as a rim, as in "24K gold banded, or rimmed." A typical method of finishing or decorating a plate, bell or stein is to band it in gold, platinum or silver. The firing process allows the precious material to adhere to the piece.

BAS-RELIEF. A technique in which the collectible has a raised design. This design may be achieved by pouring liquid material into a mold before firing, or by applying material to the flat surface of a plate, figurine, stein or other "blank" piece.

BAVARIA. A section of Germany known as one of the world's richest sources of kaolin clay—an essential component for fine porcelain production. Bavaria is home to a number of renowned porcelain factories.

BEDROOM DEALER. Slang term for an individual who functions as a small-scale seller of limited edition collectibles, usually from his or her home. Often unable to purchase at wholesale direct from manufacturers, these dealers may buy items at a discount from a larger dealer and then resell at a small profit.

BISQUE OR BISCUIT. A fired ware which has neither a glaze nor enamel applied to it. Bisque may be white or colored. It gets its name from its biscuit-like, matte texture.

BLUE CHIP. Slang for a well-established series that some believe represents a safe and sound collectibles investment. An interesting play on words in that many of the plate series that fall into this category are Copenhagen or Cobalt blue.

BODY. The basic form of a plate, figurine, bell or other item, or its component materials.

BONE ASH. By means of heat, animal bones are reduced to powder as an ingredient for bone china or porcelain. The name of the resulting powder is calcium phosphate, or bone ash.

BONE CHINA/BONE PORCELAIN. Bone porcelain is similar to hard porcelain in its ingredients, except that calcined bone ash comprises a large percentage of the mix and is the primary contributor to the vitrification and translucency. Bone clay allows for extreme thinness and translucency without the sacrifice of strength and durability.

BOTTOMSTAMP. Same idea as the backstamp, but usually refers to documentation material which appears on the bottom of a figurine or stein. On a bell, such information may appear on the inside.

BYE-LO BABY. Grace Storey Putnam copyrighted this life-sized baby (three days old) in 1922. This style of baby doll is much in fashion today among limited edition collectors.

CAMEO. Relief decoration with a flat surface around it, similar to the look of a jeweler's cameo. A technique used by Wedgwood, Incolay and Avondale among others.

CAST. When liquid clay, or slip, is poured into a mold and hardened. Most often used for figurines, bells, and many other forms.

CERAMIC. The generic term for a piece which is made of some form of clay and finished by firing at high temperatures.

CERTIFICATE/CERTIFICATE OF AUTHENTICITY. A document which accompanies a limited edition item to establish its place within the limited edition. Such a Certificate may include information such as the series name, item title, artist's name and/or signature, brief description of the item and its subject, signatures of sponsoring and marketing organization representatives, and other documentation material along with the item's in-dividual number or a statement of the edition limit.

CHARACTER DOLLS. Usually made of bisque or composition, these dolls are created to resemble a real person, usually an actor or other celebrity.

"Juliet," from Gorham, is an example of a character doll.

CHARACTER STEIN. A stein with a shape designed to represent an object, person, or an animal.

CHINA. Originally "china" referred to all wares which came from China. Now this term means products which are fired at a high temperature. China usually is comprised of varying percentages of kaolin clay, feldspar and quartz. Also known as "porcelain."

CHRISTMAS SERIES. Plates, figurines, bells, and other collectible items which are issued to commemorate this yearly holiday, but which normally are sold and displayed all year.

CINNABAR. A red mineral found in volcanic regions, and a principal ingredient in mercury. This material is frequently used to create collectors' items.

CIRE PERDUE. See lost wax.

CLAY. A general term for the materials used to make ceramic items. Malleable when moist, clay becomes hard and strong when fired. It may be composed of any number of earthen materials.

CLOISONNE. An enameling process in which thin metal strips are soldered in place on a base to create a pattern, and then enamel is poured in to provide the color.

CLOSED-END SERIES. A group of limited edition plates, figurines or other collectibles which comprise a specific number—be it 2, 4, 6, 8, 12 or more. This number normally is disclosed when the series begins.

COBALT BLUE. Also known as Copenhagen blue, this rich color is a favorite of ceramicists because it can withstand high firing temperatures. Cobalt oxide is a black powder when applied, but fires to a deep blue.

COLD CAST. A metal powder and a binder are forced into a mold or die under high pressure, and thus a forging process occurs. Allows for exceptional detail and creates pieces which take well to handpainting.

COLLECTOR PLATE. A limited edition plate which is created with the expressed intent that it be collected.

COMMEMORATIVE. An item created to mark a special date, holiday or event.

DEALER. The individual or store from whom a collector purchases plates, bells, and other items at retail.

DECAL. Also known as a transfer, this is a lithographic or silkscreen rendering of a piece of artwork, which is applied to a ceramic, metal, glass or other material and then fired on to fuse it to the surface.

DELFTWARE. Heavy earthenware with a tin glaze. First developed in Delft, Holland in the 16th century.

DISTRIBUTOR. A person in the collectibles market who buys from a manufacturer and sells to dealers, who in turn sell to individual collectors.

EARTHENWARE. A non-vitrified ceramic, composed of ball clay, kaolin, and pegmatite. Most often glazed and fired.

EDITION. The term which refers to the number of items created with the same name and decoration.

ETCHED. Refers to a stein. The name commonly given to a type of stoneware that used colored clays or colored clay slips to form a smooth matte-finished decora-

tion; this decoration was probably applied from the inside, with a distinctive incised black outlining of uniformly colored areas.

FAIENCE. Named after an Italian town called Faenza, faience is similar to Delftware in that it is a tin-glazed earthenware. Also similar to Majolica.

FELDSPAR. When decomposed, this mineral becomes kaolin, which is the essential ingredient in china and porcelain. When left in its undecomposed form, feldspar adds hardness to a ware.

FIRE. To heat, and thus harden, a ceramic ware in a kiln.

FIRING PERIOD. A time period—usuall 10 to 100 days—which serves to limit an edition, usually of plates. The number of items made is limited to the capacity of the manufacturer over that 10-to-100-day period.

FIRST ISSUE. The premiere item in a series, whether closed-ended or open-ended.

FRENCH BRONZE. Also known as "spelter," this is zinc refined to 99.97% purity. This material has been used as an alternate to bronze for casting for more than a century.

GLAZE. The liquid material which is applied to a ware to serve various purposes: cosmetically, it provides shine and decorative value. It also makes the item more durable. Decorations may be applied before or after glaze is applied.

GRAPHIC. A print produced by one of the "original" print processes such as etchings, engravings, woodblocks, lithographs and serigraphs.

HALLMARK. The mark or logo of the manufacturer of an item.

HARD PASTE PORCELAIN. The hardest porcelain made, this material uses feldspar to enhance vitrification and translucency, and is fired at about 2642 degrees Farenheit.

INCISED. Writing or design which is cut into the piece—may provide a backstamp or a decorative purpose.

INCOLAY STONE. A man-made material combining minerals including carnelain and crystal quartz. Used to make cameo-style plates by Incolay Studios.

INLAY. To fill an etched or incised design with another material such as enamel, metal or jewels.

INLAID. In reference to steins, a theory that proposes that the colored clays or clay slips used in the production of etched stonewares were applied from the outside.

IN STOCK. Refers to prints in a given edition which are still available from the publisher's inventory.

ISSUE. As a verb, to introduce. As a noun, this term means an item within a series or edition.

ISSUE PRICE. The original price upon introduction of a limited edition, established by its manufacturer or principle marketer.

JASPER WARE. Josiah Wedgwood's unglazed stoneware material, first introduced in the 1770s. Although Jasper is white in its original form, it can be stained throughout in various colors. Wedgwood typically offers Jasper in the medium blue called "Wedgwood Blue," as well as a darker blue, black, green, lilac, yellow, brown and grey. Some other colors have resulted through continued experimentation. Colored Wedgwood "bodies" often are decorated with white bas-relief, or vice-versa.

KAOLIN. The essential ingredient in china and porcelain, this special clay is found in quantity at several spots throughout the world—and it is there that many famous porcelain houses have developed. These areas include Bavaria in Germany, and the Limoges region of France.

LEAD CRYSTAL. Lead oxide gives this glass its weight and brilliance, as well as its clear ring. Lead crystal has a lead oxide content of 24%, while "full" lead crystal contains more than 30%.

LIMITED EDITION. An item produced only in a certain quantity or only during a certain time period. The typical ways in which collectibles editions are limited include: limited by number; limited by year; limited by specific time period; limited by firing period.

LIMOGES. A town in France which boasts a large deposit of kaolin clay, the essential ingredient in china and porcelain. Home of a number of top porcelain manufacturers.

LOST WAX. A wax "positive" is created by a sculptor, and used to create a ceramic "negative" shell. Then the ceramic shell becomes the original mold—basis for working molds used in the creation of an edition. A classic method of creating three-dimensional pieces.

LOW INVENTORY. Is the classification given an edition which has been 85% or more sold out by the publisher.

MAJOLICA. Similar to Delftware and Faience, this is a glazed earthenware first made on the Spanish island, Majorca.

MARKET. The buy-sell medium for collectibles.

MARKS OR MARKINGS. The logo or insignia which certifies that an item is made by a particular firm.

MINT CONDITION. A term originally related to the coin collecting hobby, this means that a limited edition item is still in its original, like-new condition, with all accompanying documents.

MOLD. The form which supplies the shape for a plate, figurine, bell, doll, or other item.

OCCUPATIONAL STEIN. A stein with a decoration or shape that depicts or symbolizes an occupation, probably the occupation of the original owner of the stein.

OPEN-ENDED SERIES. A collection of plates or other limited editions which appear at intervals, usually annually, with no limit as to the number of years in which they will be produced. As an example, the Bing & Grondahl Christmas series has been produced annually since 1895, with no end in sight.

OVERGLAZE. A decoration which is applied to an item after its original glazing and firing.

PASTE. The raw material of porcelain before shaping and firing.

PEWTER. A material composed of 80% tin and 20% antimony and brass or copper (fine pewter) or lesser amounts of copper and antimony (pewter).

PORCELAIN. Made of kaolin, quartz and feldspar, porcelain is fired at up to 1450 degrees Centigrade. Porcelain is noted for

its translucency and its true ring. Also called "china".

POTTERY. Ceramic ware, more specifically that which is earthenware or non-vitrified. Also a term for the manufacturing plant where such objects are made and fired.

PRIMARY MARKET. The buy-sell arrangement whereby individuals purchase collectibles direct from their manufacturer, or through a dealer, at issue price.

PRINTED REMARQUE. A hand drawn image by the artist that is photomechanically reproduced in the margin of a print.

A Simon Combes remarque that was drawn on his print "Wildebeest Migration." Each remarque is individually drawn by the artist.

PRINT. A photomechanical reproduction process such as offset lithography, collotypes and letterpress.

QUEEN'S WARE. Cream-colored earthenware developed by Josiah Wedgwood, now used as a generic term for similar materials.

QUOTE. The average selling price of a collectible at any given time—may be at issue, or above or below.

REGIMENTAL, RESERVIST'S OR MILITARY STEIN. A stein that was purchased as a souvenir of the service in the Imperial German Armies, generally dated between 1890 and 1914.

RELEASE PRICE. Is that price for which each print in the edition is sold until the edition is Sold Out and a secondary market (collector price) is established.

This Lladro annual Christmas bell is decorated in bas-relief with a trio of carolers reveling in the falling snow.

RELIEF. A raised design in various levels above a background.

REMARQUE. A hand drawn original image by the artist, either pencil, pen & ink, watercolor or oil that is drawn in the margin of a limited edition print.

SECOND. An item which is not first quality, and should not be included in the limited edition. Normally such items should be destroyed or at least marked on the backstamp or bottomstamp to indicate that they are not first quality.

SECONDARY MARKET. Once the original edition has been sold out, the buying and selling among collectors, through dealers or exchanges, takes place on the "secondary" market.

SECONDARY MARKET PRICE. The retail price that a customer is willing to sell/buy a print that is no longer available from the publisher. These prices will vary from one territory to another depending upon the popularity and demand for the subject in each particular area.

SERIGRAPHY. A direct printing process whereby the artist designs, makes and prints his own stencils. A serigraph differs from other prints in that its images are created with paint films instead of printing inks.

SIGNED & NUMBERED. Each individual print is signed and consecutively numbered by the artist, in pencil, either in the image area or in the margin. Edition size is limited.

SIGNED IN THE PLATE. The only signature on the print is printed from the artist's original signature. Not necessarily limited in edition size.

SIGNED ONLY. Usually refers to a print that is signed without consecutive numbers. Not limited in edition size.

SOLD OUT. Is the classification given an edition which has been 100% sold out by the publisher.

STEIN. A drinking vessel with a handle and an attached lid. Sometimes similar vessels without lids are still called steins. Stein literally means 'stone' and is probably a shortened form of 'Steinzeugkruge,' or 'stoneware tankard.'

STONEWARE. A vitrified ceramic material, usually a silicate clay that is very hard, rather heavy and impervious to liquids and most stains.

TERRA COTTA. A reddish earthenware, or a general term for any fired clay.

TIN GLAZE. The glaze used on Delftware, Faience or Majolica, this material allows for a heavy, white and opaque surfce after firing.

TRANSFER. See Decal.

TRANSLUCENCY. Allowing light to shine through a non-transparent object. A positive quality of fine porcelain or china.

TRIPTYCH. a three-panel art piece, often of religious significance.

UNDERGLAZE. A decoration which is applied before the final glazing and firing of a plate or other item. Most often, such a decoration is painted by hand.

VITRIFICATION. The process by which a ceramic body becomes vitrified, or totally non-poros, at high temperaturs.

Collectors' Information Bureau

PRICE INDEX

To Limited-Edition Plates, Figurines, Bells, Graphics, Steins and Dolls

1988

This index includes several thousand of the most widely-traded limited editions in today's collectibles market. It is based upon interviews with more than a score of the most experienced and well-informed limited edition dealers in the United States, as well as several independent market advisors.

If you should find that a specific, contemporary limited edition, plate, figurine, bell, graphic, stein or doll in which you are interested is not included in the Index, write the Collectors' Information Bureau. We will do our best to provide a current quote. The address is: 2059 Edgewood S.E., Grand Rapids, MI 49506

HOW TO USE THIS INDEX

Listings are set up using the following format:

Company	Series
Company Name	Series Name

Number*	Name	Artist	Edition Limit	Issue Price	Current Price
See Below	Item Name	First Initial Last Name	Number or Time Period	In U.S. Dollars	Average of Input

Number

Each item in the index has been assigned an individual number for ease of access on computer. Here is how to interpret these numbers: Sample Number: 70-P-BG-03-002
Interpretation:

70 = 1970 (year of issue)

P = Plate (category) - others are F for Figurine, B for Bell, G for Graphic, S for Stein, D for Doll.

BG = Maker, Bing & Grongahl. Each firm is assigned a two-letter code.

03 = Series number for Bing & Grondahl plates. Each series within a category has a series number, but they are not necessarily chronological.

002 = Item number within series 3 of Bing & Grondahl. Each item has a sequential number within its series.

A Special Note to All Precious Moments Collectors:

Each ENESCO Precious Moments subject is engraved with a special annual mark. This emblem changes with each production year. The Collector value for each piece varies because of these distinctive yearly markings. Our pricing reflects an average for all years.

TERMS AND ABBREVIATIONS

Annual - Issued once a year
Closed - An item or series no longer in production
Happy Traveler 190/11 - The numbers refer to the Goebel mold code in the figurine section
Open - Not limited by number or time—available until manufacturer stops production, "retires" or "closes" the item or series
Retrd - Retired
Set - Refers to two or more items issued together for a single price

Suspd - Suspended (not currently being produced; may be produced in the future)
Time — Limited to a specific production or reservation period, usually defined by a closing date
Undis. - Undisclosed
Unkn. - Unknown
Yr. Iss. - Year of issue (limited to a calendar year)
28-day, 10-day, etc. - limited to this number of production (or firing) days—usually not consecutive

Number	Name	Artist	Edition limit	Issue Price	Quote
Company		**Series**			
Anri		**Anri Wooden Christmas Bells**			
76-B-AO-01-001	Christmas	J. Ferrandiz	Yr.Iss	6.00	50.00
77-B-AO-01-002	Christmas	J. Ferrandiz	Yr.Iss	7.00	42.00
78-B-AO-01-003	Christmas	J. Ferrandiz	Yr.Iss	10.00	40.00
79-B-AO-01-004	Christmas	J. Ferrandiz	Yr.Iss	13.00	30.00
80-B-AO-01-005	The Christmas King	J. Ferrandiz	Yr.Iss	17.50	18.50
81-B-AO-01-006	Lighting The Way	J. Ferrandiz	Yr.Iss	18.50	18.50
82-B-AO-01-007	Caring	J. Ferrandiz	Yr.Iss	18.50	18.50
83-B-AO-01-008	Behold	J. Ferrandiz	Yr.Iss	18.50	18.50
85-B-AO-01-009	Nature's Dream	J. Ferrandiz	Yr.Iss	18.50	18.50
Anri		**Juan Ferrandiz Musical Christmas Bells**			
76-B-AO-02-001	Christmas	J. Ferrandiz	Yr.Iss	25.00	80.00
77-B-AO-02-002	Christmas	J. Ferrandiz	Yr.Iss	25.00	80.00
78-B-AO-02-003	Christmas	J. Ferrandiz	Yr.Iss	35.00	75.00
79-B-AO-02-004	Christmas	J. Ferrandiz	Yr.Iss	47.50	60.00
80-B-AO-02-005	Little Drummer Boy	J. Ferrandiz	Yr.Iss	60.00	63.00
81-B-AO-02-006	The Good Shepherd Boy	J. Ferrandiz	Yr.Iss	63.00	63.00
82-B-AO-02-007	Spreading the Word	J. Ferrandiz	Yr.Iss	63.00	63.00
83-B-AO-02-008	Companions	J. Ferrandiz	Yr.Iss	63.00	63.00
84-B-AO-02-009	With Love	J. Ferrandiz	Yr.Iss	55.00	55.00
Artists of the World		**DeGrazia Bells**			
80-B-AW-01-001	Los Ninos	T. DeGrazia	7,500	40.00	65.00
80-B-AW-01-002	Festival of Lights	T. DeGrazia	5,000	40.00	55.00
Brown & Bigelow Inc.		**Brown & Bigelow Bells**			
79-B-BP-01-001	The Runaway	N. Rockwell	9,800	30.00	30.00
Brown & Bigelow Inc.		**A Boy and His Dog Silver Bells**			
80-B-BP-02-001	Mysterious Malady	N. Rockwell	9,800	60.00	60.00
80-B-BP-02-002	Pride of Parenthood	N. Rockwell	9,800	60.00	60.00
Crown & Rose		**12 Days of Christmas**			
78-B-CI-01-001	Partridge in a Pear Tree	M. Dinkel	7,500	50.00	300.00
79-B-CI-01-002	Two Turtle Doves	M. Dinkel	7,500	55.00	78.00
80-B-CI-01-003	Three French Hens	M. Dinkel	7,500	60.00	78.00
81-B-CI-01-004	Four Calling Birds	J. Spouse	7,500	70.00	78.00
82-B-CI-01-005	Five Golden Rings	J. Bergdahl	7,500	75.00	78.00
83-B-CI-01-006	Six Geese a' laying	J. Bergdahl	7,500	75.00	78.00
84-B-CI-01-007	Seven Swans a' Swimming	J. Bergdahl	7,500	78.00	78.00
Curator Collection		**Bells**			
87-B-CX-01-001	Newborn Bell	R. Sauber	Unkn.	25.00	25.00
87-B-CX-01-002	Motherhood Bell	R. Sauber	Unkn.	25.00	25.00
87-B-CX-01-003	Fatherhood Bell	R. Sauber	Unkn.	25.00	25.00
87-B-CX-01-004	Sweet Sixteen Bell	R. Sauber	Unkn.	25.00	25.00
Danbury Mint		**Various**			
75-B-DA-01-001	Doctor and Doll	N. Rockwell	None	27.50	54.00
76-B-DA-01-002	Grandpa Snowman	N. Rockwell	None	27.50	44.00
76-B-DA-01-003	Freedom From Want	N. Rockwell	None	27.50	44.00
76-B-DA-01-004	No Swimming	N. Rockwell	None	27.50	44.00
76-B-DA-01-005	Saying Grace	N. Rockwell	None	27.50	44.00
76-B-DA-01-006	The Discovery	N. Rockwell	None	27.50	44.00
77-B-DA-01-007	The Runaway	N. Rockwell	None	27.50	40.00
77-B-DA-01-008	Knuckles Down	N. Rockwell	None	27.50	40.00
77-B-DA-01-009	Tom Sawyer	N. Rockwell	None	27.50	40.00
77-B-DA-01-010	Puppy Love	N. Rockwell	None	27.50	40.00
77-B-DA-01-011	Santa's Mail	N. Rockwell	None	27.50	40.00
77-B-DA-01-012	The Remedy	N. Rockwell	None	27.50	40.00
Danbury Mint		**The Wonderful World of Norman Rockwell**			
79-B-DA-02-001	Grandpa's Girl	N. Rockwell	None	27.50	29.50
79-B-DA-02-002	Leapfrog	N. Rockwell	None	27.50	29.50
79-B-DA-02-003	Baby-Sitter	N. Rockwell	None	27.50	29.50
79-B-DA-02-004	Batter Up	N. Rockwell	None	27.50	29.50
79-B-DA-02-005	Back to School	N. Rockwell	None	27.50	29.50
79-B-DA-02-006	Gramps at the Reins	N. Rockwell	None	27.50	29.50
79-B-DA-02-007	Friend in Need	N. Rockwell	None	27.50	29.50
79-B-DA-02-008	Puppy in the Pocket	N. Rockwell	None	27.50	29.50
Danbury Mint		**The Norman Rockwell Commemorative Bell**			
79-B-DA-03-001	Triple Self-Portrait	N. Rockwell	None	29.50	35.00
Enesco Imports Corporation		**Annual Bells**			
83-B-EA-01-001	Surrounded With Joy - E-0522	S. Butcher	Open	18.00	18.00
82-B-EA-01-002	I'll Play My Drum for Him - E-2358	S. Butcher	Open	17.00	17.00
84-B-EA-01-003	Wishing You a Merry Christmas - E-5393	S. Butcher	Open	19.00	19.00
81-B-EA-01-004	Let the Heaven's Rejoice - E-5622	S. Butcher	Open	15.00	15.00
85-B-EA-01-005	God Sent His Love - 15873	S. Butcher	Open	19.00	19.00
Enesco Imports Corporation		**Various Bells**			
81-B-EA-02-001	Jesus Loves Me - E-5208	S. Butcher	Suspd.	15.00	38.00
81-B-EA-02-002	Jesus Loves Me - E-5209	S. Butcher	Suspd.	15.00	38.00
81-B-EA-02-003	Prayer Changes Things - E-5210	S. Butcher	Suspd.	15.00	38.00
81-B-EA-02-004	God Understands - E-5211	S. Butcher	Retrd.	15.00	55-85.00
81-B-EA-02-005	We Have Seen His Star - E-5620	S. Butcher	Suspd.	15.00	19.00
81-B-EA-02-006	Jesus Is Born - E-5623	S. Butcher	Suspd.	15.00	19.00
82-B-EA-02-007	The Lord Bless You and Keep You - E-7175	S. Butcher	Suspd.	17.00	19.00
82-B-EA-02-008	The Lord Bless You and Keep You - E-7176	S. Butcher	Suspd.	17.00	19.00
82-B-EA-02-009	The Lord Bless You and Keep You - E-7179	S. Butcher	Open	22.50	30.00
82-B-EA-02-010	Mother Sew Dear - E-7181	S. Butcher	Open	17.00	22.50
82-B-EA-02-011	The Purr-fect Grandma - E-7183	S. Butcher	Open	17.00	22.50
86-B-EA-02-012	Wishing You a Cozy Christmas - 102318	S. Butcher	Open	20.00	20.00
Goebel		**M. I. Hummel Collectibles Annual Bells**			
78-B-GG-01-001	Let's Sing 700	M. I. Hummel	Annual	50.00	145.00
79-B-GG-01-002	Farewell 701	M. I. Hummel	Annual	70.00	70.00
80-B-GG-01-003	Thoughtful 702	M. I. Hummel	Annual	85.00	85.00
81-B-GG-01-004	In Tune 703	M. I. Hummel	Annual	85.00	85.00
82-B-GG-01-005	She Loves Me, She Loves Me Not 704	M. I. Hummel	Annual	90.00	90.00
83-B-GG-01-006	Knit One 705	M. I. Hummel	Annual	90.00	90.00
84-B-GG-01-007	Mountaineer 706	M. I. Hummel	Annual	90.00	90.00
85-B-GG-01-008	Sweet Song	M. I. Hummel	Annual	90.00	90.00
86-B-GG-01-009	Sing Along	M. I. Hummel	Annual	100.00	100.00
87-B-GG-01-010	With Loving Greetings 709	M. I. Hummel	Yr.Iss	110.00	110.00
87-B-GG-01-011	Busy Student (Hum 710)	M. I. Hummel	Annual	Unknown	Unknown
Gorham		**Various**			
75-B-GO-01-001	Sweet Song So Young	N. Rockwell	Annual	19.50	50.00
75-B-GO-01-002	Santa's Helpers	N. Rockwell	Annual	19.50	30.00
75-B-GO-01-003	Tavern Sign Painter	N. Rockwell	Annual	19.50	30.00
76-B-GO-01-004	Flowers in Tender Bloom	N. Rockwell	Annual	19.50	40.00
76-B-GO-01-005	Snow Sculpture	N. Rockwell	Annual	19.50	45.00
77-B-GO-01-006	Fondly Do We Remember	N. Rockwell	Annual	19.50	55.00
77-B-GO-01-007	Chilling Chore (Christmas)	N. Rockwell	Annual	19.50	35.00
78-B-GO-01-008	Gaily Sharing Vintage Times	N. Rockwell	Annual	22.50	22.50
78-B-GO-01-009	Gay Blades (Christmas)	N. Rockwell	Annual	22.50	22.50
79-B-GO-01-010	Beguiling Buttercup	N. Rockwell	Annual	24.50	26.50
79-B-GO-01-011	A Boy Meets His Dog (Christmas)	N. Rockwell	Annual	24.50	30.00
80-B-GO-01-012	Flying High	N. Rockwell	Annual	27.50	27.50
80-B-GO-01-013	Chilly Reception (Christmas)	N. Rockwell	Annual	27.50	27.50
81-B-GO-01-014	Sweet Serenade	N. Rockwell	Annual	27.50	27.50
81-B-GO-01-015	Ski Skills (Christmas)	N. Rockwell	Annual	27.50	27.50
82-B-GO-01-016	Young Mans Fancy	N. Rockwell	Annual	29.50	29.50
82-B-GO-01-017	Coal Season's Coming	N. Rockwell	Annual	29.50	29.50
83-B-GO-01-018	Christmas Medley	N. Rockwell	Annual	29.50	29.50
83-B-GO-01-019	The Milkmaid	N. Rockwell	Annual	29.50	29.50
84-B-GO-01-020	Tiny Tim	N. Rockwell	Annual	29.50	29.50
84-B-GO-01-021	Young Love	N. Rockwell	Annual	29.50	29.50
84-B-GO-01-022	Marriage License	N. Rockwell	Open	32.50	32.50
85-B-GO-01-023	Yuletide Reflections	N. Rockwell	5,000	32.50	32.50
84-B-GO-01-024	Yarn Spinner	N. Rockwell	5,000	32.50	32.50
86-B-GO-01-025	Home For The Holidays	N. Rockwell	5,000	32.50	32.50
86-B-GO-01-026	On Top of the World	N. Rockwell	5,000	32.50	32.50
87-B-GO-01-027	Merry Christmas Grandma	N. Rockwell	5,000	32.50	32.50
87-B-GO-01-028	The Artist	N. Rockwell	5,000	32.50	32.50
Gorham		**Currier & Ives - Mini Bells**			
76-B-GO-02-001	Christmas Sleigh Ride	Currier & Ives	Annual	9.95	35.00
77-B-GO-02-002	American Homestead	Currier & Ives	Annual	9.95	25.00
78-B-GO-02-003	Yule Logs	Currier & Ives	Annual	12.95	20.00
79-B-GO-02-004	Sleigh Ride	Currier & Ives	Annual	14.95	20.00
80-B-GO-02-005	Christmas in the Country	Currier & Ives	Annual	14.95	20.00
81-B-GO-02-006	Christmas Tree	Currier & Ives	Annual	14.95	17.50
82-B-GO-02-007	Christmas Visitation	Currier & Ives	Annual	16.50	17.50
83-B-GO-02-008	Winter Wonderland	Currier & Ives	Annual	16.50	17.50
84-B-GO-02-009	Hitching Up	Currier & Ives	Annual	16.50	17.50
85-B-GO-02-010	Skaters Holiday	Currier & Ives	Annual	17.50	17.50
86-B-GO-02-011	Central Park in Winter	Currier & Ives	Annual	17.50	17.50
87-B-GO-02-012	Early Winter	Currier & Ives	Annual	19.00	19.00
Gorham		**Mini Bells**			
81-B-GO-03-001	Tiny Tim	N. Rockwell	Annual	19.75	19.75
82-B-GO-03-002	Planning Christmas Visit	N. Rockwell	Annual	20.00	20.00
Hamilton Mint		**Four Seasons Silver Bells**			
80-B-HJ-01-001	Adventurers Between Adventures	N. Rockwell	9,800	57.00	57.00
80-B-HJ-01-002	The Mysterious Malady	N. Rockwell	9,800	57.00	57.00
80-B-HJ-01-003	Pride of Parenthood	N. Rockwell	9,800	57.00	57.00
80-B-HJ-01-004	A Boy Meets His Dog	N. Rockwell	9,800	57.00	57.00
Kaiser		**Kaiser Christmas Bells**			
78-B-KA-01-001	The Nativity	T. Schoener	15,000	60.00	60.00
79-B-KA-01-002	Eskimo Christmas	N. Peter	15,000	60.00	60.00
80-B-KA-01-003	Sleigh Ride at Christmas	K. Bauer	15,000	60.00	60.00
81-B-KA-01-004	Snowman	K. Bauer	15,000	60.00	60.00
Kaiser		**Kaiser Tree Ornament Bells**			
79-B-KA-02-001	The Carolers	K. Bauer	Yr.Iss	27.50	27.50
80-B-KA-02-002	Holiday Snowman	K. Bauer	Yr.Iss	30.00	30.00
81-B-KA-02-003	Christmas at Home	K. Bauer	Yr.Iss	30.00	30.00
82-B-KA-02-004	Christmas in the City	K. Bauer	Yr.Iss	30.00	30.00
Lladro		**Lladro Christmas Bell**			
87-B-LL-01-001	Christmas Bell - L5458	Lladro	Annual	29.50	29.50
Lincoln Mint		**Lincoln Bells**			
75-B-LM-01-001	Downhill Daring	N. Rockwell	None	25.00	70.00
Norman Rockwell Museum		**Collectors Bells**			
82-B-NO-01-001	Wedding/Anniversary	N. Rockwell	Open	45.00	45.00
82-B-NO-01-002	25th Anniversary	N. Rockwell	Open	45.00	45.00
82-B-NO-01-003	50th Anniversary	N. Rockwell	Open	45.00	45.00
82-B-NO-01-004	For A Good Boy	N. Rockwell	Open	45.00	45.00
Pickard		**Christmas Carol Bell Series**			
77-B-PI-01-001	The First Noel	Unknown	3,000	75.00	75.00
78-B-PI-01-002	O Little Town of Bethlehem	Unknown	3,000	75.00	75.00
79-B-PI-01-003	Silent Night	Unknown	3,000	80.00	80.00
80-B-PI-01-004	Hark! The Herald Angels Sing	Unknown	3,000	80.00	80.00
Reco International		**Joyous Moments**			
80-B-RA-01-001	I Love You	J. McClelland	5,000	25.00	25.00
81-B-RA-01-002	Sea Echoes	J. McClelland	5,000	25.00	25.00
82-B-RA-01-003	Talk to Me	J. McClelland	5,000	25.00	25.00
River Shore		**Rockwell Children Series I**			
77-B-RG-01-001	School Play	N. Rockwell	7,500	30.00	75.00
77-B-RG-01-002	First Day of School	N. Rockwell	7,500	30.00	75.00
77-B-RG-01-003	Football Hero	N. Rockwell	7,500	30.00	75.00
77-B-RG-01-004	Flowers for Mother	N. Rockwell	7,500	30.00	60.00
River Shore		**Rockwell Children Series II**			
78-B-RG-02-001	Dressing Up	N. Rockwell	15,000	35.00	50.00
78-B-RG-02-002	Future All American	N. Rockwell	15,000	35.00	52.00
78-B-RG-02-003	Garden Girl	N. Rockwell	15,000	35.00	40.00
78-B-RG-02-004	Five Cents A Glass	N. Rockwell	15,000	35.00	40.00
River Shore		**World of Children Bell Collection**			
79-B-RG-03-001	Allison	R. Brown	15,000	50.00	50.00
79-B-RG-03-002	Rei-Ling	Y. R. Hicks	15,000	50.00	50.00
80-B-RG-03-003	Katrina	R. Brown	15,000	50.00	50.00
80-B-RG-03-004	Kuluk	Y. R. Hicks	15,000	50.00	50.00
River Shore		**Norman Rockwell Single Issues**			
81-B-RG-04-001	Looking Out to Sea	N. Rockwell	7,000	45.00	95.00
81-B-RG-04-002	Spring Flowers	N. Rockwell	347	175.00	175.00
82-B-RG-04-003	Grandpa's Guardian	N. Rockwell	7,000	45.00	45.00
River Shore		**Grant Wood Bell**			
82-B-RG-05-001	American Gothic	G. Wood	7,000	50.00	50.00
Roman, Inc.		**The Masterpiece Collection**			
79-B-RO-01-001	Adoration	F. Lippe	Open	20.00	20.00
80-B-RO-01-002	Madonna with Grapes	P. Mignard	Open	25.00	25.00
81-B-RO-01-003	The Holy Family	G. Notti	Open	25.00	25.00
82-B-RO-01-004	Madonna of the Streets	R. Ferruzzi	Open	25.00	25.00
Roman, Inc.		**F. Hook Bells**			
85-B-RO-02-001	Beach Buddies	F. Hook	15,000	25.00	25.00
86-B-RO-02-002	Sounds of the Sea	F. Hook	15,000	25.00	25.00
87-B-RO-02-003	Bear Hug	F. Hook	15,000	25.00	25.00
Sandstone Creations		**A Fantasy Edition**			
80-B-SB-01-001	Little Prayer	T. DeGrazia	7,500	40.00	40.00
81-B-SB-01-002	Flower Vendor	T. DeGrazia	7,500	40.00	40.00

Number	Name	Artist	Edition limit	Issue Price	Quote
Company		**Series**			
XX-B-SB-01-003	Wee Three	T. DeGrazia	7,500	40.00	40.00
XX-B-SB-01-004	Party Time	T. DeGrazia	7,500	40.00	40.00
Schmid		**Berta Hummel Christmas Bells**			
72-B-SC-02-001	Angel with Flute	B. Hummel	Yr.Iss	20.00	75.00
73-B-SC-02-002	Nativity	B. Hummel	Yr.Iss	15.00	80.00
74-B-SC-02-003	The Guardian Angel	B. Hummel	Yr.Iss	17.50	45.00
75-B-SC-02-004	The Christmas Child	B. Hummel	Yr.Iss	22.50	45.00
76-B-SC-02-005	Sacred Journey	B. Hummel	Yr.Iss	22.50	25.00
77-B-SC-02-006	Herald Angel	B. Hummel	Yr.Iss	22.50	50.00
78-B-SC-02-007	Heavenly Trio	B. Hummel	Yr.Iss	27.50	40.00
79-B-SC-02-008	Starlight Angel	B. Hummel	Yr.Iss	38.00	45.00
80-B-SC-02-009	Parade into Toyland	B. Hummel	Yr.Iss	45.00	55.00
81-B-SC-02-010	A Time to Remember	B. Hummel	Yr.Iss	45.00	55.00
82-B-SC-02-011	Angelic Procession	B. Hummel	Yr.Iss	45.00	50.00
83-B-SC-02-012	Angelic Messenger	B. Hummel	Yr.Iss	45.00	55.00
84-B-SC-02-013	A Gift from Heaven	B. Hummel	Yr.Iss	45.00	75.00
85-B-SC-02-014	Heavenly Light	B. Hummel	Yr.Iss	45.00	75.00
86-B-SC-02-015	Tell the Heavens	B. Hummel	Yr.Iss	45.00	45.00
87-B-SC-02-016	Angelic Gifts	B. Hummel	Yr.Iss	47.50	47.50
Schmid		**Berta Hummel Mother's Day Bells**			
76-B-SC-03-001	Devotion for Mothers	B. Hummel	Yr.Iss	22.50	55.00
77-B-SC-03-002	Moonlight Return	B. Hummel	Yr.Iss	22.50	45.00
78-B-SC-03-003	Afternoon Stroll	B. Hummel	Yr.Iss	27.50	45.00
79-B-SC-03-004	Cherub's Gift	B. Hummel	Yr.Iss	38.00	45.00
80-B-SC-03-005	Mother's Little Helper	B. Hummel	Yr.Iss	45.00	45.00
81-B-SC-03-006	Playtime	B. Hummel	Yr.Iss	45.00	45.00
82-B-SC-03-007	The Flower Basket	B. Hummel	Yr.Iss	45.00	45.00
83-B-SC-03-008	Spring Bouquet	B. Hummel	Yr.Iss	45.00	45.00
84-B-SC-03-009	A Joy to Share	B. Hummel	Yr.Iss	45.00	45.00
Schmid		**Peanuts Annual Bells**			
79-B-SC-06-001	A Special Letter	C. Schulz	10,000	15.00	25.00
80-B-SC-06-002	Waiting For Santa	C. Schulz	10,000	15.00	25.00
81-B-SC-06-003	Mission For Mom	C. Schulz	10,000	17.50	20.00
82-B-SC-06-004	Perfect Performance	C. Schulz	10,000	18.50	18.50
83-B-SC-06-005	Peanuts in Concert	C. Schulz	10,000	12.50	12.50
84-B-SC-06-006	Snoopy and the Beagle Scouts	C. Schulz	10,000	12.50	12.50
Schmid		**Peanuts Christmas Bells**			
75-B-SC-07-001	Woodstock, Santa Claus	C. Schulz	Yr.Iss	10.00	25.00
76-B-SC-07-002	Woodstock's Christmas	C. Schulz	Yr.Iss	10.00	25.00
77-B-SC-07-003	Deck the Doghouse	C. Schulz	Yr.Iss	10.00	20.00
78-B-SC-07-004	Filling the Stocking	C. Schulz	Yr.Iss	13.00	15.00
Schmid		**Peanuts Mother's Day Bells**			
73-B-SC-08-001	Mom?	C. Schulz	Yr.Iss	5.00	15.00
74-B-SC-08-002	Snoppy/Woodstock/Parade	C. Schulz	Yr.Iss	5.00	15.00
76-B-SC-08-003	Linus and Snoopy	C. Schulz	Yr.Iss	10.00	15.00
77-B-SC-08-004	Dear Mom	C. Schulz	Yr.Iss	10.00	15.00
78-B-SC-08-005	Thoughts That Count	C. Schulz	Yr.Iss	13.00	15.00
Schmid		**Peanuts Special Edition Bell**			
76-B-SC-09-001	Bi-Centennial	C. Schulz	Yr.Iss	10.00	20.00
Schmid/B.F.A.		**RFD Bell**			
79-B-SD-01-001	Blossom	L. Davis	Closed	65.00	135.00
79-B-SD-01-002	Kate	L. Davis	Closed	65.00	135.00
79-B-SD-01-003	Willy	L. Davis	Closed	65.00	135.00
79-B-SD-01-004	Caruso	L. Davis	Closed	65.00	135.00
79-B-SD-01-005	Wilbur	L. Davis	Closed	65.00	135.00
79-B-SD-01-006	Old Blue Lead	L. Davis	Closed	65.00	135.00
Swarovski America		**Bells**			
XX-B-SW-01-001	Large Dinner Bell	Unknown	Open	80.00	100.00
87-B-SW-01-002	Medium Dinner Bell	Unknown	Open	80.00	80.00
87-B-SW-01-003	Small Dinner Bell	Unknown	Open	60.00	60.00
Vague Shadows		**Annual Bell Ornament**			
85-B-VC-01-001	Home Sweet Wigwam	G. Perillo	Open	14.00	14.00
86-B-VC-01-002	Peek-A-Boo	G. Perillo	Open	15.00	15.00
87-B-VC-01-003	Annual Bell Ornament	G. Perillo	Open	15.00	15.00
Vague Shadows		**Sagebrush Kids**			
85-B-VC-02-001	Hail to the Chief	G. Perillo	Open	19.50	19.50
85-B-VC-02-002	Dressing Up	G. Perillo	Open	19.50	19.50
85-B-VC-02-003	Favorite Kachina	G. Perillo	Open	19.50	19.50
85-B-VC-02-004	Message of Joy	G. Perillo	Open	19.50	19.50
85-B-VC-02-005	Boots	G. Perillo	Open	19.50	19.50
85-B-VC-02-006	Stay Awhile	G. Perillo	Open	19.50	19.50
85-B-VC-02-007	Room for Two?	G. Perillo	Open	19.50	19.50
85-B-VC-02-008	Blue Bird	G. Perillo	Open	19.50	19.50
85-B-VC-02-009	Ouch!	G. Perillo	Closed	19.50	19.50
85-B-VC-02-010	Take One	G. Perillo	Closed	19.50	19.50
86-B-VC-02-011	The Long Wait	G. Perillo	Open	19.50	19.50
86-B-VC-02-012	Westward Ho!	G. Perillo	Open	19.50	19.50
86-B-VC-02-013	Finishing Touches	G. Perillo	Open	19.50	19.50
86-B-VC-02-014	Deputies	G. Perillo	Open	19.50	19.50
86-B-VC-02-015	Country Music	G. Perillo	Open	19.50	19.50
86-B-VC-02-016	Practice Makes Perfect	G. Perillo	Open	19.50	19.50
86-B-VC-02-017	The Hiding Place	G. Perillo	Open	19.50	19.50
86-B-VC-02-018	Prarie Prayers	G. Perillo	Open	19.50	19.50
87-B-VC-02-019	Just Picked	G. Perillo	Open	19.50	19.50
87-B-VC-02-020	Row, Row	G. Perillo	Open	19.50	19.50
87-B-VC-02-021	My Papoose	G. Perillo	Open	19.50	19.50
87-B-VC-02-022	Playing House	G. Perillo	Open	19.50	19.50
87-B-VC-02-023	Wagon Train	G. Perillo	Open	19.50	19.50
87-B-VC-02-024	Small Talk	G. Perillo	Open	19.50	19.50
Vague Shadows		**Sagebrush Kids Bell Ornament**			
87-B-VC-03-001	The Fiddler	G. Perillo	Open	9.00	9.00
87-B-VC-03-002	The Harpist	G. Perillo	Open	9.00	9.00
87-B-VC-03-003	Christmas Horn	G. Perillo	Open	9.00	9.00
87-B-VC-03-004	The Gift	G. Perillo	Open	9.00	9.00
87-B-VC-03-005	Christmas Candle	G. Perillo	Open	9.00	9.00
87-B-VC-03-006	The Carolers	G. Perillo	Open	9.00	9.00
Vague Shadows		**Sagebrush Kids Christmas Caravan**			
87-B-VC-04-001	Leading the Way	G. Perillo	Open	90.00	90.00
87-B-VC-04-002	Sleepy Sentinels	G. Perillo	Open	45.00	45.00
87-B-VC-04-003	Singing Praises	G. Perillo	Open	45.00	45.00
87-B-VC-04-004	Gold, Frankincense & Presents	G. Perillo	Open	35.00	35.00
87-B-VC-04-005	Complete Set	G. Perillo	Open	185.00	185.00
Wedgwood		**New Year Bells**			
79-B-WE-01-001	Penguins	Unknown	Annual	40.00	40.00
80-B-WE-01-002	Polar Bears	Unknown	Annual	50.00	50.00
81-B-WE-01-003	Moose	Unknown	Annual	55.00	55.00
82-B-WE-01-004	Fur Seals	Unknown	Annual	60.00	60.00

Number	Name	Artist	Edition limit	Issue Price	Quote
Company		**Series**			
83-B-WE-01-005	Ibex	Unknown	Annual	64.00	64.00
84-B-WE-01-006	Puffin	Unknown	Annual	64.00	64.00
85-B-WE-01-007	Ermine	Unknown	Annual	64.00	64.00

Dolls

Number	Name	Artist	Edition limit	Issue Price	Quote
Annalee Mobilitee		**Annalee Mobilitee Dolls**			
83-D-AP-01-001	18″ Bob Cratchett and Tiny Tim	Annalee Thorndike	1770	49.95	400.00
57-D-AP-01-002	10″ Boy Building a Boat	Annalee Thorndike	Unkn.	9.95	500.00
74-D-AP-01-003	7″ Black Santa	Annalee Thorndike	1,157	5.50	250.00
68-D-AP-01-004	7″ Scuba Diver	Annalee Thorndike	Unkn.	3.00	225.00
76-D-AP-01-005	10″ Uncle Sam	Annalee Thorndike	1,095	6.00	300.00
77-D-AP-01-006	8″ Purple Rooster	Annalee Thorndike	1,642	6.00	250.00
75-D-AP-01-007	8″ White Rooster	Annalee Thorndike	1,767	5.50	300.00
72-D-AP-01-008	10″ Mushroom with 7″ Santa	Annalee Thorndike	540	7.00	325.00
76-D-AP-01-009	10″ Donkey	Annalee Thorndike	1,202	6.00	175.00
76-D-AP-01-010	10″ Elephant	Annalee Thorndike	1,232	6.00	175.00
82-D-AP-01-011	22″ Christmas Giraffe with 10″ Elf	Annalee Thorndike	488	44.00	250.00
74-D-AP-01-012	12″ Granny Mouse	Annalee Thorndike	1,135	13.50	225.00
74-D-AP-01-013	12″ Grandpa Mouse	Annalee Thorndike	1,103	13.50	225.00
76-D-AP-01-014	18″ Scarecrow	Annalee Thorndike	916	13.50	175.00
74-D-AP-01-015	36″ Reindeer with 18″ Santa's Helper	Annalee Thorndike	388	58.00	350.00
76-D-AP-01-016	29″ Donkey	Annalee Thorndike	119	35.00	375.00
78-D-AP-01-017	29″ Caroller Mouse	Annalee Thorndike	658	50.00	750.00
83-D-AP-01-018	Johnny Appleseed Fok Hero Poll	Annalee Thorndike	1,500	85.00	1200.00
79-D-AP-01-019	30″ Artist Bunny	Annalee Thorndike	179	43.00	300.00
80-D-AP-01-020	18″ Diam. Balloon with two 18″ Frogs	Annalee Thorndike	268	100.00	450.00
76-D-AP-01-021	42″ Scarecrow	Annalee Thorndike	134	58.00	325.00
81-D-AP-01-022	18″ Escort Fox	Annalee Thorndike	639	28.50	500.00
81-D-AP-01-023	18″ Foxy Lady	Annalee Thorndike	639	28.50	600.00
79-D-AP-01-024	8″ Artist Bunny	Annalee Thorndike	2,809	7.50	200.00
75-D-AP-01-025	12″ Mama Duck	Annalee Thorndike	476	11.00	175.00
75-D-AP-01-026	5″ Baby Duck	Annalee Thorndike	1,333	4.00	125.00
80-D-AP-01-027	10″ Diam. Balloon with two 10″ Frogs	Annalee Thorndike	837	50.00	250.00
76-D-AP-01-028	18″ Colonial Drummer Boy	Annalee Thorndike	1,090	12.00	275.00
82-D-AP-01-029	12″ Skunk with Sno-ball	Annalee Thorndike	1,304	19.00	225.00
82-D-AP-01-030	12″ Girl Skunk	Annalee Thorndike	936	28.00	200.00
82-D-AP-01-031	12″ Boy Skunk	Annalee Thorndike	936	28.00	200.00
79-D-AP-01-032	10″ Girl Frog	Annalee Thorndike	5,970	8.50	125.00
79-D-AP-01-033	10″ Boy Frog	Annalee Thorndike	5,642	8.50	125.00
75-D-AP-01-034	7″ Boy Biyclist Mouse	Annalee Thorndike	1,561	5.50	150.00
81-D-AP-01-035	12″ Santa Monkey	Annalee Thorndike	1,800	24.00	250.00
68-D-AP-01-036	6″ Myrtle Turtle	Annalee Thorndike	Unkn.	4.50	425.00
82-D-AP-01-037	10″ Butterfly with Elf	Annalee Thorndike	882	28.00	275.00
81-D-AP-01-038	12″ Boy Frog	Annalee Thorndike	727	24.00	125.00
76-D-AP-01-039	7″ Weight Watcher Mouse	Annalee Thorndike	1,921	5.50	200.00
67-D-AP-01-040	10″ Nun	Annalee Thorndike	Unkn.	3.00	200.00
74-D-AP-01-041	7″ Vacationer Mouse	Annalee Thorndike	340	5.50	175.00
82-D-AP-01-042	7″ Santa Fox	Annalee Thorndike	3,622	13.00	250.00
76-D-AP-01-043	16″ Donkey	Annalee Thorndike	219	13.00	275.00
76-D-AP-01-044	16″ Elephant	Annalee Thorndike	806	17.00	275.00
76-D-AP-01-045	8″ Donkey	Annalee Thorndike	1,202	6.00	125.00
76-D-AP-01-046	8″ Elephant	Annalee Thorndike	1,223	6.00	125.00
83-D-AP-01-047	7″ Cowboy Mouse	Annalee Thorndike	2,175	13.00	125.00
83-D-AP-01-048	7″ Equestrienne Mouse	Annalee Thorndike	2,185	13.00	150.00
81-D-AP-01-049	7″ Santa Monkey	Annalee Thorndike	4,606	10.00	150.00
79-D-AP-01-050	7″ White Hare	Annalee Thorndike	Unkn.	Unknown	450.00
57-D-AP-01-051	8″ Crippled Child	Annalee Thorndike	Unkn.	Unknown	825.00
57-D-AP-01-052	10″ Potentate Doll	Annalee Thorndike	Unkn.	Unknown	825.00
57-D-AP-01-053	8″ Crippled Child	Annalee Thorndike	Unkn.	Unknown	825.00
76-D-AP-01-054	7″ Colonial Mouse	Annalee Thorndike	5,457	5.50	300.00
52-D-AP-01-055	10″ Girl Skier with Hand-signed Skis	Annalee Thorndike	Unkn.	10.95	1000.00
XX-D-AP-01-056	Mark Twain Folk Hero Doll	Annalee Thorndike	Unkn.	Unknown	1500.00
52-D-AP-01-057	10″ Boy Skier	Annalee Thorndike	Unkn.	15.00	850.00
XX-D-AP-01-058	Third Doll Society Annalee Animal-Unicorn	Annalee Thorndike	Unkn.	Unknown	1050.00
86-D-AP-01-059	The Logo Kid	Annalee Thorndike	Unkn.	Unknown	575.00
82-D-AP-01-060	4′ Country Boy Bunny	Annalee Thorndike	186	190.00	450.00
82-D-AP-01-061	4′ Country Girl Bunny	Annalee Thorndike	186	190.00	450.00
79-D-AP-01-062	42″ Frog	Annalee Thorndike	269	90.00	300.00
79-D-AP-01-063	18″ Gnome	Annalee Thorndike	9,048	17.00	325.00
84-D-AP-01-064	10″ Shrine Doll	Annalee Thorndike	1,000	Unknown	500.00
70-D-AP-01-065	18″ Clown, Daisy in Hat	Annalee Thorndike	542	10.00	525.00
68-D-AP-01-066	8″ Elephant in Bathing Trunks	Annalee Thorndike	Unkn.	5.00	200.00
68-D-AP-01-067	10″ Elephant with Uncle Sam	Annalee Thorndike	Unkn.	7.00	350.00
70-D-AP-01-068	10″ Elf Skier	Annalee Thorndike	597	4.00	175.00
63-D-AP-01-069	10″ Ski Doll	Annalee Thorndike	Unkn.	15.00	200.00
67-D-AP-01-070	10″ Tennis Player	Annalee Thorndike	Unkn.	5.00	200.00
81-D-AP-01-071	7″ Cross-Country Skier Santa	Annalee Thorndike	5,180	10.00	200.00
69-D-AP-01-072	7″ Bathtime Baby with Sponge	Annalee Thorndike	Unkn.	3.00	275.00
67-D-AP-01-073	3″ Pig-Jogging Joe	Annalee Thorndike	Unkn.	5.00	375.00
70-D-AP-01-074	7″ Baby Bunting in a Basket	Annalee Thorndike	568	4.00	375.00
63-D-AP-01-075	10″ Male Bathing Beauty	Annalee Thorndike	Unkn.	Unknown	225.00
71-D-AP-01-076	7″ Mt Wash MV Cruise Ship Mse in Sailor Suit	Annalee Thorndike	Unkn.	Unknown	225.00
73-D-AP-01-077	12″ Girl Monkey	Annalee Thorndike	Unkn.	Unknown	350.00
68-D-AP-01-078	10″ Donkey wearing Santa Hat	Annalee Thorndike	Unkn.	5.00	375.00
74-D-AP-01-079	5″ Baby Duck	Annalee Thorndike	1,171	4.00	150.00
57-D-AP-01-080	10″ Holiday Doll-Valentines Day	Annalee Thorndike	Unkn.	10.00	500.00
66-D-AP-01-081	10″ Go-Go Kid	Annalee Thorndike	Unkn.	4.00	200.00
67-D-AP-01-082	10″ Girl Putter	Annalee Thorndike	Unkn.	Unknown	250.00
82-D-AP-01-083	8″ Barbecue Pig	Annalee Thorndike	1,044	11.95	55.00
81-D-AP-01-084	10″ Groom Frog	Annalee Thorndike	2,061	14.95	145.00
72-D-AP-01-085	30″ Election Elephant	Annalee Thorndike	113	23.95	550.00
72-D-AP-01-086	30″ Election Donkey	Annalee Thorndike	120	23.95	559.00
85-D-AP-01-087	7″ Dressup Girl	Annalee Thorndike	1,536	18.95	75.00
85-D-AP-01-088	7″ Dressup Boy	Annalee Thorndike	1,174	18.95	75.00
71-D-AP-01-089	30″ White Boy Bunny with Carrot	Annalee Thorndike	172	24.95	165.00
80-D-AP-01-090	7″ Pilot Mouse	Annalee Thorndike	2,011	9.50	100.00
81-D-AP-01-091	7″ Girl Ice Skater Mouse	Annalee Thorndike	1,429	10.95	125.00
80-D-AP-01-092	7″ Girl Card Player Mouse	Annalee Thorndike	1,826	9.50	125.00
76-D-AP-01-093	42″ Scarecrow	Annalee Thorndike	134	57.95	375.00
86-D-AP-01-094	7″ Boating Mouse	Annalee Thorndike	2,320	16.95	55.00
75-D-AP-01-095	7″ Fisherman Mouse	Annalee Thorndike	1,343	5.50	200.00
82-D-AP-01-096	7″ Football Mouse	Annalee Thorndike	2,164	10.95	75.00
82-D-AP-01-097	12″ Nighshirt Mouse	Annalee Thorndike	2,319	25.95	125.00
57-D-AP-01-098	10″ Skier with Hand-signed Skis	Annalee Thorndike	Unkn.	10.95	1000.00
85-D-AP-01-099	5″ Pilot Duck	Annalee Thorndike	1,306	15.95	50.00
73-D-AP-01-100	18″ Mrs. Santa Cardholder	Annalee Thorndike	3,900	8.95	150.00
75-D-AP-01-101	10″ Caroller Boy	Annalee Thorndike	Unkn.	5.50	50.00
84-D-AP-01-102	10″ Aerobic Dancer	Annalee Thorndike	4,785	17.95	65.00

Company	Series				
Number	**Name**	**Artist**	**Edition limit**	**Issue Price**	**Quote**
85-D-AP-01-103	10″ Groom	Annalee Thorndike	264	31.95	150.00
85-D-AP-01-104	30″ Boy Bunny with Wheelbarrow	Annalee Thorndike	Unkn.	119.50	200.00
81-D-AP-01-105	18″ Clown	Annalee Thorndike	2,742	24.95	125.00
86-D-AP-01-106	5″ Duck Raincoat and Umbrella	Annalee Thorndike	Unkn.	18.50	65.00
85-D-AP-01-107	7″ Logo Kid	Annalee Thorndike	3,562	17.90	100.00
Dolls by Jerri	**Dolls by Jerri**				
84-D-DJ-01-001	Clara	J. McCloud	1,000	320.00	775.00
84-D-DJ-01-002	Emily	J. McCloud	1,000	330.00	2700.00
85-D-DJ-01-003	Scotty	J. McCloud	1,000	340.00	750.00
85-D-DJ-01-004	Uncle Joe	J. McCloud	1,000	160.00	250.00
85-D-DJ-01-005	Miss Nanny	J. McCloud	1,000	160.00	250.00
85-D-DJ-01-006	Bride	J. McCloud	1,000	350.00	350.00
86-D-DJ-01-007	David-2 Years Old	J. McCloud	1,000	330.00	330.00
86-D-DJ-01-008	Princess and the Unicorn	J. McCloud	1,000	370.00	370.00
86-D-DJ-01-009	Charlotte	J. McCloud	1,000	330.00	330.00
86-D-DJ-01-010	Cane	J. McCloud	1,000	350.00	350.00
86-D-DJ-01-011	Clown-David 3 Yrs. Old	J. McCloud	1,000	340.00	340.00
86-D-DJ-01-012	Tammy	J. McCloud	1,000	350.00	350.00
86-D-DJ-01-013	Samantha	J. McCloud	1,000	350.00	350.00
86-D-DJ-01-014	Elizabeth	J. McCloud	1,000	340.00	340.00
86-D-DJ-01-015	Audrey	J. McCloud	300	550.00	550.00
86-D-DJ-01-016	Yvonne	J. McCloud	300	500.00	500.00
86-D-DJ-01-017	Annabelle	J. McCloud	300	600.00	600.00
86-D-DJ-01-018	Ashley	J. McCloud	1,000	350.00	350.00
86-D-DJ-01-019	Allison	J. McCloud	1,000	350.00	350.00
86-D-DJ-01-020	Nobody	J. McCloud	1,000	350.00	350.00
86-D-DJ-01-021	Somebody	J. McCloud	1,000	350.00	350.00
86-D-DJ-01-022	Danielle	J. McCloud	1,000	350.00	350.00
86-D-DJ-01-023	Helenjean	J. McCloud	1,000	350.00	350.00
86-D-DJ-01-024	David-Magician	J. McCloud	1,000	350.00	350.00
86-D-DJ-01-025	Amber	J. McCloud	1,000	350.00	350.00
86-D-DJ-01-026	Joy	J. McCloud	1,000	350.00	350.00
86-D-DJ-01-027	Mary Beth	J. McCloud	1,000	350.00	350.00
86-D-DJ-01-028	Jacqueline	J. McCloud	300	500.00	500.00
86-D-DJ-01-029	Lucianna	J. McCloud	300	500.00	500.00
86-D-DJ-01-030	Bridgette	J. McCloud	300	500.00	500.00
86-D-DJ-01-031	The Fool	J. McCloud	1,000	350.00	350.00
86-D-DJ-01-032	Alfalfa	J. McCloud	1,000	350.00	350.00
Enesco Imports Corporation	**Dolls**				
83-D-EA-01-001	Katie Lynne, 16″- E-0539	S. Butcher	Open	165.00	175.00
84-D-EA-01-002	Mother Sew Dear, 18″- E-2850	S. Butcher	Retrd.	350.00	350.00
84-D-EA-01-003	Kristy, 12″ - E-2851	S. Butcher	Open	150.00	160.00
84-D-EA-01-004	Timmy, 12″ - E-5397	S. Butcher	Open	125.00	135.00
81-D-EA-01-005	Mikey, 18″ - E-6214B	S. Butcher	Suspd.	150.00	200.00
81-D-EA-01-006	Debbie, 18″- E-6214G	S. Butcher	Suspd.	150.00	200.00
82-D-EA-01-007	Cubby, 18″ - E-7267B	S. Butcher	5,000	200.00	380.00
82-D-EA-01-008	Tammy, 18″ - E-7267G	S. Butcher	5,000	300.00	500.00
85-D-EA-01-009	Aaron, 12″ - 12424	S. Butcher	Suspd.	135.00	135.00
85-D-EA-01-010	Bethany, 12″ - 12432	S. Butcher	Suspd.	135.00	135.00
85-D-EA-01-011	P.D., 7″, 12475	S. Butcher	Suspd.	50.00	50.00
85-D-EA-01-012	Trish, 7″, 12483	S. Butcher	Suspd.	50.00	50.00
86-D-EA-01-013	Bong Bong, 13″ - 100455	S. Butcher	12,000	150.00	150.00
86-D-EA-01-014	Candy, 13″ - 100463	S. Butcher	12,000	150.00	150.00
86-D-EA-01-015	Connie, 12″ - 102253	S. Butcher	7,500	160.00	160.00
Goebel	**M. I. Hummel Collectibles Dolls**				
01-D-GG-01-001	Gretel 1901	M. I. Hummel	Closed	55.00	55.00
02-D-GG-01-002	Hansel 1902	M. I. Hummel	Closed	55.00	55.00
04-D-GG-01-003	Rosa-Blue Baby 1904/B	M. I. Hummel	Closed	45.00	45.00
04-D-GG-01-004	Rosa-Pink Baby 1904/P	M. I. Hummel	Closed	45.00	45.00
05-D-GG-01-005	Little Knitter 1905	M. I. Hummel	Closed	55.00	55.00
06-D-GG-01-006	Merry Wanderer 1906	M. I. Hummel	Closed	55.00	55.00
08-D-GG-01-007	Chimney Sweep 1908	M. I. Hummel	Closed	55.00	55.00
09-D-GG-01-008	School Girl 1909	M. I. Hummel	Closed	55.00	55.00
10-D-GG-01-009	School Boy 1910	M. I. Hummel	Closed	55.00	55.00
14-D-GG-01-010	Goose Girl 1914	M. I. Hummel	Closed	55.00	55.00
17-D-GG-01-011	For Father 1917	M. I. Hummel	Closed	55.00	55.00
25-D-GG-01-012	Merry Wanderer 1925	M. I. Hummel	Closed	55.00	55.00
26-D-GG-01-013	Lost Stocking 1926	M. I. Hummel	Closed	55.00	55.00
27-D-GG-01-014	Visiting and Invalid 1927	M. I. Hummel	Closed	55.00	55.00
28-D-GG-01-015	On Secret Path 1928	M. I. Hummel	Closed	55.00	55.00
Goebel	**M. I. Hummel Porcelain Dolls**				
84-D-GG-02-001	Birthday Serenade/Boy	M. I. Hummel	Open	175.00	225.00
84-D-GG-02-002	Birthday Serenade/Girl	M. I. Hummel	Open	175.00	225.00
84-D-GG-02-003	On Holiday	M. I. Hummel	Open	175.00	225.00
84-D-GG-02-004	Postman	M. I. Hummel	Open	175.00	225.00
85-D-GG-02-005	Carnival	M. I. Hummel	Open	175.00	225.00
85-D-GG-02-006	Easter Greetings	M. I. Hummel	Open	175.00	225.00
85-D-GG-02-007	Lost Sheep	M. I. Hummel	Open	175.00	225.00
85-D-GG-02-008	Signs of Spring	M. I. Hummel	Open	175.00	225.00
Gorham	**Gorham Dolls**				
81-D-GO-01-001	Jillian, 16″	Unknown	Open	200.00	275.00
81-D-GO-01-002	Alexandria, 19″	Unknown	Open	250.00	350.00
81-D-GO-01-003	Christopher, 19″	Unknown	Open	250.00	600.00
81-D-GO-01-004	Stephanie, 10″	Unknown	Open	250.00	1,250.00
81-D-GO-01-005	Cecile, 16″	Unknown	Open	200.00	850.00
81-D-GO-01-006	Christina, 16″	Unknown	Open	200.00	275.00
81-D-GO-01-007	Daniella, 14″	Unknown	Open	150.00	275.00
81-D-GO-01-008	Melinda, 14″	Unknown	Open	150.00	275.00
81-D-GO-01-009	Elena, 14″	Unknown	Open	150.00	450.00
81-D-GO-01-010	Rosemond, 19″	Unknown	Open	250.00	350.00
82-D-GO-01-011	Mlle. Monique, 12″	Unknown	Open	125.00	275.00
82-D-GO-01-012	Mlle. Jeanette, 12″	Unknown	Open	125.00	175.00
82-D-GO-01-013	Mlle. Lucille, 12″	Unknown	Open	125.00	350.00
82-D-GO-01-014	Benjamin, 18″	Unknown	Open	200.00	300.00
82-D-GO-01-015	Ellice, 18″	Unknown	Open	200.00	300.00
82-D-GO-01-016	Corrine, 21″	Unknown	Open	250.00	400.00
82-D-GO-01-017	Baby in Blue Dress, 12″	Unknown	Open	150.00	225.00
82-D-GO-01-018	Baby in Apricot Dress, 16″	Unknown	Open	175.00	250.00
82-D-GO-01-019	Baby in White Dress, 18″	Unknown	Open	250.00	300.00
82-D-GO-01-020	Melanie, 23″	Unknown	Open	300.00	500.00
82-D-GO-01-021	Jeremy, 23″	Unknown	Open	300.00	550.00
82-D-GO-01-023	Mlle. Yvonne, 12″	Unknown	Open	125.00	350.00
82-D-GO-01-024	M. Anton, 12″	Unknown	Open	125.00	175.00
82-D-GO-01-025	Mlle. Marsella, 12″	Unknown	Open	125.00	275.00
82-D-GO-01-026	Kristen, 23″	Unknown	Open	300.00	500.00

Company	Series				
Number	**Name**	**Artist**	**Edition limit**	**Issue Price**	**Quote**
83-D-GO-01-027	Blue Girl	Unknown	Open	80.00	130.00
83-D-GO-01-028	Christmas Morning	Unknown	Open	80.00	130.00
83-D-GO-01-029	Heather, 14″	Unknown	Open	80.00	130.00
83-D-GO-01-030	Little Amy, 14″	Unknown	Open	80.00	130.00
83-D-GO-01-031	Robbie, 14″	Unknown	Open	80.00	130.00
83-D-GO-01-032	Sweet Valentine, 16″	Unknown	Open	100.00	165.00
83-D-GO-01-033	Yesterday's Memories, 18″	Unknown	Open	125.00	225.00
83-D-GO-01-034	Sunday Best, 18″	Unknown	Open	115.00	175.00
83-D-GO-01-035	Blue Girl, 18″	Unknown	Open	115.00	175.00
83-D-GO-01-036	Beth, 16″	Unknown	Open	225.00	475.00
83-D-GO-01-038	Meg, 19″	Unknown	Open	275.00	575.00
83-D-GO-01-039	Jo, 19″	Unknown	Open	275.00	475.00
83-D-GO-01-040	Jennifer, 19″ Bridal Doll	Unknown	Open	325.00	475.00
85-D-GO-01-041	Linda, 19″	Gorham	Open	275.00	275.00
85-D-GO-01-042	Odette, 19″	Gorham	Open	250.00	250.00
85-D-GO-01-043	Amelia, 19″	Gorham	Open	275.00	275.00
85-D-GO-01-044	Nanette, 19″	Gorham	Open	275.00	275.00
85-D-GO-01-045	Alexander, 19″	Gorham	Open	275.00	275.00
85-D-GO-01-046	Gabrielle, 19″	Gorham	Open	225.00	225.00
86-D-GO-01-047	Julia, 16″	Gorham	Open	225.00	225.00
86-D-GO-01-048	Lauren, 14″	Gorham	Open	175.00	175.00
86-D-GO-01-049	Emily, 14″	Gorham	Open	175.00	175.00
86-D-GO-01-050	Fleur, 19″	Gorham	Open	300.00	300.00
87-D-GO-01-051	Juliet	S. Stone Aiken	Open	325.00	325.00
86-D-GO-01-052	Meredith	Unknown	Open	275.00	275.00
86-D-GO-01-053	Alissa	Unknown	Open	225.00	225.00
86-D-GO-01-054	Jessica	Unknown	Open	175.00	175.00
Gorham	**Limited Edition Dolls**				
82-D-GO-02-001	Allison	Gorham	1,000	300.00	2500.00
83-D-GO-02-002	Ashley	Gorham	2,500	350.00	900.00
84-D-GO-02-003	Nicole	Gorham	2,500	350.00	500.00
84-D-GO-02-004	Holly (Christmas)	Gorham	2,500	300.00	750.00
85-D-GO-02-005	Lydia 19″	Gorham	1,500	550.00	1250.00
85-D-GO-02-006	Joy 19″ (Christmas)	Gorham	2,500	350.00	500.00
85-D-GO-02-007	Colette 19″	Gorham	2,500	400.00	850.00
86-D-GO-02-008	Noel (Christmas)	S. Stone Aiken	2,500	400.00	400.00
87-D-GO-02-009	Jacqueline	S. Stone Aiken	1,500	500.00	500.00
87-D-GO-02-010	Charlotte	S. Stone Aiken	2,500	425.00	425.00
87-D-GO-02-011	Merrie (Christmas)	S. Stone Aiken	2,500	500.00	500.00
Gorham	**Gorham Holly Hobbie Childhood Memories**				
85-D-GO-03-001	Mother's Helper	Gorham	Open	45.00	55.00
85-D-GO-03-002	Best Friends	Gorham	Open	45.00	45.00
85-D-GO-03-003	First Day of School	Gorham	Open	45.00	45.00
85-D-GO-03-004	Christmas Wishes	Gorham	Open	45.00	45.00
Gorham	**Gorham Holly Hobbie For All Seasons**				
84-D-GO-04-001	Summer Holly 12″	Gorham	Open	42.50	50.00
84-D-GO-04-002	Fall Holly 12″	Gorham	Open	42.50	42.50
84-D-GO-04-003	Winter Holly 12″	Gorham	Open	42.50	55.00
84-D-GO-04-004	Spring Holly 12″	Gorham	Open	42.50	42.50
Gorham	**Kezi Doll For All Seasons**				
85-D-GO-09-001	Ariel 16″	Kezi	2 yr.	135.00	175.00
85-D-GO-09-002	Aubrey 16″	Kezi	2 yr.	135.00	175.00
85-D-GO-09-003	Amber 16″	Kezi	2 yr.	135.00	175.00
85-D-GO-09-004	Adrienne 16″	Kezi	2 yr.	135.00	175.00
Gorham	**Kezi Golden Gifts**				
84-D-GO-10-001	Faith 18″	Kezi	2 yr.	95.00	145.00
84-D-GO-10-002	Felicity 18″	Kezi	2 yr.	95.00	145.00
84-D-GO-10-003	Patience 18″	Kezi	2 yr.	95.00	145.00
84-D-GO-10-004	Prudence 18″	Kezi	2 yr.	85.00	145.00
84-D-GO-10-005	Hope 16″	Kezi	2 yr.	85.00	145.00
84-D-GO-10-006	Grace 16″	Kezi	2 yr.	85.00	145.00
84-D-GO-10-007	Charity 16″	Kezi	2 yr.	85.00	145.00
84-D-GO-10-008	Merrie 16″	Kezi	2 yr.	85.00	145.00
Gorham	**Southern Belles**				
85-D-GO-12-001	Amanda, 19″	Gorham	Open	300.00	375.00
86-D-GO-12-002	Veronica, 19″	Gorham	Open	325.00	325.00
87-D-GO-12-003	Rachel	S. Stone Aiken	Open	375.00	375.00
Gorham	**Valentine Ladies**				
87-D-GO-13-001	Jane	P. Valentine	2,500	145.00	145.00
87-D-GO-13-002	Lee Ann	P. Valentine	2,500	145.00	145.00
87-D-GO-13-003	Elizabeth	P. Valentine	2,500	145.00	145.00
87-D-GO-13-004	Rebecca	P. Valentine	2,500	145.00	145.00
87-D-GO-13-005	Patrice	P. Valentine	2,500	145.00	145.00
87-D-GO-13-006	Anabella	P. Valentine	2,500	145.00	145.00
87-D-GO-13-007	Sylvia	P. Valentine	2,500	160.00	160.00
87-D-GO-13-008	Rosanne	P. Valentine	2,500	145.00	145.00
87-D-GO-13-009	Marianna	P. Valentine	2,500	160.00	160.00
Gorham	**Gorham Baby Doll Collection**				
87-D-GO-16-001	Christening Day	Aiken/Matthews	Open	245.00	245.00
87-D-GO-16-002	Leslie	Aiken/Matthews	Open	245.00	245.00
87-D-GO-16-003	Matthew	Aiken/Matthews	Open	245.00	245.00
Gorham	**Beverly Port Designer Collection**				
87-D-GO-17-001	Silver Bell 17″	B. Port	2,500	175.00	175.00
87-D-GO-17-002	Kristobear Kringle 17″	B. Port	2,500	200.00	200.00
87-D-GO-17-003	Tedwina Kimelina Bearkin 10″	B. Port	2,500	95.00	95.00
87-D-GO-17-004	Christopher Paul Bearkin 10″	B. Port	2,500	95.00	95.00
87-D-GO-17-005	Molly Melinda Bearkin 10″	B. Port	2,500	95.00	95.00
87-D-GO-17-006	Tedward Jonathan Bearkin 10″	B. Port	2,500	95.00	95.00
Hamilton Collection	**Maidens of the Changing Seasons Hakata Dolls**				
81-D-HC-01-001	Peony Maiden	Unknown	7,500	75.00	155.00
81-D-HC-01-002	Maple Leaf Maiden	Unknown	7,500	75.00	105.00
81-D-HC-01-003	Snowflake Maiden	Unknown	7,500	75.00	95.00
81-D-HC-01-004	Cherry Blossom Maiden	Unknown	7,500	75.00	85.00
Hamilton Collection	**The Art of Kabuki Hakata Doll Collection**				
82-D-HC-02-001	Wisteria Maiden	Togo San	9,800	75.00	105.00
82-D-HC-02-002	Male Lion Dancer	Togo San	9,800	75.00	89.00
82-D-HC-02-003	White Heron Dancer	Togo San	9,800	75.00	75.00
82-D-HC-02-004	The Marionette	Togo San	9,800	75.00	75.00
82-D-HC-02-005	Dojo Temple Maiden	Togo San	9,800	75.00	75.00
82-D-HC-02-006	Female Lion Dancer	Togo San	9,800	75.00	75.00
Hamilton Collection	**American Fashion Doll Collection**				
85-D-HC-03-001	Victoria	Unknown	9,800	125.00	125.00
85-D-HC-03-002	Heather	Unknown	9,800	125.00	125.00

Dolls/Figurines

Company / Number	Series / Name	Artist	Edition limit	Issue Price	Quote
85-D-HC-03-003	Melanie	Unknown	9,800	125.00	125.00
85-D-HC-03-004	Roxanne	Unknown	9,800	125.00	125.00
Hamilton Collection	**Royal Princess Doll Collection**				
85-D-HC-04-001	Princess Victoria	J. Bromley	9,800	174.00	174.00
85-D-HC-04-002	Princess Margarita	J. Bromley	9,800	174.00	174.00
85-D-HC-04-003	Princess Catherine	J. Bromley	9,800	174.00	174.00
85-D-HC-04-004	Princess Marie-Therese	J. Bromley	9,800	174.00	174.00
85-D-HC-04-005	Princess Luisa	J. Bromley	9,800	174.00	174.00
85-D-HC-04-006	Princess Christina	J. Bromley	9,800	174.00	174.00
Hamilton Collection	**Songs of the Seasons Hakata Doll Collection**				
85-D-HC-05-001	Winter Song Maiden	T. Murakami	9,800	75.00	75.00
85-D-HC-05-002	Spring Song Maiden	T. Murakami	9,800	75.00	75.00
85-D-HC-05-003	Summer Song Maiden	T. Murakami	9,800	75.00	75.00
85-D-HC-05-004	Autumn Song Maiden	T. Murakami	9,800	75.00	75.00
Edna Hibel Studios	**Child's Fancy**				
85-D-HG-01-001	Jenny's Lady Jennifer	E. Hibel	800	395.00	750.00
Edna Hibel Studios	**Wax Doll Collection**				
86-D-HG-02-001	Wax Doll	E. Hibel	12	2500.00	3000.00
Lenox	**Lenox China Dolls**				
84-D-LE-01-001	Maryanne, 20″	J. Grammer	Unkn.	425.00	1500.00
84-D-LE-01-002	Abigail, 20″	J. Grammer	Unkn.	425.00	1500.00
84-D-LE-01-003	Jessica, 20″	J. Grammer	Unkn.	450.00	1500.00
84-D-LE-01-004	Rebecca, 16″	J. Grammer	Unkn.	375.00	1500.00
84-D-LE-01-005	Amanda, 16″	J. Grammer	Unkn.	385.00	1500.00
84-D-LE-01-006	Maggie, 16″	J. Grammer	Unkn.	375.00	1500.00
84-D-LE-01-007	Melissa	J. Grammer	Unkn.	450.00	2500.00
84-D-LE-01-008	Samantha	J. Grammer	Unkn.	500.00	2200.00
Lenox	**China Dolls - Cloth Bodies**				
85-D-LE-02-001	Amy, 14″	T. Grammer	250	250.00	950.00
85-D-LE-02-002	Elizabeth, 14″	T. Grammer	250	250.00	950.00
85-D-LE-02-003	Sarah, 14″	T. Grammer	250	250.00	950.00
85-D-LE-02-004	Annabelle, 14″	T. Grammer	250	250.00	950.00
85-D-LE-02-005	Miranda, 14″	T. Grammer	250	250.00	950.00
85-D-LE-02-006	Jennifer, 14″	T. Grammer	250	250.00	950.00
Pemberton & Oakes	**Zolan's Children**				
84-D-PO-01-003	Sabina in the Grass	D. Zolan	880	98.00	98.00
Sally-Lynne Dolls	**French Replicas**				
85-D-SA-01-001	Victoria, 30″	S. Beatty	100	1050.00	1500.00
85-D-SA-01-002	Charles, 30″	S. Beatty	100	1050.00	1400.00
85-D-SA-01-003	Annabelle, 28″	S. Beatty	100	950.00	1400.00
85-D-SA-01-004	Candice	S. Beatty	100	950.00	1250.00
86-D-SA-01-005	Victoria at Christmas, 30″	S. Beatty	Unkn.	2500.00	2850.00
U.S. Historical Society	**Living Image Dolls**				
82-D-US-01-001	Benjamin Franklin	R. Lamb	2,500	525.00	625.00
82-D-US-01-002	George Washington	R. Lamb	2,500	525.00	625.00
83-D-US-01-003	Abigail Adams	R. Lamb	2,500	525.00	625.00
83-D-US-01-004	Thomas Jefferson	R. Lamb	2,500	525.00	625.00
83-D-US-01-005	Abraham Lincoln	R. Lamb	2,500	525.00	525.00
83-D-US-01-006	Mary Todd Lincoln	R. Lamb	2,500	525.00	525.00
84-D-US-01-007	Robert E. Lee	R. Lamb	2,500	525.00	525.00
84-D-US-01-008	Mary Custis Lee	R. Lamb	2,500	525.00	525.00
84-D-US-01-009	Martha Washington	R. Lamb	2,500	525.00	525.00
85-D-US-01-010	John Paul Jones	V. Davis	2,500	525.00	525.00
85-D-US-01-011	Franklin Roosevelt	V. Davis	2,500	525.00	525.00
85-D-US-01-012	Eleanor Roosevelt	V. Davis	2,500	525.00	525.00
U.S. Historical Society	**Children of the Past**				
84-D-US-02-001	Holly	F. Zeller	950	625.00	625.00
85-D-US-02-002	Michael	P. Wright	950	350.00	350.00
Vague Shadows	**Dolls**				
86-D-VC-01-001	Morning Star, 17-1/2″	G. Perillo	1,000	250.00	250.00

Figurines

Company / Number	Series / Name	Artist	Edition limit	Issue Price	Quote
American Artists	**Fred Stone Figurines**				
85-F-AA-01-001	The Black Stallion, porcelain	F. Stone	Unkn.	125.00	150.00
85-F-AA-01-002	The Black Stallion, bronze	F. Stone	Unkn.	150.00	150.00
86-F-AA-01-003	Arab Mare & Foal	F. Stone	Unkn.	150.00	175.00
86-F-AA-01-004	Tranquility	F. Stone	Unkn.	175.00	195.00
Anri	**Anri Woodcarvings Ferrandiz**				
76-F-AO-06-001	Cowboy	J. Ferrandiz	1,500	75.00	700.00
83-F-AO-06-002	Cowboy	J. Ferrandiz	7,500	45.00	50.00
76-F-AO-06-003	Harvest Girl	J. Ferrandiz	1,500	75.00	800.00
77-F-AO-06-004	Leading the Way	J. Ferrandiz	1,500	100.00	400.00
77-F-AO-06-005	Friendship	J. Ferrandiz	Unkn.	110.00	400.00
77-F-AO-06-006	Friendship	J. Ferrandiz	Unkn.	53.50	190.00
77-F-AO-06-007	Friendship	J. Ferrandiz	250	2350.00	2350.00
78-F-AO-06-008	Spreading the Word	J. Ferrandiz	Unkn.	350.00	390.00
78-F-AO-06-009	Spreading the Word	J. Ferrandiz	Unkn.	140.00	395.00
78-F-AO-06-010	Peace Pipe	J. Ferrandiz	1,500	150.00	400.00
83-F-AO-06-011	Peace Pipe	J. Ferrandiz	7,500	45.00	45.00
83-F-AO-06-012	Peace Pipe	J. Ferrandiz	250	2200.00	2200.00
78-F-AO-06-013	Basket of Joy	J. Ferrandiz	1,500	140.00	350.00
83-F-AO-06-014	Basket of Joy	J. Ferrandiz	7,500	45.00	45.00
79-F-AO-06-015	Drummer Boy	J. Ferrandiz	Unkn.	325.00	390.00
79-F-AO-06-016	Drummer Boy	J. Ferrandiz	Unkn.	140.00	175.00
79-F-AO-06-017	Drummer Boy	J. Ferrandiz	1,000	80.00	175.00
79-F-AO-06-018	Drummer Boy	J. Ferrandiz	1,000	220.00	300.00
79-F-AO-06-019	First Blossom	J. Ferrandiz	2,250	135.00	285.00
79-F-AO-06-020	Happy Strummer	J. Ferrandiz	2,250	160.00	300.00
80-F-AO-06-021	Melody for Two	J. Ferrandiz	2,250	200.00	300.00
83-F-AO-06-022	Melody for Two	J. Ferrandiz	7,500	45.00	45.00
80-F-AO-06-023	Friends	J. Ferrandiz	2,250	200.00	300.00
80-F-AO-06-024	Freedom Bound	J. Ferrandiz	1,000	225.00	300.00
80-F-AO-06-025	Freedom Bound	J. Ferrandiz	1,000	90.00	175.00
83-F-AO-06-026	Freedom Bound	J. Ferrandiz	250	2200.00	2200.00
81-F-AO-06-027	Tiny Sounds	J. Ferrandiz	2,250	220.00	300.00
81-F-AO-06-028	Merry Melody	J. Ferrandiz	2,250	220.00	300.00
81-F-AO-06-029	Jolly Piper	J. Ferrandiz	2,250	225.00	275.00
82-F-AO-06-030	Star Struck	J. Ferrandiz	250	2400.00	2400.00
82-F-AO-06-031	The Choral	J. Ferrandiz	250	2200.00	2200.00
82-F-AO-06-032	Companions	J. Ferrandiz	2,250	220.00	220.00
82-F-AO-06-033	The Guiding Light	J. Ferrandiz	2,250	225.00	225.00
82-F-AO-06-034	To Market	J. Ferrandiz	2,250	220.00	220.00
77-F-AO-06-035	Tracker	J. Ferrandiz	1,500	100.00	400.00

Company / Number	Series / Name	Artist	Edition limit	Issue Price	Quote
83-F-AO-06-036	Tracker	J. Ferrandiz	7,500	45.00	45.00
83-F-AO-06-037	Girl With Dove	J. Ferrandiz	7,500	45.00	45.00
83-F-AO-06-038	Bewildered	J. Ferrandiz	2,250	196.00	196.00
83-F-AO-06-039	Good Samaritan	J. Ferrandiz	2,250	220.00	220.00
83-F-AO-06-040	Admiration	J. Ferrandiz	2,250	220.00	220.00
80-F-AO-06-041	Good Shepherd	J. Ferrandiz	120	1750.00	1750.00
80-F-AO-06-042	Talk to the Animals	J. Ferrandiz	120	1750.00	1750.00
81-F-AO-06-043	Trumpeter	J. Ferrandiz	250	2350.00	2350.00
81-F-AO-06-044	Spring Arrivals	J. Ferrandiz	250	2350.00	2350.00
82-F-AO-06-045	Adoration	J. Ferrandiz	250	3200.00	3200.00
83-F-AO-06-046	Treasure Chest M/B	J. Ferrandiz	10,000	300.00	300.00
84-F-AO-06-047	Friendly Faces, 6″	J. Ferrandiz	2,250	210.00	210.00
84-F-AO-06-048	Friendly Faces, 3″	J. Ferrandiz	2,250	93.00	93.00
84-F-AO-06-049	Wanderer's Return, 6″	J. Ferrandiz	2,250	196.00	196.00
84-F-AO-06-050	Wanderer's Return, 3″	J. Ferrandiz	2,250	93.00	93.00
84-F-AO-06-051	Devotion, 1984 Shepherd of the Year, 6″	J. Ferrandiz	2,250	180.00	180.00
84-F-AO-06-052	Devotion, 1984 Shepherd of the Year, 3″	J. Ferrandiz	2,250	82.50	82.50
84-F-AO-06-053	Cowboy, 20″	J. Ferrandiz	250	2,100.00	2,100.00
84-F-AO-06-054	Edelweiss, 40″	J. Ferrandiz	50	8,300.00	8,300.00
85-F-AO-06-055	Butterfly Boy, 6″	J. Ferrandiz	2,250	220.00	220.00
85-F-AO-06-056	Butterfly Boy, 3″	J. Ferrandiz	2,250	95.00	95.00
86-F-AO-06-057	Swiss Boy 6″	J. Ferrandiz	Unkn.	245.00	245.00
86-F-AO-06-058	Swiss Boy 3″	J. Ferrandiz	Unkn.	122.50	122.50
86-F-AO-06-059	Swiss Girl 6″	J. Ferrandiz	Unkn.	245.00	245.00
86-F-AO-06-060	Swiss Girl 3″	J. Ferrandiz	Unkn.	122.50	122.50
86-F-AO-06-061	God's Little Helper 4″	J. Ferrandiz	2,000	425.00	425.00
86-F-AO-06-062	God's Little Helper 2″	J. Ferrandiz	3,500	170.00	170.00
86-F-AO-06-063	Edelweiss 10″	J. Ferrandiz	Unkn.	500.00	500.00
86-F-AO-06-064	Edelweiss 20″	J. Ferrandiz	250	3300.00	3300.00
86-F-AO-06-065	Golden Blossom 10″	J. Ferrandiz	Unkn.	500.00	500.00
86-F-AO-06-066	Golden Blossom 20″	J. Ferrandiz	250	3300.00	3300.00
86-F-AO-06-067	Golden Blossom 40″	J. Ferrandiz	50	8300.00	8300.00
86-F-AO-06-068	Musical Ride 7-1/2″	J. Ferrandiz	Unkn.	395.00	395.00
86-F-AO-06-069	Musical Ride 4″	J. Ferrandiz	Unkn.	165.00	165.00
86-F-AO-06-070	Celebration March 11″	J. Ferrandiz	Unkn.	450.00	450.00
86-F-AO-06-071	Celebration March 20″	J. Ferrandiz	Unkn.	2200.00	2200.00
87-F-AO-06-072	Gloria Angel 6″	J. Ferrandiz	Unkn.	125.00	125.00
87-F-AO-06-073	Gloria Angel 3″	J. Ferrandiz	Unkn.	60.00	60.00
87-F-AO-06-074	Serenity 6″	J. Ferrandiz	3,000	245.00	245.00
87-F-AO-06-075	Serenity 3″	J. Ferrandiz	3,000	125.00	125.00
87-F-AO-06-076	Nature's Wonder 6″	J. Ferrandiz	3,000	245.00	245.00
87-F-AO-06-077	Nature's Wonder 3″	J. Ferrandiz	3,000	125.00	125.00
87-F-AO-06-078	Black Forest Girl 6″	J. Ferrandiz	3,000	250.00	250.00
87-F-AO-06-079	Black Forest Girl 3″	J. Ferrandiz	3,000	125.00	125.00
87-F-AO-06-080	Black Forest Boy 6″	J. Ferrandiz	3,000	250.00	250.00
87-F-AO-06-081	Black Forest Boy 3″	J. Ferrandiz	3,000	125.00	125.00
87-F-AO-06-082	Among Friends 6″	J. Ferrandiz	3,000	245.00	245.00
87-F-AO-06-083	Among Friends 3″	J. Ferrandiz	3,000	125.00	125.00
87-F-AO-06-084	Heavenly Concert 4″	J. Ferrandiz	2,000	450.00	450.00
87-F-AO-06-085	Heavenly Concert 2″	J. Ferrandiz	3,500	200.00	200.00
87-F-AO-06-086	Clown with Bow Tie 5″	J. Ferrandiz	3,000	175.00	175.00
87-F-AO-06-087	Clown with Boe Tie 2-1/2″	J. Ferrandiz	Unkn.	80.00	80.00
87-F-AO-06-088	Clown with Sun 5″	J. Ferrandiz	3,000	175.00	175.00
87-F-AO-06-089	Clown with Sun 2-1/2″	J. Ferrandiz	Unkn.	80.00	80.00
Anri	**Ferrandiz Mini Nativity Set**				
86-F-AO-08-001	Mini Melchoir	J. Ferrandiz	Unkn.	45.00	49.50
86-F-AO-08-002	Mini Caspar	J. Ferrandiz	Unkn.	45.00	49.50
86-F-AO-08-003	Mini Balthasar	J. Ferrandiz	Unkn.	45.00	49.50
86-F-AO-08-004	Mini Angel	J. Ferrandiz	Unkn.	45.00	49.50
86-F-AO-08-005	Mini Free Ride, plus Mini Lamb	J. Ferrandiz	Unkn.	45.00	49.50
86-F-AO-08-006	Mini Weary Traveller	J. Ferrandiz	Unkn.	45.00	49.50
86-F-AO-08-007	Mini The Stray	J. Ferrandiz	Unkn.	45.00	49.50
86-F-AO-08-008	Mini The Hiker	J. Ferrandiz	Unkn.	45.00	49.50
86-F-AO-08-009	Mini Star Struck	J. Ferrandiz	Unkn.	45.00	49.50
Anri	**Sarah Kay Figurines**				
83-F-AO-10-001	Morning Chores	S. Kay	2,000	210.00	300.00
83-F-AO-10-002	Morning Chores	S. Kay	7,500	45.00	49.50
83-F-AO-10-003	Helping Mother	S. Kay	2,000	210.00	210.00
83-F-AO-10-004	Helping Mother	S. Kay	7,500	45.00	49.50
83-F-AO-10-005	Sweeping	S. Kay	4,000	195.00	300.00
83-F-AO-10-006	Sweeping	S. Kay	7,500	45.00	49.50
83-F-AO-10-007	Playtime	S. Kay	4,000	195.00	220.00
83-F-AO-10-008	Playtime	S. Kay	7,500	45.00	49.50
83-F-AO-10-009	Feeding the Chickens	S. Kay	4,000	195.00	220.00
83-F-AO-10-010	Feeding the Chickens	S. Kay	7,500	45.00	49.50
83-F-AO-10-011	Waiting for Mother	S. Kay	4,000	195.00	195.00
83-F-AO-10-012	Waiting for Mother	S. Kay	7,500	45.00	45.00
83-F-AO-10-013	Bedtime	S. Kay	4,000	195.00	195.00
83-F-AO-10-014	Bedtime	S. Kay	7,500	45.00	49.50
83-F-AO-10-015	From the Garden	S. Kay	4,000	195.00	220.00
83-F-AO-10-016	From the Garden	S. Kay	7,500	45.00	45.00
83-F-AO-10-017	Wake Up Kiss, 6″	S. Kay	2,000	210.00	210.00
83-F-AO-10-018	Wake Up Kiss, 4″	S. Kay	4,000	95.00	110.00
84-F-AO-10-019	Wake Up Kiss, mini	S. Kay	7,500	45.00	49.50
84-F-AO-10-020	Finding R Way, 6″	S. Kay	2,000	210.00	250.00
84-F-AO-10-021	Finding R Way, 4″	S. Kay	4,000	95.00	110.00
84-F-AO-10-022	Finding R Way, mini	S. Kay	7,500	45.00	49.50
84-F-AO-10-023	Daydreaming, 6″	S. Kay	4,000	195.00	220.00
84-F-AO-10-024	Daydreaming, 4″	S. Kay	4,000	95.00	130.00
84-F-AO-10-025	Daydreaming, mini	S. Kay	7,500	45.00	49.50
84-F-AO-10-026	Off to School, 6″	S. Kay	4,000	195.00	220.00
84-F-AO-10-027	Off to School, 4″	S. Kay	4,000	95.00	110.00
84-F-AO-10-028	Off to School, mini	S. Kay	7,500	45.00	49.50
84-F-AO-10-029	Flowers for You, 6″	S. Kay	4,000	195.00	220.00
84-F-AO-10-030	Flowers for You, 4″	S. Kay	4,000	95.00	110.00
84-F-AO-10-031	Flowers for You, mini	S. Kay	7,500	45.00	49.50
84-F-AO-10-032	Watchful Eye, 6″	S. Kay	4,000	195.00	220.00
84-F-AO-10-033	Watchful Eye, 4″	S. Kay	4,000	95.00	110.00
84-F-AO-10-034	Watchful Eye, mini	S. Kay	7,500	45.00	49.50
84-F-AO-10-035	Special Delivery, 6″	S. Kay	4,000	195.00	220.00
84-F-AO-10-036	Special Delivery, 4″	S. Kay	4,000	95.00	110.00
84-F-AO-10-037	Special Delivery, mini	S. Kay	7,500	45.00	49.50
84-F-AO-10-038	Tag Along, 6″	S. Kay	4,000	195.00	220.00

Figurines

Number	Name	Artist	Edition limit	Issue Price	Quote
84-F-AO-10-039	Tag Along, 4″	S. Kay	4,000	95.00	110.00
84-F-AO-10-040	Tag Along, mini	S. Kay	7,500	45.00	45.00
85-F-AO-10-041	Waiting for Mother, 11″	S. Kay	750	495.00	650.00
85-F-AO-10-042	A Special Day, 6″	S. Kay	4,000	195.00	220.00
85-F-AO-10-043	A Special Day, 4″	S. Kay	4,000	95.00	110.00
85-F-AO-10-044	Afternoon Tea, 6″	S. Kay	4,000	195.00	245.00
85-F-AO-10-045	Afternoon Tea, 4″	S. Kay	4,000	95.00	110.00
85-F-AO-10-046	Nightie Night, 6″	S. Kay	4,000	195.00	195.00
85-F-AO-10-047	Nightie Night, 4″	S. Kay	4,000	95.00	95.00
85-F-AO-10-048	Yuletide Cheer, 6″	S. Kay	2,000	210.00	240.00
85-F-AO-10-049	Yuletide Cheer, 4″	S. Kay	4,000	95.00	110.00
85-F-AO-10-050	'Tis the Season, 6″	S. Kay	2,000	210.00	240.00
85-F-AO-10-051	'Tis the Season, 4″	S. Kay	4,000	95.00	110.00
85-F-AO-10-052	Giddyap!, 6″	S. Kay	4,000	195.00	195.00
85-F-AO-10-053	Giddyap!, 4″	S. Kay	4,000	95.00	95.00
86-F-AO-10-054	Our Puppy 4″	S. Kay	4,000	95.00	95.00
86-F-AO-10-055	Our Puppy 6″	S. Kay	2,000	210.00	210.00
86-F-AO-10-056	Our Puppy 1-1/2″	S. Kay	7,500	45.00	45.00
86-F-AO-10-057	Always By My Side 4″	S. Kay	4,000	95.00	95.00
86-F-AO-10-058	Always By My Side 6″	S. Kay	4,000	195.00	195.00
86-F-AO-10-059	Always By My Side 1-1/2″	S. Kay	7,500	45.00	45.00
86-F-AO-10-060	Finishing Touch 4″	S. Kay	4,000	95.00	95.00
86-F-AO-10-061	Finishing Touch 6″	S. Kay	4,000	195.00	195.00
86-F-AO-10-062	Finishing Touch 1-1/2″	S. Kay	7,500	45.00	45.00
86-F-AO-10-063	Good As New 4″	S. Kay	4,000	95.00	95.00
86-F-AO-10-064	Good As New 6″	S. Kay	4,000	195.00	195.00
86-F-AO-10-065	Good As New 1-1/2″	S. Kay	7,500	45.00	45.00
86-F-AO-10-066	Bunny Hug 4″	S. Kay	4,000	95.00	95.00
86-F-AO-10-067	Bunny Hug 6″	S. Kay	2,000	210.00	210.00
86-F-AO-10-068	Bunny Hug 1-1/2″	S. Kay	7,500	45.00	45.00
86-F-AO-10-069	Sweet Treat 4″	S. Kay	4,000	95.00	95.00
86-F-AO-10-070	Sweet Treat 6″	S. Kay	4,000	195.00	195.00
86-F-AO-10-071	Sweet Treat 1-1/2″	S. Kay	7,500	45.00	45.00
86-F-AO-10-072	To Love And To Cherish 4″	S. Kay	4,000	95.00	95.00
86-F-AO-10-073	To Love And To Cherish 6″	S. Kay	4,000	195.00	195.00
86-F-AO-10-074	To Love And To Cherish 1-1/2″	S. Kay	7,500	45.00	45.00
86-F-AO-10-075	With This Ring 4″	S. Kay	4,000	95.00	95.00
86-F-AO-10-076	With This Ring 6″	S. Kay	4,000	195.00	195.00
86-F-AO-10-077	With This Ring 1-1/2″	S. Kay	7,500	45.00	45.00
87-F-AO-10-078	All Aboard 6″	S. Kay	2,000	265.00	265.00
87-F-AO-10-079	All Aboard 4″	S. Kay	4,000	130.00	130.00
87-F-AO-10-080	All Aboard 1-1/2″	S. Kay	7,500	49.50	49.50
87-F-AO-10-081	Let's Play 6″	S. Kay	2,000	265.00	265.00
87-F-AO-10-082	Let's Play 4″	S. Kay	4,000	130.00	130.00
87-F-AO-10-083	Let's Play 1-1/2″	S. Kay	7,500	49.50	49.50
87-F-AO-10-084	A Loving Spoonful 6″	S. Kay	4,000	295.00	295.00
87-F-AO-10-085	A Loving Spoonful 4″	S. Kay	4,000	150.00	150.00
87-F-AO-10-086	A Loving Spoonful 1-1/2″	S. Kay	7,500	49.50	49.50
87-F-AO-10-087	Little Nanny 6″	S. Kay	4,000	295.00	295.00
87-F-AO-10-088	Little Nanny 4″	S. Kay	4,000	150.00	150.00
87-F-AO-10-089	Little Nanny 1-1/2″	S. Kay	7,500	49.50	49.50
87-F-AO-10-090	All Mine 6″	S. Kay	4,000	245.00	245.00
87-F-AO-10-091	All Mine 4″	S. Kay	4,000	130.00	130.00
87-F-AO-10-092	All Mine 1-1/2″	S. Kay	7,500	49.50	49.50
87-F-AO-10-093	Cuddles 6″	S. Kay	4,000	245.00	245.00
87-F-AO-10-094	Cuddles 4″	S. Kay	4,000	130.00	130.00
87-F-AO-10-095	Cuddles 1-1/2″	S. Kay	7,500	49.50	49.50
87-F-AO-10-096	Afternoon Tea 11″	S. Kay	750	590.00	590.00
87-F-AO-10-097	Afternoon Tea 20″	S. Kay	100	2790.00	2790.00
Anri	**Club Anri**				
83-F-AO-14-001	Welcome 4″	J. Ferrandiz	Yr.Iss	110.00	180.00
84-F-AO-14-002	My Friend 4″	J. Ferrandiz	Yr.Iss	110.00	180.00
84-F-AO-14-003	Apple of My Eye 4-1/2″	S. Kay	Yr.Iss	135.00	150.00
85-F-AO-14-004	Harvest Time 4″	J. Ferrandiz	Yr.Iss	125.00	125.00
85-F-AO-14-005	Dad's Helper 4-1/2″	S. Kay	Yr.Iss	135.00	150.00
86-F-AO-14-006	Harvest's Helper 4″	J. Ferrandiz	Yr.Iss	135.00	135.00
86-F-AO-14-007	Romantic Notions 4″	S. Kay	Yr.Iss	135.00	135.00
86-F-AO-14-008	Celebration March 5″	J. Ferrandiz	Yr.Iss	165.00	165.00
86-F-AO-14-009	Will You Be Mine	J. Ferrandiz	Yr.Iss	135.00	135.00
86-F-AO-14-010	Make A Wish	S. Kay	Yr.Iss	165.00	165.00
86-F-AO-14-011	A Young Man's Fancy	S. Kay	Yr.Iss	135.00	135.00
Anri	**Annual Limited Edition Girl**				
85-F-AO-15-001	Tender Love, 6″	J. Ferrandiz	2,250	225.00	245.00
85-F-AO-15-002	Tender Love, 3″	J. Ferrandiz	2,250	100.00	125.00
86-F-AO-15-003	Golden Sheaves 6″	J. Ferrandiz	2,250	240.00	245.00
86-F-AO-15-004	Golden Sheaves 3″	J. Ferrandiz	2,250	120.00	125.00
86-F-AO-15-005	For My Sweetheart 6″	J. Ferrandiz	2,250	250.00	250.00
86-F-AO-15-006	For My Sweetheart 3″	J. Ferrandiz	2,250	130.00	130.00
Anri	**Limited Edition Couples**				
85-F-AO-16-001	Springtime Stroll, 8″	J. Ferrandiz	750	590.00	700.00
85-F-AO-16-002	First Kiss, 8″	J. Ferrandiz	750	590.00	700.00
86-F-AO-16-003	A Tender Touch 8″	J. Ferrandiz	750	590.00	590.00
86-F-AO-16-004	My Heart Is Yours 8″	J. Ferrandiz	750	590.00	590.00
86-F-AO-16-005	Heart to Heart 8″	J. Ferrandiz	750	590.00	650.00
Armstrong's	**Pro Autographed Ceramic Baseball Card Plaques**				
85-F-AT-06-001	Brett, Garvey, Jackson, Rose, Seaver, auto,3-1/4″ X 5″	Unknown	1,000	149.75	149.75
Armstrong's	**Pro Classic Ceramic Baseball Card Plaques**				
85-F-AT-07-001	George Brett, 2-1/2″ X 3-1/2″	Unknown	Open	9.95	9.95
85-F-AT-07-002	Steve Garvey, 2-1/2″ X 3-1/2″	Unknown	Open	9.95	9.95
85-F-AT-07-003	Reggie Jackson, 2-1/2″ X 3-1/2″	Unknown	Open	9.95	9.95
85-F-AT-07-004	Pete Rose, 2-1/2″ X 3-1/2″	Unknown	Open	9.95	9.95
85-F-AT-07-005	Tom Seaver, 2-1/2″ X 3-1/2″	Unknown	Open	9.95	9.95
Boehm Studios	**Boehm**				
83-F-BJ-01-001	Great Egret	Boehm	Yr.Iss	1200.00	1500.00
84-F-BJ-01-002	Whooping Crane	Boehm	Yr.Iss	1800.00	1800.00
85-F-BJ-01-003	Trumpeter Swan	Boehm	Yr.Iss	1500.00	1500.00
Boehm Studios	**Bird Sculptures**				
57-F-BJ-09-001	American Eagle, large	Boehm	31	225.00	11000.00
57-F-BJ-09-002	American Eagle, small	Boehm	76	225.00	9200.00
58-F-BJ-09-003	American Redstarts	Boehm	500	350.00	2000.00
80-F-BJ-09-004	Arctic Tern	Boehm	350	1400.00	2600.00
69-F-BJ-09-005	Black-headed Grosbeak	Boehm	675	1250.00	1525.00
56-F-BJ-09-006	Black-tailed Bantams,pair	Boehm	57	350.00	4700.00
58-F-BJ-09-007	Black-throated Blue Warbler	Boehm	500	400.00	1875.00
76-F-BJ-09-008	Black-throated Blue Warbler	Boehm	200	900.00	1100.00
67-F-BJ-09-009	Blue Grosbeak	Boehm	750	1050.00	1500.00
62-F-BJ-09-010	Blue Jays, pair	Boehm	250	2000.00	12750.00
64-F-BJ-09-011	Bobolink	Boehm	500	550.00	1550.00
53-F-BJ-09-012	Bob White Quail, pair	Boehm	750	400.00	2600.00
72-F-BJ-09-013	Brown Pelican	Boehm	100	10500.00	14500.00
73-F-BJ-09-014	Brown Thrasher	Boehm	260	1850.00	1875.00
72-F-BJ-09-015	Cactus Wren	Boehm	225	3000.00	3300.00
57-F-BJ-09-016	California Quail, pair	Boehm	500	400.00	2900.00
78-F-BJ-09-017	Canada Geese, pair	Boehm	100	4200.00	4200.00
77-F-BJ-09-018	Cape May Warbler	Boehm	400	825.00	950.00
55-F-BJ-09-019	Cardinals, pair	Boehm	500	550.00	3750.00
77-F-BJ-09-020	Cardinals	Boehm	200	3500.00	3500.00
57-F-BJ-09-021	Carolina Wrens	Boehm	100	750.00	5500.00
65-F-BJ-09-022	Catbird	Boehm	500	900.00	2135.00
56-F-BJ-09-023	Cedar Waxwings, pair	Boehm	100	600.00	7750.00
57-F-BJ-09-024	Cerulean Warblers	Boehm	100	800.00	4335.00
68-F-BJ-09-025	Common Tern	Boehm	500	1400.00	6200.00
67-F-BJ-09-026	Crested Flycatcher	Boehm	500	1650.00	2925.00
57-F-BJ-09-027	Downy Woodpeckers	Boehm	500	450.00	1775.00
76-F-BJ-09-028	Eagle of Freedom I	Boehm	15	35000.00	53000.00
59-F-BJ-09-029	Eastern Bluebirds, pair	Boehm	100	1800.00	12000.00
75-F-BJ-09-030	Eastern Kingbird	Boehm	100	3500.00	3900.00
73-F-BJ-09-031	Everglades Kites	Boehm	50	5800.00	7200.00
77-F-BJ-09-032	Fledgling Brown Thrashers	Boehm	400	500.00	655.00
67-F-BJ-09-033	Fledgling Canada Warbler	Boehm	750	550.00	2275.00
65-F-BJ-09-034	Fledgling Great Horned Owl	Boehm	750	350.00	1475.00
71-F-BJ-09-035	Flicker	Boehm	250	2400.00	2950.00
56-F-BJ-09-036	Golden-crowned Kinglets	Boehm	500	1400.00	2400.00
54-F-BJ-09-037	Golden Pheasant,decorated	Boehm	7	350.00	19000.00
54-F-BJ-09-038	Golden Pheasant,bisque	Boehm	7	200.00	11250.00
61-F-BJ-09-039	Goldfinches	Boehm	500	400.00	1800.00
66-F-BJ-09-040	Green Jays, pair	Boehm	400	1850.00	4200.00
74-F-BJ-09-041	Hooded Warbler	Boehm	100	2400.00	3150.00
73-F-BJ-09-042	Horned Larks	Boehm	200	3800.00	5000.00
68-F-BJ-09-043	Kestrels, pair	Boehm	460	2300.00	3000.00
64-F-BJ-09-044	Killdeer, pair	Boehm	300	1750.00	4500.00
74-F-BJ-09-045	Lark Sparrow	Boehm	150	2100.00	2200.00
73-F-BJ-09-046	Lazuli Buntings	Boehm	250	1800.00	2300.00
79-F-BJ-09-047	Least Tern	Boehm	350	1275.00	3100.00
62-F-BJ-09-048	Lesser Prairie Chickens, pair	Boehm	300	1200.00	2400.00
52-F-BJ-09-049	Mallards, pair	Boehm	500	650.00	1700.00
57-F-BJ-09-050	Meadowlark	Boehm	750	350.00	3100.00
63-F-BJ-09-051	Mearn's Quail, pair	Boehm	350	950.00	3450.00
68-F-BJ-09-052	Mergansers, pair	Boehm	440	2200.00	2825.00
61-F-BJ-09-053	Mockingbirds, pair	Boehm	500	650.00	3800.00
78-F-BJ-09-054	Mockingbirds	Boehm	None	2200.00	2800.00
63-F-BJ-09-055	Mountain Bluebirds	Boehm	300	1900.00	5850.00
58-F-BJ-09-056	Mourning Doves	Boehm	500	550.00	1250.00
71-F-BJ-09-057	Mute swans, life-size, pair	Boehm	3	Unknown	Unknown
71-F-BJ-09-058	Mute Swans, small size, pair	Boehm	400	4000.00	7900.00
74-F-BJ-09-059	Myrtle Warblers	Boehm	210	1850.00	2075.00
58-F-BJ-09-060	Nonpareil Buntings	Boehm	750	250.00	1075.00
67-F-BJ-09-061	Northern Water Thrush	Boehm	500	800.00	1400.00
70-F-BJ-09-062	Orchard Orioles	Boehm	550	1750.00	2200.00
70-F-BJ-09-063	Oven-bird	Boehm	450	1400.00	1800.00
65-F-BJ-09-064	Parula Warblers	Boehm	400	1500.00	3150.00
75-F-BJ-09-065	Pekin Robins	Boehm	100	7000.00	8550.00
62-F-BJ-09-066	Ptarmigan, pair	Boehm	350	800.00	3575.00
74-F-BJ-09-067	Purple Martins	Boehm	50	6700.00	8450.00
75-F-BJ-09-068	Red-billed Blue Magpie	Boehm	100	4600.00	5950.00
57-F-BJ-09-069	Red-winged Blackbirds, pair	Boehm	100	700.00	5250.00
54-F-BJ-09-070	Ringed-necked Pheasants, pair	Boehm	500	650.00	1825.00
68-F-BJ-09-071	Roadrunner	Boehm	500	2600.00	3700.00
64-F-BJ-09-072	Robin (Daffodils)	Boehm	500	600.00	5700.00
77-F-BJ-09-073	Robin (nest)	Boehm	350	1650.00	1840.00
60-F-BJ-09-074	Ruffed Grouse, pair	Boehm	250	950.00	4950.00
66-F-BJ-09-075	Rufous Hummingbirds	Boehm	500	850.00	1900.00
77-F-BJ-09-076	Scarlet Tanager	Boehm	4	1800.00	4000.00
77-F-BJ-09-077	Scissor-tailed Flycatcher	Boehm	100	3200.00	3200.00
79-F-BJ-09-078	Scops Owl	Boehm	300	975.00	1300.00
80-F-BJ-09-079	Screech Owl	Boehm	350	2100.00	3100.00
70-F-BJ-09-080	Slate-colored Junco	Boehm	None	1600.00	2000.00
81-F-BJ-09-081	Snow Buntings	Boehm	350	2400.00	2950.00
56-F-BJ-09-082	Song Sparrows, pair	Boehm	50	2000.00	38000.00
61-F-BJ-09-083	Sugarbirds	Boehm	100	2500.00	13250.00
63-F-BJ-09-084	Towhee	Boehm	500	350.00	2600.00
65-F-BJ-09-085	Tufted Titmice	Boehm	500	600.00	2000.00
65-F-BJ-09-086	Varied Buntings	Boehm	300	2200.00	4500.00
74-F-BJ-09-087	Varied Thrush	Boehm	None	2500.00	3000.00
69-F-BJ-09-088	Verdins	Boehm	575	1150.00	1525.00
69-F-BJ-09-089	Western Bluebirds	Boehm	300	5500.00	6600.00
71-F-BJ-09-090	Western Meadowlark	Boehm	350	1425.00	1675.00
54-F-BJ-09-091	Woodcock	Boehm	500	300.00	1950.00
51-F-BJ-09-092	Wood Thrush	Boehm	2	375.00	Unknown
66-F-BJ-09-093	Wood Thrushes, pair	Boehm	400	4200.00	8400.00
72-F-BJ-09-094	Yellow-bellied Sapsucker	Boehm	None	2700.00	3200.00
74-F-BJ-09-095	Yellow-bellied Cuckoo	Boehm	None	2800.00	3000.00
74-F-BJ-09-096	Yellow-headed Blackbird	Boehm	75	3200.00	3600.00
73-F-BJ-09-097	Young American Eagle, Inaugural	Boehm	100	1500.00	2100.00
69-F-BJ-09-098	Young American Eagle	Boehm	850	700.00	1400.00
75-F-BJ-09-099	Young & Spirited 1976	Boehm	1,121	950.00	1800.00
79-F-BJ-09-100	Avocet	Boehm	175	1200.00	1200.00
72-F-BJ-09-101	Barn Owl	Boehm	350	3600.00	5600.00
73-F-BJ-09-102	Blackbirds, pair	Boehm	75	5400.00	6300.00
72-F-BJ-09-103	Black Grouse	Boehm	175	2800.00	3025.00
73-F-BJ-09-104	Blue Tits	Boehm	300	3000.00	3000.00
74-F-BJ-09-105	Chaffinch	Boehm	125	2000.00	2200.00
74-F-BJ-09-106	Crested Tit	Boehm	400	1150.00	1250.00
75-F-BJ-09-107	European Goldfinch	Boehm	225	1150.00	1350.00
72-F-BJ-09-108	Goldcrest	Boehm	500	650.00	1200.00
73-F-BJ-09-109	Green Woodpeckers	Boehm	50	4200.00	4800.00
79-F-BJ-09-110	Grey Wagtail	Boehm	150	1050.00	1260.00
76-F-BJ-09-111	Kingfishers	Boehm	200	1900.00	2300.00
73-F-BJ-09-112	Lapwing	Boehm	100	2600.00	2975.00

Figurines

Company		Series			
Number	Name	Artist	Edition limit	Issue Price	Quote
71-F-BJ-09-113	Little Owl	Boehm	350	700.00	1325.00
73-F-BJ-09-114	Long Tail Tits	Boehm	200	2600.00	2900.00
71-F-BJ-09-115	Nuthatch	Boehm	350	650.00	1100.00
73-F-BJ-09-116	Peregrine Falcon	Boehm	350	4400.00	5450.00
76-F-BJ-09-117	Rivoli's Hummingbird	Boehm	350	950.00	1550.00
74-F-BJ-09-118	Ruby-throated Hummingbird	Boehm	200	1900.00	2650.00
73-F-BJ-09-119	Screech Owl	Boehm	50	850.00	1425.00
74-F-BJ-09-120	Song Thrushes	Boehm	100	2800.00	3350.00
74-F-BJ-09-121	Stonechats	Boehm	150	2200.00	2400.00
74-F-BJ-09-122	Swallows	Boehm	125	3400.00	4100.00
72-F-BJ-09-123	Tree Creepers	Boehm	200	3200.00	4200.00
71-F-BJ-09-124	Winter Robin	Boehm	225	1150.00	1440.00
73-F-BJ-09-125	Yellowhammers	Boehm	350	3300.00	4200.00
Boehm Studios		**Animal Sculptures**			
69-F-BJ-10-001	Adios	Boehm	130	1500.00	1800.00
52-F-BJ-10-002	Hunter	Boehm	250	600.00	1300.00
57-F-BJ-10-003	Polo Player	Boehm	100	850.00	4450.00
78-F-BJ-10-004	Thoroughbred with Jockey	Boehm	25	2600.00	2800.00
77-F-BJ-10-005	African Elephant	Boehm	50	9500.00	14400.00
76-F-BJ-10-006	American Mustangs	Boehm	75	3700.00	5700.00
80-F-BJ-10-007	Asian Lion	Boehm	100	1500.00	1500.00
78-F-BJ-10-008	Black Rhinoceros	Boehm	50	9500.00	9500.00
71-F-BJ-10-009	Bobcats	Boehm	200	1600.00	2000.00
78-F-BJ-10-010	Camel & Calf	Boehm	50	3500.00	3900.00
80-F-BJ-10-011	Cheetah	Boehm	100	2700.00	2700.00
79-F-BJ-10-012	Fallow Deer	Boehm	30	7500.00	7500.00
71-F-BJ-10-013	Foxes	Boehm	200	1800.00	2550.00
75-F-BJ-10-014	Giant Panda	Boehm	100	3800.00	6350.00
78-F-BJ-10-015	Gorilla	Boehm	50	3800.00	4400.00
79-F-BJ-10-016	Hunter Chase	Boehm	20	4000.00	4000.00
73-F-BJ-10-017	Nyala Antelope	Boehm	100	4700.00	6500.00
76-F-BJ-10-018	Otter	Boehm	75	1100.00	1450.00
75-F-BJ-10-019	Puma	Boehm	50	5700.00	6800.00
71-F-BJ-10-020	Raccoons	Boehm	200	1600.00	2250.00
72-F-BJ-10-021	Red Squirrels	Boehm	100	2600.00	2800.00
78-F-BJ-10-022	Snow Leopard	Boehm	75	3500.00	4950.00
79-F-BJ-10-023	Young & Free Fawns	Boehm	160	1875.00	1875.00
Boehm Studios		**Floral Sculptures**			
79-F-BJ-11-001	Cactus Dahlia	Boehm	300	800.00	960.00
72-F-BJ-11-002	Chrysanthemums	Boehm	350	1100.00	1950.00
71-F-BJ-11-003	Daisies	Boehm	350	600.00	975.00
74-F-BJ-11-004	Debutante Camellia	Boehm	500	625.00	800.00
73-F-BJ-11-005	Dogwood	Boehm	250	625.00	975.00
78-F-BJ-11-006	Double Clematis Centerpiece	Boehm	150	1500.00	1950.00
74-F-BJ-11-007	Double Peony	Boehm	275	575.00	1050.00
75-F-BJ-11-008	Emmett Barnes Camellia	Boehm	425	550.00	780.00
74-F-BJ-11-009	Gentians	Boehm	350	425.00	725.00
79-F-BJ-11-010	Grand Floral Centerpiece	Boehm	15	7500.00	8700.00
78-F-BJ-11-011	Helen Boehm Camellia	Boehm	500	600.00	1050.00
78-F-BJ-11-012	Helen Boehm Daylily	Boehm	175	975.00	1160.00
78-F-BJ-11-013	Helen Boehm Iris	Boehm	175	975.00	1175.00
79-F-BJ-11-014	Honeysuckle	Boehm	200	900.00	1080.00
75-F-BJ-11-015	Magnolia Grandiflora	Boehm	750	650.00	1350.00
76-F-BJ-11-016	Orchid Cactus	Boehm	100	650.00	975.00
76-F-BJ-11-017	Queen of the Night Cactus	Boehm	125	650.00	850.00
78-F-BJ-11-018	Rhododendron Centerpiece	Boehm	350	1150.00	1750.00
80-F-BJ-11-019	Rose, Alec's Red	Boehm	500	1050.00	1300.00
78-F-BJ-11-020	Rose, Blue Moon	Boehm	500	650.00	900.00
78-F-BJ-11-021	Rose, Pascali	Boehm	500	950.00	1375.00
76-F-BJ-11-022	Rose, Supreme Peace	Boehm	250	850.00	1575.00
76-F-BJ-11-023	Rose, Supreme Yellow	Boehm	250	850.00	1575.00
78-F-BJ-11-024	Rose, Tropicana	Boehm	500	475.00	1085.00
78-F-BJ-11-025	Spanish Iris	Boehm	500	600.00	600.00
73-F-BJ-11-026	Streptocalyx Poeppigii	Boehm	50	3400.00	4300.00
71-F-BJ-11-027	Swan Centerpiece	Boehm	135	1950.00	2725.00
76-F-BJ-11-028	Swan Lake Camellia	Boehm	750	825.00	1725.00
71-F-BJ-11-029	Sweet Viburnum	Boehm	35	650.00	1425.00
74-F-BJ-11-030	Waterlily	Boehm	350	400.00	660.00
78-F-BJ-11-031	Watsonii Magnolia	Boehm	250	575.00	690.00
Boehm Studios		**Figurines**			
77-F-BJ-12-180	Beverly Sills	Boehm	100	950.00	1500.00
77-F-BJ-12-181	Jerome Hines	Boehm	12	825.00	1000.00
Brantwood/Treins		**Various**			
80-F-BN-01-001	Doctor and the Doll	N. Rockwell	15,000	89.50	70.00
80-F-BN-01-002	Toymaker	N. Rockwell	15,000	79.50	90.00
Brown & Bigelow Inc.		**Various**			
79-F-BP-01-001	The Runaway	N. Rockwell	None	90.00	90.00
Burgues		**Animals**			
76-F-BU-01-001	American Wild Goat	I. Burgues	10	10000.00	14500.00
XX-F-BU-01-002	Big Horn Sheep	I. Burgues	250	2500.00	4500.00
XX-F-BU-01-003	Black Tailed Prairie Dog	I. Burgues	950	225.00	425.00
82-F-BU-01-004	Brown Bears	I. Burgues	250	550.00	650.00
XX-F-BU-01-005	Bunny, sitting	I. Burgues	950	75.00	120.00
XX-F-BU-01-006	Bunny, standing	I. Burgues	950	85.00	120.00
XX-F-BU-01-007	Big Horn Sheep, glazed	I. Burgues	25	2750.00	4575.00
XX-F-BU-01-008	Chipmunk	I. Burgues	750	150.00	450.00
XX-F-BU-01-009	Chipmunk w/Fly Amanita	I. Burgues	450	400.00	625.00
83-F-BU-01-010	Oscar, cat	I. Burgues	950	75.00	100.00
XX-F-BU-01-011	Albert, cat	I. Burgues	950	75.00	100.00
XX-F-BU-01-012	Natasha, cat	I. Burgues	950	75.00	95.00
XX-F-BU-01-013	Mimi, cat	I. Burgues	950	75.00	95.00
XX-F-BU-01-014	Felix, cat	I. Burgues	950	75.00	110.00
XX-F-BU-01-015	Isis, cat	I. Burgues	950	75.00	110.00
XX-F-BU-01-016	Caramella, cat	I. Burgues	950	75.00	100.00
XX-F-BU-01-017	Tabu, cat	I. Burgues	950	75.00	110.00
XX-F-BU-01-018	Princess, cat	I. Burgues	950	75.00	100.00
XX-F-BU-01-019	Ginger, cat	I. Burgues	950	75.00	105.00
XX-F-BU-01-020	Ebony, cat	I. Burgues	950	75.00	120.00
72-F-BU-01-021	Cab Eater Seals	I. Burgues	200	1250.00	1400.00
76-F-BU-01-022	Horse, dec. Spirit of Freedom	I. Burgues	50	1500.00	2250.00
76-F-BU-01-023	Horse, white, Spirit of Freedom	I. Burgues	50	1000.00	2100.00
84-F-BU-01-024	Horse, Conquest	I. Burgues	25	3500.00	4300.00
XX-F-BU-01-025	Horse, Lady	I. Burgues	950	75.00	85.00
XX-F-BU-01-026	Horse, Samy	I. Burgues	950	75.00	85.00
XX-F-BU-01-027	Hare, summer	I. Burgues	950	95.00	110.00
XX-F-BU-01-028	Hare, winter	I. Burgues	950	95.00	110.00
76-F-BU-01-029	Polar Bear, fem	I. Burgues	950	280.00	325.00
XX-F-BU-01-030	Polar Bear, cub	I. Burgues	950	235.00	295.00
XX-F-BU-01-031	Polar Bear, cub male	I. Burgues	950	245.00	315.00
76-F-BU-01-032	Red Squirrel	I. Burgues	950	230.00	250.00
XX-F-BU-01-033	White tailed Prairie Dog	I. Burgues	350	550.00	750.00
XX-F-BU-01-034	Young African Elephant	I. Burgues	950	225.00	260.00
78-F-BU-01-035	Young Cottontail	I. Burgues	950	225.00	325.00
XX-F-BU-01-036	Young Mountain Goat	I. Burgues	950	195.00	200.00
XX-F-BU-01-037	Young Burro	I. Burgues	950	1250.00	1600.00
76-F-BU-01-038	Young Walrus	I. Burgues	Unkn.	225.00	425.00
Burgues		**Birds**			
71-F-BU-02-001	Am. Goldfinches	I. Burgues	150	1250.00	2100.00
XX-F-BU-02-002	Belted Kingfisher	I. Burgues	750	350.00	650.00
XX-F-BU-02-003	Blue Jay	I. Burgues	Open	125.00	175.00
72-F-BU-02-004	Baltimore Oriole	I. Burgues	200	725.00	995.00
76-F-BU-02-005	Bay breasted Warbler	I. Burgues	950	175.00	245.00
76-F-BU-02-006	Black capped Chickadee	I. Burgues	950	160.00	220.00
XX-F-BU-02-007	Black chinned Hummingbirds w/Trumpet Vine	I. Burgues	250	1800.00	1900.00
XX-F-BU-02-008	Black throated Green Warbler	I. Burgues	250	750.00	850.00
XX-F-BU-02-009	Carolina Wren	I. Burgues	350	750.00	950.00
XX-F-BU-02-010	Cassin's Kingbird	I. Burgues	350	750.00	950.00
XX-F-BU-02-011	Cave Swallows	I. Burgues	500	750.00	2900.00
71-F-BU-02-012	Chanticleer	I. Burgues	100	1300.00	2100.00
71-F-BU-02-013	Chickadee on Dogwood	I. Burgues	75	950.00	1375.00
72-F-BU-02-014	Canon Wren	I. Burgues	250	750.00	980.00
XX-F-BU-02-015	Cardinal, juv.	I. Burgues	500	225.00	290.00
76-F-BU-02-016	Chestnut backed Chickadee	I. Burgues	950	175.00	245.00
76-F-BU-02-017	Chestnut sided Warbler	I. Burgues	950	175.00	225.00
XX-F-BU-02-018	Duckling w/Spiderwort	I. Burgues	950	225.00	240.00
74-F-BU-02-019	Golden crowned Kinglet	I. Burgues	450	450.00	725.00
71-F-BU-02-020	Golden winged Warbler	I. Burgues	100	1100.00	1750.00
XX-F-BU-02-021	Junco on Snow	I. Burgues	250	550.00	700.00
XX-F-BU-02-022	King Penguins	I. Burgues	350	850.00	950.00
76-F-BU-02-023	Lucy's Warbler	I. Burgues	950	175.00	225.00
76-F-BU-02-024	Magnolia Warbler	I. Burgues	950	160.00	225.00
76-F-BU-02-025	Parula Warbler	I. Burgues	950	160.00	225.00
XX-F-BU-02-026	Penguins, male & female	I. Burgues	950 ea	125.00	150.00
76-F-BU-02-027	Piliated Woodpecker	I. Burgues	350	275.00	350.00
XX-F-BU-02-028	Red headed Woodpecker	I. Burgues	350	1100.00	1250.00
XX-F-BU-02-029	Ruby throated Hummingbird	I. Burgues	300	700.00	950.00
XX-F-BU-02-030	Red breasted Nuthatch	I. Burgues	950	225.00	325.00
XX-F-BU-02-031	Robin, adult	I. Burgues	500	550.00	650.00
XX-F-BU-02-032	Robin, juv.	I. Burgues	950	150.00	350.00
XX-F-BU-02-033	Rufus Hummingbird	I. Burgues	350	275.00	380.00
XX-F-BU-02-034	Snowy Owl	I. Burgues	500	450.00	500.00
XX-F-BU-02-035	Saw whet Owl	I. Burgues	350	265.00	350.00
XX-F-BU-02-036	Snow Bunting	I. Burgues	500	250.00	425.00
XX-F-BU-02-037	Snow Bunting, juv.	I. Burgues	950	150.00	225.00
XX-F-BU-02-038	Snow Bunting w/Holly	I. Burgues	950	165.00	260.00
XX-F-BU-02-039	White breasted Nuthatches	I. Burgues	75	3500.00	4750.00
73-F-BU-02-040	White throated Sparrow	I. Burgues	250	725.00	1025.00
XX-F-BU-02-041	Wood Duckling	I. Burgues	950	175.00	225.00
XX-F-BU-02-042	Woodthrush, juv.	I. Burgues	500	250.00	350.00
XX-F-BU-02-043	Yellow billed Cuckoo	I. Burgues	500	400.00	600.00
XX-F-BU-02-044	Yellow billed Cuckoo, juv.	I. Burgues	950	175.00	250.00
XX-F-BU-02-045	Yellow Warbler	I. Burgues	75	700.00	950.00
Burgues		**Various**			
XX-F-BU-03-001	Peter and his goose	I. Burgues	250	275.00	395.00
XX-F-BU-03-002	Clown, Andy	I. Burgues	200	550.00	625.00
XX-F-BU-03-003	Lollipop Louie	I. Burgues	250	550.00	625.00
XX-F-BU-03-004	Lollipop Louie, green	I. Burgues	Spec.	750.00	1000.00
XX-F-BU-03-005	Lollipop Louie, orange	I. Burgues	25	650.00	875.00
XX-F-BU-03-006	Pierrot	I. Burgues	250	425.00	585.00
XX-F-BU-03-007	Joey	I. Burgues	150	350.00	1750.00
XX-F-BU-03-008	Morning	I. Burgues	200	450.00	750.00
81-F-BU-03-009	Joy	I. Burgues	Unkn.	85.00	95.00
XX-F-BU-03-010	Jason	I. Burgues	150	385.00	825.00
XX-F-BU-03-011	Fabian	I. Burgues	250	525.00	550.00
70-F-BU-03-012	Madonna	I. Burgues	30	125.00	3570.00
XX-F-BU-03-013	Madonna, dec	I. Burgues	200	250.00	350.00
XX-F-BU-03-014	Madonna, white	I. Burgues	350	175.00	295.00
82-F-BU-03-015	Frosty	I. Burgues	500	50.00	75.00
83-F-BU-03-016	Crystal	I. Burgues	500	65.00	95.00
XX-F-BU-03-017	The Prince	I. Burgues	950	50.00	95.00
83-F-BU-03-018	Lazy Days	I. Burgues	500	75.00	150.00
72-F-BU-03-019	Veiltail Goldfish	I. Burgues	150	975.00	1550.00
72-F-BU-03-020	Veiltail Goldfish, glazed	I. Burgues	150	875.00	1800.00
Burgues		**Flowers**			
XX-F-BU-04-001	Anemone	I. Burgues	350	550.00	750.00
76-F-BU-04-002	Anniversary Orchid	I. Burgues	Spec.	75.00	120.00
XX-F-BU-04-003	Barrel Cactus	I. Burgues	500	225.00	265.00
XX-F-BU-04-004	Begonia, yellow	I. Burgues	150	275.00	450.00
XX-F-BU-04-005	Begonia, pink	I. Burgues	150	275.00	450.00
84-F-BU-04-006	Cymbidium, Pink Blush	I. Burgues	200	65.00	95.00
XX-F-BU-04-007	Cymbidium, lav.	I. Burgues	200	75.00	150.00
XX-F-BU-04-008	Cymbidium, orange	I. Burgues	200	75.00	150.00
XX-F-BU-04-009	Camellia, Snow Cap	I. Burgues	250	750.00	950.00
XX-F-BU-04-010	Camellia, Anniversary	I. Burgues	250	75.00	95.00
XX-F-BU-04-011	Camellia, Memories	I. Burgues	250	75.00	95.00
XX-F-BU-04-012	Carnation, My Love	I. Burgues	300	90.00	90.00
XX-F-BU-04-013	Carnation, Affection	I. Burgues	300	90.00	90.00
XX-F-BU-04-014	Carnation, Innocence	I. Burgues	300	90.00	90.00
XX-F-BU-04-015	Clematis, Sieboldi	I. Burgues	500	175.00	250.00
XX-F-BU-04-016	Daffodil	I. Burgues	500	120.00	160.00
XX-F-BU-04-017	Dainty Bess	I. Burgues	200	165.00	195.00
XX-F-BU-04-018	Daffodil, Manco	I. Burgues	250	450.00	850.00
XX-F-BU-04-019	Desert Spring	I. Burgues	5	15000.00	19500.00
XX-F-BU-04-020	Double Hibiscus, yellow	I. Burgues	150	325.00	395.00
XX-F-BU-04-021	Double Hibiscus, red	I. Burgues	150	325.00	395.00
XX-F-BU-04-022	Flower Basket w/handle, red	I. Burgues	100	550.00	685.00
XX-F-BU-04-023	Flower Basket w/handle, salmon	I. Burgues	100	550.00	685.00
XX-F-BU-04-024	Flower Basket w/handle, yellow	I. Burgues	100	550.00	685.00
XX-F-BU-04-025	Flower Basket w/handle, pink	I. Burgues	100	550.00	685.00

Number	Name	Artist	Edition limit	Issue Price	Quote
XX-F-BU-04-026	Floribunda, My Treasure	I. Burgues	300	75.00	75.00
XX-F-BU-04-027	Floribunda, Darling	I. Burgues	300	75.00	75.00
XX-F-BU-04-028	Flower Basket, open, June Bouquet	I. Burgues	100	550.00	695.00
XX-F-BU-04-029	Flower Basket, Country Spice	I. Burgues	100	550.00	695.00
XX-F-BU-04-030	Flower Basket, Golden Treasure	I. Burgues	100	550.00	695.00
XX-F-BU-04-031	Gardenia	I. Burgues	500	65.00	75.00
XX-F-BU-04-032	Hibiscus, pink	I. Burgues	200	75.00	100.00
XX-F-BU-04-033	Hibiscus, yellow	I. Burgues	200	75.00	100.00
XX-F-BU-04-034	Hibiscus, flame	I. Burgues	200	75.00	100.00
XX-F-BU-04-035	Hibiscus, white	I. Burgues	200	75.00	100.00
XX-F-BU-04-036	Hibiscus, Fantasy	I. Burgues	300	95.00	95.00
XX-F-BU-04-037	Hibiscus, Passion	I. Burgues	300	95.00	110.00
XX-F-BU-04-038	Hibiscus, Paradise	I. Burgues	300	95.00	95.00
XX-F-BU-04-039	Harmony Rose	I. Burgues	250	125.00	150.00
XX-F-BU-04-040	Harmony Yellow	I. Burgues	250	125.00	150.00
XX-F 'U-04-041	Harmony Pink	I. Burgues	250	125.00	150.00
XX-F-BU-04-042	Heavenly Blue Morning Glory	I. Burgues	300	175.00	250.00
XX-F-BU-04-043	Imperial Gold Lily	I. Burgues	200	225.00	325.00
XX-F-BU-04-044	Lily Harlequin	I. Burgues	250	550.00	750.00
XX-F-BU-04-045	Lilac Charm Rose	I. Burgues	75	700.00	825.00
XX-F-BU-04-046	Lily, Gypsy	I. Burgues	250	110.00	110.00
XX-F-BU-04-047	Lily, Pink Pearl	I. Burgues	250	110.00	110.00
XX-F-BU-04-048	Lily, Dreams	I. Burgues	250	110.00	110.00
XX-F-BU-04-049	Magnolia, Soulangeana	I. Burgues	150	1600.00	1850.00
XX-F-BU-04-050	Magnolia w/Butterfly	I. Burgues	50	325.00	650.00
XX-F-BU-04-051	Miniature Rose, Love You	I. Burgues	250	75.00	175.00
XX-F-BU-04-052	Oriental Poppy	I. Burgues	300	125.00	175.00
XX-F-BU-04-053	Paphiopedilium Orchid, Ecstasy	I. Burgues	200	85.00	120.00
XX-F-BU-04-054	Paphiopedilium Orchid, Perfection	I. Burgues	200	85.00	120.00
XX-F-BU-04-055	Paphiopedilium Orchid, Sunny Glow	I. Burgues	200	85.00	120.00
XX-F-BU-04-056	Paphiopedilium Orchid, Spring Time	I. Burgues	200	85.00	120.00
XX-F-BU-04-057	Pink Poppy	I. Burgues	300	125.00	160.00
XX-F-BU-04-058	Prickly Pear Cactus	I. Burgues	250	900.00	1200.00
XX-F-BU-04-059	Peony, cream	I. Burgues	300	130.00	160.00
XX-F-BU-04-060	Peony, pink	I. Burgues	300	130.00	160.00
XX-F-BU-04-061	Pink Lady's Slipper Orchid	I. Burgues	300	750.00	1100.00
XX-F-BU-04-062	Pink Glory Lily	I. Burgues	200	225.00	300.00
XX-F-BU-04-063	Rhododendron	I. Burgues	200	425.00	550.00
XX-F-BU-04-064	Roses: Floribunda, violet	I. Burgues	950	185.00	250.00
XX-F-BU-04-065	Roses: Floribunda, yellow	I. Burgues	950	185.00	250.00
XX-F-BU-04-066	Roses: Floribunda, pink	I. Burgues	950	185.00	250.00
XX-F-BU-04-067	Roses: Tea, small, yellow	I. Burgues	200	225.00	275.00
XX-F-BU-04-068	Roses: Tea, small, pink	I. Burgues	200	225.00	275.00
XX-F-BU-04-069	Roses: Tea, large, yellow	I. Burgues	200	225.00	340.00
XX-F-BU-04-070	Roses: Tea, large, pink	I. Burgues	200	275.00	340.00
XX-F-BU-04-071	Tea Rose, Honey	I. Burgues	300	85.00	100.00
XX-F-BU-04-072	Tea Rose, Be Mine	I. Burgues	300	85.00	95.00
XX-F-BU-04-073	Rose, Sea Shell	I. Burgues	250	125.00	125.00
XX-F-BU-04-074	Spring Gold	I. Burgues	200	145.00	175.00
XX-F-BU-04-075	Sterling Silver	I. Burgues	250	125.00	150.00
XX-F-BU-04-076	Sweetheart Rose, pink	I. Burgues	200	150.00	175.00
XX-F-BU-04-077	Sweetheart Rose, yellow	I. Burgues	200	150.00	175.00
XX-F-BU-04-078	Sweetheart Rose, nectarine	I. Burgues	200	150.00	175.00
XX-F-BU-04-079	Sweetheart Rose, white	I. Burgues	200	150.00	175.00
XX-F-BU-04-080	Tea Rose on Base, Promise	I. Burgues	150	165.00	195.00
XX-F-BU-04-081	Tea Rose on Base, Antiqua	I. Burgues	150	165.00	225.00
XX-F-BU-04-082	Tea Rose on Base, Angel Face	I. Burgues	150	165.00	195.00
XX-F-BU-04-083	Tea Rose on Base, Butterscotch	I. Burgues	150	165.00	230.00
XX-F-BU-04-084	Tea Rose on Base, Dawn	I. Burgues	150	165.00	200.00

Chilmark — **Western Americana-Pewter**

Number	Name	Artist	Edition limit	Issue Price	Quote
74-F-CE-01-001	Cheyenne	D. Polland	2,800	200.00	2750.00
74-F-CE-01-002	Counting Coup	D. Polland	2,800	225.00	1500.00
74-F-CE-01-003	Crow Scout	D. Polland	3,000	175.00	900.00
75-F-CE-01-004	Maverick Calf	D. Polland	2,500	250.00	900.00
75-F-CE-01-005	Cold Saddles	D. Polland	2,800	335.00	365.00
75-F-CE-01-006	The Outlaws	D. Polland	2,500	450.00	525.00
76-F-CE-01-007	Buffalo Hunt	D. Polland	2,250	300.00	1150.00
76-F-CE-01-008	Rescue	D. Polland	2,500	275.00	1750.00
76-F-CE-01-009	Painting the Town	D. Polland	2,250	300.00	950.00
76-F-CE-01-010	Monday Morning Wash	D. Polland	2,500	350.00	900.00
77-F-CE-01-011	Spring-Mustangs	D. Polland	3,500	120.00	120.00
77-F-CE-01-012	Summer-Mustangs	D. Polland	3,500	120.00	120.00
77-F-CE-01-013	Fall-Mustangs	D. Polland	3,500	120.00	120.00
77-F-CE-01-014	Winter-Mustangs	D. Polland	3,500	120.00	120.00
79-F-CE-01-015	Border Rustlers	D. Polland	500	1295.00	1350.00
79-F-CE-01-016	Mandan Hunter	D. Polland	5,000	95.00	250.00
79-F-CE-01-017	Getting Acquainted	D. Polland	Unkn.	240.00	325.00
79-F-CE-01-018	Elephant	D. Polland	Unkn.	315.00	450.00
79-F-CE-01-019	Giraffe	D. Polland	Unkn.	145.00	145.00
79-F-CE-01-020	Kudu	D. Polland	Unkn.	160.00	160.00
79-F-CE-01-021	Rhino	D. Polland	Unkn.	135.00	135.00
81-F-CE-01-022	Buffalo Robe	D. Polland	2,500	235.00	265.00
81-F-CE-01-023	When War Chiefs Meet	D. Polland	2,500	350.00	425.00
81-F-CE-01-024	War Party	D. Polland	2,500	550.00	650.00
81-F-CE-01-025	Dog Soldier	D. Polland	2,500	235.00	265.00
81-F-CE-01-026	Enemy Tracks	D. Polland	2,500	265.00	300.00
81-F-CE-01-027	Ambushed	D. Polland	500	2370.00	2650.00
81-F-CE-01-028	U.S. Marshal	D. Polland	1,500	115.00	250.00
82-F-CE-01-029	Last Arrow	D. Polland	2,500	95.00	100.00
82-F-CE-01-030	Sioux War Chief	D. Polland	2,500	95.00	100.00
82-F-CE-01-031	Navajo Kachina	D. Polland	2,500	95.00	100.00
82-F-CE-01-032	Arapaho Drummer	D. Polland	2,500	95.00	100.00
82-F-CE-01-033	Apache Hostile	D. Polland	2,500	95.00	100.00
82-F-CE-01-034	Buffalo Prayer	D. Polland	2,500	95.00	100.00
82-F-CE-01-035	Eagle Dancer	D. Polland	2,500	95.00	100.00
82-F-CE-01-036	Flathead War Dancer	D. Polland	2,500	95.00	100.00
82-F-CE-01-037	Hopi Kachina	D. Polland	2,500	95.00	100.00
82-F-CE-01-038	Apache Gan Dancer	D. Polland	2,500	95.00	100.00
82-F-CE-01-039	Crow Medicine Dancer	D. Polland	2,500	95.00	100.00
82-F-CE-01-040	Comanche Drummer	D. Polland	2,500	95.00	100.00
82-F-CE-01-041	Yakima Salmon Fisherman	D. Polland	2,500	200.00	285.00
82-F-CE-01-042	Mustanger	D. Polland	2,500	425.00	495.00
83-F-CE-01-043	The Chief	D. Polland	Yr.Iss	275.00	1800.00
83-F-CE-01-044	Line Rider	D. Polland	2,500	195.00	245.00
83-F-CE-01-045	Bounty Hunter	D. Polland	2,500	250.00	250.00
83-F-CE-01-046	The Wild Bunch	D. Polland	2,500	200.00	250.00
83-F-CE-01-047	Too Many Aces	D. Polland	2,500	400.00	425.00
83-F-CE-01-048	Eye to Eye	D. Polland	2,500	350.00	400.00
83-F-CE-01-049	Now or Never	D. Polland	2,500	265.00	325.00
84-F-CE-01-050	The Guidon	D. Polland	Unkn.	Unknown	Unknown
85-F-CE-01-051	Saddle Bronc Rider	D. Polland	2,500	250.00	265.00
85-F-CE-01-052	Bareback Rider	D. Polland	2,500	225.00	245.00
85-F-CE-01-053	Bull Rider	D. Polland	2,500	265.00	275.00
85-F-CE-01-054	Steer Wrestling	D. Polland	2,500	500.00	525.00
85-F-CE-01-055	Team Roping	D. Polland	2,500	500.00	550.00
85-F-CE-01-056	Calf Roper	D. Polland	2,500	300.00	325.00
85-F-CE-01-057	Barrel Racer	D. Polland	2,500	275.00	245.00
Z5-F-CE-01-058	Fighting Stallions	D. Polland	2,500	225.00	265.00
Z5-F-CE-01-059	Wild Stallion	D. Polland	2,500	145.00	150.00
Z5-F-CE-01-060	Oh Great Sperit	D. Polland	Yr.Iss	300.00	450.00

Creative World — **Woodcarvings**

Number	Name	Artist	Edition limit	Issue Price	Quote
79-F-CW-01-001	Little Leaguer	N. Rockwell	2,500	175.00	180.00
79-F-CW-01-002	First Formal	N. Rockwell	2,500	190.00	195.00

Curator Collection — **Heavenly Blessings**

Number	Name	Artist	Edition limit	Issue Price	Quote
85-F-CX-01-001	First Step	Unknown	Open	15.00	15.00
85-F-CX-01-002	Heaven Scent	Unknown	Open	15.00	15.00
85-F-CX-01-003	Bubbles	Unknown	Open	15.00	15.00
85-F-CX-01-004	So Soft	Unknown	Open	15.00	15.00
85-F-CX-01-005	See!	Unknown	Open	15.00	15.00
85-F-CX-01-006	Listen!	Unknown	Open	15.00	15.00
85-F-CX-01-007	Happy Birthday	Unknown	Open	15.00	15.00
85-F-CX-01-008	Day Dreams	Unknown	Open	15.00	15.00
85-F-CX-01-009	Just Up	Unknown	Open	15.00	15.00
85-F-CX-01-010	Beddy Bye	Unknown	Open	15.00	15.00
85-F-CX-01-011	Race You!	Unknown	Open	15.00	15.00
85-F-CX-01-012	Yum, Yum!	Unknown	Open	15.00	15.00

Curator Collection — **Musical Figurines**

Number	Name	Artist	Edition limit	Issue Price	Quote
84-F-CX-02-001	The Wedding	R. Sauber	Open	65.00	65.00
86-F-CX-02-002	The Anniversary	R. Sauber	Open	65.00	65.00
87-F-CX-02-003	Home Sweet Home	R. Sauber	Open	65.00	65.00
87-F-CX-02-004	Newborn	R. Sauber	Open	65.00	65.00
87-F-CX-02-005	Motherhood	R. Sauber	Open	65.00	65.00
87-F-CX-02-006	Fatherhood	R. Sauber	Open	65.00	65.00
87-F-CX-02-007	Sweet Sixteen	R. Sauber	Open	65.00	65.00

Curator Collection — **Curator Christian Collection**

Number	Name	Artist	Edition limit	Issue Price	Quote
87-F-CX-03-001	Bring to Me the Children	A. Tobey	Open	75.00	100.00

Cybis — **Animal Kingdom**

Number	Name	Artist	Edition limit	Issue Price	Quote
71-F-CY-01-001	American Bullfrog	Cybis	Closed	250.00	600.00
75-F-CY-01-002	American White Buffalo	Cybis	250	1250.00	4000.00
71-F-CY-01-003	Appaloosa Colt	Cybis	Closed	150.00	300.00
80-F-CY-01-004	Arctic White Fox	Cybis	100	4500.00	4700.00
84-F-CY-01-005	Australian Greater Sulpher Crested Cockatoo	Cybis	25	9850.00	9850.00
85-F-CY-01-006	Baxter and Doyle	Cybis	400	450.00	450.00
68-F-CY-01-007	Bear	Cybis	Closed	85.00	400.00
85-F-CY-01-008	Beagles, Branigan and Clancy	Cybis	Open	375.00	375.00
81-F-CY-01-009	Beavers, Egbert and Brewster	Cybis	400	285.00	335.00
68-F-CY-01-010	Buffalo	Cybis	Closed	115.00	185.00
XX-F-CY-01-011	Bull	Cybis	100	150.00	4500.00
76-F-CY-01-012	Bunny, Muffet	Cybis	Closed	85.00	125.00
77-F-CY-01-013	Bunny Pat-a-Cake	Cybis	Closed	90.00	110.00
85-F-CY-01-014	Bunny, Snowflake	Cybis	Open	65.00	65.00
84-F-CY-01-015	Chantilly, Kitten	Cybis	Open	175.00	175.00
76-F-CY-01-016	Chipmunk w/Bloodroot	Cybis	225	625.00	675.00
69-F-CY-01-017	Colts, Darby and Joan	Cybis	Closed	295.00	475.00
82-F-CY-01-018	Dall Sheep	Cybis	50	Unknown	4250.00
86-F-CY-01-019	Dapple Grey Foal	Cybis	Open	195.00	195.00
70-F-CY-01-020	Deer Mouse in Clover	Cybis	Closed	65.00	150.00
78-F-CY-01-021	Dormouse, Maximilian	Cybis	Closed	250.00	285.00
78-F-CY-01-022	Dormouse, Maxine	Cybis	Closed	195.00	225.00
68-F-CY-01-023	Elephant	Cybis	100	600.00	5000.00
85-F-CY-01-024	Elephant, Willoughby	Cybis	Open	195.00	195.00
61-F-CY-01-025	Horse	Cybis	100	150.00	2000.00
86-F-CY-01-026	Huey, the Harmonious Hare	Cybis	Open	175.00	175.00
67-F-CY-01-027	Kitten, Blue Ribbon	Cybis	Closed	95.00	500.00
75-F-CY-01-028	Kitten, Tabitha	Cybis	Closed	90.00	150.00
75-F-CY-01-029	Kitten, Topaz	Cybis	Closed	90.00	150.00
86-F-CY-01-030	Mick, The Melodious Mutt	Cybis	Open	175.00	175.00
85-F-CY-01-031	Monday, Rhinoceros	Cybis	Open	85.00	95.00
71-F-CY-01-032	Nashua	Cybis	100	2000.00	3000.00
78-F-CY-01-033	Pinky Bunny/Carrot	Cybis	200	200.00	265.00
72-F-CY-01-034	Pinto Colt	Cybis	Closed	175.00	250.00
76-F-CY-01-035	Prairie Dog	Cybis	Closed	245.00	345.00
65-F-CY-01-036	Raccoon, Raffles	Cybis	Closed	110.00	365.00
68-F-CY-01-038	Snail, Sir Escargot	Cybis	Closed	50.00	300.00
65-F-CY-01-039	Squirrel, Mr. Fluffy Tail	Cybis	Closed	90.00	350.00
80-F-CY-01-040	Squirrel, Highrise	Cybis	400	475.00	525.00
68-F-CY-01-041	Stallion	Cybis	350	475.00	850.00
66-F-CY-01-042	Thoroughbred	Cybis	350	425.00	1500.00
86-F-CY-01-043	White Tailed Deer	Cybis	50	9500.00	9800.00

Cybis — **Biblical**

Number	Name	Artist	Edition limit	Issue Price	Quote
60-F-CY-02-001	Exodus	Cybis	50	350.00	2600.00
60-F-CY-02-002	Flight Into Egypt	Cybis	50	175.00	2500.00
56-F-CY-02-003	Holy Child of Prague	Cybis	10	1500.00	75000.00
XX-F-CY-02-004	Holywater Font "Holy Ghost"	Cybis	Closed	15.00	90.00
57-F-CY-02-005	Madonna, House of Gold	Cybis	8	125.00	4000.00
60-F-CY-02-006	Madonna Lace & Rose	Cybis	Open	15.00	295.00
63-F-CY-02-007	Moses, The Great Lawgiver	Cybis	750	250.00	3500.00
84-F-CY-02-008	Nativity, Angel, color	Cybis	Open	395.00	495.00
84-F-CY-02-009	Nativity, Camel, color	Cybis	Open	625.00	695.00
85-F-CY-02-010	Nativity Cow, color	Cybis	Open	175.00	175.00
85-F-CY-02-011	Nativity Cow, white	Cybis	Open	125.00	125.00
85-F-CY-02-012	Nativity Donkey, color	Cybis	Open	195.00	195.00
85-F-CY-02-013	Nativity Donkey, white	Cybis	Open	130.00	130.00
85-F-CY-02-014	Nativity Lamb, color	Cybis	Open	150.00	150.00
85-F-CY-02-015	Nativity Lamb, white	Cybis	Open	115.00	115.00
84-F-CY-02-016	Nativity, Shepherd, color	Cybis	Open	395.00	445.00
76-F-CY-02-017	Noah	Cybis	500	975.00	2400.00
64-F-CY-02-018	St. Peter	Cybis	500	Unknown	1250.00
60-F-CY-02-019	The Prophet	Cybis	50	250.00	3500.00

Company / Number	Series / Name	Artist	Edition limit	Issue Price	Quote
Cybis	**Birds & Flowers**				
85-F-CY-03-001	American Bald Eagle	Cybis	300	2900.00	2900.00
72-F-CY-03-002	American Crested Iris	Cybis	400	975.00	1150.00
76-F-CY-03-003	American White Turkey	Cybis	75	1450.00	1600.00
76-F-CY-03-004	American Wild Turkey	Cybis	75	1950.00	2200.00
77-F-CY-03-005	Apple Blossoms	Cybis	400	350.00	550.00
72-F-CY-03-006	Autumn Dogwood w/Chickadees	Cybis	350	1100.00	1200.00
XX-F-CY-03-007	Birds & Flowers	Cybis	250	500.00	4500.00
61-F-CY-03-008	Blue-Gray Gnatcatchers, pair	Cybis	200	400.00	2500.00
60-F-CY-03-009	Blue Headed Virio Building Nest	Cybis	Closed	60.00	1100.00
60-F-CY-03-010	Blue Headed Virio with Lilac	Cybis	275	1200.00	2200.00
XX-F-CY-03-011	Butterfly w/ Dogwood	Cybis	200	Unknown	350.00
68-F-CY-03-012	Calla Lily	Cybis	500	750.00	1750.00
65-F-CY-03-013	Christmas Rose	Cybis	500	250.00	750.00
77-F-CY-03-014	Clematis	Cybis	Closed	210.00	315.00
69-F-CY-03-015	Clematis with House Wren	Cybis	350	1300.00	1400.00
76-F-CY-03-016	Colonial Basket	Cybis	100	2750.00	5000.00
76-F-CY-03-017	Constancy Flower Basket	Cybis	Closed	345.00	400.00
64-F-CY-03-018	Dahlia, Yellow	Cybis	350	450.00	1800.00
76-F-CY-03-019	Devotion Flower Basket	Cybis	Closed	345.00	400.00
62-F-CY-03-020	Duckling "Baby Brother"	Cybis	Closed	35.00	140.00
77-F-CY-03-021	Duckling "Buttercup and Daffodil"	Cybis	Closed	165.00	295.00
70-F-CY-03-022	Dutch Crocus	Cybis	350	550.00	750.00
76-F-CY-03-023	Felicity Flower Basket	Cybis	Closed	325.00	345.00
61-F-CY-03-024	Golden Clarion Lily	Cybis	100	250.00	4500.00
74-F-CY-03-025	Golden Winged Warbler	Cybis	200	1075.00	1150.00
75-F-CY-03-026	Great Horned Owl, color	Cybis	50	3250.00	7500.00
75-F-CY-03-027	Great Horned Owl, white	Cybis	150	1950.00	4500.00
64-F-CY-03-028	Great White Heron	Cybis	350	850.00	3750.00
77-F-CY-03-029	Hermit Thrush	Cybis	150	1450.00	1450.00
59-F-CY-03-030	Hummingbird	Cybis	Closed	95.00	950.00
63-F-CY-03-031	Iris	Cybis	250	500.00	4500.00
77-F-CY-03-032	Krestrel	Cybis	175	1875.00	1925.00
78-F-CY-03-033	Kinglets on Pyracantha	Cybis	175	900.00	1100.00
71-F-CY-03-034	Little Blue Heron	Cybis	500	425.00	1500.00
63-F-CY-03-035	Magnolia	Cybis	Closed	350.00	450.00
76-F-CY-03-036	Majesty Flower Basket	Cybis	Closed	345.00	400.00
70-F-CY-03-037	Mushroom with Butterfly	Cybis	Closed	225.00	450.00
68-F-CY-03-038	Narcissus	Cybis	500	350.00	550.00
78-F-CY-03-039	Nestling Bluebirds	Cybis	Closed	235.00	250.00
72-F-CY-03-040	Pansies, China Maid	Cybis	1,000	275.00	350.00
75-F-CY-03-041	Pansies, Chinolina Lady	Cybis	750	295.00	400.00
60-F-CY-03-042	Pheasant	Cybis	150	750.00	5000.00
XX-F-CY-03-043	Sandpipers	Cybis	400	700.00	1500.00
85-F-CY-03-044	Screech Owl & Siblings	Cybis	100	3250.00	3250.00
XX-F-CY-03-045	Skylarks	Cybis	350	330.00	1800.00
62-F-CY-03-046	Sparrow on a Log	Cybis	Closed	35.00	450.00
82-F-CY-03-047	Spring Bouquet	Cybis	200	750.00	750.00
57-F-CY-03-048	Turtle Doves	Cybis	500	350.00	5000.00
68-F-CY-03-049	Wood Duck	Cybis	500	325.00	800.00
80-F-CY-03-050	Yellow Rose	Cybis	Closed	80.00	450.00
80-F-CY-03-051	Yellow Condesa Rose	Cybis	Closed	Unknown	255.00
Cybis	**Children to Cherish**				
64-F-CY-05-001	Alice in Wonderland	Cybis	Closed	50.00	700.00
78-F-CY-05-002	Alice (seated)	Cybis	Closed	350.00	365.00
78-F-CY-05-003	Allegra	Cybis	Closed	310.00	325.00
63-F-CY-05-004	Ballerina on Cue	Cybis	Closed	150.00	700.00
68-F-CY-05-005	Ballerina, Little Princess	Cybis	Closed	125.00	700.00
85-F-CY-05-006	Ballerina, Recital	Cybis	Open	275.00	275.00
60-F-CY-05-007	Ballerina Red Shoes	Cybis	Closed	75.00	1200.00
85-F-CY-05-008	Ballerina, Swanilda	Cybis	Open	450.00	450.00
68-F-CY-05-009	Baby Bust	Cybis	239	375.00	1000.00
85-F-CY-05-010	Beth	Cybis	Open	235.00	235.00
77-F-CY-05-011	Boys Playing Marbles	Cybis	Closed	285.00	325.00
84-F-CY-05-012	The Choirboy	Cybis	Open	325.00	345.00
85-F-CY-05-013	Clara	Cybis	Open	395.00	395.00
86-F-CY-05-014	Clarissa	Cybis	Open	165.00	165.00
78-F-CY-05-015	Edith	Cybis	Closed	310.00	325.00
76-F-CY-05-016	Elizabeth Ann	Cybis	Closed	195.00	275.00
85-F-CY-05-017	Felicia	Cybis	Open	425.00	425.00
86-F-CY-05-017	'Encore' Figure Skater	Cybis	750	625.00	625.00
85-F-CY-05-018	Figure Eight	Cybis	750	625.00	625.00
XX-F-CY-05-019	First Bouquet	Cybis	250	150.00	300.00
66-F-CY-05-020	First Flight	Cybis	Closed	50.00	395.00
81-F-CY-05-021	Fleurette	Cybis	1,000	725.00	765.00
73-F-CY-05-022	Goldilocks	Cybis	Closed	145.00	350.00
74-F-CY-05-023	Gretel	Cybis	Closed	260.00	395.00
74-F-CY-05-024	Hansel	Cybis	Closed	270.00	450.00
62-F-CY-05-025	Heidi, white	Cybis	Closed	165.00	495.00
62-F-CY-05-026	Heidi, color	Cybis	Closed	165.00	475.00
84-F-CY-05-027	Jack in the Beanstalk	Cybis	750	575.00	575.00
85-F-CY-05-028	Jody	Cybis	Open	235.00	235.00
86-F-CY-05-029	Kitri	Cybis	Open	450.00	450.00
78-F-CY-05-030	Lisa and Lynette	Cybis	Open	395.00	425.00
78-F-CY-05-031	Little Boy Blue	Cybis	Closed	425.00	445.00
84-F-CY-05-032	Little Champ	Cybis	Open	325.00	375.00
80-F-CY-05-033	Little Miss Muffet	Cybis	Closed	335.00	365.00
73-F-CY-05-034	Little Red Riding Hood	Cybis	Closed	110.00	425.00
86-F-CY-05-035	Lullaby, pink	Cybis	Open	125.00	125.00
86-F-CY-05-036	Lullaby, blue	Cybis	Open	125.00	125.00
86-F-CY-05-037	Lullaby, ivory	Cybis	Open	125.00	125.00
85-F-CY-05-038	Marguerite	Cybis	Open	425.00	425.00
74-F-CY-05-039	Mary, Mary	Cybis	500	475.00	750.00
76-F-CY-05-040	Melissa	Cybis	Closed	285.00	425.00
84-F-CY-05-041	Michael	Cybis	Open	235.00	235.00
67-F-CY-05-042	Pandora Blue	Cybis	Closed	265.00	300.00
58-F-CY-05-043	Peter Pan	Cybis	Closed	80.00	975.00
71-F-CY-05-044	Polyanna	Cybis	Closed	195.00	400.00
75-F-CY-05-045	Rapunzel, apricot	Cybis	1,500	475.00	1000.00
78-F-CY-05-046	Rapunzel, lilac	Cybis	1,000	675.00	775.00
72-F-CY-05-047	Rapunzel, pink	Cybis	1,000	425.00	975.00
64-F-CY-05-048	Rebecca	Cybis	Closed	110.00	360.00
85-F-CY-05-049	Recital	Cybis	Open	275.00	275.00
82-F-CY-05-050	Robin	Cybis	1,000	475.00	475.00
82-F-CY-05-051	Sleeping Beauty	Cybis	750	695.00	695.00
63-F-CY-05-052	Springtime	Cybis	Closed	45.00	600.00
57-F-CY-05-053	Thumbelina	Cybis	Closed	45.00	475.00
59-F-CY-05-054	Tinkerbell	Cybis	Closed	95.00	1350.00
85-F-CY-05-055	Vanessa	Cybis	Open	425.00	425.00
75-F-CY-05-056	Wendy with Flowers	Cybis	Unkn.	250.00	300.00
75-F-CY-05-057	Yankee Doodle Dandy	Cybis	Closed	275.00	325.00
Cybis	**Commemorative**				
81-F-CY-06-001	Arion, Dolphin Rider	Cybis	1,000	575.00	675.00
69-F-CY-06-002	Apollo II Moon Mission	Cybis	111	1500.00	2500.00
72-F-CY-06-003	Chess Set	Cybis	10	30000.00	60000.00
67-F-CY-06-004	Columbia	Cybis	200	1000.00	2500.00
86-F-CY-06-005	1986 Commemorative Egg	Cybis	Open	365.00	365.00
67-F-CY-06-006	Conductor's Hands	Cybis	250	250.00	1500.00
71-F-CY-06-007	Cree Indian	Cybis	100	2500.00	5500.00
84-F-CY-06-008	Cree Indian "Magic Boy"	Cybis	200	4250.00	4250.00
75-F-CY-06-009	George Washington Bust	Cybis	Closed	275.00	350.00
85-F-CY-06-010	Holiday Ornament	Cybis	Open	75.00	75.00
81-F-CY-06-011	Kateri Takakwitha	Cybis	100	2875.00	2975.00
86-F-CY-06-012	Little Miss Liberty	Cybis	Open	295.00	295.00
77-F-CY-06-013	Oceania	Cybis	200	1250.00	1500.00
81-F-CY-06-014	Phoenix	Cybis	100	950.00	950.00
80-F-CY-06-015	The Bride	Cybis	100	6500.00	7250.00
84-F-CY-06-016	1984 Cybis Holiday	Cybis	Open	145.00	145.00
85-F-CY-06-017	Liberty	Cybis	100	1875.00	2500.00
Cybis	**Fantasia**				
74-F-CY-07-001	Cybele	Cybis	500	675.00	800.00
81-F-CY-07-002	Desiree, White Deer	Cybis	400	575.00	595.00
84-F-CY-07-003	Flight and Fancy	Cybis	1,000	975.00	975.00
80-F-CY-07-004	Pegasus	Cybis	500	1450.00	3750.00
80-F-CY-07-005	Pegaus, Free Spirit	Cybis	1,000	675.00	775.00
81-F-CY-07-006	Prince Brocade Unicorn	Cybis	500	2200.00	2300.00
78-F-CY-07-007	'Satin' Horse Head	Cybis	500	1100.00	2400.00
77-F-CY-07-008	Sea King's Steed "Oceania"	Cybis	200	1250.00	1450.00
78-F-CY-07-009	'Sharmaine' Sea Nymph	Cybis	250	1450.00	1525.00
82-F-CY-07-010	Theron	Cybis	350	675.00	850.00
69-F-CY-07-011	Unicorn	Cybis	500	1250.00	3750.00
77-F-CY-07-012	Unicorns, Gambol and Frolic	Cybis	1,000	425.00	1400.00
85-F-CY-07-013	Dore'	Cybis	1,000	575.00	825.00
Cybis	**Land of Chemeric**				
77-F-CY-08-001	Marigold	Cybis	Closed	185.00	400.00
81-F-CY-08-002	Melody	Cybis	1,000	725.00	765.00
79-F-CY-08-003	Pip, Elfin Player	Cybis	1,000	450.00	665.00
77-F-CY-08-004	Queen Titania	Cybis	750	725.00	2100.00
77-F-CY-08-005	Tiffin	Cybis	Closed	175.00	400.00
85-F-CY-08-006	Oberon	Cybis	750	825.00	825.00
Cybis	**North American Indian**				
74-F-CY-09-001	Apache, "Chato"	Cybis	350	1950.00	2775.00
69-F-CY-09-002	Blackfeet "Beaverhead Medicine Man"	Cybis	500	2000.00	2775.00
82-F-CY-09-003	Choctaw "Tasculusa"	Cybis	200	2475.00	2675.00
77-F-CY-09-004	Crow Dancer	Cybis	200	3875.00	6500.00
69-F-CY-09-005	Dakota "Minnehaha Laughing Water"	Cybis	500	1500.00	2250.00
73-F-CY-09-006	Eskimo Mother	Cybis	200	1875.00	2500.00
79-F-CY-09-007	Great Spirit "Wankan Tanka"	Cybis	200	3500.00	4150.00
73-F-CY-09-008	Iriquois "At the Council Fire"	Cybis	500	4250.00	4975.00
69-F-CY-09-009	Onondaga "Hiawatha"	Cybis	500	1500.00	2250.00
71-F-CY-09-010	Shoshone "Sacajawea"	Cybis	500	2250.00	2775.00
85-F-CY-09-011	Yaqui "Deer Dancer"	Cybis	200	2095.00	2095.00
Cybis	**Portraits in Porcelain**				
76-F-CY-10-001	Abigail Adams	Cybis	600	875.00	1175.00
84-F-CY-10-002	Bathsheba	Cybis	500	1975.00	1975.00
65-F-CY-10-003	Beatrice	Cybis	700	225.00	1500.00
79-F-CY-10-004	Berengaria	Cybis	500	1450.00	3250.00
82-F-CY-10-005	Desdemona	Cybis	500	1850.00	2500.00
71-F-CY-10-006	Eleanor of Aquitaine	Cybis	750	875.00	3750.00
67-F-CY-10-007	Folk Singer	Cybis	283	300.00	850.00
78-F-CY-10-008	Good Queen Anne	Cybis	350	975.00	1300.00
67-F-CY-10-009	Guinevere	Cybis	600	250.00	1695.00
68-F-CY-10-010	Hamlet	Cybis	500	350.00	1750.00
81-F-CY-10-011	Jane Eyre	Cybis	500	975.00	1275.00
65-F-CY-10-012	Juliet	Cybis	800	175.00	4000.00
85-F-CY-10-013	King David	Cybis	350	1475.00	1475.00
72-F-CY-10-014	Kwan Yin	Cybis	350	1250.00	2000.00
82-F-CY-10-015	Lady Godiva	Cybis	200	1875.00	2500.00
75-F-CY-10-016	Lady Macbeth	Cybis	750	850.00	1125.00
79-F-CY-10-017	Nefertiti	Cybis	500	2100.00	2750.00
69-F-CY-10-018	Ophelia	Cybis	800	750.00	3500.00
85-F-CY-10-019	Pagliacci	Cybis	Open	325.00	325.00
82-F-CY-10-020	Persephone	Cybis	200	3250.00	3350.00
73-F-CY-10-021	Portia	Cybis	750	825.00	3250.00
73-F-CY-10-022	Ballet - Prince Florimund	Cybis	200	975.00	1100.00
73-F-CY-10-023	Ballet - Princess Aurora	Cybis	200	1125.00	1500.00
76-F-CY-10-024	Priscilla	Cybis	500	825.00	1125.00
74-F-CY-10-025	Queen Esther	Cybis	750	925.00	1600.00
68-F-CY-10-026	Scarlett	Cybis	500	450.00	3000.00
85-F-CY-10-027	Tristan and Isolde	Cybis	200	2200.00	2200.00
85-F-CY-10-028	King Arthur	Cybis	350	2350.00	2350.00
85-F-CY-10-029	Romeo and Juliet	Cybis	300	2200.00	2200.00
86-F-CY-10-030	Carmen	Cybis	500	1675.00	1675.00
Cybis	**Theatre of Porcelain**				
81-F-CY-11-001	Columbine	Cybis	250	2250.00	2250.00
78-F-CY-11-002	Court Jester	Cybis	250	1450.00	1750.00
80-F-CY-11-003	Harlequin	Cybis	250	1575.00	1875.00
81-F-CY-11-004	Puck	Cybis	250	2300.00	2450.00
Cybis	**Carousel-Circus**				
75-F-CY-12-001	'Barnaby' Bear	Cybis	Closed	165.00	325.00
81-F-CY-12-002	Bear, "Bernhard"	Cybis	325	1125.00	1150.00
75-F-CY-12-003	Bicentennial Horse Ticonderoga	Cybis	350	925.00	3200.00
75-F-CY-12-004	'Bosun' Monkey	Cybis	Closed	195.00	375.00
81-F-CY-12-005	Bull, Plutus	Cybis	325	1125.00	1150.00
85-F-CY-12-006	Carousel Unicorn	Cybis	325	1275.00	1275.00
79-F-CY-12-007	Circus Rider "Equestrienne Extraordinaire"	Cybis	150	2275.00	3000.00
77-F-CY-12-008	'Dandy' Dancing Dog	Cybis	Closed	145.00	295.00
81-F-CY-12-009	Frollo	Cybis	1,000	750.00	775.00
76-F-CY-12-010	'Funny Face' Child Head/Holly	Cybis	Closed	325.00	500.00

Figurines

Number	Name	Artist	Edition limit	Issue Price	Quote
Company	**Series**				
82-F-CY-12-011	Giraffe	Cybis	750	Unknown	1150.00
73-F-CY-12-012	Carousel Goat	Cybis	325	875.00	1200.00
73-F-CY-12-013	Carousel Horse	Cybis	325	925.00	3200.00
74-F-CY-12-014	Lion	Cybis	325	1025.00	1200.00
76-F-CY-12-015	Performing Pony "Poppy"	Cybis	1,000	325.00	1000.00
84-F-CY-12-016	Phineas, Circus Elephant	Cybis	Open	325.00	325.00
86-F-CY-12-017	Pierre, the Performing Poodle	Cybis	Open	225.00	225.00
81-F-CY-12-018	Pony	Cybis	750	975.00	975.00
76-F-CY-12-019	'Sebastian' Seal	Cybis	Closed	195.00	200.00
74-F-CY-12-020	Tiger	Cybis	325	925.00	1150.00
85-F-CY-12-021	Jumbles and Friend	Cybis	750	675.00	675.00
85-F-CY-12-022	Valentine	Cybis	Open	335.00	335.00
Cybis	**Children of the World**				
72-F-CY-13-001	Eskimo Child Head	Cybis	Closed	165.00	400.00
75-F-CY-13-002	Indian Girl Head	Cybis	Closed	325.00	900.00
75-F-CY-13-003	Indian Boy Head	Cybis	Closed	425.00	675.00
78-F-CY-13-004	Jason	Cybis	Closed	285.00	325.00
78-F-CY-13-005	Jennifer	Cybis	Closed	325.00	350.00
77-F-CY-13-006	Jeremy	Cybis	Closed	315.00	375.00
79-F-CY-13-007	Jessica	Cybis	Closed	325.00	350.00
Cybis	**Sport Scenes**				
80-F-CY-14-001	Jogger, Female	Cybis	Closed	345.00	425.00
80-F-CY-14-002	Jogger, Male	Cybis	Closed	395.00	475.00
Cybis	**Everyone's Fun Time (Limnettes)**				
72-F-CY-15-001	Country Fair	Cybis	500	125.00	200.00
72-F-CY-15-001	Country Fair	Cybis	500	125.00	200.00
72-F-CY-15-002	Windy Day	Cybis	500	125.00	200.00
72-F-CY-15-003	The Pond	Cybis	500	125.00	200.00
72-F-CY-15-004	The Seashore	Cybis	500	125.00	200.00
Cybis	**The Wonderful Seasons (Limnettes)**				
72-F-CY-16-001	Autumn	Cybis	500	125.00	200.00
72-F-CY-16-002	Spring	Cybis	500	125.00	200.00
72-F-CY-16-003	Summer	Cybis	500	125.00	200.00
72-F-CY-16-004	Winter	Cybis	500	125.00	200.00
Cybis	**When Bells are Ringing (Limnettes)**				
72-F-CY-17-001	Easter Egg Hunt	Cybis	500	125.00	200.00
72-F-CY-17-002	Independence Celebration	Cybis	500	125.00	200.00
72-F-CY-17-003	Merry Christmas	Cybis	500	125.00	200.00
72-F-CY-17-004	Sabbath Morning	Cybis	500	125.00	200.00
Danbury Mint	**Rockwell Figurines**				
80-F-DA-01-001	Trick or Treat	N. Rockwell	Unkn.	55.00	60.00
80-F-DA-01-002	Gramps at the Reins	N. Rockwell	Unkn.	55.00	60.00
80-F-DA-01-003	Grandpa Snowman	N. Rockwell	Unkn.	55.00	60.00
80-F-DA-01-004	Caught in the Act	N. Rockwell	Unkn.	55.00	60.00
80-F-DA-01-005	Boy on Stilts	N. Rockwell	Unkn.	55.00	60.00
80-F-DA-01-006	Young Love	N. Rockwell	Unkn.	55.00	60.00
Duncan Royale	**History of Santa Claus I**				
83-F-DR-01-001	St. Nicholas	P. Apsit	10,000	175.00	185.00
83-F-DR-01-002	Dedt Moroz	P. Apsit	10,000	145.00	155.00
83-F-DR-01-003	Black Peter	P. Apsit	10,000	145.00	155.00
83-F-DR-01-004	Victorian	P. Apsit	10,000	120.00	130.00
83-F-DR-01-005	Medieval	P. Apsit	10,000	220.00	230.00
83-F-DR-01-006	Russian	P. Apsit	10,000	145.00	155.00
83-F-DR-01-007	Wassail	P. Apsit	10,000	90.00	100.00
83-F-DR-01-008	Kris Kringle	P. Apsit	10,000	165.00	175.00
83-F-DR-01-009	Soda Pop	P. Apsit	10,000	145.00	155.00
83-F-DR-01-010	Pioneer	P. Apsit	10,000	145.00	155.00
83-F-DR-01-011	Civil War	P. Apsit	10,000	145.00	155.00
83-F-DR-01-012	Nast	P. Apsit	10,000	90.00	130.00
83-F-DR-01-013	Collection of 12	P. Apsit	10,000	1730.00	1880.00
Duncan Royale	**History of Santa Claus II**				
86-F-DR-02-001	Odin	P. Apsit	10,000	200.00	200.00
86-F-DR-02-002	Lord of Misrule	P. Apsit	10,000	160.00	160.00
86-F-DR-02-003	Mongolian/Asian	P. Apsit	10,000	240.00	240.00
86-F-DR-02-004	The Magi	P. Apsit	10,000	350.00	350.00
86-F-DR-02-005	St. Lucia	P. Apsit	10,000	180.00	180.00
86-F-DR-02-006	Befana	P. Apsit	10,000	200.00	200.00
86-F-DR-02-007	Babouska	P. Apsit	10,000	170.00	170.00
86-F-DR-02-008	Bavarian	P. Apsit	10,000	250.00	250.00
86-F-DR-02-009	Alsace Angel	P. Apsit	10,000	250.00	250.00
86-F-DR-02-010	Frau Holda	P. Apsit	10,000	160.00	160.00
86-F-DR-02-011	Sir Christmas	P. Apsit	10,000	150.00	150.00
86-F-DR-02-012	The Pixie	P. Apsit	10,000	140.00	140.00
86-F-DR-02-013	Collection of 12	P. Apsit	10,000	2450.00	2450.00
Enesco Imports Corporation	**Special Edition**				
81-F-EA-01-001	Hello, Lord, It's Me Again - PM-811	S. Butcher	Closed	25.00	400.00
82-F-EA-01-002	Smile, God Loves You - PM-821	S. Butcher	Closed	25.00	235.00
83-F-EA-01-003	Put on a Happy Face - PM-822	S. Butcher	Closed	25.00	185.00
83-F-EA-01-004	Dawn's Early Light - PM-831	S. Butcher	Closed	27.50	80.00
84-F-EA-01-005	God's Ray of Mercy - PM-841	S. Butcher	Closed	25.00	50.00
84-F-EA-01-006	Trust in the Lord to the Finish - PM-842	S. Butcher	Closed	25.00	75.00
85-F-EA-01-007	The Lord is My Shepherd - PM-851	S. Butcher	Closed	25.00	50.00
85-F-EA-01-008	I Love to Tell the Story - PM-852	S. Butcher	Closed	27.50	50.00
86-F-EA-01-009	Grandma's Prayer - PM-861	S. Butcher	Closed	25.00	40.00
Enesco Imports Corporation	**Special Club Welcome Gift**				
81-F-EA-02-001	But Love Goes on Forever - E-0001	S. Butcher	Yr.Iss	Unknown	150.00
82-F-EA-02-002	Let Us Call the Club to Order - E-0303	S. Butcher	Yr.Iss	Unknown	55.00
84-F-EA-02-003	Join in on the Blessings - E-0404	S. Butcher	Yr.Iss	Unknown	55.00
85-F-EA-02-004	Seek and Ye Shall Find - E-0005	S. Butcher	Yr.Iss	Unknown	50.00
86-F-EA-02-005	Birds of a Feather Collect Together-E-0006	S. Butcher	Yr.Iss	Unknown	50.00
Enesco Imports Corporation	**Inscribed Charter Member Renewal Gift**				
83-F-EA-03-001	Let Us Call the Club to Order - E-0103	S. Butcher	Yr.Iss	Unknown	55.00
84-F-EA-03-002	Join in on the Blessings - E-0104	S. Butcher	Yr.Iss	Unknown	55.00
85-F-EA-03-003	Seek and Ye Shall Find - E-0105	S. Butcher	Yr.Iss	Unknown	50.00
86-F-EA-03-004	Birds of a Feather Collect Together-E-0106	S. Butcher	Yr.Iss	Unknown	50.00
Enesco Imports Corporation	**Precious Moments Figurines**				
83-F-EA-04-001	Sharing Our Season Together - E-0501	S. Butcher	Suspd.	50.00	100.00
83-F-EA-04-002	Jesus is the Light that Shines - E-0502	S. Butcher	Suspd.	23.00	23.00
83-F-EA-04-003	Blessings from My House to Yours - E-0503	S. Butcher	Suspd.	27.00	27.00
83-F-EA-04-004	Christmastime is for Sharing - E-0504	S. Butcher	Open	37.00	40.00
83-F-EA-04-005	Surrounded with Joy - E-0506	S. Butcher	Open	21.00	23.00
83-F-EA-04-006	God Sent His Son - E-0507	S. Butcher	Suspd.	32.50	37.00
83-F-EA-04-007	Prepare Ye the Way of the Lord - E-0508	S. Butcher	Suspd.	75.00	75.00
83-F-EA-04-008	Bringing God's Blessing to You - E-0509	S. Butcher	Open	35.00	38.50
83-F-EA-04-009	Tubby's First Christmas - E-0511	S. Butcher	Open	12.00	13.50
83-F-EA-04-010	It's a Perfect Boy - E-0512	S. Butcher	Open	18.50	21.00
83-F-EA-04-011	Onward Christian Soldiers - E-0523	S. Butcher	Open	24.00	30.00
83-F-EA-04-012	You Can't Run Away from God - E-0525	S. Butcher	Open	28.50	35.00
83-F-EA-04-013	He Upholdeth Those Who Fall - E-0526	S. Butcher	Suspd.	35.00	35.00
83-F-EA-04-013	His Eye is on the Sparrow - E-0530	S. Butcher	Retrd.	28.50	32.50
79-F-EA-04-015	Jesus Loves Me - E-1372B	S. Butcher	Open	7.00	21.00
79-F-EA-04-016	Jesus Loves Me - E-1372G	S. Butcher	Open	7.00	21.00
79-F-EA-04-018	Jesus is the Light - E-1373G	S. Butcher	Open	7.00	21.00
79-F-EA-04-020	Make a Joyful Noise - E-1374G	S. Butcher	Open	8.00	23.00
79-F-EA-04-021	Love Lifted Me - E-1375A	S. Butcher	Open	11.00	30.00
79-F-EA-04-022	Prayer Changes Things - E-1375B	S. Butcher	Suspd	11.00	65-95.00
79-F-EA-04-023	Love One Another - E-1376	S. Butcher	Open	10.00	30.00
79-F-EA-04-024	He Leadeth Me - E-1377A	S. Butcher	Suspd.	9.00	40.00
79-F-EA-04-025	He Careth For You - E-1377B	S. Butcher	Suspd.	9.00	40.00
79-F-EA-04-027	Love is Kind - E-1379A	S. Butcher	Suspd.	8.00	38.00
79-F-EA-04-028	God Understands - E-1379B	S. Butcher	Suspd.	8.00	38.00
79-F-EA-04-031	Jesus is the Answer - E-1381	S. Butcher	Suspd.	11.50	45.00
79-F-EA-04-032	We Have Seen His Star - E-2010	S. Butcher	Suspd.	8.00	38.00
79-F-EA-04-034	Jesus is Born - E-2012	S. Butcher	Suspd.	12.00	50.00
79-F-EA-04-035	Unto Us a Child is Born - E-2013	S. Butcher	Suspd.	12.00	50.00
82-F-EA-04-036	May Your Christmas Be Cozy - E-2345	S. Butcher	Suspd.	23.00	50.00
82-F-EA-04-037	May Your Christmas Be Warm - E-2348	S. Butcher	Suspd.	30.00	37.00
82-F-EA-04-038	Tell Me the Story of Jesus - E-2349	S. Butcher	Suspd.	30.00	66.00
82-F-EA-04-039	Dropping in for Christmas - E-2350	S. Butcher	Suspd.	18.00	36.00
82-F-EA-04-040	Holy Smokes - E-2351	S. Butcher	Retrd.	27.00	33.50
82-F-EA-04-042	I'll Play My Drum for Him - E-2356	S. Butcher	Suspd.	30.00	60.00
82-F-EA-04-043	I'll Play My Drum for Him - E-2360	S. Butcher	Open	16.00	19.00
82-F-EA-04-044	Christmas Joy from Head to Toe - E-2361	S. Butcher	Suspd.	25.00	37.50
82-F-EA-04-045	Camel Figurine - E-2363	S. Butcher	Open	20.00	25.00
82-F-EA-04-046	Goat Figurine - E-2364	S. Butcher	Open	10.00	12.00
82-F-EA-04-047	The First Noel - E-2365	S. Butcher	Suspd.	16.00	34.00
82-F-EA-04-048	The First Noel - E-2366	S. Butcher	Suspd.	16.00	34.00
82-F-EA-04-049	Bundles of Joy - E-2374	S. Butcher	Open	27.50	33.50
82-F-EA-04-050	Dropping Over for Christmas - E-2375	S. Butcher	Open	30.00	37.00
82-F-EA-04-051	Our First Christmas Together - E-2377	S. Butcher	Suspd.	35.00	75.00
82-F-EA-04-052	3Mini.Nativity Houses & Palm Tree - E-2387	S. Butcher	Open	45.00	55.00
82-F-EA-04-053	Come Let Us Adore Him - E-2395 (11 pc.set)	S. Butcher	Open	80.00	95.00
80-F-EA-04-054	Come Let Us Adore Him - E-2800 (9 pc. set)	S. Butcher	Open	70.00	90.00
80-F-EA-04-055	Jesus is Born - E-2801	S. Butcher	Suspd.	37.00	100.00
80-F-EA-04-056	Christmas is a Time to Share - E-2802	S. Butcher	Suspd.	20.00	55.00
80-F-EA-04-057	Crown Him Lord of All - E-2803	S. Butcher	Suspd.	20.00	55.00
80-F-EA-04-058	Peace on Earth - E-2804	S. Butcher	Suspd.	20.00	55.00
84-F-EA-04-060	You Have Touched So Many Hearts - E-2821	S. Butcher	Open	25.00	30.00
84-F-EA-04-061	This is Your Day to Shine - E-2822	S. Butcher	Open	37.50	40.00
84-F-EA-04-062	To God Be the Glory - E-2823	S. Butcher	Suspd.	40.00	45.00
84-F-EA-04-063	To a Very Special Mom - E-2824	S. Butcher	Open	27.50	32.50
84-F-EA-04-064	To a Very Special Sister - E-2825	S. Butcher	Open	37.50	40.00
84-F-EA-04-065	May Your Birthday Be a Blessing - E-2826	S. Butcher	Suspd.	37.50	47.50
84-F-EA-04-066	I Get a Kick Out of You - E-2827	S. Butcher	Suspd.	50.00	65.00
84-F-EA-04-067	Precious Memories - E-2828	S. Butcher	Open	45.00	50.00
84-F-EA-04-068	I'm Sending You a White Christmas - E-2829	S. Butcher	Open	37.50	40.00
84-F-EA-04-069	God Bless the Bride - E-2832	S. Butcher	Open	35.00	40.00
86-F-EA-04-070	Sharing Our Joy Together - E-2834	S. Butcher	Open	30.00	36.00
84-F-EA-04-071	Baby Figurines (6 styles)- E-2852	S. Butcher	Open	12.00	14.00
80-F-EA-04-072	Blessed Are the Pure in Heart - E-3104	S. Butcher	Open	9.00	16.00
80-F-EA-04-073	He Watches Over Us All - E-3105	S. Butcher	Susp.d	11.00	40-65.00
80-F-EA-04-074	Mother Sew Dear - E-3106	S. Butcher	Open	13.00	22.50
80-F-EA-04-076	The Hand that Rocks the Future - E-3108	S. Butcher	Suspd.	13.00	38-60.00
80-F-EA-04-077	The Purr-fect Grandma - E-3109	S. Butcher	Open	13.00	23.00
80-F-EA-04-078	Loving is Sharing - E-3110B	S. Butcher	Open	13.00	24.00
80-F-EA-04-079	Loving is Sharing - E-3110G	S. Butcher	Open	13.00	24.00
80-F-EA-04-082	Thou Art Mine - E-3113	S. Butcher	Open	16.00	30.00
80-F-EA-04-083	The Lord Bless You and Keep You - E-3114	S. Butcher	Open	16.00	32.50
80-F-EA-04-084	But Love Goes on Forever - E-3115	S. Butcher	Open	16.50	30.00
80-F-EA-04-085	Thee I Love - E-3116	S. Butcher	Open	16.50	32.50
80-F-EA-04-086	Walking By Faith - E-3117	S. Butcher	Open	35.00	60.00
80-F-EA-04-088	It's What's Inside that Counts - E-3119	S. Butcher	Suspd.	13.00	38.00
80-F-EA-04-089	To Thee With Love - E-3120	S. Butcher	Suspd.	13.00	38.00
81-F-EA-04-090	The Lord Bless You and Keep You - E-4720	S. Butcher	Suspd.	14.00	22.50
81-F-EA-04-091	The Lord Bless You and Keep You - E-4721	S. Butcher	Open	14.00	24.00
81-F-EA-04-092	Love Cannot Break a True Friendship - E-4722	S. Butcher	Suspd.	22.50	55.00
81-F-EA-04-093	Peace Amid the Storm - E-4723	S. Butcher	Suspd.	22.50	33.50
81-F-EA-04-094	Rejoicing with You - E-4724	S. Butcher	Open	25.00	37.50
81-F-EA-04-095	Peace on Earth - E-4725	S. Butcher	Suspd.	25.00	50.00
81-F-EA-04-096	Bear Ye One Another's Burdens - E-5200	S. Butcher	Suspd.	20.00	50.00
81-F-EA-04-097	Love Lifted Me - E-5201	S. Butcher	Suspd.	25.00	66.00
81-F-EA-04-098	Thank You for Coming to My Ade - E-5202	S. Butcher	Suspd.	22.50	60.00
81-F-EA-04-099	Let Not the Sun Go Down Upon Your Wrath-E5203	S. Butcher	Suspd.	22.50	60.00
81-F-EA-04-100	To A Special Dad - E-5212	S. Butcher	Open	20.00	30.00
81-F-EA-04-101	God is Love - E-5213	S. Butcher	Open	17.00	27.00
81-F-EA-04-102	Prayer Changes Things - E-5214	S. Butcher	Suspd.	35.00	75.00
84-F-EA-04-103	May Your Christmas Be Blessed - E-5376	S. Butcher	Suspd.	37.50	75.00
84-F-EA-04-104	Love is Kind - E-5377	S. Butcher	Retrd.	27.50	30.00
84-F-EA-04-105	Joy to the World - E-5378	S. Butcher	Open	18.00	20.00

Figurines

Company Number	Name	Artist	Edition limit	Issue Price	Quote
Series					
84-F-EA-04-106	Isn't He Precious? - E-5379	S. Butcher	Open	20.00	22.50
84-F-EA-04-107	A Monarch is Born - E-5380	S. Butcher	Suspd.	33.00	43.00
84-F-EA-04-108	His Name is Jesus - E-5381	S. Butcher	Suspd.	45.00	50.00
84-F-EA-04-109	For God So Love the World - E-5382	S. Butcher	Suspd.	70.00	85.00
84-F-EA-04-110	Wishing You a Merry Christmas - E-5383	S. Butcher	Yr.Iss.	17.00	30.00
84-F-EA-04-111	I'll Play My Drum for Him - E-5384	S. Butcher	Open	10.00	11.00
84-F-EA-04-112	Oh Worship the Lord - E-5385	S. Butcher	Suspd.	10.00	20.00
84-F-EA-04-113	Oh Worship the Lord - E-5386	S. Butcher	Suspd.	10.00	20.00
81-F-EA-04-114	Come Let Us Adore Him - E-5619	S. Butcher	Suspd.	10.00	22.00
81-F-EA-04-115	Donkey Figurine - E-5621	S. Butcher	Open	6.00	10.00
81-F-EA-04-116	They Followed the Star - E-5624	S. Butcher	Open	130.00	175.00
81-F-EA-04-117	Wee Three King's - E-5635	S. Butcher	Open	40.00	60.00
81-F-EA-04-118	Rejoice O Earth - E-5636	S. Butcher	Open	15.00	22.50
81-F-EA-04-119	The Heavenly Light - E-5637	S. Butcher	Open	15.00	21.00
81-F-EA-04-120	Cow with Bell Figurine - E-5638	S. Butcher	Open	16.00	25.00
81-F-EA-04-121	Isn't He Wonderful - E-5639	S. Butcher	Suspd.	12.00	34.00
81-F-EA-04-122	Isn't He Wonderful - E-5640	S. Butcher	Suspd.	12.00	34.00
81-F-EA-04-123	They Followed the Star - E-5641	S. Butcher	Suspd.	75.00	150.00
84-F-EA-04-124	God Sends the Gift of His Love - E-6613	S. Butcher	Suspd.	22.50	50.00
82-F-EA-04-125	God is Love, Dear Valentine - E-7153	S. Butcher	Suspd.	16.00	34.00
82-F-EA-04-126	God is Love, Dear Valentine - E-7154	S. Butcher	Suspd.	16.00	32.50
82-F-EA-04-127	Thanking Him for You - E-7155	S. Butcher	Suspd.	16.00	34.00
82-F-EA-04-128	I Believe in Miracles - E-7156	S. Butcher	Suspd.	17.00	38.00
82-F-EA-04-130	Love Beareth All Things - E-7158	S. Butcher	Open	25.00	32.50
82-F-EA-04-131	Lord Give Me Patience - E-7159	S. Butcher	Suspd.	25.00	27.50
82-F-EA-04-132	The Perfect Grandpa - E-7160	S. Butcher	Suspd.	25.00	40.00
82-F-EA-04-133	His Sheep Am I - E-7161	S. Butcher	Suspd.	25.00	45.00
82-F-EA-04-134	Love is Sharing - E-7162	S. Butcher	Suspd.	25.00	60-90.00
82-F-EA-04-135	God is Watching Over You - E-7163	S. Butcher	Suspd.	27.50	30.00
82-F-EA-04-136	Bless This House - E-7164	S. Butcher	Suspd.	45.00	100.00
82-F-EA-04-137	Let the Whole World Know - E-7165	S. Butcher	Suspd.	45.00	55.00
83-F-EA-04-138	Love is Patient - E-9251	S. Butcher	Suspd.	35.00	70.00
83-F-EA-04-139	Forgiving is Forgetting - E-9252	S. Butcher	Open	37.50	42.50
83-F-EA-04-140	The End is in Sight - E-9253	S. Butcher	Suspd.	25.00	35.00
83-F-EA-04-141	Praise the Lord Anyhow - E-9254	S. Butcher	Open	35.00	40.00
83-F-EA-04-142	Bless You Two - E-9255	S. Butcher	Open	21.00	25.00
83-F-EA-04-143	We are God's Workmanship - E-9258	S. Butcher	Open	19.00	22.50
83-F-EA-04-144	We're In It Together - E-9259	S. Butcher	Open	24.00	30.00
83-F-EA-04-145	God's Promises are Sure - E-9260	S. Butcher	Suspd.	30.00	33.50
83-F-EA-04-146	Seek Ye the Lord - E-9261	S. Butcher	Suspd.	21.00	42.00
83-F-EA-04-147	Seek Ye the Lord - E-9262	S. Butcher	Suspd.	21.00	42.00
83-F-EA-04-148	How Can 2 Wlk Together Excpt They Agree-E9263	S. Butcher	Suspd.	35.00	70.00
83-F-EA-04-149	Press On - E-9265	S. Butcher	Open	40.00	45.00
83-F-EA-04-150	Animal Collection - E-9267	S. Butcher	Open	6.50	8.50
83-F-EA-04-151	Nobody's Perfect - E-9268	S. Butcher	Open	21.00	24.00
83-F-EA-04-152	Let Love Reign - E-9273	S. Butcher	Retrd.	27.50	30.00
83-F-EA-04-154	Jesus Loves Me - E-9278	S. Butcher	Open	9.00	12.50
83-F-EA-04-155	Jesus Loves Me - E-9279	S. Butcher	Open	9.00	12.50
83-F-EA-04-156	If God Be for Us, Who Can Be Against Us-E9285	S. Butcher	Suspd.	27.50	35.00
83-F-EA-04-157	Peace on Earth - E-9287	S. Butcher	Suspd.	37.50	75.00
83-F-EA-04-158	Sending You a Rainbow - E-9288	S. Butcher	Suspd.	22.50	32.50
83-F-EA-04-159	Trust In the Lord - E-9289	S. Butcher	Suspd.	21.00	23.00
85-F-EA-04-160	Love Covers All - 12009	S. Butcher	Open	27.50	32.50
85-F-EA-04-161	Part of Me Wants to be Good - 12149	S. Butcher	Open	19.00	22.50
85-F-EA-04-162	Get into the Habit of Prayer - 12203	S. Butcher	Suspd.	19.00	19.00
85-F-EA-04-163	Miniature Clown Figurines - 12238	S. Butcher	Open	13.50	16.00
85-F-EA-04-164	It is Better to Give than to Receive - 12297	S. Butcher	Suspd.	19.00	21.00
85-F-EA-04-165	Love Never Fails - 12300	S. Butcher	Open	25.00	30.00
85-F-EA-04-166	God Bless Our Home - 12319	S. Butcher	Open	40.00	45.00
86-F-EA-04-167	You Can Fly - 12335	S. Butcher	Open	25.00	30.00
85-F-EA-04-168	Jesus is Coming Soon - 12343	S. Butcher	Suspd.	22.50	32.50
85-F-EA-04-169	Halo, and Merry Christmas - 12351	S. Butcher	Open	40.00	45.00
85-F-EA-04-170	May Your Christmas Be Delightful - 15482	S. Butcher	Open	25.00	27.50
85-F-EA-04-171	Honk if You Love Jesus - 15490	S. Butcher	Open	13.00	15.00
85-F-EA-04-172	Baby's First Christmas - 15539	S. Butcher	Yr.Iss	13.00	33.00
85-F-EA-04-173	Baby's First Christmas - 15547	S. Butcher	Yr.Iss	13.00	33.00
85-F-EA-04-174	God Sent His Love - 15881	S. Butcher	Yr.Iss	17.00	25.00
86-F-EA-04-175	To My Favorite Paw - 100021	S. Butcher	Open	22.50	27.00
86-F-EA-04-176	Sending My Love - 100056	S. Butcher	Open	22.50	27.00
86-F-EA-04-177	O Worship the Lord - 100064	S. Butcher	Open	24.00	30.00
86-F-EA-04-178	To My Forever Friend - 100072	S. Butcher	Open	33.00	40.00
86-F-EA-04-179	Lord I'm Coming Home - 100110	S. Butcher	Open	22.50	27.00
86-F-EA-04-180	Lord, Keep Me On My Toes - 100129	S. Butcher	Open	22.50	27.00
86-F-EA-04-181	The Joy of the Lord is My Strength - 100137	S. Butcher	Open	35.00	40.00
86-F-EA-04-182	God Bless the Day We Found You - 100145	S. Butcher	Open	37.50	47.50
86-F-EA-04-183	God Bless the Day We Found You - 100153	S. Butcher	Open	37.50	47.50
86-F-EA-04-184	Serving the Lord - 100161	S. Butcher	Open	19.00	22.50
86-F-EA-04-185	I'm a Possibility - 100188	S. Butcher	Open	21.00	27.00
86-F-EA-04-186	Friends Never Drift Apart - 100250	S. Butcher	Open	35.00	42.50
86-F-EA-04-187	Help, Lord, I'm in a Spot - 100269	S. Butcher	Open	18.50	22.50
86-F-EA-04-188	He Cleansed My Soul - 100277	S. Butcher	Open	24.00	30.00
86-F-EA-04-189	Serving the Lord - 100293	S. Butcher	Open	19.00	22.50
86-F-EA-04-190	Brotherly Love - 100544	S. Butcher	Open	37.00	42.50
86-F-EA-04-191	O Worship the Lord - 102229	S. Butcher	Open	24.00	30.00
86-F-EA-04-192	Shepherd of Love - 102261	S. Butcher	Open	10.00	11.00
86-F-EA-04-193	Three Mini Animals - 102296	S. Butcher	Open	13.50	15.00
86-F-EA-04-194	Wishing You a Cozy Christmas - 102342	S. Butcher	Yr.Iss	17.00	34.00
86-F-EA-04-195	Love Rescued Me - 102393	S. Butcher	Open	21.00	27.00
86-F-EA-04-196	Angel of Mercy - 102482	S. Butcher	Open	19.00	22.50
86-F-EA-04-197	Sharing our Christmas Together - 102490	S. Butcher	Open	35.00	40.00
86-F-EA-04-198	God Bless America - 102938	S. Butcher	Yr.Iss	30.00	65.00
86-F-EA-04-199	It's the Birthday of a King - 102962	S. Butcher	Open	18.50	21.00
86-F-EA-04-200	I Believe in the Old Rugged Cross - 103632	S. Butcher	Open	25.00	30.00

Company Number	Name	Artist	Edition limit	Issue Price	Quote
Enesco Imports Corporation	**Bridal Party**				
84-F-EA-05-001	Bridesmaid - E-2831	S. Butcher	Open	13.50	16.00
85-F-EA-05-002	Ringbearer - E-2833	S. Butcher	Open	11.00	13.00
85-F-EA-05-003	Flower Girl - E-2835	S. Butcher	Open	11.00	13.00
84-F-EA-05-004	Groomsman - E-2836	S. Butcher	Open	13.50	16.00
86-F-EA-05-005	Groom - E-2837	S. Butcher	Open	13.50	18.00
85-F-EA-05-006	Junior Bridesmaid - E-2845	S. Butcher	Open	12.50	15.00
Enesco Imports Corporation	**Baby's First**				
84-F-EA-06-001	Baby's First Step - E-2840	S. Butcher	Open	35.00	40.00
84-F-EA-06-002	Baby's First Picture - E-2841	S. Butcher	Retrd.	45.00	45-60.00
85-F-EA-06-003	Baby's First Haircut - 12211	S.Butcher	Suspd.	32.50	37.00
86-F-EA-06-004	Baby's First Trip - 16012	S. Butcher	Open	32.50	40.00
Enesco Imports Corporation	**God Blessed Our Years Together**				
84-F-EA-07-001	Anniversary - E-2853	S. Butcher	Open	35.00	40.00
84-F-EA-07-002	First Anniversary - E-2854	S. Butcher	Open	35.00	40.00
84-F-EA-07-003	Fifth Anniversary - E-2855	S. Butcher	Open	35.00	40.00
84-F-EA-07-004	Tenth Anniversary - E-2856	S. Butcher	Open	35.00	40.00
84-F-EA-07-005	Twenty-Fifth Anniversary - E-2857	S. Butcher	Open	35.00	40.00
84-F-EA-07-006	Fortieth Anniversary - E-2859	S. Butcher	Open	35.00	40.00
84-F-EA-07-007	Fiftieth Anniversary - E-2860	S. Butcher	Open	35.00	40.00
Enesco Imports Corporation	**The Four Seasons**				
85-F-EA-08-001	The Voice of Spring - 12068	S. Butcher	Yr.Iss	30.00	80.00
85-F-EA-08-002	Summer's Joy - 12076	S. Butcher	Yr.Iss	30.00	80.00
86-F-EA-08-003	Autumn's Praise - 12084	S. Butcher	Yr.Iss	30.00	60.00
86-F-EA-08-004	Winter's Song - 12092	S. Butcher	Yr.Iss	30.00	62.50
Enesco Imports Corporation	**Rejoice in the Lord**				
85-F-EA-09-001	There's a Song in My Heart - 12173	S. Butcher	Open	11.00	13.00
85-F-EA-09-002	Happiness is the Lord - 12378	S. Butcher	Open	15.00	18.00
85-F-EA-09-003	Lord Give Me a Song - 12386	S. Butcher	Open	15.00	18.00
85-F-EA-09-004	He is My Song - 12394	S. Butcher	Open	17.50	22.50
Enesco Imports Corporation	**All the World Loves a Clown**				
XX-F-EA-10-001	I Get a Bang Out of You - 12262	S. Butcher	Open	30.00	35.00
86-F-EA-10-002	Lord Keep Me On the Ball - 12270	S. Butcher	Open	30.00	35.00
86-F-EA-10-003	Waddle I Do Without You - 12459	S. Butcher	Open	30.00	35.00
86-F-EA-10-004	The Lord Will Carry You Through - 12467	S. Butcher	Open	30.00	35.00
Enesco Imports Corporation	**Fifth Anniversary Commemorative Edition**				
85-F-EA-11-001	God Bless Our Years Together - 12440	S. Butcher	Closed	175.00	275.00
Enesco Imports Corporation	**Family Christmas Scene**				
85-F-EA-12-001	May You Have the Sweetest Christmas - 15776	S. Butcher	Open	17.00	19.00
85-F-EA-12-002	The Story of God's Love - 15784	S. Butcher	Open	22.50	25.00
85-F-EA-12-003	Tell Me a Story - 15792	S. Butcher	Open	10.00	11.00
85-F-EA-12-004	God Gave His Best - 15806	S. Butcher	Open	13.00	15.00
Enesco Imports Corporation	**Retired Precious Moments Figurines**				
79-F-EA-13-001	Smile, God Loves You - E-1373B	S. Butcher	Retrd.	7.00	60-90.00
79-F-EA-13-002	Praise the Lord Anyhow - E-1374B	S. Butcher	Retrd.	8.00	80-110.0
79-F-EA-13-003	God Loveth a Cheerful Giver - E-1378	S. Butcher	Retrd.	11.00	575.00
79-F-EA-13-004	O, How I Love Jesus - E-1380B	S. Butcher	Retrd.	8.00	45-75.00
79-F-EA-13-005	His Burden Is Light - E-1380G	S. Butcher	Retrd.	8.00	45-75.00
79-F-EA-13-006	Come Let Us Adore Him - E-2011	S. Butcher	Retrd.	10.00	250.00
80-F-EA-13-007	Wishing You a Season Filled with Joy - E-2805	S. Butcher	Retrd.	20.00	50-80.00
84-F-EA-13-008	Mother Sew Dear - E-2850	S. Butcher	Retrd.	350.00	350.00
80-F-EA-13-009	Blessed are the Peacemakers - E-3107	S. Butcher	Retrd.	13.00	45-75.00
80-F-EA-13-010	Be Not Weary In Well Doing - E-3111	S. Butcher	Retrd.	14.00	50-80.00
80-F-EA-13-011	God's Speed - E-3112	S. Butcher	Retrd.	14.00	65-95.00
80-F-EA-13-012	Eggs Over Easy - E-3118	S. Butcher	Retrd.	12.00	65-95.00
82-F-EA-13-014	O Come All Ye Faithful - E-2353	S. Butcher	Retrd.	27.50	33-60.00
82-F-EA-13-015	There is Joy in Serving Jesus - E-7157	S. Butcher	Retrd.	17.00	30-40.00
83-F-EA-13-016	Taste and See that the Lord is Good - E-9274	S. Butcher	Retrd.	22.50	42.50
Ernst Enterprises	**Little Misses Young and Fair**				
82-F-EB-01-001	Heart of a Child	A. Murray	5,000	65.00	65.00
83-F-EB-01-002	Where Wild Flowers Grow	A. Murray	2,000	65.00	65.00
85-F-EB-01-003	Whispered Memories	A. Murray	5,000	75.00	75.00
85-F-EB-01-004	Final Touch	A. Murray	2,000	75.00	75.00
Ernst Enterprises	**My Fair Ladies**				
82-F-EB-02-001	Lady Sabrina	R. Money	5,000	85.00	85.00
Ernst Enterprises	**Seems Like Yesterday**				
81-F-EB-03-001	Stop and Smell the Roses	R. Money	5,000	45.00	45.00
82-F-EB-03-002	Home by Lunch	R. Money	5,000	45.00	45.00
82-F-EB-03-003	Lisa's Creek	R. Money	5,000	45.00	45.00
82-F-EB-03-004	It's Got My Name on It	R. Money	5,000	45.00	45.00
82-F-EB-03-005	My Magic Hat	R. Money	2,000	45.00	45.00
Ernst Enterprises	**Yesterdays**				
82-F-EB-04-001	Amber	Glenice	5,000	45.00	45.00
84-F-EB-04-002	Elmer	Glenice	5,000	45.00	45.00
85-F-EB-04-003	Katie	Glenice	600	45.00	45.00
Flambro Imports	**Emmett Kelly, Jr. Figurines**				
81-F-FD-01-001	Looking Out To See	Undis.	12,000	75.00	700.00
81-F-FD-01-002	Sweeping Up	Undis.	12,000	75.00	500.00
82-F-FD-01-003	Wet Paint	Undis.	15,000	80.00	350.00
82-F-FD-01-004	The Thinker	Undis.	15,000	60.00	725.00
82-F-FD-01-005	Why Me?	Undis.	15,000	65.00	150.00
83-F-FD-01-006	The Balancing Act	Undis.	10,000	75.00	300.00
83-F-FD-01-007	Wishful Thinking	Undis.	10,000	65.00	150.00
83-F-FD-01-008	Hole In The Sole	Undis.	10,000	75.00	150.00
83-F-FD-01-009	Balloons For Sale	Undis.	10,000	75.00	300.00
83-F-FD-01-010	Spirit of Christmas I	Undis.	3,500	125.00	850.00
84-F-FD-01-011	Eating Cabbage	Undis.	12,000	75.00	150.00
84-F-FD-01-012	Big Business	Undis.	9,500	110.00	110.00
84-F-FD-01-013	Piano Player	Undis.	9,500	160.00	160.00
84-F-FD-01-014	Spirit of Christmas II	Undis.	3,500	270.00	270.00
85-F-FD-01-015	Man's Best Friend	Undis.	9,500	98.00	98.00
85-F-FD-01-016	No Strings Attached	Undis.	9,500	98.00	98.00
85-F-FD-01-017	In The Spotlight	Undis.	12,000	103.00	103.00
85-F-FD-01-018	Emmett's Fan	Undis.	12,000	80.00	120.00
85-F-FD-01-019	Spirit of Christmas III	Undis.	3,500	220.00	220.00
86-F-FD-01-020	The Entertainers	Undis.	12,000	120.00	120.00
86-F-FD-01-021	Cotton Candy	Undis.	12,000	98.00	98.00
86-F-FD-01-022	Bedtime	Undis.	12,000	98.00	98.00
86-F-FD-01-023	Making New Friends	Undis.	9,500	140.00	140.00

Figurines

Company		Series			
Number	Name	Artist	Edition limit	Issue Price	Quote

86-F-FD-01-024	Fair Game	Undis.	2,500	450.00	450.00
86-F-FD-01-025	Spirit of Christmas IV	Undis.	3,500	150.00	150.00
87-F-FD-01-026	On The Road Again	Undis.	9,500	109.00	109.00
87-F-FD-01-027	My Favorite Things	Undis.	9,500	109.00	109.00
87-F-FD-01-028	Saturday Night	Undis.	7,500	153.00	153.00
87-F-FD-01-029	Toothache	Undis.	12,000	98.00	98.00
87-F-FD-01-030	Spirit of Christmas V	Undis.	2,500	170.00	170.00
88-F-FD-01-031	Over a Barrel	Undis.	9,500	120.00	120.00
88-F-FD-01-032	Wheeler Dealer	Undis.	7,500	160.00	160.00
88-F-FD-01-033	Dining Out	Undis.	12,000	110.00	110.00
88-F-FD-01-034	Amen	Undis.	12,000	110.00	110.00

Flambro Imports — Circus World Museum Clowns

85-F-FD-02-001	Paul Jerome (Hobo)	Undis.	9,500	80.00	80.00
85-F-FD-02-002	Paul Jung (Neat)	Undis.	9,500	80.00	80.00
85-F-FD-02-003	Felix Adler (Grotesque)	Undis.	9,500	80.00	80.00
87-F-FD-02-004	Paul Jerome with Dog	Undis.	7,500	90.00	90.00
87-F-FD-02-005	Paul Jung, Sitting	Undis.	7,500	90.00	90.00
87-F-FD-02-006	Felix Adler with Balloon	Undis.	7,500	90.00	90.00
87-F-FD-02-007	Abe Goldstein, Keystone Kop	Undis.	7,500	90.00	90.00

Flambro Imports — Emmett Kelly, Jr. Miniatures

86-F-FD-03-001	Looking Out To See	Undis.	Numb.	25.00	25.00
86-F-FD-03-002	Sweeping Up	Undis.	Numb.	25.00	25.00
86-F-FD-03-003	Wet Paint	Undis.	Numb.	25.00	25.00
86-F-FD-03-004	Why Me?	Undis.	Numb.	25.00	25.00
86-F-FD-03-005	The Thinker	Undis.	Numb.	25.00	25.00
86-F-FD-03-006	Balancing Act	Undis.	Numb.	25.00	25.00
86-F-FD-03-007	Hole in the Sole	Undis.	Numb.	25.00	25.00
86-F-FD-03-008	Balloons for Sale	Undis.	Numb.	25.00	25.00
86-F-FD-03-009	Wishful Thinking	Undis.	Numb.	25.00	25.00

Franklin Mint — Joys of Childhood

76-F-FM-01-001	Hopscotch	N. Rockwell	3,700	120.00	175.00
76-F-FM-01-002	The Fishing Hole	N. Rockwell	3,700	120.00	175.00
76-F-FM-01-003	Dressing Up	N. Rockwell	3,700	120.00	175.00
76-F-FM-01-004	The Stilt Walker	N. Rockwell	3,700	120.00	175.00
76-F-FM-01-005	Trick or Treat	N. Rockwell	3,700	120.00	175.00
76-F-FM-01-006	Time Out	N. Rockwell	3,700	120.00	175.00
76-F-FM-01-007	The Marble Champ	N. Rockwell	3,700	120.00	175.00
76-F-FM-01-008	The Nurse	N. Rockwell	3,700	120.00	175.00
76-F-FM-01-009	Ride 'Em Cowboy	N. Rockwell	3,700	120.00	175.00
76-F-FM-01-010	Coasting Along	N. Rockwell	3,700	120.00	175.00

Gartlan USA — Plaques

85-F-GB-01-001	Pete Rose - "Desire to Win"	T. Sizemore	4,192	75.00	75.00
86-F-GB-01-002	George Brett - "Royalty in Motion"	J. Martin	2,000	85.00	85.00
86-F-GB-01-003	Reggie Jackson - "The Roundtripper"	J. Martin	500	150.00	150.00
86-F-GB-01-004	Reggie Jackson Artist Prf "The Round- tripper"	J. Martin	44	200.00	200.00
87-F-GB-01-005	Roger Staubach	C. Soileau	1,979	85.00	85.00

Gartlan USA — Pete Rose Platinum Edition

| 85-F-GB-02-001 | Pete Rose - "For the Record" | H. Reed | 4,192 | 125.00 | 125.00 |

Gartlan USA — Baseball/Football Series

85-F-GB-03-001	Pete Rose Ceramic Baseball Card	T. Sizemore	Open	9.95	9.95
85-F-GB-03-002	Pete Rose Ceramic Baseball Card	T. Sizemore	4,192	39.00	39.00
86-F-GB-03-003	George Brett Baseball Rounder	J. Martin	Open	9.95	9.95
86-F-GB-03-004	George Brett Baseball Rounder	J. Martin	2,000	29.95	29.95
86-F-GB-03-005	George Brett Ceramic Baseball	J. Martin	Open	19.95	19.95
86-F-GB-03-006	George Brett Ceramic Baseball	J. Martin	2,000	49.50	49.50
87-F-GB-03-007	Roger Staubach Ceramic Football Card	C. Soileau	Open	9.95	9.95
87-F-GB-03-008	Roger Staubach Ceramic Football Card	C. Soileau	1,979	39.00	39.00

Goebel — Goebel Figurines

63-F-GG-01-001	Little Veterinarian (Mysterious Malady)	N. Rockwell	Closed	15.00	400.00
63-F-GG-01-002	Boyhood Dreams (Adventurers between Adventure	N. Rockwell	Closed	12.00	400.00
63-F-GG-01-003	Mother's Helper (Pride of Parent-hood)	N. Rockwell	Closed	15.00	400.00
63-F-GG-01-004	His First Smoke	N. Rockwell	Closed	9.00	400.00
63-F-GG-01-005	My New Pal (A Boy Meets His Dog)	N. Rockwell	Closed	12.00	400.00
63-F-GG-01-006	Home Cure	N. Rockwell	Closed	16.00	400.00
63-F-GG-01-007	Timely Assistance (Love Aid)	N. Rockwell	Closed	16.00	40.00
63-F-GG-01-008	She Loves Me (Day Dreamer)	N. Rockwell	Closed	8.00	400.00
63-F-GG-01-009	Buttercup Test (Beguiling Buttercup)	N. Rockwell	Closed	10.00	400.00
63-F-GG-01-010	First Love (A Scholarly Pace)	N. Rockwell	Closed	30.00	400.00
63-F-GG-01-012	Patient Anglers (Fisherman's Paradise)	N. Rockwell	Open	18.00	400.00
63-F-GG-01-013	Advertising Plaque	N. Rockwell	Open	Unknown	600.00

Goebel — M. I. Hummel Collectibles Figurines

XX-F-GG-02-001	A Fair Measure 345	M. I. Hummel	Open	Unknown	165.00
XX-F-GG-02-002	A Gentle Glow 439	M. I. Hummel	Open	Unknown	120.00
XX-F-GG-02-003	Accordian Boy 185	M. I. Hummel	Open	Unknown	105.00
XX-F-GG-02-004	Adoration 23/1	M. I. Hummel	Open	Unknown	210.00
XX-F-GG-02-004	Adoration 23/111	M. I. Hummel	Open	Unknown	315.00
XX-F-GG-02-006	Adventure Bound 347	M. I. Hummel	Open	Unknown	2400.00
XX-F-GG-02-007	Angel Duet 261	M. I. Hummel	Open	Unknown	125.00
XX-F-GG-02-008	Angel Serenade 214D	M. I. Hummel	Open	Unknown	48.00
XX-F-GG-02-009	Angel Serenade with Lamb 83	M. I. Hummel	Open	Unknown	120.00
XX-F-GG-02-010	Angel with Accordian 238/B	M. I. Hummel	Open	Unknown	29.00
XX-F-GG-02-011	Angel with Lute 238/A	M. I. Hummel	Open	Unknown	29.00
XX-F-GG-02-012	Angel with Trumpet 238/C	M. I. Hummel	Open	Unknown	29.00
XX-F-GG-02-013	Angelic Song 144	M. I. Hummel	Open	Unknown	90.00
XX-F-GG-02-014	Apple Tree Boy 142/3/0	M. I. Hummel	Open	Unknown	79.00
XX-F-GG-02-015	Apple Tree Boy 142/1	M. I. Hummel	Open	Unknown	155.00
XX-F-GG-02-016	Apple Tree Boy 142/V	M. I. Hummel	Open	Unknown	720.00
XX-F-GG-02-017	Apple Tree Boy 142/X	M. I. Hummel	Open	Unknown	16500.00
XX-F-GG-02-018	Apple Tree Girl 141/3/0	M. I. Hummel	Open	Unknown	79.00
XX-F-GG-02-019	Apple Tree Girl 141/1	M. I. Hummel	Open	Unknown	155.00
XX-F-GG-02-020	Apple Tree Girl 141/V	M. I. Hummel	Open	Unknown	720.00
XX-F-GG-02-021	Apple Tree Girl 141/X	M. I. Hummel	Open	Unknown	16500.00
XX-F-GG-02-022	Artist 304	M. I. Hummel	Open	Unknown	140.00
XX-F-GG-02-023	Auf Wiedersehen 153/0	M. I. Hummel	Open	Unknown	140.00
XX-F-GG-02-024	Auf Wiedersehen 153/1	M. I. Hummel	Open	Unknown	180.00
XX-F-GG-02-025	Autumn Harvest 355	M. I. Hummel	Open	Unknown	125.00
XX-F-GG-02-026	Baker 128	M. I. Hummel	Open	Unknown	105.00
XX-F-GG-02-027	Baking Day 330	M. I. Hummel	Open	Unknown	135.00
XX-F-GG-02-028	Band Leader 129	M. I. Hummel	Open	Unknown	125.00
XX-F-GG-02-029	Bandleader 129/4/0	M. I. Hummel	Open	Unknown	55.00
XX-F-GG-02-030	Barnyard Hero 195/2/0	M. I. Hummel	Open	Unknown	105.00
XX-F-GG-02-031	Barnyard Herd 195/1	M. I. Hummel	Open	Unknown	180.00

Company		Series			
Number	Name	Artist	Edition limit	Issue Price	Quote

XX-F-GG-02-032	Bashful 377	M. I. Hummel	Open	Unknown	118.00
XX-F-GG-02-033	Begging his Share 9	M. I. Hummel	Open	Unknown	130.00
XX-F-GG-02-034	Be Patient 197/2/0	M. I. Hummel	Open	Unknown	118.00
XX-F-GG-02-035	Be Patient 197/1	M. I. Hummel	Open	Unknown	155.00
XX-F-GG-02-036	Big Housecleaning 363	M. I. Hummel	Open	Unknown	160.00
XX-F-GG-02-037	Bird Duet 169	M. I. Hummel	Open	Unknown	90.00
XX-F-GG-02-038	Bird Watcher 300	M. I. Hummel	Open	Unknown	135.00
XX-F-GG-02-039	Birthday Serenade 218/2/0	M. I. Hummel	Open	Unknown	110.00
XX-F-GG-02-040	Birthday Serenade 218/0	M. I. Hummel	Open	Unknown	180.00
XX-F-GG-02-041	Blessed Event 333	M. I. Hummel	Open	Unknown	29.00
XX-F-GG-02-042	Blessed Child 78/1/11	M. I. Hummel	Open	Unknown	35.00
XX-F-GG-02-043	Blessed Child 78/11/11	M. I. Hummel	Open	Unknown	45.00
XX-F-GG-02-044	Blessed Child 78/111/11	M. I. Hummel	Open	Unknown	210.00
XX-F-GG-02-045	Bookworm 8	M. I. Hummel	Open	Unknown	130.00
XX-F-GG-02-046	Bookworm 3/1	M. I. Hummel	Open	Unknown	185.00
XX-F-GG-02-047	Bookworm 3/11	M. I. Hummel	Open	Unknown	850.00
XX-F-GG-02-048	Bookworm 3/111	M. I. Hummel	Open	Unknown	910.00
XX-F-GG-02-049	Boots 143/0	M. I. Hummel	Open	Unknown	110.00
XX-F-GG-02-050	Boots 143/1	M. I. Hummel	Open	Unknown	160.00
XX-F-GG-02-051	Botanist 351	M. I. Hummel	Open	Unknown	125.00
XX-F-GG-02-052	Boy with Accordian 390	M. I. Hummel	Open	Unknown	45.00
XX-F-GG-02-053	Boy with Horse 239C	M. I. Hummel	Open	Unknown	35.00
XX-F-GG-02-054	Boy with Toothache 217	M. I. Hummel	Open	Unknown	118.00
XX-F-GG-02-055	Brother 95	M. I. Hummel	Open	Unknown	98.00
XX-F-GG-02-056	Builder 305	M. I. Hummel	Open	Unknown	140.00
XX-F-GG-02-057	Busy Student 367	M. I. Hummel	Open	Unknown	105.00
XX-F-GG-02-058	Carnival 328	M. I. Hummel	Open	Unknown	118.00
XX-F-GG-02-059	Celestial Musician 188/0	M. I. Hummel	Open	Unknown	118.00
XX-F-GG-02-060	Celestial Musician 188	M. I. Hummel	Open	Unknown	160.00
XX-F-GG-02-062	Chick Girl 57/0	M. I. Hummel	Open	Unknown	95.00
XX-F-GG-02-063	Chick Girl 57/1	M. I. Hummel	Open	Unknown	155.00
XX-F-GG-02-064	Chick Girl 57/2	M. I. Hummel	Open	Unknown	85.00
XX-F-GG-02-065	Chicken-Licken 385	M. I. Hummel	Open	Unknown	175.00
XX-F-GG-02-066	Chimney Sweep 12/2/0	M. I. Hummel	Open	Unknown	60.00
XX-F-GG-02-067	Chimney Sweep 12/1	M. I. Hummel	Open	Unknown	110.00
XX-F-GG-02-068	Christ Child 18	M. I. Hummel	Open	Unknown	75.00
XX-F-GG-02-069	Christmas Song 343	M. I. Hummel	Open	Unknown	125.00
XX-F-GG-02-070	Cinderella 337	M. I. Hummel	Open	Unknown	165.00
XX-F-GG-02-071	Close Harmony 336	M. I. Hummel	Open	Unknown	175.00
XX-F-GG-02-072	Confidentially 314	M. I. Hummel	Open	Unknown	140.00
XX-F-GG-02-073	Congratulations 17/0	M. I. Hummel	Open	Unknown	98.00
XX-F-GG-02-074	Coquettes 179	M. I. Hummel	Open	Unknown	155.00
XX-F-GG-02-075	Crossroads 331	M. I. Hummel	Open	Unknown	260.00
XX-F-GG-02-076	Culprits 56/A	M. I. Hummel	Open	Unknown	155.00
XX-F-GG-02-077	Doctor 127	M. I. Hummel	Open	Unknown	90.00
XX-F-GG-02-078	Doll Bath 319	M. I. Hummel	Open	Unknown	140.00
XX-F-GG-02-079	Doll Mother 67	M. I. Hummel	Open	Unknown	140.00
XX-F-GG-02-080	Duet 130	M. I. Hummel	Open	Unknown	155.00
XX-F-GG-02-081	Easter Greetings 378	M. I. Hummel	Open	Unknown	120.00
XX-F-GG-02-082	Easter Time 384	M. I. Hummel	Open	Unknown	175.00
XX-F-GG-02-083	Eventide 99	M. I. Hummel	Open	Unknown	190.00
XX-F-GG-02-084	Farewell 65	M. I. Hummel	Open	Unknown	155.00
XX-F-GG-02-085	Farm Boy 66	M. I. Hummel	Open	Unknown	130.00
XX-F-GG-02-086	Favorite Pet 361	M. I. Hummel	Open	Unknown	155.00
XX-F-GG-02-087	Feathered Friend 344	M. I. Hummel	Open	Unknown	160.00
XX-F-GG-02-088	Feeding Time 199/0	M. I. Hummel	Open	Unknown	125.00
XX-F-GG-02-089	Feeding Time 199/1	M. I. Hummel	Open	Unknown	140.00
XX-F-GG-02-090	Festival Harmony, with Mandolin 172/0	M. I. Hummel	Open	Unknown	160.00
XX-F-GG-02-092	Festival Harmony, with Flute 173/0	M. I. Hummel	Open	Unknown	160.00
XX-F-GG-02-094	Flower Vendor 381	M. I. Hummel	Open	Unknown	145.00
XX-F-GG-02-095	Follow the Leader 369	M. I. Hummel	Open	Unknown	660.00
XX-F-GG-02-096	For Father 87	M. I. Hummel	Open	Unknown	120.00
XX-F-GG-02-097	For Mother 257	M. I. Hummel	Open	Unknown	95.00
XX-F-GG-02-098	For Mother 257/2/0	M. I. Hummel	Open	Unknown	72.00
XX-F-GG-02-099	Forest Shrine 183	M. I. Hummel	Open	Unknown	350.00
XX-F-GG-02-100	Friends 136/I	M. I. Hummel	Open	Unknown	120.00
XX-F-GG-02-101	Friends 136/V	M. I. Hummel	Open	Unknown	720.00
XX-F-GG-02-102	Gay Adventure 356	M. I. Hummel	Open	Unknown	105.00
XX-F-GG-02-103	Girl with Doll 239/B	M. I. Hummel	Open	Unknown	35.00
XX-F-GG-02-104	Girl with Music 389	M. I. Hummel	Open	Unknown	45.00
XX-F-GG-02-105	Girl with Nosegay 239A	M. I. Hummel	Open	Unknown	35.00
XX-F-GG-02-106	Girl with Trumpet 391	M. I. Hummel	Open	Unknown	45.00
XX-F-GG-02-107	Globe Trotter 79	M. I. Hummel	Open	Unknown	110.00
XX-F-GG-02-108	Going Home 383	M. I. Hummel	Open	Unknown	180.00
XX-F-GG-02-109	Going to Grandma's 52/0	M. I. Hummel	Open	Unknown	145.00
XX-F-GG-02-111	Good Friends 182	M. I. Hummel	Open	Unknown	120.00
XX-F-GG-02-112	Good Hunting 307	M. I. Hummel	Open	Unknown	140.00
XX-F-GG-02-113	Good Night 214C	M. I. Hummel	Open	Unknown	55.00
XX-F-GG-02-114	Good Shepherd 42/0	M. I. Hummel	Open	Unknown	98.00
XX-F-GG-02-115	Goose Girl 47/3/0	M. I. Hummel	Open	Unknown	95.00
XX-F-GG-02-116	Goose Girl 47/0	M. I. Hummel	Open	Unknown	130.00
XX-F-GG-02-117	Goose Girl 47/II	M. I. Hummel	Open	Unknown	260.00
XX-F-GG-02-118	Guiding Angel 357	M. I. Hummel	Open	Unknown	55.00
XX-F-GG-02-119	Happiness 86	M. I. Hummel	Open	Unknown	75.00
XX-F-GG-02-120	Happy Birthday 176/0	M. I. Hummel	Open	Unknown	135.00
XX-F-GG-02-121	Happy Birthday 176/I	M. I. Hummel	Open	Unknown	190.00
XX-F-GG-02-122	Happy Days 150/2/0	M. I. Hummel	Open	Unknown	110.00
XX-F-GG-02-123	Happy Days 150/0	M. I. Hummel	Open	Unknown	175.00
XX-F-GG-02-124	Happy Days 150/I	M. I. Hummel	Open	Unknown	325.00
XX-F-GG-02-125	Happy Pastime 69	M. I. Hummel	Open	Unknown	95.00
XX-F-GG-02-126	Happy Traveller 109/0	M. I. Hummel	Open	Unknown	79.00
XX-F-GG-02-127	Hear Ye! Hear Ye! 15/0	M. I. Hummel	Open	Unknown	125.00
XX-F-GG-02-128	Hear Ye! Hear Ye! 15/I	M. I. Hummel	Open	Unknown	145.00
iX-F-GG-02-129	Hear Ye! Hear Ye! 15/II	M. I. Hummel	Open	Unknown	275.00
XX-F-GG-02-130	Hear Ye! Hear Ye! 15/2	M. I. Hummel	Open	Unknown	85.00
XX-F-GG-02-131	Heavenly Angel 21/0	M. I. Hummel	Open	Unknown	64.00
XX-F-GG-02-132	Heavenly Angel 21/0 1/2	M. I. Hummel	Open	Unknown	105.00
XX-F-GG-02-133	Heavenly Angel 21/I	M. I. Hummel	Open	Unknown	130.00
XX-F-GG-02-134	Heavenly Angel 21/II	M. I. Hummel	Open	Unknown	250.00
XX-F-GG-02-135	Heavenly Lullaby 262	M. I. Hummel	Open	Unknown	110.00
XX-F-GG-02-136	Heavenly Protection 88/I	M. I. Hummel	Open	Unknown	250.00
XX-F-GG-02-137	Heavenly Protection 88/II	M. I. Hummel	Open	Unknown	380.00
XX-F-GG-02-138	Hello 124/0	M. I. Hummel	Open	Unknown	118.00
XX-F-GG-02-140	Holy Child 70	M. I. Hummel	Open	Unknown	95.00
XX-F-GG-02-141	Home from Market 198/2/0	M. I. Hummel	Open	Unknown	75.00
XX-F-GG-02-142	Home from Market 198/1	M. I. Hummel	Open	Unknown	125.00

Number	Name	Artist	Edition limit	Issue Price	Quote
XX-F-GG-02-143	Homeward Bound 334	M. I. Hummel	Open	Unknown	220.00
XX-F-GG-02-145	Infant of Krumbad 78/1/11	M. I. Hummel	Open	Unknown	21.00
XX-F-GG-02-146	Infant of Krumbad 78/11/11	M. I. Hummel	Open	Unknown	26.50
XX-F-GG-02-147	Infant of Krumbad 78/111/11	M. I. Hummel	Open	Unknown	31.50
XX-F-GG-02-148	In The Meadow 459	M. I. Hummel	Open	Unknown	120.00
XX-F-GG-02-149	In Tune 414	M. I. Hummel	Open	Unknown	165.00
XX-F-GG-02-150	Joyful 53	M. I. Hummel	Open	Unknown	65.00
XX-F-GG-02-151	Joyous News 27/III	M. I. Hummel	Open	Unknown	130.00
XX-F-GG-02-152	Just Fishing 373	M. I. Hummel	Open	Unknown	125.00
XX-F-GG-02-153	Just Resting 112/3/0	M. I. Hummel	Open	Unknown	90.00
XX-F-GG-02-154	Just Resting 112/I	M. I. Hummel	Open	Unknown	140.00
XX-F-GG-02-155	Kiss Me 311	M. I. Hummel	Open	Unknown	140.00
XX-F-GG-02-156	Knitting Lesson 256	M. I. Hummel	Open	Unknown	310.00
XX-F-GG-02-157	Knit One, Purl One 432	M. I. Hummel	Open	Unknown	75.00
XX-F-GG-02-158	Latest News 184/0	M. I. Hummel	Open	Unknown	160.00
XX-F-GG-02-159	Let's Sing 110/0	M. I. Hummel	Open	Unknown	75.00
XX-F-GG-02-160	Let's Sing 110/I	M. I. Hummel	Open	Unknown	105.00
XX-F-GG-02-161	Letter to Santa Claus 340	M. I. Hummel	Open	Unknown	195.00
XX-F-GG-02-162	Little Bank 392	M. I. Hummel	Open	Unknown	132.00
XX-F-GG-02-163	Little Bookkeeper 306	M. I. Hummel	Open	Unknown	160.00
XX-F-GG-02-164	Little Cellist 89/I	M. I. Hummel	Open	Unknown	125.00
XX-F-GG-02-165	Little Cellist 89/II	M. I. Hummel	Open	Unknown	275.00
XX-F-GG-02-166	Little Drummer 240	M. I. Hummel	Open	Unknown	75.00
XX-F-GG-02-167	Little Fiddler 2/4/0	M. I. Hummel	Open	Unknown	55.00
XX-F-GG-02-168	Little Fiddler 4	M. I. Hummel	Open	Unknown	110.00
XX-F-GG-02-169	Little Fiddler 2/0	M. I. Hummel	Open	Unknown	130.00
XX-F-GG-02-170	Little Fiddler 2/I	M. I. Hummel	Open	Unknown	260.00
XX-F-GG-02-171	Little Fiddler 2/II	M. I. Hummel	Open	Unknown	850.00
XX-F-GG-02-172	Little Fiddler 2/III	M. I. Hummel	Open	Unknown	910.00
XX-F-GG-02-173	Little Gabriel 32	M. I. Hummel	Open	Unknown	75.00
XX-F-GG-02-174	Little Gardener 74	M. I. Hummel	Open	Unknown	75.00
XX-F-GG-02-175	Little Goat Herder 200/0	M. I. Hummel	Open	Unknown	120.00
XX-F-GG-02-176	Little Goat Herder 200/1	M. I. Hummel	Open	Unknown	140.00
XX-F-GG-02-177	Little Guardian 145	M. I. Hummel	Open	Unknown	90.00
XX-F-GG-02-178	Little Helper 73	M. I. Hummel	Open	Unknown	75.00
XX-F-GG-02-179	Little Hiker 16/2/0	M. I. Hummel	Open	Unknown	65.00
XX-F-GG-02-180	Little Hiker 16/I	M. I. Hummel	Open	Unknown	115.00
XX-F-GG-02-181	Little Nurse 376	M. I. Hummel	Open	Unknown	145.00
XX-F-GG-02-182	Little Pharmacist 322	M. I. Hummel	Open	Unknown	145.00
XX-F-GG-02-183	Little Scholar 80	M. I. Hummel	Open	Unknown	110.00
XX-F-GG-02-184	Little Shopper 96	M. I. Hummel	Open	Unknown	75.00
XX-F-GG-02-185	Little Sweeper 171	M. I. Hummel	Open	Unknown	75.00
XX-F-GG-02-186	Little Tailor 308	M. I. Hummel	Open	Unknown	150.00
XX-F-GG-02-187	Little Thrifty 118	M. I. Hummel	Open	Unknown	90.00
XX-F-GG-02-188	Little Tooter 214H	M. I. Hummel	Open	Unknown	72.00
XX-F-GG-02-189	Lost Sheep 68/2/0	M. I. Hummel	Open	Unknown	79.00
XX-F-GG-02-190	Lost Sheep 68/0	M. I. Hummel	Open	Unknown	118.00
XX-F-GG-02-191	Lost Stocking 374	M. I. Hummel	Open	Unknown	90.00
XX-F-GG-02-192	Mail is Here 226	M. I. Hummel	Open	Unknown	360.00
XX-F-GG-02-193	March Winds 43	M. I. Hummel	Open	Unknown	79.00
XX-F-GG-02-194	Max and Moritz 123	M. I. Hummel	Open	Unknown	118.00
XX-F-GG-02-195	Meditation 13/2/0	M. I. Hummel	Open	Unknown	75.00
XX-F-GG-02-196	Meditation 13/0	M. I. Hummel	Open	Unknown	115.00
XX-F-GG-02-198	Meditation 13V	M. I. Hummel	Open	Unknown	910.00
XX-F-GG-02-199	Merry Wanderer 11/2/0	M. I. Hummel	Open	Unknown	75.00
XX-F-GG-02-200	Merry Wanderer 11/0	M. I. Hummel	Open	Unknown	105.00
XX-F-GG-02-201	Merry Wanderer 7/0	M. I. Hummel	Open	Unknown	145.00
XX-F-GG-02-202	Merry Wanderer 7/I	M. I. Hummel	Open	Unknown	260.00
XX-F-GG-02-203	Merry Wanderer 7/II	M. I. Hummel	Open	Unknown	850.00
XX-F-GG-02-204	Merry Wanderer 7/III	M. I. Hummel	Open	Unknown	910.00
XX-F-GG-02-205	Merry Wanderer 7X	M. I. Hummel	Open	Unknown	16500.00
XX-F-GG-02-206	Mischief Maker 342	M. I. Hummel	Open	Unknown	160.00
XX-F-GG-02-207	Mother's Darling 175	M. I. Hummel	Open	Unknown	125.00
XX-F-GG-02-208	Mother's Helper 133	M. I. Hummel	Open	Unknown	120.00
XX-F-GG-02-209	Mountaineer 315	M. I. Hummel	Open	Unknown	140.00
XX-F-GG-02-210	Not for You 317	M. I. Hummel	Open	Unknown	140.00
XX-F-GG-02-211	On Holiday 350	M. I. Hummel	Open	Unknown	120.00
XX-F-GG-02-212	On Secret Path 386	M. I. Hummel	Open	Unknown	155.00
XX-F-GG-02-213	Out of Danger 56/B	M. I. Hummel	Open	Unknown	155.00
XX-F-GG-02-214	Photographer 178	M. I. Hummel	Open	Unknown	155.00
XX-F-GG-02-215	Playmates 58/2/0	M. I. Hummel	Open	Unknown	85.00
XX-F-GG-02-216	Playmates 58/0	M. I. Hummel	Open	Unknown	95.00
XX-F-GG-02-217	Playmates 58/I	M. I. Hummel	Open	Unknown	155.00
XX-F-GG-02-218	Pleasant Journey 406	M. I. Hummel	Yr.Iss	500.00	500.00
XX-F-GG-02-219	Postman 119	M. I. Hummel	Open	Unknown	120.00
XX-F-GG-02-220	Prayer Before Battle 20	M. I. Hummel	Open	Unknown	105.00
XX-F-GG-02-221	Puppy Love 1	M. I. Hummel	Open	Unknown	115.00
XX-F-GG-02-222	Retreat to Safety 201/2/0	M. I. Hummel	Open	Unknown	105.00
XX-F-GG-02-223	Retreat to Safety 201/1	M. I. Hummel	Open	Unknown	185.00
XX-F-GG-02-224	Ride into Christmas 396/2/0	M. I. Hummel	Open	Unknown	145.00
XX-F-GG-02-225	Ride into Christmas 396/I	M. I. Hummel	Open	Unknown	260.00
XX-F-GG-02-226	Ring Around the Rosie 348	M. I. Hummel	Open	Unknown	1750.00
XX-F-GG-02-227	Run-A-Way 327	M. I. Hummel	Open	Unknown	155.00
XX-F-GG-02-228	St. George 55	M. I. Hummel	Open	Unknown	195.00
XX-F-GG-02-229	St. Jopseph, color, 214/B/11	M. I. Hummel	Open	Unknown	115.00
XX-F-GG-02-230	School Boy 82/2/0	M. I. Hummel	Open	Unknown	75.00
XX-F-GG-02-231	School Boy 82/0	M. I. Hummel	Open	Unknown	110.00
XX-F-GG-02-232	School Boy 82/II	M. I. Hummel	Open	Unknown	275.00
XX-F-GG-02-233	School Boys 17/0/I	M. I. Hummel	Open	Unknown	725.00
XX-F-GG-02-234	School Girl 81/2/0	M. I. Hummel	Open	Unknown	75.00
XX-F-GG-02-235	School Girl 81/0	M. I. Hummel	Open	Unknown	110.00
XX-F-GG-02-236	School Girls 177/I	M. I. Hummel	Open	Unknown	725.00
XX-F-GG-02-237	Sensitive Hunter 6/0	M. I. Hummel	Open	Unknown	105.00
XX-F-GG-02-238	Sensitive Hunter 6/I	M. I. Hummel	Open	Unknown	140.00
XX-F-GG-02-240	Sensitive Hunter 6/2/0	M. I. Hummel	Open	Unknown	85.00
XX-F-GG-02-241	Serenade 85/0	M. I. Hummel	Open	Unknown	75.00
XX-F-GG-02-242	Serenade 85/II	M. I. Hummel	Open	Unknown	275.00
XX-F-GG-02-243	Serenade 85/4/0	M. I. Hummel	Open	Unknown	55.00
XX-F-GG-02-244	Shepherd's Boy 64	M. I. Hummel	Open	Unknown	130.00
XX-F-GG-02-245	She Loves Me, She Loves Me Not 174	M. I. Hummel	Open	Unknown	105.00
XX-F-GG-02-246	Shining Light 358	M. I. Hummel	Open	Unknown	55.00
XX-F-GG-02-247	Signs of Spring 203/2/0	M. I. Hummel	Open	Unknown	105.00
XX-F-GG-02-248	Signs of Spring 203/I	M. I. Hummel	Open	Unknown	140.00
XX-F-GG-02-249	Sing Along 433	M. I. Hummel	Open	Unknown	160.00
XX-F-GG-02-250	Singing Lesson 63	M. I. Hummel	Open	Unknown	75.00
XX-F-GG-02-251	Sing With Me 405	M. I. Hummel	Open	Unknown	180.00
XX-F-GG-02-252	Sister 98/2/0	M. I. Hummel	Open	Unknown	75.00
XX-F-GG-02-253	Sister 98/0	M. I. Hummel	Open	Unknown	98.00
XX-F-GG-02-254	Skier 59	M. I. Hummel	Open	Unknown	125.00
XX-F-GG-02-255	Smart Little Sister 346	M. I. Hummel	Open	Unknown	135.00
XX-F-GG-02-256	Soldier Boy 332	M. I. Hummel	Open	Unknown	105.00
XX-F-GG-02-257	Soloist 135/4/0	M. I. Hummel	Open	Unknown	55.00
XX-F-GG-02-258	Soloist 135	M. I. Hummel	Open	Unknown	79.00
XX-F-GG-02-260	Spring Dance 353/0	M. I. Hummel	Open	Unknown	160.00
XX-F-GG-02-261	Spring Dance 353/1	M. I. Hummel	Open	Unknown	265.00
XX-F-GG-02-262	Star Gazer 132	M. I. Hummel	Open	Unknown	125.00
XX-F-GG-02-263	Stitch in Time 255	M. I. Hummel	Open	Unknown	140.00
XX-F-GG-02-264	Stormy Weather 71/I	M. I. Hummel	Open	Unknown	275.00
XX-F-GG-02-265	Stormy Weather 71/2/0	M. I. Hummel	Open	Unknown	165.00
XX-F-GG-02-266	Street Singer 131	M. I. Hummel	Open	Unknown	98.00
XX-F-GG-02-267	Strolling Along 5	M. I. Hummel	Open	Unknown	118.00
XX-F-GG-02-268	Surprise 94/3/0	M. I. Hummel	Open	Unknown	95.00
XX-F-GG-02-269	Surprise 94/I	M. I. Hummel	Open	Unknown	140.00
XX-F-GG-02-270	Sweet Greetings 352	M. I. Hummel	Open	Unknown	125.00
XX-F-GG-02-271	Sweet Music 186	M. I. Hummel	Open	Unknown	120.00
XX-F-GG-02-272	Telling Her Secret 196/0	M. I. Hummel	Open	Unknown	180.00
XX-F-GG-02-273	Telling Her Secret 196/1	M. I. Hummel	Open	Unknown	240.00
XX-F-GG-02-274	The Kindergartner 467	M. I. Hummel	Open	Unknown	100.00
XX-F-GG-02-275	Thoughtful 415	M. I. Hummel	Open	Unknown	150.00
XX-F-GG-02-276	Timid Little Sister 394	M. I. Hummel	Open	Unknown	260.00
XX-F-GG-02-277	To Market 49/3/0	M. I. Hummel	Open	Unknown	110.00
XX-F-GG-02-278	To Market 49/0	M. I. Hummel	Open	Unknown	165.00
XX-F-GG-02-279	To Market 49/1	M. I. Hummel	Open	Unknown	240.00
XX-F-GG-02-280	Trumpet Boy 97	M. I. Hummel	Open	Unknown	75.00
XX-F-GG-02-281	Tuneful Angel 359	M. I. Hummel	Open	Unknown	55.00
XX-F-GG-02-282	Umbrella Boy 152/0A	M. I. Hummel	Open	Unknown	360.00
XX-F-GG-02-283	Umbrella Boy 152/IIA	M. I. Hummel	Open	Unknown	990.00
XX-F-GG-02-284	Umbrella Girl 152/0B	M. I. Hummel	Open	Unknown	360.00
XX-F-GG-02-285	Umbrella Girl 152/IIB	M. I. Hummel	Open	Unknown	990.00
XX-F-GG-02-286	Village Boy 51/3/0	M. I. Hummel	Open	Unknown	60.00
XX-F-GG-02-287	Village Boy 51/2/0	M. I. Hummel	Open	Unknown	79.00
XX-F-GG-02-288	Village Boy 51/0	M. I. Hummel	Open	Unknown	130.00
XX-F-GG-02-289	Village Boy 51/1	M. I. Hummel	Open	Unknown	110.00
XX-F-GG-02-290	Visiting an Invalid 382	M. I. Hummel	Open	Unknown	130.00
XX-F-GG-02-291	Volunteers 50/2/0	M. I. Hummel	Open	Unknown	140.00
XX-F-GG-02-292	Volunteers 50/0	M. I. Hummel	Open	Unknown	185.00
XX-F-GG-02-293	Volunteers 50/1	M. I. Hummel	Open	Unknown	240.00
XX-F-GG-02-294	Waiter 154/0	M. I. Hummel	Open	Unknown	125.00
XX-F-GG-02-295	Waiter 154/I	M. I. Hummel	Open	Unknown	160.00
XX-F-GG-02-296	Wash Day 321	M. I. Hummel	Open	Unknown	140.00
XX-F-GG-02-297	Watchful Angel 194	M. I. Hummel	Open	Unknown	195.00
XX-F-GG-02-298	Wayside Devotion 28/II	M. I. Hummel	Open	Unknown	240.00
XX-F-GG-02-299	Wayside Devotion 28/III	M. I. Hummel	Open	Unknown	315.00
XX-F-GG-02-300	Wayside Harmony 111/3/0	M. I. Hummel	Open	Unknown	90.00
XX-F-GG-02-301	Wayside Harmony 111/I	M. I. Hummel	Open	Unknown	140.00
XX-F-GG-02-302	Weary Wanderer 204	M. I. Hummel	Open	Unknown	130.00
XX-F-GG-02-303	We Congratulate 214/E	M. I. Hummel	Open	Unknown	95.00
XX-F-GG-02-304	We Congratulate 220	M. I. Hummel	Open	Unknown	98.00
XX-F-GG-02-305	Which Hand? 258	M. I. Hummel	Open	Unknown	95.00
XX-F-GG-02-306	Whitsuntide 163	M. I. Hummel	Open	Unknown	175.00
XX-F-GG-02-307	With Loving Greetings 309	M. I. Hummel	Open	Unknown	118.00
XX-F-GG-02-308	Worship 84/0	M. I. Hummel	Open	Unknown	98.00
XX-F-GG-02-309	Worship 84/V	M. I. Hummel	Open	Unknown	790.00
Goebel	**M. I. Hummel's Temp. Out of Production**				
86-F-GG-03-001	Chapel Time 442	M. I. Hummel	Yr.Iss	500.00	500.00
XX-F-GG-03-002	Festival Harmony, with Mandolin 172/11	M. I. Hummel	Open	Unknown	Unknown
XX-F-GG-03-003	Festival Harmony, with Flute 173/11	M. I. Hummel	Open	Unknown	220.00
XX-F-GG-03-004	Going to Grandma's 52/1	M. I. Hummel	Open	Unknown	240.00
XX-F-GG-03-005	Hello 124/1	M. I. Hummel	Open	Unknown	110.00
XX-F-GG-03-006	'Hummel' Display Plaque 187/C	M. I. Hummel	Open	Unknown	46.00
XX-F-GG-03-007	Meditation 13/11	M. I. Hummel	Open	Unknown	200.00
XX-F-GG-03-008	Sensitive Hunter 6/11	M. I. Hummel	Open	Unknown	175.00
XX-F-GG-03-009	Spring Cheer 72	M. I. Hummel	Open	Unknown	55.00
XX-F-GG-03-010	Flower Madonna, color 10/111/11	M. I. Hummel	Open	Unknown	315.00
XX-F-GG-03-011	Flower Madonna, white 10/111/W	M. I. Hummel	Open	Unknown	175.00
XX-F-GG-03-012	Madonna with Halo, color 45/0/6	M. I. Hummel	Open	Unknown	42.00
XX-F-GG-03-013	Madonna with Halo 45/111/W	M. I. Hummel	Open	Unknown	70.00
XX-F-GG-03-014	Madonna with Halo 45/111/6	M. I. Hummel	Open	Unknown	105.00
XX-F-GG-03-015	Madonna Praying, color 46/0/6	M. I. Hummel	Open	Unknown	42.00
XX-F-GG-03-016	Madonna Praying, color 46/111/6	M. I. Hummel	Open	Unknown	105.00
XX-F-GG-03-017	Madonna Praying, white 46/0/W	M. I. Hummel	Open	Unknown	26.50
XX-F-GG-03-018	Madonna Praying, white 46/111/W	M. I. Hummel	Open	Unknown	73.50
Goebel	**M. I. Hummel Collectibles Figurines**				
XX-F-GG-04-001	Happy Traveler 109/11	M. I. Hummel	Closed	Unknown	Unknown
XX-F-GG-04-002	Jubilee 416	M. I. Hummel	Closed	Unknown	Unknown
XX-F-GG-04-003	School Boys 170/111	M. I. Hummel	Closed	Unknown	Unknown
XX-F-GG-04-004	School Girls 177/111	M. I. Hummel	Closed	Unknown	Unknown
XX-F-GG-04-005	Supreme Protection 362	M. I. Hummel	Closed	Unknown	Unknown
Goebel	**M. I. Hummel Collectibles Nativity Components**				
XX-F-GG-05-002	Madonna 214/A/M/11	M. I. Hummel	Open	Unknown	115.00
XX-F-GG-05-003	Infant Jesus 214/A/K	M. I. Hummel	Open	Unknown	35.00
XX-F-GG-05-004	St. Joseph color 214/B/11	M. I. Hummel	Open	Unknown	115.00
XX-F-GG-05-005	Goodnight 214/C/11	M. I. Hummel	Open	Unknown	55.00
XX-F-GG-05-006	Angel Serenade 214/D/11	M. I. Hummel	Open	Unknown	48.00
XX-F-GG-05-007	We Congratulate 214/E/11	M. I. Hummel	Open	Unknown	95.00
XX-F-GG-05-008	Shepherd with Sheep 214/F/11 1 Piece	M. I. Hummel	Open	Unknown	120.00
XX-F-GG-05-009	Shepherd Boy 214/G/11	M. I. Hummel	Open	Unknown	84.00
XX-F-GG-05-010	Little Tooter 214/H/11	M. I. Hummel	Open	Unknown	72.00
XX-F-GG-05-011	Donkey 214/J/11	M. I. Hummel	Open	Unknown	40.00
XX-F-GG-05-012	Ox 214/K/11	M. I. Hummel	Open	Unknown	40.00
XX-F-GG-05-013	King (standing) 214/L/11	M. I. Hummel	Open	Unknown	118.00
XX-F-GG-05-014	King (kneeling on one knee) 214/M/11	M. I. Hummel	Open	Unknown	115.00
XX-F-GG-05-015	King (kneeling on two knees) 214/N/11	M. I. Hummel	Open	Unknown	105.00
XX-F-GG-05-016	Lamb 214/0/11	M. I. Hummel	Open	Unknown	14.00
XX-F-GG-05-017	Flying Angel/color 366	M. I. Hummel	Open	Unknown	79.00
XX-F-GG-05-018	Madonna 260A	M. I. Hummel	Open	Unknown	410.00
XX-F-GG-05-019	St. Joseph 260B	M. I. Hummel	Open	Unknown	410.00
XX-F-GG-05-020	Infant Jesus 260C	M. I. Hummel	Open	Unknown	85.00
XX-F-GG-05-021	Good Night 260D	M. I. Hummel	Open	Unknown	105.00
XX-F-GG-05-022	Angel Serenade 260E	M. I. Hummel	Open	Unknown	95.00
XX-F-GG-05-023	We Congratulate 260F	M. I. Hummel	Open	Unknown	290.00

Number	Name	Artist	Edition limit	Issue Price	Quote
Company	**Series**				
XX-F-GG-05-024	Shepherd, standing 260G	M. I. Hummel	Open	Unknown	440.00
XX-F-GG-05-025	Sheep (standing) with Lamb 260H	M. I. Hummel	Open	Unknown	75.00
XX-F-GG-05-026	Shepherd Boy (kneeling) 260J	M. I. Hummel	Open	Unknown	250.00
XX-F-GG-05-027	Little Tooter 260K	M. I. Hummel	Open	Unknown	120.00
XX-F-GG-05-028	Donkey 260L	M. I. Hummel	Open	Unknown	95.00
XX-F-GG-05-029	Ox 260M	M. I. Hummel	Open	Unknown	120.00
XX-F-GG-05-030	Moorish King 260N	M. I. Hummel	Open	Unknown	415.00
XX-F-GG-05-031	King (standing) 290 0	M. I. Hummel	Open	Unknown	415.00
XX-F-GG-05-032	King (kneeling) 260P	M. I. Hummel	Open	Unknown	415.00
XX-F-GG-05-033	Sheep (lying) 260R	M. I. Hummel	Open	Unknown	35.00
XX-F-GG-05-034	Holy Family 3 Pieces 214/A & B/11	M. I. Hummel	Open	Unknown	265.00
XX-F-GG-05-035	12-Set,Figs.Only,Color,214/A-B,F-G,J-0/11 366	M. I. Hummel	Open	Unknown	980.00
XX-F-GG-05-036	16-Set,Figs.only,Color,214/A-H,J-0/11 366	M. I. Hummel	Open	Unknown	1250.00
XX-F-GG-05-037	17 Pc Set Large Color 16 Figs. &Stable260 A-S	M. I. Hummel	Open	Unknown	4100.00
XX-F-GG-05-038	Stable only fit 12 or 16 pc HUM214 Set 214 S1	M. I. Hummel	Open	Unknown	72.00
XX-F-GG-05-039	Stable only to fit 3 pc HUM214 Set 214/S11	M. I. Hummel	Open	Unknown	40.00
XX-F-GG-05-040	Stable only to fit 16 piece HUM260 Set 260/S	M. I. Hummel	Open	Unknown	350.00
Goebel	**M. I. Hummel Collectibles Madonna Figurines**				
XX-F-GG-06-001	Flower Madonna,color, 10/I/11	M. I. Hummel	Open	Unknown	195.00
XX-F-GG-06-002	Flower Madonna, white 10/I/W	M. I. Hummel	Open	Unknown	98.00
XX-F-GG-06-006	Madonna with Halo, color 45/I/6	M. I. Hummel	Open	Unknown	72.00
XX-F-GG-06-007	Madonna with Halo, white 45/I/W	M. I. Hummel	Open	Unknown	42.50
XX-F-GG-06-008	Madonna with Halo, white 45/1/W	M. I. Hummel	Open	Unknown	31.50
XX-F-GG-06-012	Madonna Praying, color 46/1/6	M. I. Hummel	Open	Unknown	64.00
XX-F-GG-06-015	Madonna Praying, white 46/1/W	M. I. Hummel	Open	Unknown	38.00
XX-F-GG-06-017	Madonna Holding Child, color 151/II	M. I. Hummel	Open	Unknown	640.00
XX-F-GG-06-018	Madonna Holding Child, white 151/W	M. I. Hummel	Open	Unknown	240.00
XX-F-GG-06-019	Madonna 214/A/M 11	M. I. Hummel	Open	Unknown	115.00
XX-F-GG-06-020	Madonna - Supreme Protection 364	M. I. Hummel	Closed	150.00	150.00
Goebel	**Goebel Collectors Club Exclusives**				
77-F-GG-07-001	Valentine Gift 387	M. I. Hummel	Closed	45.00	275.00
78-F-GG-07-002	Smiling Through Plaque 690	M. I. Hummel	Closed	50.00	85.00
79-F-GG-07-003	Bust of Sister M. I. Hummel HU-3	G. Skrobek	Closed	75.00	125.00
80-F-GG-07-004	Valentine Joy 399	M. I. Hummel	Closed	95.00	95.00
81-F-GG-07-005	Daisies Don't Tell 380	M. I. Hummel	Closed	80.00	95.00
82-F-GG-07-006	It's Cold 421	M. I. Hummel	Closed	80.00	95.00
83-F-GG-07-007	What Now? 422	M. I. Hummel	Closed	90.00	105.00
83-F-GG-07-008	Valentine Gift Mini Pendant	R. Olszewski	Closed	85.00	195.00
84-F-GG-07-009	Coffee Break 409	M. I. Hummel	Closed	90.00	110.00
85-F-GG-07-010	Smiling Through 408/0	M. I. Hummel	Closed	125.00	125.00
86-F-GG-07-011	Birthday Candle 440	M. I. Hummel	Open	95.00	95.00
86-F-GG-07-012	What Now? Mini Pendant	R. Olszewski	Open	125.00	125.00
Goebel	**Blumenkinder-First Edition**				
66-F-GG-08-001	Her First Bouquet	Lore	2,000	30.00	Unknown
66-F-GG-08-002	A Butterfly's Kiss	Lore	2,000	27.50	Unknown
66-F-GG-08-003	St. Valentine's Messenger	Lore	2,000	30.00	Unknown
66-F-GG-08-004	Nature's Treasures	Lore	2,000	25.00	Unknown
66-F-GG-08-005	Flute Recital	Lore	2,000	25.00	Unknown
66-F-GG-08-006	Bearer of Gifts	Lore	2,000	27.50	Unknown
66-F-GG-08-007	Apronful of Flowers	Lore	2,000	25.00	Unknown
66-F-GG-08-008	The Flower Farmer	Lore	2,000	30.00	Unknown
66-F-GG-08-009	Tender Loving Care	Lore	2,000	30.00	Unknown
66-F-GG-08-010	Garden Romance	Lore	2,000	50.00	Unknown
66-F-GG-08-011	Barefoot Lad	Lore	2,000	27.50	Unknown
66-F-GG-08-012	Her Kitten	Lore	2,000	27.50	Unknown
66-F-GG-08-013	Display Plaque	Lore	2,000	4.00	Unknown
Goebel	**Blumenkinder-Second Edition**				
69-F-GG-09-001	Summer Magic	Lore	2,000	50.00	Unknown
69-F-GG-09-002	Garden Princes	Lore	2,000	50.00	Unknown
69-F-GG-09-003	First Journey	Lore	2,000	25.00	Unknown
69-F-GG-09-004	First Love	Lore	2,000	25.00	Unknown
71-F-GG-09-005	Country Lad	Lore	2,000	35.00	Unknown
71-F-GG-09-006	Country Maiden	Lore	2,000	35.00	Unknown
71-F-GG-09-007	The Boy Friend	Lore	2,000	65.00	Unknown
71-F-GG-09-008	Bird Song	Lore	2,000	65.00	Unknown
71-F-GG-09-009	Cello Recital	Lore	2,000	80.00	Unknown
71-F-GG-09-010	Courting Country Style	Lore	2,000	80.00	Unknown
Goebel	**Blumenkinder-Third Edition**				
72-F-GG-10-001	Party Guest	Lore	2,000	95.00	Unknown
72-F-GG-10-002	First Date	Lore	2,000	95.00	Unknown
73-F-GG-10-003	The Patient	Lore	2,000	95.00	Unknown
73-F-GG-10-004	The Hitchhiker	Lore	2,000	80.00	Unknown
73-F-GG-10-005	The Accompanyist	Lore	2,000	95.00	Unknown
73-F-GG-10-006	By A Garden Pond	Lore	2,000	75.00	Unknown
73-F-GG-10-007	Kittens	Lore	2,000	75.00	Unknown
73-F-GG-10-008	Easter Time	Lore	2,000	80.00	Unknown
Goebel	**Blumenkinder-Fourth Edition**				
75-F-GG-11-001	The Lucky One	Lore	2,000	150.00	Unknown
75-F-GG-11-002	With Love	Lore	2,000	150.00	Unknown
75-F-GG-11-003	Both In Harmony	Lore	2,000	95.00	Unknown
75-F-GG-11-004	Happy Minstrel	Lore	2,000	95.00	Unknown
75-F-GG-11-005	Springtime	Lore	2,000	95.00	Unknown
75-F-GG-11-006	For You—With Love	Lore	2,000	95.00	Unknown
75-F-GG-11-007	Companions	Lore	2,000	85.00	Unknown
75-F-GG-11-008	Loyal Friend	Lore	2,000	85.00	Unknown
Goebel	**Blumenkinder-Fifth Edition**				
79-F-GG-12-001	Garden Friends	Lore	2,000	175.00	Unknown
79-F-GG-12-002	Farmhouse Companions	Lore	2,000	175.00	Unknown
79-F-GG-12-003	Harvest Treat	Lore	2,000	149.00	Unknown
79-F-GG-12-004	Sweet Treat	Lore	2,000	149.00	Unknown
79-F-GG-12-005	Loving Touch	Lore	2,000	201.00	Unknown
79-F-GG-12-006	Birthday Morning	Lore	2,000	201.00	Unknown
Goebel	**Blumenkinder-Sixth Edition**				
80-F-GG-13-001	Flutist	Lore	2,000	175.00	Unknown
80-F-GG-13-002	Drummer Boy	Lore	2,000	180.00	Unknown
80-F-GG-13-003	Violinist	Lore	2,000	180.00	Unknown
80-F-GG-13-004	Spring Song	Lore	2,000	180.00	Unknown
80-F-GG-13-005	Dancing Song	Lore	2,000	175.00	Unknown
80-F-GG-13-006	Romance	Lore	2,000	175.00	Unknown

Number	Name	Artist	Edition limit	Issue Price	Quote
Company	**Series**				
Goebel	**Blumenkinder-Seventh Edition**				
82-F-GG-14-001	Happy Sailing	Lore	2,000	150.00	Unknown
82-F-GG-14-002	The Spinning Top	Lore	2,000	150.00	Unknown
82-F-GG-14-003	Mail Call	Lore	2,000	165.00	Unknown
82-F-GG-14-004	Little Mommy	Lore	2,000	165.00	Unknown
82-F-GG-14-005	Autumn Delight	Lore	2,000	165.00	Unknown
82-F-GG-14-006	Play Ball	Lore	2,000	165.00	Unknown
Goebel	**Goebel Miniatures: Childrens Series**				
80-F-GG-15-001	Blumenkinder—Courting 630-P	R. Olszewski	Open	55.00	290.00
81-F-GG-15-002	Summer Days 631-P	R. Olszewski	Open	65.00	225.00
82-F-GG-15-003	Out and About 632-P	R. Olszewski	Closed	85.00	235.00
83-F-GG-15-004	Backyard Frolic 633-P	R. Olszewski	Open	75.00	75.00
84-F-GG-15-005	Grandpa 634-P	R. Olszewski	Open	75.00	75.00
85-F-GG-15-006	Snow Holiday 635-P	R. Olszewski	Open	75.00	75.00
86-F-GG-15-007	Clowning Around 636-P	R. Olszewski	Open	85.00	85.00
87-F-GG-15-008	Carrousel Days 637-P	R. Olszewski	Open	85.00	85.00
Goebel	**Goebel Miniatures: Wildlife Series**				
80-F-GG-16-001	Chipping Sparrow 620-P	R. Olszewski	Open	55.00	280.00
81-F-GG-16-002	Owl—Daylight Encounter 621-P	R. Olszewski	Open	65.00	195.00
82-F-GG-16-003	Western Bluebird 622-P	R. Olszewski	Open	65.00	120.00
83-F-GG-16-004	Red-Winged Blackbird 623-P	R. Olszewski	Closed	65.00	95.00
84-F-GG-16-005	Winter Cardinal 624-P	R. Olszewski	Open	65.00	65.00
85-F-GG-16-006	American Goldfinch 625-P	R. Olszewski	Open	65.00	65.00
86-F-GG-16-007	Autumn Blue Jay 626-P	R. Olszewski	Open	65.00	65.00
87-F-GG-16-008	Mallard Duck 627-P	R. Olszewski	Open	75.00	75.00
Goebel	**Goebel Miniatures: Women's Series**				
80-F-GG-17-001	Dresden Dancer 610-P	R. Olszewski	Open	55.00	325.00
81-F-GG-17-002	The Hunt With Hounds 611-P	R. Olszewski	Open	75.00	215.00
82-F-GG-17-003	Precious Years 612-P	R. Olszewski	Closed	65.00	190.00
83-F-GG-17-004	On The Avenue 613-P	R. Olszewski	Open	65.00	65.00
84-F-GG-17-005	Roses 614-P	R. Olszewski	Open	65.00	65.00
86-F-GG-17-006	I Do 615-P	R. Olszewski	Open	85.00	85.00
Goebel	**Goebel Miniatures: Historical Series**				
80-F-GG-18-001	Capodimonte 600-P	R. Olszewski	Open	90.00	320.00
81-F-GG-18-002	Masquerade--St. Petersburg 601-P	R. Olszewski	Closed	75.00	245.00
83-F-GG-18-003	Cherry Pickers 602-P	R. Olszewski	Open	85.00	85.00
84-F-GG-18-004	Moor With Spanish Horse 603-P	R. Olszewski	Open	85.00	85.00
85-F-GG-18-005	Floral Bouquet Pompadour 604-P	R. Olszewski	Open	85.00	85.00
87-F-GG-18-006	Meissen Parrot 605-P	R. Olszweski	Open	85.00	85.00
Goebel	**Goebel Miniatures: Oriental Series**				
80-F-GG-19-001	Kuan Yin 640-P	R. Olszewski	Open	40.00	195.00
82-F-GG-19-002	The Geisha 641-P	R. Olszewski	Open	65.00	115.00
85-F-GG-19-003	Tang Horse 642-P	R. Olszewski	Open	65.00	65.00
86-F-GG-19-004	The Blind Men and the Elephant 643-P	R. Olszewski	Open	70.00	70.00
87-F-GG-19-005	Chinese Water Dragon 644-P	R. Olszewski	Open	70.00	70.00
Goebel	**Goebel Miniatures: Americana Series**				
81-F-GG-20-001	The Plainsman 660-B	R. Olszewski	Open	40.00	175.00
82-F-GG-20-002	American Bald Eagle 661-B	R. Olszewski	Closed	45.00	150.00
83-F-GG-20-003	She Sounds the Deep 662-B	R. Olszewski	Open	45.00	45.00
84-F-GG-20-004	Eyes on the Horizon 663-B	R. Olszewski	Open	45.00	45.00
85-F-GG-20-005	Central Park Sunday 664-B	R. Olszewski	Open	45.00	45.00
86-F-GG-20-006	Carousel Ride 665-B	R. Olszewski	Open	45.00	45.00
87-F-GG-20-007	To The Bandstand 666-B	R. Olszewski	Open	45.00	45.00
Goebel	**Goebel Miniatures: DeGrazia**				
85-F-GG-21-001	Flower Boy 501-P	R. Olszewski	Open	80.00	85.00
85-F-GG-21-002	Flower Girl 502-P	R. Olszewski	Open	80.00	85.00
85-F-GG-21-003	Flower Girl Pendant 561-P	R. Olszewski	Open	125.00	125.00
85-F-GG-21-004	My First Horse 503-P	R. Olszewski	Open	80.00	85.00
85-F-GG-21-005	Sunflower Boy 551-P	R. Olszewski	7,500	87.50	92.50
85-F-GG-21-006	White Dove 504-P	R. Olszewski	Open	75.00	80.00
85-F-GG-21-007	Wondering 505-P	R. Olszewski	Open	87.50	92.50
86-F-GG-21-008	Little Madonna 552-P	R. Olszewski	7,500	92.50	92.50
86-F-GG-21-009	Pima Drummer Boy 506-P	R. Olszewski	Open	85.00	85.00
86-F-GG-21-010	Festival of Lights 507-P	R. Olszewski	Open	85.00	85.00
87-F-GG-21-011	Merry Little Indian 508-P	R. Olszewski	7,500	95.00	95.00
Goebel	**Special Release -- Alice in Wonderland**				
82-F-GG-22-001	Alice in the Garden 670-P	R. Olszewski	5,000	60.00	575.00
83-F-GG-22-002	Down the Rabbit Hole 671-P	R. Olszewski	5,000	75.00	245.00
84-F-GG-22-003	The Cheshire Cat 672-P	R. Olszewski	5,000	75.00	195.00
Goebel	**Special Release -- Wizard of Oz**				
85-F-GG-23-001	Scarecrow 673-P	R. Olszewski	5,000	75.00	175.00
85-F-GG-23-002	Tinman 674-P	R. Olszewski	5,000	80.00	95.00
86-F-GG-23-003	The Cowardly Lion 675-P	R. Olszewski	5,000	85.00	85.00
Goebel	**Co-Boy**				
71-F-GG-24-001	Robby the Vegetarian	G. Skrobek	Closed	16.00	Unknown
71-F-GG-24-002	Mike the Jam Maker	G. Skrobek	Closed	16.00	Unknown
71-F-GG-24-003	Bit the Bachelor	G. Skrobek	Closed	16.00	Unknown
71-F-GG-24-004	Tom the Honey Lover	G. Skrobek	Closed	16.00	Unknown
71-F-GG-24-005	Sam the Gourmet	G. Skrobek	Closed	16.00	Unknown
71-F-GG-24-006	Plum the Pastry Chef	G. Skrobek	Closed	16.00	Unknown
71-F-GG-24-007	Wim the Court Supplier	G. Skrobek	Closed	16.00	Unknown
71-F-GG-24-008	Fips the Foxy Fisherman	G. Skrobek	Closed	16.00	Unknown
72-F-GG-24-009	Porz the Mushroom Muncher	G. Skrobek	Closed	20.00	Unknown
72-F-GG-24-010	Sepp the Beer Buddy	G. Skrobek	Closed	20.00	Unknown
72-F-GG-24-011	Kuni the Big Dripper	G. Skrobek	Closed	20.00	Unknown
Goebel	**Co-Boy**				
71-F-GG-25-001	Fritz the Happy Boozer	G. Skrobek	Open	16.00	50.00
72-F-GG-25-002	Bob the Bookworm	G. Skrobek	Open	20.00	50.00
72-F-GG-25-003	Brum the Lawyer	G. Skrobek	Open	20.00	50.00
72-F-GG-25-004	Utz the Banker	G. Skrobek	Open	20.00	50.00
72-F-GG-25-005	Co-Boy Plaque P	G. Skrobek	Open	20.00	50.00
XX-F-GG-25-006	Jack the Village Pharmacist	G. Skrobek	Open	Unknown	50.00
XX-F-GG-25-007	John the Hawkeye Hunter	G. Skrobek	Open	Unknown	50.00
XX-F-GG-25-008	Petri the Village Angler	G. Skrobek	Open	Unknown	50.00
XX-F-GG-25-009	Conny the Night Watchman	G. Skrobek	Open	Unknown	50.00
XX-F-GG-25-010	Ed the Wine Cellar Steward	G. Skrobek	Open	Unknown	50.00
XX-F-GG-25-011	Toni the Skier	G. Skrobek	Open	Unknown	50.00
XX-F-GG-25-012	Candy the Baker's Delight	G. Skrobek	Open	Unknown	50.00
XX-F-GG-25-013	Mark—Safety First	G. Skrobek	Open	Unknown	50.00
XX-F-GG-25-014	Bert the Soccer Star	G. Skrobek	Open	Unknown	50.00
XX-F-GG-25-015	Jim the Bowler	G. Skrobek	Open	Unknown	50.00
XX-F-GG-25-016	Max the Boxing Champ	G. Skrobek	Open	Unknown	50.00
78-F-GG-25-017	Gil the Goalie	G. Skrobek	Open	34.00	50.00
78-F-GG-25-018	Pat the Pitcher	G. Skrobek	Open	34.00	50.00

Figurines

Company		Series			
Number	Name	Artist	Edition limit	Issue Price	Quote
78-F-GG-25-019	Tommy Touchdown	G. Skrobek	Open	34.00	50.00
80-F-GG-25-020	Ted the Tennis Player	G. Skrobek	Open	49.00	50.00
80-F-GG-25-021	Herb the Horseman	G. Skrobek	Open	49.00	50.00
80-F-GG-25-022	Monty the Mountain Climber	G. Skrobek	Open	49.00	50.00
80-F-GG-25-023	Carl the Chef	G. Skrobek	Open	49.00	50.00
80-F-GG-25-024	Doc the Doctor	G. Skrobek	Open	49.00	50.00
80-F-GG-25-025	Gerd the Diver	G. Skrobek	Open	49.00	50.00
81-F-GG-25-026	George the Gourmand	G. Skrobek	Open	45.00	50.00
81-F-GG-25-027	Greg the Gourmet	G. Skrobek	Open	45.00	50.00
81-F-GG-25-028	Ben the Blacksmith	G. Skrobek	Open	45.00	50.00
81-F-GG-25-029	Al the Trumpet Player	G. Skrobek	Open	45.00	50.00
81-F-GG-25-030	Peter the Accordianist	G. Skrobek	Open	45.00	50.00
81-F-GG-25-031	Niels the Strummer	G. Skrobek	Open	45.00	50.00
81-F-GG-25-032	Greta the Happy Housewife	G. Skrobek	Open	45.00	50.00
81-F-GG-25-033	Nick the Nightclub Singer	G. Skrobek	Open	45.00	50.00
81-F-GG-25-034	Walter the Jogger	G. Skrobek	Open	45.00	50.00
84-F-GG-25-035	Rudy the World Traveler	G. Skrobek	Open	45.00	50.00
84-F-GG-25-036	Sid the Vintner	G. Skrobek	Open	45.00	50.00
84-F-GG-25-037	Herman the Butcher	G. Skrobek	Open	45.00	50.00
84-F-GG-25-038	Rick the Fireman	G. Skrobek	Open	45.00	50.00
84-F-GG-25-039	Chuck the Chimney Sweep	G. Skrobek	Open	45.00	50.00
84-F-GG-25-040	Chris the Shoemaker	G. Skrobek	Open	45.00	50.00
84-F-GG-25-041	Felix the Baker	G. Skrobek	Open	45.00	50.00
84-F-GG-25-042	Marthe the Nurse	G. Skrobek	Open	45.00	50.00
84-F-GG-25-043	Paul the Dentist	G. Skrobek	Open	45.00	50.00
84-F-GG-25-044	Homer the Driver	G. Skrobek	Open	45.00	50.00
84-F-GG-25-045	Brad the Clockmaker	G. Skrobek	Open	75.00	95.00
87-F-GG-25-046	Pete the Pirate Bank	G. Skrobek	Open	75.00	75.00
87-F-GG-25-047	Utz the Moneybag Bank	G. Skrobek	Open	75.00	75.00
87-F-GG-25-048	Cony the Watchman Clock	G. Skrobek	Open	110.00	110.00
87-F-GG-25-049	Sepp and the Beerkeg Clock	G. Skrobek	Open	110.00	110.00
87-F-GG-25-050	Chuck on a Pig	G. Skrobek	Open	70.00	70.00
Goebel		**Fashions on Parade**			
82-F-GG-26-001	The Garden Fancier	G. Bochmann	Open	30.00	45.00
82-F-GG-26-002	The Visitor	G. Bochmann	Open	30.00	45.00
82-F-GG-26-003	The Cosmopolitan	G. Bochmann	Open	30.00	45.00
82-F-GG-26-004	At The Tea Dance	G. Bochmann	Open	30.00	45.00
82-F-GG-26-005	Strolling On The Avenue	G. Bochmann	Open	30.00	45.00
82-F-GG-26-006	Edwardian Grace	G. Bochmann	Open	30.00	45.00
83-F-GG-26-007	Gentle Thoughts	G. Bochmann	Open	32.50	45.00
83-F-GG-26-008	Demure Elegance	G. Bochmann	Open	32.50	45.00
83-F-GG-26-009	Reflection	G. Bochmann	Open	32.50	45.00
83-F-GG-26-010	Impatience	G. Bochmann	Open	32.50	45.00
83-F-GG-26-011	Waiting For His Love	G. Bochmann	Open	32.50	45.00
83-F-GG-26-012	Her Treasured Day	G. Bochmann	Open	32.50	45.00
83-F-GG-26-013	Bride and Groom	G. Bochmann	Open	65.00	90.00
84-F-GG-26-014	On The Fairway	G. Bochmann	Open	32.50	45.00
84-F-GG-26-015	Center Court	G. Bochmann	Open	32.50	45.00
84-F-GG-26-016	Skimming Gently	G. Bochmann	Open	32.50	45.00
85-F-GG-26-017	A Lazy Day	G. Bochmann	Open	22.50	35.00
85-F-GG-26-018	A Gentle Moment	G. Bochmann	Open	22.50	35.00
85-F-GG-26-019	Afternoon Tea	G. Bochmann	Open	32.50	45.00
85-F-GG-26-020	River Outing	G. Bochmann	Open	32.50	45.00
85-F-GG-26-021	To The Hunt	G. Bochmann	Open	32.50	45.00
85-F-GG-26-022	Gentle Breezes	G. Bochmann	Open	32.50	45.00
86-F-GG-26-023	Equestrian	G. Bochmann	Open	36.00	45.00
86-F-GG-26-024	Southern Belle	G. Bochmann	Open	36.00	45.00
86-F-GG-26-025	Fashions on Parade Plaque	G. Bochmann	Open	10.00	12.50
87-F-GG-26-026	Say Please	G. Bochmann	Open	45.00	45.00
87-F-GG-26-027	The Viscountess Diane	G. Bochmann	Open	45.00	45.00
87-F-GG-26-028	The Shepherdess	G. Bochmann	Open	45.00	45.00
87-F-GG-26-029	Paris in Fall	G. Bochmann	Open	45.00	45.00
87-F-GG-26-030	Promenade in Nice	G. Bochmann	Open	45.00	45.00
87-F-GG-26-031	Silver Lace and Rhinestones	G. Bochmann	Open	45.00	45.00
Goebel		**DeGrazia Figurines**			
84-F-GG-27-001	Flower Girl	T. DeGrazia	Open	65.00	80.00
84-F-GG-27-002	Flower Boy	T. DeGrazia	Open	65.00	80.00
84-F-GG-27-003	Sunflower Boy	T. DeGrazia	Closed	65.00	225.00
84-F-GG-27-004	My First Horse	T. DeGrazia	Open	65.00	80.00
84-F-GG-27-005	White Dove	T. DeGrazia	Open	45.00	60.00
84-F-GG-27-006	Wondering	T. DeGrazia	Open	85.00	105.00
84-F-GG-27-007	Display Plaque	T. DeGrazia	Closed	45.00	85.00
85-F-GG-27-008	Little Madonna	T. DeGrazia	Open	80.00	95.00
85-F-GG-27-009	Mary	T. DeGrazia	Open	55.00	65.00
85-F-GG-27-010	Joseph	T. DeGrazia	Open	55.00	65.00
85-F-GG-27-011	Child	T. DeGrazia	Open	25.00	30.00
85-F-GG-27-012	Nativity Set - 3 pieces	T. DeGrazia	Open	135.00	160.00
86-F-GG-27-013	The Blue Boy	T. DeGrazia	Open	70.00	90.00
86-F-GG-27-014	Festival Lights	T. DeGrazia	Open	75.00	95.00
86-F-GG-27-015	Merry Little Indian	T. DeGrazia	12,500	175.00	195.00
87-F-GG-27-016	Luv Me	T. DeGrazia	Open	90.00	90.00
87-F-GG-27-017	We Three	T. DeGrazia	Open	165.00	165.00
87-F-GG-27-018	Angel from Christmas Prayer	T. DeGrazia	Open	60.00	60.00
85-F-GG-27-019	Pima Drummer Boy	T. DeGrazia	Open	Unknown	80.00
Gorham		**A Boy And His Dog (Four Seasons)**			
72-F-GO-01-001	A Boy Meets His Dog	N. Rockwell	2,500	200.00	1575.00
72-F-GO-01-002	Adventurers Betweeen Adventurers	N. Rockwell	2,500	set	set
72-F-GO-01-003	The Mysterious Malady	N. Rockwell	2,500	set	set
72-F-GO-01-004	Pride of Parenthood	N. Rockwell	2,500	set	set
Gorham		**Young Love (Four Seasons)**			
73-F-GO-02-001	Downhill Daring	N. Rockwell	2,500	250.00	1100.00
73-F-GO-02-002	Beguiling Buttercup	N. Rockwell	2,500	set	set
73-F-GO-02-003	Flying High	N. Rockwell	2,500	set	set
73-F-GO-02-004	A Scholarly Pace	N. Rockwell	2,500	set	set
Gorham		**Four Ages of Love (Four Seasons)**			
74-F-GO-03-001	Gaily Sharing Vintage Times	N. Rockwell	2,500	300.00	1250.00
74-F-GO-03-002	Sweet Song So Young	N. Rockwell	2,500	set	set
74-F-GO-03-003	Flowers in Tender Bloom	N. Rockwell	2,500	set	set
74-F-GO-03-004	Fondly Do We Remember	N. Rockwell	2,500	set	set
Gorham		**Grandpa and Me (Four Seasons)**			
75-F-GO-04-001	Gay Blades	N. Rockwell	2,500	300.00	925.00
75-F-GO-04-002	Day Dreamers	N. Rockwell	2,500	set	set
75-F-GO-04-003	Goin' Fishing	N. Rockwell	2,500	set	set
75-F-GO-04-004	Pensive Pals	N. Rockwell	2,500	set	set
Gorham		**Me and My Pal (Four Seasons)**			
76-F-GO-05-001	A Licking Good Bath	N. Rockwell	2,500	300.00	900.00
76-F-GO-05-002	Young Man's Fancy	N. Rockwell	2,500	set	set
76-F-GO-05-003	Fisherman's Paradise	N. Rockwell	2,500	set	set
76-F-GO-05-004	Disastrous Daring	N. Rockwell	2,500	set	set
Gorham		**Grand Pals (Four Seasons)**			
77-F-GO-06-001	Snow Sculpturing	N. Rockwell	2,500	350.00	675.00
77-F-GO-06-002	Soaring Spirits	N. Rockwell	2,500	set	set
77-F-GO-06-003	Fish Finders	N. Rockwell	2,500	set	set
77-F-GO-06-004	Ghostly Gourds	N. Rockwell	2,500	set	set
Gorham		**Going On Sixteen (Four Seasons)**			
78-F-GO-07-001	Chilling Chore	N. Rockwell	2,500	400.00	675.00
78-F-GO-07-002	Sweet Serenade	N. Rockwell	2,500	set	set
78-F-GO-07-003	Shear Agony	N. Rockwell	2,500	set	set
78-F-GO-07-004	Pilgrimage	N. Rockwell	2,500	set	set
Gorham		**Tender Years (Four Seasons)**			
79-F-GO-08-001	New Year Look	N. Rockwell	2,500	500.00	550.00
79-F-GO-08-002	Spring Tonic	N. Rockwell	2,500	set	set
79-F-GO-08-003	Cool Aid	N. Rockwell	2,500	set	set
79-F-GO-08-004	Chilly Reception	N. Rockwell	2,500	set	set
Gorham		**A Helping Hand (Four Seasons)**			
80-F-GO-09-001	Year End Court	N. Rockwell	2,500	650.00	700.00
80-F-GO-09-002	Closed For Business	N. Rockwell	2,500	set	set
80-F-GO-09-003	Swatter's Right	N. Rockwell	2,500	set	set
80-F-GO-09-004	Coal Seasons Coming	N. Rockwell	2,500	set	set
Gorham		**'Dad's Boy' (Four Seasons)**			
81-F-GO-10-001	Ski Skills	N. Rockwell	2,500	750.00	800.00
81-F-GO-10-002	In His Spirit	N. Rockwell	2,500	set	set
81-F-GO-10-003	Trout Dinner	N. Rockwell	2,500	set	set
81-F-GO-10-004	Careful Aim	N. Rockwell	2,500	set	set
Gorham		**Rockwell**			
74-F-GO-11-001	Weighing In	N. Rockwell	None	40.00	80.00
74-F-GO-11-002	Missing Tooth	N. Rockwell	None	30.00	70.00
74-F-GO-11-003	Tiny Tim	N. Rockwell	None	30.00	75.00
74-F-GO-11-004	At The Vets	N. Rockwell	None	25.00	65.00
74-F-GO-11-005	Fishing	N. Rockwell	None	50.00	100.00
74-F-GO-11-006	Batter Up	N. Rockwell	None	40.00	90.00
74-F-GO-11-007	Skating	N. Rockwell	None	37.50	85.00
74-F-GO-11-008	Captain	N. Rockwell	None	45.00	95.00
75-F-GO-11-009	Boy And His Dog	N. Rockwell	None	37.50	85.00
75-F-GO-11-010	No Swimming	N. Rockwell	None	35.00	80.00
75-F-GO-11-011	Old Mill Pond	N. Rockwell	None	45.00	95.00
76-F-GO-11-012	Saying Grace	N. Rockwell	None	75.00	120.00
76-F-GO-11-013	God Rest Ye Merry Gentlemen	N. Rockwell	None	50.00	800.00
76-F-GO-11-014	Tackled (Ad Stand)	N. Rockwell	None	35.00	55.00
76-F-GO-11-015	Independence	N. Rockwell	None	40.00	150.00
76-F-GO-11-016	Marriage License	N. Rockwell	None	50.00	110.00
76-F-GO-11-017	The Occultist	N. Rockwell	None	50.00	175.00
81-F-GO-11-018	Day in the Life Boy II	N. Rockwell	None	75.00	85.00
81-F-GO-11-019	Wet Sport	N. Rockwell	None	85.00	85.00
82-F-GO-11-020	April Fool's (At The Curiosity Shop)	N. Rockwell	None	55.00	110.00
82-F-GO-11-021	Tackled (Rockwell Name Signed)	N. Rockwell	None	45.00	70.00
82-F-GO-11-022	A Day in the Life Boy III	N. Rockwell	None	85.00	85.00
82-F-GO-11-023	A Day in the Life Girl III	N. Rockwell	None	85.00	85.00
81-F-GO-11-024	Christmas Dancers	N. Rockwell	7,500	130.00	130.00
82-F-GO-11-025	Marriage License	N. Rockwell	5,000	110.00	400.00
82-F-GO-11-026	Saying Grace	N. Rockwell	5,000	110.00	450.00
82-F-GO-11-027	Triple Self Portrait	N. Rockwell	5,000	300.00	500.00
80-F-GO-11-028	Jolly Coachman	N. Rockwell	7,500	75.00	125.00
82-F-GO-11-029	Merrie Christmas	N. Rockwell	7,500	75.00	75.00
83-F-GO-11-030	Facts of Life	N. Rockwell	7,500	110.00	110.00
83-F-GO-11-031	Antique Dealer	N. Rockwell	7,500	130.00	130.00
83-F-GO-11-032	Christmas Goose	N. Rockwell	7,500	75.00	75.00
84-F-GO-11-033	Serenade	N. Rockwell	7,500	95.00	95.00
84-F-GO-11-034	Card Tricks	N. Rockwell	7,500	110.00	110.00
84-F-GO-11-035	Santa's Friend	N. Rockwell	7,500	75.00	75.00
85-F-GO-11-036	Puppet Maker	N. Rockwell	7,500	130.00	130.00
85-F-GO-11-037	The Old Sign Painter	N. Rockwell	7,500	130.00	130.00
86-F-GO-11-038	Drum For Tommy	N. Rockwell	Annual	90.00	90.00
87-F-GO-11-039	Santa Planning His Annual Visit	N. Rockwell	7,500	95.00	95.00
Gorham		**Miniature Christmas Figurines**			
79-F-GO-12-001	Tiny Tim	N. Rockwell	Yr.Iss	15.00	15.00
80-F-GO-12-002	Santa Plans His Trip	N. Rockwell	Yr.Iss	15.00	15.00
81-F-GO-12-003	Yuletide Reckoning	N. Rockwell	Yr.Iss	20.00	20.00
82-F-GO-12-004	Checking Good Deeds	N. Rockwell	Yr.Iss	20.00	20.00
83-F-GO-12-005	Santa's Friend	N. Rockwell	Yr.Iss	20.00	20.00
84-F-GO-12-006	Downhill Daring	N. Rockwell	Yr.Iss	20.00	20.00
85-F-GO-12-007	Christmas Santa	T. Nast	Yr.Iss	20.00	20.00
86-F-GO-12-008	Christmas Santa	T. Nast	Yr.Iss	25.00	25.00
87-F-GO-12-009	Annual Thomas Nast Santa	T. Nast	Yr.Iss	25.00	25.00
Gorham		**Miniatures**			
81-F-GO-13-001	Young Man's Fancy	N. Rockwell	Open	55.00	55.00
81-F-GO-13-002	Beguiling Buttercup	N. Rockwell	Open	45.00	45.00
81-F-GO-13-003	Gay Blades	N. Rockwell	Open	45.00	45.00
81-F-GO-13-004	Sweet Song So Young	N. Rockwell	Open	55.00	55.00
81-F-GO-13-005	Snow Sculpture	N. Rockwell	Open	45.00	45.00
81-F-GO-13-006	Sweet Serenade	N. Rockwell	Open	45.00	45.00
81-F-GO-13-007	At the Vets	N. Rockwell	Open	27.50	27.50
81-F-GO-13-008	Boy Meets His Dog	N. Rockwell	Open	37.50	37.50
81-F-GO-13-009	Downhill Daring	N. Rockwell	Open	45.00	45.00
81-F-GO-13-010	Flowers in Tender Bloom	N. Rockwell	Open	60.00	60.00
82-F-GO-13-011	Triple Self Portrait	N. Rockwell	Open	60.00	60.00
82-F-GO-13-012	Marriage License	N. Rockwell	Open	60.00	60.00
82-F-GO-13-013	The Runaway	N. Rockwell	Open	50.00	50.00
82-F-GO-13-014	Vintage Times	N. Rockwell	Open	50.00	50.00
82-F-GO-13-015	The Annual Visit	N. Rockwell	Open	50.00	50.00
83-F-GO-13-016	Trout Dinner	N. Rockwell	15,000	60.00	60.00
84-F-GO-13-017	Ghostly Gourds	N. Rockwell	Open	60.00	60.00
84-F-GO-13-018	Years End Court	N. Rockwell	Open	60.00	60.00
84-F-GO-13-019	Shear Agony	N. Rockwell	Open	60.00	60.00
84-F-GO-13-020	Pride of Parenthood	N. Rockwell	Open	50.00	50.00
84-F-GO-13-021	Goin Fishing	N. Rockwell	Open	60.00	60.00
84-F-GO-13-022	Careful Aims	N. Rockwell	Open	55.00	55.00
84-F-GO-13-023	In His Spirit	N. Rockwell	Open	60.00	60.00

223

Figurines

Company Number	Name	Series Artist	Edition limit	Issue Price	Quote
85-F-GO-13-024	To Love & Cherish	N. Rockwell	Open	32.50	32.50
85-F-GO-13-025	Spring Checkup	N. Rockwell	Open	60.00	60.00
85-F-GO-13-026	Engineer	N. Rockwell	Open	55.00	55.00
85-F-GO-13-027	Best Friends	N. Rockwell	Open	27.50	27.50
85-F-GO-13-028	Muscle Bound	N. Rockwell	Open	30.00	30.00
85-F-GO-13-029	New Arrival	N. Rockwell	Open	32.50	32.50
85-F-GO-13-030	Little Red Truck	N. Rockwell	Open	25.00	25.00
86-F-GO-13-031	The Old Sign Painter	N. Rockwell	Open	70.00	70.00
86-F-GO-13-032	The Graduate	N. Rockwell	Open	30.00	30.00
86-F-GO-13-033	Football Season	N. Rockwell	Open	60.00	60.00
86-F-GO-13-034	Lemonade Stand	N. Rockwell	Open	60.00	60.00
86-F-GO-13-035	Welcome Mat	N. Rockwell	Open	70.00	70.00
86-F-GO-13-036	Shoulder Ride	N. Rockwell	Open	50.00	50.00
86-F-GO-13-037	Morning Walk	N. Rockwell	Open	60.00	60.00
86-F-GO-13-038	Little Angel	N. Rockwell	Open	60.00	60.00
87-F-GO-13-039	Starstruck	N. Rockwell	15,000	75.00	75.00
87-F-GO-13-040	The Prom Dress	N. Rockwell	15,000	75.00	75.00
87-F-GO-13-041	The Milkmaid	N. Rockwell	15,000	80.00	80.00
87-F-GO-13-042	Cinderella	N. Rockwell	15,000	70.00	70.00
87-F-GO-13-043	Springtime	N. Rockwell	15,000	65.00	65.00
87-F-GO-13-044	Babysitter	N. Rockwell	15,000	75.00	75.00
87-F-GO-13-045	Between The Acts	N. Rockwell	15,000	60.00	60.00
Gorham		**Old Timers (Four Seasons Miniatures)**			
82-F-GO-14-001	Canine Solo	N. Rockwell	2,500	250.00	250.00
82-F-GO-14-002	Sweet Surprise	N. Rockwell	2,500	set	set
82-F-GO-14-003	Lazy Days	N. Rockwell	2,500	set	set
82-F-GO-14-004	Fancy Footwork	N. Rockwell	2,500	set	set
Gorham		**Life With Father (Four Seasons Miniatures)**			
83-F-GO-15-001	Big Decision	N. Rockwell	2,500	250.00	250.00
83-F-GO-15-002	Blasting Out	N. Rockwell	2,500	set	set
83-F-GO-15-003	Cheering The Champs	N. Rockwell	2,500	set	set
83-F-GO-15-004	A Tough One	N. Rockwell	2,500	set	set
Gorham		**Old Buddies (Four Seasons)**			
84-F-GO-17-001	Shared Sucess	N. Rockwell	2,500	250.00	250.00
84-F-GO-17-002	Hasty Retreat	N. Rockwell	2,500	set	set
84-F-GO-17-003	Final Speech	N. Rockwell	2,500	set	set
84-F-GO-17-004	Endless Debate	N. Rockwell	2,500	set	set
Gorham		**Traveling Salesman (Four Seasons)**			
85-F-GO-18-001	Horse Trader	N. Rockwell	2,500	275.00	275.00
85-F-GO-18-002	Expert Salesman	N. Rockwell	2,500	set	set
85-F-GO-18-003	Traveling Salesman	N. Rockwell	2,500	set	set
85-F-GO-18-004	Country Pedlar	N. Rockwell	2,500	set	set
Gorham		**Vasari Figurines**			
71-F-GO-22-001	Mercenary Warrior	Vasari	250	250.00	500.00
71-F-GO-22-002	Ming Warrior	Vasari	250	200.00	400.00
71-F-GO-22-003	Swiss Warrior	Vasari	250	250.00	1000.00
73-F-GO-22-004	Austrian Hussar	Vasari	250	300.00	600.00
73-F-GO-22-005	D'Artagnan	Vasari	250	250.00	800.00
73-F-GO-22-006	English Crusader	Vasari	250	250.00	500.00
73-F-GO-22-007	French Crusader	Vasari	250	250.00	500.00
73-F-GO-22-008	German Hussar	Vasari	250	250.00	500.00
73-F-GO-22-009	German Mercenary	Vasari	250	250.00	500.00
73-F-GO-22-010	Italian Crusader	Vasari	250	250.00	500.00
73-F-GO-22-011	Pirate	Vasari	250	200.00	400.00
73-F-GO-22-012	Porthos	Vasari	250	250.00	500.00
73-F-GO-22-013	Roman Centurion	Vasari	250	200.00	400.00
73-F-GO-22-014	Spanish Grandee	Vasari	250	200.00	400.00
73-F-GO-22-015	The Cossack	Vasari	250	250.00	500.00
73-F-GO-22-016	Venetian Nobleman	Vasari	250	200.00	400.00
73-F-GO-22-017	Viking	Vasari	250	200.00	400.00
73-F-GO-22-018	Cellini	Vasari	250	400.00	800.00
73-F-GO-22-019	Christ	Vasari	250	250.00	500.00
73-F-GO-22-020	Creche	Vasari	250	500.00	1000.00
73-F-GO-22-021	Leonardo Da Vinci	Vasari	200	250.00	500.00
73-F-GO-22-022	Michelangelo	Vasari	200	250.00	500.00
73-F-GO-22-023	Three Kings, set of 3	Vasari	200	750.00	1500.00
73-F-GO-22-024	Three Musketeers, set of 3	Vasari	200	750.00	1500.00
Granget		**Granget Porcelains**			
74-F-GR-02-001	Blue Titmouse, Lively Fellow	G. Granget	750	1295.00	1295.00
74-F-GR-02-002	Caffinch, Spring Melody	G. Granget	750	1675.00	1675.00
74-F-GR-02-003	Goldfinch, Morning Hour	G. Granget	750	1250.00	1250.00
74-F-GR-02-004	Great Titmouse Adults, Busy Activity	G. Granget	750	2175.00	2175.00
74-F-GR-02-005	Robin, A Day Begins	G. Granget	750	1795.00	1795.00
76-F-GR-02-006	American Bald Eagle, Freedom in Flight	G. Granget	200	3400.00	3400.00
XX-F-GR-02-007	Woodcocks, A Family Affair	G. Granget	200	Unknown	1500.00
76-F-GR-02-008	American Robin, It's Spring Again	G. Granget	150	1950.00	1950.00
XX-F-GR-02-009	Canadian Geese, Heading South	G. Granget	150	4650.00	4650.00
XX-F-GR-02-010	Great Blue Herons, The Challenge	G. Granget	150	Unknown	74-9000.
XX-F-GR-02-011	Red Deer Stag, The Royal Stag	G. Granget	150	4850.00	4850.00
XX-F-GR-02-012	Ruffed Grouse	G. Granget	150	2000.00	2000.00
XX-F-GR-02-013	Spring Bok, The Sentinel	G. Granget	150	2000.00	2000.00
76-F-GR-02-014	Bluebirds, Reluctant Fledgling	G. Granget	350	1750.00	1750.00
XX-F-GR-02-015	Pintail Ducks, Safe at Home	G. Granget	350	Unknown	4000.00
77-F-GR-02-016	Reluctant Fledgling	G. Granget	350	1750.00	1750.00
XX-F-GR-02-017	Bobwhite Quail, Off Season	G. Granget	350	Unknown	27-3300.
XX-F-GR-02-018	Dolphin Group	G. Granget	350	Unknown	17-1900.
XX-F-GR-02-019	Halla	G. Granget	350	Unknown	13-1400.
XX-F-GR-02-020	Stag	G. Granget	350	Unknown	40-4850.
XX-F-GR-02-021	California Sea Lions, Sea Frolic	G. Granget	500	1375.00	1375.00
XX-F-GR-02-022	Dolphins, Play Time, Undecorated	G. Granget	500	3500.00	30-3500.
XX-F-GR-02-023	Open Jumper, The Champion	G. Granget	500	1350.00	1350.00
XX-F-GR-02-024	Cedar Waxwings, Anxious Moments	G. Granget	175	2675.00	2675.00
XX-F-GR-02-025	Meadowlark, Spring Is Here	G. Granget	175	2450.00	2450.00
XX-F-GR-02-027	Screech Owl With Chickadees, Distain	G. Granget	175	Unknown	22-3150.
XX-F-GR-02-028	Dolphins, Play Time, decorated	G. Granget	100	9000.00	Unknown
76-F-GR-02-029	Secretary Bird, The Contest	G. Granget	100	6000.00	6000.00
76-F-GR-02-030	Double Eagle, 24k Gold Vermeil On Pewter	G. Granget	1,200	250.00	250.00
74-F-GR-02-031	Golden-Crested Wrens, Tiny Acrobats	G. Granget	700	2060.00	2060.00
74-F-GR-02-032	Kingerfisher, Detected Prey	G. Granget	600	1975.00	1975.00
XX-F-GR-02-033	Mourning Doves, Engaged	G. Granget	250	Unknown	12-1750.
XX-F-GR-02-034	Peregrine Falcon, wood, 20 inches	G. Granget	250	2000.00	2000.00
XX-F-GR-02-035	Peregrine Falcon, wood, 10 inches	G. Granget	2,500	500.00	500.00
XX-F-GR-02-036	Peregrine Falcon, wood, 12.5 inches	G. Granget	1,500	700.00	700.00
XX-F-GR-02-037	Ring-necked Pheasants, Take Cover	G. Granget	125	Unknown	38-6350.
XX-F-GR-02-038	Crowned Cranes, The Dance	G. Granget	25	20000.00	20000.00
Granget		**Granget Wood Carvings**			
XX-F-GR-03-001	Barn Owl, 20 inches	G. Granget	250	2000.00	2000.00
73-F-GR-03-002	Black Grouse, large	G. Granget	250	2800.00	3500.00
73-F-GR-03-003	Golden Eagle, large	G. Granget	250	2000.00	2500.00
73-F-GR-03-004	Lynx, large	G. Granget	250	1600.00	2000.00
73-F-GR-03-005	Mallard, large	G. Granget	250	2000.00	2250.00
XX-F-GR-03-006	Peregrine Falcon, large	G. Granget	250	2250.00	2250.00
73-F-GR-03-007	Rooster, large	G. Granget	250	2400.00	2800.00
73-F-GR-03-008	Black Grouse, small	G. Granget	1,000	700.00	700.00
73-F-GR-03-009	Fox, small	G. Granget	1,000	650.00	650.00
73-F-GR-03-010	Golden Eagle, small	G. Granget	1,000	550.00	750.00
73-F-GR-03-011	Lynx, small	G. Granget	1,000	400.00	400.00
73-F-GR-03-012	Mallard, small	G. Granget	1,000	500.00	500.00
73-F-GR-03-013	Patridge, small	G. Granget	1,000	550.00	550.00
XX-F-GR-03-014	Peregrine Falcon, small	G. Granget	1,000	500.00	500.00
73-F-GR-03-015	Rooster, small	G. Granget	1,000	600.00	650.00
73-F-GR-03-016	Wild Boar, small	G. Granget	1,000	275.00	275.00
XX-F-GR-03-017	Wild Sow with Young, large	G. Granget	1,000	2800.00	2800.00
73-F-GR-03-018	Fox, large	G. Granget	200	2800.00	28-3200.
73-F-GR-03-019	Partridge, large	G. Granget	200	2400.00	2800.00
73-F-GR-03-020	Wild Boar, large	G. Granget	200	2400.00	2400.00
XX-F-GR-03-021	Wild Sow with Young, small	G. Granget	200	600.00	600.00
XX-F-GR-03-022	Barn Owl, 10 inches	G. Granget	2,500	600.00	600.00
XX-F-GR-03-023	Barn Owl, 12.5 inches	G. Granget	1,500	700.00	700.00
XX-F-GR-03-024	Peregrine Falcon, medium	G. Granget	1,500	700.00	700.00
XX-F-GR-03-025	Ring-Necked Pheasant, large	G. Granget	Unkn.	2250.00	2250.00
XX-F-GR-03-026	Ring-Necked Pheasant, small	G. Granget	Unkn.	500.00	500.00
Hamilton/Boehm		**Classic Moments in Ballet**			
81-F-HB-01-001	Giselle	Boehm	7,500	120.00	150.00
81-F-HB-01-002	Swan Lake	Boehm	7,500	120.00	135.00
81-F-HB-01-003	Don Quixote	Boehm	7,500	120.00	120.00
81-F-HB-01-004	Nutcracker	Boehm	7,500	120.00	120.00
Hamilton/Boehm		**Annual Ballet Classics**			
82-F-HB-02-001	Firebird	Boehm	Annual	140.00	140.00
82-F-HB-02-002	Coppelia	Boehm	Annual	140.00	140.00
Hamilton/Boehm		**The First Noel Nativity Figurines**			
82-F-HB-03-001	The Holy Family	Boehm	Time	135.00	135.00
82-F-HB-03-002	The Three Kings	Boehm	Time	135.00	135.00
82-F-HB-03-003	The Divine Vigil	Boehm	Time	135.00	135.00
Hamilton/Boehm		**Roses of Distinction**			
83-F-HB-04-001	Peace Rose	Boehm	9,800	135.00	195.00
83-F-HB-04-002	White Masterpiece Rose	Boehm	9,800	135.00	180.00
83-F-HB-04-003	Angel Face Rose	Boehm	9,800	135.00	175.00
83-F-HB-04-004	Queen Elizabeth Rose	Boehm	9,800	135.00	175.00
83-F-HB-04-005	Elegance Rose	Boehm	9,800	135.00	175.00
83-F-HB-04-006	Royal Highness Rose	Boehm	9,800	135.00	175.00
83-F-HB-04-007	Tropicana Rose	Boehm	9,800	135.00	175.00
83-F-HB-04-008	Mr. Lincoln Rose	Boehm	9,800	135.00	175.00
Hamilton/Boehm		**Favorite Garden Flowers**			
85-F-HB-05-001	Morning Glory	Boehm	9,800	195.00	195.00
85-F-HB-05-002	Hibiscus	Boehm	9,800	195.00	195.00
85-F-HB-05-003	Tulip	Boehm	9,800	195.00	195.00
85-F-HB-05-004	Sweet Pea	Boehm	9,800	195.00	195.00
85-F-HB-05-005	Rose	Boehm	9,800	195.00	195.00
85-F-HB-05-006	Carnation	Boehm	9,800	195.00	195.00
85-F-HB-05-007	California Poppy	Boehm	9,800	195.00	195.00
85-F-HB-05-008	Daffodil	Boehm	9,800	195.00	195.00
Hamilton Collection		**American Wildlife Bronze Collection**			
79-F-HC-01-001	Cougar	H./N. Deaton	7,500	60.00	125.00
79-F-HC-01-002	White-Tailed Deer	H./N. Deaton	7,500	60.00	105.00
79-F-HC-01-003	Bobcat	H./N. Deaton	7,500	60.00	75.00
80-F-HC-01-004	Beaver	H./N. Deaton	7,500	60.00	65.00
80-F-HC-01-005	Polar Bear	H./N. Deaton	7,500	60.00	65.00
80-F-HC-01-006	Sea Otter	H./N. Deaton	7,500	60.00	65.00
Hamilton Collection		**The Art Of The Carousel**			
80-F-HC-02-001	Lead Horse	P. Cozzolino	7,500	135.00	175.00
80-F-HC-02-002	Majestic Lion	P. Cozzolino	7,500	135.00	140.00
80-F-HC-02-003	Laughing Horse	P. Cozzolino	7,500	135.00	135.00
81-F-HC-02-004	White Rabbit	P. Cozzolino	7,500	135.00	135.00
81-F-HC-02-005	Patriotic Horse	P. Cozzolino	7,500	135.00	135.00
81-F-HC-02-006	Dancing Bear	P. Cozzolino	7,500	135.00	135.00
Hamilton Collection		**Rockwell Home of The Brave**			
82-F-HC-03-001	Reminiscing	N. Rockwell	7,500	75.00	85.00
82-F-HC-03-002	Hero's Welcome	N. Rockwell	7,500	75.00	75.00
82-F-HC-03-003	Uncle Sam Takes Wings	N. Rockwell	7,500	75.00	75.00
82-F-HC-03-004	Back to His Old Job	N. Rockwell	7,500	75.00	75.00
82-F-HC-03-005	Willie Gillis in Church	N. Rockwell	7,500	75.00	75.00
82-F-HC-03-006	Taking Mother over the Top	N. Rockwell	7,500	75.00	75.00
Hamilton Collection		**Ringling Bros. Circus Animals**			
83-F-HC-04-001	Miniature Show Horse	P. Cozzolino	9,800	49.50	68.00
83-F-HC-04-002	Baby Elephant	P. Cozzolino	9,800	49.50	55.00
83-F-HC-04-003	Acrobatic Seal	P. Cozzolino	9,800	49.50	49.50
83-F-HC-04-004	Skating Bear	P. Cozzolino	9,800	49.50	49.50
83-F-HC-04-005	Mr. Chimpanzee	P. Cozzolino	9,800	49.50	49.50
83-F-HC-04-006	Performing Poodles	P. Cozzolino	9,800	49.50	49.50
84-F-HC-04-007	Roaring Lion	P. Cozzolino	9,800	49.50	49.50
84-F-HC-04-008	Parade Camel	P. Cozzolino	9,800	49.50	49.50
Hamilton Collection		**Great Animals of the American Wilderness**			
83-F-HC-05-001	Mountain Lion	H. Deaton	7,500	75.00	75.00
83-F-HC-05-002	Grizzly Bear	H. Deaton	7,500	75.00	75.00
83-F-HC-05-003	Timber Wolf	H. Deaton	7,500	75.00	75.00
83-F-HC-05-004	Pronghorn Antelope	H. Deaton	7,500	75.00	75.00
83-F-HB-05-005	Plains Bison	H. Deaton	7,500	75.00	75.00
83-F-HC-05-006	Elk	H. Deaton	7,500	75.00	75.00
83-F-HC-05-007	Mustang	H. Deaton	7,500	75.00	75.00
83-F-HC-05-008	Bighorn Sheep	H. Deaton	7,500	75.00	75.00
Hamilton Collection		**Splendor of the Ballet**			
87-F-HC-06-001	Juliet	E. Daub	15,000	75.00	75.00
87-F-HC-06-002	Odette	E. Daub	15,000	75.00	75.00
87-F-HC-06-003	Giselle	E. Daub	15,000	75.00	75.00

Figurines

Number	Name	Artist	Edition limit	Issue Price	Quote
Hamilton Collection		**Exotic Birds of the World**			
84-F-HC-08-001	The Cockatoo	Francesco	7,500	75.00	115.00
84-F-HC-08-002	The Budgerigar	Francesco	7,500	75.00	105.00
84-F-HC-08-003	The Rubenio Parakeet	Francesco	7,500	75.00	95.00
84-F-HC-08-004	The Quetzal	Francesco	7,500	75.00	95.00
84-F-HC-08-005	The Red Lorg	Francesco	7,500	75.00	95.00
84-F-HC-08-006	The Fisher's Whydah	Francesco	7,500	75.00	95.00
84-F-HC-08-007	The Diamond Dove	Francesco	7,500	75.00	95.00
84-F-HC-08-008	The Peach-faced Lovebird	Francesco	7,500	75.00	95.00
Hamilton Collection		**Majestic Wildlife of North America**			
85-F-HC-09-001	White-tailed Deer	H. Deaton	7,500	75.00	75.00
85-F-HC-09-002	Ocelot	H. Deaton	7,500	75.00	75.00
85-F-HC-09-003	Alaskan Moose	H. Deaton	7,500	75.00	75.00
85-F-HC-09-004	Black Bear	H. Deaton	7,500	75.00	75.00
85-F-HC-09-005	Mountain Goat	H. Deaton	7,500	75.00	75.00
85-F-HC-09-006	Coyote	H. Deaton	7,500	75.00	75.00
85-F-HC-09-007	Barren Ground Caribou	H. Deaton	7,500	75.00	75.00
85-F-HC-09-008	Harbour Seal	H. Deaton	7,500	75.00	75.00
Hamilton Collection		**Magnificent Birds of Paradise**			
85-F-HC-10-001	Emperor of Germany	Francesco	12,500	75.00	95.00
85-F-HC-10-002	Greater Bird of Paradise	Francesco	12,500	75.00	95.00
85-F-HC-10-003	Magnificent Bird of Paradise	Francesco	12,500	75.00	95.00
85-F-HC-10-004	Raggiana Bird of Paradise	Francesco	12,500	75.00	95.00
85-F-HC-10-005	Princess Stephanie Bird of Paradise	Francesco	12,500	75.00	95.00
85-F-HC-10-006	Goldie's Bird of Paradise	Francesco	12,500	75.00	95.00
85-F-HC-10-007	Blue Bird of Paradise	Francesco	12,500	75.00	95.00
85-F-HC-10-008	Black Sickle-Billed Bird of Paradise	Francesco	12,500	75.00	95.00
Hamilton Collection		**Legendary Flowers of the Orient**			
85-F-HC-11-001	Iris	Ito	15,000	55.00	55.00
85-F-HC-11-002	Lotus	Ito	15,000	55.00	55.00
85-F-HC-11-003	Chinese Peony	Ito	15,000	55.00	55.00
85-F-HC-11-004	Gold Band Lily	Ito	15,000	55.00	55.00
85-F-HC-11-005	Chrysanthemum	Ito	15,000	55.00	55.00
85-F-HC-11-006	Cherry Blossom	Ito	15,000	55.00	55.00
85-F-HC-11-007	Japanese Orchid	Ito	15,000	55.00	55.00
85-F-HC-11-008	Wisteria	Ito	15,000	55.00	55.00
Hamilton Collection		**American Garden Flowers**			
87-F-HC-12-001	Camellia	D. Fryer	9,800	55.00	55.00
87-F-HC-12-002	Gardenia	D. Fryer	9,800	55.00	55.00
87-F-HC-12-003	Azalea	D. Fryer	9,800	55.00	55.00
87-F-HC-12-004	Rose	D. Fryer	9,800	55.00	55.00
Hamilton Collection		**The Noble Swan**			
85-F-HC-13-001	The Noble Swan	G. Granget	5,000	295.00	295.00
Hamilton Collection		**The Gibson Girls**			
86-F-HC-14-001	The Actress	Unknown	Open	55.00	75.00
87-F-HC-14-002	The Career Girl	Unknown	Open	55.00	75.00
87-F-HC-14-003	The College Girl	Unknown	Open	55.00	75.00
87-F-HC-14-004	The Bride	Unknown	Open	55.00	75.00
87-F-HC-14-005	The Sportswoman	Unknown	Open	55.00	75.00
John Hine N.A. Ltd.		**David Winter Cottages**			
80-F-HI-01-001	The Wine Merchant	D. Winter	Open	Unknown	33.30
80-F-HI-01-002	Little Market	D. Winter	Open	Unknown	33.30
80-F-HI-01-003	Rose Cottage	D. Winter	Open	Unknown	33.30
80-F-HI-01-004	Market Street	D. Winter	Open	Unknown	56.30
81-F-HI-01-005	Single Oast	D. Winter	Open	Unknown	25.40
81-F-HI-01-006	Triple Oast	D. Winter	Open	Unknown	69.00
81-F-HI-01-007	Tudor Manor House	D. Winter	Open	Unknown	56.30
81-F-HI-01-008	Stratford House	D. Winter	Open	Unknown	86.00
81-F-HI-01-009	The Village	D. Winter	Open	Unknown	420.00
82-F-HI-01-010	Drover's Cottage	D. Winter	Open	Unknown	25.40
82-F-HI-01-011	Ivy Cottage	D. Winter	Open	Unknown	25.40
82-F-HI-01-012	Sussex Cottage	D. Winter	Open	Unknown	25.40
82-F-HI-01-013	The Village Shop	D. Winter	Open	Unknown	25.40
82-F-HI-01-014	The Dower House	D. Winter	Open	Unknown	25.40
82-F-HI-01-015	Cotswold Cottage	D. Winter	Open	Unknown	25.40
82-F-HI-01-016	Cotswold Village	D. Winter	Open	Unknown	69.00
82-F-HI-01-017	Brookside Hamlet	D. Winter	Open	Unknown	86.00
82-F-HI-01-018	The House on Top	D. Winter	Open	Unknown	106.50
82-F-HI-01-019	Fairytale Castle	D. Winter	Open	Unknown	133.20
82-F-HI-01-020	The Old Distillery	D. Winter	Open	Unknown	385.00
83-F-HI-01-021	Cornish Tin Mine	D. Winter	Open	Unknown	25.40
83-F-HI-01-022	The Bakehouse	D. Winter	Open	Unknown	36.30
83-F-HI-01-023	The Bothy	D. Winter	Open	Unknown	36.30
83-F-HI-01-024	Fisherman's Wharf	D. Winter	Open	Unknown	36.30
83-F-HI-01-025	The Green Dragon Inn	D. Winter	Open	Unknown	36.30
83-F-HI-01-026	The Cotton Mill	D. Winter	Open	Unknown	47.60
83-F-HI-01-027	Pilgrim's Rest	D. Winter	Open	Unknown	56.30
83-F-HI-01-028	Hertford Court	D. Winter	Open	Unknown	100.00
83-F-HI-01-029	Woodcutter's Cottage	D. Winter	Open	Unknown	100.00
84-F-HI-01-030	Spinner's Cottage	D. Winter	Open	Unknown	33.30
84-F-HI-01-031	The Chapel	D. Winter	Open	Unknown	56.30
84-F-HI-01-032	Snow Cottage	D. Winter	Open	Unknown	86.00
84-F-HI-01-033	Tollkeeper's Cottage	D. Winter	Open	Unknown	100.00
84-F-HI-01-034	House of the Master Mason	D. Winter	Open	Unknown	86.00
84-F-HI-01-035	Castle Gate	D. Winter	Open	Unknown	179.00
84-F-HI-01-036	The Parsonage	D. Winter	Open	Unknown	450.00
85-F-HI-01-037	Suffolk House	D. Winter	Open	Unknown	56.30
85-F-HI-01-038	The Cooper's Cottage	D. Winter	Open	Unknown	69.00
85-F-HI-01-039	Kent Cottage	D. Winter	Open	Unknown	56.30
85-F-HI-01-040	Hermit's Humble Home	D. Winter	Open	Unknown	100.00
85-F-HI-01-041	Squires Hall	D. Winter	Open	Unknown	106.50
85-F-HI-01-042	The Schoolhouse	D. Winter	Open	Unknown	27.80
85-F-HI-01-043	Craftsmen's Cottages	D. Winter	Open	Unknown	27.80
85-F-HI-01-044	The Vicarage	D. Winter	Open	Unknown	27.80
85-F-HI-01-045	The Hogs Head Tavern	D. Winter	Open	Unknown	27.80
85-F-HI-01-046	Blackfriars Grange	D. Winter	Open	Unknown	27.80
85-F-HI-01-047	Shirehall	D. Winter	Open	Unknown	27.80
85-F-HI-01-048	The Apothecary Shop	D. Winter	Open	Unknown	27.80
85-F-HI-01-049	Yeoman's Farmhouse	D. Winter	Open	Unknown	27.80
85-F-HI-01-050	Meadowbank Cottages	D. Winter	Open	Unknown	27.80
85-F-HI-01-051	St. George's Church	D. Winter	Open	Unknown	27.80
86-F-HI-01-052	Falstaff's Manor	D. Winter	Open	Unknown	279.00
86-F-HI-01-053	Crofter's Cottage	D. Winter	Open	Unknown	56.30
87-F-HI-01-054	Smuggler's Cove	D. Winter	Open	Unknown	Unknown
87-F-HI-01-055	Devon Cottage	D. Winter	Open	Unknown	Unknown
87-F-HI-01-056	Cornish Farmhouse	D. Winter	Open	Unknown	Unknown
87-F-HI-01-057	There was a Crooked House	D. Winter	Open	Unknown	Unknown
John Hine N.A. Ltd.		**Collectors Guild Exclusives**			
87-F-HI-02-001	Robin Hood's Hideaway	D. Winter	Open	Unknown	Unknown
John Hine N.A. Ltd.		**David Winter Retired Cottages**			
80-F-HI-03-001	Mill House	D. Winter	Closed	Unknown	Unknown
80-F-HI-03-002	Little Mill	D. Winter	Closed	Unknown	Unknown
80-F-HI-03-003	Three Ducks Inn	D. Winter	Closed	Unknown	Unknown
80-F-HI-03-004	Dove Cottage	D. Winter	Closed	Unknown	Unknown
80-F-HI-03-005	The Forge	D. Winter	Closed	Unknown	Unknown
80-F-HI-03-006	Little Forge	D. Winter	Closed	Unknown	Unknown
80-F-HI-03-007	Mill House - remodeled	D. Winter	Closed	Unknown	Unknown
80-F-HI-03-008	Little Mill - remodeled	D. Winter	Closed	Unknown	Unknown
80-F-HI-03-009	The Coaching Inn	D. Winter	Closed	Unknown	Unknown
80-F-HI-03-010	Quayside	D. Winter	Closed	Unknown	Unknown
81-F-HI-03-011	St. Paul's Cathedral	D. Winter	Closed	Unknown	Unknown
81-F-HI-03-012	Castle Keep	D. Winter	Closed	Unknown	Unknown
81-F-HI-03-013	Chichester Cross	D. Winter	Closed	Unknown	Unknown
81-F-HI-03-014	Double Oast	D. Winter	Closed	Unknown	Unknown
81-F-HI-03-015	The Old Curiosity Shop	D. Winter	Closed	Unknown	Unknown
81-F-HI-03-016	Tythe Barn	D. Winter	Closed	Unknown	Unknown
82-F-HI-03-017	Sabrina's Cottage	D. Winter	Closed	Unknown	Unknown
82-F-HI-03-018	William Shakespeare's Birthplace (large)	D. Winter	Closed	Unknown	Unknown
82-F-HI-03-019	Cornish Cottage	D. Winter	Closed	Unknown	Unknown
82-F-HI-03-020	Blacksmith's Cottage	D. Winter	Closed	Unknown	Unknown
82-F-HI-03-021	Moorland Cottage	D. Winter	Closed	Unknown	25.40
82-F-HI-03-022	The Haybarn	D. Winter	Closed	Unknown	25.40
82-F-HI-03-023	Miner's Cottage	D. Winter	Closed	Unknown	25.40
83-F-HI-03-024	The Alms Houses	D. Winter	Closed	Unknown	Unknown
John Hine N.A. Ltd.		**David Winter Retired Cottages - Tiny Series**			
80-F-HI-04-001	William Shakespeare's Birthplace	D. Winter	Closed	Unknown	Unknown
80-F-HI-04-002	Ann Hathaway's Cottage	D. Winter	Closed	Unknown	Unknown
80-F-HI-04-003	Sulgrave Manor	D. Winter	Closed	Unknown	Unknown
80-F-HI-04-004	Cotswold Farmhouse	D. Winter	Closed	Unknown	Unknown
80-F-HI-04-005	Crown Inn	D. Winter	Closed	Unknown	Unknown
80-F-HI-04-006	St. Nicholas' Church	D. Winter	Closed	Unknown	Unknown
Hoyle Products		**Various**			
82-F-HP-02-001	The Horsetrader	N. Rockwell	1,500	180.00	Unknown
80-F-HP-02-002	The Country Pedlar	N. Rockwell	1,500	160.00	220.00
81-F-HP-02-003	The Traveling Salesman	N. Rockwell	1,500	175.00	175.00
Hutschenreuther		**Portrait Figurines**			
77-F-HU-01-001	Catherine The Great	D. Valenza	500	500.00	875.00
77-F-HU-01-002	Helen of Troy	D. Valenza	500	500.00	925.00
77-F-HU-01-003	Jennie Churchhill	D. Valenza	500	500.00	925.00
77-F-HU-01-004	Queen Isabelle	D. Valenza	500	500.00	925.00
77-F-HU-01-005	Judith	D. Valenza	500	500.00	1400.00
77-F-HU-01-006	Isolde	D. Valenza	500	500.00	2650.00
77-F-HU-01-007	Lillian Russell	D. Valenza	500	500.00	1825.00
Hutschenreuther		**American Limited Edition Collection**			
XX-F-HU-02-001	A Family Affair	Granget	200	Unknown	1875.00
XX-F-HU-02-002	Take Cover	Granget	125	Unknown	7950.00
XX-F-HU-02-003	The Challenge	Granget	150	Unknown	9000.00
XX-F-HU-02-004	Heading South	Granget	150	Unknown	5800.00
XX-F-HU-02-005	First Lesson	Granget	175	Unknown	3550.00
XX-F-HU-02-006	Safe at Home	Granget	350	Unknown	3400.00
XX-F-HU-02-007	Off Season	Granget	125	Unknown	4125.00
XX-F-HU-02-008	Disdain	Granget	175	Unknown	3780.00
XX-F-HU-02-009	Friendly Enemies	Granget	175	Unknown	3750.00
XX-F-HU-02-010	Engaged	Granget	250	Unknown	1750.00
XX-F-HU-02-011	Spring is Here	Granget	175	Unknown	4500.00
XX-F-HU-02-012	Anxious Moment	Granget	175	Unknown	5225.00
XX-F-HU-02-013	It's Spring Again	Granget	250	Unknown	3475.00
XX-F-HU-02-014	Freedom in Flight	Granget	200	Unknown	3400.00
XX-F-HU-02-015	Reluctant Fledgling	Granget	350	Unknown	3475.00
XX-F-HU-02-016	Proud Parent	Granget	250	Unknown	13750.00
XX-F-HU-02-017	Joe	Granget	150	Unknown	9350.00
XX-F-HU-02-018	Olympic Champion	Granget	500	Unknown	3650.00
XX-F-HU-02-019	The Sentinel	Granget	150	Unknown	3575.00
XX-F-HU-02-020	Sea Frolic	Granget	500	Unknown	2700.00
XX-F-HU-02-021	The Dance	Granget	25	Unknown	25000.00
XX-F-HU-02-022	The Contest	Granget	100	Unknown	11000.00
XX-F-HU-02-023	The Fish Hawk	Granget	500	Unknown	12000.00
XX-F-HU-02-024	To Ride the Wind	Granget	500	Unknown	8650.00
XX-F-HU-02-025	Decorated Sea Lions	Granget	100	Unknown	3850.00
XX-F-HU-02-026	Decorated Dolphin Group	Granget	10	Unknown	4000.00
XX-F-HU-02-027	Silver Heron	Granget	500	Unknown	5000.00
XX-F-HU-02-028	Sparrowhawk w/Kingbird	Granget	500	Unknown	8250.00
XX-F-HU-02-029	Saw Whet Owl	Granget	750	Unknown	3575.00
XX-F-HU-02-030	Pygmy Owls	Granget	650	Unknown	6225.00
XX-F-HU-02-031	Arabian Stallion	Achtziger	300	Unknown	8525.00
XX-F-HU-02-032	Whopping Cranes	Netzsch	300	Unknown	8000.00
XX-F-HU-02-033	Wren on Wild Rose	Netzsch	250	Unknown	1675.00
XX-F-HU-02-034	Redstart on Quince Branch	Netzsch	250	Unknown	1300.00
XX-F-HU-02-035	Linnet on Ear of Rye	Netzsch	250	Unknown	1175.00
XX-F-HU-02-036	Quince	Netzsch	375	Unknown	2850.00
XX-F-HU-02-037	Water Lily	O'Hara	375	Unknown	4150.00
XX-F-HU-02-038	Christmas Rose	O'Hara	375	Unknown	3050.00
XX-F-HU-02-039	Blue Dolphins	Granget	100	Unknown	6545.00
Hutschenreuther		**Ballet Impressions**			
82-F-HU-03-001	Gran Finale, decorated	W. Stefan	Open	Unknown	550.00
82-F-HU-03-002	Gran Finale, matte finish	W. Stefan	Open	Unknown	325.00
82-F-HU-03-003	Hour of Ballet, decorated	W. Stefan	Open	Unknown	525.00
82-F-HU-03-004	Hour of Ballet, matte finish	W. Stefan	Open	Unknown	320.00
82-F-HU-03-005	Odette, decorated	W. Stefan	Open	Unknown	1450.00
82-F-HU-03-006	Odette, matte finish	W. Stefan	Open	Unknown	975.00
82-F-HU-03-007	In the Practice Room, decorated	W. Stefan	Open	Unknown	800.00
82-F-HU-03-008	In the Practice Room, matte finish	W. Stefan	Open	Unknown	550.00
82-F-HU-03-009	Before the Performance, decorated	W. Stefan	Open	Unknown	400.00
82-F-HU-03-010	Before the Performance, matte finish	W. Stefan	Open	Unknown	250.00
Ispanky		**Ispanky Porcelains**			
67-F-IS-01-001	Drummer Boy, white	L. Ispanky	600	150.00	185.00
75-F-IS-01-002	Healing Hand, decorated	L. Ispanky	600	750.00	1250.00
75-F-IS-01-003	Healing Hand, white	L. Ispanky	600	650.00	800.00

Figurines

Company Number	Series Name	Artist	Edition limit	Issue Price	Quote
75-F-IS-01-004	Spring Fever	L. Ispanky	600	650.00	1050.00
XX-F-IS-01-005	Princess of the Nile	L. Ispanky	500	275.00	275.00
67-F-IS-01-006	Artist Girl	L. Ispanky	500	200.00	1800.00
67-F-IS-01-007	Ballerina	L. Ispanky	500	350.00	1000.00
67-F-IS-01-008	Ballet Dancers	L. Ispanky	500	350.00	1000.00
67-F-IS-01-009	Morning	L. Ispanky	500	300.00	1500.00
71-F-IS-01-009	Beauty and the Beast	L. Ispanky	15	4500.00	4500.00
67-F-IS-01-010	Romeo and Juliet, decorated	L. Ispanky	500	375.00	950.00
67-F-IS-01-011	King Arthur	L. Ispanky	500	300.00	750.00
69-F-IS-01-012	Autumn Wind	L. Ispanky	500	300.00	1500.00
69-F-IS-01-013	Storm	L. Ispanky	500	400.00	950.00
71-F-IS-01-014	Debutante	L. Ispanky	500	350.00	625.00
71-F-IS-01-015	Mr. and Mrs. Otter	L. Ispanky	500	250.00	600.00
72-F-IS-01-016	Princess and the Frog	L. Ispanky	500	675.00	675.00
72-F-IS-01-017	Annabel Lee	L. Ispanky	500	750.00	750.00
73-F-IS-01-018	Abraham	L. Ispanky	500	600.00	1400.00
73-F-IS-01-019	Lorelei	L. Ispanky	500	550.00	650.00
74-F-IS-01-020	Dianne	L. Ispanky	500	500.00	900.00
74-F-IS-01-021	Belle of the Ball	L. Ispanky	500	550.00	950.00
74-F-IS-01-022	Second Base	L. Ispanky	500	650.00	1100.00
75-F-IS-01-023	Madonna, The Blessed Saint, decorated	L. Ispanky	500	295.00	350.00
75-F-IS-01-024	Madonna, The Blessed Saint, white	L. Ispanky	500	195.00	250.00
67-F-IS-01-025	Cavalry Scout, white	L. Ispanky	150	675.00	900.00
67-F-IS-01-026	Great Spirit, white	L. Ispanky	150	750.00	750.00
67-F-IS-01-027	Hunt, white	L. Ispanky	150	1200.00	1485.00
67-F-IS-01-028	On The Trail, white	L. Ispanky	150	750.00	1125.00
67-F-IS-01-029	Pack Horse, white	L. Ispanky	150	500.00	350.00
67-F-IS-01-030	Pioneer Woman, white	L. Ispanky	150	225.00	350.00
67-F-IS-01-031	Cavalry Scout, decorated	L. Ispanky	200	1000.00	1200.00
67-F-IS-01-032	Drummer Boy, decorated	L. Ispanky	200	250.00	285.00
67-F-IS-01-033	Forty-Niner, decorated	L. Ispanky	200	450.00	650.00
67-F-IS-01-034	Hunt, decorated	L. Ispanky	200	2000.00	3850.00
67-F-IS-01-035	Pack Horse, decorated	L. Ispanky	200	700.00	1250.00
67-F-IS-01-036	Pilgrim Family, decorated	L. Ispanky	200	500.00	750.00
67-F-IS-01-037	Pioneer Scout, decorated	L. Ispanky	200	1000.00	1000.00
67-F-IS-01-038	Pioneer Scout, white	L. Ispanky	200	675.00	405.00
67-F-IS-01-039	Pioneer Woman, decorated	L. Ispanky	200	350.00	550.00
68-F-IS-01-040	Queen of Spring	L. Ispanky	200	750.00	1200.00
69-F-IS-01-041	Great Spirit, decorated	L. Ispanky	200	1500.00	1850.00
69-F-IS-01-042	Mermaid Group, decorated	L. Ispanky	200	1000.00	1800.00
69-F-IS-01-043	Mermaid Group, white	L. Ispanky	200	950.00	950.00
70-F-IS-01-044	Celeste	L. Ispanky	200	475.00	500.00
70-F-IS-01-045	On the Trail, decorated	L. Ispanky	200	1700.00	1700.00
70-F-IS-01-046	Reverie	L. Ispanky	200	200.00	850.00
67-F-IS-01-047	Bird of Paradise	L. Ispanky	250	1500.00	1500.00
67-F-IS-01-048	Dutch Iris	L. Ispanky	250	1400.00	1500.00
69-F-IS-01-049	Daffodils	L. Ispanky	250	950.00	950.00
70-F-IS-01-050	King and Queen, pair	L. Ispanky	250	750.00	1200.00
71-F-IS-01-051	Freedom	L. Ispanky	250	300.00	500.00
74-F-IS-01-052	King Lear and Cordelia	L. Ispanky	250	1250.00	1250.00
75-F-IS-01-053	Apotheosis of the Sculptor	L. Ispanky	250	495.00	1000.00
66-F-IS-01-054	Orchids	L. Ispanky	250	1000.00	1500.00
67-F-IS-01-055	Love	L. Ispanky	300	375.00	950.00
67-F-IS-01-056	Meditation	L. Ispanky	300	350.00	700.00
68-F-IS-01-057	Horse	L. Ispanky	300	300.00	600.00
68-F-IS-01-058	Pegasus, decorated	L. Ispanky	300	375.00	800.00
68-F-IS-01-059	Pegasus, white	L. Ispanky	300	300.00	800.00
69-F-IS-01-060	Isaiah	L. Ispanky	300	475.00	1100.00
70-F-IS-01-061	Dawn	L. Ispanky	300	500.00	1000.00
70-F-IS-01-062	Evening	L. Ispanky	300	375.00	650.00
70-F-IS-01-063	Thrasher	L. Ispanky	300	1000.00	1000.00
71-F-IS-01-064	Christine	L. Ispanky	300	350.00	800.00
71-F-IS-01-065	Eternal Love	L. Ispanky	300	400.00	650.00
71-F-IS-01-066	Swan Lake	L. Ispanky	300	1000.00	2500.00
72-F-IS-01-067	Madame Butterfly	L. Ispanky	300	1500.00	1500.00
73-F-IS-01-068	Rebekah	L. Ispanky	300	400.00	675.00
XX-F-IS-01-069	Owl	L. Ispanky	300	750.00	825.00
67-F-IS-01-070	Forty-Niner, white	L. Ispanky	350	250.00	250.00
67-F-IS-01-071	Pilgrim Family, white	L. Ispanky	350	350.00	350.00
69-F-IS-01-072	Maria	L. Ispanky	350	750.00	1000.00
70-F-IS-01-073	Icarus	L. Ispanky	350	350.00	650.00
71-F-IS-01-074	Betsy Ross	L. Ispanky	350	750.00	1325.00
73-F-IS-01-075	Aaron	L. Ispanky	350	1200.00	2400.00
73-F-IS-01-076	Maid of the Mist	L. Ispanky	350	450.00	850.00
74-F-IS-01-077	Banbury Cross	L. Ispanky	350	550.00	1025.00
74-F-IS-01-078	Hamlet and Ophelia	L. Ispanky	350	1250.00	12-1500.
75-F-IS-01-079	Joshua	L. Ispanky	350	750.00	1200.00
XX-F-IS-01-080	Rosh Hashana, White Beard	L. Ispanky	400	275.00	1300.00
67-F-IS-01-081	Moses	L. Ispanky	400	400.00	1800.00
71-F-IS-01-082	David	L. Ispanky	400	450.00	600.00
71-F-IS-01-083	Jessamy 1	L. Ispanky	400	450.00	600.00
72-F-IS-01-084	Cinderella	L. Ispanky	400	375.00	375.00
72-F-IS-01-085	Spring Ballet	L. Ispanky	400	450.00	600.00
73-F-IS-01-086	Texas Rangers	L. Ispanky	400	1650.00	1650.00
76-F-IS-01-087	Lydia	L. Ispanky	400	450.00	835.00
XX-F-IS-01-088	Exodus, bronze	L. Ispanky	100	1500.00	1500.00
67-F-IS-01-089	Promises	L. Ispanky	100	225.00	2500.00
70-F-IS-01-090	Horsepower	L. Ispanky	100	1650.00	3250.00
70-F-IS-01-091	Peace, decorated	L. Ispanky	100	375.00	750.00
70-F-IS-01-092	Peace, white	L. Ispanky	100	300.00	450.00
73-F-IS-01-093	Emerald Dragon	L. Ispanky	100	2500.00	3250.00
77-F-IS-01-094	Serene Highness	L. Ispanky	100	2500.00	4250.00
67-F-IS-01-095	Tulips, Red	L. Ispanky	50	1800.00	4500.00
67-F-IS-01-096	Tulips, Yellow	L. Ispanky	50	1800.00	4500.00
72-F-IS-01-097	Spring Bouquet	L. Ispanky	50	3000.00	15000.00
71-F-IS-01-098	Peace Riders	L. Ispanky	1	35000.00	35000.00
71-F-IS-01-100	Exacalibur	L. Ispanky	15	3500.00	3500.00
71-F-IS-01-101	Felicia	L. Ispanky	15	2500.00	2500.00
71-F-IS-01-102	Quest	L. Ispanky	15	1500.00	1500.00
71-F-IS-01-103	Tekieh	L. Ispanky	15	1800.00	1800.00
72-F-IS-01-104	Spirit of the Sea	L. Ispanky	450	500.00	500.00
73-F-IS-01-105	Love Letters	L. Ispanky	450	750.00	850.00
74-F-IS-01-106	Holy Family, decorated	L. Ispanky	450	900.00	1595.00
74-F-IS-01-107	Holy Family, white	L. Ispanky	450	750.00	700.00
73-F-IS-01-108	Messiah	L. Ispanky	750	450.00	500.00
75-F-IS-01-109	Madonna with Halo, decorated	L. Ispanky	500	350.00	495.00
75-F-IS-01-110	Madonna with Halo, white	L. Ispanky	500	250.00	250.00
75-F-IS-01-111	Memories	L. Ispanky	500	600.00	900.00
77-F-IS-01-112	Thunder	L. Ispanky	500	500.00	795.00
78-F-IS-01-113	Romance	L. Ispanky	500	800.00	1200.00
78-F-IS-01-114	Ten Commandments, decorated	L. Ispanky	500	950.00	1525.00
78-F-IS-01-115	Little Mermaid	L. Ispanky	800	350.00	520.00
76-F-IS-01-116	Piano Girl	L. Ispanky	800	300.00	725.00
76-F-IS-01-117	Sophistication	L. Ispanky	800	350.00	575.00
77-F-IS-01-118	Daisy	L. Ispanky	1,000	325.00	575.00
77-F-IS-01-119	Day Dreams	L. Ispanky	1,000	300.00	520.00
77-F-IS-01-120	Morning Glory	L. Ispanky	1,000	325.00	620.00
77-F-IS-01-121	Poppy	L. Ispanky	1,000	325.00	575.00
77-F-IS-01-122	Snow Drop	L. Ispanky	1,000	325.00	430.00
76-F-IS-01-123	Swanilda	L. Ispanky	1,000	285.00	650.00
77-F-IS-01-124	Water Lily	L. Ispanky	1,000	325.00	620.00
78-F-IS-01-125	My Name Is Iris	L. Ispanky	700	500.00	785.00
78-F-IS-01-126	Narcissus	L. Ispanky	700	500.00	620.00
78-F-IS-01-127	Ten Commandments, white	L. Ispanky	700	600.00	850.00
XX-F-IS-01-128	Rosh Hashana, Gray Beard	L. Ispanky	2	275.00	10000.00
Kaiser	**The Birds Of America Collection**				
70-F-KA-01-001	Cardinal, color	Unknown	1,500	60.00	425.00
70-F-KA-01-002	Owl, color	Unknown	1,500	150.00	350.00
70-F-KA-01-003	Pigeon Group, color	Unknown	1,500	150.00	550.00
70-F-KA-01-004	Wild Ducks, color	Unknown	1,500	150.00	500.00
71-F-KA-01-005	Cardinal, wood base, color	Unknown	1,500	60.00	425.00
72-F-KA-01-006	Kingfisher, color	Unknown	1,500	140.00	350.00
74-F-KA-01-007	Blue Jay, wood base	Unknown	1,500	475.00	900.00
74-F-KA-01-008	Hummingbirds, wood base	Unknown	1,500	450.00	875.00
75-F-KA-01-009	Peregrine Falcon, color, wood base	Unknown	1,500	850.00	1300.00
75-F-KA-01-010	Sparrow, color, wood base.	Unknown	1,500	300.00	350.00
77-F-KA-01-011	Arabian Stallion, One Leg Up, white	Unknown	1,500	250.00	825.00
77-F-KA-01-012	Canadian Geese	Unknown	1,500	1500.00	2400.00
77-F-KA-01-013	Pheasant	Unknown	1,500	3200.00	4300.00
77-F-KA-01-014	Robin	Unknown	1,500	340.00	500.00
XX-F-KA-01-015	Owl, horned	Unknown	2,000	650.00	1500.00
70-F-KA-01-016	Baltimore Oriole, color	Unknown	2,000	60.00	500.00
70-F-KA-01-017	Blue Jay, color	Unknown	2,000	60.00	100.00
70-F-KA-01-018	Robin and Worm, color	Unknown	2,000	60.00	90.00
70-F-KA-01-019	Scarlet Tanager, color	Unknown	2,000	60.00	90.00
71-F-KA-01-020	Kingfisher, white	Unknown	2,000	45.00	60.00
71-F-KA-01-021	Wild Ducks, white	Unknown	2,000	75.00	175.00
72-F-KA-01-022	Owl, white	Unknown	2,000	70.00	160.00
72-F-KA-01-023	Pigeon Group, white	Unknown	2,000	60.00	140.00
77-F-KA-01-024	German Shepherd, white	Unknown	2,000	185.00	185.00
77-F-KA-01-025	Irish Setter, white	Unknown	2,000	185.00	185.00
77-F-KA-01-026	Screech Owl, white	Unknown	2,000	85.00	85.00
XX-F-KA-01-027	Titmouse	Unknown	1,200	265.00	265.00
70-F-KA-01-028	Eagle, white	Unknown	1,200	250.00	250.00
74-F-KA-01-029	Baby Titmice, white	Unknown	1,200	200.00	200.00
75-F-KA-01-030	Mare and Colt, wood base	Unknown	1,200	650.00	775.00
75-F-KA-01-031	Owl, white, wood base	Unknown	1,200	300.00	400.00
76-F-KA-01-032	Mother Bear and Cub, white, wood base	Unknown	1,200	125.00	160.00
77-F-KA-01-033	Pelican	Unknown	1,200	925.00	925.00
70-F-KA-01-034	Eagle, color	Unknown	400	500.00	500-650.
71-F-KA-01-035	Porpoises, group of 3, white	Unknown	5,000	85.00	375.00
72-F-KA-01-036	Pony Group, white	Unknown	5,000	50.00	150.00
72-F-KA-01-037	Arabian Stallion, color	Unknown	3,000	250.00	825.00
XX-F-KA-01-038	American Eagle, 11 inches	Unknown	1,000	Unknown	Unknown
72-F-KA-01-039	Pony Group, color	Unknown	1,000	150.00	350.00
73-F-KA-01-040	Roadrunner, color	Unknown	1,000	350.00	500.00
74-F-KA-01-041	Robin, Wood base	Unknown	1,000	260.00	390.00
77-F-KA-01-042	Baltimore Oriole	Unknown	1,000	280.00	500.00
77-F-KA-01-043	German Shepherd, color	Unknown	1,000	250.00	290.00
77-F-KA-01-044	Irish Setter, color	Unknown	1,000	290.00	290.00
77-F-KA-01-045	Screech Owl, color	Unknown	1,000	175.00	175.00
XX-F-KA-01-046	American Eagle, 16.5 inches	Unknown	800	1850.00	1850.00
XX-F-KA-01-047	Titmouse, baby, color	Unknown	800	Unknown	Unknown
73-F-KA-01-048	Goshawk, color	Unknown	800	1200.00	2900.00
73-F-KA-01-049	Seagull, color	Unknown	800	850.00	1150.00
73-F-KA-01-050	Tay-Kaiser Eagle, color	Unknown	800	1300.00	1300.00
74-F-KA-01-051	Baby Titmice, color	Unknown	800	400.00	500.00
75-F-KA-01-052	Lipizzaner Horse, color, wood base	Unknown	800	625.00	800.00
75-F-KA-01-053	Owl, color, wood base	Unknown	800	850.00	1150.00
75-F-KA-01-054	Wood Ducks, color, wood base	Unknown	800	1450.00	1675.00
75-F-KA-01-055	Woodpeckers, color, wood base	Unknown	800	900.00	1000.00
76-F-KA-01-056	Mother Bear and Cub, color,wood base	Unknown	800	400.00	550.00
76-F-KA-01-057	Porpoises, group of 5, white, wood base	Unknown	800	850.00	1100.00
73-F-KA-01-058	Encroachment, color	Unknown	950	900.00	1100.00
73-F-KA-01-059	Flushed, color	Unknown	950	1000.00	1150.00
73-F-KA-01-060	Waiting for Mother, color	Unknown	950	550.00	650.00
73-F-KA-01-061	Goshawk, white	Unknown	700	550.00	800.00
73-F-KA-01-062	Seagull, white	Unknown	700	550.00	850.00
73-F-KA-01-063	Bluebird, color	Unknown	2,500	120.00	225.00
77-F-KA-01-064	Victorian Lady with Dog	Unknown	2,500	450.00	450.00
77-F-KA-01-065	Victorian Lady with Tennis Racket	Unknown	2,500	450.00	450.00
77-F-KA-01-066	Victorian Lady with Umbrella	Unknown	2,500	450.00	450.00
75-F-KA-01-067	Lipizzaner Horse, white, wood base	Unknown	2,500	275.00	350.00
75-F-KA-01-068	Porpoises, group of 4, white, wood base	Unknown	3,000	75.00	460.00
76-F-KA-01-069	Four Dolphins	Unknown	3,000	Unknown	Unknown
77-F-KA-01-070	Eagle	Unknown	3,000	450.00	500.00
77-F-KA-01-071	Arabian Stallion, one leg up, color	Unknown	500	600.00	600.00
77-F-KA-01-072	Seated Poodle	Unknown	1,060	160.00	160.00
XX-F-KA-01-073	American Eagle, 11 inches, white	Unknown	4,000	260.00	260.00
XX-F-KA-01-074	Hummingbird, pair, wood base, color	Unknown	3,000	650.00	650.00
XX-F-KA-01-075	Mother and Child, bust, wood base, color	Unknown	7,500	500.00	500.00
XX-F-KA-01-076	Mother and Child, bust, wood base, white	Unknown	7,500	225.00	225.00
XX-F-KA-01-077	Eagle, wood base, color	Unknown	7,500	500.00	500.00
84-F-KA-01-078	Pheasant, wood base, color	Unknown	1,500	1000.00	1000.00
84-F-KA-01-079	Screech Owl, wood base, color	Unknown	1,500	225.00	225.00
85-F-KA-01-080	Goshawk, wood base, color	Unknown	1,500	2400.00	2400.00
85-F-KA-01-081	Goshawk, wood base, white	Unknown	1,500	850.00	850.00
86-F-KA-01-082	American Bald Eagle	Unknown	3,000	700.00	700.00

Company	Series				
Number	**Name**	**Artist**	**Edition limit**	**Issue Price**	**Quote**
86-F-KA-01-083	American Bald Eagle	Unknown	2,000	800.00	800.00
86-F-KA-01-084	Kingfisher	Unknown	3,000	425.00	425.00
86-F-KA-01-085	Sparrowhawk	Unknown	3,000	575.00	575.00
86-F-KA-01-086	Pike	Unknown	Open	350.00	350.00
86-F-KA-01-087	Brook Trout	Unknown	Open	250.00	250.00
86-F-KA-01-088	Rainbow Trout	Unknown	Open	250.00	250.00
86-F-KA-01-089	Trout	Unknown	Open	95.00	95.00
86-F-KA-01-090	The American Bald Eagle	Unknown	2,000	400.00	400.00
87-F-KA-01-091	Pintails, color, base	Unknown	3,000	Unknown	495.00
87-F-KA-01-092	Pintails, white, base	Unknown	3,000	Unknown	195.00
Lladro	**Lladro Porcelains**				
XX-F-LL-01-001	Allegory for Peace	Lladro	150	550.00	550.00
XX-F-LL-01-002	Eagle Owl	Lladro	750	650.00	1500.00
XX-F-LL-01-003	Girl with Guitar	Lladro	750	650.00	1265.00
XX-F-LL-01-004	Hamlet	Lladro	750	350.00	2250.00
XX-F-LL-01-005	Peasant Woman	Lladro	750	500.00	500.00
XX-F-LL-01-006	Soccer Players	Lladro	750	2750.00	4750.00
XX-F-LL-01-007	Eve at the Tree	Lladro	600	450.00	600.00
XX-F-LL-01-008	The Forest	Lladro	500	1500.00	1500.00
XX-F-LL-01-009	Seabirds with Nest	Lladro	500	600.00	600.00
XX-F-LL-01-010	Three Graces	Lladro	500	950.00	1100.00
XX-F-LL-01-011	Hunting Scene	Lladro	800	850.00	1960.00
XX-F-LL-01-012	Judge	Lladro	1,200	325.00	325.00
XX-F-LL-01-013	Lyric Huse	Lladro	400	750.00	1325.00
XX-F-LL-01-014	Man from La Mancha	Lladro	1,500	800.00	800.00
86-F-LL-01-015	A Stitch in Time	Lladro	Open	425.00	425.00
86-F-LL-01-016	A New Hat	Lladro	Open	200.00	200.00
86-F-LL-01-017	Nature Girl	Lladro	Open	450.00	450.00
86-F-LL-01-018	Bedtime	Lladro	Open	300.00	300.00
86-F-LL-01-019	Hindu Children	Lladro	Open	250.00	250.00
86-F-LL-01-020	Eskimo Riders	Lladro	Open	150.00	150.00
86-F-LL-01-021	A Ride in the Country	Lladro	Open	225.00	225.00
86-F-LL-01-022	Consideration	Lladro	Open	100.00	100.00
86-F-LL-01-023	Oration	Lladro	Open	170.00	170.00
86-F-LL-01-024	Little Sculptor	Lladro	Open	160.00	160.00
86-F-LL-01-025	El Greco	Lladro	Open	300.00	300.00
86-F-LL-01-026	Sewing Circle	Lladro	Open	600.00	600.00
86-F-LL-01-027	Try This One	Lladro	Open	225.00	225.00
86-F-LL-01-028	Still Life	Lladro	Open	180.00	180.00
86-F-LL-01-029	Litter of Fun	Lladro	Open	275.00	275.00
86-F-LL-01-030	Sunday in the Park	Lladro	Open	375.00	375.00
86-F-LL-01-031	Can Can	Lladro	Open	700.00	700.00
86-F-LL-01-032	Family Roots	Lladro	Open	575.00	575.00
86-F-LL-01-033	Lolita	Lladro	Open	120.00	120.00
86-F-LL-01-034	Carmencita	Lladro	Open	120.00	120.00
86-F-LL-01-035	Pepita	Lladro	Open	120.00	120.00
86-F-LL-01-036	Teresita	Lladro	Open	120.00	120.00
86-F-LL-01-037	This One's Mine	Lladro	Open	300.00	300.00
86-F-LL-01-038	A Touch of Class	Lladro	Open	475.00	475.00
86-F-LL-01-039	Time for Reflection	Lladro	Open	425.00	425.00
86-F-LL-01-040	Children's Games	Lladro	Open	325.00	325.00
86-F-LL-01-041	Sweet Harvest	Lladro	Open	450.00	450.00
86-F-LL-01-042	Serenade	Lladro	Open	450.00	450.00
86-F-LL-01-043	Lovers Serenade	Lladro	Open	350.00	350.00
86-F-LL-01-044	Petite Maiden	Lladro	Open	110.00	110.00
86-F-LL-01-045	Petite Pair	Lladro	Open	225.00	225.00
86-F-LL-01-046	Scarecrow and the Lady	Lladro	Open	350.00	350.00
86-F-LL-01-047	St. Vincent	Lladro	Open	190.00	190.00
86-F-LL-01-048	Sidewalk Serenade	Lladro	Open	750.00	750.00
86-F-LL-01-049	Deep in Thought	Lladro	Open	170.00	170.00
86-F-LL-01-050	Spanish Dancer	Lladro	Open	170.00	170.00
86-F-LL-01-051	A Time to Rest	Lladro	Open	170.00	170.00
86-F-LL-01-052	Valencian Boy	Lladro	Open	200.00	200.00
86-F-LL-01-053	The Puppet Painter	Lladro	Open	500.00	500.00
86-F-LL-01-054	The Poet	Lladro	Open	425.00	425.00
86-F-LL-01-055	At the Ball	Lladro	Open	375.00	375.00
86-F-LL-01-056	On the Scent	Lladro	Open	45.00	45.00
86-F-LL-01-057	Relaxing	Lladro	Open	45.00	45.00
86-F-LL-01-058	On Gard	Lladro	Open	50.00	50.00
86-F-LL-01-059	Woe is Me	Lladro	Open	45.00	45.00
86-F-LL-01-060	Wolf Hound	Lladro	Open	45.00	45.00
86-F-LL-01-061	Balancing Act	Lladro	Open	35.00	35.00
86-F-LL-01-062	Curiosity	Lladro	Open	25.00	25.00
86-F-LL-01-063	Poor Puppy	Lladro	Open	25.00	25.00
86-F-LL-01-064	The New World	Lladro	4,000	700.00	700.00
86-F-LL-01-065	Lady of the East	Lladro	Open	625.00	625.00
86-F-LL-01-066	Valencian Children	Lladro	Open	700.00	700.00
86-F-LL-01-067	My Wedding Day	Lladro	Open	800.00	800.00
86-F-LL-01-068	A Lady of Taste	Lladro	Open	575.00	575.00
86-F-LL-01-069	Don Quixote and the Windmill	Lladro	Open	1100.00	1100.00
86-F-LL-01-070	Tahitian Dancing Girls	Lladro	Open	750.00	750.00
86-F-LL-01-071	Dressed Family	Lladro	Open	200.00	200.00
86-F-LL-01-072	Ragamuffin	Lladro	Open	125.00	125.00
86-F-LL-01-073	Rag Doll	Lladro	Open	125.00	125.00
86-F-LL-01-074	Forgotten	Lladro	Open	125.00	125.00
86-F-LL-01-075	Neglected	Lladro	Open	125.00	125.00
86-F-LL-01-076	The Reception	Lladro	Open	625.00	625.00
86-F-LL-01-077	Nature Boy	Lladro	Open	100.00	100.00
86-F-LL-01-078	A New Friend	Lladro	Open	110.00	110.00
86-F-LL-01-079	Bouquet	Lladro	Open	90.00	90.00
86-F-LL-01-080	In The Meadow	Lladro	Open	100.00	100.00
86-F-LL-01-081	Spring Flowers	Lladro	Open	100.00	100.00
86-F-LL-01-082	Fantasia	Lladro	5,000	1500.00	1500.00
86-F-LL-01-083	Floral Offering	Lladro	3,000	2500.00	2500.00
86-F-LL-01-084	Three Sisters	Lladro	3,000	1850.00	1850.00
86-F-LL-01-085	At the Stroke of Twelve	Lladro	1,500	4250.00	4250.00
86-F-LL-01-086	The Puppet Painter L5396	Lladro	Open	500.00	550.00
86-F-LL-01-087	Sidewalk Serenade L5388	Lladro	Open	750.00	850.00
86-F-LL-01-088	Petite Pair L5384	Lladro	Open	225.00	250.00
86-F-LL-01-089	Petite Maiden L5383	Lladro	Open	110.00	125.00
86-F-LL-01-090	Lovers Serenade L5382	Lladro	Open	350.00	390.00
86-F-LL-01-091	Sunday in the Park L5365	Lladro	Open	375.00	410.00
86-F-LL-01-092	Can Can L5370	Lladro	Open	700.00	770.00
86-F-LL-01-093	Family Roots L5371	Lladro	Open	575.00	630.00
86-F-LL-01-094	Time for Reflection L5378	Lladro	Open	425.00	475.00
73-F-LL-01-095	Three Graces LL2028	Lladro	Closed	950.00	1100.00
XX-F-LL-01-096	Allegory for Peace	Lladro	150	550.00	550.00

Company	Series				
Number	**Name**	**Artist**	**Edition limit**	**Issue Price**	**Quote**
Lladro	**Historical Figurines**				
83-F-LL-02-002	Queen Elizabeth II LL1275	Lladro	Closed	3650.00	4200.00
86-F-LL-02-003	The New World LL1486	Lladro	4,000	700.00	800.00
XX-F-LL-02-004	Henry VIII LL1384	Lladro	1,200	650.00	675.00
XX-F-LL-02-005	Columbus LL1432	Lladro	1,200	575.00	650.00
85-F-LL-02-006	Napoleon Planning Battle LL1459	Lladro	1,500	875.00	900.00
85-F-LL-02-007	Napoleon Bonaparte LL5338	Lladro	5,000	275.00	280.00
85-F-LL-02-008	Beethoven LL5339	Lladro	3,000	800.00	810.00
86-F-LL-02-009	El Greco L5359	Lladro	Open	300.00	330.00
Lladro	**Literary Figurines**				
71-F-LL-03-001	Hamlet LL1144	Lladro	Closed	250.00	3000.00
71-F-LL-03-002	Othello and Desdemona LL1145	Lladro	Closed	275.00	3000.00
75-F-LL-03-003	Man from LaMancha LL1269	Lladro	Closed	700.00	5000.00
77-F-LL-03-004	Impossible Dream LL1318	Lladro	Closed	2400.00	3300.00
85-F-LL-03-005	I Have Found Thee, Dulcinea LL5341	Lladro	750	1550.00	1600.00
XX-F-LL-03-006	Letters to Dulcinea, numbered LL3509	Lladro	Open	1275.00	1400.00
87-F-LL-03-007	I Am Don Quixote! L1522	Lladro	Open	2600.00	2600.00
87-F-LL-03-008	Listen to Don Quixote LL1520	Lladro	750	1800.00	1800.00
74-F-LL-03-009	Lovers from Verona L1250	Lladro	Open	330.00	900.00
74-F-LL-03-010	Hamlet and Yorick L1254	Lladro	Open	325.00	825.00
71-F-LL-03-011	Romeo and Juliet L4750	Lladro	Open	150.00	750.00
78-F-LL-03-012	Don Quixote and Sancho L4998	Lladro	Open	875.00	1375.00
86-F-LL-03-013	Don Quijote & The Windmill L1497	Lladro	Open	1100.00	1250.00
86-F-LL-03-014	Oration L5357	Lladro	Open	170.00	190.00
84-F-LL-03-015	Reflections of Hamlet L1455	Lladro	Open	1000.00	1150.00
Lladro	**Animals and Birds**				
73-F-LL-04-001	Oriental Horse LL2030	Lladro	Closed	1100.00	2500.00
81-F-LL-04-002	Successful Hunt LL5098	Lladro	1,000	5200.00	5550.00
83-F-LL-04-003	Flight of Gazelles LL1352	Lladro	1,500	2450.00	2850.00
83-F-LL-04-004	Turtledove Nest LL3519	Lladro	1,200	3600.00	3900.00
83-F-LL-04-005	Turtle Doves LL3520	Lladro	750	6800.00	7200.00
83-F-LL-04-006	Nest of Eagles LL3523	Lladro	300	6900.00	7300.00
73-F-LL-04-007	Eagles LL1189	Lladro	Closed	900.00	2575.00
73-F-LL-04-008	Sea Birds LL1174	Lladro	Closed	600.00	2500.00
73-F-LL-04-009	Turkey Group LL1196	Lladro	Closed	650.00	2500.00
73-F-LL-04-010	Eagle Owl LL1223	Lladro	Closed	450.00	1500.00
74-F-LL-04-011	Hunting Scene LL1238	Lladro	Closed	800.00	2000.00
74-F-LL-04-012	Turtle Doves LL1240	Lladro	Closed	500.00	3000.00
74-F-LL-04-013	The Hunt LL1308	Lladro	Closed	4750.00	6300.00
77-F-LL-04-014	Ducks at Pond LL1317	Lladro	Closed	4250.00	6300.00
XX-F-LL-04-015	Fox Hunt LL3562	Lladro	1,000	5200.00	5700.00
85-F-LL-04-016	Pack of Hunting Dogs LL5342	Lladro	3,000	925.00	1000.00
85-F-LL-04-017	Thoroughbred Horse LL5340	Lladro	1,000	625.00	650.00
XX-F-LL-04-018	Elk LL3501	Lladro	500	1000.00	1050.00
XX-F-LL-04-019	Flying Partridges LL2064	Lladro	1,500	3675.00	3900.00
85-F-LL-04-020	Flock of Birds LL1462	Lladro	1,500	1125.00	1150.00
71-F-LL-04-021	Horse Group L1022	Lladro	Open	465.00	1375.00
79-F-LL-04-022	Spring Birds L1368	Lladro	Open	1600.00	2150.00
71-F-LL-04-023	Shepherdess with Lamb L2005	Lladro	Open	100.00	650.00
79-F-LL-04-024	Jockey with Lass L5036	Lladro	Open	950.00	1375.00
87-F-LL-04-025	Desert Tour L5402	Lladro	Open	950.00	950.00
87-F-LL-04-026	Short Eared Owl L5418	Lladro	Open	200.00	200.00
87-F-LL-04-027	Great Gray Owl L5419	Lladro	Open	190.00	190.00
87-F-LL-04-028	Horned Owl L5420	Lladro	Open	150.00	150.00
87-F-LL-04-029	Barn Owl L5421	Lladro	Open	120.00	120.00
87-F-LL-04-030	Hawk Owl L5422	Lladro	Open	120.00	120.00
80-F-LL-04-031	IBIS L1319	Lladro	Open	1550.00	1850.00
84-F-LL-04-032	Cranes L1456	Lladro	Open	1000.00	1150.00
83-F-LL-04-033	Winter Wonderland L1429	Lladro	Open	1025.00	1225.00
74-F-LL-04-034	The Race L1249	Lladro	Open	450.00	1210.00
71-F-LL-04-035	Elephants (3) L1150	Lladro	Open	100.00	475.00
71-F-LL-04-036	Playful Horses L4597	Lladro	Open	240.00	975.00
71-F-LL-04-037	Horses L4655	Lladro	Open	110.00	490.00
71-F-LL-04-038	Elephants (2) L1151	Lladro	Open	45.00	260.00
85-F-LL-04-039	Antelope Drinking L5302	Lladro	Open	215.00	250.00
84-F-LL-04-040	'How Do You Do!' L1439	Lladro	Open	185.00	210.00
84-F-LL-04-041	Kitty Confrontation L1442	Lladro	Open	155.00	175.00
Lladro	**Nudes**				
78-F-LL-05-001	Native L3502	Lladro	Open	700.00	1550.00
73-F-LL-05-002	Lyric Muse LL2031	Lladro	Closed	750.00	1325.00
79-F-LL-05-003	Nude with Dove LL3503	Lladro	Closed	500.00	1000.00
82-F-LL-05-004	Venus and Cupid LL1392	Lladro	750	1100.00	1200.00
86-F-LL-05-005	Pastoral Scene LL5386	Lladro	750	1100.00	1225.00
85-F-LL-05-006	Youthful Beauty LL1461	Lladro	5,000	800.00	825.00
85-F-LL-05-007	Classic Spring LL1465	Lladro	1,500	650.00	675.00
85-F-LL-05-008	Classic Fall LL1466	Lladro	1,500	650.00	675.00
86-F-LL-05-009	Nature Girl L5346	Lladro	Open	450.00	490.00
87-F-LL-05-010	Artist's Model L5417	Lladro	Open	425.00	425.00
Lladro	**Vehicular Figurines**				
87-F-LL-06-001	A Sunday Drive LL1510	Lladro	1,000	2600.00	2600.00
79-F-LL-06-002	Car in Trouble LL1375	Lladro	1,500	3000.00	4100.00
82-F-LL-06-003	First Date LL1393	Lladro	1,500	3800.00	4200.00
71-F-LL-06-004	Antique Auto LL1146	Lladro	Closed	1000.00	15000.00
73-F-LL-06-005	Hansom Carriage LL1225	Lladro	Closed	1250.00	12000.00
XX-F-LL-06-006	Coach XVIII Century LL1485	Lladro	500	15500.00	16000.00
XX-F-LL-06-007	Her Ladyship, numbered L5097	Lladro	Open	5250.00	5300.00
XX-F-LL-06-008	In the Gondola, numbered L1350	Lladro	Open	1850.00	2050.00
85-F-LL-06-009	Love Boat LL5343	Lladro	3,000	825.00	875.00
87-F-LL-06-010	The Landau Carriage L1521	Lladro	Open	2500.00	2500.00
87-F-LL-06-011	A Happy Encounter LL1523	Lladro	1,500	2900.00	2900.00
84-F-LL-06-012	Venetian Serenade LL1433	Lladro	750	2600.00	2900.00
87-F-LL-06-013	Carnival Time LL5423	Lladro	1,000	2400.00	2400.00
Lladro	**Flowers**				
74-F-LL-07-001	Floral LL1184	Lladro	Closed	400.00	1450.00
74-F-LL-07-002	Floral LL1186	Lladro	Closed	575.00	1575.00
83-F-LL-07-003	Three Pink Roses L5179	Lladro	Open	70.00	80.00
83-F-LL-07-004	Dahlia L5180	Lladro	Open	65.00	75.00
83-F-LL-07-005	Japanese Camelia L1581	Lladro	Open	60.00	70.00
83-F-LL-07-006	White Peony L5182	Lladro	Open	85.00	95.00
83-F-LL-07-007	Two Yellow Roses L5183	Lladro	Open	57.50	65.00
83-F-LL-07-008	White Carnation L5184	Lladro	Open	65.00	75.00
83-F-LL-07-009	Lactiflora Peony L5185	Lladro	Open	65.00	75.00
83-F-LL-07-010	Begonia L5186	Lladro	Open	67.50	75.00
83-F-LL-07-011	Rhododendrom L5187	Lladro	Open	67.50	75.00
83-F-LL-07-012	Miniature Begonia L5188	Lladro	Open	80.00	90.00
83-F-LL-07-013	Chrysanthemum L5189	Lladro	Open	100.00	110.00
83-F-LL-07-014	California Poppy L5190	Lladro	Open	97.50	110.00

Company / Number	Name	Series / Artist	Edition limit	Issue Price	Quote
Lladro		**Valencian Figurines**			
85-F-LL-08-001	Festival in Valencia LL1457	Lladro	3,000	1475.00	1500.00
85-F-LL-08-002	Valencian Couple on Horse LL1472	Lladro	3,000	950.00	1000.00
XX-F-LL-08-003	Floral Offering LL1490	Lladro	3,000	2500.00	2750.00
86-F-LL-08-004	Lolita L5372	Lladro	Open	120.00	120.00
86-F-LL-08-005	Carmencita L5373	Lladro	Open	120.00	120.00
86-F-LL-08-006	Pepita L5374	Lladro	Open	120.00	120.00
86-F-LL-08-007	Teresita L5375	Lladro	Open	120.00	120.00
86-F-LL-08-008	Valencian Boy L5395	Lladro	Open	200.00	225.00
86-F-LL-08-009	Valencian Children L1489	Lladro	Open	700.00	775.00
87-F-LL-08-010	Valencian Garden L1518	Lladro	Open	1100.00	1100.00
87-F-LL-08-011	Valencian Bouquet L1524	Lladro	Open	250.00	250.00
87-F-LL-08-012	Valencian Dreams L1525	Lladro	Open	240.00	240.00
87-F-LL-08-013	Valencian Flowers L1526	Lladro	Open	375.00	375.00
Lladro		**Religious Figurines**			
73-F-LL-09-001	Madonna with Child LL2018	Lladro	Closed	450.00	1350.00
73-F-LL-09-002	Eve at Tree LL2029	Lladro	Closed	450.00	3000.00
73-F-LL-09-003	Madonna and Child LL2043	Lladro	Closed	400.00	1000.00
XX-F-LL-09-004	St. Theresa LL2061	Lladro	1,200	825.00	900.00
XX-F-LL-09-005	St. Michael LL3515	Lladro	1,500	2300.00	2550.00
XX-F-LL-09-006	Jesus in Tiberias LL3557	Lladro	1,200	2700.00	2800.00
XX-F-LL-09-007	Holy Mary, numbered L1394	Lladro	Open	1050.00	1075.00
71-F-LL-09-008	King Gaspar L1018	Lladro	Open	345.00	1250.00
71-F-LL-09-009	King Melchor L1019	Lladro	Open	345.00	1250.00
71-F-LL-09-010	King Baltasar L1020	Lladro	Open	345.00	1250.00
87-F-LL-09-011	Gaspar L1514	Lladro	Open	275.00	275.00
87-F-LL-09-012	Melchor L1515	Lladro	Open	290.00	290.00
87-F-LL-09-013	Baltasar L1516	Lladro	Open	275.00	275.00
87-F-LL-09-014	Saint Nicholas L5427	Lladro	Open	425.00	425.00
86-F-LL-09-015	Blessed Family L1499	Lladro	Open	200.00	225.00
86-F-LL-09-016	St. Vincent L5387	Lladro	Open	190.00	225.00
86-F-LL-09-017	Consideration L5355	Lladro	Open	100.00	125.00
86-F-LL-09-018	Sewing Circle L5360	Lladro	Open	600.00	690.00
Lladro		**Fantasy Figurines**			
85-F-LL-10-001	Camelot LL1458	Lladro	3,000	1000.00	1025.00
86-F-LL-10-002	Rey De Copas LL8368	Lladro	2,000	325.00	360.00
86-F-LL-10-003	Rey De Oros LL5367	Lladro	2,000	325.00	360.00
86-F-LL-10-004	Rey De Espadas LL5368	Lladro	2,000	325.00	360.00
86-F-LL-10-005	Rey De Bastos LL5369	Lladro	2,000	325.00	360.00
XX-F-LL-10-006	At the Stroke of Twelve LL1493	Lladro	1,500	4250.00	4675.00
Lladro		**Foreign Figurines**			
82-F-LL-11-001	Drum Beats LL3524	Lladro	1,500	1875.00	2000.00
83-F-LL-11-002	Desert People LL3555	Lladro	750	1680.00	1950.00
83-F-LL-11-003	Road to Mandalay LL3556	Lladro	750	1390.00	1600.00
XX-F-LL-11-004	Blue God LL3552	Lladro	1,500	950.00	975.00
XX-F-LL-11-005	Fire Bird LL3553	Lladro	1,500	850.00	875.00
82-F-LL-11-006	Philippine Folklore LL3522	Lladro	1,500	1450.00	1600.00
86-F-LL-11-007	Hawaiian Festival LL1496	Lladro	4,000	1850.00	2025.00
86-F-LL-11-008	A Time to Rest L5391	Lladro	Open	170.00	190.00
86-F-LL-11-009	Deep in Thought L5389	Lladro	Open	170.00	190.00
86-F-LL-11-010	Spanish Dancer L5390	Lladro	Open	170.00	190.00
86-F-LL-11-011	Tahitian Dancing Girls L1498	Lladro	Open	750.00	850.00
86-F-LL-11-012	Hindu Children L5352	Lladro	Open	250.00	275.00
86-F-LL-11-013	Eskimo Riders L5353	Lladro	Open	150.00	170.00
86-F-LL-11-014	A Ride in the Country L5354	Lladro	Open	225.00	260.00
87-F-LL-11-015	Hawaiian Beauty L1512	Lladro	Open	575.00	575.00
87-F-LL-11-016	Momi L1529	Lladro	Open	275.00	275.00
87-F-LL-11-017	Leilani L1530	Lladro	Open	275.00	275.00
87-F-LL-11-018	Malia L1531	Lladro	Open	275.00	275.00
87-F-LL-11-019	Lehua L1532	Lladro	Open	275.00	275.00
87-F-LL-11-020	Mexican Dancers L5415	Lladro	Open	800.00	800.00
Lladro		**Asso Figurines**			
77-F-LL-12-001	My Baby LL1331	Lladro	Closed	550.00	1125.00
73-F-LL-12-002	Girl with Guitar LL2016	Lladro	Closed	650.00	1265.00
73-F-LL-12-003	Oriental Man LL2021	Lladro	Closed	500.00	1500.00
74-F-LL-12-004	Peasant Woman LL2049	Lladro	Closed	400.00	1180.00
74-F-LL-12-005	Passionate Dance LL2051	Lladro	Closed	450.00	2500.00
81-F-LL-12-006	The Rescue LL3506	Lladro	1,500	3500.00	4050.00
82-F-LL-12-007	Concerto LL2063	Lladro	1,200	1000.00	1125.00
83-F-LL-12-008	Fearful Flight LL1377	Lladro	750	7000.00	8100.00
73-F-LL-12-009	Peace LL1202	Lladro	Closed	550.00	5000.00
74-F-LL-12-010	The Forest LL1243	Lladro	Closed	1250.00	2400.00
77-F-LL-12-011	Comforting Baby LL1329	Lladro	Closed	700.00	2000.00
77-F-LL-12-012	Mountain Country Lady LL1330	Lladro	Closed	900.00	1700.00
XX-F-LL-12-013	Card Players, numbered L1327	Lladro	Open	3800.00	4175.00
XX-F-LL-12-014	Mother and Son, numbered L2131	Lladro	Open	850.00	930.00
XX-F-LL-12-015	Fantasia LL1487	Lladro	5,000	1500.00	1650.00
71-F-LL-12-016	Violinist and Girl L1039	Lladro	Open	120.00	750.00
76-F-LL-12-017	Victorian Girl on Swing L1297	Lladro	Open	520.00	1175.00
87-F-LL-12-018	Inspiration LL5413	Lladro	500	1200.00	1200.00
Lladro		**Lladro Sculptures**			
XX-F-LL-13-001	Dawn LL3000	Lladro	300	325.00	360.00
XX-F-LL-13-002	Monks LL3001	Lladro	300	1675.00	1800.00
XX-F-LL-13-003	Waiting LL3002	Lladro	125	1550.00	1700.00
XX-F-LL-13-004	Indolence LL3003	Lladro	150	1465.00	1600.00
XX-F-LL-13-005	Venus in the Bath LL3005	Lladro	200	1175.00	1300.00
XX-F-LL-13-006	Togetherness LL3527	Lladro	75	750.00	825.00
XX-F-LL-13-007	Wrestling LL3528	Lladro	50	950.00	1025.00
XX-F-LL-13-008	Companionship LL3529	Lladro	65	1000.00	1075.00
XX-F-LL-13-009	Anxiety LL3530	Lladro	125	1075.00	1175.00
XX-F-LL-13-010	Victory LL3531	Lladro	90	1500.00	1650.00
XX-F-LL-13-011	Plentitude LL3532	Lladro	50	1000.00	1250.00
XX-F-LL-13-012	Observer LL353?	Lladro	115	900.00	1050.00
XX-F-LL-13-013	In the Distance LL3534	Lladro	75	525.00	650.00
XX-F-LL-13-014	Slave LL3535	Lladro	50	950.00	1050.00
XX-F-LL-13-015	Relaxation LL3536	Lladro	100	Unknown	Unknown
XX-F-LL-13-016	Dreaming LL3537	Lladro	250	950.00	1025.00
XX-F-LL-13-017	Youth LL3538	Lladro	250	525.00	575.00
XX-F-LL-13-018	Dantiness LL3529	Lladro	100	Unknown	Unknown
XX-F-LL-13-019	Pose LL3540	Lladro	100	1250.00	1350.00
XX-F-LL-13-020	Tranquility LL3541	Lladro	75	Unknown	Unknown
XX-F-LL-13-021	Yoga LL3542	Lladro	125	650.00	725.00
XX-F-LL-13-022	Demure LL3543	Lladro	100	1250.00	Unknown
XX-F-LL-13-023	Reflections LL3544	Lladro	75	650.00	725.00
XX-F-LL-13-024	Adoration LL3545	Lladro	150	1050.00	1200.00

Company / Number	Name	Series / Artist	Edition limit	Issue Price	Quote
XX-F-LL-13-025	African Woman LL3546	Lladro	50	Unknown	Unknown
XX-F-LL-13-026	Reclining Nude LL3547	Lladro	75	Unknown	Unknown
XX-F-LL-13-027	Serenity LL3548	Lladro	300	925.00	990.00
XX-F-LL-13-028	Reposing LL3549	Lladro	80	425.00	Unknown
XX-F-LL-13-029	Boxer LL3550	Lladro	300	850.00	925.00
XX-F-LL-13-030	Bather LL3551	Lladro	300	975.00	1050.00
Lladro		**Lladro Collectors Society**			
85-F-LL-14-001	Little Pals S7600	Lladro	Closed	95.00	1000.00
86-F-LL-14-002	Little Traveler S7602	Lladro	Closed	95.00	95.00
87-F-LL-14-003	Spring Bouquets S7603	Lladro	Closed	125.00	125.00
Lladro		**Gres Figurines**			
75-F-LL-15-001	The Wind L1279	Lladro	Open	250.00	575.00
76-F-LL-15-002	The Helmsman L1325	Lladro	Open	600.00	1200.00
75-F-LL-15-003	Thailandia L2058	Lladro	Open	650.00	1250.00
79-F-LL-15-004	A New Hairdo L2070	Lladro	Open	1060.00	1300.00
77-F-LL-15-005	Graceful Duo L2073	Lladro	Open	775.00	1100.00
77-F-LL-15-006	Thai Dancer L2069	Lladro	Open	300.00	475.00
83-F-LL-15-007	The Whaler L2121	Lladro	Open	820.00	950.00
78-F-LL-15-008	Native L3502	Lladro	Open	700.00	1550.00
82-F-LL-15-009	Mother's Love L3521	Lladro	Open	1000.00	1050.00
XX-F-LL-15-010	Innocence/Green L3558/3	Lladro	Open	Unknown	1200.00
XX-F-LL-15-011	Innocence/Red L3558 M	Lladro	Open	Unknown	1100.00
82-F-LL-15-012	American Heritage L2127	Lladro	Open	525.00	600.00
82-F-LL-15-013	Venus L2128	Lladro	Open	650.00	775.00
XX-F-LL-15-014	Nautical Watch L2134	Lladro	Open	Unknown	525.00
XX-F-LL-15-015	Mystical Joseph L2135	Lladro	Open	Unknown	500.00
XX-F-LL-15-016	The King L2136	Lladro	Open	Unknown	650.00
XX-F-LL-15-017	Fairy Ballerina L2137	Lladro	Open	Unknown	575.00
XX-F-LL-15-018	Aztec Indian L2139	Lladro	Open	Unknown	630.00
XX-F-LL-15-019	Sea Harvest L2142	Lladro	Open	Unknown	625.00
XX-F-LL-15-020	Aztec Dancer L2143	Lladro	Open	Unknown	525.00
83-F-LL-15-021	Stormy Sea L3554	Lladro	Open	675.00	800.00
79-F-LL-15-022	Pensive L3514	Lladro	Open	500.00	700.00
80-F-LL-15-023	A Wintry Day L3513	Lladro	Open	525.00	575.00
XX-F-LL-15-024	A Tribute to Peace L2150	Lladro	Open	Unknown	550.00
XX-F-LL-15-025	Young Madonna L2149	Lladro	Open	Unknown	475.00
Lladro		**Children's Themes**			
87-F-LL-16-001	Circus Train L1517	Lladro	Open	2900.00	2900.00
87-F-LL-16-002	Time To Rest L5399	Lladro	Open	175.00	175.00
87-F-LL-16-003	The Wanderer L5400	Lladro	Open	150.00	150.00
87-F-LL-16-004	My Best Friend L5401	Lladro	Open	150.00	150.00
87-F-LL-16-005	The Drummer Boy L5403	Lladro	Open	225.00	225.00
87-F-LL-16-006	Cadet Captain L5404	Lladro	Open	175.00	175.00
87-F-LL-16-007	The Flag Bearer L5405	Lladro	Open	200.00	200.00
87-F-LL-16-008	The Bugler L5406	Lladro	Open	175.00	175.00
87-F-LL-16-009	At Attention L5407	Lladro	Open	175.00	175.00
87-F-LL-16-010	Studying in the Park L5425	Lladro	Open	675.00	675.00
87-F-LL-16-011	One, Two, Three L5426	Lladro	Open	240.00	240.00
87-F-LL-16-012	Feeding the Pigeons L5428	Lladro	Open	490.00	490.00
87-F-LL-16-013	Happy Birthday L5429	Lladro	Open	100.00	100.00
87-F-LL-16-014	Music Time L5430	Lladro	Open	500.00	500.00
87-F-LL-16-015	Sleepy Trio L5443	Lladro	Open	190.00	190.00
87-F-LL-16-016	Naptime L5448	Lladro	Open	135.00	135.00
87-F-LL-16-017	Good Night L5449	Lladro	Open	225.00	225.00
87-F-LL-16-018	I Hope She Does L5450	Lladro	Open	190.00	190.00
87-F-LL-16-019	Tenderness L1527	Lladro	Open	260.00	260.00
87-F-LL-16-020	Poetry of Love L5442	Lladro	Open	500.00	500.00
87-F-LL-16-021	Courting Time L5409	Lladro	Open	425.00	425.00
87-F-LL-16-022	In the Garden L5416	Lladro	Open	200.00	200.00
86-F-LL-16-023	Neglected L1503	Lladro	Open	125.00	150.00
86-F-LL-16-024	Forgotten L1502	Lladro	Open	125.00	150.00
86-F-LL-16-025	Rag Doll L1501	Lladro	Open	125.00	150.00
86-F-LL-16-026	Ragamuffin L1500	Lladro	Open	125.00	150.00
86-F-LL-16-027	This One's Mine L5376	Lladro	Open	300.00	330.00
86-F-LL-16-028	Children's Games L5379	Lladro	Open	325.00	360.00
86-F-LL-16-029	Nature Boy L1505	Lladro	Open	100.00	120.00
86-F-LL-16-030	A New Friend L1506	Lladro	Open	110.00	120.00
86-F-LL-16-031	Boy & His Bunny L1507	Lladro	Open	90.00	105.00
86-F-LL-16-032	In the Meadow L1508	Lladro	Open	100.00	125.00
86-F-LL-16-033	Spring Flowers L1509	Lladro	Open	100.00	125.00
86-F-LL-16-034	A Stitch in Time L5344	Lladro	Open	425.00	475.00
86-F-LL-16-035	Bedtime L5347	Lladro	Open	300.00	350.00
86-F-LL-16-036	Little Sculptor L5358	Lladro	Open	160.00	180.00
86-F-LL-16-037	Try This One L5361	Lladro	Open	225.00	250.00
86-F-LL-16-038	Still Life L5363	Lladro	Open	180.00	225.00
86-F-LL-16-039	Litter of Fun L5364	Lladro	Open	275.00	300.00
86-F-LL-16-040	Sweet Harvest L5380	Lladro	Open	450.00	500.00
86-F-LL-16-041	Scarecrow & the Lady L5385	Lladro	Open	350.00	390.00
85-F-LL-16-042	Boy on Carousel Horse L14700	Lladro	Open	470.00	550.00
85-F-LL-16-043	Girl on Carousel Horse L1469	Lladro	Open	470.00	550.00
Lladro		**Llardo Miniatures**			
86-F-LL-17-001	On Guard L5350	Lladro	Open	50.00	60.00
86-F-LL-17-002	Woe is Me L5351	Lladro	Open	45.00	55.00
86-F-LL-17-003	Wolf Hound L5356	Lladro	Open	45.00	50.00
86-F-LL-17-004	Balancing Act L5392	Lladro	Open	35.00	40.00
86-F-LL-17-005	Curiosity L5393	Lladro	Open	25.00	30.00
86-F-LL-17-006	Poor Puppy L5394	Lladro	Open	25.00	30.00
87-F-LL-17-007	Monkey L5432	Lladro	Open	60.00	60.00
87-F-LL-17-008	Kangaroo L5433	Lladro	Open	65.00	65.00
87-F-LL-17-009	Polar Bear L5434	Lladro	Open	65.00	65.00
87-F-LL-17-010	Cougar L5435	Lladro	Open	65.00	65.00
87-F-LL-17-011	Lion L5436	Lladro	Open	50.00	50.00
87-F-LL-17-012	Rhino L5437	Lladro	Open	50.00	50.00
87-F-LL-17-013	Elephant L5438	Lladro	Open	50.00	50.00
Lladro		**Period Figurines**			
86-F-LL-18-001	At the Ball L1504	Lladro	Open	375.00	410.00
86-F-LL-18-002	A Lady of Taste L1495	Lladro	Open	575.00	625.00
86-F-LL-18-003	The Reception	Lladro	Open	625.00	675.00
86-F-LL-18-004	Serenade L5381	Lladro	Open	450.00	500.00
86-F-LL-18-005	A New Hat L5345	Lladro	Open	200.00	225.00
87-F-LL-18-006	Cafe De Paris L1511	Lladro	Open	1900.00	1900.00
87-F-LL-18-007	A Flower for My Lady L1513	Lladro	Open	1150.00	1150.00
87-F-LL-18-008	Will You Marry Me? L5447	Lladro	Open	750.00	750.00
87-F-LL-18-009	Intermezzo L5424	Lladro	Open	325.00	325.00
87-F-LL-18-010	Pilar L5410	Lladro	Open	200.00	200.00

Company		Series			
Number	**Name**	**Artist**	**Edition limit**	**Issue Price**	**Quote**
87-F-LL-18-011	Teresa L5411	Lladro	Open	225.00	225.00
87-F-LL-18-012	Isabel L5412	Lladro	Open	225.00	225.00
87-F-LL-18-013	Sunday Stroll L5408	Lladro	Open	250.00	250.00
87-F-LL-18-014	Stroll in the Park L1519	Lladro	Open	1600.00	1600.00
86-F-LL-18-015	A Touch of Class L5377	Lladro	Open	475.00	525.00
76-F-LL-18-016	Lovers in the Park L1274	Lladro	Open	450.00	950.00
84-F-LL-18-017	On the Town L1452	Lladro	Open	Unknown	260.00
86-F-LL-18-018	Serenade L5381	Lladro	Open	450.00	500.00
85-F-LL-18-019	Medieval Courtship L5300	Lladro	Open	735.00	825.00
85-F-LL-18-020	English Lady L5324	Lladro	Open	225.00	250.00
Lladro		**Period Figurines**			
85-F-LL-18-021	Milanese Lady L5323	Lladro	Open	180.00	210.00
85-F-LL-18-022	Viennese Lady L5322	Lladro	Open	160.00	180.00
85-F-LL-18-023	Parisian Lady L5321	Lladro	Open	192.50	225.00
85-F-LL-18-024	Socialite of the Twenties L5283	Lladro	Open	175.00	210.00
83-F-LL-18-025	Roaring 20's L5174	Lladro	Open	172.50	200.00
83-F-LL-18-026	Flapper L5175	Lladro	Open	185.00	225.00
80-F-LL-18-027	Reading L5000	Lladro	Open	150.00	180.00
76-F-LL-18-028	Spring Breeze L4936	Lladro	Open	145.00	275.00
76-F-LL-18-029	'My Dog' L4893	Lladro	Open	85.00	170.00
71-F-LL-18-030	Dressmaker L47000	Lladro	Open	45.00	230.00
74-F-LL-18-031	Lady with Dog L4761	Lladro	Open	60.00	175.00
80-F-LL-18-032	Sunny Day L50003	Lladro	Open	192.50	240.00
75-F-LL-18-033	Lady with Shawl L4914	Lladro	Open	220.00	440.00
79-F-LL-18-034	Anniversary Waltz L1372	Lladro	Open	260.00	375.00
74-F-LL-18-035	Lady with Parasol L4879	Lladro	Open	48.00	200.00
86-F-LL-18-036	Three Sisters LL1492	Lladro	3,000	1850.00	2050.00
Lladro		**Oriental Figurines**			
86-F-LL-19-001	Oriental Musica LL1491	Lladro	5,000	1350.00	1475.00
85-F-LL-19-002	Nippon Lady L5327	Lladro	Open	325.00	360.00
86-F-LL-19-003	Lady of the East L1488	Lladro	Open	625.00	675.00
83-F-LL-19-004	Mariko L1421	Lladro	Open	860.00	990.00
84-F-LL-19-005	Springtime in Japan L1445	Lladro	Open	965.00	1100.00
80-F-LL-19-006	A Rickshaw Ride L1383	Lladro	Open	1500.00	1525.00
84-F-LL-19-007	Michiko L1447	Lladro	Open	235.00	275.00
84-F-LL-19-008	Yuki L1448	Lladro	Open	285.00	330.00
84-F-LL-19-009	Mayumi L1449	Lladro	Open	235.00	275.00
84-F-LL-19-010	Kiyoko L1450	Lladro	Open	235.00	275.00
84-F-LL-19-011	Teruko L1451	Lladro	Open	235.00	275.00
77-F-LL-19-012	Geisha L4807	Lladro	Open	190.00	330.00
73-F-LL-19-013	Oriental Flower Arranger L4840	Lladro	Open	90.00	350.00
82-F-LL-19-014	August Moom L5122	Lladro	Open	185.00	210.00
82-F-LL-19-015	My Precious Bundle L5123	Lladro	Open	150.00	170.00
83-F-LL-19-016	Fish A' Plenty L5172	Lladro	Open	190.00	230.00
78-F-LL-19-017	Chrysanthemum L4990	Lladro	Open	125.00	220.00
78-F-LL-19-018	Butterfly L4991	Lladro	Open	125.00	210.00
78-F-LL-19-019	Sayonara L4989	Lladro	Open	125.00	210.00
78-F-LL-19-020	Oriental Spring L4988	Lladro	Open	125.00	210.00
Lladro		**Sports Figurines**			
74-F-LL-20-001	Soccer Players LL1266	Lladro	Closed	2000.00	6000.00
83-F-LL-20-002	Male Tennis Player L1426	Lladro	Open	200.00	250.00
83-F-LL-20-003	Female Tennis Player L1427	Lladro	Open	200.00	250.00
84-F-LL-20-004	Golfing Couple L1453	Lladro	Open	248.00	300.00
72-F-LL-20-005	Female Equestrian L4516	Lladro	Open	170.00	425.00
74-F-LL-20-006	Lady Golfer L4851	Lladro	Open	70.00	175.00
73-F-LL-20-007	Male Golfer L4824	Lladro	Open	66.00	220.00
73-F-LL-20-008	Young Sailor L4810	Lladro	Open	33.00	115.00
73-F-LL-20-009	'Going Fishing' L4809	Lladro	Open	33.00	115.00
83-F-LL-20-010	Yachtsman L5206	Lladro	Open	110.00	130.00
83-F-LL-20-011	Male Soccer Player L5200	Lladro	Open	155.00	170.00
84-F-LL-20-012	Torch Bearer L5251	Lladro	Open	100.00	120.00
85-F-LL-20-013	Racing Motor Cyclist L5270	Lladro	Open	360.00	425.00
85-F-LL-20-014	Biking in the Country L5272	Lladro	Open	295.00	360.00
85-F-LL-20-015	Gentleman Equestrian L5329	Lladro	Open	160.00	190.00
85-F-LL-20-016	Lady L5328	Lladro	Open	160.00	190.00
85-F-LL-20-017	Waiting to Tee Off L5301	Lladro	Open	145.00	165.00
85-F-LL-20-018	Hiker L5280	Lladro	Open	195.00	225.00
Lladro		**Bridal Figurines**			
87-F-LL-21-001	The Bride L5439	Lladro	Open	250.00	250.00
87-F-LL-21-002	I Love You Truly L1528	Lladro	Open	375.00	375.00
85-F-LL-21-003	Over the Threshold L5282	Lladro	Open	150.00	170.00
85-F-LL-21-004	Wedding Day L5274	Lladro	Open	240.00	275.00
XX-F-LL-21-005	Matrimony L1404	Lladro	Open	Unknown	385.00
75-F-LL-21-006	Wedding L4808	Lladro	Open	50.00	125.00
86-F-LL-21-007	My Wedding Day L1494	Lladro	Open	800.00	875.00
84-F-LL-21-008	'Here Comes the Bride' L1446	Lladro	Open	517.50	600.00
Lladro		**Professional Figurines**			
87-F-LL-22-001	Midwife L5431	Lladro	Open	175.00	175.00
86-F-LL-22-002	The Poet L5397	Lladro	Open	425.00	475.00
84-F-LL-22-003	Artistic Endeavor L5234	Lladro	Open	225.00	275.00
83-F-LL-22-004	Lamplighter L5205	Lladro	Open	170.00	225.00
83-F-LL-22-005	Sharpening the Cutlery L5204	Lladro	Open	210.00	275.00
84-F-LL-22-006	Wine Taster L5239	Lladro	Open	190.00	220.00
83-F-LL-22-007	Professor L5208	Lladro	Open	205.00	275.00
83-F-LL-22-008	School Marm L5209	Lladro	Open	205.00	275.00
83-F-LL-22-009	Lawyer L5213	Lladro	Open	250.00	320.00
83-F-LL-22-010	'Maestro, Music Please!' L5196	Lladro	Open	135.00	160.00
83-F-LL-22-011	Female Physician L5197	Lladro	Open	120.00	140.00
83-F-LL-22-012	Architect L5214	Lladro	Open	140.00	175.00
85-F-LL-22-013	The Tailor L5326	Lladro	Open	335.00	390.00
85-F-LL-22-014	Concert Violinist L5330	Lladro	Open	220.00	250.00
71-F-LL-22-015	Obstetrician L4763-3	Lladro	Open	40.00	160.00
71-F-LL-22-016	Nurse - L4603-3	Lladro	Open	35.00	130.00
71-F-LL-22-017	Doctor L4602-3	Lladro	Open	33.00	120.00
83-F-LL-22-018	Say "Cheese!" L5195	Lladro	Open	170.00	200.00
75-F-LL-22-019	Judge LL1281	Lladro	Closed	325.00	1200.00
Lynell Studios		**Rockwell**			
81-F-LS-01-001	Snow Queen	N. Rockwell	10,000	85.00	85.00
81-F-LS-01-002	Cradle of Love	N. Rockwell	10,000	85.00	85.00
81-F-LS-01-003	Scotty	N. Rockwell	7,500	125.00	125.00
Maruri USA		**Birds of Prey**			
81-F-MC-01-001	Screech Owl	W. Gaither	300	960.00	960.00
81-F-MC-01-002	American Bald Eagle I	W. Gaither	Closed	165.00	600.00
82-F-MC-01-003	American Bald Eagle II	W. Gaither	Closed	245.00	390.00

Company		Series			
Number	**Name**	**Artist**	**Edition limit**	**Issue Price**	**Quote**
83-F-MC-01-004	American Bald Eagle III	W. Gaither	950	445.00	445.00
84-F-MC-01-005	American Bald Eagle IV	W. Gaither	950	360.00	360.00
86-F-MC-01-006	American Bald Eagle V	W. Gaither	950	325.00	325.00
Maruri USA		**North American Waterfowl I**			
81-F-MC-02-001	Blue Winged Teal	W. Gaither	200	980.00	980.00
81-F-MC-02-002	Wood Duck, decoy	W. Gaither	950	480.00	480.00
81-F-MC-02-003	Flying Wood Ducks	W. Gaither	Closed	880.00	880.00
81-F-MC-02-004	Canvasback Ducks	W. Gaither	300	780.00	780.00
81-F-MC-02-005	Mallard Drake	W. Gaither	Closed	2380.00	2380.00
Maruri USA		**North American Waterfowl II**			
81-F-MC-03-001	Mallard Ducks Pair	W. Gaither	1,500	225.00	225.00
82-F-MC-03-002	Goldeneye Ducks Pair	W. Gaither	1,500	225.00	225.00
82-F-MC-03-003	Bufflehead Ducks Pair	W. Gaither	1,500	225.00	225.00
82-F-MC-03-004	Widgeon, male	W. Gaither	Closed	225.00	225.00
82-F-MC-03-005	Widgeon, female	W. Gaither	Closed	225.00	225.00
82-F-MC-03-006	Pintail Ducks Pair	W. Gaither	1,500	225.00	225.00
83-F-MC-03-007	Loon	W. Gaither	1,500	245.00	245.00
Maruri USA		**North American Songbirds**			
82-F-MC-05-001	Cardinal, male	W. Gaither	Closed	95.00	95.00
82-F-MC-05-002	Chicadee	W. Gaither	Closed	95.00	95.00
82-F-MC-05-003	Bluebird	W. Gaither	Closed	95.00	95.00
82-F-MC-05-004	Mockingbird	W. Gaither	Closed	95.00	95.00
82-F-MC-05-005	Carolina Wren	W. Gaither	Closed	95.00	95.00
83-F-MC-05-006	Cardinal, female	W. Gaither	Closed	95.00	95.00
83-F-MC-05-007	Robin	W. Gaither	Closed	95.00	95.00
Maruri USA		**North American Game Birds**			
81-F-MC-06-001	Canadian Geese, pair	W. Gaither	Closed	2000.00	2000.00
81-F-MC-06-002	Eastern Wild Turkey	W. Gaither	Closed	300.00	300.00
82-F-MC-06-003	Ruffed Grouse	W. Gaither	200	1745.00	1745.00
83-F-MC-06-004	Bobtail Quail, male	W. Gaither	Closed	375.00	375.00
83-F-MC-06-005	Bobtail Quail, female	W. Gaither	Closed	375.00	375.00
83-F-MC-06-006	Wild Turkey Hen with Chicks	W. Gaither	480	300.00	300.00
Maruri USA		**Baby Animals**			
81-F-MC-07-001	African Lion Cubs	W. Gaither	1,500	195.00	195.00
81-F-MC-07-002	Wolf Cubs	W. Gaither	1,500	195.00	195.00
81-F-MC-07-003	Black Bear Cubs	W. Gaither	1,500	195.00	195.00
Maruri USA		**Upland Birds**			
81-F-MC-08-001	Mourning Doves	W. Gaither	350	780.00	780.00
Maruri USA		**Americana**			
81-F-MC-09-001	Grizzly Bear and Indian	W. Gaither	Closed	650.00	650.00
82-F-MC-09-002	Sioux Brave and Bisen	W. Gaither	300	985.00	985.00
Maruri USA		**Stump Animals**			
82-F-MC-10-001	Red Fox	W. Gaither	1,200	175.00	175.00
83-F-MC-10-002	Raccoon	W. Gaither	1,200	175.00	175.00
83-F-MC-10-003	Owl	W. Gaither	1,200	175.00	175.00
84-F-MC-10-004	Gray Squirrel	W. Gaither	1,200	175.00	175.00
84-F-MC-10-005	Chipmunk	W. Gaither	1,200	175.00	175.00
84-F-MC-10-006	Bob Cat	W. Gaither	1,200	175.00	175.00
Maruri USA		**Shore Birds**			
84-F-MC-11-001	Pelican	W. Gaither	1,500	260.00	260.00
84-F-MC-11-002	Sand Piper	W. Gaither	1,500	285.00	285.00
Maruri USA		**North American Game Animals**			
84-F-MC-12-001	White Tail Deer	W. Gaither	950	285.00	285.00
Maruri USA		**African Safari Animals**			
83-F-MC-13-001	African Elephant	W. Gaither	150	3500.00	3500.00
83-F-MC-13-002	Southern White Rhino	W. Gaither	150	3200.00	3200.00
83-F-MC-13-003	Cape Buffalo	W. Gaither	300	2200.00	2200.00
83-F-MC-13-004	Black Maned Lion	W. Gaither	300	1450.00	1450.00
83-F-MC-13-005	Southern Leopard	W. Gaither	300	1450.00	1450.00
83-F-MC-13-006	Southern Greater Kudu	W. Gaither	300	1800.00	1800.00
83-F-MC-13-007	Southern Impala	W. Gaither	300	1200.00	1200.00
83-F-MC-13-008	Nyala	W. Gaither	300	1450.00	1450.00
83-F-MC-13-009	Sable	W. Gaither	500	1200.00	1200.00
83-F-MC-13-010	Grant's Zebras, pair	W. Gaither	500	1200.00	1200.00
Maruri USA		**Special Commissions**			
81-F-MC-14-001	White Bengal Tiger	W. Gaither	240	340.00	340.00
82-F-MC-14-002	Cheetah	W. Gaither	200	995.00	995.00
83-F-MC-14-003	Orange Bengal Tiger	W. Gaither	240	340.00	340.00
Maruri USA		**Signature Collection**			
85-F-MC-15-001	American Bald Eagle	W. Gaither	Closed	60.00	60.00
85-F-MC-15-002	Canada Goose	W. Gaither	Closed	60.00	60.00
85-F-MC-15-003	Hawk	W. Gaither	Closed	60.00	60.00
85-F-MC-15-004	Snow Goose	W. Gaither	Closed	60.00	60.00
85-F-MC-15-005	Pintail Duck	W. Gaither	Closed	60.00	60.00
85-F-MC-15-006	Swallow	W. Gaither	Closed	60.00	60.00
Maruri USA		**Legendary Flowers of the Orient**			
85-F-MC-16-001	Iris	Ito	15,000	45.00	55.00
85-F-MC-16-002	Lotus	Ito	15,000	45.00	45.00
85-F-MC-16-003	Chinese Peony	Ito	15,000	45.00	55.00
85-F-MC-16-004	Lily	Ito	15,000	45.00	55.00
85-F-MC-16-005	Chrysanthemum	Ito	15,000	45.00	55.00
85-F-MC-16-006	Cherry Blossom	Ito	15,000	45.00	55.00
85-F-MC-16-007	Orchid	Ito	15,000	45.00	55.00
85-F-MC-16-008	Wisteria	Ito	15,000	45.00	55.00
Maruri USA		**American Eagle Gallery**			
85-F-MC-17-001	E-8501	Maruri Studios	Open	45.00	45.00
85-F-MC-17-002	E-8502	Maruri Studios	Open	55.00	55.00
85-F-MC-17-003	E-8503	Maruri Studios	Open	60.00	60.00
85-F-MC-17-004	E-8504	Maruri Studios	Open	65.00	65.00
85-F-MC-17-005	E-8505	Maruri Studios	Open	65.00	65.00
85-F-MC-17-006	E-8506	Maruri Studios	Open	75.00	75.00
85-F-MC-17-007	E-8507	Maruri Studios	Open	75.00	75.00
85-F-MC-17-008	E-8508	Maruri Studios	Open	75.00	75.00
85-F-MC-17-009	E-8509	Maruri Studios	Open	85.00	85.00
85-F-MC-17-010	E-8510	Maruri Studios	Open	85.00	85.00
85-F-MC-17-011	E-8511	Maruri Studios	Open	85.00	85.00
85-F-MC-17-012	E-8512	Maruri Studios	Open	147.50	147.50
87-F-MC-17-013	E-8721	Maruri Studios	Open	40.00	40.00
87-F-MC-17-014	E-8722	Maruri Studios	Open	45.00	45.00
87-F-MC-17-015	E-8723	Maruri Studios	Open	55.00	55.00
87-F-MC-17-016	E-8724	Maruri Studios	Open	175.00	175.00

Company Number	Name	Series Artist	Edition limit	Issue Price	Quote
Maruri USA		**Wings of Love Doves**			
87-F-MC-18-001	D-8701 Single Dove	Maruri Studios	Open	45.00	45.00
87-F-MC-18-002	D-8702 Double Dove	Maruri Studios	Open	55.00	55.00
87-F-MC-18-003	D-8703 Single Dove	Maruri Studios	Open	65.00	65.00
87-F-MC-18-004	D-8704 Double Dove	Maruri Studios	Open	75.00	75.00
87-F-MC-18-005	D-8705 Single Dove	Maruri Studios	Open	95.00	95.00
87-F-MC-18-006	D-8706 Double Dove	Maruri Studios	Open	175.00	175.00
Maruri USA		**Majestic Owls of the Night**			
87-F-MC-19-001	Barn Owl	D. Lyttleton	15,000	55.00	55.00
87-F-MC-19-002	Great Horned Owl	D. Lyttleton	15,000	55.00	55.00
87-F-MC-19-003	Snowy Owl	D. Lyttleton	15,000	55.00	55.00
87-F-MC-19-004	Tawny Owl	D. Lyttleton	15,000	55.00	55.00
87-F-MC-19-005	Screech Owl	D. Lyttleton	15,000	55.00	55.00
87-F-MC-19-006	Burrowing Owl	D. Littleton	15,000	55.00	55.00
Mill Pond Press		**Bateman Sculptures**			
87-F-MF-01-001	Peregrine in Flight	R. Bateman	90	850.00	Unknown
87-F-MF-01-002	Red-Tailed Hawk Study	R. Bateman	250	950.00	Unknown
87-F-MF-01-003	Merganser Duckling	R. Bateman	250	695.00	Unknown
Moussalli		**Moussalli Porcelains**			
69-F-MO-01-001	Black-Capped Chickadee	Moussalli	250	550.00	3500.00
XX-F-MO-01-002	American Redstart with Cherries	Moussalli	500	60.00	150.00
73-F-MO-01-003	Canadian Warbler	Moussalli	500	180.00	350.00
72-F-MO-01-004	Hummingbird in Forsythia	Moussalli	500	250.00	375.00
XX-F-MO-01-005	Hummingbird and Honeysuckle	Moussalli	500	250.00	275-325.
XX-F-MO-01-006	Olive Warbler	Moussalli	500	200.00	325.00
74-F-MO-01-007	Slate-Colored Junco	Moussalli	500	180.00	325.00
73-F-MO-01-008	Wren on a Rock	Moussalli	500	170.00	750.00
69-F-MO-01-009	Eastern Bluebird on Rock	Moussalli	500	250.00	1100.00
69-F-MO-01-010	Yellow-Throated Warbler	Moussalli	500	120.00	1100.00
72-F-MO-01-011	American RedStart with Flowers	Moussalli	500	600.00	1350.00
72-F-MO-01-012	House Wren	Moussalli	500	250.00	500.00
XX-F-MO-01-013	Baltimore Oriole	Moussalli	300	650.00	625.00
74-F-MO-01-014	Bay-Breasted Warbler	Moussalli	300	325.00	350.00
75-F-MO-01-015	Cardinal	Moussalli	300	600.00	900.00
74-F-MO-01-016	Flycatcher	Moussalli	300	360.00	360.00
71-F-MO-01-017	Redbreasted Grosbeak	Moussalli	300	435.00	435.00
74-F-MO-01-018	Red-Faced Warbler	Moussalli	300	435.00	435.00
XX-F-MO-01-019	Red-Winged Blackbird	Moussalli	300	700.00	1200.00
XX-F-MO-01-020	Say's Phoebe	Moussalli	300	360.00	360.00
75-F-MO-01-021	Scarlet Tanager	Moussalli	300	360.00	360.00
74-F-MO-01-022	Wheatear	Moussalli	300	350.00	375.00
72-F-MO-01-023	Wren on Magnolia Branch	Moussalli	300	600.00	900.00
XX-F-MO-01-024	Golden Finch	Moussalli	150	550.00	900.00
72-F-MO-01-025	Indigo Bunting	Moussalli	150	700.00	900.00
72-F-MO-01-026	Tufted Titmouse	Moussalli	150	650.00	2100.00
74-F-MO-01-027	Golden-Crowned Kinglet	Moussalli	400	225.00	650.00
XX-F-MO-01-028	Redheaded Woodpecker	Moussalli	200	450.00	650.00
74-F-MO-01-029	Snow Bunting	Moussalli	200	830.00	830.00
73-F-MO-01-030	Anna's Hummingbird	Moussalli	200	250.00	375.00
72-F-MO-01-031	Baltimore Oriole with Snake	Moussalli	100	1250.00	2500.00
79-F-MO-01-032	Bluebird on Crabapple Tree	Moussalli	150	475.00	3500.00
Norman Rockwell Museum		**American Family I**			
79-F-NO-01-001	Baby's First Step	N. Rockwell	22,500	90.00	120.00
80-F-NO-01-002	Happy Birthday, Dear Mother	N. Rockwell	22,500	90.00	125.00
80-F-NO-01-003	Sweet Sixteen	N. Rockwell	22,500	90.00	90.00
80-F-NO-01-004	First Haircut	N. Rockwell	22,500	90.00	90.00
80-F-NO-01-005	First Prom	N. Rockwell	22,500	90.00	90.00
80-F-NO-01-006	Wrapping Christmas Presents	N. Rockwell	22,500	90.00	110.00
80-F-NO-01-007	The Student	N. Rockwell	22,500	110.00	140.00
80-F-NO-01-008	Birthday Party	N. Rockwell	22,500	110.00	110.00
80-F-NO-01-009	Little Mother	N. Rockwell	22,500	110.00	110.00
80-F-NO-01-010	Washing Our Dog	N. Rockwell	22,500	110.00	110.00
81-F-NO-01-011	Mother's Little Helpers	N. Rockwell	22,500	110.00	110.00
81-F-NO-01-012	Bride and Groom	N. Rockwell	22,500	110.00	110.00
Norman Rockwell Museum		**Christmas**			
80-F-NO-02-001	Checking His List	N. Rockwell	Yr.Iss	65.00	65.00
81-F-NO-02-002	Ringing in Good Cheer	N. Rockwell	Yr.Iss	95.00	95.00
82-F-NO-02-003	Waiting for Santa	N. Rockwell	Yr.Iss	95.00	95.00
83-F-NO-02-004	High Hopes	N. Rockwell	Yr.Iss	95.00	95.00
84-F-NO-02-005	Space Age Santa	N. Rockwell	Yr.Iss	65.00	65.00
Norman Rockwell Museum		**Classic**			
80-F-NO-03-001	Lighthouse Keeper's Daughter	N. Rockwell	Open	65.00	65.00
80-F-NO-03-002	The Cobbler	N. Rockwell	Open	65.00	65.00
80-F-NO-03-003	The Toymaker	N. Rockwell	Open	65.00	65.00
80-F-NO-03-004	Bedtime	N. Rockwell	Open	65.00	65.00
80-F-NO-03-005	Memories	N. Rockwell	Open	65.00	65.00
80-F-NO-03-006	For A Good Boy	N. Rockwell	Open	65.00	65.00
81-F-NO-03-007	A Dollhouse for Sis	N. Rockwell	Open	65.00	65.00
81-F-NO-03-008	Music Master	N. Rockwell	Open	65.00	65.00
81-F-NO-03-009	The Music Lesson	N. Rockwell	Open	65.00	65.00
81-F-NO-03-010	Puppy Love	N. Rockwell	Open	65.00	65.00
81-F-NO-03-011	While The Audience Waits	N. Rockwell	Open	65.00	65.00
81-F-NO-03-012	Off to School	N. Rockwell	Open	65.00	65.00
82-F-NO-03-013	The Country Doctor	N. Rockwell	Open	65.00	65.00
82-F-NO-03-014	Spring Fever	N. Rockwell	Open	65.00	65.00
82-F-NO-03-015	Words of Wisdom	N. Rockwell	Open	65.00	65.00
82-F-NO-03-016	The Kite Maker	N. Rockwell	Open	65.00	65.00
82-F-NO-03-017	Dreams in the Antique Shop	N. Rockwell	Open	65.00	65.00
83-F-NO-03-018	Winter Fun	N. Rockwell	Open	65.00	65.00
83-F-NO-03-019	A Special Treat	N. Rockwell	Open	65.00	65.00
83-F-NO-03-020	High Stepping	N. Rockwell	Open	65.00	65.00
83-F-NO-03-021	Bored of Education	N. Rockwell	Open	65.00	65.00
83-F-NO-03-022	A Final Touch	N. Rockwell	Open	65.00	65.00
83-F-NO-03-023	Braving the Storm	N. Rockwell	Open	65.00	65.00
84-F-NO-03-024	Goin' Fishin'	N. Rockwell	Open	65.00	65.00
84-F-NO-03-025	The Big Race	N. Rockwell	Open	65.00	65.00
84-F-NO-03-026	Saturday's Hero	N. Rockwell	Open	65.00	65.00
84-F-NO-03-027	All Wrapped Up	N. Rockwell	Open	65.00	65.00
Norman Rockwell Museum		**Commemorative**			
81-F-NO-06-001	Norman Rockwell Display	N. Rockwell	5,000	125.00	150.00
82-F-NO-06-002	Spirit of America	N. Rockwell	5,000	125.00	125.00
83-F-NO-06-003	Norman Rockwell, America's Artist	N. Rockwell	5,000	125.00	125.00
84-F-NO-06-004	Outward Bound	N. Rockwell	5,000	125.00	125.00
85-F-NO-06-005	Another Masterpiece by Norman Rockwell	N. Rockwell	5,000	125.00	125.00
86-F-NO-06-006	The Painter and the Pups	N. Rockwell	5,000	125.00	125.00

Company Number	Name	Series Artist	Edition limit	Issue Price	Quote
Pemberton & Oakes		**Zolan's Children**			
82-F-PO-01-001	Erik and the Dandelion	D. Zolan	17,000	48.00	48.00
83-F-PO-01-002	Sabina in the Grass	D. Zolan	6,800	48.00	48.00
84-F-PO-01-003	Winter Angel	D. Zolan	8,000	28.00	28.00
85-F-PO-01-004	Tender Moment	D. Zolan	10,000	29.00	29.00
Polland Studios		**Collectible Bronzes**			
67-F-PQ-01-001	Bull Session	D. Polland	11	200.00	1200.00
69-F-PQ-01-002	Blowin' Cold	D. Polland	30	375.00	950.00
69-F-PQ-01-003	The Breed	D. Polland	30	350.00	900.00
69-F-PQ-01-004	Buffalo Hunt	D. Polland	30	450.00	1100.00
69-F-PQ-01-005	Comanchero	D. Polland	30	350.00	350.00
69-F-PQ-01-006	Dancing Indian with Lance	D. Polland	50	250.00	700.00
69-F-PQ-01-007	Dancing Indian with Tomahawk	D. Polland	50	250.00	700.00
69-F-PQ-01-008	Dancing Medicine Man	D. Polland	50	250.00	700.00
69-F-PQ-01-009	Drawn Sabers	D. Polland	50	2000.00	5500.00
69-F-PQ-01-010	Lookouts	D. Polland	30	375.00	1200.00
69-F-PQ-01-011	Top Money	D. Polland	30	275.00	700.00
69-F-PQ-01-012	Trail Hazard	D. Polland	30	700.00	1600.00
69-F-PQ-01-013	War Cry	D. Polland	30	350.00	900.00
69-F-PQ-01-014	When Enemies Meet	D. Polland	30	700.00	2200.00
70-F-PQ-01-015	Coffee Time	D. Polland	50	1200.00	2700.00
70-F-PQ-01-016	The Lost Dispatch	D. Polland	50	1200.00	2800.00
70-F-PQ-01-017	Wanted	D. Polland	50	500.00	1000.00
71-F-PQ-01-018	Ambush at Rock Canyon	D. Polland	5	20000.00	45000.00
71-F-PQ-01-019	Oh Sugar!	D. Polland	40	700.00	1400.00
71-F-PQ-01-020	Shakin' Out a Loop	D. Polland	40	500.00	950.00
72-F-PQ-01-021	Buffalo Robe	D. Polland	50	1000.00	2200.00
73-F-PQ-01-022	Bunch Quitter	D. Polland	60	750.00	1800.00
73-F-PQ-01-023	Challenge	D. Polland	60	750.00	1800.00
73-F-PQ-01-024	War Party	D. Polland	60	1500.00	4000.00
75-F-PQ-01-025	Cheyenne	D. Polland	6	1300.00	1600.00
75-F-PQ-01-026	Counting Coup	D. Polland	6	1450.00	1750.00
75-F-PQ-01-027	Crow Scout	D. Polland	6	1300.00	1600.00
76-F-PQ-01-028	Buffalo Hunt	D. Polland	6	2200.00	3500.00
76-F-PQ-01-029	Rescue	D. Polland	6	2400.00	3000.00
76-F-PQ-01-030	Painting the Town	D. Polland	6	3000.00	4200.00
76-F-PQ-01-031	Monday Morning Wish	D. Polland	6	2000.00	2600.00
76-F-PQ-01-032	Mandan Hunter	D. Polland	12	375.00	450.00
Polland Studios		**Collector Society Specials**			
87-F-PQ-02-001	I Come In Peace	D. Polland	Yr.Iss	35.00	35.00
87-F-PQ-02-002	Silent Trail	D. Polland	Yr.Iss	300.00	300.00
Polland Studios		**Pewter Collection**			
87-F-PQ-03-001	Federal Stallion	D. Polland	1,500	145.00	145.00
87-F-PQ-03-002	Hunting Cougar	D. Polland	1,500	145.00	145.00
87-F-PQ-03-003	Running Free	D. Polland	1,500	250.00	250.00
Reco International		**Granget Crystal Sculpture**			
73-F-RA-01-001	Long Earred Owl, Asio Otus	G. Granget	350	2250.00	2250.00
XX-F-RA-01-002	Ruffed Grouse	G. Granget	3,500	1000.00	1000.00
Reco International		**Porcelains in Miniature by John McClelland**			
XX-F-RA-02-001	John	J. McClelland	10,000	34.50	34.50
XX-F-RA-02-002	Alice	J. McClelland	10,000	34.50	34.50
XX-F-RA-02-003	Chimney Sweep	J. McClelland	10,000	34.50	34.50
XX-F-RA-02-004	Dressing Up	J. McClelland	10,000	34.50	34.50
XX-F-RA-02-005	Autumn Dreams	J. McClelland	Open	29.50	29.50
XX-F-RA-02-006	Tuck-Me-In	J. McClelland	Open	29.50	29.50
XX-F-RA-02-007	Country Lass	J. McClelland	Open	29.50	29.50
XX-F-RA-02-008	Sudsie Suzie	J. McClelland	Open	29.50	29.50
XX-F-RA-02-009	Smooth Smailing	J. McClelland	Open	29.50	29.50
XX-F-RA-02-010	The Clown	J. McClelland	Open	29.50	29.50
XX-F-RA-02-011	The Baker	J. McClelland	Open	29.50	29.50
XX-F-RA-02-012	Quiet Moments	J. McClelland	Open	29.50	29.50
XX-F-RA-02-013	The Farmer	J. McClelland	Open	29.50	29.50
XX-F-RA-02-014	The Nurse	J. McClelland	Open	29.50	29.50
XX-F-RA-02-015	The Policeman	J. McClelland	Open	29.50	29.50
XX-F-RA-02-016	The Fireman	J. McClelland	Open	29.50	29.50
XX-F-RA-02-017	Winter Fun	J. McClelland	Open	29.50	29.50
XX-F-RA-02-018	Cowgirl	J. McClelland	Open	29.50	29.50
XX-F-RA-02-019	Cowboy	J. McClelland	Open	29.50	29.50
XX-F-RA-02-020	Doc	J. McClelland	Open	29.50	29.50
XX-F-RA-02-021	Lawyer	J. McClelland	Open	29.50	29.50
XX-F-RA-02-022	Farmer's Wife	J. McClelland	Open	29.50	29.50
XX-F-RA-02-023	First Outing	J. McClelland	Open	29.50	29.50
XX-F-RA-02-024	Club Pro	J. McClelland	Open	29.50	29.50
XX-F-RA-02-025	Batter Up	J. McClelland	Open	29.50	29.50
XX-F-RA-02-026	Love 40	J. McClelland	Open	29.50	29.50
XX-F-RA-02-027	The Painter	J. McClelland	Open	29.50	29.50
XX-F-RA-02-028	Special Delivery	J. McClelland	Open	29.50	29.50
XX-F-RA-02-029	Center Ice	J. McClelland	Open	29.50	29.50
XX-F-RA-02-030	First Solo	J. McClelland	Open	29.50	29.50
XX-F-RA-02-031	Highland Fling	J. McClelland	7,500	34.50	34.50
XX-F-RA-02-032	Cheerleader	J. McClelland	Open	29.50	29.50
Reco International		**The Reco Clown Collection**			
85-F-RA-03-001	Whoopie	J. McClelland	Open	12.00	12.00
85-F-RA-03-002	The Professor	J. McClelland	Open	12.00	12.00
85-F-RA-03-003	Top Hat	J. McClelland	Open	12.00	12.00
85-F-RA-03-004	Winkie	J. McClelland	Open	12.00	12.00
85-F-RA-03-005	Scamp	J. McClelland	Open	12.00	12.00
85-F-RA-03-006	Curly	J. McClelland	Open	12.00	12.00
85-F-RA-03-007	Bow Jangles	J. McClelland	Open	12.00	12.00
85-F-RA-03-008	Sparkles	J. McClelland	Open	12.00	12.00
85-F-RA-03-009	Ruffles	J. McClelland	Open	12.00	12.00
85-F-RA-03-010	Arabesque	J. McClelland	Open	12.00	12.00
85-F-RA-03-011	Hobo	J. McClelland	Open	12.00	12.00
85-F-RA-03-012	Sad Eyes	J. McClelland	Open	12.00	12.00
87-F-RA-03-013	Love	J. McClelland	Open	12.00	12.00
87-F-RA-03-014	Mr. Big	J. McClelland	Open	12.00	12.00
87-F-RA-03-015	Twinkle	J. McClelland	Open	12.00	12.00
87-F-RA-03-016	Disco Dan	J. McClelland	Open	12.00	12.00
87-F-RA-03-017	Smiley	J. McClelland	Open	12.00	12.00
87-F-RA-03-018	The Joker	J. McClelland	Open	12.00	12.00
87-F-RA-03-019	Jolly Joe	J. McClelland	Open	12.00	12.00
87-F-RA-03-020	Zany Jack	J. McClelland	Open	12.00	12.00
87-F-RA-03-021	Domino	J. McClelland	Open	12.00	12.00
87-F-RA-03-022	Happy George	J. McClelland	Open	12.00	12.00
87-F-RA-03-023	Tramp	J. McClelland	Open	12.00	12.00
87-F-RA-03-024	Wistful	J. McClelland	Open	12.00	12.00
Reco International		**King's Porcelain Figurines**			
74-F-RA-04-001	Blue Jay	A. Falchi	200	900.00	900.00
74-F-RA-04-002	Weasel	A. Falchi	200	325.00	325.00

Company / Number	Name	Series / Artist	Edition limit	Issue Price	Quote
74-F-RA-04-003	European Roller	A. Falchi	350	500.00	500.00
74-F-RA-04-004	Hummingbird	A. Falchi	300	700.00	700.00
74-F-RA-04-005	Robins	A. Falchi	300	650.00	650.00
74-F-RA-04-006	Titmouse	A. Falchi	250	700.00	700.00
74-F-RA-04-007	White Or Western Pelican	A. Falchi	100	975.00	975.00
74-F-RA-04-008	Woodcock	A. Falchi	100	900.00	900.00
74-F-RA-04-009	Wood Ducks, Pair	A. Falchi	100	1350.00	1350.00
Reco International		**Mousetown U.S.A. Collection**			
85-F-RA-05-001	The Duchess	Dolli Tingle	Open	12.00	12.00
85-F-RA-05-002	Miz Miggles & Mary Jane	Dolli Tingle	Open	15.00	15.00
85-F-RA-05-003	Miss Rosebud	Dolli Tingle	Open	12.00	12.00
85-F-RA-05-004	Patches	Dolli Tingle	Open	12.00	12.00
85-F-RA-05-005	Mr. Tickmouse	Dolli Tingle	Open	12.00	12.00
85-F-RA-05-006	Fun Loving Sam	Dolli Tingle	Open	12.00	12.00
85-F-RA-05-007	Emily Woolsey	Dolli Tingle	Open	12.00	12.00
85-F-RA-05-008	Nanny Nursemaid	Dolli Tingle	Open	15.00	15.00
85-F-RA-05-009	Count de Monnaie	Dolli Tingle	Open	12.00	12.00
85-F-RA-05-010	Sally Trinket	Dolli Tingle	Open	15.00	15.00
85-F-RA-05-011	Matilda Twig	Dolli Tingle	Open	12.00	12.00
85-F-RA-05-012	The Duke	Dolli Tingle	Open	15.00	15.00
Reco International		**The Reco Angel Collection**			
86-F-RA-06-001	Innocence	J. McClelland	Open	12.00	12.00
86-F-RA-06-002	Harmony	J. McClelland	Open	12.00	12.00
86-F-RA-06-003	Love	J. McClelland	Open	12.00	12.00
86-F-RA-06-003	Love	J. McClelland	Open	12.00	12.00
86-F-RA-06-004	Gloria	J. McClelland	Open	12.00	12.00
86-F-RA-06-005	Praise	J. McClelland	Open	18.00	18.00
86-F-RA-06-006	Devotion	J. McClelland	Open	14.50	14.50
86-F-RA-06-007	Faith	J. McClelland	Open	21.50	21.50
86-F-RA-06-008	Joy	J. McClelland	Open	14.50	14.50
86-F-RA-06-009	Adoration	J. McClelland	Open	21.50	21.50
86-F-RA-06-010	Peace	J. McClelland	Open	18.00	18.00
86-F-RA-06-011	Serenity	J. McClelland	Open	21.50	21.50
86-F-RA-06-012	Hope	J. McClelland	Open	21.50	21.50
Reco International		**Sophisticated Ladies Figurines**			
87-F-RA-07-001	Felicia	A. Fazio	9,500	29.50	29.50
87-F-RA-07-002	Samantha	A. Fazio	9,500	29.50	29.50
87-F-RA-07-003	Phoebe	A. Fazio	9,500	29.50	29.50
87-F-RA-07-004	Cleo	A. Fazio	9,500	29.50	29.50
87-F-RA-07-005	Cerissa	A. Fazio	9,500	29.50	29.50
87-F-RA-07-006	Natasha	A. Fazio	9,500	29.50	29.50
87-F-RA-07-007	Bianka	A. Fazio	9,500	29.50	29.50
87-F-RA-07-008	Chelsea	A. Fazio	9,500	29.50	29.50
Reco International		**Clown Figurines by John McClelland**			
87-F-RA-08-001	Mr. Tip	J. McClelland	9,500	29.50	29.50
87-F-RA-08-002	Mr. Cure-All	J. McClelland	9,500	29.50	29.50
87-F-RA-08-003	Mr. One-Note	J. McClelland	9,500	29.50	29.50
87-F-RA-08-004	Mr. Lovable	J. McClelland	9,500	29.50	29.50
Reco International		**The Reco Angel Collection Miniatures**			
87-F-RA-09-001	Innocence	J. McClelland	Open	7.00	7.00
87-F-RA-09-002	Harmony	J. McClelland	Open	7.00	7.00
87-F-RA-09-003	Love	J. McClelland	Open	7.00	7.00
87-F-RA-09-004	Gloria	J. McClelland	Open	7.00	7.00
87-F-RA-09-005	Devotion	J. McClelland	Open	7.00	7.00
87-F-RA-09-006	Joy	J. McClelland	Open	7.00	7.00
87-F-RA-09-007	Adoration	J. McClelland	Open	9.50	9.50
87-F-RA-09-008	Peace	J. McClelland	Open	9.50	9.50
87-F-RA-09-009	Serenity	J. McClelland	Open	9.50	9.50
87-F-RA-09-010	Hope	J. McClelland	Open	9.50	9.50
Reco International		**The Reco Clown Collection Hang-Ups**			
87-F-RA-10-001	Whoopie	J. McClelland	Open	8.00	8.00
87-F-RA-10-002	The Professor	J. McClelland	Open	8.00	8.00
87-F-RA-10-003	Top Hat	J. McClelland	Open	8.00	8.00
87-F-RA-10-004	Winkie	J. McClelland	Open	8.00	8.00
87-F-RA-10-005	Scamp	J. McClelland	Open	8.00	8.00
87-F-RA-10-006	Curly	J. McClelland	Open	8.00	8.00
87-F-RA-10-007	Bow Jangles	J. McClelland	Open	8.00	8.00
87-F-RA-10-008	Sparkles	J. McClelland	Open	8.00	8.00
87-F-RA-10-009	Ruffles	J. McClelland	Open	8.00	8.00
87-F-RA-10-010	Arabesque	J. McClelland	Open	8.00	8.00
87-F-RA-10-011	Hobo	J. McClelland	Open	8.00	8.00
87-F-RA-10-012	Sad Eyes	J. McClelland	Open	8.00	8.00
Reco International		**The Reco Angel Collection Hang-Ups**			
87-F-RA-11-001	Innocence	J. McClelland	Open	7.50	7.50
87-F-RA-11-002	Harmony	J. McClelland	Open	7.50	7.50
87-F-RA-11-003	Love	J. McClelland	Open	7.50	7.50
87-F-RA-11-004	Gloria	J. McClelland	Open	7.50	7.50
87-F-RA-11-005	Devotion	J. McClelland	Open	7.50	7.50
87-F-RA-11-006	Joy	J. McClelland	Open	7.50	7.50
87-F-RA-11-007	Adoration	J. McClelland	Open	10.00	10.00
87-F-RA-11-008	Peace	J. McClelland	Open	10.00	10.00
87-F-RA-11-009	Serenity	J. McClelland	Open	10.00	10.00
87-F-RA-11-010	Hope	J. McClelland	Open	10.00	10.00
River Shore		**Loveable-Baby Animals**			
78-F-RG-01-001	Akiku-Seal	R. Brown	15,000	37.50	150.00
78-F-RG-01-002	Alfred-Raccoon	R. Brown	15,000	42.50	45.00
79-F-RG-01-003	Scooter-Chipmunk	R. Brown	15,000	45.00	55.00
79-F-RG-01-004	Matilda-Koala	R. Brown	15,000	45.00	45.00
River Shore		**Wildlife Baby Animals**			
78-F-RG-02-001	Fanny-Fawn	R. Brown	15,000	45.00	90.00
79-F-RG-02-002	Roosevelt-Bear	R. Brown	15,000	50.00	65.00
79-F-RG-02-003	Roscoe-Red Fox	R. Brown	15,000	50.00	50.00
80-F-RG-02-004	Priscilla-Skunk	R. Brown	15,000	50.00	50.00
River Shore		**Farm Baby Animals**			
80-F-RG-03-001	Buddy-Foal	R. Brown	15,000	50.00	60.00
80-F-RG-03-002	Clover-Lamb	R. Brown	15,000	50.00	65.00
80-F-RG-03-003	Clementine-Calf	R. Brown	15,000	50.00	50.00
80-F-RG-03-004	Zeke-Piglet	R. Brown	15,000	50.00	50.00
River Shore		**Safari Baby Animals**			
81-F-RG-04-001	Bakuba-Lion Cub	R. Brown	15,000	50.00	70.00
81-F-RG-04-002	Kimbundo-Chimp	R. Brown	15,000	50.00	58.00
81-F-RG-04-003	Zuela-Elephant	R. Brown	15,000	50.00	65.00
81-F-RG-04-004	Kalina-Tiger Cub	R. Brown	15,000	50.00	50.00
River Shore		**Rockwell Single Issues**			
81-F-RG-05-001	Looking Out To Sea	N. Rockwell	9,500	85.00	145.00
82-F-RG-05-002	Grandpa's Guardian	N. Rockwell	9,500	125.00	125.00
River Shore		**Grant Wood Figurines**			
82-F-RG-06-001	American Gothic	G. Wood	9,500	185.00	185.00
River Shore		**Vignette**			
82-F-RG-07-001	Broken Window	N. Rockwell	9,500	150.00	150.00
River Shore		**Christmas After Christmas**			
82-F-RG-08-001	Kay's Doll	B. Timberlake	5,000	95.00	95.00
River Shore		**Babies of Endangered Species**			
84-F-RG-09-001	Sidney (Cougar)	R. Brown	15,000	45.00	45.00
84-F-RG-09-002	Baxter (Bear)	R. Brown	15,000	45.00	45.00
84-F-RG-09-003	Caroline (Antelope)	R. Brown	15,000	45.00	45.00
84-F-RG-09-004	Webster (Timberwolf)	R. Brown	15,000	45.00	45.00
84-F-RG-09-005	Violet (Otter)	R. Brown	15,000	45.00	45.00
84-F-RG-09-006	Chester (Prairie Dog)	R. Brown	15,000	45.00	45.00
84-F-RG-09-007	Trevor (Fox)	R. Brown	15,000	45.00	45.00
84-F-RG-09-008	Daisy (Wood Bison)	R. Brown	15,000	45.00	45.00
River Shore		**Wilderness Babies**			
85-F-RG-10-001	Penelope (Deer)	R. Brown	15,000	45.00	45.00
85-F-RG-10-002	Carmen (Burro)	R. Brown	15,000	45.00	45.00
85-F-RG-10-003	Rocky (Bobcat)	R. Brown	15,000	45.00	45.00
85-F-RG-10-004	Abercrombie (Polar Bear)	R. Brown	15,000	45.00	45.00
85-F-RG-10-005	Elrod (Fox)	R. Brown	15,000	45.00	45.00
85-F-RG-10-006	Reggie (Racoon)	R. Brown	15,000	45.00	45.00
85-F-RG-10-007	Arianne (Rabbie)	R. Brown	15,000	45.00	45.00
85-F-RG-10-008	Annabel (Mountain Goat)	R. Brown	15,000	45.00	45.00
Rohn		**Around the World**			
71-F-RL-01-001	Coolie	E. Rohn	100	700.00	1200.00
72-F-RL-01-002	Gypsy	E. Rohn	125	1450.00	1850.00
73-F-RL-01-003	Matador	E. Rohn	90	2400.00	3100.00
73-F-RL-01-004	Sherif	E. Rohn	100	1500.00	1900.00
74-F-RL-01-005	Aussie-Hunter	E. Rohn	90	1000.00	1300.00
Rohn		**Clowns-Big Top Series**			
79-F-RL-02-001	White Face	E. Rohn	100	1000.00	1700.00
80-F-RL-02-002	Tramp	E. Rohn	100	1200.00	1700.00
81-F-RL-02-003	Auguste	E. Rohn	100	1400.00	1700.00
83-F-RL-02-004	Sweetheart	E. Rohn	200	925.00	925.00
Rohn		**Famous People**			
75-F-RL-03-001	Harry S. Truman	E. Rohn	75	2400.00	3000.00
79-F-RL-03-002	Norman Rockwell	E. Rohn	200	1950.00	2300.00
81-F-RL-03-003	Ronald Reagan	E. Rohn	200	3000.00	3000.00
86-F-RL-03-004	Sherlock Holmes	E. Rohn	2,210	155.00	190.00
Rohn		**Remember When**			
71-F-RL-04-001	Riverboat Captain	E. Rohn	100	1000.00	2400.00
71-F-RL-04-002	American GI	E. Rohn	100	600.00	1000.00
73-F-RL-04-003	Apprentice	E. Rohn	175	500.00	850.00
74-F-RL-04-004	Recruit (set w/FN-5)	E. Rohn	250	250.00	360.00
74-F-RL-04-005	Missy	E. Rohn	250	250.00	360.00
77-F-RL-04-006	Flapper	E. Rohn	500	325.00	325.00
77-F-RL-04-007	Sou' Wester	E. Rohn	450	300.00	300.00
77-F-RL-04-008	Casey	E. Rohn	300	275.00	275.00
77-F-RL-04-009	Wally	E. Rohn	250	250.00	250.00
73-F-RL-04-010	Jazz Man	E. Rohn	150	750.00	1000.00
80-F-RL-04-011	Showman (W.C. Fields)	E. Rohn	300	220.00	400.00
81-F-RL-04-012	Clown Prince	E. Rohn	25	2000.00	2400.00
Rohn		**Religious and Biblical**			
77-F-RL-05-001	Zaide	E. Rohn	70	1950.00	2900.00
78-F-RL-05-002	Sabbath	E. Rohn	70	1825.00	2300.00
85-F-RL-05-003	The Mentor	E. Rohn	15	9500.00	9500.00
Rohn		**Small World Series**			
74-F-RL-06-001	Big Brother	E. Rohn	250	90.00	90.00
74-F-RL-06-002	Burglers	E. Rohn	250	120.00	120.00
74-F-RL-06-003	Quackers	E. Rohn	250	75.00	75.00
74-F-RL-06-004	Knee Deep	E. Rohn	500	60.00	60.00
75-F-RL-06-005	Field Mushrooms	E. Rohn	250	90.00	90.00
75-F-RL-06-006	Oyster Mushroom	E. Rohn	250	140.00	140.00
XX-F-RL-06-007	Johnnie's	E. Rohn	1,500	90.00	90.00
Rohn		**Western**			
71-F-RL-07-001	Trail-Hand	E. Rohn	100	1200.00	1600.00
71-F-RL-07-002	Crow Indian	E. Rohn	100	800.00	800.00
71-F-RL-07-003	Apache Indian	E. Rohn	125	800.00	1150.00
71-F-RL-07-004	Chosen One (Indian Maid)	E. Rohn	125	850.00	1350.00
Roman, Inc.		**Fontanini, The Collectible Creche**			
73-F-RO-01-001	10cm., 15 piece set	E. Simonetti	Open	63.60	63.60
73-F-RO-01-002	12cm., 15 piece set	E. Simonetti	Open	76.50	76.50
79-F-RO-01-003	16cm., 15 piece set	E. Simonetti	Open	178.50	178.50
82-F-RO-01-004	17cm., 15 piece set	E. Simonetti	Open	189.00	189.00
73-F-RO-01-005	19cm., 15 piece set	E. Simonetti	Open	175.50	175.50
80-F-RO-01-006	30 cm., 15 piece set	E. Simonetti	Open	670.00	670.00
Roman, Inc.		**A Child's World 1st Edition**			
80-F-RO-02-001	Nighttime Thoughts	F. Hook	15,000	25.00	50.00
80-F-RO-02-002	Kiss Me Good Night	F. Hook	15,000	29.00	29.00
80-F-RO-02-003	Sounds of the Sea	F. Hook	15,000	45.00	125.00
80-F-RO-02-004	Beach Buddies, signed	F. Hook	15,000	29.00	500.00
80-F-RO-02-005	My Big Brother	F. Hook	15,000	39.00	135.00
80-F-RO-02-006	Helping Hands	F. Hook	15,000	45.00	45.00
80-F-RO-02-007	Beach Buddies, unsigned	F. Hook	15,000	29.00	400.00
Roman, Inc.		**A Child's World 2nd Edition**			
81-F-RO-03-001	Making Friends	F. Hook	15,000	42.00	42.00
81-F-RO-03-002	Cat Nap	F. Hook	15,000	42.00	42.00
81-F-RO-03-003	The Sea and Me	F. Hook	15,000	39.00	39.00
81-F-RO-03-004	Sunday School	F. Hook	15,000	39.00	39.00
81-F-RO-03-005	I'll Be Good	F. Hook	15,000	36.00	36.00
81-F-RO-03-006	All Dressed Up	F. Hook	15,000	36.00	36.00
Roman, Inc.		**A Child's World 3rd Edition**			
81-F-RO-04-001	Pathway to Dreams	R. Hook	15,000	47.00	47.00
81-F-RO-04-002	Road to Adventure	R. Hook	15,000	47.00	47.00
81-F-RO-04-003	Sisters	R. Hook	15,000	64.00	64.00
81-F-RO-04-004	Bear Hug	R. Hook	15,000	42.00	42.00
81-F-RO-04-005	Spring Breeze	R. Hook	15,000	37.50	37.50
81-F-RO-04-006	Youth	R. Hook	15,000	37.50	37.50

Number	Name	Artist	Edition limit	Issue Price	Quote
Company	**Series**				
Roman, Inc.	**A Child's World 4th Edition**				
82-F-RO-05-001	All Bundled Up	F. Hook	15,000	37.50	37.50
82-F-RO-05-002	Bedtime	F. Hook	15,000	35.00	35.00
82-F-RO-05-003	Birdie	F. Hook	15,000	37.50	37.50
82-F-RO-05-004	My Dolly !	F. Hook	15,000	39.00	39.00
82-F-RO-05-005	Ring Bearer	F. Hook	15,000	39.00	39.00
82-F-RO-05-006	Flower Girl	F. Hook	15,000	42.00	42.00
Roman, Inc.	**A Child's World 5th Edition**				
83-F-RO-06-001	Ring Around the Rosie	F. Hook	15,000	99.00	99.00
83-F-RO-06-002	Handful of Happiness	F. Hook	15,000	36.00	36.00
83-F-RO-06-003	He Loves Me...	F. Hook	15,000	49.00	49.00
83-F-RO-06-004	Finish Line	F. Hook	15,000	39.00	39.00
83-F-RO-06-005	Brothers	F. Hook	15,000	64.00	64.00
83-F-RO-06-006	Puppy's Pal	F. Hook	15,000	39.00	39.00
Roman, Inc.	**A Child's World 6th Edition**				
84-F-RO-07-001	Good Doggie	F. Hook	15,000	47.00	47.00
84-F-RO-07-002	Sand Castles	F. Hook	15,000	37.50	37.50
84-F-RO-07-003	Nature's Wonders	F. Hook	15,000	29.00	29.00
84-F-RO-07-004	Let's Play Catch	F. Hook	15,000	33.00	33.00
84-F-RO-07-005	Can I Help?	F. Hook	15,000	37.50	37.50
84-F-RO-07-006	Future Artist	F. Hook	15,000	42.00	42.00
Roman, Inc.	**A Child's World 7th Edition**				
85-F-RO-08-001	Art Class	F. Hook	15,000	99.00	99.00
85-F-RO-08-002	Please Hear Me	F. Hook	15,000	29.00	29.00
85-F-RO-08-003	Don't Tell Anyone	F. Hook	15,000	49.00	49.00
85-F-RO-08-004	Mother's Helper	F. Hook	15,000	45.00	45.00
85-F-RO-08-005	Yummm!	F. Hook	15,000	36.00	36.00
85-F-RO-08-006	Look at Me!	F. Hook	15,000	42.00	42.00
Roman, Inc.	**A Child's World-8th Edition**				
85-F-RO-09-001	Private Ocean	F. Hook	15,000	29.00	29.00
85-F-RO-09-002	Just Stopped By	F. Hook	15,000	36.00	36.00
85-F-RO-09-003	Dress Rehearsal	F. Hook	15,000	33.00	33.00
85-F-RO-09-004	Chance of Showers	F. Hook	15,000	33.00	33.00
85-F-RO-09-005	Engine ffl1	F. Hook	15,000	36.00	36.00
85-F-RO-09-006	Puzzling	F. Hook	15,000	36.00	36.00
Roman, Inc.	**A Child's World-9th Edition**				
87-F-RO-10-001	Li'l Brother	F. Hook	15,000	60.00	60.00
87-F-RO-10-002	Hopscotch	F. Hook	15,000	67.50	67.50
Roman, Inc.	**Rohn's Clowns**				
84-F-RO-15-001	White Face	E. Rohn	7,500	95.00	95.00
84-F-RO-15-002	Auguste	E. Rohn	7,500	95.00	95.00
84-F-RO-15-003	Hobo	E. Rohn	7,500	95.00	95.00
Roman, Inc.	**The Masterpiece Collection**				
79-F-RO-16-001	Adoration, Sculpture	F. Lippe	5,000	73.00	73.00
80-F-RO-16-002	Madonna with Grapes	P. Mignard	5,000	85.00	85.00
81-F-RO-16-003	The Holy Family	G. delle Notti	5,000	98.00	98.00
82-F-RO-16-004	Madonna of the Streets	R. Ferruzzi	5,000	65.00	65.00
Roman, Inc.	**Ceramica Excelsis**				
77-F-RO-17-001	Madonna and Child with Angels	Unknown	5,000	60.00	60.00
77-F-RO-17-002	What Happened to your Hand?	Unknown	5,000	60.00	60.00
77-F-RO-17-003	Madonna with Child	Unknown	5,000	65.00	65.00
77-F-RO-17-004	St. Francis	Unknown	5,000	60.00	60.00
77-F-RO-17-005	Christ Knocking at the Door	Unknown	5,000	60.00	60.00
78-F-RO-17-006	Infant of Prague	Unknown	5,000	37.50	60.00
78-F-RO-17-007	Christ in the Garden of Gethsemane	Unknown	5,000	40.00	60.00
78-F-RO-17-008	Flight into Egypt	Unknown	5,000	59.00	90.00
78-F-RO-17-009	Christ Entering Jerusalem	Unknown	5,000	96.00	96.00
78-F-RO-17-010	Holy Family at Work	Unknown	5,000	96.00	96.00
78-F-RO-17-011	Assumption Madonna	Unknown	5,000	56.00	56.00
78-F-RO-17-012	Guardian Angel with Girl	Unknown	5,000	69.00	69.00
78-F-RO-17-013	Guardian Angel with Boy	Unknown	5,000	69.00	69.00
79-F-RO-17-014	Moses	Unknown	5,000	77.00	77.00
79-F-RO-17-015	Noah	Unknown	5,000	77.00	77.00
79-F-RO-17-016	Jesus Speaks in Parables	Unknown	5,000	90.00	90.00
80-F-RO-17-017	Way to Emmaus	Unknown	5,000	155.00	155.00
80-F-RO-17-018	Daniel in the Lion's Den	Unknown	5,000	80.00	80.00
80-F-RO-17-019	David	Unknown	5,000	77.00	77.00
81-F-RO-17-020	Innocence	Unknown	5,000	95.00	95.00
81-F-RO-17-021	Journey to Bethlehem	Unknown	5,000	89.00	89.00
81-F-RO-17-022	Way to the Cross	Unknown	5,000	59.00	59.00
81-F-RO-17-023	Sermon on the Mount	Unknown	5,000	56.00	56.00
83-F-RO-17-024	Good Shepherd	Unknown	5,000	49.00	49.00
83-F-RO-17-025	Holy Family	Unknown	5,000	72.00	72.00
83-F-RO-17-026	St. Francis	Unknown	5,000	59.50	59.50
83-F-RO-17-027	St. Anne	Unknown	5,000	49.00	49.00
83-F-RO-17-028	Jesus with Children	Unknown	5,000	74.00	74.00
83-F-RO-17-029	Kneeling Santa	Unknown	5,000	95.00	95.00
Roman, Inc.	**Hook**				
82-F-RO-18-001	Sailor Mates	F. Hook	2,000	290.00	290.00
82-F-RO-18-002	Sun Shy	F. Hook	2,000	290.00	290.00
Roman, Inc.	**Frances Hooks' Four Seasons**				
84-F-RO-19-001	Winter	F. Hook	12,500	95.00	95.00
85-F-RO-19-002	Spring	F. Hook	12,500	95.00	95.00
85-F-RO-19-003	Summer	F. Hook	12,500	95.00	95.00
85-F-RO-19-004	Fall	F. Hook	12,500	95.00	95.00
Roman, Inc.	**Jam Session**				
85-F-RO-20-001	Trombone Player	E. Rohn	7,500	145.00	145.00
85-F-RO-20-002	Bass Player	E. Rohn	7,500	145.00	145.00
85-F-RO-20-003	Banjo Player	E. Rohn	7,500	145.00	145.00
85-F-RO-20-004	Coronet Player	E. Rohn	7,500	145.00	145.00
85-F-RO-20-005	Clarinet Player	E. Rohn	7,500	145.00	145.00
85-F-RO-20-006	Drummer	E. Rohn	7,500	145.00	145.00
Roman, Inc.	**Spencer**				
85-F-RO-21-001	Moon Goddess	I. Spencer	5,000	195.00	195.00
85-F-RO-21-002	Flower Princess	I. Spencer	5,000	195.00	195.00
Roman, Inc.	**Hook**				
86-F-RO-22-001	Carpenter Bust	F. Hook	Yr.Iss	95.00	95.00
86-F-RO-22-002	Carpenter Bust - Heirloom Edition	F. Hook	Yr.Iss	95.00	95.00
87-F-RO-22-003	Madonna and Child	F. Hook	15,000	39.50	39.50
87-F-RO-22-004	Little Children, Come to Me	F. Hook	15,000	45.00	45.00
Roman, Inc.	**Catnippers**				
85-F-RO-23-001	The Paw that Refreshes	I. Spencer	15,000	45.00	45.00
85-F-RO-23-002	A Christmas Mourning	I. Spencer	15,000	45.00	45.00
85-F-RO-23-003	A Tail of Two Kitties	I. Spencer	15,000	45.00	45.00
85-F-RO-23-004	Sandy Claws	I. Spencer	15,000	45.00	45.00
85-F-RO-23-005	Can't We Be Friends	I. Spencer	15,000	45.00	45.00
85-F-RO-23-006	A Baffling Yarn	I. Spencer	15,000	45.00	45.00
85-F-RO-23-007	Flying Tiger - Retired	I. Spencer	15,000	45.00	45.00
85-F-RO-23-008	Flora and Felina	I. Spencer	15,000	45.00	45.00
Roman, Inc.	**Heartbeats**				
86-F-RO-24-001	Miracle	I. Spencer	5,000	145.00	145.00
87-F-RO-24-002	Storytime	I. Spencer	5,000	145.00	145.00
Royal Doulton	**Royal Doulton Figurines**				
67-F-RU-01-001	Indian Brave	P. Davies	500	2500.00	4000.00
71-F-RU-01-002	The Palio	P. Davies	500	2500.00	7000.00
69-F-RU-01-003	HRH Prince Charles Bust	J. Bromley	150	400.00	400.00
74-F-RU-01-004	Black-Throated Loon	R. Jefferson	150	1750.00	1850.00
74-F-RU-01-005	King Eider Drake	R. Jefferson	150	1400.00	1500.00
74-F-RU-01-006	Snowy Owl, female	R. Jefferson	150	1500.00	1600.00
71-F-RU-01-007	Lady Musicians, Cello	P. Davies	750	250.00	1000.00
71-F-RU-01-008	Lady Musicians, Virginals	P. Davies	750	250.00	1500.00
72-F-RU-01-009	Lady Musicians, Lute	P. Davies	750	250.00	900.00
72-F-RU-01-010	Lady Musicians, Violin	P. Davies	750	250.00	1000.00
72-F-RU-01-011	Queen Elizabeth and HRH Duke of Edinburgh	E. Griffiths	750	1000.00	Unknown
73-F-RU-01-012	Lady Musicians, Flute	P. Davies	750	250.00	900.00
73-F-RU-01-013	Lady Musicians, Harp	P. Davies	750	275.00	1500.00
74-F-RU-01-014	Lady Musicians, Chitter one	P. Davies	750	350.00	700.00
74-F-RU-01-015	Lady Musicians, Cymbals	P. Davies	750	325.00	600.00
75-F-RU-01-016	Lady Musicians, Dulcimer	P. Davies	750	375.00	700.00
75-F-RU-01-017	Lady Musicians, Hurdy-Gurdy	P. Davies	750	375.00	700.00
76-F-RU-01-018	Lady Musicians, French Horn	P. Davies	750	400.00	750.00
76-F-RU-01-019	Lady Musicians, Viola D'amore	P. Davies	750	400.00	750.00
77-F-RU-01-020	Dancers, Flamenco	P. Davies	750	400.00	1500.00
77-F-RU-01-022	General Washington at Prayer	L. Ispanky	750	875.00	2000.00
78-F-RU-01-023	Dancers Philippine	P. Davies	750	400.00	1000.00
78-F-RU-01-024	Dancers, Scottish	P. Davies	750	400.00	1000.00
74-F-RU-01-025	Roseate Tern	R. Jefferson	100	1850.00	2000.00
74-F-RU-01-026	Colorado Chipmunks	R. Jefferson	75	1800.00	1800.00
74-F-RU-01-027	Snowy Owl, male	R. Jefferson	75	1800.00	1800.00
75-F-RU-01-028	Harbor Seal	R. Jefferson	75	1200.00	1200.00
75-F-RU-01-029	Snowshoe Hare	R. Jefferson	75	2000.00	2000.00
74-F-RU-01-030	White-Winged Crossbills	R. Jefferson	250	1000.00	1000.00
74-F-RU-01-031	Puffins	R. Jefferson	250	1200.00	1200.00
76-F-RU-01-032	Fledgling Bluebird	R. Jefferson	250	450.00	450.00
75-F-RU-01-033	Soldiers,Corporal,1st N.Hampshire Reg.1778	E. Griffiths	350	750.00	900.00
75-F-RU-01-034	Soldiers, Major 3rd New Jersey Reg. 1776	E. Griffiths	350	750.00	2000.00
75-F-RU-01-035	Soldiers, Private, 1st Georgia Reg. 1777	E. Griffiths	350	750.00	1200.00
75-F-RU-01-036	Soldiers,Private,2nd S.Carolina, Reg. 1781	E. Griffiths	350	750.00	1600.00
76-F-RU-01-037	Soldiers, Captain, 2nd New York Reg. 1775	E. Griffiths	350	750.00	900.00
76-F-RU-01-038	Soldiers,Private,3rd N. Carolina Reg. 1778	E. Griffiths	350	750.00	900.00
76-F-RU-01-039	Soldiers, Sergeant 6th Maryland Reg. 1777	E. Griffiths	350	750.00	900.00
77-F-RU-01-040	Soldiers, Private, Mass. Reg. 1778	E. Griffiths	350	750.00	900.00
77-F-RU-01-041	Soldiers, Private, Delaware Reg. 1776	E. Griffiths	350	750.00	900.00
77-F-RU-01-042	Soldiers, Private, Rhode Island Reg. 1781	E. Griffiths	350	750.00	750.00
77-F-RU-01-043	Soldiers, Sergeant, Virginia 1777	E. Griffiths	350	1200.00	3000.00
76-F-RU-01-044	Chipping Sparrow	R. Jefferson	200	750.00	900.00
78-F-RU-01-045	Soldiers, Private, Penn. Rifle Battalion	E. Griffiths	350	750.00	900.00
78-F-RU-01-046	Soldiers, Private, Conn. Reg. 1777	E. Griffiths	350	750.00	1600.00
74-F-RU-01-047	Winston Churchill Bust	E. Griffiths	750	Unknown	Unknown
73-F-RU-01-048	HRH Princess Anne	E. Griffiths	750	Unknown	Unknown
79-F-RU-01-049	Femmes Fatales, Cleopatra	P. Davies	750	750.00	1200.00
81-F-RU-01-050	Femmes Fatales, Helen of Troy	P. Davies	750	1250.00	1250.00
82-F-RU-01-051	Femmes Fatales, Queen of Sheba	P. Davies	750	1250.00	1250.00
83-F-RU-01-052	Femmes Fatales, Tz'w Hsi	P. Davies	750	1250.00	1250.00
84-F-RU-01-053	Femmes Fatales, Eve	P. Davies	750	1250.00	1250.00
85-F-RU-01-054	Femmes Fatales, Lucrezia Borgia	P. Davies	750	1250.00	1250.00
82-F-RU-01-055	Myths and Maidens, Lady and the Unicorn	R. Jefferson	300	2500.00	2500.00
83-F-RU-01-056	Myths and Maidens, Leda and the Swan	R. Jefferson	300	2500.00	2500.00
84-F-RU-01-057	Myths and Maidens, Juno and the Peacock	R. Jefferson	300	2500.00	2500.00
85-F-RU-01-058	Myths and Maidens, Europa and Bull	R. Jefferson	300	2500.00	2500.00
84-F-RU-01-059	Gentle Arts, Spinning	P. Davies	750	1250.00	1250.00
82-F-RU-01-060	Sweet and Twenties, Monte Carlo	P. Davies	1,500	195.00	195.00
82-F-RU-01-061	Sweet and Twenties, Deauville	P. Davies	1,500	195.00	195.00
82-F-RU-01-062	Ships Figureheads, Chieftain	S. Keenan	950	950.00	950.00
82-F-RU-01-063	Ships Figureheads, Pocahontas	S. Keenan	950	950.00	950.00
81-F-RU-01-064	Ships Figureheads, Nelson	S. Keenan	950	950.00	950.00
81-F-RU-01-065	Ships Figureheads, Lalla Roolch	S. Keenan	950	950.00	950.00
80-F-RU-01-066	Ships Figureheads, Benmore	S. Keenan	950	750.00	750.00
80-F-RU-01-067	Ships Figureheads, HMS Ajax	S. Keenan	950	750.00	750.00
82-F-RU-01-068	Ships Figureheads, Mary Queen of Scots	S. Keenan	950	750.00	750.00
82-F-RU-01-069	Ships Figureheads, Hibernia	S. Keenan	950	950.00	950.00
82-F-RU-01-070	HRH Princess of Wales	E. Griffiths	1,500	1200.00	1200.00
82-F-RU-01-071	Lady Diana Spencer	E. Griffiths	1,500	750.00	750.00
81-F-RU-01-072	HRH Princess of Wales, HN 2883	E. Griffiths	1,500	750.00	750.00
81-F-RU-01-073	HRH Prince of Wales, HN 2884	E. Griffiths	1,500	750.00	750.00
79-F-RU-01-074	Dancers of the World-Mexican	P. Davies	750	500.00	800.00
79-F-RU-01-075	Dancers of the World-Kurdish	P. Davies	750	500.00	800.00
80-F-RU-01-076	Dancers of the World-Chinese	P. Davies	750	750.00	750.00
80-F-RU-01-077	Dancers of the World-Polish	P. Davies	750	750.00	750.00
82-F-RU-01-078	Dancers of the World-Balinese	P. Davies	750	950.00	950.00
82-F-RU-01-079	Dancers of the World-North American Indian	P. Davies	750	950.00	950.00
81-F-RU-01-080	Dancers of the World-Breton	P. Davies	750	950.00	950.00
81-F-RU-01-081	Dancers of the World-West Indian	P. Davies	750	850.00	850.00
81-F-RU-01-082	Dancers of the World-Indian Temple	P. Davies	750	400.00	1000.00
85-F-RU-01-083	Gentle Arts, Tapestry Weaving	P. Parsons	750	1250.00	1250.00
85-F-RU-01-084	Richard III/Sir Lawrence Olivier	E. Griffiths	750	650.00	650.00

Figurines

Company / Number	Series / Name	Artist	Edition limit	Issue Price	Quote
77-F-RU-01-085	Winter Wren	R. Jefferson	Open	300.00	375.00
77-F-RU-01-086	Golden Crowned Knight	R. Jefferson	Open	400.00	525.00
77-F-RU-01-087	Downy Woodpecker	R. Jefferson	Open	400.00	525.00
86-F-RU-01-088	Automne HN3068	R. Jefferson	300	795.00	795.00
Royal Worcester	**Dorothy Doughty Porcelains**				
35-F-RZ-01-001	American Redstarts and Hemlock	D. Doughty	66	Unknown	5500.00
41-F-RZ-01-002	Apple Blossoms	D. Doughty	250	400.00	14-3750.
63-F-RZ-01-003	Audobon Warblers	D. Doughty	500	1350.00	21-4200.
38-F-RZ-01-004	Baltimore Orioles	D. Doughty	250	350.00	Unknown
56-F-RZ-01-005	Bewick's Wrens & Yellow Jasmine	D. Doughty	500	600.00	21-3800.
36-F-RZ-01-006	Bluebirds	D. Doughty	350	500.00	85-9000.
64-F-RZ-01-007	Blue Tits & Pussy Willow	D. Doughty	500	250.00	3000.00
40-F-RZ-01-008	Bobwhite Quail	D. Doughty	22	275.00	11000.
59-F-RZ-01-009	Cactus Wrens	D. Doughty	500	1250.00	17-4500.
60-F-RZ-01-010	Canyon Wrens	D. Doughty	500	750.00	2-4,000.
37-F-RZ-01-011	Cardinals	D. Doughty	500	500.00	20-9250.
68-F-RZ-01-012	Carolina Paroquet, Color	D. Doughty	350	1200.00	19-2200.
68-F-RZ-01-013	Carolina Paroquet, White	D. Doughty	75	600.00	Unknown
65-F-RZ-01-014	Cerulean Warblers & Red Maple	D. Doughty	500	1350.00	14-3000.
38-F-RZ-01-015	Chickadees & Larch	D. Doughty	300	350.00	85-8900.
65-F-RZ-01-016	Chuffchaff	D. Doughty	500	1500.00	13-2900.
42-F-RZ-01-017	Crabapple Blossom Sprays And A Butterfly	D. Doughty	250	Unknown	800.00
40-F-RZ-01-018	Crabapples	D. Doughty	250	400.00	37-4250.
67-F-RZ-01-019	Downy Woodpecker & Pecan, Color	D. Doughty	400	1500.00	1-2400.
67-F-RZ-01-020	Downy Woodpecker & Pecan, White	D. Doughty	75	1000.00	1900.00
59-F-RZ-01-021	Elf Owl	D. Doughty	500	875.00	Unknown
55-F-RZ-01-022	Gnatcatchers	D. Doughty	500	600.00	27-4900.
72-F-RZ-01-023	Goldcrests, Pair	D. Doughty	500	4200.00	Unknown
36-F-RZ-01-024	Goldfinches & Thistle	D. Doughty	250	350.00	2-7,000.
68-F-RZ-01-025	Gray Wagtail	D. Doughty	500	600.00	Unknown
61-F-RZ-01-026	Hooded Warblers	D. Doughty	500	950.00	4300.00
50-F-RZ-01-027	Hummingbirds And Fuchsia	D. Doughty	500	Unknown	2800.00
42-F-RZ-01-028	Indigo Bunting And Plum Twig	D. Doughty	5,000	Unknown	Unknown
42-F-RZ-01-029	Indigo Buntings, Blackberry Sprays	D. Doughty	500	375.00	17-3500.
65-F-RZ-01-030	Kingfisher Cock & Autumn Beech	D. Doughty	500	1250.00	19-2300.
52-F-RZ-01-031	Kinglets & Noble Pine	D. Doughty	500	450.00	13-4800.
66-F-RZ-01-032	Lark Sparrow	D. Doughty	500	750.00	Unknown
62-F-RZ-01-033	Lazuli Bunting & Chokecherries, Color	D. Doughty	500	1350.00	3-4,500.
62-F-RZ-01-034	Lazuli Bunting & Chokecherries, White	D. Doughty	100	1350.00	26-3000.
64-F-RZ-01-035	Lesser Whitethroats	D. Doughty	500	350.00	12-4000.
50-F-RZ-01-036	Magnolia Warbler	D. Doughty	150	1100.00	19-3600.
77-F-RZ-01-037	Meadow Pipit	D. Doughty	500	1800.00	1800.00
50-F-RZ-01-038	Mexican Feijoa	D. Doughty	250	600.00	26-4900.
40-F-RZ-01-039	Mockingbirds	D. Doughty	500	450.00	72-7750.
42-F-RZ-01-040	Mockingbirds And Peach Blossom	D. Doughty	500	Unknown	Unknown
64-F-RZ-01-041	Moorhen Chick	D. Doughty	500	1000.00	Unknown
64-F-RZ-01-042	Mountain Bluebirds	D. Doughty	500	950.00	17-2300.
55-F-RZ-01-043	Myrtle Warblers	D. Doughty	500	550.00	13-4000.
71-F-RZ-01-044	Nightingale & Honeysuckle	D. Doughty	500	2500.00	11-2750.
47-F-RZ-01-045	Orange Blossoms & Butterfly	D. Doughty	250	500.00	42-4500.
57-F-RZ-01-046	Ovenbirds	D. Doughty	250	650.00	4500.00
57-F-RZ-01-047	Parula Warblers	D. Doughty	500	600.00	17-3600.
58-F-RZ-01-048	Phoebes On Flame Vine	D. Doughty	500	750.00	22-5500.
52-F-RZ-01-049	Red-Eyed Vireos	D. Doughty	500	450.00	2000.00
68-F-RZ-01-050	Redstarts & Gorse	D. Doughty	500	1900.00	2300.00
64-F-RZ-01-051	Robin	D. Doughty	500	750.00	Unknown
56-F-RZ-01-052	Scarlet Tanagers	D. Doughty	500	675.00	3-4,200.
62-F-RZ-01-053	Scissor-Tailed Flycatcher, Color	D. Doughty	250	950.00	Unknown
62-F-RZ-01-054	Scissor-Tailed Flycatcher, White	D. Doughty	75	950.00	13-1600.
63-F-RZ-01-055	Vermillion Flycatchers	D. Doughty	500	250.00	11-3400.
64-F-RZ-01-056	Wrens & Burnet Rose	D. Doughty	500	650.00	1000.00
52-F-RZ-01-057	Yellow-Headed Blackbirds	D. Doughty	350	650.00	2-2,400.
58-F-RZ-01-058	Yellowthroats on Water Hyacinth	D. Doughty	350	750.00	17-4000.
Royal Worcester	**Frederick Gertner and Neal French Porcelains**				
63-F-RZ-02-001	Colonel Of The Noble Guard	Gertner/French	350	600.00	Unknown
65-F-RZ-02-002	Officer Of The Palatine Guard	Gertner/French	150	500.00	Unknown
67-F-RZ-02-003	Papal Gendarme	Gertner/French	150	450.00	Unknown
59-F-RZ-02-004	Privy Chamberlain Of The Sword & Cape	Gertner/French	150	500.00	Unknown
56-F-RZ-02-005	Trooper Of The Papal Swiss Guard	Gertner/French	150	500.00	Unknown
Royal Worcester	**James Alder Porcelain Sculptures**				
77-F-RZ-03-001	British Bird, Dipper	J. Alder	500	1595.00	1595.00
77-F-RZ-03-002	British Bird, Wall Creeper	J. Alder	500	995.00	995.00
76-F-RZ-03-003	English Bird, Bearded Reedling	J. Alder	500	995.00	995.00
76-F-RZ-03-004	English Bird, Dartford Warbler	J. Alder	500	995.00	995.00
76-F-RZ-03-005	English Bird, Hobby and Swallow	J. Alder	250	6950.00	6950.00
76-F-RZ-03-006	English Bird, Shore Lark	J. Alder	500	995.00	995.00
76-F-RZ-03-007	English Bird, Snow Bunting	J. Alder	500	995.00	995.00
76-F-RZ-03-008	English Bird, Sparrow Hawk & Bullfinch	J. Alder	250	6000.00	6000.00
76-F-RZ-03-009	English Bird, Sparrow Hawk & Bullfinch, Whit	J. Alder	150	3500.00	3500.00
78-F-RZ-03-010	North American Bird, Carolina Wren	J. Alder	150	995.00	995.00
78-F-RZ-03-011	North American Bird,Chestnut Collar Longspurr	J. Alder	150	1900.00	1900.00
78-F-RZ-03-012	North American Bird, Dickeissel	J. Alder	15	1500.00	1500.00
78-F-RZ-03-013	North American Bird, Red-Breasted Nuthatch	J. Alder	150	1250.00	1250.00
78-F-RZ-03-014	North American Bird, Ruby-Crowned Kinglet	J. Alder	150	1250.00	1250.00
78-F-RZ-03-015	North American Bird, Rufous Hummingbird	J. Alder	150	1500.00	1500.00
Royal Worcester	**Doris Lindner Porcelains**				
73-F-RZ-04-001	American Saddle Horse	D. Lindner	750	1450.00	Unknown
61-F-RZ-04-002	Angus Bull	D. Lindner	500	350.00	Unknown
69-F-RZ-04-003	Appaloosa	D. Lindner	750	550.00	12-1500.
63-F-RZ-04-004	Arab Stallion	D. Lindner	500	450.00	Unknown
67-F-RZ-04-005	Arkle	D. Lindner	500	525.00	825.00
68-F-RZ-04-006	Brahma Bull	D. Lindner	500	400.00	Unknown
64-F-RZ-04-007	British Friesian Bull	D. Lindner	500	400.00	800-900.
68-F-RZ-04-008	Bulldog	D. Lindner	500	Unknown	Unknown
68-F-RZ-04-009	Charolais Bull	D. Lindner	500	400.00	800-875.
77-F-RZ-04-010	Clydesdale	D. Lindner	500	1250.00	1250.00
66-F-RZ-04-011	Dairy Shorthorn Bull	D. Lindner	500	475.00	875-900.
68-F-RZ-04-012	Duke of Edinburgh	D. Lindner	750	100.00	Unknown
76-F-RZ-04-013	Duke of Marlborough	D. Lindner	350	5200.00	5200.00
60-F-RZ-04-014	Fox Hunter	D. Lindner	500	500.00	Unknown
75-F-RZ-04-015	Galloping Ponies, Colored	D. Lindner	500	3300.00	Unknown
75-F-RZ-04-016	Galloping, Classic	D. Lindner	250	2500.00	Unknown
76-F-RZ-04-017	Galloping In Winter	D. Lindner	250	3500.00	Unknown
77-F-RZ-04-018	Grundy	D. Lindner	500	1800.00	1800.00
76-F-RZ-04-019	Hackney	D. Lindner	500	1500.00	1500.00
59-F-RZ-04-020	Hereford Bull	D. Lindner	1000	350.00	650-775.
77-F-RZ-04-021	Highland Bull	D. Lindner	500	900.00	900.00
65-F-RZ-04-022	Hyperion	D. Lindner	500	525.00	850.00
64-F-RZ-04-023	Jersey Bull	D. Lindner	500	400.00	900-975.
61-F-RZ-04-024	Jersey Cow	D. Lindner	500	300.00	550-600.
70-F-RZ-04-025	Marion Coakes-Mould	D. Lindner	750	750.00	1500.00
63-F-RZ-04-026	Merano	D. Lindner	500	500.00	1375.00
76-F-RZ-04-027	Mill Reef	D. Lindner	500	2000.00	2000.00
76-F-RZ-04-028	New Born, Color	D. Lindner	500	1800.00	1800.00
76-F-RZ-04-029	New Born, White	D. Lindner	150	1250.00	1250.00
72-F-RZ-04-030	Nijinsky	D. Lindner	500	2000.00	2000.00
61-F-RZ-04-031	Officer of Royal Horse Guards	D. Lindner	150	500.00	Unknown
61-F-RZ-04-032	Officer of The Life Guards	D. Lindner	150	500.00	Unknown
71-F-RZ-04-033	Palomino	D. Lindner	750	975.00	Unknown
66-F-RZ-04-034	Percheron Stallion	D. Lindner	500	725.00	Unknown
71-F-RZ-04-035	Prince's Grace & Foal, Color	D. Lindner	750	1500.00	15-1700.
71-F-RZ-04-036	Prince's Grace & Foal, White	D. Lindner	250	1400.00	14-1600.
73-F-RZ-04-037	Princess Anne On Doublet	D. Lindner	750	4250.00	4250.00
62-F-RZ-04-038	Quarter Horse	D. Lindner	500	400.00	Unknown
47-F-RZ-04-039	Queen Elizabeth on Tommy	D. Lindner	100	275.00	13200.00
76-F-RZ-04-040	Red Rum	D. Lindner	250	2000.00	2000.00
76-F-RZ-04-041	Richard Meade	D. Lindner	500	2450.00	2450.00
66-F-RZ-04-042	Royal Canadian Mounty	D. Lindner	500	875.00	14-1600.
61-F-RZ-04-043	Santa Gertrudis Bull	D. Lindner	500	350.00	675-700.
64-F-RZ-04-044	Shire Stallion	D. Lindner	500	700.00	13-1400.
69-F-RZ-04-045	Suffolk Punch	D. Lindner	500	650.00	975.00
66-F-RZ-04-046	Welsh Mountain Pony	D. Lindner	500	3000.00	25-3000.
Royal Worcester	**Norbert E. J. Roessler Bronzes**				
76-F-RZ-05-001	Hummer, With Fushsia	N. Roessler	500	225.00	225.00
76-F-RZ-05-002	Marlin	N. Roessler	500	250.00	250.00
Royal Worcester	**Van Ruyckevelt Porcelains**				
XX-F-RZ-06-001	Alice	R. Van Ruyckevelt	500	1875.00	1875.00
70-F-RZ-06-002	American Pintail, Pair	R. Van Ruyckevelt	500	Unknown	3000.00
69-F-RZ-06-003	Argenteuil A-108	R. Van Ruyckevelt	338	Unknown	Unknown
60-F-RZ-06-004	Beatrice	R. Van Ruyckevelt	500	125.00	Unknown
68-F-RZ-06-005	Blue Angel Fish	R. Van Ruyckevelt	500	375.00	900.00
67-F-RZ-06-006	Bluefin Tuna	R. Van Ruyckevelt	500	500.00	Unknown
65-F-RZ-06-007	Blue Marlin	R. Van Ruyckevelt	500	500.00	1000.00
69-F-RZ-06-008	Bobwhite Quail, Pair	R. Van Ruyckevelt	500	Unknown	2000.00
69-F-RZ-06-009	Bridget	R. Van Ruyckevelt	500	300.00	600-700.
67-F-RZ-06-010	Butterfly Fish	R. Van Ruyckevelt	500	375.00	1600.00
60-F-RZ-06-011	Caroline	R. Van Ruyckevelt	500	125.00	Unknown
69-F-RZ-06-012	Castelneau Pink	R. Van Ruyckevelt	429	Unknown	825-875.
69-F-RZ-06-013	Castelneau Yellow	R. Van Ruyckevelt	163	Unknown	825-875.
XX-F-RZ-06-014	Cecilia	R. Van Ruyckevelt	500	1875.00	1875.00
68-F-RZ-06-015	Charlotte & Jane	R. Van Ruyckevelt	500	1000.00	15-1650.
68-F-RZ-06-016	Dolphin	R. Van Ruyckevelt	500	500.00	900.00
71-F-RZ-06-017	Elaine	R. Van Ruyckevelt	750	600.00	600-650.
67-F-RZ-06-018	Elizabeth	R. Van Ruyckevelt	750	300.00	750-800.
69-F-RZ-06-019	Emily	R. Van Ruyckevelt	500	300.00	600.00
78-F-RZ-06-020	Esther	R. Van Ruyckevelt	500	Unknown	Unknown
71-F-RZ-06-021	Felicity	R. Van Ruyckevelt	750	600.00	600.00
62-F-RZ-06-022	Flying Fish	R. Van Ruyckevelt	300	400.00	450.00
71-F-RZ-06-023	Green-Winged Teal	R. Van Ruyckevelt	500	1450.00	1450.00
62-F-RZ-06-024	Hibiscus	R. Van Ruyckevelt	500	300.00	350.00
56-F-RZ-06-025	Hogfish & Sergeant Major	R. Van Ruyckevelt	500	375.00	650.00
68-F-RZ-06-026	Honfleur A-105	R. Van Ruyckevelt	290	Unknown	600.00
68-F-RZ-06-027	Honfleur A-106	R. Van Ruyckevelt	290	Unknown	600.00
71-F-RZ-06-028	Languedoc	R. Van Ruyckevelt	216	Unknown	1150.00
59-F-RZ-06-029	Lisette	R. Van Ruyckevelt	500	100.00	Unknown
62-F-RZ-06-030	Louisa	R. Van Ruyckevelt	500	400.00	975.00
68-F-RZ-06-031	Madelaine	R. Van Ruyckevelt	500	300.00	750-800.
68-F-RZ-06-032	Mallards	R. Van Ruyckevelt	500	Unknown	2000.00
68-F-RZ-06-033	Marion	R. Van Ruyckevelt	500	275.00	575-625.
64-F-RZ-06-034	Melanie	R. Van Ruyckevelt	500	150.00	Unknown
68-F-RZ-06-035	Mennecy A-101	R. Van Ruyckevelt	338	Unknown	675-725.
68-F-RZ-06-036	Mennecy A-102	R. Van Ruyckevelt	334	Unknown	675-725.
61-F-RZ-06-037	Passionflower	R. Van Ruyckevelt	500	300.00	400.00
59-F-RZ-06-038	Penelope	R. Van Ruyckevelt	500	100.00	Unknown
76-F-RZ-06-039	Picnic	R. Van Ruyckevelt	250	2850.00	2850.00
76-F-RZ-06-040	Queen Elizabeth I	R. Van Ruyckevelt	250	3850.00	3850.00
77-F-RZ-06-041	Queen Elizabeth II	R. Van Ruyckevelt	250	Unknown	Unknown
76-F-RZ-06-042	Queen Mary I	R. Van Ruyckevelt	250	4850.00	4850.00
68-F-RZ-06-043	Rainbow Parrot Fish	R. Van Ruyckevelt	500	1500.00	1500.00
58-F-RZ-06-044	Red Hind	R. Van Ruyckevelt	500	375.00	900.00
68-F-RZ-06-045	Ring-Necked Pheasants	R. Van Ruyckevelt	500	Unknown	32-3400.
64-F-RZ-06-046	Rock Beauty	R. Van Ruyckevelt	500	425.00	850.00
64-F-RZ-06-047	Rosalind	R. Van Ruyckevelt	500	150.00	Unknown
62-F-RZ-06-048	Sailfish	R. Van Ruyckevelt	500	400.00	550.00
69-F-RZ-06-049	Saint Denis A-109	R. Van Ruyckevelt	500	Unknown	925-950.
63-F-RZ-06-050	Sister Of London Hospital	R. Van Ruyckevelt	500	Unknown	475-500.
63-F-RZ-06-051	Sister Of St. Thomas' Hospital	R. Van Ruyckevelt	500	Unknown	475-500.
70-F-RZ-06-052	Sister Of The Red Cross	R. Van Ruyckevelt	750	Unknown	525-550.
66-F-RZ-06-053	Sister Of University College Hospital	R. Van Ruyckevelt	500	Unknown	475-500.
61-F-RZ-06-054	Squirrelfish	R. Van Ruyckevelt	500	400.00	9000.00
66-F-RZ-06-055	Swordfish	R. Van Ruyckevelt	500	575.00	650.00
64-F-RZ-06-056	Tarpon	R. Van Ruyckevelt	500	500.00	975.00
64-F-RZ-06-057	Tea Party	R. Van Ruyckevelt	250	1000.00	22-2400.
72-F-RZ-06-058	White Doves	R. Van Ruyckevelt	25	3600.00	27,850.
Royal Worcester	**Bernard Winskill Porcelains**				
77-F-RZ-07-001	By A Short Head	B. Winskill	100	5000.00	5000.00
76-F-RZ-07-002	Duke Of Marlborough	B. Winskill	350	5200.00	Unknown
70-F-RZ-07-003	Duke Of Wellington	B. Winskill	750	4500.00	Unknown
76-F-RZ-07-004	Exmoor Pony	B. Winskill	500	895.00	Unknown
76-F-RZ-07-005	George Washington, Bronze	B. Winskill	15	6000.00	Unknown
76-F-RZ-07-006	George Washington, Horseback	B. Winskill	750	4000.00	Unknown
69-F-RZ-07-007	Napoleon Bonaparte	B. Winskill	750	3500.00	3500.00
76-F-RZ-07-008	Shetland Pony	B. Winskill	500	795.00	795.00

Number	Name	Artist	Edition limit	Issue Price	Quote
Royal Worcester		**Birds and Flowers of America Sculptures**			
84-F-RZ-08-001	The Swallow and Wild Rose	D. Friar	9800	135.00	135.00
84-F-RZ-08-002	The Robin and Narcissus	D. Friar	9800	135.00	135.00
84-F-RZ-08-003	The Cardinal and Downy Hawthorne	D. Friar	9800	135.00	135.00
84-F-RZ-08-004	The Bluebird and Fir	D. Friar	9800	135.00	135.00
84-F-RZ-08-005	The Goldfinch and Dogwood	D. Friar	9800	135.00	135.00
84-F-RZ-08-006	The Chickadee and Daisy	D. Friar	9800	135.00	135.00
84-F-RZ-08-007	The Kingfisher and Water Lily	D. Friar	9800	135.00	135.00
84-F-RZ-08-008	The Wren and Blackberry	D. Friar	9800	135.00	135.00
Royal Worcester		**Royal Worcester Great American Birds of Prey**			
85-F-RZ-09-001	Bald Eagle	D. Friar	9800	195.00	195.00
85-F-RZ-09-002	Peregrine Falcon	D. Friar	9800	195.00	195.00
85-F-RZ-09-003	Screech Owl	D. Friar	9800	195.00	195.00
85-F-RZ-09-004	American Kestral	D. Friar	9800	195.00	195.00
85-F-RZ-09-005	Coopers Hawk	D. Friar	9800	195.00	195.00
85-F-RZ-09-006	Gyrfalcon	D. Friar	9800	195.00	195.00
85-F-RZ-09-007	Red Tail Hawk	D. Friar	9800	195.00	195.00
85-F-RZ-09-008	Great Horned Owl	D. Friar	9800	195.00	195.00
Schmid/B.F.A.		**Don Polland Figurines I**			
83-F-SD-01-001	Young Bull	D. Polland	2,750	125.00	125.00
83-F-SD-01-002	Escape	D. Polland	2,500	175.00	175.00
83-F-SD-01-003	Fighting Bulls	D. Polland	2,500	200.00	200.00
83-F-SD-01-004	Hot Pursuit	D. Polland	2,500	225.00	225.00
83-F-SD-01-005	The Hunter	D. Polland	2,500	225.00	225.00
83-F-SD-01-006	Downed	D. Polland	2,500	250.00	250.00
83-F-SD-01-007	Challenge	D. Polland	2,000	275.00	275.00
83-F-SD-01-008	A Second Chance	D. Polland	2,000	350.00	350.00
83-F-SD-01-009	Dangerous Moment	D. Polland	2,000	250.00	250.00
83-F-SD-01-010	The Great Hunt	D. Polland	350	3750.00	3750.00
86-F-SD-01-011	Running Wolf - War Chief	D. Polland	2,500	170.00	170.00
86-F-SD-01-012	Eagle Dancer	D. Polland	2,500	170.00	170.00
86-F-SD-01-013	Plains Warrior	D. Polland	1,250	350.00	350.00
86-F-SD-01-014	Second Chance	D. Polland	2,000	125.00	125.00
86-F-SD-01-015	Shooting The Rapids	D. Polland	2,500	195.00	195.00
86-F-SD-01-016	Down From The High Country	D. Polland	2,250	225.00	225.00
86-F-SD-01-017	War Trophy	D. Polland	2,250	225.00	225.00
Schmid/B.F.A.		**Davis Country Pride Figurines**			
81-F-SD-10-001	Surprise in the Cellar	L. Davis	2,500	100.00	250.00
81-F-SD-10-002	Plum Tuckered Out	L. Davis	2,500	100.00	250.00
81-F-SD-10-003	Duke's Mixture	L. Davis	2,500	100.00	150.00
81-F-SD-10-004	Bustin' with Pride	L. Davis	2,500	100.00	100.00
Schmid/B.F.A.		**Lowell Davis Figurines**			
79-F-SD-11-001	Country Road	L. Davis	Closed	120.00	275.00
79-F-SD-11-002	Ignorance is Bliss	L. Davis	Closed	165.00	350.00
79-F-SD-11-003	Blossom	L. Davis	Closed	180.00	700.00
79-F-SD-11-004	Fowl Play	L. Davis	Closed	100.00	250.00
79-F-SD-11-005	Slim Pickins	L. Davis	Closed	185.00	275.00
82-F-SD-11-006	Broken Dreams	L. Davis	Closed	185.00	225.00
82-F-SD-11-007	Up To No Good	L. Davis	900	200.00	250.00
82-F-SD-11-008	Punkin Seeds	L. Davis	750	250.00	550.00
82-F-SD-11-009	Moon Raiders	L. Davis	900	180.00	200.00
82-F-SD-11-010	Blossom and Calf	L. Davis	1,000	250.00	275.00
83-F-SD-11-011	Treed	L. Davis	1,250	155.00	165.00
83-F-SD-11-012	Hi Girls/Call Me Big Jack	L. Davis	2,500	200.00	210.00
83-F-SD-11-013	City Slicker	L. Davis	1,500	150.00	165.00
83-F-SD-11-014	Happy Hunting Ground	L. Davis	1,750	160.00	175.00
83-F-SD-11-015	Stirring Up Trouble	L. Davis	2,500	160.00	175.00
83-F-SD-11-016	Eyes Bigger Than Stomach	L. Davis	2,250	235.00	250.00
84-F-SD-11-017	Anybody Home	L. Davis	Unkn.	35.00	37.50
84-F-SD-11-018	Headed Home	L. Davis	Unkn.	25.00	27.50
84-F-SD-11-019	One for the Road	L. Davis	Unkn.	37.50	41.25
84-F-SD-11-020	Huh?	L. Davis	Unkn.	40.00	42.50
84-F-SD-11-021	Gonna Pay for His Sins	L. Davis	Unkn.	27.50	30.00
84-F-SD-11-022	His Master's Dog	L. Davis	Unkn.	45.00	47.50
84-F-SD-11-023	Pasture Pals	L. Davis	Unkn.	52.00	55.00
84-F-SD-11-024	Country Kitty	L. Davis	Unkn.	52.00	55.00
84-F-SD-11-025	Catnapping Too	L. Davis	Unkn.	70.00	75.00
84-F-SD-11-026	Gossips	L. Davis	Unkn.	110.00	115.00
84-F-SD-11-027	Prairie Chorus	L. Davis	950	135.00	250.00
84-F-SD-11-028	Mad as a Wet Hen	L. Davis	950	185.00	195.00
85-F-SD-11-029	Country Crooner	L. Davis	Unkn.	25.00	27.50
85-F-SD-11-030	Barn Cats	L. Davis	Unkn.	39.50	42.50
85-F-SD-11-031	Don't Play with Your Food	L. Davis	Unkn.	28.50	30.00
85-F-SD-11-032	Out-of-Step	L. Davis	Unkn.	45.00	47.50
85-F-SD-11-033	Renoir	L. Davis	Unkn.	45.00	47.50
85-F-SD-11-034	Too Good to Waste on Kids	L. Davis	Unkn.	70.00	75.00
85-F-SD-11-035	Will You Respect Me in the Morning	L. Davis	Unkn.	35.00	37.50
85-F-SD-11-036	Country Cousins	L. Davis	Unkn.	42.50	45.00
85-F-SD-11-037	Love at First Sight	L. Davis	Unkn.	70.00	75.00
85-F-SD-11-038	Furs Gonna Fly	L. Davis	950	145.00	150.00
85-F-SD-11-039	Hog Heaven	L. Davis	950	165.00	175.00
85-F-SD-11-040	Home from Market	L. Davis	1,200	400.00	450.00
86-F-SD-11-041	Comfy?	L. Davis	Unkn.	39.00	40.00
86-F-SD-11-042	Feelin' His Oats	L. Davis	1,500	150.00	165.00
86-F-SD-11-043	Mama?	L. Davis	Unkn.	15.00	16.50
86-F-SD-11-044	Bit Off More Than He Could Chew	L. Davis	Unkn.	15.00	16.50
87-F-SD-11-045	Mail Order Bride	L. Davis	Unkn.	150.00	150.00
87-F-SD-11-046	Glutton for Punishment	L. Davis	Unkn.	95.00	95.00
87-F-SD-11-047	Easy Pickins	L. Davis	Unkn.	45.00	45.00
87-F-SD-11-048	Bottoms Up	L. Davis	Unkn.	80.00	80.00
87-F-SD-11-049	The Orphans	L. Davis	Unkn.	50.00	50.00
87-F-SD-11-050	When the Cat's Away	L. Davis	Unkn.	40.00	40.00
87-F-SD-11-051	Two in the Bush	L. Davis	Unkn.	150.00	150.00
87-F-SD-11-052	Chicken Thief	L. Davis	Unkn.	200.00	200.00
80-F-SD-11-053	Country Crook	L. Davis	Closed	37.50	60.00
80-F-SD-11-054	Forbidden Fruit	L. Davis	Closed	32.50	32.50
80-F-SD-11-055	Milking Time	L. Davis	Closed	32.50	32.50
80-F-SD-11-056	Sunday Afternoon	L. Davis	Closed	32.50	32.50
80-F-SD-11-057	Wilbur	L. Davis	Closed	110.00	110.00
80-F-SD-11-058	Creek Bank Bandit	L. Davis	Closed	50.00	50.00
80-F-SD-11-059	Idle Hours	L. Davis	Closed	37.50	37.50
80-F-SD-11-060	Licking Good	L. Davis	Closed	35.00	35.00
80-F-SD-11-061	False Alarm	L. Davis	Closed	65.00	65.00
80-F-SD-11-063	Courtin	L. Davis	Closed	50.00	50.00
80-F-SD-11-064	Two's Company	L. Davis	Closed	43.50	45.00

Number	Name	Artist	Edition limit	Issue Price	Quote
80-F-SD-11-065	A Shoe to Fill	L. Davis	Closed	37.50	40.00
80-F-SD-11-066	Waiting for His Master	L. Davis	Closed	50.00	50.00
80-F-SD-11-067	Split Decision	L. Davis	Closed	45.00	65.00
80-F-SD-11-068	Double Trouble	L. Davis	Closed	42.50	100.00
80-F-SD-11-069	Country Boy	L. Davis	Closed	45.00	65.00
80-F-SD-11-070	Hightailing It	L. Davis	Closed	50.00	65.00
80-F-SD-11-071	Studio Mouse	L. Davis	Closed	60.00	85.00
80-F-SD-11-072	Dry as a Bone	L. Davis	Closed	45.00	60.00
80-F-SD-11-073	Baby Bobs	L. Davis	Closed	47.50	65.00
80-F-SD-11-074	Moving Day	L. Davis	Closed	43.50	60.00
80-F-SD-11-075	Brand New Day	L. Davis	Closed	23.50	60.00
80-F-SD-11-076	When Mama Gets Mad	L. Davis	Closed	37.50	55.00
Schmid/B.F.A.		**Farm Set**			
85-F-SD-12-001	Privy	L. Davis	Unkn.	12.50	12.50
85-F-SD-12-002	Windmill	L. Davis	Unkn.	25.00	25.00
85-F-SD-12-003	Remus' Cabin	L. Davis	Unkn.	42.50	42.50
85-F-SD-12-004	Main House	L. Davis	Unkn.	42.50	42.50
85-F-SD-12-005	Barn	L. Davis	Unkn.	47.50	47.50
85-F-SD-12-006	Goat Yard and Studio	L. Davis	Unkn.	32.50	32.50
85-F-SD-12-007	Corn Crib and Sheep Pen	L. Davis	Unkn.	25.00	25.00
85-F-SD-12-008	Hog House	L. Davis	Unkn.	27.50	27.50
85-F-SD-12-009	Hen House	L. Davis	Unkn.	32.50	32.50
85-F-SD-12-010	Smoke House	L. Davis	Unkn.	12.50	12.50
85-F-SD-12-011	Chicken House	L. Davis	Unkn.	19.00	19.00
85-F-SD-12-012	Garden and Wood Shed	L. Davis	Unkn.	25.00	25.00
Schmid/B.F.A.		**Davis Cat Tales Figurines**			
82-F-SD-13-001	Right Church, Wrong Pew	L. Davis	4,000	70.00	85.00
82-F-SD-13-002	Company's Coming	L. Davis	4,000	60.00	85.00
82-F-SD-13-003	On the Move	L. Davis	4,000	70.00	85.00
82-F-SD-13-004	Flew the Coop	L. Davis	4,000	60.00	85.00
Schmid/B.F.A.		**Davis Special Edition Figurines**			
83-F-SD-14-001	The Critics	L. Davis	1,200	400.00	500.00
85-F-SD-14-002	Home from Market	L. Davis	1,200	400.00	495.00
Schmid/B.F.A.		**Davis Christmas Figurine**			
83-F-SD-15-001	Country Christmas	L. Davis	2,500	80.00	100.00
84-F-SD-15-002	Country Christmas	L. Davis	2,500	80.00	85.00
85-F-SD-15-003	Country Christmas	L. Davis	2,500	80.00	80.00
86-F-SD-15-004	Country Christmas	L. Davis	2,500	80.00	80.00
87-F-SD-15-005	Blossom's Gift	L. Davis	2,500	150.00	150.00
Schmid/B.F.A.		**Foxfire Farm Club**			
85-F-SD-17-001	The Bride	L. Davis	Unkn.	45.00	45.00
87-F-SD-17-002	The Party's Over	L. Davis	Unkn.	50.00	50.00
Schmid/B.F.A.		**Country Pride**			
79-F-SD-18-001	Surprise in the Cellar	L. Davis	2,500	100.00	225.00
79-F-SD-18-002	Plum Tuckered Out	L. Davis	2,500	100.00	275.00
79-F-SD-18-003	Bustin' with Pride	L. Davis	2,500	100.00	225.00
79-F-SD-18-004	Duke's Mixture	L. Davis	2,500	100.00	200.00
Schmid/B.F.A.		**Uncle Remus**			
79-F-SD-19-001	Brer Fox	L. Davis	Closed	70.00	150.00
79-F-SD-19-002	Brer Bear	L. Davis	Closed	80.00	150.00
79-F-SD-19-003	Brer Rabbit	L. Davis	Closed	85.00	175.00
79-F-SD-19-004	Brer Wolf	L. Davis	Closed	85.00	150.00
79-F-SD-19-005	Brer Weasel	L. Davis	Closed	80.00	150.00
79-F-SD-19-006	Brer Coyote	L. Davis	Closed	80.00	150.00
Swarovski America		**Mini Animal Series**			
XX-F-SW-01-001	Sparrow	Unknown	Open	16.00	20.00
XX-F-SW-01-002	Chicken	Unknown	Open	16.00	20.00
XX-F-SW-01-003	Rabbit	Unknown	Open	16.00	20.00
XX-F-SW-01-004	Duck	Unknown	Open	16.00	20.00
XX-F-SW-01-005	Owl	Unknown	Open	16.00	20.00
XX-F-SW-01-006	Mouse	Unknown	Open	16.00	20.00
XX-F-SW-01-007	Pig	Unknown	Open	16.00	20.00
XX-F-SW-01-008	Swan	Unknown	Open	16.00	20.00
XX-F-SW-01-009	Cat	Unknown	Open	16.00	20.00
XX-F-SW-01-010	Drake	Unknown	Open	20.00	30.00
XX-F-SW-01-011	Penguin	Unknown	Open	16.00	22.00
XX-F-SW-01-012	Squirrel	Unknown	Open	20.00	30.00
XX-F-SW-01-013	Baby Seal	Unknown	Open	20.00	30.00
XX-F-SW-01-014	Swimming Duck	Unknown	Open	16.00	22.00
XX-F-SW-01-015	Bear	Unknown	Open	16.00	22.00
XX-F-SW-01-016	Butterfly	Unknown	Open	20.00	30.00
XX-F-SW-01-017	Dachshund	Unknown	Open	20.00	30.00
86-F-SW-01-018	Standing Duck	Unknown	Open	21.00	22.00
87-F-SW-01-019	Blowfish	Unknown	Open	22.00	22.00
Swarovski America		**Animal Series**			
XX-F-SW-02-001	Small Hedgehog	Unknown	Open	38.00	40.00
XX-F-SW-02-002	Medium Hedgehog	Unknown	Open	44.00	50.00
XX-F-SW-02-003	Large Hedgehog	Unknown	Open	65.00	65.00
XX-F-SW-02-004	King Size Hedgehog	Unknown	Open	98.00	100.00
XX-F-SW-02-005	Small Mouse	Unknown	Open	38.00	38.00
XX-F-SW-02-006	Medium Mouse	Unknown	Open	48.00	50.00
XX-F-SW-02-007	Large Mouse	Unknown	Open	69.00	70.00
XX-F-SW-02-008	King Size Mouse	Unknown	Open	95.00	100.00
XX-F-SW-02-009	Small Turtle	Unknown	Open	38.00	38.00
XX-F-SW-02-010	Large Turtle	Unknown	Open	48.00	55.00
XX-F-SW-02-011	King Size Turtle	Unknown	Open	58.00	70.00
XX-F-SW-02-012	Small Swan	Unknown	Open	35.00	35.00
XX-F-SW-02-013	Medium Swan	Unknown	Open	44.00	44.00
XX-F-SW-02-014	Large Swan	Unknown	Open	55.00	60.00
XX-F-SW-02-015	Medium Cat	Unknown	Open	38.00	38.00
XX-F-SW-02-016	Large Cat	Unknown	Open	44.00	44.00
XX-F-SW-02-017	Dog	Unknown	Open	44.00	44.00
XX-F-SW-02-018	Small Owl	Unknown	Open	59.00	59.00
XX-F-SW-02-019	Large Owl	Unknown	Open	90.00	90.00
XX-F-SW-02-020	Small Bear	Unknown	Open	44.00	44.00
XX-F-SW-02-021	Large Bear	Unknown	Open	75.00	75.00
XX-F-SW-02-022	King Size Bear	Unknown	Open	95.00	100.00
XX-F-SW-02-023	Giant Size Bear	Unknown	Open	125.00	170.00
XX-F-SW-02-024	Medium Pig	Unknown	Open	35.00	35.00
XX-F-SW-02-025	Large Pig	Unknown	Open	65.00	65.00
XX-F-SW-02-026	Butterfly	Unknown	Open	44.00	55.00
XX-F-SW-02-027	Elephant	Unknown	Open	90.00	90.00
XX-F-SW-02-028	Dachshund	Unknown	Open	48.00	50.00
XX-F-SW-02-029	Frog	Unknown	Open	30.00	35.00

Figurines

Company Number	Name	Series Artist	Edition limit	Issue Price	Quote
XX-F-SW-02-030	Large Penguin	Unknown	Open	44.00	60.00
XX-F-SW-02-031	Large Blowfish	Unknown	Open	40.00	55.00
XX-F-SW-02-032	Falcon Head	Unknown	Open	600.00	600.00
XX-F-SW-02-033	Large Sparrow	Unknown	Open	38.00	38.00
XX-F-SW-02-034	Large Rabbit	Unknown	Open	38.00	38.00
XX-F-SW-02-035	Medium Duck	Unknown	Open	38.00	38.00
XX-F-SW-02-036	Large Duck	Unknown	Open	48.00	48.00
XX-F-SW-02-037	Large Seal	Unknown	Open	44.00	55.00
86-F-SW-02-038	Mallard	Unknown	Open	80.00	80.00
86-F-SW-02-039	Small Blowfish	Unknown	Open	35.00	35.00
86-F-SW-02-040	Snail	Unknown	Open	35.00	35.00
87-F-SW-02-041	Togetherness - Lovebirds	M. Schreck	Yr.Iss	150.00	150.00
87-F-SW-02-042	Small Falcon Head	Unknown	Open	60.00	60.00
87-F-SW-02-043	Large Polar Bear	Unknown	Open	140.00	140.00
Swarovski America		**Giant Series**			
XX-F-SW-03-001	Turtle	Unknown	Open	2500.00	3000.00
XX-F-SW-03-002	Owl	Unknown	Open	1200.00	1500.00
XX-F-SW-03-003	Pineapple	Unknown	Open	1750.00	2400.00
87-F-SW-03-004	Mallard	Unknown	Open	2,000.00	2,000.00
Swarovski America		**Various**			
XX-F-SW-04-001	Small Apple	Unknown	Open	40.00	50.00
XX-F-SW-04-002	Large Apple	Unknown	Open	80.00	100.00
XX-F-SW-04-003	King Size Apple	Unknown	Open	120.00	130.00
XX-F-SW-04-004	Large Pinapple	Unknown	Open	150.00	150.00
XX-F-SW-04-005	Small Grapes	Unknown	Open	200.00	200.00
XX-F-SW-04-006	Medium Grapes	Unknown	Open	300.00	300.00
XX-F-SW-04-007	Large Grapes	Unknown	Open	250.00	250.00
XX-F-SW-04-008	Chess Set	Unknown	Open	950.00	950.00
XX-F-SW-04-009	Butterfly	Unknown	Open	200.00	200.00
XX-F-SW-04-010	Hummingbird	Unknown	Open	200.00	200.00
XX-F-SW-04-011	Bee	Unknown	Open	200.00	200.00
XX-F-SW-04-012	Bird Bath	Unknown	Open	150.00	150.00
86-F-SW-04-013	Small Pineapple	Unknown	Open	55.00	55.00
87-F-SW-04-014	Birds' Nest	Unknown	Open	90.00	90.00
Tay Porcelains		**Tay Porcelains**			
XX-F-TA-01-001	Turtledoves, group of two, 10 inches	Unknown	500	Unknown	500.00
70-F-TA-01-002	Blue Jay, 13 inches	Unknown	500	375.00	675.00
70-F-TA-01-003	Eagle, 12 inches x 15 inches	Unknown	500	1000.00	1650.00
70-F-TA-01-004	European Woodcock 10.5 inches	Unknown	500	325.00	550.00
70-F-TA-01-005	Limpkin, 20 inches	Unknown	500	600.00	1100.00
71-F-TA-01-006	Falcon, 13 inches	Unknown	500	500.00	925.00
71-F-TA-01-007	Pheasant, 30 inches	Unknown	500	1500.00	2-2700.
71-F-TA-01-008	Quail Group, 10 inches	Unknown	500	400.00	725.00
71-F-TA-01-009	Roadrunner, 10 x 19 inches	Unknown	500	800.00	Unknown
72-F-TA-01-010	Gray Partridge, 11.5 inches	Unknown	500	800.00	1400.00
74-F-TA-01-011	American Woodcock, 10.5 inches	Unknown	500	625.00	700.00
74-F-TA-01-012	Mallard Duck, 13.5 inches	Unknown	500	900.00	1050.00
74-F-TA-01-013	Mallard Duck, Flying, 15 inches	Unknown	500	550.00	675.00
74-F-TA-01-014	Owl, 10.5 inches	Unknown	500	350.00	450.00
74-F-TA-01-015	Turtledoves on Roof Tile, 9.5 inches	Unknown	500	335.00	375.00
75-F-TA-01-016	Carolina Ducks, group of two, 13 inches	Unknown	500	1350.00	1500.00
75-F-TA-01-017	Smergos Ducks, group of two, 10 inches	Unknown	500	1000.00	1100.00
75-F-TA-01-018	White-Throated Sparrow, 5.5 inches	Unknown	500	360.00	400.00
76-F-TA-01-019	Bluebirds, group of two, 9.5 inches	Unknown	500	500.00	550.00
76-F-TA-01-020	Custer on Horse, 13 x 14.5 inches	Unknown	500	1500.00	1500.00
73-F-TA-01-021	Austrian Officer on Horseback	Unknown	100	1200.00	12-1500.
74-F-TA-01-022	Gyrfalcon, 18 inches	Unknown	300	1250.00	1500.00
74-F-TA-01-023	Boreal Chickadee, 7 inches	Unknown	5,000	275.00	360.00
74-F-TA-01-024	Great Crested Flycatcher, 9 inches	Unknown	1,000	300.00	360.00
75-F-TA-01-025	Oriole, 9.5 inches	Unknown	1,000	300.00	325.00
76-F-TA-01-026	Indian on Horse, 13 x 14.5 inches	Unknown	500	1500.00	1500.00
76-F-TA-01-027	Robin, 8 inches	Unknown	500	400.00	450.00
Tengra		**Romantic Figures**			
86-F-TE-01-001	Girl - 985	Unknown	Open	200.00	200.00
86-F-TE-01-002	Girl with Doves - 953	Unknown	Open	125.00	125.00
78-F-TE-01-003	Dancing Couple - 963	Unknown	Open	235.00	235.00
86-F-TE-01-004	Woman - 986	Unknown	Open	165.00	165.00
87-F-TE-01-005	Ballerina - 991	Unknown	Open	235.00	235.00
87-F-TE-01-006	Sitting Thinking - 1021	Unknown	Open	270.00	270.00
87-F-TE-01-007	Sitting Distracted - 1022	Unknown	Open	270.00	270.00
87-F-TE-01-008	Sitting Relaxed - 1023	Unknown	Open	270.00	270.00
Tengra		**Country Style**			
82-F-TE-02-001	Shepherd - 909	Unknown	Open	100.00	100.00
82-F-TE-02-002	Shepherdess - 910	Unknown	Open	90.00	90.00
78-F-TE-02-003	Hunter - 588	Unknown	Open	110.00	110.00
Tengra		**Clowns**			
84-F-TE-03-001	Clown with Violin - 796	Unknown	Open	190.00	190.00
84-F-TE-03-002	Clown with Fiddle - 800	Unknown	Open	190.00	190.00
87-F-TE-03-003	Clown with Saxophone - 1001	Unknown	Open	125.00	125.00
87-F-TE-03-004	Clown with Fiddle - 1003	Unknown	Open	125.00	125.00
87-F-TE-03-005	Clown with Accordion - 1008	Unknown	Open	125.00	125.00
87-F-TE-03-006	Clown with Cymbals - 1009	Unknown	Open	125.00	125.00
87-F-TE-03-007	Clown with Parrot - 997	Unknown	Open	220.00	220.00
87-F-TE-03-008	Clown with Monkee - 1007	Unknown	Open	210.00	210.00
Tengra		**Contemporary Style**			
87-F-TE-04-001	Contemporary Style A - 2011	Unknown	Open	200.00	200.00
87-F-TE-04-002	Contemporary Style B - 2012	Unknown	Open	245.00	245.00
87-F-TE-04-003	Contemporary Style B - 2013	Unknown	Open	290.00	290.00
87-F-TE-04-004	Oval Style A - 2041	Unknown	Open	260.00	260.00
87-F-TE-04-005	Oval Style B - 2043	Unknown	Open	260.00	260.00
87-F-TE-04-006	Babylonian Group - 2032	Unknown	Open	1075.00	1075.00
87-F-TE-04-007	Babylonian Kneeling - 2033	Unknown	Open	495.00	495.00
87-F-TE-04-008	Babylonian Open Arms - 2034	Unknown	Open	585.00	585.00
87-F-TE-04-009	Fantasy G - 2035	Unknown	Open	220.00	220.00
87-F-TE-04-010	Fantasy M - 2036	Unknown	Open	200.00	200.00
87-F-TE-04-011	Fantasy P - 2037	Unknown	Open	180.00	180.00
87-F-TE-04-012	Fantasy B - 2038	Unknown	Open	180.00	180.00
Tengra		**Contemporary Style:The White Series**			
87-F-TE-05-001	Clown with Parrot - 998	Unknown	Open	240.00	240.00
87-F-TE-05-002	Woman - 999	Unknown	Open	185.00	185.00
87-F-TE-05-003	Clown with Saxophone - 1002	Unknown	Open	145.00	145.00
87-F-TE-05-004	Clown with Fiddle - 1004	Unknown	Open	145.00	145.00
87-F-TE-05-005	Girl - 1000	Unknown	Open	220.00	220.00

Figurines/Graphics

Company Number	Name	Series Artist	Edition limit	Issue Price	Quote
87-F-TE-05-006	Clown with Accordion - 1010	Unknown	Open	145.00	145.00
87-F-TE-05-007	Clown with Cymbals - 1011	Unknown	Open	145.00	145.00
Vague Shadows		**Single Issue**			
84-F-VC-01-001	Babysitter Musical Fig.	G. Perillo	2,500	65.00	90.00
Vague Shadows		**The Professionals**			
80-F-VC-02-001	The Big Leaguer	G. Perillo	10,000	65.00	120.00
80-F-VC-02-002	Ballerina's Dilemma	G. Perillo	10,000	65.00	65.00
81-F-VC-02-003	The Quarterback	G. Perillo	10,000	65.00	65.00
82-F-VC-02-004	Rodeo Joe	G. Perillo	10,000	65.00	65.00
82-F-VC-02-005	Major Leaguer	G. Perillo	10,000	65.00	100.00
83-F-VC-02-006	Hockey Player	G. Perillo	10,000	65.00	100.00
Vague Shadows		**The Storybook Collection**			
80-F-VC-03-001	Little Red Ridinghood	G. Perillo	10,000	65.00	65.00
81-F-VC-03-002	Cinderella	G. Perillo	10,000	65.00	65.00
82-F-VC-03-003	Hansel and Gretel	G. Perillo	10,000	80.00	80.00
82-F-VC-03-004	Goldilocks & 3 Bears	G. Perillo	10,000	80.00	80.00
Vague Shadows		**The Princesses**			
84-F-VC-04-001	Lily of the Mohawks	G. Perillo	1,500	65.00	100.00
84-F-VC-04-002	Pocahontas	G. Perillo	1,500	65.00	75.00
84-F-VC-04-003	Minnehaha	G. Perillo	1,500	65.00	75.00
84-F-VC-04-004	Sacajawea	G. Perillo	1,500	65.00	75.00
Vague Shadows		**The Chieftains**			
83-F-VC-05-001	Sitting Bull	G. Perillo	5,000	65.00	375.00
83-F-VC-05-002	Joseph	G. Perillo	5,000	65.00	100.00
83-F-VC-05-003	Red Cloud	G. Perillo	5,000	65.00	135.00
83-F-VC-05-004	Geronimo	G. Perillo	5,000	65.00	80.00
83-F-VC-05-005	Crazy Horse	G. Perillo	5,000	65.00	140.00
Vague Shadows		**Child Life**			
83-F-VC-06-001	Siesta	G. Perillo	2,500	65.00	65.00
84-F-VC-06-002	Sweet Dreams	G. Perillo	1,500	65.00	65.00
Vague Shadows		**Special Issue**			
85-F-VC-07-001	Lovers	G. Perillo	Unkn.	70.00	70.00
Vague Shadows		**Special Issue**			
84-F-VC-08-001	Papoose	G. Perillo	325	500.00	500.00
Vague Shadows		**Special Issue**			
82-F-VC-09-001	The Peaceable Kingdom	G. Perillo	950	750.00	1000.00
Vague Shadows		**Perillo Collector Club Piece**			
83-F-VC-10-001	Apache Brave	G. Perillo	Unkn.	50.00	130.00
Vague Shadows		**The Little Indians**			
82-F-VC-11-001	Blue Spruce	G. Perillo	10,000	50.00	50.00
82-F-VC-11-002	White Rabbit	G. Perillo	10,000	50.00	50.00
82-F-VC-11-003	Tender Love	G. Perillo	10,000	65.00	65.00
Vague Shadows		**Special Issue**			
84-F-VC-12-001	Apache Boy Bust	G. Perillo	Unkn.	40.00	40.00
84-F-VC-12-002	Navajo Girl Bust	G. Perillo	Unkn.	40.00	40.00
Vague Shadows		**The War Pony**			
83-F-VC-13-001	Sioux War Pony	G. Perillo	495	150.00	200.00
83-F-VC-13-002	Nez Perce Pony	G. Perillo	495	150.00	200.00
83-F-VC-13-003	Apache War Pony	G. Perillo	495	150.00	200.00
Vague Shadows		**The Tribal Ponies**			
84-F-VC-14-001	Arapaho	G. Perillo	1,500	65.00	65.00
84-F-VC-14-002	Comanche	G. Perillo	1,500	65.00	65.00
84-F-VC-14-003	Crow	G. Perillo	1,500	65.00	95.00
Vague Shadows		**Annual Christmas Ornament Figurines**			
85-F-VC-15-001	Papoose Ornament	G. Perillo	Unkn.	14.00	14.00
86-F-VC-15-002	Christmas Cactus	G. Perillo	Unkn.	15.00	15.00
87-F-VC-15-003	Annual Ornament	G. Perillo	Unkn.	15.00	15.00

Graphics

Company Number	Name	Series Artist	Edition limit	Issue Price	Quote
American Legacy		**Etem**			
XX-G-AL-01-001	Indiana Summer	S. Etem	Closed	150.00	150.00
XX-G-AL-01-002	Little Bandit	S. Etem	Closed	150.00	150.00
XX-G-AL-01-003	The Fountain	S. Etem	Closed	150.00	150.00
Anna-Perenna		**Krumeich Hector's Window**			
XX-G-AN-01-001	Genuine Stone Litho	T. Krumeich	325	175.00	225.00
XX-G-AN-01-002	13-Color Litho, framed	T. Krumeich	995	95.00	95.00
Arabia Annual		**Various**			
XX-G-AR-01-001	Navajo Portrait	O. Weighorst	1,000	75.00	150.00
XX-G-AR-01-002	Buffalo Scout	O. Weighorst	1,000	100.00	350.00
XX-G-AR-01-003	California Wrangler	O. Weighorst	1,000	100.00	200.00
XX-G-AR-01-004	Missing in the Roundup	O. Weighorst	1,000	100.00	200.00
XX-G-AR-01-005	Packing In	O. Weighorst	1,000	100.00	200.00
XX-G-AR-01-006	Corralling the Cavvy	O. Weighorst	1,000	100.00	200.00
XX-G-AR-01-007	Boys in the Bunkhouse	O. Weighorst	1,000	150.00	200.00
Blue River Mill Publishing Company, Inc.		**The Old Road Series**			
73-G-BH-01-001	Mail Pouch Barn, S/N	R. Day	500	15.00	175.00
73-G-BH-01-002	Mail Pouch Barn, signed	R. Day	2,000	10.00	75.00
74-G-BH-01-003	Rock City Barn, S/N	R. Day	500	15.00	75.00
74-G-BH-01-004	Rock City Barn, signed	R. Day	2,000	10.00	75.00
75-G-BH-01-005	Burma-Shave Country, S/N	R. Day	500	15.00	50.00
75-G-BH-01-006	Burma-Shave Country, signed	R. Day	2,000	10.00	Unknown
77-G-BH-01-007	Coca Cola Country, S/N	R. Day	750	20.00	175.00
77-G-BH-01-008	Coca Cola Country, signed	R. Day	1,250	15.00	50.00
79-G-BH-01-009	Country General Store, S/N	R. Day	1,000	25.00	70.00
80-G-BH-01-010	The Old Mill, S/N	R. Day	1,000	25.00	100.00
81-G-BH-01-011	An Old Covered Bridge, S/N	R. Day	1,000	35.00	70.00
81-G-BH-01-012	Country Station, S/N	R. Day	1,000	35.00	70.00
82-G-BH-01-013	Mail Pouch, Mail Pouch S/N	R. Day	1,000	35.00	250.00
82-G-BH-01-014	Country Church, S/N	R. Day	1,000	35.00	70.00
83-G-BH-01-015	Reel Refreshing, S/N	R. Day	1,000	35.00	35.00
84-G-BH-01-016	Country Schoolhouse, S/N	R. Day	1,000	40.00	40.00
85-G-BH-01-017	Ruby Falls, S/N	R. Day	1,000	40.00	40.00
85-G-BH-01-018	Rust of Ages, S/N	R. Day	1,000	40.00	40.00
86-G-BH-01-019	Summer Coolers, S/N	R. Day	1,000	40.00	40.00
86-G-BH-01-020	Back Road Bargins, S/N	R. Day	1,000	40.00	40.00
Blue River Mill Publishing Company, Inc.		**The Seasons Series**			
83-G-BH-02-001	Rural Church in Autumn, S/N	R. Day	1,000	20.00	20.00
83-G-BH-02-002	Grist Mill in Winter, S/N	R. Day	1,000	20.00	20.00
84-G-BH-02-003	Covered Bridge in Spring, S/N	R. Day	1,000	20.00	20.00
84-G-BH-02-004	Farmstead in Summer, S/N	R. Day	1,000	20.00	20.00

Company / Number	Series / Name	Artist	Edition limit	Issue Price	Quote
Blue River Mill Publishing Company, Inc.	**The Country Cousins Series**				
76-G-BH-03-001	Pops Corn, S/N	R. Day	500	10.00	45.00
76-G-BH-03-002	Pops Corn, signed	R. Day	500	7.50	45.00
76-G-BH-03-003	Mother's Basket, S/N	R. Day	500	10.00	45.00
76-G-BH-03-004	Mother's Basket, signed	R. Day	500	7.50	45.00
78-G-BH-03-005	Strawberries and Daisies, S/N	R. Day	1,000	25.00	140.00
79-G-BH-03-006	Eggs in the Basket, S/N	R. Day	1,000	25.00	25.00
80-G-BH-03-007	Pumpkins and Jugs, S/N	R. Day	1,000	30.00	50.00
81-G-BH-03-008	Gernamiums, S/N	R. Day	1,000	30.00	30.00
81-G-BH-03-009	The Collection, S/N	R. Day	1,000	30.00	30.00
82-G-BH-03-010	Peaches on the Porch, S/N	R. Day	1,000	30.00	30.00
83-G-BH-03-011	Honeysuckle and Roses, S/N	R. Day	1,000	30.00	30.00
84-G-BH-03-012	Strawberry Days, S/N	R. Day	1,000	30.00	30.00
85-G-BH-03-013	October Patch, S/N	R. Day	1,000	30.00	30.00
Blue River Mill Publishing Company, Inc.	**The Medart Series**				
80-G-BH-04-01	Articles of Administration, S/N	R. Day	3,000	35.00	35.00
84-G-BH-04-02	Commitment to Life, S/N	R. Day	1,500	50.00	50.00
Brad Bennett Studio	**Kenosha**				
81-G-BL-01-001	Monument	B. Bennett	1,000	30.00	30.00
81-G-BL-01-002	Monument, proof	B. Bennett	25	30.00	30.00
81-G-BL-01-003	First Ship of the Season	B. Bennett	1,000	30.00	30.00
81-G-BL-01-004	First Ship of the Season, proof	B. Bennett	25	30.00	30.00
81-G-BL-01-005	Evolution/Saltwater Port	B. Bennett	1,000	30.00	30.00
81-G-BL-01-006	Evolution/Saltwater Port, proof	B. Bennett	25	30.00	30.00
81-G-BL-01-007	North Shore Trolley	B. Bennett	1,000	30.00	30.00
81-G-BL-01-008	North Shore Trolley, proof	B. Bennett	25	30.00	30.00
81-G-BL-01-009	Petrifying Springs	B. Bennett	1,000	30.00	30.00
81-G-BL-01-010	Petrifying Springs, proof	B. Bennett	25	30.00	30.00
81-G-BL-01-011	Stormy Harbor	B. Bennett	1,000	30.00	30.00
81-G-BL-01-012	Stormy Harbor,proof	B. Bennett	25	30.00	30.00
81-G-BL-01-013	Harvest Time	B. Bennett	1,000	30.00	30.00
81-G-BL-01-014	Harvest Time, proof	B. Bennett	25	30.00	30.00
81-G-BL-01-015	Winter Cannon	B. Bennett	1,000	30.00	30.00
81-G-BL-01-016	Winter Cannon, proof	B. Bennett	25	30.00	30.00
81-G-BL-01-017	Kemper Center	B. Bennett	1,000	30.00	30.00
81-G-BL-01-018	Kemper Center, proof	B. Bennett	25	30.00	30.00
81-G-BL-01-019	See How They Run	B. Bennett	1,000	30.00	30.00
81-G-BL-01-020	See How They Run, proof	B. Bennett	25	30.00	30.00
81-G-BL-01-021	Bike Races	B. Bennett	1,000	30.00	30.00
81-G-BL-01-022	Bike Races, proof	Kenosha	25	30.00	30.00
81-G-BL-01-023	Cohorama	B. Bennett	1,000	30.00	30.00
81-G-BL-01-024	Cohorama, proof	B. Bennett	25	30.00	30.00
Brad Bennett Studio	**King Richard's Faire**				
82-G-BL-02-001	King Richard & His Court	B. Bennett	1,000	30.00	30.00
82-G-BL-02-002	King Richard & His Court, proof	B. Bennett	25	30.00	30.00
82-G-BL-02-003	Toothsome Wench	B. Bennett	1,000	30.00	30.00
82-G-BL-02-004	Toothsome Wench, proof	B. Bennett	25	30.00	30.00
82-G-BL-02-005	The Queen's Dancers	B. Bennett	1,000	30.00	30.00
82-G-BL-02-006	The Queen's Dancers, proof	B. Bennett	25	30.00	30.00
82-G-BL-02-007	The Sorcerer	B. Bennett	1,000	30.00	30.00
82-G-BL-02-008	The Sorcerer, proof	B. Bennett	25	30.00	30.00
82-G-BL-02-009	Dressing for Battle	B. Bennett	1,000	30.00	30.00
82-G-BL-02-010	Dressing for Battle, proof	B. Bennett	25	30.00	30.00
82-G-BL-02-011	Village Jesters	B. Bennett	1,000	30.00	30.00
82-G-BL-02-012	Village Jesters, proof	B. Bennett	25	30.00	30.00
82-G-BL-02-013	Absolution	B. Bennett	1,000	30.00	30.00
82-G-BL-02-014	Absolution, proof	B. Bennett	25	30.00	30.00
82-G-BL-02-015	Human Chess Game	B. Bennett	1,000	30.00	30.00
82-G-BL-02-016	Human Chess Game, proof	B. Bennett	25	30.00	30.00
82-G-BL-02-017	Baptism of the Beggars	B. Bennett	1,000	30.00	30.00
82-G-BL-02-018	Baptism of the Beggars, proof	B. Bennett	25	30.00	30.00
82-G-BL-02-019	The Joust	B. Bennett	1,000	30.00	30.00
82-G-BL-02-020	The Joust, proof	B. Bennett	25	30.00	30.00
Brad Bennett Studio	**Chicago**				
83-G-BL-03-001	Michigan Avenue	B. Bennett	1,000	30.00	120.00
83-G-BL-03-002	Michgan Avenue, proof	B. Bennett	25	30.00	30.00
83-G-BL-03-003	Buckingham Fountain	B. Bennett	1,000	30.00	30.00
83-G-BL-03-004	Buckingham Fountain, proof	B. Bennett	25	30.00	30.00
83-G-BL-03-005	Oak Street Beach	B. Bennett	1,000	30.00	30.00
83-G-BL-03-006	Oak Street Beach, proof	B. Bennett	25	30.00	30.00
83-G-BL-03-007	Mack Race	B. Bennett	1,000	30.00	30.00
83-G-BL-03-008	Mack Race, proof	B. Bennett	25	30.00	30.00
83-G-BL-03-009	Wrigley Field	B. Bennett	1,000	30.00	120.00
83-G-BL-03-010	Wrigley Field, proof	B. Bennett	25	30.00	30.00
83-G-BL-03-011	Chicago Elevated Railway	B. Bennett	1,000	30.00	30.00
83-G-BL-03-012	Chicago Elevated Railway, proof	B. Bennett	25	30.00	30.00
83-G-BL-03-013	Chicago Mercantile Exchange	B. Bennett	1,000	30.00	30.00
83-G-BL-03-014	Chicago Mercantile Exchange, proof	B. Bennett	25	30.00	30.00
83-G-BL-03-015	St. Patrick's Day Parade	B. Bennett	1,000	30.00	30.00
83-G-BL-03-016	St. Patrick's Day Parade, proof	B. Bennett	25	30.00	30.00
83-G-BL-03-017	Lincoln Park Zoo	B. Bennett	1,000	30.00	30.00
83-G-BL-03-018	Lincoln Park Zoo, proof	B. Bennett	25	30.00	30.00
83-G-BL-03-019	Art Institute of Chicago	B. Bennett	1,000	30.00	30.00
83-G-BL-03-020	Art Institute of Chicago, proof	B. Bennett	25	30.00	30.00
83-G-BL-03-021	Chinese New Year	B. Bennett	1,000	30.00	30.00
83-G-BL-03-022	Chinese New Year, proof	B. Bennett	25	30.00	30.00
83-G-BL-03-023	Burnham Park	B. Bennett	1,000	30.00	30.00
83-G-BL-03-024	Burnham Park, proof	B. Bennett	25	30.00	30.00
Brad Bennett Studio	**Houston**				
83-G-BL-04-001	Sam Houston	B. Bennett	1,000	30.00	30.00
83-G-BL-04-002	Sam Houston, proof	B. Bennett	25	30.00	30.00
83-G-BL-04-003	Highways and Skyways	B. Bennett	1,000	30.00	30.00
83-G-BL-04-004	Highways and Skyways, proof	B. Bennett	25	30.00	30.00
83-G-BL-04-005	Houston Ship Channel	B. Bennett	1,000	30.00	30.00
83-G-BL-04-006	Houston Ship Channel, proof	B. Bennett	25	30.00	30.00
83-G-BL-04-007	Green Tug Churning	B. Bennett	1,000	30.00	30.00
83-G-BL-04-008	Green Tug Churning, proof	B. Bennett	25	30.00	30.00
83-G-BL-04-009	The Refinery	B. Bennett	1,000	30.00	30.00
83-G-BL-04-010	The Refinery, proof	B. Bennett	25	30.00	30.00
83-G-BL-04-011	Tranquility Park	B. Bennett	1,000	30.00	30.00
83-G-BL-04-012	Tranquility Park, proof	B. Bennett	25	30.00	30.00
83-G-BL-04-013	Galleria	B. Bennett	1,000	30.00	30.00
83-G-BL-04-014	Galleria, proof	B. Bennett	25	30.00	30.00
83-G-BL-04-015	N.A.S.A.	B. Bennett	1,000	30.00	30.00
83-G-BL-04-016	N.A.S.A., proof	B. Bennett	25	30.00	30.00

Company / Number	Series / Name	Artist	Edition limit	Issue Price	Quote
83-G-BL-04-017	Let's Rodeo	B. Bennett	1,000	30.00	30.00
83-G-BL-04-018	Let's Rodeo, proof	B. Bennett	25	30.00	30.00
83-G-BL-04-019	Trail Rider	B. Bennett	1,000	30.00	30.00
83-G-BL-04-020	Trail Rider, proof	B. Bennett	25	30.00	30.00
83-G-BL-04-021	Azalea Trail-Bayou Bend	B. Bennett	1,000	30.00	30.00
83-G-BL-04-022	Azalea Trail-Bayou Bend, proof	B. Bennett	25	30.00	30.00
83-G-BL-04-023	Houston Festival	B. Bennett	1,000	30.00	30.00
83-G-BL-04-024	Houston Festival, proof	B. Bennett	25	30.00	30.00
Brad Bennett Studio	**Ireland**				
84-G-BL-05-001	Adare Cottages	B. Bennett	500	85.00	85.00
84-G-BL-05-002	Dingle at Low Tide	B. Bennett	500	85.00	85.00
84-G-BL-05-003	Creamery	B. Bennett	500	85.00	85.00
84-G-BL-05-004	O'Donoghue's Pub	B. Bennett	500	85.00	85.00
Brad Bennett Studio	**University of Wisconsin**				
84-G-BL-06-001	Bascom Hall	B. Bennett	1,000	75.00	75.00
84-G-BL-06-002	Carillon Tower	B. Bennett	1,000	75.00	75.00
84-G-BL-06-003	Union Terrace	B. Bennett	1,000	75.00	75.00
84-G-BL-06-004	Wisconsin Crew	B. Bennett	1,000	75.00	75.00
Brad Bennett Studio	**Bennett**				
84-G-BL-07-001	Chicago Mercantile Exchange	B. Bennett	500	95.00	95.00
84-G-BL-07-002	Wrigley Field II	B. Bennett	2,000	100.00	125.00
Brad Bennett Studio	**World Trading Centers**				
85-G-BL-08-001	Chicago Board of Trade	B. Bennett	2,500	125.00	125.00
85-G-BL-08-002	Midwest Stock Exchange	B. Bennett	2,500	125.00	125.00
Brad Bennett Studio	**Special Issue**				
85-G-BL-09-001	Al's Run	B. Bennett	1,000	75.00	75.00
Brad Bennett Studio	**Chicago Collection**				
83-G-BL-10-001	Chicago (lithographs, narratives)	B. Bennett	1,000	350.00	410.00
Brad Bennett Studio	**King Richard's Faire Collection**				
82-G-BL-11-001	King Richard's Faire (lithographs, narrative)	B. Bennett	1,000	250.00	300.00
Brad Bennett Studio	**Kenosha Collection**				
82-G-BL-12-001	Kenosha (lithographs, narratives)	B. Bennett	1,000	240.00	350.00
Brad Bennett Studio	**Houston Collection**				
83-G-BL-13-001	Houston (lithographs, narrative)	B. Bennett	1,000	300.00	300.00
Brad Bennett Studio	**The United States of America: Volume I**				
86-G-BL-14-001	Fourth of July	B. Bennett	5,000	1000.00	1000.00
86-G-BL-14-002	Mount Rushmore	B. Bennett	5,000	Suite	Suite
86-G-BL-14-003	Washington, D.C., Jefferson Memorial	B. Bennett	5,000	Suite	Suite
86-G-BL-14-004	Black Sands of Hawaii	B. Bennett	5,000	Suite	Suite
86-G-BL-14-005	Michigan Avenue, Chicago	B. Bennett	5,000	Suite	Suite
86-G-BL-14-006	San Francisco Cable Car	B. Bennett	5,000	Suite	Suite
86-G-BL-14-007	Refinery, Houston	B. Bennett	5,000	Suite	Suite
86-G-BL-14-008	Pennsylvania Amish Farmer	B. Bennett	5,000	Suite	Suite
86-G-BL-14-009	Keywest Shrimp Boats	B. Bennett	5,000	Suite	Suite
86-G-BL-14-010	Main Lobster Trap Floats	B. Bennett	5,000	Suite	Suite
86-G-BL-14-011	The Grand Canyon	B. Bennett	5,000	Suite	Suite
86-G-BL-14-012	Blizzard	B. Bennett	5,000	Suite	Suite
Brad Bennett Studio	**The United States of America: Volume II**				
87-G-BL-15-001	USA (lithographs, narratives)	B. Bennett	5,000	1000.00	1000.00
Circle Fine Arts	**Neiman**				
XX-G-CF-01-001	Pool Room	L. Neiman	350	Unknown	1500.00
XX-G-CF-01-002	Deuce	L. Neiman	275	Unknown	1950.00
XX-G-CF-01-003	Sailing	L. Neiman	275	Unknown	1400.00
XX-G-CF-01-004	Chipping On	L. Neiman	275	Unknown	1200.00
XX-G-CF-01-005	In the Stretch	L. Neiman	250	Unknown	1100.00
XX-G-CF-01-006	Punchinello	L. Neiman	250	Unknown	1100.00
XX-G-CF-01-007	Pierrot	L. Neiman	250	Unknown	850.00
XX-G-CF-01-008	Harlequin with Sword	L. Neiman	250	Unknown	850.00
XX-G-CF-01-009	Ocelot	L. Neiman	250	Unknown	1700.00
XX-G-CF-01-010	Sudden Death	L. Neiman	250	Unknown	2050.00
XX-G-CF-01-011	Hommage to Boucher	L. Neiman	250	Unknown	1100.00
XX-G-CF-01-012	12 Meter Yacht Race	L. Neiman	250	Unknown	1500.00
XX-G-CF-01-013	Roulette	L. Neiman	40	Unknown	4200.00
XX-G-CF-01-014	Pierrot the Juggler	L. Neiman	200	Unknown	850.00
XX-G-CF-01-015	Harlequin	L. Neiman	200	Unknown	850.00
XX-G-CF-01-016	Punchinello with Text	L. Neiman	200	Unknown	1300.00
XX-G-CF-01-017	Harlequin with Text	L. Neiman	200	Unknown	850.00
XX-G-CF-01-019	Tiger	L. Neiman	300	Unknown	4800.00
XX-G-CF-01-020	Tennis Player	L. Neiman	300	Unknown	1200.00
XX-G-CF-01-021	The Race	L. Neiman	300	Unknown	1000.00
XX-G-CF-01-022	Stock Market	L. Neiman	300	Unknown	7600.00
XX-G-CF-01-023	Jockey	L. Neiman	300	Unknown	1300.00
XX-G-CF-01-024	Casino	L. Neiman	300	Unknown	1800.00
XX-G-CF-01-025	Paddock	L. Neiman	300	Unknown	1300.00
XX-G-CF-01-026	Sliding Home	L. Neiman	300	Unknown	1600.00
XX-G-CF-01-027	Skier	L. Neiman	300	Unknown	1200.00
XX-G-CF-01-028	Four Aces	L. Neiman	300	Unknown	1200.00
XX-G-CF-01-029	Slalom	L. Neiman	300	Unknown	1200.00
XX-G-CF-01-030	Leopard	L. Neiman	300	Unknown	8100.00
XX-G-CF-01-031	Al Capone	L. Neiman	300	Unknown	1100.00
XX-G-CF-01-032	Hockey Player	L. Neiman	300	Unknown	2500.00
XX-G-CF-01-033	Tee Shot	L. Neiman	300	Unknown	1550.00
XX-G-CF-01-034	End Around	L. Neiman	300	Unknown	1400.00
XX-G-CF-01-035	Lion Pride	L. Neiman	300	Unknown	6700.00
XX-G-CF-01-036	Marathon	L. Neiman	300	Unknown	1500.00
XX-G-CF-01-037	Scramble	L. Neiman	300	Unknown	1500.00
XX-G-CF-01-038	Downhill	L. Neiman	300	Unknown	1500.00
XX-G-CF-01-039	Innsbruck	L. Neiman	300	Unknown	1500.00
XX-G-CF-01-040	Doubles	L. Neiman	300	Unknown	2850.00
XX-G-CF-01-041	Trotters	L. Neiman	300	Unknown	1550.00
XX-G-CF-01-042	Goal	L. Neiman	300	Unknown	1200.00
XX-G-CF-01-043	Backhand	L. Neiman	300	Unknown	1150.00
XX-G-CF-01-044	Slapshot	L. Neiman	300	Unknown	1300.00
XX-G-CF-01-045	Fox Hunt	L. Neiman	300	Unknown	1200.00
XX-G-CF-01-046	Smash	L. Neiman	300	Unknown	1450.00
Curator Collection	**Sauber**				
82-G-CX-01-001	Butterfly	R. Sauber	3,000	45.00	45.00
Derby Collection	**Etem**				
XX-G-DD-01-001	Picnickin'	S. Etem	350	125.00	125.00
XX-G-DD-01-002	Lisa's Loving Arms	S. Etem	350	150.00	150.00
85-G-DD-01-003	On Your Mark	S. Etem	350	80.00	80.00
85-G-DD-01-004	Susan	S. Etem	350	95.00	95.00

Number	Name	Artist	Edition limit	Issue Price	Quote
Ernst Enterprises		**Rockwell**			
XX-G-EB-01-001	Little League	N. Rockwell	2,000	65.00	65.00
Ernst Enterprises		**Money**			
XX-G-EB-02-001	Somedays I Just Don't Feel Loved	R. Money	675	95.00	95.00
XX-G-EB-02-002	Scarlet Ribbons	R. Money	675	95.00	95.00
Ernst Enterprises		**Morton**			
XX-G-EB-03-001	John Wayne	S. Morton	2,000	50.00	50.00
Frame House Gallery		**Harrison**			
XX-G-FG-01-001	American Byways, S/N	J. Harrison	1,500	40.00	220.00
XX-G-FG-01-002	Brush and Bucket, S/N	J. Harrison	300	300.00	Unknown
XX-G-FG-01-003	Bull of the Woods, S/N	J. Harrison	1,500	75.00	125.00
XX-G-FG-01-004	Burma Shave, S/N	J. Harrison	1,500	50.00	200.00
XX-G-FG-01-005	Clabber Girl	J. Harrison	1,500	75.00	200.00
XX-G-FG-01-006	Coca-Cola	J. Harrison	Open	12.00	12.00
XX-G-FG-01-007	Coca-Cola Bridge, S/N	J. Harrison	975	135.00	135.00
XX-G-FG-01-008	Community Church, S/N	J. Harrison	1,500	50.00	100.00
XX-G-FG-01-009	Country Seasonin', S/N	J. Harrison	1,500	40.00	225.00
XX-G-FG-01-010	Disappearing America, S/N	J. Harrison	1,500	40.00	950.00
XX-G-FG-01-011	Dr. Pepper, S/N	J. Harrison	1,500	50.00	200.00
XX-G-FG-01-012	Fallow and Forgotten, S/N	J. Harrison	1,500	50.00	85.00
XX-G-FG-01-013	Fillin' Station, S/N	J. Harrison	1,500	80.00	110.00
XX-G-FG-01-014	Fishing Village, S/N	J. Harrison	975	135.00	200.00
XX-G-FG-01-015	Fishing Village Remarque	J. Harrison	Open	195.00	260.00
XX-G-FG-01-016	Fresh Grits, S/N	J. Harrison	1,500	80.00	400.00
XX-G-FG-01-017	Fresh Grits, exclusive S/N	J. Harrison	100	Unknown	Unknown
XX-G-FG-01-018	Gold Dust Twins, S/N	J. Harrison	1,500	55.00	75.00
XX-G-FG-01-019	Goody's S/N	J. Harrison	1,500	50.00	100.00
XX-G-FG-01-020	House and Barn, pair, S/N	J. Harrison	1,500	50.00	80.00
XX-G-FG-01-021	Lee Overalls	J. Harrison	Unkn.	7.50	Unknown
XX-G-FG-01-022	Lighthouse, S/N	J. Harrison	975	135.00	200.00
XX-G-FG-01-023	Lighthouse Remarque	J. Harrison	Unkn.	195.00	260.00
XX-G-FG-01-024	Lucky Strike, S/N	J. Harrison	1,500	50.00	200.00
XX-G-FG-01-025	Memories I, S/N	J. Harrison	408	90.00	150.00
XX-G-FG-01-026	Memories I, S/NR	J. Harrison	342	135.00	235.00
XX-G-FG-01-027	Memories II, S/N	J. Harrison	431	90.00	150.00
XX-G-FG-01-028	Memories II, S/NR	J. Harrison	319	135.00	235.00
XX-G-FG-01-029	Morton Salt and Rock City, S/N	J. Harrison	1,500	135.00	200.00
XX-G-FG-01-030	Mountain Bridge, S/N	J. Harrison	1,500	80.00	130.00
XX-G-FG-01-031	Old Dutch Cleanser, S/N	J. Harrison	1,500	75.00	125.00
XX-G-FG-01-032	Old Stone Barn, S/N	J. Harrison	1,500	90.00	110.00
XX-G-FG-01-033	Peanuts and Pepsi pr., S/N	J. Harrison	1,500	60.00	160.00
XX-G-FG-01-034	Philip Morris, S/N	J. Harrison	1,500	50.00	185.00
XX-G-FG-01-035	Railroad Crossing, S/N	J. Harrison	1,500	75.00	130.00
XX-G-FG-01-036	Red Covered Bridge, S/N	J. Harrison	1,500	50.00	150.00
XX-G-FG-01-037	Red Goose Shoes, S/N	J. Harrison	1,500	90.00	110.00
XX-G-FG-01-038	Road, The S/N	J. Harrison	500	250.00	Unknown
XX-G-FG-01-039	Rural Americana, S/N	J. Harrison	1,500	40.00	300.00
XX-G-FG-01-040	Rural Delivery, S/N	J. Harrison	1,500	40.00	325.00
XX-G-FG-01-041	Sand Dunes and Inlet Marsh pr.,S/N	J. Harrison	1,500	75.00	Unknown
XX-G-FG-01-042	7-Up and Blackeyed Susans, S/N	J. Harrison	1,500	75.00	125.00
XX-G-FG-01-043	Signs of the Times, S	J. Harrison	3,000	45.00	Unknown
XX-G-FG-01-044	666 Cold Tablets, S/N	J. Harrison	1,500	50.00	150.00
XX-G-FG-01-045	Shrine Circus, S/N	J. Harrison	1,500	80.00	135.00
XX-G-FG-01-046	Shrine Circus Exclusive, S/N	J. Harrison	1,000	Unknown	Unknown
XX-G-FG-01-047	Spring Clouds, S/N	J. Harrison	1,500	90.00	110.00
XX-G-FG-01-048	Tonic and Liniment (pr.), S/N	J. Harrison	1,500	85.00	140.00
XX-G-FG-01-049	Tools, S/N	J. Harrison	300	275.00	400.00
XX-G-FG-01-050	Tools (artist proof), S/N	J. Harrison	50	325.00	450.00
XX-G-FG-01-051	Tube Rose Snuff, S/N	J. Harrison	1,500	60.00	100.00
XX-G-FG-01-052	Unpainted Covered Bridge, S/N	J. Harrison	1,500	60.00	100.00
XX-G-FG-01-053	Windmill, S/N	J. Harrison	1,500	75.00	90.00
XX-G-FG-01-054	Woodpile, S/N	J. Harrison	1,500	75.00	90.00
XX-G-FG-01-055	Yesteryear, S/N	J. Harrison	1,500	50.00	120.00
Frame House Gallery		**Hunt**			
XX-G-FG-02-001	Canada Goose, S/N	A. Hunt	1,500	65.00	Unknown
XX-G-FG-02-002	Fox in Reeds, S/N	A. Hunt	1,500	75.00	135.00
XX-G-FG-02-003	Lazy Afternoon, S/N	A. Hunt	1,500	75.00	175.00
XX-G-FG-02-004	Mallards, S/N	A. Hunt	1,500	75.00	Unknown
XX-G-FG-02-005	Mandarin-Ducklings, S/N	A. Hunt	1,500	35.00	Unknown
XX-G-FG-02-006	Red-tailed Hawk, S/N	A. Hunt	1,500	75.00	150.00
XX-G-FG-02-007	Snow Leopard, S/N	A. Hunt	1,000	150.00	Unknown
XX-G-FG-02-008	Solitaire, S/N	A. Hunt	1,500	90.00	Unknown
XX-G-FG-02-009	Tender Moment, S/N	A. Hunt	1,500	75.00	150.00
XX-G-FG-02-010	Tiger Cub, S/N	A. Hunt	1,500	45.00	Unknown
Gartlan USA		**Lithograph**			
86-G-GB-01-001	George Brett - "The Swing"	J. Martin	2,000	85.00	85.00
87-G-GB-01-002	Roger Staubach	C. Soileau	1,979	85.00	85.00
Graphics Buying Service		**Stone**			
79-G-GT-03-001	Mare and Foal	F. Stone	500	90.00	400.00
79-G-GT-03-002	Affirmed, Steve Cauthen Up	F. Stone	750	100.00	400.00
79-G-GT-03-003	The Rivals-Affirmed & Alydar	F. Stone	500	90.00	500.00
79-G-GT-03-004	Patience	F. Stone	1,000	90.00	750.00
79-G-GT-03-005	One, Two, Three	F. Stone	500	100.00	775.00
79-G-GT-03-006	The Moment After	F. Stone	500	90.00	300.00
80-G-GT-03-007	Genuine Risk	F. Stone	500	100.00	550.00
80-G-GT-03-008	The Belmont - Bold Forbes	F. Stone	500	100.00	315.00
80-G-GT-03-009	The Kentucky Derby	F. Stone	750	100.00	650.00
80-G-GT-03-010	The Pasture Pest	F. Stone	500	100.00	495.00
80-G-GT-03-011	Exceller - Bill Shoemaker	F. Stone	500	90.00	700.00
80-G-GT-03-012	Spectacular Bid	F. Stone	500	65.00	350.00
80-G-GT-03-013	Kidnapped Mare - Franfreluche	F. Stone	750	115.00	490.00
81-G-GT-03-014	The Shoe - 8,000 Wins	F. Stone	395	200.00	2000.00
81-G-GT-03-015	The Arabians	F. Stone	750	115.00	400.00
81-G-GT-03-016	The Thoroughbreds	F. Stone	750	115.00	350.00
81-G-GT-03-017	Contentment	F. Stone	750	115.00	350.00
81-G-GT-03-018	John Henry	F. Stone	595	160.00	900.00
82-G-GT-03-019	Off and Running	F. Stone	750	125.00	350.00
82-G-GT-03-020	The Water Trough	F. Stone	750	125.00	400.00
82-G-GT-03-021	The Power Horses	F. Stone	750	125.00	200.00
82-G-GT-03-022	Man O' War	F. Stone	750	175.00	1800.00
83-G-GT-03-023	For Only a Moment - Ruffian	F. Stone	750	175.00	400.00
83-G-GT-03-024	The Duel	F. Stone	750	150.00	350.00
83-G-GT 03-025	The Andalusian	F. Stone	Unkn.	150.00	325.00
83-G-GT-03-026	Tranquility	F. Stone	Unkn.	150.00	350.00
83-G-GT-03-027	Secretariat	F. Stone	Unkn.	175.00	500.00
84-G-GT-03-028	Turning for Home	F. Stone	Unkn.	150.00	370.00
84-G-GT-03-029	Northern Dancer	F. Stone	Unkn.	175.00	300.00
85-G-GT-03-030	John Henry-McCarron Up	F. Stone	Unkn.	175.00	450.00
85-G-GT-03-031	The Legacy	F. Stone	Unkn.	175.00	225.00

Number	Name	Artist	Edition limit	Issue Price	Quote
85-G-GT-03-032	Fred Stone Paints the Sport of Kings	F. Stone	Unkn.	265.00	265.00
85-G-GT-03-033	Kelso	F. Stone	Unkn.	175.00	250.00
86-G-GT-03-034	Ruffian & Foolish Pleasure	F. Stone	Unkn.	175.00	250.00
86-G-GT-03-035	Nijinski II	F. Stone	Unkn.	175.00	200.00
86-G-GT-03-036	Forever Friends	F. Stone	Unkn.	175.00	275.00
86-G-GT-03-037	Lady's Secret	F. Stone	Unkn.	175.00	225.00
Greenwich Workshop		**Doolittle**			
80-G-GW-01-001	Bugged Bear	B. Doolittle	Closed	85.00	265.00
83-G-GW-01-002	Christmas Day, Give or Take a Week	B. Doolittle	Closed	80.00	185.00
82-G-GW-01-003	Eagle's Flight	B. Doolittle	Closed	185.00	1015.00
83-G-GW-01-004	Escape by a Hare	B. Doolittle	Closed	80.00	170.00
84-G-GW-01-005	Forest Has Eyes, The	B. Doolittle	Closed	175.00	750.00
80-G-GW-01-006	Good Omen, The	B. Doolittle	Closed	85.00	1155.00
87-G-GW-01-007	Guardian Spirits	B. Doolittle	13,238	295.00	295.00
84-G-GW-01-008	Let My Spirit Soar	B. Doolittle	Closed	195.00	500.00
79-G-GW-01-009	Pintos	B. Doolittle	Closed	65.00	3500.00
83-G-GW-01-010	Runs With Thunder	B. Doolittle	Closed	150.00	390.00
83-G-GW-01-011	Rushing War Eagle	B. Doolittle	Closed	150.00	395.00
81-G-GW-01-012	Spirit of the Grizzly	B. Doolittle	Closed	150.00	1000.00
86-G-GW-01-013	Two Bears of the Blackfeet	B. Doolittle	2,650	225.00	350.00
85-G-GW-01-014	Two Indian Horses	B. Doolittle	12,253	225.00	850.00
81-G-GW-01-015	Unknown Presence	B. Doolittle	Closed	150.00	575.00
86-G-GW-01-016	Where Silence Speaks,The Art of Bev Doolittle	B. Doolittle	3,500	650.00	850.00
80-G-GW-01-017	Whoo!?	B. Doolittle	Closed	75.00	200.00
85-G-GW-01-018	Wolves of the Crow	B. Doolittle	Closed	225.00	465.00
81-G-GW-01-019	Woodland Encounter	B. Doolittle	Closed	145.00	3500.00
Greenwich Workshop		**McCarthy**			
84-G-GW-02-001	After the Dust Storm	F. McCarthy	Closed	145.00	Unknown
82-G-GW-02-002	Alert	F. McCarthy	Closed	135.00	185.00
84-G-GW-02-003	Along the West Fork	F. McCarthy	Closed	175.00	205.00
78-G-GW-02-004	Ambush, The	F. McCarthy	Closed	125.00	330.00
82-G-GW-02-005	Apache Scout	F. McCarthy	Closed	165.00	275.00
82-G-GW-02-006	Attack on the Wagon Train	F. McCarthy	Closed	150.00	230.00
77-G-GW-02-007	Beaver Men, The	F. McCarthy	Closed	75.00	440.00
80-G-GW-02-008	Before the Charge	F. McCarthy	Closed	115.00	250.00
78-G-GW-02-009	Before the Norther	F. McCarthy	Closed	90.00	540.00
83-G-GW-02-010	Blackfoot Raiders	F. McCarthy	Closed	90.00	170.00
86-G-GW-02-011	Buffalo Runners, The	F. McCarthy	1,000	195.00	195.00
83-G-GW-02-012	Burning the Way Station	F. McCarthy	Closed	175.00	375.00
82-G-GW-02-013	Challenge, The	F. McCarthy	Closed	175.00	275.00
85-G-GW-02-014	Charging the Challenger	F. McCarthy	Closed	150.00	Unknown
86-G-GW-02-015	Children of the Raven	F. McCarthy	1,000	185.00	185.00
77-G-GW-02-016	Comanche Moon	F. McCarthy	Closed	75.00	355.00
86-G-GW-02-017	Comanche War Trail	F. McCarthy	1,000	165.00	185.00
81-G-GW-02-018	Coup, The	F. McCarthy	Closed	125.00	360.00
84-G-GW-02-019	Decoys, The	F. McCarthy	Closed	325.00	475.00
77-G-GW-02-020	Distant Thunder	F. McCarthy	Closed	75.00	675.00
86-G-GW-02-021	Drive, The	F. McCarthy	1,000	95.00	95.00
77-G-GW-02-022	Dust Stained Posse	F. McCarthy	Closed	75.00	695.00
85-G-GW-02-023	Fireboat, The	F. McCarthy	Closed	175.00	Unknown
80-G-GW-02-024	Forbidden Land	F. McCarthy	Closed	125.00	325.00
78-G-GW-02-025	Fording, The	F. McCarthy	Closed	75.00	440.00
83-G-GW-02-026	In the Land of the Sparrow Hawk People	F. McCarthy	Closed	165.00	185.00
78-G-GW-02-027	In the Pass	F. McCarthy	Closed	90.00	275.00
81-G-GW-02-028	Headed North	F. McCarthy	Closed	150.00	260.00
76-G-GW-02-029	Hostiles, The	F. McCarthy	Closed	75.00	685.00
74-G-GW-02-030	Hunt, The	F. McCarthy	Closed	75.00	695.00
85-G-GW-02-031	Last Crossing, The	F. McCarthy	550	350.00	420.00
74-G-GW-02-032	Lone Sentinel	F. McCarthy	Closed	55.00	1525.00
79-G-GW-02-033	Loner, The	F. McCarthy	Closed	75.00	425.00
74-G-GW-02-034	Long Column	F. McCarthy	Closed	75.00	975.00
85-G-GW-02-035	Long Knives, The	F. McCarthy	Closed	175.00	Unknown
83-G-GW-02-036	Moonlit Trail	F. McCarthy	Closed	90.00	185.00
78-G-GW-02-037	Night Crossing	F. McCarthy	Closed	75.00	290.00
74-G-GW-02-038	Night They Needed a Good Ribbon Man, The	F. McCarthy	Closed	65.00	365.00
77-G-GW-02-039	Old-Time Mountain Man, An	F. McCarthy	Closed	65.00	365.00
79-G-GW-02-040	On the Warpath	F. McCarthy	Closed	75.00	250.00
83-G-GW-02-041	Out of the Mist They Came	F. McCarthy	Closed	165.00	240.00
76-G-GW-02-042	Packing In	F. McCarthy	Closed	65.00	350.00
79-G-GW-02-043	Prayer, The	F. McCarthy	Closed	90.00	585.00
81-G-GW-02-044	Race with the Hostiles	F. McCarthy	Closed	135.00	220.00
86-G-GW-02-045	Red Bull's War Party	F. McCarthy	1,000	165.00	165.00
79-G-GW-02-046	Retreat to Higher Ground	F. McCarthy	Closed	90.00	280.00
75-G-GW-02-047	Returning Raiders	F. McCarthy	Closed	75.00	495.00
80-G-GW-02-048	Roar of the Norther	F. McCarthy	Closed	90.00	270.00
77-G-GW-02-049	Robe Signal	F. McCarthy	Closed	60.00	445.00
84-G-GW-02-050	Savage Taunt, The	F. McCarthy	Closed	225.00	325.00
78-G-GW-02-051	Single File	F. McCarthy	Closed	75.00	380.00
76-G-GW-02-052	Sioux Warriors	F. McCarthy	Closed	55.00	445.00
75-G-GW-02-053	Smoke Was Their Ally	F. McCarthy	Closed	75.00	395.00
80-G-GW-02-054	Snow Moon	F. McCarthy	Closed	115.00	515.00
81-G-GW-02-055	Surrounded	F. McCarthy	Closed	150.00	265.00
75-G-GW-02-056	Survivor, The	F. McCarthy	Closed	65.00	460.00
80-G-GW-02-057	Time of Decision, A	F. McCarthy	Closed	125.00	285.00
80-G-GW-02-058	The Trooper	F. McCarthy	Closed	90.00	255.00
78-G-GW-02-059	To Battle	F. McCarthy	Closed	75.00	360.00
85-G-GW-02-060	Traders, The	F. McCarthy	1,000	195.00	220.00
83-G-GW-02-061	Under Attack	F. McCarthy	Closed	125.00	190.00
81-G-GW-02-062	Under Hostile Fire	F. McCarthy	Closed	150.00	285.00
75-G-GW-02-063	Waiting for the Escort	F. McCarthy	Closed	75.00	220.00
76-G-GW-02-064	Warrior, The	F. McCarthy	Closed	50.00	500.00
82-G-GW-02-065	Warriors, The	F. McCarthy	Closed	150.00	215.00
84-G-GW-02-066	Watching the Wagons	F. McCarthy	Closed	175.00	245.00
86-G-GW-02-067	Where Tracks Will Be Lost	F. McCarthy	550	350.00	350.00
84-G-GW-02-068	Whirling He Raced to Meet the Challenge	F. McCarthy	Closed	175.00	280.00
Greenwich Workshop		**Wysocki**			
83-G-GW-03-001	Amish Neighbors	C. Wysocki	Closed	150.00	160.00
83-G-GW-03-002	Applebutter Makers	C. Wysocki	Closed	135.00	160.00
84-G-GW-03-003	Bird House	C. Wysocki	Closed	85.00	95.00
79-G-GW-03-004	Butternut Farms	C. Wysocki	Closed	75.00	405.00
80-G-GW-03-005	Caleb's Buggy Barn	C. Wysocki	Closed	80.00	105.00
84-G-GW-03-006	Cape Cod Cold Fish Party	C. Wysocki	Closed	150.00	150.00
81-G-GW-03-007	Carver Coggins	C. Wysocki	Closed	145.00	220.00
82-G-GW-03-008	Christmas Print, 1982	C. Wysocki	Closed	80.00	435.00
85-G-GW-03-009	Clammers at Hodge's Horn	C. Wysocki	Closed	150.00	Unknown

Number	Name	Artist	Edition limit	Issue Price	Quote
83-G-GW-03-010	Commemorative Print, 1983	C. Wysocki	2,000	55.00	55.00
84-G-GW-03-011	Cotton Country	C. Wysocki	1,000	150.00	150.00
83-G-GW-03-012	Country Race	C. Wysocki	Closed	150.00	170.00
86-G-GW-03-013	Daddy's Coming Home	C. Wysocki	1,250	150.00	150.00
86-G-GW-03-014	Dancing Pheasant Farms	C. Wysocki	1,750	165.00	165.00
80-G-GW-03-015	Derby Square	C. Wysocki	Closed	90.00	255.00
86-G-GW-03-016	Devilbelly Bay	C. Wysocki	1,000	145.00	145.00
79-G-GW-03-017	Fairhaven by the Sea	C. Wysocki	Closed	75.00	265.00
79-G-GW-03-018	Fox Run	C. Wysocki	Closed	75.00	605.00
84-G-GW-03-019	Foxy Fox Outfoxes the Fox Hunters, The	C. Wysocki	Closed	150.00	Unknown
86-G-GW-03-020	Hickory Haven Canal	C. Wysocki	1,500	165.00	165.00
80-G-GW-03-021	Jolly Hill Farms	C. Wysocki	Closed	75.00	250.00
86-G-GW-03-022	Lady Lib. Ind. Day Enterprising Immigrants	C. Wysocki	1,500	140.00	140.00
86-G-GW-03-023	Mr. Swallobark	C. Wysocki	2,000	145.00	145.00
82-G-GW-03-024	Nantucket, The	C. Wysocki	1,000	145.00	145.00
81-G-GW-03-025	Olde America	C. Wysocki	Closed	125.00	165.00
81-G-GW-03-026	Page's Bake Shoppe	C. Wysocki	Closed	115.00	190.00
81-G-GW-03-027	Prairie Wind Flowers	C. Wysocki	Closed	125.00	225.00
85-G-GW-03-028	Salty Witch Bay	C. Wysocki	Closed	350.00	Unknown
79-G-GW-03-029	Shall We?	C. Wysocki	Closed	75.00	140.00
82-G-GW-03-030	Sleepy Town West	C. Wysocki	1,500	150.00	150.00
84-G-GW-03-031	Storin Up	C. Wysocki	Closed	325.00	Unknown
84-G-GW-03-032	Sweetheart Chessmate	C. Wysocki	Closed	95.00	105.00
83-G-GW-03-033	Tea by the Sea	C. Wysocki	Closed	145.00	225.00
84-G-GW-03-034	Warm Christmas Love, A	C. Wysocki	Closed	80.00	120.00
84-G-GW-03-035	Yankee Wink Hollow	C. Wysocki	Closed	95.00	235.00
87-G-GW-03-036	Yearning For My Captain	C. Wysocki	2,000	150.00	150.00
Hackett American		**Etem**			
XX-G-HA-01-001	First Dance	S. Etem	Closed	125.00	200.00
XX-G-HA-01-002	The Faucet	S. Etem	Closed	125.00	200.00
XX-G-HA-01-003	Little Boast	S. Etem	Closed	125.00	200.00
XX-G-HA-01-004	The Winner	S. Etem	Closed	100.00	200.00
XX-G-HA-01-005	Second Place	S. Etem	Closed	set	set
XX-G-HA-01-006	Just Fishin'	S. Etem	Closed	150.00	250.00
XX-G-HA-01-007	The Wagon	S. Etem	Closed	150.00	175.00
XX-G-HA-01-008	Round 'N Round	S. Etem	Closed	150.00	175.00
XX-G-HA-01-009	Tag A Long	S. Etem	Closed	150.00	175.00
XX-G-HA-01-010	A Little Chilly	S. Etem	Closed	150.00	175.00
Edna Hibel Studios		**Hibel Stone Lithography**			
74-G-HG-01-001	Mother and Four Children	E. Hibel	Closed	150.00	1090.00
75-G-HG-01-002	Sandy (Kissing Baby)	E. Hibel	Closed	75.00	1250.00
77-G-HG-01-003	Museum Suite	E. Hibel	Closed	1900.00	9200.00
81-G-HG-01-004	The Little Emperor	E. Hibel	Closed	695.00	795.00
82-G-HG-01-005	Bettina and Children	E. Hibel	Closed	310.00	900.00
Edna Hibel Studios		**Hibel Lithography on Porcelain**			
80-G-HG-02-001	Cheryll and Wendy	E. Hibel	Closed	3900.00	9000.00
78-G-HG-02-002	Lenore and Child	E. Hibel	Closed	600.00	1600.00
Mill Pond Press		**Bateman**			
86-G-MF-01-001	A Resting Place - Cape Buffalo	R. Bateman	950	265.00	325.00
82-G-MF-01-002	Above the River - Trumpeter Swans	R. Bateman	950	200.00	475.00
84-G-MF-01-003	Across the Sky - Snow Geese	R. Bateman	950	220.00	325.00
80-G-MF-01-004	African Amber - Lioness Pair	R. Bateman	950	175.00	425.00
79-G-MF-01-005	Afternoon Glow - Snowy Owl	R. Bateman	950	125.00	400.00
84-G-MF-01-006	Along the Ridge - Grizzly Bears	R. Bateman	950	200.00	300.00
84-G-MF-01-007	American Goldfinch - Winter Dress	R. Bateman	950	75.00	175.00
79-G-MF-01-008	Among the Leaves - Cottontail Rabbit	R. Bateman	950	75.00	900.00
80-G-MF-01-009	Antarctic Elements	R. Bateman	950	125.00	175.00
82-G-MF-01-010	Arctic Evening - White Wolf	R. Bateman	950	185.00	650.00
80-G-MF-01-011	Arctic Family - Polar Bears	R. Bateman	950	150.00	800.00
82-G-MF-01-012	Arctic Portrait - White Gyrfalcon	R. Bateman	950	175.00	250.00
85-G-MF-01-013	Arctic Tern Pair	R. Bateman	950	175.00	225.00
81-G-MF-01-014	Artist and His Dog	R. Bateman	950	150.00	225.00
80-G-MF-01-015	Asleep in the Hemlock - Screech Owl	R. Bateman	950	125.00	825.00
82-G-MF-01-016	At the Roadside - Red-Tailed Hawk	R. Bateman	950	185.00	325.00
80-G-MF-01-017	Autumn Overture - Moose	R. Bateman	950	245.00	900.00
80-G-MF-01-018	Awesome Land - American Elk	R. Bateman	950	245.00	850.00
83-G-MF-01-019	Bald Eagle Portrait	R. Bateman	950	185.00	250.00
82-G-MF-01-020	Baobab Tree and Impala	R. Bateman	950	245.00	275.00
80-G-MF-01-021	Barn Owl in the Churchyard	R. Bateman	950	125.00	400.00
82-G-MF-01-022	Barn Swallows in August	R. Bateman	950	245.00	325.00
85-G-MF-01-023	Beaver Pond Reflections	R. Bateman	950	185.00	225.00
84-G-MF-01-024	Big Country - Pronghorn Antelope	R. Bateman	950	185.00	200.00
86-G-MF-01-025	Black Eagle	R. Bateman	950	200.00	200.00
86-G-MF-01-026	Black-Tailed Deer in the Olympics	R. Bateman	950	245.00	245.00
86-G-MF-01-027	Blacksmith Plover	R. Bateman	950	185.00	185.00
80-G-MF-01-028	Bluffing Bull - African Elephant	R. Bateman	950	135.00	600.00
81-G-MF-01-029	Bright Day - Atlantic Puffins	R. Bateman	950	175.00	300.00
80-G-MF-01-030	Brown Pelican and Pilings	R. Bateman	950	165.00	875.00
79-G-MF-01-031	Bull Moose	R. Bateman	950	125.00	1100.00
78-G-MF-01-032	By the Tracks - Killdeer	R. Bateman	950	75.00	550.00
83-G-MF-01-033	Call of the Wild - Bald Eagle	R. Bateman	950	200.00	225.00
81-G-MF-01-034	Canada Geese - Nesting	R. Bateman	950	295.00	1500.00
85-G-MF-01-035	Canada Geese Family (stone lithograph)	R. Bateman	260	350.00	1075.00
85-G-MF-01-036	Canada Geese Over the Escarpment	R. Bateman	950	135.00	200.00
86-G-MF-01-037	Canada Geese With Young	R. Bateman	950	195.00	350.00
80-G-MF-01-038	Chapel Doors	R. Bateman	950	135.00	225.00
86-G-MF-01-039	Charging Rhino	R. Bateman	950	325.00	325.00
82-G-MF-01-040	Cheetah Profile	R. Bateman	950	245.00	350.00
78-G-MF-01-041	Cheetah With Cubs	R. Bateman	950	95.00	350.00
81-G-MF-01-042	Clear Night - Wolves	R. Bateman	950	245.00	2800.00
84-G-MF-01-043	Cougar Portrait	R. Bateman	950	95.00	195.00
79-G-MF-01-044	Country Lane - Pheasants	R. Bateman	950	85.00	355.00
81-G-MF-01-045	Courting Pair - Whistling Swans	R. Bateman	950	245.00	525.00
81-G-MF-01-046	Courtship Display - Wild Turkey	R. Bateman	950	175.00	175.00
80-G-MF-01-047	Coyote in Winter Sage	R. Bateman	950	245.00	2400.00
80-G-MF-01-048	Curious Glance - Red Fox	R. Bateman	950	135.00	850.00
86-G-MF-01-049	Dark Gyfalcon	R. Bateman	950	225.00	350.00
82-G-MF-01-050	Dipper By the Waterfall	R. Bateman	950	165.00	200.00
84-G-MF-01-051	Down for a Drink - Morning Dove	R. Bateman	950	135.00	225.00
78-G-MF-01-052	Downy Woodpecker on Goldenrod Gall	R. Bateman	950	50.00	900.00
86-G-MF-01-053	Driftwood Perch - Striped Swallows	R. Bateman	950	195.00	225.00
83-G-MF-01-054	Early Snowfall - Ruffed Grouse	R. Bateman	950	195.00	295.00
83-G-MF-01-055	Early Spring - Bluebird	R. Bateman	950	185.00	325.00
81-G-MF-01-056	Edge of the Ice - Ermine	R. Bateman	950	175.00	475.00
82-G-MF-01-057	Edge of the Woods - Whitetail Deer	R. Bateman	950	745.00	1300.00
86-G-MF-01-058	Elephant Herd and Sandgrouse	R. Bateman	950	235.00	300.00
85-G-MF-01-059	Entering the Water Common Gulls	R. Bateman	950	195.00	195.00
86-G-MF-01-060	European Robin and Hydrangeas	R. Bateman	950	130.00	175.00

Number	Name	Artist	Edition limit	Issue Price	Quote
80-G-MF-01-061	Evening Grosbeak	R. Bateman	950	125.00	850.00
83-G-MF-01-062	Evening Idyll - Mute Swans	R. Bateman	950	245.00	350.00
81-G-MF-01-063	Evening Light - White Gyrfalcon	R. Bateman	950	245.00	450.00
79-G-MF-01-064	Evening Snowfall - American Elk	R. Bateman	950	150.00	1000.00
80-G-MF-01-065	Fallen Willow - Snowy Owl	R. Bateman	950	200.00	700.00
86-G-MF-01-066	Fence Post and Burdock	R. Bateman	950	130.00	130.00
80-G-MF-01-067	Flying High - Golden Eagle	R. Bateman	950	150.00	600.00
82-G-MF-01-068	Fox at the Granary	R. Bateman	950	165.00	175.00
82-G-MF-01-069	Frosty Morning - Blue Jay	R. Bateman	950	185.00	1000.00
82-G-MF-01-070	Gallinule Family	R. Bateman	950	135.00	150.00
81-G-MF-01-071	Galloping Herd - Giraffes	R. Bateman	950	175.00	400.00
85-G-MF-01-072	Gambel's Quail Pair	R. Bateman	950	95.00	200.00
82-G-MF-01-073	Gentoo Penguins and Whale Bones	R. Bateman	950	205.00	245.00
83-G-MF-01-074	Ghost of the North - Great Gray Owl	R. Bateman	950	200.00	1200.00
82-G-MF-01-075	Golden Crowned Kinglet and Rhododendron	R. Bateman	950	150.00	2000.00
79-G-MF-01-076	Golden Eagle	R. Bateman	950	150.00	295.00
85-G-MF-01-077	Golden Eagle Portrait	R. Bateman	950	115.00	175.00
83-G-MF-01-078	Goshawk and Ruffed Grouse	R. Bateman	950	185.00	325.00
81-G-MF-01-079	Gray Squirrel	R. Bateman	950	180.00	795.00
79-G-MF-01-080	Great Blue Heron	R. Bateman	950	125.00	750.00
83-G-MF-01-081	Great Horned Owl in the White Pine	R. Bateman	950	225.00	500.00
80-G-MF-01-082	Heron on the Rocks	R. Bateman	950	75.00	250.00
81-G-MF-01-083	High Camp at Dusk	R. Bateman	950	245.00	275.00
79-G-MF-01-084	High Country - Stone Sheep	R. Bateman	950	125.00	250.00
87-G-MF-01-085	High Kingdom - Snow Leopard	R. Bateman	950	325.00	325.00
84-G-MF-01-086	Hooded Mergansers in Winter	R. Bateman	950	210.00	450.00
84-G-MF-01-087	House Finch and Yucca	R. Bateman	950	95.00	150.00
86-G-MF-01-088	House Sparrow	R. Bateman	950	125.00	125.00
86-G-MF-01-089	Hummingbird Pair Diptych	R. Bateman	950	330.00	330.00
81-G-MF-01-090	In for the Evening	R. Bateman	950	150.00	650.00
84-G-MF-01-091	In the Brier Patch - Cottontail	R. Bateman	950	165.00	275.00
86-G-MF-01-092	In the Grass - Lioness	R. Bateman	950	245.00	245.00
85-G-MF-01-093	In the Highlands - Golden Eagle	R. Bateman	950	235.00	325.00
85-G-MF-01-094	In the Mountains - Osprey	R. Bateman	950	95.00	125.00
85-G-MF-01-095	Irish Cottage and Wagtail	R. Bateman	950	175.00	175.00
79-G-MF-01-096	King of the Realm	R. Bateman	950	125.00	375.00
81-G-MF-01-097	Kingfisher and Aspen	R. Bateman	950	225.00	400.00
80-G-MF-01-098	Kingfisher in Winter	R. Bateman	950	175.00	500.00
80-G-MF-01-099	Kittiwake Greeting	R. Bateman	950	75.00	450.00
81-G-MF-01-100	Last Look - Bighorn Sheep	R. Bateman	950	195.00	295.00
87-G-MF-01-101	Late Winter - Black Squirrel	R. Bateman	950	165.00	165.00
81-G-MF-01-102	Laughing Gull and Horseshoe Crab	R. Bateman	950	125.00	150.00
82-G-MF-01-103	Leopard Ambush	R. Bateman	950	245.00	350.00
85-G-MF-01-104	Leopard at Seronera	R. Bateman	950	175.00	295.00
80-G-MF-01-105	Leopard in a Sausage Tree	R. Bateman	950	150.00	800.00
84-G-MF-01-106	Lily Pads and Loon	R. Bateman	950	200.00	800.00
80-G-MF-01-107	Lion at Tsavo	R. Bateman	950	150.00	275.00
78-G-MF-01-108	Lion Cubs	R. Bateman	950	125.00	350.00
87-G-MF-01-109	Lioness at Serengeti	R. Bateman	950	325.00	325.00
85-G-MF-01-110	Lions in the Grass	R. Bateman	950	265.00	875.00
81-G-MF-01-111	Little Blue Heron	R. Bateman	950	95.00	285.00
82-G-MF-01-112	Lively Pair - Chickadees	R. Bateman	950	160.00	400.00
83-G-MF-01-113	Loon Family	R. Bateman	950	200.00	695.00
78-G-MF-01-114	Majesty on the Wing - Bald Eagle	R. Bateman	950	150.00	2800.00
86-G-MF-01-115	Mallard Family - Misty Marsh	R. Bateman	950	130.00	130.00
86-G-MF-01-116	Mallard Pair - Early Winter	R. Bateman	41,740	135.00	135.00
86-G-MF-01-117	Mallard Pair - Early Winter Gold Plated	R. Bateman	7,691	250.00	250.00
85-G-MF-01-118	Mallard Pair - Early Winter 24K Gold	R. Bateman	950	1650.00	1650.00
86-G-MF-01-119	Marginal Meadow	R. Bateman	950	220.00	400.00
79-G-MF-01-120	Master of the Herd - African Buffalo	R. Bateman	950	150.00	1100.00
84-G-MF-01-121	May Maple - Scarlet Tanager	R. Bateman	950	175.00	425.00
82-G-MF-01-122	Meadow's Edge - Mallard	R. Bateman	950	175.00	875.00
82-G-MF-01-123	Merganser Family in Hiding	R. Bateman	950	200.00	350.00
80-G-MF-01-124	Mischief on the Prowl - Raccoon	R. Bateman	950	85.00	300.00
80-G-MF-01-125	Misty Coast - Gulls	R. Bateman	950	135.00	375.00
84-G-MF-01-126	Misty Lake - Osprey	R. Bateman	950	95.00	200.00
81-G-MF-01-127	Misty Morning - Loons	R. Bateman	950	150.00	1900.00
86-G-MF-01-128	Moose at Water's Edge	R. Bateman	950	130.00	175.00
85-G-MF-01-129	Morning Dew - Roe Deer	R. Bateman	950	175.00	175.00
83-G-MF-01-130	Morning on the Flats - Bison	R. Bateman	950	200.00	275.00
84-G-MF-01-131	Morning on the River - Trumpeter Swans	R. Bateman	950	185.00	225.00
86-G-MF-01-132	Mule Deer in Aspen	R. Bateman	950	175.00	300.00
83-G-MF-01-133	Mule Deer in Winter	R. Bateman	950	200.00	275.00
83-G-MF-01-134	New Season - American Robin	R. Bateman	950	200.00	400.00
86-G-MF-01-135	Northern Reflections - Loon Family	R. Bateman	8,631	255.00	255.00
85-G-MF-01-136	Old Whaling Base and Fur Seals	R. Bateman	950	195.00	450.00
80-G-MF-01-137	On the Alert - Chipmunk	R. Bateman	950	60.00	525.00
85-G-MF-01-138	On the Garden Wall	R. Bateman	950	115.00	250.00
85-G-MF-01-139	Orca Procession	R. Bateman	950	245.00	1650.00
81-G-MF-01-140	Osprey Family	R. Bateman	950	245.00	325.00
83-G-MF-01-141	Osprey in the Rain	R. Bateman	950	110.00	350.00
83-G-MF-01-141	Osprey in the Rain	R. Bateman	950	110.00	350.00
81-G-MF-01-142	Pair of Skimmers	R. Bateman	950	150.00	175.00
84-G-MF-01-143	Peregrine and Ruddy Turnstones	R. Bateman	950	200.00	250.00
85-G-MF-01-144	Peregrine Falcon and White-Throated Swifts	R. Bateman	950	245.00	350.00
87-G-MF-01-145	Peregrine Falcon on the Cliff - Stone Lith	R. Bateman	525	350.00	350.00
83-G-MF-01-146	Pheasant in Cornfield	R. Bateman	950	200.00	375.00
82-G-MF-01-147	Pileated Woodpecker on Beech Tree	R. Bateman	950	175.00	250.00
82-G-MF-01-148	Pioneer Memories - Magpie Pair	R. Bateman	950	175.00	175.00
82-G-MF-01-149	Polar Bear Profile	R. Bateman	950	210.00	1400.00
82-G-MF-01-150	Polar Bears at Bafin Island	R. Bateman	950	245.00	650.00
80-G-MF-01-151	Prairie Evening - Short-Eared Owl	R. Bateman	950	150.00	175.00
86-G-MF-01-152	Proud Swimmer - Snow Goose	R. Bateman	950	185.00	185.00
82-G-MF-01-153	Queen Anne's Lace and American Goldfinch	R. Bateman	950	150.00	850.00
84-G-MF-01-154	Ready for Flight - Peregrine Falcon	R. Bateman	950	185.00	275.00
82-G-MF-01-155	Ready for the Hunt - Snowy Owl	R. Bateman	950	245.00	400.00
84-G-MF-01-156	Red Fox on the Prowl	R. Bateman	950	245.00	1000.00
82-G-MF-01-157	Red Squirrel	R. Bateman	950	175.00	500.00
86-G-MF-01-158	Red Wolf	R. Bateman	950	250.00	500.00
81-G-MF-01-159	Red-Tailed Hawk by the Cliff	R. Bateman	950	245.00	450.00
81-G-MF-01-160	Red-Winged Blackbird and Rail Fence	R. Bateman	950	195.00	225.00
84-G-MF-01-161	Reeds	R. Bateman	950	185.00	300.00
86-G-MF-01-162	Robins at the Nest	R. Bateman	950	185.00	350.00
80-G-MF-01-163	Rocky Wilderness - Cougar	R. Bateman	950	175.00	900.00
81-G-MF-01-164	Rough-Legged Hawk in the Elm	R. Bateman	950	175.00	175.00

Company Number	Series Name	Artist	Edition limit	Issue Price	Quote
81-G-MF-01-165	Royal Family - Mute Swans	R. Bateman	950	245.00	450.00
83-G-MF-01-166	Ruby Throat and Columbine	R. Bateman	950	150.00	1000.00
81-G-MF-01-167	Sarah E. with Gulls	R. Bateman	950	245.00	1850.00
81-G-MF-01-168	Sheer Drop - Mountain Goats	R. Bateman	950	245.00	1500.00
84-G-MF-01-169	Smallwood	R. Bateman	950	200.00	350.00
85-G-MF-01-170	Snowy Hemlock - Barred Owl	R. Bateman	950	245.00	450.00
87-G-MF-01-171	Snowy Owl and Milkweed	R. Bateman	950	235.00	300.00
83-G-MF-01-172	Snowy Owl on Driftwood	R. Bateman	950	245.00	700.00
83-G-MF-01-173	Spirits of the Forest	R. Bateman	950	170.00	500.00
86-G-MF-01-174	Split Rails - Snow Buntings	R. Bateman	950	220.00	220.00
80-G-MF-01-175	Spring Cardinal	R. Bateman	950	125.00	450.00
82-G-MF-01-176	Spring Marsh - Pintail Pair	R. Bateman	950	200.00	300.00
80-G-MF-01-177	Spring Thaw - Killdeer	R. Bateman	950	85.00	200.00
82-G-MF-01-178	Still Morning - Herring Gulls	R. Bateman	950	200.00	250.00
87-G-MF-01-179	Stone Sheep Ram	R. Bateman	950	175.00	175.00
85-G-MF-01-180	Stream Bank June	R. Bateman	950	160.00	175.00
84-G-MF-01-181	Stretching - Canada Goose	R. Bateman	950	225.00	1300.00
85-G-MF-01-182	Strutting - Ring-Necked Pheasant	R. Bateman	950	225.00	345.00
85-G-MF-01-183	Sudden Blizzard - Red-Tailed Hawk	R. Bateman	950	245.00	600.00
84-G-MF-01-184	Summer Morning - Loon	R. Bateman	950	185.00	595.00
86-G-MF-01-185	Summertime - Polar Bears	R. Bateman	950	225.00	600.00
79-G-MF-01-186	Surf and Sanderlings	R. Bateman	950	65.00	300.00
81-G-MF-01-187	Swift Fox	R. Bateman	950	175.00	325.00
86-G-MF-01-188	Swift Fox Study	R. Bateman	950	115.00	115.00
87-G-MF-01-189	Sylvan Stream - Mute Swans	R. Bateman	950	125.00	125.00
84-G-MF-01-190	Tadpole Time	R. Bateman	950	135.00	250.00
84-G-MF-01-191	Tiger at Dawn	R. Bateman	950	225.00	1750.00
83-G-MF-01-192	Tiger Portrait	R. Bateman	950	130.00	225.00
85-G-MF-01-193	Trumpeter Swans and Aspen	R. Bateman	950	245.00	325.00
79-G-MF-01-194	Up in the Pine - Great Horned Owl	R. Bateman	950	150.00	550.00
80-G-MF-01-195	Vantage Point	R. Bateman	950	245.00	850.00
81-G-MF-01-196	Watchful Repose - Black Bear	R. Bateman	950	245.00	400.00
85-G-MF-01-197	Weathered Branch - Bald Eagle	R. Bateman	950	115.00	275.00
80-G-MF-01-198	White Encounter - Polar Bear	R. Bateman	950	245.00	2800.00
82-G-MF-01-199	White-Footed Mouse on Aspen	R. Bateman	950	90.00	200.00
82-G-MF-01-200	White World - Dall Sheep	R. Bateman	950	200.00	400.00
85-G-MF-01-201	White-Breasted Nuthatch on a Beech Tree	R. Bateman	950	175.00	275.00
80-G-MF-01-202	White-Footed Mouse in Wintergreen	R. Bateman	950	60.00	400.00
84-G-MF-01-203	White-Throated Sparrow and Pussy Willow	R. Bateman	950	750.00	450.00
86-G-MF-01-204	Wildebeest	R. Bateman	950	185.00	185.00
82-G-MF-01-205	Willet on the Shore	R. Bateman	950	125.00	175.00
79-G-MF-01-206	Wily and Wary - Red Fox	R. Bateman	950	125.00	1275.00
84-G-MF-01-207	Window into Ontario	R. Bateman	950	265.00	600.00
79-G-MF-01-208	Winter - Snowshoe Hare	R. Bateman	950	95.00	750.00
83-G-MF-01-209	Winter Barn	R. Bateman	950	170.00	345.00
79-G-MF-01-210	Winter Cardinal	R. Bateman	950	75.00	3100.00
85-G-MF-01-211	Winter Companion	R. Bateman	950	175.00	250.00
80-G-MF-01-212	Winter Elm - American Kestrel	R. Bateman	950	135.00	400.00
86-G-MF-01-213	Winter in the Mountains - Raven	R. Bateman	950	200.00	200.00
81-G-MF-01-214	Winter Mist - Great Horned Owl	R. Bateman	950	245.00	600.00
80-G-MF-01-215	Winter Song–Chickadees	R. Bateman	950	95.00	775.00
84-G-MF-01-216	Winter Sunset–Moose	R. Bateman	950	245.00	1800.00
81-G-MF-01-217	Winter Wren	R. Bateman	950	135.00	250.00
83-G-MF-01-218	Winter–Lady Cardinal	R. Bateman	950	200.00	800.00
87-G-MF-01-219	Wise One	R. Bateman	950	325.00	325.00
79-G-MF-01-220	Wolf Pack in Moonlight	R. Bateman	950	95.00	2300.00
83-G-MF-01-221	Wolves on the Trail	R. Bateman	950	225.00	600.00
85-G-MF-01-222	Wood Bison Portrait	R. Bateman	950	165.00	175.00
83-G-MF-01-223	Woodland Drumer–Ruffed Grouse	R. Bateman	950	185.00	225.00
81-G-MF-01-224	Wrangler's Campsite–Gray Jay	R. Bateman	950	195.00	500.00
79-G-MF-01-225	Yellow-Rumped Warbler	R. Bateman	950	50.00	325.00
78-G-MF-01-226	Young Barn Swallow	R. Bateman	950	75.00	600.00
83-G-MF-01-227	Young Elf Owl–Old Saguaro	R. Bateman	950	95.00	200.00
Mill Pond Press	Reece				
74-G-MF-02-001	A Burst of Color–Ring-Neck Pheasant	M. Reece	950	75.00	175.00
75-G-MF-02-002	Afternoon Shadows–Bobwhites	M. Reece	950	100.00	350.00
72-G-MF-02-003	Against the Wind–Canvasbacks	M. Reece	950	60.00	450.00
80-G-MF-02-004	Along the Shore–Redheads	M. Reece	950	160.00	160.00
86-G-MF-02-005	Autumn Marsh–Mallards	M. Reece	950	125.00	125.00
76-G-MF-02-006	Autumn Trio–Ring-Necked Pheasants	M. Reece	950	85.00	250.00
64-G-MF-02-007	Bobwhites Stone Lithographs	M. Reece	950	20.00	650.00
74-G-MF-02-008	Bufflehead Duck Stamp Print-Third Edition S/N	M. Reece	350	250.00	275.00
76-G-MF-02-009	Canada Geese - Coming In	M. Reece	950	85.00	175.00
74-G-MF-02-010	Courtship Flight - Pintails	M. Reece	950	75.00	175.00
77-G-MF-02-011	Covey Rise - Bobwhites	M. Reece	950	150.00	625.00
78-G-MF-02-012	Crescent Lake - Mallards	M. Reece	950	125.00	175.00
77-G-MF-02-013	Dark Shadows - Whitetail Deer	M. Reece	950	85.00	125.00
79-G-MF-02-014	Dark Sky - Bobwhites	M. Reece	950	225.00	400.00
78-G-MF-02-015	Dark Sky - Canada Geese	M. Reece	950	175.00	325.00
80-G-MF-02-016	Dark Sky - Canvasbacks	M. Reece	950	195.00	225.00
76-G-MF-02-017	Dark Sky - Mallards	M. Reece	950	85.00	675.00
83-G-MF-02-018	Dark Sky - Pheasants	M. Reece	950	125.00	125.00
81-G-MF-02-019	Dark Sky - Ruffed Grouse	M. Reece	950	245.00	300.00
80-G-MF-02-020	Diamond Island - Mallards	M. Reece	950	195.00	275.00
74-G-MF-02-021	Early Arrivals - Mallards	M. Reece	950	50.00	125.00
77-G-MF-02-022	Easy Landing - Pintails	M. Reece	950	95.00	200.00
70-G-MF-02-023	Edge of the Hedgerow - Bobwhites	M. Reece	950	60.00	700.00
81-G-MF-02-024	Escape - Ring-Necked Pheasants	M. Reece	950	195.00	195.00
48-G-MF-02-025	Federal Duck Stamp - Buffleheads	M. Reece	200	15.00	1200.00
51-G-MF-02-026	Federal Duck Stamp - Gadwalls	M. Reece	250	15.00	1200.00
59-G-MF-02-027	Federal Duck Stamp - Retriever	M. Reece	400	15.00	4000.00
69-G-MF-02-028	Federal Duck Stamp - White-Winged Scoters	M. Reece	750	50.00	1000.00
71-G-MF-02-029	Federal Duck Stamp - Cinnamon Teal	M. Reece	950	75.00	5000.00
73-G-MF-02-030	Feeding Time - Canada Geese S/N	M. Reece	550	75.00	400.00
76-G-MF-02-031	Flight - Canada Geese	M. Reece	950	50.00	100.00
74-G-MF-02-032	Flooded Oaks - Mallards S/N	M. Reece	850	150.00	300.00
81-G-MF-02-033	Frosty Morning - Canada Geese	M. Reece	950	175.00	275.00
76-G-MF-02-034	Gentoo Penquins S/N (stone litho)	M. Reece	260	125.00	175.00
76-G-MF-02-035	Good Fetch - Labrador Retriever	M. Reece	950	150.00	200.00
77-G-MF-02-036	Graceful Pair - Ring-Necked Pheasants	M. Reece	950	50.00	125.00
75-G-MF-02 037	Hazy Day - Bobwhites	M. Reece	950	150.00	400.00
77-G-MF-02-038	Jumping Greenwings - Green-Winged Teal	M. Reece	950	85.00	150.00
80-G-MF-02-039	Landing - Canada Geese	M. Reece	950	125.00	150.00
73-G-MF-02-040	Late Afternoon - Mallards S/N	M. Reece	450	150.00	175.00
69-G-MF-02-041	Mallards - Pitching In S/N	M. Reece	500	40.00	600.00
74-G-MF-02-042	Mallards - Dropping In	M. Reece	950	75.00	150.00
64-G-MF-02-043	Mallards Stone Lithographs	M. Reece	950	20.00	650.00
73-G-MF-02-044	Marshlander Mallards S/N	M. Reece	600	60.00	125.00
82-G-MF-02-045	Miniature Series I - Mallards	M. Reece	950	75.00	125.00
82-G-MF-02-046	Miniature Series II - Wood Ducks	M. Reece	950	75.00	125.00
80-G-MF-02-047	Mountain Snow	M. Reece	950	95.00	225.00
78-G-MF-02-048	New Snow - Whitetail Deer	M. Reece	950	95.00	110.00
77-G-MF-02-049	Nine Travelers - Canada Geese	M. Reece	950	95.00	175.00
78-G-MF-02-050	Oak Forest - Turkey	M. Reece	950	125.00	225.00
81-G-MF-02-051	Out of the Pines - Bobwhites	M. Reece	950	245.00	300.00
78-G-MF-02-052	Over the Point - Lesser Scaups	M. Reece	950	125.00	140.00
73-G-MF-02-053	Pheasant Country S/N	M. Reece	550	60.00	200.00
79-G-MF-02-054	Pheasant Cover	M. Reece	950	175.00	325.00
80-G-MF-02-055	Pointers and Bobwhites	M. Reece	950	245.00	300.00
80-G-MF-02-056	Quail Country	M. Reece	950	250.00	350.00
74-G-MF-02-057	Quail Cover S/N	M. Reece	750	150.00	350.00
82-G-MF-02-058	Quail Covey - Bobwhites	M. Reece	950	245.00	295.00
77-G-MF-02-059	Quiet Pond - Mallards	M. Reece	950	95.00	150.00
79-G-MF-02-060	Regal Flight - Whistling Swans	M. Reece	950	125.00	150.00
77-G-MF-02-061	Resting - Wood Ducks	M. Reece	950	50.00	100.00
78-G-MF-02-062	Rough Water - Canvasbacks	M. Reece	950	150.00	200.00
76-G-MF-02-063	Shallow Pond - Mallards	M. Reece	950	125.00	250.00
74-G-MF-02-064	Snow Geese - Blue Geese S/N	M. Reece	750	150.00	200.00
74-G-MF-02-065	Snowy Creek - Mallards	M. Reece	950	75.00	200.00
74-G-MF-02-066	Solitude - Whitetail Deer	M. Reece	950	85.00	150.00
77-G-MF-02-067	Stick Pond - Mallards	M. Reece	950	125.00	175.00
79-G-MF-02-068	Sunrise - Green-Winged Teal	M. Reece	950	150.00	200.00
79-G-MF-02-069	The Marsh	M. Reece	950	75.00	100.00
74-G-MF-02-070	The Passing Storm - Canvasbacks	M. Reece	950	50.00	100.00
80-G-MF-02-071	The Quiet Place - Canada Geese	M. Reece	950	175.00	275.00
76-G-MF-02-072	The Rail Fence - Bobwhites	M. Reece	950	85.00	200.00
74-G-MF-02-073	The Sandbar - Canada Geese	M. Reece	950	50.00	100.00
77-G-MF-02-074	The Sentinal - Whitetail Deer	M. Reece	950	150.00	175.00
82-G-MF-02-075	The Splash - Smallmouth Bass	M. Reece	950	95.00	95.00
79-G-MF-02-076	The Valley - Pintails	M. Reece	950	150.00	175.00
80-G-MF-02-077	The Willow - Green-Winged Teal	M. Reece	950	160.00	200.00
77-G-MF-02-078	Through the Trees - Wood Ducks	M. Reece	950	95.00	400.00
76-G-MF-02-079	Thunderhead - Canada Geese S/N (stone litho)	M. Reece	260	125.00	300.00
80-G-MF-02-080	Timber - Wood Ducks	M. Reece	950	160.00	200.00
80-G-MF-02-081	Tundra - Black Brant	M. Reece	950	85.00	100.00
80-G-MF-02-082	Twilight - American Widgeon	M. Reece	950	75.00	100.00
76-G-MF-02-083	Weathered Wood - Bobwhites	M. Reece	950	50.00	150.00
79-G-MF-02-084	Windy Day - Mallards	M. Reece	950	150.00	200.00
74-G-MF-02-085	Winging South - Canada Geese S/N	M. Reece	750	150.00	275.00
79-G-MF-02-086	Winter - Ring-Necked Pheasants	M. Reece	950	125.00	150.00
78-G-MF-02-087	Winter Covey - Bobwhites	M. Reece	950	225.00	600.00
73-G-MF-02-088	Wood Ducks S/N	M. Reece	550	125.00	250.00
74-G-MF-02-089	Wooded Seclusion - Turkey	M. Reece	950	75.00	125.00
Mill Pond Press	Calle				
84-G-MF-03-001	A Brace for the Spit	P. Calle	950	110.00	110.00
83-G-MF-03-002	A Winter Surprise	P. Calle	950	195.00	275.00
81-G-MF-03-003	Almost Home (Color)	P. Calle	950	150.00	175.00
81-G-MF-03-004	And Still Miles to Go	P. Calle	950	245.00	400.00
81-G-MF-03-005	Andrew At The Falls	P. Calle	950	150.00	175.00
80-G-MF-03-006	Caring for the Herd	P. Calle	950	110.00	125.00
81-G-MF-03-007	Chief High Pipe (Color)	P. Calle	950	265.00	400.00
80-G-MF-03-008	Chief High Pipe (Pencil)	P. Calle	950	75.00	200.00
80-G-MF-03-009	Chief Joseph - Man of Peace	P. Calle	950	135.00	150.00
81-G-MF-03-010	End of a Long Day	P. Calle	950	150.00	175.00
84-G-MF-03-011	Fate of the Late Migrant	P. Calle	950	110.00	110.00
83-G-MF-03-012	Free Sprits	P. Calle	950	195.00	195.00
83-G-MF-03-013	Free Trapper Study S/N	P. Calle	550	75.00	125.00
81-G-MF-03-015	Fresh Tracks	P. Calle	950	150.00	175.00
83-G-MF-03-016	In Search of Beaver	P. Calle	950	225.00	325.00
81-G-MF-03-017	Just Over the Ridge	P. Calle	950	245.00	325.00
80-G-MF-03-018	Landmark Tree	P. Calle	950	125.00	250.00
81-G-MF-03-019	One With The Land	P. Calle	950	245.00	325.00
81-G-MF-03-020	Pause at the Lower Falls	P. Calle	950	110.00	150.00
80-G-MF-03-021	Prayer to the Great Mystery	P. Calle	950	245.00	400.00
82-G-MF-03-022	Return to Camp	P. Calle	950	245.00	400.00
80-G-MF-03-023	Sioux Chief	P. Calle	950	85.00	100.00
80-G-MF-03-024	Something for the Pot	P. Calle	950	175.00	950.00
85-G-MF-03-025	Storyteller of the Mountains	P. Calle	950	225.00	225.00
83-G-MF-03-026	Strays from the Flyway	P. Calle	950	195.00	275.00
81-G-MF-03-027	Teton Friends	P. Calle	950	150.00	225.00
82-G-MF-03-028	Two from the Flock	P. Calle	950	245.00	400.00
80-G-MF-03-029	View from the Heights	P. Calle	950	245.00	400.00
80-G-MF-03-030	When Snow Came Early	P. Calle	950	85.00	250.00
84-G-MF-03-031	When Trails Cross	P. Calle	950	245.00	300.00
81-G-MF-03-032	Winter Hunter (Color)	P. Calle	950	245.00	525.00
80-G-MF-03-033	Winter Hunter (Pencil)	P. Calle	950	65.00	475.00
Mill Pond Press	Peterson				
76-G-MF-04-001	Adelie Penguins	R. Peterson	950	35.00	35.00
74-G-MF-04-002	Bald Eagle	R. Peterson	950	150.00	500.00
73-G-MF-04-003	Baltimore Oriole S/N	R. Peterson	450	150.00	300.00
76-G-MF-04-005	Barn Owl	R. Peterson	950	225.00	275.00
74-G-MF-04-006	Barn Swallow S/N	R. Peterson	750	150.00	200.00
76-G-MF-04-008	Blue Jays	R. Peterson	950	150.00	200.00
77-G-MF-04-009	BlueBird	R. Peterson	950	75.00	200.00
74-G-MF-04-010	Bobolink S/N	R. Peterson	750	150.00	200.00
75-G-MF-04-012	Bobwhites	R. Peterson	950	150.00	400.00
73-G-MF-04-013	Cardinal S/N	R. Peterson	450	150.00	600.00
73-G-MF-04-015	Flicker	R. Peterson	450	150.00	300.00
76-G-MF-04-017	Golden Eagle	R. Peterson	950	200.00	250.00
74-G-MF-04-018	Great Horned Owl	R. Peterson	950	150 00	800.00
79-G-MF-04-020	Gyrfalcon	R. Peterson	950	225.00	325.00
78-G-MF-04-021	Mockingbird	R. Peterson	950	125.00	275.00
77-G-MF-04-022	Peregrine Falcon	R. Peterson	950	175.00	300.00
78-G-MF-04-023	Ring-Necked Pheasant	R. Peterson	950	200.00	250.00
78-G-MF-04-024	Robin	R. Peterson	950	125.00	325.00
78-G-MF-04-025	Rose-Breasted Grosbeak	R. Peterson	950	125.00	125.00
75-G-MF-04-026	Ruffed Grouse	R. Peterson	950	150.00	425.00
77-G-MF-04-027	Scarlet Tanager	R. Peterson	950	125.00	200.00
75-G-MF-04-028	Sea Otters	R. Peterson	950	25.00	100.00
76-G-MF-04-029	Snowy Owl	R. Peterson	950	175.00	600.00
77-G-MF-04-030	Sooty Terns S/N	R. Peterson	450	50.00	85.00
77-G-MF-04-032	Willets S/N	R. Peterson	450	50.00	85.00
73-G-MF-04-034	Wood Thrush	R. Peterson	450	150.00	400.00

Company Number	Name	Series Artist	Edition limit	Issue Price	Quote
Mill Pond Press		**Machetanz**			
79-G-MF-05-001	Beginnings	F. Machetanz	950	175.00	425.00
79-G-MF-05-002	Decision on the Ice Field	F. Machetanz	950	150.00	425.00
84-G-MF-05-003	End of a Long Day	F. Machetanz	950	200.00	275.00
78-G-MF-05-004	Face to Face	F. Machetanz	950	150.00	1500.00
81-G-MF-05-005	Golden Years	F. Machetanz	950	245.00	350.00
78-G-MF-05-006	Hunter's Dawn	F. Machetanz	950	125.00	500.00
78-G-MF-05-007	Into the Home Stretch	F. Machetanz	950	175.00	700.00
80-G-MF-05-008	King of the Mountain	F. Machetanz	950	200.00	300.00
86-G-MF-05-009	Kyrok - Eskimo Seamstress	F. Machetanz	950	225.00	225.00
85-G-MF-05-010	Land of the Midnight Sun	F. Machetanz	950	245.00	295.00
85-G-MF-05-011	Leaving the Nest	F. Machetanz	950	245.00	245.00
86-G-MF-05-012	Lone Musher	F. Machetanz	950	245.00	245.00
84-G-MF-05-013	Many Miles Together	F. Machetanz	950	245.00	245.00
81-G-MF-05-014	Midday Moonlight	F. Machetanz	950	265.00	425.00
84-G-MF-05-015	Midnight Watch	F. Machetanz	950	250.00	250.00
82-G-MF-05-016	Mighty Hunter	F. Machetanz	950	265.00	400.00
82-G-MF-05-017	Moonlit Stakeout	F. Machetanz	950	265.00	400.00
82-G-MF-05-018	Moose Tracks	F. Machetanz	950	265.00	300.00
86-G-MF-05-019	Mt. Blackburn-Sovereign of the Wrangells	F. Machetanz	950	245.00	245.00
80-G-MF-05-020	Nelchina Trail	F. Machetanz	950	245.00	375.00
79-G-MF-05-021	Pick of the Litter	F. Machetanz	950	165.00	450.00
79-G-MF-05-022	Reaching the Campsite	F. Machetanz	950	200.00	400.00
85-G-MF-05-023	Reaching the Pass	F. Machetanz	950	265.00	2000.00
80-G-MF-05-024	Sourdough	F. Machetanz	950	245.00	400.00
84-G-MF-05-025	Story of the Beads	F. Machetanz	950	245.00	245.00
84-G-MF-05-026	The Heritage of Alaska	F. Machetanz	950	400.00	800.00
82-G-MF-05-027	The Tender Arctic	F. Machetanz	950	295.00	475.00
83-G-MF-05-028	They Opened the North Country	F. Machetanz	950	245.00	245.00
81-G-MF-05-029	What Every Hunter Fears	F. Machetanz	950	245.00	375.00
80-G-MF-05-030	When Three's a Crowd	F. Machetanz	950	225.00	400.00
81-G-MF-05-031	Where Men and Dogs Seem Small	F. Machetanz	950	245.00	400.00
81-G-MF-05-032	Winter Harvest	F. Machetanz	950	265.00	265.00
Mill Pond Press		**Parker**			
86-G-MF-06-001	Above the Breakers	R. Parker	950	150.00	200.00
86-G-MF-06-002	At End of Day - Wolves	R. Parker	950	235.00	300.00
86-G-MF-06-003	Autumn Foraging - Moose	R. Parker	950	175.00	425.00
86-G-MF-06-004	Autumn Leaves - Red Fox	R. Parker	950	95.00	150.00
86-G-MF-06-005	Autumn Meadow - Elk	R. Parker	950	195.00	275.00
86-G-MF-06-006	Cardinal In Blue Spruce	R. Parker	950	125.00	Unknown
86-G-MF-06-007	Cardinal In Brambles	R. Parker	950	125.00	Unknown
86-G-MF-06-012	Just Resting - Sea Otter	R. Parker	950	85.00	Unknown
85-G-MF-06-022	Spring Arrivals - Canada Geese	R. Parker	950	120.00	Unknown
86-G-MF-06-027	Whitetail and Wolves	R. Parker	950	180.00	275.00
87-G-MF-06-029	Winter Creek and Whitetails	R. Parker	950	185.00	Unknown
87-G-MF-06-031	Winter Encounter - Wolf	R. Parker	950	235.00	Unknown
Mill Pond Press		**Engle**			
81-G-MF-07-001	House by the Sea	N. Engle	950	75.00	250.00
84-G-MF-07-002	Island Lake	N. Engle	950	95.00	150.00
83-G-MF-07-003	Morning on the Yellowdog River	N. Engle	950	75.00	75.00
83-G-MF-07-004	Quiet Waters	N. Engle	950	75.00	175.00
83-G-MF-07-005	Summer River	N. Engle	950	75.00	75.00
81-G-MF-07-006	Wilderness Marsh	N. Engle	950	75.00	250.00
83-G-MF-07-007	Winter Brook	N. Engle	950	75.00	75.00
Mill Pond Press		**Seerey-Lester**			
86-G-MF-08-001	Above the Treeline - Cougar	J. Seerey-Lester	950	130.00	130.00
84-G-MF-08-002	Among the Cattails - Canada Geese	J. Seerey-Lester	950	130.00	165.00
85-G-MF-08-003	Children of the Forest - Red Fox Kits	J. Seerey-Lester	950	110.00	150.00
85-G-MF-08-004	Children of the Tundra - Artic Wolf Pup	J. Seerey-Lester	950	110.00	150.00
85-G-MF-08-005	Fallen Birch - Chipmunk	J. Seerey-Lester	950	60.00	200.00
85-G-MF-08-006	First Light - Gray Jays	J. Seerey-Lester	950	130.00	225.00
83-G-MF-08-007	First Snow - Grizzly Bears	J. Seerey-Lester	950	95.00	175.00
86-G-MF-08-008	Hidden Admirer - Moose	J. Seerey-Lester	950	165.00	165.00
86-G-MF-08-009	High Country Champion - Grizzly	J. Seerey-Lester	950	175.00	250.00
84-G-MF-08-010	High Ground - Wolves	J. Seerey-Lester	950	130.00	185.00
83-G-MF-08-011	Lone Fisherman - Great Blue Heron	J. Seerey-Lester	950	85.00	150.00
84-G-MF-08-012	Lying Low - Cougar	J. Seerey-Lester	950	85.00	200.00
86-G-MF-08-013	Racing the Storm—Artic Wolves	J. Seerey-Lester	950	200.00	250.00
84-G-MF-08-014	Spirit of the North—White Wolf	J. Seerey-Lester	950	130.00	130.00
86-G-MF-08-015	Spring Mist Chickadees	J. Seerey-Lester	950	105.00	150.00
83-G-MF-08-016	The Refuge—Raccoons	J. Seerey-Lester	950	85.00	160.00
85-G-MF-08-017	Under the Pines—Bobcat	J. Seerey-Lester	950	95.00	150.00
83-G-MF-08-018	Winter Lookout—Cougar	J. Seerey-Lester	950	85.00	225.00
86-G-MF-08-019	Winter Perch—Cardinal	J. Seerey-Lester	950	85.00	85.00
85-G-MF-08-020	Winter Rendezvous—Coyotes	J. Seerey-Lester	950	140.00	200.00
Mill Pond Press		**Zemsky**			
79-G-MF-09-001	When the Then and the Now Hold Hands	J. Zemsky	950	65.00	175.00
79-G-MF-09-002	Jordan's Dolly	J. Zemsky	950	65.00	65.00
79-G-MF-09-003	Love at First Sight	J. Zemsky	950	75.00	75.00
79-G-MF-09-004	Come See the New Colt	J. Zemsky	950	65.00	65.00
79-G-MF-09-005	Jordan at the Wedding	J. Zemsky	950	65.00	125.00
Mill Pond Press		**Utz**			
81-G-MF-10-001	Pink Lady	T. Utz	450	85.00	110.00
81-G-MF-10-002	Melanie	T. Utz	450	85.00	100.00
81-G-MF-10-003	The Greenhouse Nude	T. Utz	550	95.00	125.00
81-G-MF-10-004	Picnic	T. Utz	550	110.00	110.00
81-G-MF-10-005	Lavender Lace	T. Utz	950	75.00	75.00
81-G-MF-10-006	The Soft Wind	T. Utz	950	75.00	75.00
Moss Portfolio		**Moss**			
XX-G-MS-01-001	Apple Picker	P. Moss	1,000	30.00	70.00
XX-G-MS-01-002	Barelimbed Reflections	P. Moss	1,000	25.00	70.00
XX-G-MS-01-003	Becky and Tom	P. Moss	1,000	10.00	40.00
XX-G-MS-01-004	Canada Geese	P. Moss	1,000	60.00	140.00
XX-G-MS-01-005	Family Outing	P. Moss	1,000	65.00	300.00
XX-G-MS-01-006	Flag Boy	P. Moss	1,000	16.00	40.00
XX-G-MS-01-007	Four Little Girls	P. Moss	1,000	30.00	80.00
XX-G-MS-01-008	Frosty Frolic	P. Moss	1,000	75.00	400.00
XX-G-MS-01-009	Ginny and Chris with Lambs	P. Moss	1,000	35.00	100.00
XX-G-MS-01-010	Golden Winter	P. Moss	1,000	150.00	400.00
XX-G-MS-01-011	Gossip	P. Moss	1,000	45.00	95.00
XX-G-MS-01-012	Hungry Baby Bird	P. Moss	1,000	15.00	40.00
XX-G-MS-01-013	Joy	P. Moss	1,000	10.00	40.00
XX-G-MS-01-014	Little Fellow	P. Moss	1,000	57.00	115.00
XX-G-MS-01-015	Love	P. Moss	1,000	10.00	40.00
XX-G-MS-01-016	Mary's Lamb, large	P. Moss	1,000	75.00	200.00
XX-G-MS-01-017	Moonlit Skater I, large	P. Moss	1,000	75.00	200.00
XX-G-MS-01-018	Muffet Boy I	P. Moss	1,000	10.00	40.00
XX-G-MS-01-019	Muffet Girl I	P. Moss	1,000	10.00	40.00
XX-G-MS-01-020	Orchard Helpers	P. Moss	1,000	75.00	250.00
XX-G-MS-01-021	Public Gardens and Beacon Street	P. Moss	1,000	50.00	200.00
XX-G-MS-01-022	Quilting Dreams	P. Moss	1,000	40.00	55.00
XX-G-MS-01-023	Reluctant Ballerina	P. Moss	1,000	15.00	40.00
XX-G-MS-01-024	Shenandoah Silhouette	P. Moss	1,000	25.00	60.00
XX-G-MS-01-025	Sisters	P. Moss	1,000	20.00	60.00
XX-G-MS-01-026	Skating Lesson	P. Moss	1,000	50.00	400.00
XX-G-MS-01-027	Snowy Birches	P. Moss	1,000	60.00	160.00
XX-G-MS-01-028	Spirit of Equus	P. Moss	1,000	100.00	150.00
XX-G-MS-01-029	Tarry Not	P. Moss	1,000	35.00	100.00
XX-G-MS-01-030	Wayside Inn	P. Moss	1,000	65.00	440.00
XX-G-MS-01-031	Wedding	P. Moss	1,000	80.00	300.00
XX-G-MS-01-032	Winter Cameo	P. Moss	1,000	30.00	80.00
XX-G-MS-01-033	Workday's O'er	P. Moss	1,000	110.00	350.00
XX-G-MS-01-034	Together	P. Moss	99	450.00	2000.00
New Masters Publishing		**Bannister**			
80-G-ND-01-001	Dust of Autumn	P. Bannister	200	200.00	600.00
80-G-ND-01-002	Faded Glory	P. Bannister	200	200.00	600.00
80-G-ND-01-003	Gift of Happiness	P. Bannister	200	200.00	600.00
80-G-ND-01-004	Girl on the Beach	P. Bannister	200	200.00	600.00
80-G-ND-01-005	The Silver Bell	P. Bannister	200	200.00	600.00
81-G-ND-01-006	April	P. Bannister	300	285.00	300.00
81-G-ND-01-007	Crystal	P. Bannister	300	285.00	300.00
81-G-ND-01-008	Easter	P. Bannister	300	285.00	300.00
81-G-ND-01-009	Juliet	P. Bannister	300	285.00	625.00
81-G-ND-01-010	My Special Place	P. Bannister	300	285.00	600.00
81-G-ND-01-011	Porcelain Rose	P. Bannister	300	285.00	600.00
81-G-ND-01-012	Rehearsal	P. Bannister	300	285.00	300.00
81-G-ND-01-013	Sea Haven	P. Bannister	300	285.00	300.00
81-G-ND-01-014	Titania	P. Bannister	350	285.00	300.00
82-G-ND-01-015	Amaryllis	P. Bannister	500	260.00	600.00
82-G-ND-01-016	Cinderella	P. Bannister	500	260.00	285.00
82-G-ND-01-017	Emily	P. Bannister	500	260.00	285.00
82-G-ND-01-018	Ivy	P. Bannister	500	260.00	285.00
82-G-ND-01-019	Jasmine	P. Bannister	500	260.00	285.00
82-G-ND-01-020	Lily	P. Bannister	500	235.00	235.00
82-G-ND-01-021	Mail Order Brides	P. Bannister	500	325.00	325.00
82-G-ND-01-022	Memories	P. Bannister	500	235.00	235.00
82-G-ND-01-023	Nuance	P. Bannister	500	235.00	235.00
82-G-ND-01-024	Parasols	P. Bannister	500	235.00	235.00
82-G-ND-01-025	The Present	P. Bannister	500	260.00	285.00
83-G-ND-01-026	The Duchess	P. Bannister	500	250.00	250.00
84-G-ND-01-027	The Fan Window	P. Bannister	950	195.00	195.00
84-G-ND-01-028	Window Seat	P. Bannister	950	150.00	150.00
84-G-ND-01-029	Scarlet Ribbons	P. Bannister	950	150.00	150.00
84-G-ND-01-030	April Light	P. Bannister	950	150.00	150.00
Pemberton & Oakes		**Zolan's Children**			
82-G-PO-01-001	Erik and the Dandelion	D. Zolan	880	98.00	250.00
83-G-PO-01-002	By Myself	D. Zolan	880	98.00	130.00
84-G-PO-01-003	Sabina in the Grass	D. Zolan	880	98.00	200.00
Reco International		**Limited Edition Print**			
84-G-RA-02-001	Jessica, signed	S. Kuck	500	60.00	60.00
85-G-RA-02-002	Heather	S. Kuck	500	75.00	75.00
86-G-RA-02-003	Ashley	S. Kuck	500	85.00	85.00
Reco International		**McClelland**			
XX-G-RA-50-001	Olivia	J. McClelland	300	175.00	175.00
XX-G-RA-50-002	Sweet Dreams	J. McClelland	300	145.00	145.00
XX-G-RA-50-003	Just for You	J. McClelland	300	155.00	155.00
XX-G-RA-50-004	Reverie	J. McClelland	300	110.00	110.00
XX-G-RA-50-005	I Love Tammy	J. McClelland	500	75.00	75.00
Roman, Inc.		**Hook**			
81-G-RO-01-001	The Carpenter	F. Hook	Unkn.	100.00	1000.00
81-G-RO-01-002	The Carpenter, remarqued	F. Hook	Yr.Iss	100.00	2000.00
82-G-RO-01-003	Frolicking	F. Hook	1,150	60.00	120.00
82-G-RO-01-004	Gathering	F. Hook	1,150	60.00	120.00
82-G-RO-01-005	Poulets	F. Hook	1,150	60.00	120.00
82-G-RO-01-006	Bouquet	F. Hook	1,150	70.00	140.00
82-G-RO-01-007	Surprise	F. Hook	1,150	50.00	125.00
82-G-RO-01-008	Posing	F. Hook	1,150	70.00	140.00
82-G-RO-01-009	Little Children, Come to Me	F. Hook	1,950	50.00	50.00
82-G-RO-01-010	Little Children, Come to Me, remarque	F. Hook	50	100.00	200.00
Schmid		**Lowell Davis Lithographs**			
81-G-SC-01-001	Surprise in the Cellar, remarque	L. Davis	101	100.00	300.00
81-G-SC-01-002	Surprise in the Cellar, regular edition	L. Davis	899	75.00	185.00
81-G-SC-01-003	Plum Tuckered Out, remarque	L. Davis	101	100.00	300.00
81-G-SC-01-004	Plum Tuckered Out, regular edition	L. Davis	899	75.00	185.00
81-G-SC-01-005	Duke's Mixture, remarque	L. Davis	101	150.00	250.00
81-G-SC-01-006	Duke's Mixture, regular edition	L. Davis	899	75.00	125.00
82-G-SC-01-007	Bustin' with Pride, remarque	L. Davis	101	150.00	250.00
82-G-SC-01-008	Bustin' with Pride, regular edition	L. Davis	899	75.00	125.00
82-G-SC-01-009	Birth of a Blossom, remarque	L. Davis	50	200.00	300.00
82-G-SC-01-010	Birth of Blossom, regular edition	L. Davis	400	125.00	175.00
82-G-SC-01-011	Suppertime, remarque	L. Davis	50	200.00	250.00
82-G-SC-01-012	Suppertime, regular edition	L. Davis	400	125.00	175.00
82-G-SC-01-013	Foxfire Farm, remarque	L. Davis	100	200.00	300.00
82-G-SC-01-014	Foxfire Farm, regular edition	L. Davis	800	125.00	125.00
85-G-SC-01-015	Self Portrait	L. Davis	450	75.00	75.00
Schmid		**Berta Hummel Lithographs**			
80-G-SC-02-001	Moonlight Return	B. Hummel	900	150.00	850.00
80-G-SC-02-002	1984 American Visit	B. Hummel	5	550.00	1000.00
81-G-SC-02-003	A Time to Remember	B. Hummel	720	150.00	300.00
81-G-SC-02-004	1984 American Visit	B. Hummel	5	550.00	1000.00
81-G-SC-02-005	Remarqued	B. Hummel	180	250.00	1250.00
81-G-SC-02-006	1984 American Visit	B. Hummel	2	1100.00	1600.00
82-G-SC-02-007	Poppies	B. Hummel	450	150.00	500.00
82-G-SC-02-008	1984 American Visit	B. Hummel	3	250.00	700.00
83-G-SC-02-009	Angelic Messenger, 75th Anniversary	B. Hummel	195	375.00	700.00
83-G-SC-02-010	Angelic Messenger, Christmas Message	B. Hummel	400	275.00	400.00
83-G-SC-02-011	1984 American Visit	B. Hummel	10	275.00	500.00
83-G-SC-02-012	Regular	B. Hummel	100	175.00	300.00
83-G-SC-02-013	1984 American Visit	B. Hummel	10	175.00	400.00
85-G-SC-02-014	Birthday Bouquet, Edition 1	B. Hummel	195	450.00	450.00
85-G-SC-02-015	Birthday Bouquet, Edition 2	B. Hummel	225	375.00	375.00
85-G-SC-02-016	Birthday Bouquet, Edition 3	B. Hummel	100	195.00	395.00
Schmid		**Ferrandiz Lithographs**			
81-G-SC-03-001	Most Precious Gift, remarque	J. Ferrandiz	50	225.00	2800.00
81-G-SC-03-002	Most Precious Gift, regular edition	J. Ferrandiz	425	125.00	1200.00

Graphics

Company / Number	Name	Series / Artist	Edition limit	Issue Price	Quote
81-G-SC-03-003	My Star, remarque	J. Ferrandiz	75	175.00	1800.00
81-G-SC-03-004	My Star, regular edition	J. Ferrandiz	675	100.00	575.00
81-G-SC-03-005	Heart of Seven Colors, remarque	J. Ferrandiz	75	175.00	1300.00
81-G-SC-03-006	Heart of Seven Colors, regular edition	J. Ferrandiz	600	100.00	350.00
81-G-SC-03-007	Oh Small Child, remarque	J. Ferrandiz	50	225.00	1450.00
81-G-SC-03-008	Oh Small Child, regular edition	J. Ferrandiz	450	125.00	450.00
81-G-SC-03-009	Spreading the Word, remarque	J. Ferrandiz	75	225.00	1075.00
81-G-SC-03-010	Spreading the Word, regular edition	J. Ferrandiz	675	125.00	125.00
81-G-SC-03-011	On the Threshold of Life, remarque	J. Ferrandiz	50	275.00	1250.00
81-G-SC-03-012	On the Threshold of Life, regular edition	J. Ferrandiz	425	150.00	375.00
81-G-SC-03-013	Riding Through the Rain, remarque	J. Ferrandiz	100	300.00	950.00
81-G-SC-03-014	Riding through the Rain, regular edition	J. Ferrandiz	900	165.00	165.00
81-G-SC-03-015	Mirror of the Soul, regular edition	J. Ferrandiz	225	150.00	150.00
81-G-SC-03-016	He Seems to Sleep, regular edition	J. Ferrandiz	450	150.00	600.00
81-G-SC-03-017	Friendship, remarque	J. Ferrandiz	15	1200.00	2300.00
81-G-SC-03-018	Friendship, regular edition	J. Ferrandiz	460	165.00	330.00
Irene Spencer		**Spencer**			
XX-G-SF-01-001	Hug Me	I. Spencer	350	80.00	800.00
XX-G-SF-01-002	Contentment	I. Spencer	350	125.00	190.00
XX-G-SF-01-003	No More Tears	I. Spencer	350	125.00	225.00
XX-G-SF-01-004	I Love You	I. Spencer	550	285.00	285.00
XX-G-SF-01-005	First Edition	I. Spencer	550	135.00	550.00
XX-G-SF-01-006	Precious Moment	I. Spencer	550	135.00	250.00
XX-G-SF-01-007	Flower Princess	I. Spencer	25	185.00	250.00
XX-G-SF-01-008	Storytime	I. Spencer	500	95.00	600.00
XX-G-SF-01-009	Mother's Here	I. Spencer	500	95.00	150.00
XX-G-SF-01-010	L'Envoi	I. Spencer	500	95.00	95.00
XX-G-SF-01-011	I Love Little Kitty	I. Spencer	500	95.00	150.00
XX-G-SF-01-012	Pachamama	I. Spencer	500	95.00	110.00
XX-G-SF-01-013	Sleep Little Baby	I. Spencer	500	95.00	415.00
XX-G-SF-01-014	Miracle	I. Spencer	500	125.00	600.00
XX-G-SF-01-015	Empty Saddles	I. Spencer	500	125.00	125.00
XX-G-SF-01-016	Danny's Tune	I. Spencer	50	110.00	200.00
XX-G-SF-01-017	This is What It's All About	I. Spencer	50	110.00	400.00
XX-G-SF-01-018	Lonesome Melody	I. Spencer	50	220.00	500.00
XX-G-SF-01-019	Smoke Dreams	I. Spencer	50	55.00	2000.00
XX-G-SF-01-020	Hills of Home	I. Spencer	100	110.00	450.00
XX-G-SF-01-021	Summer Afternoon	I. Spencer	100	110.00	300.00
XX-G-SF-01-022	Long, Long Days	I. Spencer	100	110.00	450.00
XX-G-SF-01-023	Dear Child	I. Spencer	100	110.00	300.00
XX-G-SF-01-024	Carefree	I. Spencer	100	110.00	300.00
XX-G-SF-01-025	Yesterday, Today & Tomorrow	I. Spencer	100	110.00	700.00
XX-G-SF-01-026	Larmette	I. Spencer	100	110.00	700.00
XX-G-SF-01-027	Sleep Little Baby	I. Spencer	100	110.00	700.00
XX-G-SF-01-028	My Devotion	I. Spencer	175	60.00	1000.00
XX-G-SF-01-029	Secrets	I. Spencer	275	60.00	1000.00
XX-G-SF-01-030	First Kiss	I. Spencer	275	15.00	450.00
XX-G-SF-01-031	Bittersweet	I. Spencer	300	150.00	500.00
XX-G-SF-01-032	Beyond the Sun	I. Spencer	400	185.00	400.00
XX-G-SF-01-033	I Love You	I. Spencer	550	285.00	285.00
XX-G-SF-01-034	First Edition	I. Spencer	550	135.00	550.00
XX-G-SF-01-035	Precious Moment	I. Spencer	550	135.00	350.00
XX-G-SF-01-036	Moon Goddess	I. Spencer	550	185.00	250.00
Irene Spencer		**Mother & Child Cats**			
80-G-SF-02-001	Christmas Mourning	I. Spencer	1,500	75.00	175.00
81-G-SF-02-002	The Paw that Refreshes	I. Spencer	1,500	85.00	115.00
81-G-SF-02-003	Sandy Claws	I. Spencer	1,500	85.00	85.00
82-G-SF-02-004	The Tail of Two Kittes	I. Spencer	1,500	85.00	85.00
Irene Spencer		**Mother & Child**			
81-G-SF-03-001	Oh, Mom!	I. Spencer	350	135.00	150.00
82-G-SF-03-002	The Greatest Gift	I. Spencer	350	135.00	150.00
Irene Spencer		**Let's Pretend**			
80-G-SF-04-001	Sir Lancelot	I. Spencer	350	185.00	210.00
81-G-SF-04-002	Queen Guinevere	I. Spencer	350	185.00	195.00
81-G-SF-04-003	Mark Antony	I. Spencer	350	225.00	265.00
82-G-SF-04-004	Cleopatra	I. Spencer	350	225.00	225.00
Irene Spencer		**Mission Madonnas**			
82-G-SF-05-001	Capistrano Madonna	I. Spencer	350	225.00	225.00
U.S. Historical Society		**Yorktown Prints**			
81-G-US-01-001	Battle of Virginia Capes	J. Woodson	575	200.00	275.00
81-G-US-01-002	George Washington Fires First Round Yorktown	J. Woodson	575	200.00	275.00
81-G-US-01-003	Historical Map of Yorktown	J. Woodson	575	200.00	275.00
Vague Shadows		**Perillo**			
77-G-VC-01-001	Madre	G. Perillo	500	125.00	425.00
78-G-VC-01-002	Madonna of the Plains	G. Perillo	500	125.00	400.00
78-G-VC-01-003	Snow Pals	G. Perillo	500	125.00	350.00
79-G-VC-01-004	Sioux Scout and Buffalo Hunt, matched set	G. Perillo	500	150.00	375.00
80-G-VC-01-005	Babysitter	G. Perillo	3,000	45.00	100.00
80-G-VC-01-006	Puppies	G. Perillo	3,000	45.00	600.00
82-G-VC-01-007	Tinker	G. Perillo	3,000	45.00	45.00
82-G-VC-01-008	Tender Love	G. Perillo	950	75.00	175.00
82-G-VC-01-009	Lonesome Cowboy	G. Perillo	950	75.00	75.00
81-G-VC-01-010	Peaceable Kingdom	G. Perillo	950	100.00	250.00
82-G-VC-01-011	Chief Pontiac	G. Perillo	950	75.00	75.00
82-G-VC-01-012	Hoofbeats	G. Perillo	950	100.00	100.00
82-G-VC-01-013	Indian Style	G. Perillo	950	75.00	75.00
82-G-VC-01-014	Maria	G. Perillo	550	150.00	150.00
82-G-VC-01-015	Butterfly	R. Sauber	3,000	45.00	45.00
83-G-VC-01-016	The Moment Poster	G. Perillo	Unkn.	20.00	20.00
85-G-VC-01-017	Chief Crazy Horse	G. Perillo	950	125.00	200.00
85-G-VC-01-018	Chief Sitting Bull	G. Perillo	500	125.00	125.00
85-G-VC-01-019	Marigold	G. Perillo	500	125.00	125.00
85-G-VC-01-020	Whirlaway	G. Perillo	950	125.00	125.00
85-G-VC-01-021	Secretariat	G. Perillo	950	125.00	125.00
86-G-VC-01-022	Pout	G. Perillo	325	150.00	150.00
86-G-VC-01-023	The Rescue	G. Perillo	325	150.00	150.00
84-G-VC-01-024	Out of the Forest	G. Perillo	Unkn.	Unknown	Unknown
84-G-VC-01-025	Navajo Love	G. Perillo	300	125.00	250.00
86-G-VC-01-026	War Pony	G. Perillo	325	150.00	150.00
86-G-VC-01-027	Learning His Ways	G. Perillo	325	150.00	150.00
86-G-VC-01-028	Pout	G. Perillo	325	150.00	150.00
Viking Import House		**Ships**			
86-G-VG-01-001	The Wanderer	R. Horton	2,800	45.00	45.00
86-G-VG-01-002	Fastnet - 1979	R. Horton	2,800	45.00	45.00

Company / Number	Name	Series / Artist	Edition limit	Issue Price	Quote
Wildlife Internationale		**John A. Ruthven**			
73-G-WF-01-001	Algonquin	J. Ruthven	750	75.00	150.00
77-G-WF-01-002	Arctic Fox	J. Ruthven	950	150.00	525.00
66-G-WF-01-003	Bald Eagle	J. Ruthven	1,000	30.00	800.00
76-G-WF-01-004	Bald Eagle	J. Ruthven	776	350.00	850.00
75-G-WF-01-005	Bengal Tiger	J. Ruthven	1,000	100.00	600.00
68-G-WF-01-006	Bengal Tiger	J. Ruthven	1,000	80.00	1800.00
70-G-WF-01-007	Bengal Tiger	J. Ruthven	5,000	65.00	850.00
74-G-WF-01-008	Black Maned Lion	J. Ruthven	5,000	65.00	200.00
XX-G-WF-01-009	Bluebirds	J. Ruthven	1,000	30.00	625.00
81-G-WF-01-010	Bluebirds	J. Ruthven	950	75.00	250.00
77-G-WF-01-011	Blue Winged Teal	J. Ruthven	500	75.00	550.00
76-G-WF-01-012	Bobwhite Quail	J. Ruthven	1,000	80.00	250.00
73-G-WF-01-013	Bobwhite Quail	J. Ruthven	750	75.00	250.00
XX-G-WF-01-014	Bobwhite Quail	J. Ruthven	1,000	30.00	575.00
XX-G-WF-01-015	Brown Pelican	J. Ruthven	500	125.00	300.00
75-G-WF-01-016	Canada Geese	J. Ruthven	1,000	95.00	250.00
70-G-WF-01-017	Canvasback on the Ohio	J. Ruthven	1,000	50.00	450.00
67-G-WF-01-018	Cardinal	J. Ruthven	1,000	30.00	875.00
78-G-WF-01-019	Cardinal	J. Ruthven	950	75.00	500.00
81-G-WF-01-020	Cardinal	J. Ruthven	950	75.00	350.00
72-G-WF-01-021	Carolina Paraquets	J. Ruthven	500	300.00	1550.00
XX-G-WF-01-022	Cedar Waxwing	J. Ruthven	950	50.00	175.00
78-G-WF-01-023	Chickadees	J. Ruthven	950	50.00	300.00
XX-G-WF-01-024	Chipmunk	J. Ruthven	500	Unknown	375.00
70-G-WF-01-025	Cinnamon Teal	J. Ruthven	1,000	30.00	200.00
79-G-WF-01-026	Decoy	J. Ruthven	750	125.00	850.00
79-G-WF-01-027	Downy Woodpecker	J. Ruthven	600	50.00	325.00
81-G-WF-01-028	Dusty	J. Ruthven	950	150.00	675.00
72-G-WF-01-029	Eagle to the Moon	J. Ruthven	500	150.00	2200.00
72-G-WF-01-030	Eastern Wild Turkey	J. Ruthven	750	75.00	375.00
67-G-WF-01-031	Eastern Wild Turkey	J. Ruthven	1,000	30.00	550.00
72-G-WF-01-032	Elephants	J. Ruthven	5,000	65.00	125.00
75-G-WF-01-033	Flickers	J. Ruthven	950	65.00	200.00
71-G-WF-01-034	Fox Masque I	J. Ruthven	1,000	30.00	200.00
71-G-WF-01-035	Fox Masque II	J. Ruthven	1,000	30.00	200.00
72-G-WF-01-036	Giant Pandas	J. Ruthven	5,000	65.00	100.00
74-G-WF-01-037	Grant's Zebra	J. Ruthven	3,500	75.00	200.00
XX-G-WF-01-038	Gray Squirrel	J. Ruthven	600	55.00	225.00
75-G-WF-01-039	Gray Fox	J. Ruthven	950	125.00	1500.00
76-G-WF-01-040	Gray Fox Family	J. Ruthven	950	150.00	1100.00
74-G-WF-01-041	Great Horned Owl	J. Ruthven	1,000	90.00	450.00
78-G-WF-01-042	Green Winged Teal	J. Ruthven	500	75.00	475.00
74-G-WF-01-043	Herring Gulls	J. Ruthven	1,000	50.00	450.00
73-G-WF-01-044	Hooded Merganser	J. Ruthven	750	70.00	150.00
74-G-WF-01-045	Ivory Billed Woodpecker	J. Ruthven	500	350.00	850.00
75-G-WF-01-046	Jaguar	J. Ruthven	950	65.00	475.00
76-G-WF-01-047	Kit Fox	J. Ruthven	500	100.00	400.00
75-G-WF-01-048	Labrador Duck	J. Ruthven	500	350.00	650.00
75-G-WF-01-049	Leopard	J. Ruthven	3,500	75.00	125.00
69-G-WF-01-050	Mallard	J. Ruthven	1,000	50.00	425.00
76-G-WF-01-051	Mallard/Wood Ducks, pair	J. Ruthven	99	750.00	1700.00
71-G-WF-01-052	Nature Center Cardinal	J. Ruthven	1,000	50.00	500.00
70-G-WF-01-053	N.Y. State Bluebird	J. Ruthven	1,000	50.00	350.00
73-G-WF-01-054	On The Hunt	J. Ruthven	1,000	90.00	200.00
73-G-WF-01-055	Passenger Pigeons	J. Ruthven	500	350.00	1550.00
79-G-WF-01-056	Peregrine Falcon	J. Ruthven	600	65.00	225.00
66-G-WF-01-057	Pheasant	J. Ruthven	1,000	30.00	600.00
77-G-WF-01-058	Pheasant, pair	J. Ruthven	99	850.00	1600.00
68-G-WF-01-059	Red Fox	J. Ruthven	1,000	90.00	1500.00
79-G-WF-01-060	Red Fox	J. Ruthven	950	150.00	550.00
71-G-WF-01-061	Red Fox Family	J. Ruthven	1,000	90.00	1100.00
60-G-WF-01-062	Redhead Ducks	J. Ruthven	400	Unknown	500.00
70-G-WF-01-063	Redheaded Woodpecker	J. Ruthven	1,000	50.00	475.00
73-G-WF-01-064	Roadrunner	J. Ruthven	1,000	50.00	400.00
71-G-WF-01-065	Robins	J. Ruthven	1,000	50.00	475.00
XX-G-WF-01-066	Robin Family	J. Ruthven	600	55.00	250.00
70-G-WF-01-067	Ruddy Ducks	J. Ruthven	1,000	50.00	475.00
XX-G-WF-01-068	Ruddy Ducks	J. Ruthven	600	55.00	300.00
69-G-WF-01-069	Ruffed Grouse	J. Ruthven	1,000	40.00	500.00
75-G-WF-01-070	Ruffed Grouse, pair	J. Ruthven	99	750.00	1950.00
80-G-WF-01-071	Rummy	J. Ruthven	950	150.00	575.00
68-G-WF-01-072	Screech Owls	J. Ruthven	1,000	30.00	750.00
77-G-WF-01-073	Screech Owls	J. Ruthven	950	50.00	350.00
70-G-WF-01-074	Snowy Owl	J. Ruthven	1,000	50.00	550.00
73-G-WF-01-075	Terns	J. Ruthven	750	150.00	375.00
70-G-WF-01-076	Wandering Brave	J. Ruthven	1,000	90.00	725.00
73-G-WF-01-077	White Tailed Deer	J. Ruthven	750	150.00	550.00
79-G-WF-01-078	White Tigers	J. Ruthven	1,000	150.00	425.00
68-G-WF-01-079	Wood Ducks	J. Ruthven	1,000	40.00	375.00
70-G-WF-01-080	Wood Ducks	J. Ruthven	1,000	90.00	500.00
XX-G-WF-01-081	Wood Ducks/Mallard, pair	J. Ruthven	99	850.00	1600.00
82-G-WF-01-082	Wood Ducks	J. Ruthven	10,000	125.00	250.00
Wild Wings		**Clymer**			
79-G-WG-01-001	By the Tundra Pond	J. Clymer	750	200.00	200.00
Wooden Bird		**Redlin**			
77-G-WJ-02-001	Apple River Mallards	T. Redlin	Closed	10.00	50.00
77-G-WJ-02-002	Over the Blowdown	T. Redlin	Closed	20.00	50.00
77-G-WJ-02-003	Winter Snows	T. Redlin	Closed	20.00	60.00
78-G-WJ-02-004	Back from the Fields	T. Redlin	720	40.00	120.00
78-G-WJ-02-005	Backwater Mallards	T. Redlin	720	40.00	500.00
78-G-WJ-02-006	Old Loggers Trail	T. Redlin	720	40.00	500.00
78-G-WJ-02-007	Quiet Afternoon	T. Redlin	720	40.00	325.00
78-G-WJ-02-008	Startled	T. Redlin	960	30.00	275.00
79-G-WJ-02-009	Aging Shoreline	T. Redlin	960	40.00	120.00
79-G-WJ-02-010	Colorful Trio	T. Redlin	960	40.00	295.00
79-G-WJ-02-011	Fighting a Headwind	T. Redlin	960	30.00	120.00
79-G-WJ-02-012	The Loner	T. Redlin	960	40.00	120.00
79-G-WJ-02-013	Morning Chores	T. Redlin	960	40.00	750.00
79-G-WJ-02-014	Whitecaps	T. Redlin	960	40.00	150.00
80-G-WJ-02-015	Autumn Run	T. Redlin	960	60.00	275.00
80-G-WJ-02-016	Breaking Away	T. Redlin	960	60.00	150.00
80-G-WJ-02-017	Clearing the Rail	T. Redlin	960	60.00	250.00
80-G-WJ-02-018	Country Road	T. Redlin	960	60.00	275.00
80-G-WJ-02-019	Drifting	T. Redlin	960	60.00	150.00
80-G-WJ-02-020	Homestead	T. Redlin	960	60.00	250.00
80-G-WJ-02-021	Intruders	T. Redlin	960	60.00	120.00
80-G-WJ-02-022	Rusty Refuge	T. Redlin	960	60.00	350.00
80-G-WJ-02-023	Secluded Pond	T. Redlin	960	60.00	120.00
80-G-WJ-02-024	Silent Sunset	T. Redlin	960	60.00	500.00

Graphics

Company		Series			
Number	Name	Artist	Edition limit	Issue Price	Quote
80-G-WJ-02-025	Spring Thaw	T. Redlin	960	60.00	300.00
80-G-WJ-02-026	Squall Line	T. Redlin	960	60.00	120.00
81-G-WJ-02-027	All Clear	T. Redlin	960	150.00	300.00
81-G-WJ-02-028	April Snow	T. Redlin	960	100.00	300.00
81-G-WJ-02-029	Broken Covey	T. Redlin	960	100.00	200.00
81-G-WJ-02-030	Sharing the Bounty	T. Redlin	960	100.00	250.00
81-G-WJ-02-031	High Country	T. Redlin	960	100.00	250.00
81-G-WJ-02-032	Hightailing	T. Redlin	960	75.00	75.00
81-G-WJ-02-033	Landmark	T. Redlin	960	100.00	250.00
81-G-WJ-02-034	Morning Retreat	T. Redlin	240	400.00	1200.00
81-G-WJ-02-035	Night Watch	T. Redlin	960	100.00	200.00
81-G-WJ-02-036	Passing Through	T. Redlin	960	100.00	300.00
81-G-WJ-02-037	Rusty Refuge II	T. Redlin	960	100.00	350.00
81-G-WJ-02-038	Soft Shadows	T. Redlin	960	100.00	100.00
81-G-WJ-02-039	Spring Run-Off	T. Redlin	1,700	125.00	125.00
82-G-WJ-02-040	The Birch Line	T. Redlin	960	100.00	300.00
82-G-WJ-02-041	Evening Retreat	T. Redlin	960	400.00	1200.00
82-G-WJ-02-042	The Landing	T. Redlin	Open	30.00	30.00
82-G-WJ-02-043	October Evening	T. Redlin	960	100.00	200.00
82-G-WJ-02-044	Spring Mapling	T. Redlin	960	100.00	300.00
82-G-WJ-02-045	Whitewater	T. Redlin	960	100.00	300.00
83-G-WJ-02-046	Autumn Shoreline	T. Redlin	Open	50.00	50.00
83-G-WJ-02-047	Backwoods Cabin	T. Redlin	960	100.00	350.00
83-G-WJ-02-048	Evening Glow	T. Redlin	960	150.00	750.00
83-G-WJ-02-049	Evening Surprise	T. Redlin	960	150.00	400.00
83-G-WJ-02-050	Hidden Point	T. Redlin	960	150.00	300.00
83-G-WJ-02-051	On the Alert	T. Redlin	960	125.00	250.00
83-G-WJ-02-052	Peaceful Evening	T. Redlin	960	100.00	250.00
83-G-WJ-02-053	Prairie Spring	T. Redlin	960	150.00	150.00
83-G-WJ-02-054	Rushing Rapids	T. Redlin	960	125.00	250.00
83-G-WJ-02-055	Seed Hunters	T. Redlin	960	100.00	250.00
84-G-WJ-02-056	Closed for the Season	T. Redlin	960	150.00	150.00
84-G-WJ-02-057	Rusty Refuge III	T. Redlin	960	150.00	300.00
84-G-WJ-02-058	Night Flight	T. Redlin	360	600.00	1000.00
84-G-WJ-02-059	Sundown	T. Redlin	960	300.00	500.00
84-G-WJ-02-060	Leaving the Sanctuary	T. Redlin	960	150.00	350.00
84-G-WJ-02-061	Rural Route	T. Redlin	960	150.00	300.00
84-G-WJ-02-062	Prairie Skyline	T. Redlin	960	150.00	400.00
84-G-WJ-02-063	Morning Glow	T. Redlin	960	150.00	700.00
84-G-WJ-02-064	1984 Quail Unlimited	T. Redlin	1,500	125.00	125.00
84-G-WJ-02-065	Silent Wings, suite of four	T. Redlin	960	200.00	400.00
84-G-WJ-02-066	Changing Seasons-Summer	T. Redlin	960	150.00	400.00
84-G-WJ-02-067	Night Harvest	T. Redlin	960	150.00	400.00
84-G-WJ-02-068	Sunny Afternoon	T. Redlin	960	150.00	300.00
84-G-WJ-02-069	Winter Windbreak	T. Redlin	960	150.00	300.00
85-G-WJ-02-070	Night Light	T. Redlin	1,500	300.00	400.00
85-G-WJ-02-071	Evening Company	T. Redlin	1,500	300.00	300.00
85-G-WJ-02-072	Clear View	T. Redlin	1,500	300.00	300.00
85-G-WJ-02-073	Delayed Departure	T. Redlin	1,500	300.00	300.00
85-G-WJ-02-074	Afternoon Glow	T. Redlin	960	150.00	600.00
85-G-WJ-02-075	Browsing	T. Redlin	960	150.00	150.00
85-G-WJ-02-076	Breaking Cover	T. Redlin	960	150.00	300.00
85-G-WJ-02-077	Rusty Refuge IV	T. Redlin	960	150.00	150.00
85-G-WJ-02-078	Riverside Pond	T. Redlin	960	150.00	300.00
85-G-WJ-02-079	Whistle Stop	T. Redlin	960	150.00	300.00
85-G-WJ-02-080	The Sharing Season	T. Redlin	Open	60.00	60.00
86-G-WJ-02-081	Stormy Weather	T. Redlin	1,500	200.00	400.00
86-G-WJ-02-082	Hazy Afternoon	T. Redlin	2,560	200.00	400.00
86-G-WJ-02-083	Silent Flight	T. Redlin	960	150.00	150.00
86-G-WJ-02-084	Back to the Sanctuary	T. Redlin	960	150.00	150.00
86-G-WJ-02-085	Changing Seasons-Autumn	T. Redlin	960	150.00	300.00

Wooden Bird — Clymer

Number	Name	Artist	Edition limit	Issue Price	Quote
78-G-WJ-03-001	Furseekers	J. Clymer	750	150.00	500.00
78-G-WJ-03-002	Nez Perce to the Buffalo	J. Clymer	750	150.00	500.00
78-G-WJ-03-003	Sacajawea at the Big Water	J. Clymer	750	150.00	650.00
78-G-WJ-03-004	Alouette	J. Clymer	750	150.00	400.00
78-G-WJ-03-005	Winter Trail	J. Clymer	975	100.00	250.00
78-G-WJ-03-006	Night Visitors	J. Clymer	750	100.00	500.00
78-G-WJ-03-007	Something for the Pot	J. Clymer	900	125.00	125.00

Wooden Bird — Raedeke

Number	Name	Artist	Edition limit	Issue Price	Quote
78-G-WJ-04-001	Broken Solitude-Grouse	J. Raedeke	580	60.00	100.00
78-G-WJ-04-002	Old Township Road-Quail	J. Raedeke	270	50.00	150.00
78-G-WJ-04-003	Prairie Homestead-Partridge	J. Raedeke	270	25.00	75.00
73-G-WJ-04-004	Empty Blind-Bluebills	J. Raedeke	580	60.00	120.00
73-G-WJ-04-005	Prairie Willow-Pheasant	J. Raedeke	380	50.00	275.00
73-G-WJ-04-006	Prairie Windmill-Blue Geese	J. Raedeke	580	20.00	20.00
80-G-WJ-04-007	Empty Blind-Canada Geese	J. Raedeke	580	60.00	150.00
81-G-WJ-04-008	Kansas Wild Trust Print	J. Raedeke	580	100.00	150.00
81-G-WJ-04-009	Pheasants on Kasota Prairie	J. Raedeke	580	50.00	100.00
81-G-WJ-04-010	Prairie Congregation AP	J. Raedeke	240	100.00	100.00
83-G-WJ-04-011	Feet Down at Dr. J's AP	J. Raedeke	300	60.00	200.00
84-G-WJ-04-012	Pair of Singles	J. Raedeke	960	15.00	15.00
84-G-WJ-04-013	Hunters Moon	J. Raedeke	4,300	60.00	60.00
85-G-WJ-04-014	Breakfast at Peterson	J. Raedeke	5,300	50.00	50.00
85-G-WJ-04-015	Loon Song	J. Raedeke	960	20.00	40.00
85-G-WJ-04-016	Wake Up Call	J. Raedeke	960	20.00	40.00
85-G-WJ-04-017	Soft and Silent	J. Raedeke	960	35.00	35.00
85-G-WJ-04-018	Sundowners	J. Raedeke	960	25.00	25.00
85-G-WJ-04-019	Sioux Tipis & Sundogs	J. Raedeke	960	45.00	45.00
85-G-WJ-04-020	Tipis on Little Grass Creek	J. Raedeke	960	25.00	25.00

Wooden Bird — Wieghorst

Number	Name	Artist	Edition limit	Issue Price	Quote
72-G-WJ-05-001	Navajo Madonna	O. Wieghorst	1,500	40.00	7000.00
73-G-WJ-05-002	Buffalo Scout	O. Wieghorst	1,000	150.00	750.00
73-G-WJ-05-003	California Wrangler	O. Wieghorst	1,000	150.00	400.00
73-G-WJ-05-004	Corraling the Cavvy	O. Wieghorst	1,000	150.00	400.00
73-G-WJ-05-005	Missing in the Roundup	O. Wieghorst	1,000	150.00	400.00
74-G-WJ-05-006	Navajo Portrait	O. Wieghorst	1,000	150.00	400.00
74-G-WJ-05-007	Packing in	O. Wieghorst	1,000	150.00	400.00
74-G-WJ-05-008	Apache Territory	O. Wieghorst	300	400.00	1200.00
79-G-WJ-05-009	Apache Renegade	O. Wieghorst	500	125.00	250.00
79-G-WJ-05-010	Arizona Range	O. Wieghorst	500	125.00	250.00
79-G-WJ-05-011	Cow Country	O. Wieghorst	500	125.00	250.00
79-G-WJ-05-012	Drifting	O. Wieghorst	500	125.00	250.00
79-G-WJ-05-013	Horse Wranglers	O. Wieghorst	500	125.00	250.00
79-G-WJ-05-014	Indian Scout	O. Wieghorst	500	125.00	1500.00
79-G-WJ-05-015	Indian Trail	O. Wieghorst	500	125.00	250.00
79-G-WJ-05-016	The Lost Trail	O. Wieghorst	500	125.00	250.00
79-G-WJ-05-017	Mogollon Trail	O. Wieghorst	500	125.00	250.00
79-G-WJ-05-018	Pleasant Creek	O. Wieghorst	500	125.00	400.00

Graphics/Plates

Company		Series			
Number	Name	Artist	Edition limit	Issue Price	Quote
79-G-WJ-05-019	Range Chuck	O. Wieghorst	500	125.00	400.00
79-G-WJ-05-020	Range Ponies	O. Wieghorst	500	125.00	400.00
79-G-WJ-05-021	Talking Sign	O. Wieghorst	500	125.00	250.00
79-G-WJ-05-022	Water Ahead	O. Wieghorst	500	125.00	650.00
80-G-WJ-05-023	Los Charros	O. Wieghorst	999	150.00	250.00
80-G-WJ-05-024	Nighthawk	O. Wieghorst	999	150.00	250.00
81-G-WJ-05-025	Wagon and Remuda	O. Wieghorst	999	150.00	350.00
82-G-WJ-05-026	Dead Cottonwood	O. Wieghorst	900	150.00	600.00
82-G-WJ-05-027	Sioux Chief Hump	O. Wieghorst	900	150.00	200.00
82-G-WJ-05-028	Tired	O. Wieghorst	900	150.00	350.00
82-G-WJ-05-029	Opening of Cherokee Strip	O. Wieghorst	900	150.00	250.00
82-G-WJ-05-030	Partners	O. Wieghorst	950	225.00	900.00
82-G-WJ-05-031	Cold Conference	O. Wieghorst	900	150.00	300.00
82-G-WJ-05-032	Canyon Trail	O. Wieghorst	900	150.00	300.00
82-G-WJ-05-033	Moonlight and Shadows	O. Wieghorst	900	150.00	300.00
82-G-WJ-05-034	Navajos at Castle Creek	O. Wieghorst	900	150.00	300.00
82-G-WJ-05-035	Rocky Mountain Trail	O. Wieghorst	900	150.00	300.00
82-G-WJ-05-036	Salt River Canyon	O. Wieghorst	900	150.00	300.00
82-G-WJ-05-037	Watering the Remuda	O. Wieghorst	900	150.00	300.00
83-G-WJ-05-038	The Navajo	O. Wieghorst	1,500	500.00	3000.00
83-G-WJ-05-039	The Wild Ones	O. Wieghorst	950	225.00	300.00
83-G-WJ-05-040	Appaloosa	O. Wieghorst	999	200.00	200.00
83-G-WJ-05-041	Indian Country	O. Wieghorst	999	200.00	200.00
83-G-WJ-05-042	Nez Perce on Appaloosa	O. Wieghorst	999	200.00	400.00
83-G-WJ-05-043	Range Boss	O. Wieghorst	999	200.00	200.00
83-G-WJ-05-044	Range Horses	O. Wieghorst	999	200.00	200.00
83-G-WJ-05-045	Tracking the Strays	O. Wieghorst	999	200.00	200.00
84-G-WJ-05-046	Nomads of the Plains	O. Wieghorst	1,500	500.00	1000.00
84-G-WJ-05-047	Beef Herd	O. Wieghorst	1,500	500.00	500.00
84-G-WJ-05-048	The Nomad	O. Wieghorst	Open	75.00	75.00
84-G-WJ-05-049	Black Canyon Trail	O. Wieghorst	1,500	250.00	250.00
84-G-WJ-05-050	No Tracks	O. Wieghorst	1,500	250.00	250.00
84-G-WJ-05-051	Watering Hole	O. Wieghorst	1,500	250.00	250.00
85-G-WJ-05-052	Scouting Party	O. Wieghorst	1,500	250.00	250.00
85-G-WJ-05-053	Superstition Trail	O. Wieghorst	1,500	250.00	250.00
85-G-WJ-05-054	When Shelter is Scarce	O. Wieghorst	1,500	250.00	250.00
86-G-WJ-05-055	Spring Rain	O. Wieghorst	1,500	250.00	750.00
86-G-WJ-05-056	His Spotted Pony	O. Wieghorst	1,500	250.00	500.00

World Art Editions — Masseria

Number	Name	Artist	Edition limit	Issue Price	Quote
80-G-WL-02-001	Eduardo	F. Masseria	300	275.00	2700.00
80-G-WL-02-002	Rosanna	F. Masseria	300	275.00	3200.00
80-G-WL-02-003	Nina	F. Masseria	300	325.00	1950.00
80-G-WL-02-004	First Kiss	F. Masseria	300	375.00	1600.00
81-G-WL-02-005	Selene	F. Masseria	300	325.00	1300.00
81-G-WL-02-006	First Flower	F. Masseria	300	325.00	1600.00
81-G-WL-02-007	Elisa with Flower	F. Masseria	300	325.00	1600.00
81-G-WL-02-008	Solange	F. Masseria	300	325.00	950.00
81-G-WL-02-009	Susan Sewing	F. Masseria	300	375.00	2300.00
81-G-WL-02-010	Jessica	F. Masseria	300	375.00	1650.00
81-G-WL-02-011	Eleanor	F. Masseria	300	375.00	900.00
81-G-WL-02-012	Julie	F. Masseria	300	375.00	950.00
82-G-WL-02-013	Robin	F. Masseria	300	425.00	975.00
82-G-WL-02-014	Jodie	F. Masseria	300	425.00	500.00
82-G-WL-02-015	Jill	F. Masseria	300	425.00	500.00
82-G-WL-02-016	Jamie	F. Masseria	300	425.00	550.00
82-G-WL-02-017	Yasmin	F. Masseria	300	425.00	525.00
82-G-WL-02-018	Yvette	F. Masseria	300	425.00	525.00
82-G-WL-02-019	Judith	F. Masseria	300	425.00	525.00
82-G-WL-02-020	Amy	F. Masseria	300	425.00	525.00
83-G-WL-02-021	Jamie	F. Masseria	300	425.00	850.00
83-G-WL-02-022	Jody	F. Masseria	300	425.00	525.00
83-G-WL-02-023	Jill	F. Masseria	300	425.00	525.00
83-G-WL-02-024	Robin	F. Masseria	300	425.00	575.00
83-G-WL-02-025	Tara	F. Masseria	300	450.00	1100.00
83-G-WL-02-026	Antonio	F. Masseria	300	450.00	1100.00
84-G-WL-02-027	Memoirs	F. Masseria	300	450.00	500.00
84-G-WL-02-028	Christopher	F. Masseria	300	450.00	500.00
84-G-WL-02-029	Bettina	F. Masseria	250	550.00	700.00
84-G-WL-02-030	Vincente	F. Masseria	300	550.00	850.00
85-G-WL-02-031	Christina	F. Masseria	300	500.00	550.00
85-G-WL-02-032	Jorgito	F. Masseria	300	500.00	550.00
84-G-WL-02-033	Regina	F. Masseria	950	395.00	495.00
84-G-WL-02-034	Peter	F. Masseria	950	395.00	495.00
85-G-WL-02-035	Marguerita	F. Masseria	950	495.00	495.00
85-G-WL-02-036	To Catch a Butterfly	F. Masseria	950	495.00	495.00

World Art Editions — Mago

Number	Name	Artist	Edition limit	Issue Price	Quote
82-G-WL-03-001	Siprario	Mago	300	325.00	325.00
82-G-WL-03-002	Deposition	Mago	300	325.00	325.00

Plates

American Artists — The Horses of Fred Stone

Number	Name	Artist	Edition limit	Issue Price	Quote
82-P-AA-01-001	Patience	F. Stone	9,500	55.00	110.00
82-P-AA-01-002	Arabian Mare and Foal	F. Stone	9,500	55.00	110.00
82-P-AA-01-003	Safe and Sound	F. Stone	9,500	55.00	70.00
83-P-AA-01-004	Contentment	F. Stone	9,500	55.00	70.00
83-P-AA-01-005	Black Stallion	F. Stone	9,500	49.50	85.00
83-P-AA-01-006	Andalusian	F. Stone	9,500	49.50	63.00
84-P-AA-01-007	Man O' War	F. Stone	9,500	65.00	80.00
84-P-AA-01-008	Secretariat	F. Stone	9,500	65.00	80.00
85-P-AA-01-009	John Henry	F. Stone	9,500	65.00	75.00
86-P-AA-01-010	Seattle Slew	F. Stone	9,500	65.00	65.00
86-P-AA-01-011	Water Trough	F. Stone	9,500	49.50	49.50
86-P-AA-01-012	Tranquility	F. Stone	9,500	49.50	49.50
86-P-AA-01-013	Pasture Pest	F. Stone	9,500	49.50	49.50
86-P-AA-01-014	The Shoe - 8,000 Wins	F. Stone	9,500	75.00	75.00

American Artists — Family Treasures

Number	Name	Artist	Edition limit	Issue Price	Quote
81-P-AA-02-001	Cora's Recital	R. Zolan	18,500	39.50	39.50
82-P-AA-02-002	Cora's Tea Party	R. Zolan	18,500	39.50	39.50
83-P-AA-02-003	Cora's Garden Party	R. Zolan	18,500	39.50	39.50

American Rose Society — All-America Rose

Number	Name	Artist	Edition limit	Issue Price	Quote
75-P-AM-01-001	Oregold	Unknown	9,800	39.00	142.00
75-P-AM-01-002	Arizona	Unknown	9,800	39.00	142.00
75-P-AM-01-003	Rose Parade	Unknown	9,800	39.00	137.00
76-P-AM-01-004	Yankee Doodle	Unknown	9,800	39.00	135.50
76-P-AM-01-005	America	Unknown	9,800	39.00	135.50
76-P-AM-01-006	Cathedral	Unknown	9,800	39.00	135.50
76-P-AM-01-007	Seashell	Unknown	9,800	39.00	135.50
77-P-AM-01-008	Double Delight	Unknown	9,800	39.00	115.00
77-P-AM-01-009	Prominent	Unknown	9,800	39.00	115.00

Number	Name	Artist	Edition limit	Issue Price	Quote
Company		**Series**			
77-P-AM-01-010	First Edition	Unknown	9,800	39.00	115.00
78-P-AM-01-011	Color Magic	Unknown	9,800	39.00	107.00
78-P-AM-01-012	Charisma	Unknown	9,800	39.00	107.00
79-P-AM-01-013	Paradise	Unknown	9,800	39.00	89.00
79-P-AM-01-014	Sundowner	Unknown	9,800	39.00	89.00
79-P-AM-01-015	Friendship	Unknown	9,800	39.00	89.00
80-P-AM-01-016	Love	Unknown	9,800	49.00	80.00
80-P-AM-01-017	Honor	Unknown	9,800	49.00	80.00
80-P-AM-01-018	Cherish	Unknown	9,800	49.00	80.00
81-P-AM-01-019	Bing Crosby	Unknown	9,800	49.00	75.00
81-P-AM-01-020	White Lightnin	Unknown	9,800	49.00	75.00
81-P-AM-01-021	Marina	Unknown	9,800	49.00	75.00
82-P-AM-01-022	Shreveport	Unknown	9,800	49.00	69.00
82-P-AM-01-023	French Lace	Unknown	9,800	49.00	69.00
82-P-AM-01-024	Brandy	Unknown	9,800	49.00	69.00
82-P-AM-01-025	Mon Cheri	Unknown	9,800	49.00	49.00
83-P-AM-01-026	Sun Flare	Unknown	9,800	49.00	69.00
83-P-AM-01-027	Sweet Surrender	Unknown	9,800	49.00	55.00
84-P-AM-01-028	Impatient	Unknown	9,800	49.00	55.00
84-P-AM-01-029	Olympiad	Unknown	9,800	49.00	55.00
84-P-AM-01-030	Intrigue	Unknown	9,800	49.00	58.00
85-P-AM-01-031	Showbiz	Unknown	9,800	49.50	49.50
85-P-AM-01-032	Peace	Unknown	9,800	49.50	49.50
85-P-AM-01-033	Queen Elizabeth	Unknown	9,800	49.50	49.50
Anna-Perenna		**Uncle Tad's Cats**			
79-P-AN-05-001	Oliver's Birthday	T. Krumeich	5,000	75.00	190.00
80-P-AN-05-002	Peaches & Cream	T. Krumeich	5,000	75.00	85.00
81-P-AN-05-003	Princess Aurora	T. Krumeich	5,000	80.00	80.00
81-P-AN-05-004	Walter's Window	T. Krumeich	5,000	85.00	85.00
Anna-Perenna		**Flowers of Count Bernadotte**			
82-P-AN-15-001	The Iris	Bernadotte	17,800	75.00	95.00
82-P-AN-15-002	Carnation	Bernadotte	17,800	75.00	95.00
82-P-AN-15-003	Freesia	Bernadotte	17,800	75.00	75.00
83-P-AN-15-004	Lily	Bernadotte	17,800	75.00	75.00
84-P-AN-15-005	Orchid	Bernadotte	17,800	75.00	75.00
84-P-AN-15-006	Rose	Bernadotte	17,800	75.00	75.00
84-P-AN-15-007	Tulip	Bernadotte	17,800	75.00	90.00
84-P-AN-15-008	Chrysanthemum	Bernadotte	17,800	75.00	75.00
Anri		**Ferrandiz Christmas**			
72-P-AO-01-001	Christ In The Manger	J. Ferrandiz	2,500	35.00	230.00
73-P-AO-01-002	Christmas	J. Ferrandiz	Unkn.	40.00	225.00
74-P-AO-01-003	Holy Night	J. Ferrandiz	Unkn.	50.00	100.00
75-P-AO-01-004	Flight into Egypt	J. Ferrandiz	Unkn.	60.00	95.00
76-P-AO-01-005	Tree of Life	J. Ferrandiz	Unkn.	60.00	60.00
76-P-AO-01-006	Girl with Flowers	J. Ferrandiz	4,000	65.00	185.00
78-P-AO-01-007	Leading the Way	J. Ferrandiz	4,000	77.50	180.00
79-P-AO-01-008	The Drummer	J. Ferrandiz	4,000	120.00	175.00
80-P-AO-01-009	Rejoice	J. Ferrandiz	4,000	150.00	160.00
81-P-AO-01-010	Spreading the Word	J. Ferrandiz	4,000	150.00	150.00
82-P-AO-01-011	The Shepherd Family	J. Ferrandiz	4,000	150.00	150.00
83-P-AO-01-012	Peace Attend Thee	J. Ferrandiz	4,000	150.00	150.00
Arabia Annual		**Kalevaia**			
76-P-AR-01-001	Vainamoinen's Sowing	R. Uosikkinen	Unkn.	30.00	230.00
77-P-AR-01-002	Aino's Fate	R. Uosikkinen	Unkn.	30.00	30.00
78-P-AR-01-003	Lemminkainen's Chase	R. Uosikkinen	2,500	39.00	40.00
79-P-AR-01-004	Kullervo's Revenge	R. Uosikkinen	Annual	39.50	40.00
80-P-AR-01-005	Vainomoinen's Rescue	R. Uosikkinen	Annual	45.00	65.00
81-P-AR-01-006	Vainomoinen's Magic	R. Uosikkinen	Annual	49.50	49.50
82-P-AR-01-007	Joukahainen Shoots the Horse	R. Uosikkinen	Annual	55.50	55.50
83-P-AR-01-008	Lemminkainen's Escape	R. Uosikkinen	Annual	60.00	90.00
84-P-AR-01-009	Lemminkainen's Magic Feathers	R. Uosikkinen	Annual	49.50	90.00
85-P-AR-01-010	Lemminkainen's Grief	R. Vosikkinen	Annual	60.00	60.00
Armstrong's		**The Three Graces**			
84-P-AT-01-001	Thalia	M. Perham	10,000	49.50	49.50
86-P-AT-01-002	Aglaia	M. Perham	10,000	49.50	49.50
87-P-AT-01-003	Euphrosyne	M. Perham	10,000	49.50	49.50
Armstrong's		**Baseball**			
85-P-AT-02-001	Pete Rose	R. Schenken	9,000	45.00	45.00
85-P-AT-02-002	Pete Rose (autographed)	R. Schenken	1,000	100.00	250.00
Armstrong's		**Infinite Love**			
87-P-AT-03-001	A Pair of Dreams	S. Etem	14-day	24.50	24.50
87-P-AT-03-002	Once Upon a Smile	S. Etem	14-day	24.50	24.50
Armstrong's		**Shakespeare**			
87-P-AT-04-001	Romeo & Juliet	M. Paredes	2,500	250.00	250.00
Arstrong's		**Statue of Liberty**			
86-P-AT-05-001	Dedication	A. D'Estrehan	10,000	39.50	39.50
86-P-AT-05-002	The Immigrants	A. D'Estrehan	10,000	39.50	39.50
86-P-AT-05-003	Independence	A. D'Estrehan	10,000	39.50	39.50
86-P-AT-05-004	Re-Dedication	A. D'Estrehan	10,000	39.50	39.50
Armstrong's		**Reflections of Innocence**			
85-P-AT-06-001	Me and My Friend	M. Paredes	10,000	37.50	37.50
85-P-AT-06-002	My Rain Beau	M. Paredes	10,000	37.50	37.50
86-P-AT-06-003	Rowboat Rendezvous	M. Paredes	10,000	37.50	37.50
87-P-AT-06-004	Hatching a Secret	M. Paredes	10,000	37.50	37.50
Armstrong's		**Lovable Kittens**			
83-P-AT-07-001	The Cat's Meow	Unknown	10,000	29.50	29.50
84-P-AT-07-002	Purr-Swayed	R. Pearcy	10,000	29.50	29.50
86-P-AT-07-003	Prince of Purrs	R. Pearcy	10,000	29.50	29.50
87-P-AT-07-004	Pet, and I'll Purr	R. Pearcy	10,000	29.50	29.50
Armstrong's		**Huggable Pupies**			
84-P-AT-08-001	Take Me Home	R. Pearcy	10,000	29.50	29.50
84-P-AT-08-002	Oh How Cute	R. Pearcy	10,000	29.50	29.50
85-P-AT-08-003	Puppy Pals	R. Pearcy	10,000	29.50	29.50
87-P-AT-08-004	Who, Me?	R. Pearcy	10,000	29.50	29.50
Armstrong's		**The Buck Hill Bears**			
86-P-AT-09-001	Tiddlywink & Pixie	R. Pearcy	10,000	29.50	29.50
87-P-AT-09-002	Rebecca & Friend (series of 4 plates)	R. Pearcy	10,000	29.50	29.50
Armstrong's		**Companion Series**			
85-P-AT-10-001	All Bark & No Bite	R. Pearcy	10,000	29.50	29.50
Armstrong's		**Commemorative Issues**			
83-P-AT-11-001	70 Years Young (10-1/2″)	R. Skelton	10,000	85.00	85.00
84-P-AT-11-002	Freddie the Torchbearer (8-1/2″)	R. Skelton	10,000	62.50	62.50
Armstrong's		**The Signature Collection**			
86-P-AT-12-001	Anyone for Tennis?	R. Skelton	9,000	62.50	62.50
86-P-AT-12-002	Anyone for Tennis? (signed)	R. Skelton	1,000	125.00	250.00
87-P-AT-12-003	Ironing the Waves	R. Skelton	9,000	62.50	62.50
87-P-AT-12-004	Ironing the Waves (signed)	R. Skelton	1,000	125.00	125.00
Armstrong's		**Happy Art Series**			
81-P-AT-13-001	Woody's Triple Self-Portrait	W. Lantz	10,000	39.50	39.50
83-P-AT-13-002	Gothic Woody	W. Lantz	10,000	39.50	39.50
84-P-AT-13-003	Blue Boy Woody	W. Lantz	10,000	39.50	39.50
Armstrong's		**Portraits of Childhood**			
83-P-AT-14-001	Miss Murray	Sir T. Lawrence	7,500	65.00	65.00
84-P-AT-14-002	Master Lambton	Sir T. Lawrence	7,500	65.00	65.00
Armstrong's/Crown Parian		**Freddie The Freeloader**			
79-P-AU-01-001	Freddie in the Bathtub	R. Skelton	10,000	60.00	325.00
80-P-AU-01-002	Freddie's Shack	R. Skelton	10,000	60.00	150.00
81-P-AU-01-003	Freddie on the Green	R. Skelton	10,000	60.00	150.00
82-P-AU-01-004	Love that Freddie	R. Skelton	10,000	60.00	85.00
Armstrong's/Crown Parian		**American Folk Heroes**			
83-P-AU-02-001	Johnny Appleseed	Unknown	Undis.	35.00	40.00
84-P-AU-02-002	Davy Crockett	Unknown	Undis.	35.00	35.00
85-P-AU-02-003	Betsy Ross	Unknown	Undis.	35.00	35.00
Armstrong's/Crown Parian		**Freddie's Adventures**			
82-P-AU-03-001	Captain Freddie	R. Skelton	15,000	60.00	150.00
82-P-AU-03-002	Bronco Freddie	R. Skelton	15,000	60.00	62.50
83-P-AU-03-003	Sir Freddie	R. Skelton	15,000	62.50	62.50
84-P-AU-03-004	Gertrude and Heathcliffe	R. Skelton	15,000	62.50	62.50
Artists of the World		**Holiday**			
76-P-AW-01-001	Festival of Lights	T. DeGrazia	9,500	45.00	250.00
77-P-AW-01-002	Bell of Hope	T. DeGrazia	9,500	45.00	100.00
78-P-AW-01-003	Little Madonna	T. DeGrazia	9,500	45.00	130.00
79-P-AW-01-004	The Nativity	T. DeGrazia	9,500	50.00	140.00
80-P-AW-01-005	Little Pima Drummer	T. DeGrazia	9,500	50.00	100.00
81-P-AW-01-006	A Little Prayer	T. DeGrazia	9,500	55.00	100.00
82-P-AW-01-007	Blue Boy	T. DeGrazia	10,000	60.00	100.00
83-P-AW-01-008	Heavenly Blessings	T. DeGrazia	10,000	65.00	85.00
84-P-AW-01-009	Navajo Madonna	T. DeGrazia	10,000	65.00	100.00
85-P-AW-01-010	Saguaro Dance	T. DeGrazia	10,000	65.00	120.00
Artists of the World		**Holiday**			
76-P-AW-02-001	Festival of Lights, signed	T. DeGrazia	500	100.00	750.00
77-P-AW-02-002	Bell of Hope, signed	T. DeGrazia	500	100.00	300.00
78-P-AW-02-003	Little Madonna, signed	T. DeGrazia	500	100.00	350.00
79-P-AW-02-004	The Nativity, signed	T. DeGrazia	500	100.00	450.00
80-P-AW-02-005	Little Pima Drummer, signed	T. DeGrazia	500	100.00	450.00
81-P-AW-02-006	A Little Prayer, signed	T. DeGrazia	500	100.00	420.00
82-P-AW-02-007	Blue Boy, signed	T. DeGrazia	96	100.00	Unknown
Artists of the World		**Children**			
76-P-AW-03-001	Los Ninos	T. DeGrazia	5,000	35.00	1800.00
77-P-AW-03-002	White Dove	T. DeGrazia	5,000	40.00	220.00
78-P-AW-03-003	Flower Girl	T. DeGrazia	9,500	45.00	190.00
79-P-AW-03-004	Flower Boy	T. DeGrazia	9,500	45.00	190.00
80-P-AW-03-005	Little Cocopah	T. DeGrazia	9,500	50.00	140.00
81-P-AW-03-006	Beautiful Burden	T. DeGrazia	9,500	50.00	130.00
82-P-AW-03-007	Merry Little Indian	T. DeGrazia	9,500	55.00	150.00
83-P-AW-03-008	Wondering	T. DeGrazia	10,000	60.00	110.00
84-P-AW-03-009	Pink Papoose	T. DeGrazia	10,000	65.00	110.00
85-P-AW-03-010	Sunflower Boy	T. DeGrazia	10,000	65.00	110.00
Artists of the World		**Children**			
78-P-AW-05-001	Los Ninos, signed	T. DeGrazia	500	100.00	1500.00
78-P-AW-05-002	White Dove, signed	T. DeGrazia	500	100.00	190.00
78-P-AW-05-003	Flower Girl, signed	T. DeGrazia	500	100.00	140.00
79-P-AW-05-004	Flower Boy, signed	T. DeGrazia	500	100.00	140.00
80-P-AW-05-005	Little Cocopah Girl, signed	T. DeGrazia	500	100.00	130.00
81-P-AW-05-006	Beautiful Burden, signed	T. DeGrazia	500	100.00	375.00
81-P-AW-05-007	Merry Little Indian, signed	T. DeGrazia	500	100.00	375.00
Artists of the World		**Children of Aberdeen**			
79-P-AW-06-001	Girl with Little Brother	Unknown	Undis.	50.00	50.00
80-P-AW-06-002	Sampan Girl	Unknown	Undis.	50.00	60.00
81-P-AW-06-003	Girl with Little Sister	Unknown	Undis.	55.00	55.00
82-P-AW-06-004	Girl with Seashells	Unknown	Undis.	60.00	65.00
83-P-AW-06-005	Girl with Seabirds	Unknown	Undis.	60.00	60.00
84-P-AW-06-006	Brother and Sister	Unknown	Undis.	60.00	75.00
Balliol Corporation		**Precious Portraits**			
87-P-BA-01-001	Sunbeam	B. P. Gutmann	14-day	24.50	24.50
87-P-BA-01-002	Mischief	B. P. Gutmann	14-day	24.50	24.50
87-P-BA-01-003	Peach Blossom	B. P. Gutmann	14-day	24.50	24.50
87-P-BA-01-004	Goldilocks	B. P. Gutmann	14-day	24.50	24.50
87-P-BA-01-005	Fairy Gold	B. P. Gutmann	14-day	24.50	24.50
87-P-BA-01-006	Bunny	B. P. Gutmann	14-day	24.50	24.50
Bareuther		**Christmas**			
67-P-BB-01-001	Stiftskirche	H. Mueller	10,000	12.00	100.00
68-P-BB-01-002	Kapplkirche	H. Mueller	10,000	12.00	35.00
69-P-BB-01-003	Christkindlesmarkt	H. Mueller	10,000	12.00	15.00
70-P-BB-01-004	Chapel in Oberndorf	H. Mueller	10,000	12.50	15.00
71-P-BB-01-005	Toys for Sale	From Drawing By L. Ricter	10,000	12.75	15.00
72-P-BB-01-006	Christmas in Munich	H. Mueller	10,000	14.50	33.00
73-P-BB-01-007	Sleigh Ride	H. Mueller	10,000	15.00	15.00
74-P-BB-01-008	Black Forest Church	H. Mueller	10,000	19.00	19.00
75-P-BB-01-009	Snowman	H. Mueller	10,000	21.50	21.50
76-P-BB-01-010	Chapel in the Hills	H. Mueller	10,000	23.50	23.50
77-P-BB-01-011	Story Time	H. Mueller	10,000	24.50	32.00
78-P-BB-01-012	Mittenwald	H. Mueller	10,000	27.50	31.00
79-P-BB-01-013	Winter Day	H. Mueller	10,000	35.00	30.00
80-P-BB-01-014	Mittenberg	H. Mueller	10,000	37.50	39.00
81-P-BB-01-015	Walk in the Forest	H. Mueller	10,000	39.50	39.50
82-P-BB-01-016	Bad Wimpfen	H. Mueller	10,000	39.50	39.50
83-P-BB-01-017	The Night before Christmas	H. Mueller	10,000	39.50	39.50
84-P-BB-01-018	Zeil on the River Main	H. Mueller	10,000	42.50	42.50
85-P-BB-01-019	Winter Wonderland	H. Mueller	10,000	42.50	42.50
86-P-BB-01-020	Christmas in Forchhe	H. Mueller	Annual	42.50	43.00
87-P-BB-01-021	Decorating the Tree	H. Mueller	10,000	42.50	46.50
Bareuther		**Danish Church**			
68-P-BB-02-001	Roskilde Cathedral Fe	Unknown	Annual	12.00	27.00
69-P-BB-02-002	Ribe Cathedral	Unknown	Annual	12.00	25.00
70-P-BB-02-003	Marmor Kirken	Unknown	Annual	13.00	13.00
71-P-BB-02-004	Ejby Church	Unknown	Annual	13.00	16.00
72-P-BB-02-005	Kalundborg Kirken	Unknown	Annual	13.00	22.00
73-P-BB-02-006	Grundtvig Kirken	Unknown	Annual	15.00	20.00
74-P-BB-02-007	Broager Kirken	Unknown	Annual	15.00	20.00
75-P-BB-02-008	St. Knuds Kirken	Unknown	Annual	20.00	20.00
76-P-BB-02-009	Osterlars Kirken	Unknown	Annual	20.00	22.00
77-P-BB-02-010	Budolfi Kirken	Unknown	Annual	15.95	23.00

Company		Series			
Number	**Name**	**Artist**	**Edition limit**	**Issue Price**	**Quote**
78-P-BB-02-011	Haderslav Cathedral	Unknown	Annual	19.95	17.00
79-P-BB-02-012	Holmens Church	Unknown	Annual	15.30	20.00
Belleck		**Christmas**			
70-P-BC-01-001	Castle Caldwell	Unknown	7,500	25.00	85.00
71-P-BC-01-002	Celtic Cross	Unknown	7,500	25.00	40.00
72-P-BC-01-003	Flight of the Earls	Unknown	7,500	30.00	44.00
73-P-BC-01-004	Tribute To Yeats	Unknown	7,500	38.50	62.00
74-P-BC-01-005	Devenish Island	Unknown	7,500	45.00	210.00
75-P-BC-01-006	The Celtic Cross	Unknown	7,500	48.00	59.00
76-P-BC-01-007	Dove of Peace	Unknown	7,500	55.00	55.00
77-P-BC-01-008	Wren	Unknown	7,500	55.00	55.00
Belleck		**Irish Wildlife**			
78-P-BC-02-001	A Leaping Salmon	Unknown	Undis.	55.00	72.00
79-P-BC-02-002	Hare at Rest	Unknown	Undis.	58.50	66.00
80-P-BC-02-003	The Hedgehog	Unknown	Undis.	66.50	66.50
81-P-BC-02-004	Red Squirrel	Unknown	Undis.	78.00	78.00
82-P-BC-02-005	Irish Seal	Unknown	Undis.	78.00	78.00
83-P-BC-02-006	Red Fox	Unknown	Undis.	85.00	85.00
Berlin Design		**Christmas**			
70-P-BD-01-001	Christmas in Bernkastel	Unknown	4,000	14.50	135.00
71-P-BD-01-002	Christmas in Rothenburg	Unknown	20,000	14.50	35.00
72-P-BD-01-003	Christmas in Michelstadt	Unknown	20,000	15.00	50.00
73-P-BD-01-004	Christmas in Wendlestein	Unknown	20,000	20.00	40.00
74-P-BD-01-005	Christmas in Bremen	Unknown	20,000	25.00	25.00
75-P-BD-01-006	Christmas in Dortland	Unknown	20,000	30.00	72.50
76-P-BD-01-007	Christmas in Augsburg	Unknown	20,000	32.00	32.00
77-P-BD-01-008	Christmas in Hamburg	Unknown	20,000	32.00	32.00
78-P-BD-01-009	Christmas in Berlin	Unknown	20,000	36.00	65.00
79-P-BD-01-010	Christmas in Greetsiel	Unknown	20,000	47.50	62.50
80-P-BD-01-011	Christmas in Mittenberg	Unknown	20,000	50.00	60.00
81-P-BD-01-012	Christmas Eve In Hahnenklee	Unknown	20,000	55.00	57.50
82-P-BD-01-013	Christmas Eve In Wasserberg	Unknown	20,000	55.00	55.00
83-P-BD-01-014	Christmas in Oberndorf	Unknown	20,000	55.00	55.00
84-P-BD-01-015	Christmas in Ramsau	Unknown	20,000	55.00	55.00
85-P-BD-01-016	Christmas Eve in Bad Wimpfen	Unknown	20,000	55.00	55.00
86-P-BD-01-017	Christmas Eve in Gelnhaus	Unknown	20,000	65.00	66.00
Berlin Design		**Historical**			
75-P-BD-02-001	Washington Crossing the Delaware	Unknown	Annual	30.00	40.00
76-P-BD-02-002	Tom Thumb	Unknown	Annual	32.00	35.00
77-P-BD-02-003	Zeppelin	Unknown	Annual	32.00	35.00
78-P-BD-02-004	Benz Motor Car Munich	Unknown	10,000	36.00	36.00
79-P-BD-02-005	Johannes Gutenberg	Unknown	10,000	47.50	48.00
Berlin Design		**Holiday Week of the Family Kappelmann**			
84-P-BD-03-001	Monday	Unknown	Undis.	33.00	40.00
84-P-BD-03-002	Tuesday	Unknown	Undis.	33.00	33.00
85-P-BD-03-003	Wednesday	Unknown	Undis.	33.00	33.00
85-P-BD-03-004	Thursday	Unknown	Undis.	35.00	35.00
85-P-BD-03-005	Friday	Unknown	Undis.	35.00	35.00
86-P-BD-03-006	Saturday	Unknown	Undis.	35.00	35.00
86-P-BD-03-007	Sunday	Unknown	Undis.	35.00	35.00
Bing & Grondahl		**Christmas**			
95-P-BG-01-001	Behind The Frozen Window	F.A. Hallin	Annual	.50	3600.00
96-P-BG-01-002	New Moon	F.A. Hallin	Annual	.50	1475.00
97-P-BG-01-003	Sparrows	F.A. Hallin	Annual	.75	1100.00
98-P-BG-01-004	Roses and Star	F. Garde	Annual	.75	600.00
99-P-BG-01-005	Crows	F. Garde	Annual	.75	900.00
00-P-BG-01-006	Church Bells	F. Garde	Annual	.75	810.00
01-P-BG-01-007	Three Wise Men	S. Sabra	Annual	1.00	500.00
02-P-BG-01-008	Gothic Church Interior	D. Jensen	Annual	1.00	300.00
03-P-BG-01-009	Expectant Children	M. Hyldahl	Annual	1.00	150.00
04-P-BG-01-010	Frederiksberg Hill	C. Olsen	Annual	1.00	127.50
05-P-BG-01-011	Christmas Night	D. Jensen	Annual	1.00	135.00
06-P-BG-01-012	Sleighing to Church	D. Jensen	Annual	1.00	90.00
07-P-BG-01-013	Little Match Girl	E. Plockross	Annual	1.00	120.00
08-P-BG-01-014	St. Petri Church	P. Jorgensen	Annual	1.00	85.00
09-P-BG-01-015	Yule Tree	Aarestrup	Annual	1.50	96.00
10-P-BG-01-016	The Old Organist	C. Ersgaard	Annual	1.50	90.00
11-P-BG-01-017	Angels and Shepherds	H. Moltke	Annual	1.50	75.00
12-P-BG-01-018	Going to Church	E. Hansen	Annual	1.50	81.00
13-P-BG-01-019	Bringing Home the Tree	T. Larsen	Annual	1.50	98.00
14-P-BG-01-020	Amalienborg Castle	T. Larsen	Annual	1.50	75.00
15-P-BG-01-021	Dog Outside Window	D. Jensen	Annual	1.50	120.00
16-P-BG-01-022	Sparrows at Christmas	P. Jorgensen	Annual	1.50	67.50
17-P-BG-01-023	Christmas Boat	A. Friis	Annual	1.50	75.00
18-P-BG-01-024	Fishing Boat	A. Friis	Annual	1.50	90.00
19-P-BG-01-025	Outside Lighted Window	A. Friis	Annual	2.00	75.00
20-P-BG-01-026	Hare in the Snow	A. Friis	Annual	2.00	75.00
21-P-BG-01-027	Pigeons	A. Friis	Annual	2.00	60.00
22-P-BG-01-028	Star of Bethlehem	A. Friis	Annual	2.00	57.00
23-P-BG-01-029	The Ermitage	A. Friis	Annual	2.00	57.00
24-P-BG-01-030	Lighthouse	A. Friis	Annual	2.50	70.00
25-P-BG-01-031	Child's Christmas	A. Friis	Annual	2.50	78.00
26-P-BG-01-032	Churchgoers	A. Friis	Annual	2.50	68.00
27-P-BG-01-033	Skating Couple	A. Friis	Annual	2.50	115.00
28-P-BG-01-034	Eskimos	A. Friis	Annual	2.50	65.00
29-P-BG-01-035	Fox Outside Farm	A. Friis	Annual	2.50	80.00
31-P-BG-01-036	Town Hall Square	H. Flugenring	Annual	2.50	96.00
30-P-BG-01-037	Christmas Train	A. Friis	Annual	2.50	85.00
32-P-BG-01-038	Life Boat	H. Flugenring	Annual	2.50	95.00
33-P-BG-01-039	Korsor-Nyborg Ferry	H. Flugenring	Annual	3.00	72.00
34-P-BG-01-040	Church Bell in Tower	H. Flugenring	Annual	3.00	75.00
35-P-BG-01-041	Lillebelt Bridge	O. Larson	Annual	3.00	60.00
36-P-BG-01-042	Royal Guard	O. Larson	Annual	3.00	78.00
37-P-BG-01-043	Arrival of Christmas Guests	O. Larson	Annual	3.00	75.00
38-P-BG-01-044	Lighting the Candles	I. Tjerne	Annual	3.00	112.00
39-P-BG-01-045	Old Lock-Eye, The Sandman	I. Tjerne	Annual	3.00	172.00
40-P-BG-01-046	Christmas Letters	O. Larson	Annual	4.00	165.00
41-P-BG-01-047	Horses Enjoying Meal	O. Larson	Annual	4.00	330.00
42-P-BG-01-048	Danish Farm	O. Larson	Annual	4.00	150.00
43-P-BG-01-049	Ribe Cathedral	O. Larson	Annual	5.00	160.00
44-P-BG-01-050	Sorgenfri Castle	O. Larson	Annual	5.00	120.00
45-P-BG-01-051	The Old Water Mill	O. Larson	Annual	5.00	130.00
46-P-BG-01-052	Commemoration Cross	M. Hyldahl	Annual	5.00	84.00
47-P-BG-01-053	Dybbol Mill	M. Hyldahl	Annual	5.00	85.00
48-P-BG-01-054	Watchman	M. Hyldahl	Annual	5.50	75.00
49-P-BG-01-055	Landsoldaten	M. Hyldahl	Annual	5.50	80.00
50-P-BG-01-056	Kronborg Castle	M. Hyldahl	Annual	5.50	150.00
51-P-BG-01-057	Jens Bang	M. Hyldahl	Annual	6.00	112.50
52-P-BG-01-058	Thorsvaldsen Museum	B. Pramvig	Annual	6.00	84.00

Company		Series			
Number	**Name**	**Artist**	**Edition limit**	**Issue Price**	**Quote**
53-P-BG-01-059	Snowman	B. Pramvig	Annual	7.50	96.00
54-P-BG-01-060	Royal Boat	K. Bonfils	Annual	7.00	105.00
55-P-BG-01-061	Kaulundorg Church	K. Bonfils	Annual	8.00	108.00
56-P-BG-01-062	Christmas in Copenhagen	K. Bonfils	Annual	8.50	144.00
57-P-BG-01-063	Christmas Candles	K. Bonfils	Annual	9.00	165.00
58-P-BG-01-064	Santa Claus	K. Bonfils	Annual	9.50	108.00
59-P-BG-01-065	Christmas Eve	K. Bonfils	Annual	10.00	127.50
60-P-BG-01-066	Village Church	K. Bonfils	Annual	10.00	180.00
61-P-BG-01-067	Winter Harmony	K. Bonfils	Annual	10.50	96.00
62-P-BG-01-068	Winter Night	K. Bonfils	Annual	11.00	85.00
63-P-BG-01-069	The Christmas Elf	H. Thelander	Annual	11.00	105.00
64-P-BG-01-070	The Fir Tree and Hare	H. Thelander	Annual	11.50	50.00
65-P-BG-01-071	Bringing Home the Tree	H. Thelander	Annual	12.00	58.00
66-P-BG-01-072	Home for Christmas	H. Thelander	Annual	12.00	45.00
67-P-BG-01-073	Sharing the Joy	H. Thelander	Annual	13.00	48.00
68-P-BG-01-074	Christmas in Church	H. Thelander	Annual	14.00	30.00
69-P-BG-01-075	Arrival of Guests	H. Thelander	Annual	14.00	27.00
70-P-BG-01-076	Pheasants in Snow	H. Thelander	Annual	14.50	19.50
71-P-BG-01-077	Christmas at Home	H. Thelander	Annual	15.00	20.00
72-P-BG-01-078	Christmas in Greenland	H. Thelander	Annual	16.50	20.00
73-P-BG-01-079	Country Christmas	H. Thelander	Annual	19.50	27.00
74-P-BG-01-080	Christmas in the Village	H. Thelander	Annual	22.00	22.00
75-P-BG-01-081	Old Water Mill	H. Thelander	Annual	27.50	27.50
76-P-BG-01-082	Christmas Welcome	H. Thelander	Annual	27.50	27.50
77-P-BG-01-083	Copenhagen Christmas	H. Thelander	Annual	29.50	29.50
78-P-BG-01-084	Christmas Tale	H. Thelander	Annual	32.00	32.00
79-P-BG-01-085	White Christmas	H. Thelander	Annual	36.50	42.00
80-P-BG-01-086	Christmas in Woods	H. Thelander	Annual	42.50	42.00
81-P-BG-01-087	Christmas Peace	H. Thelander	Annual	49.50	49.50
82-P-BG-01-088	Christmas Tree	H. Thelander	Annual	54.50	54.50
83-P-BG-01-089	Christmas in Old Town	H. Thelander	Annual	54.50	54.50
84-P-BG-01-090	The Christmas Letter	E. Jensen	Annual	54.50	54.50
85-P-BG-01-091	Christmas Eve at the Farmhouse	E. Jensen	Yr.Iss	54.50	54.50
86-P-BG-01-092	Silent Night, Holy Night	E. Jensen	Yr.Iss	54.50	54.50
87-P-BG-01-093	The Snowman's Christmas Eve	E. Jensen	Yr.Iss	59.50	59.50
Bing & Grondahl		**Jubilee-5 Year Cycle**			
15-P-BG-02-001	Frozen Window	F.A. Hallin	Annual	Unknown	225.00
20-P-BG-02-002	Church Bells	F. Garde	Annual	Unknown	60.00
25-P-BG-02-003	Dog Outside Window	D. Jensen	Annual	Unknown	300.00
30-P-BG-02-004	The Old Organist	C. Ersgaard	Annual	Unknown	225.00
35-P-BG-02-005	Little Match Girl	E. Plockross	Annual	Unknown	1000.00
40-P-BG-02-006	Three Wise Men	S. Sabra	Annual	Unknown	2000.00
45-P-BG-02-007	Amalienborg Castle	T. Larsen	Annual	Unknown	150.00
50-P-BG-02-008	Eskimos	A. Friis	Annual	Unknown	180.00
55-P-BG-02-009	Dybbol Mill	M. Hyldahl	Annual	Unknown	210.00
60-P-BG-02-010	Kronborg Castle	M. Hyldahl	Annual	25.00	90.00
65-P-BG-02-011	Churchgoers	A. Friis	Annual	25.00	39.50
70-P-BG-02-012	Amalienborg Castle	T. Larsen	Annual	30.00	35.00
75-P-BG-02-013	Horses Enjoying Meal	O. Larson	Annual	40.00	50.00
80-P-BG-02-014	Yule Tree	Aarestrup	Annual	60.00	60.00
85-P-BG-02-015	Lifeboat at Work	H. Flugenring	Annual	65.00	65.00
Bing & Grondahl		**Mother's Day**			
69-P-BG-03-001	Dogs and Puppies	H. Thelander	Annual	9.75	400.00
70-P-BG-03-002	Bird and Chicks	H. Thelander	Annual	10.00	30.00
71-P-BG-03-003	Cat and Kitten	H. Thelander	Annual	11.00	15.00
72-P-BG-03-004	Mare and Foal	H. Thelander	Annual	12.00	19.50
73-P-BG-03-005	Duck and Ducklings	H. Thelander	Annual	13.00	20.00
74-P-BG-03-006	Bear and Cubs	H. Thelander	Annual	16.50	20.00
75-P-BG-03-007	Doe and Fawns	H. Thelander	Annual	19.50	19.50
76-P-BG-03-008	Swan Family	H. Thelander	Annual	22.50	25.00
77-P-BG-03-009	Squirrel and Young	H. Thelander	Annual	23.50	25.00
78-P-BG-03-010	Heron	H. Thelander	Annual	24.50	25.00
79-P-BG-03-011	Fox and Cubs	H. Thelander	Annual	27.50	37.50
80-P-BG-03-012	Woodpecker and Young	H. Thelander	Annual	29.50	40.50
81-P-BG-03-013	Hare and Young	H. Thelander	Annual	36.50	36.50
82-P-BG-03-014	Lioness and Cubs	H. Thelander	Annual	39.50	39.50
83-P-BG-03-015	Raccoon and Young	H. Thelander	Annual	39.50	39.50
84-P-BG-03-016	Stork and Nestlings	H. Thelander	Annual	39.50	39.50
85-P-BG-03-017	Bear and Cubs	H. Thelander	Annual	39.50	39.50
86-P-BG-03-018	Elephant with Calf	H. Thelander	Annual	39.50	39.50
87-P-BG-03-019	Sheep with Lambs	H. Thelander	Annual	42.50	42.50
Bing & Grondahl		**Children's Day Plate Series**			
85-P-BG-07-001	The Magical Tea Party	C. Roller	Yr.Iss	24.50	26.00
86-P-BG-07-002	A Joyful Flight	C. Roller	Yr.Iss	26.50	28.00
86-P-BG-07-003	The Little Gardeners	C. Roller	Annual	29.50	29.50
Bing & Grondahl		**Moments of Truth**			
84-P-BG-08-001	Home is Best	Unknown	Undis.	29.50	31.50
84-P-BG-08-002	Road to Virtuosity	Unknown	Undis.	29.50	35.00
86-P-BG-08-003	First Things First	K. Ard	Undis.	29.50	35.00
86-P-BG-08-004	Unfair Competition	K. Ard	Undis.	29.50	32.00
86-P-BG-08-005	Bored Sick	K. Ard	Undis.	29.50	35.00
86-P-BG-08-006	First Crush	K. Ard	Undis.	29.50	32.00
Bing & Grondahl		**Statue of Liberty**			
85-P-BG-10-001	Statue of Liberty	Unknown	10,000	60.00	75.00
Bing & Grondahl		**Christmas in America Plate**			
86-P-BG-13-001	Christmas Eve in Williamsburg	J. Woodson	Yr.Iss	29.50	29.50
Blue River Mill Publishing Company, Inc.		**Once Upon A Barn**			
86-P-BH-01-001	Mail Pouch Barn	R. Day	5,000	45.00	45.00
87-P-BH-01-002	Rock City Barn	R. Day	5,000	45.00	45.00
87-P-BH-01-003	Meramec Caverns Barn	R. Day	5,000	45.00	45.00
88-P-BH-01-004	Coca-Cola Barn	R. Day	5,000	45.00	45.00
Boehm Studios		**Egyptian Commemorative**			
78-P-BJ-09-001	Tutankhamun	Boehm	5,000	125.00	170.00
78-P-BJ-09-002	Tutankhamun, handpainted	Boehm	225	975.00	975.00
Curator Collection		**Portraits of American Brides**			
86-P-CX-01-001	Caroline	R. Sauber	10-day	29.50	29.50
86-P-CX-01-002	Jacqueline	R. Sauber	10-day	29.50	29.50
87-P-CX-01-003	Elizabeth	R. Sauber	10-day	29.50	29.50
87-P-CX-01-004	Emily	R. Sauber	10-day	29.50	29.50
87-P-CX-01-005	Meredith	R. Sauber	10-day	29.50	29.50
87-P-CX-01-006	Laura	R. Sauber	10-day	29.50	29.50
87-P-CX-01-007	Sarah	R. Sauber	10-day	29.50	29.50
87-P-CX-01-008	Rebecca	R. Sauber	10-day	29.50	29.50
Curator Collection		**Masterpieces of Rockwell**			
80-P-CX-02-001	After the Prom	N. Rockwell	17,500	42.50	90.00
80-P-CX-02-002	The Challenger	N. Rockwell	17,500	50.00	50.00
82-P-CX-02-003	Girl at the Mirror	N. Rockwell	17,500	50.00	75.00
82-P-CX-02-004	Missing Tooth	N. Rockwell	17,500	50.00	50.00

Company / Number	Name	Series / Artist	Edition limit	Issue Price	Quote
Curator Collection		**Rockwell Americana**			
81-P-CX-03-001	Shuffleton's Barbershop	N. Rockwell	17,500	75.00	100.00
82-P-CX-03-002	Breaking Home Ties	N. Rockwell	17,500	75.00	75.00
83-P-CX-03-003	Walking to Church	N. Rockwell	17,500	75.00	75.00
Curator Collection		**Rockwell Trilogy**			
81-P-CX-04-001	Stockbridge in Winter 1	N. Rockwell	Open	35.00	35.00
82-P-CX-04-002	Stockbridge in Winter 2	N. Rockwell	Open	35.00	35.00
82-P-CX-04-003	Stockbridge in Winter 3	N. Rockwell	Open	35.00	35.00
Curator Collection		**Simpler Times Series**			
84-P-CX-05-001	Lazy Daze	N. Rockwell	7,500	35.00	35.00
84-P-CX-05-002	One for the Road	N. Rockwell	7,500	35.00	35.00
Curator Collection		**Special Occasions**			
82-P-CX-06-001	Bubbles	F. Tipton Hunter	Open	29.95	29.95
82-P-CX-06-002	Butterflies	F. Tipton Hunter	Open	29.95	29.95
Curator Collection		**Masterpieces of Impressionism**			
80-P-CX-07-001	Woman with Parasol	Monet/Cassat	17,500	35.00	50.00
81-P-CX-07-002	Young Mother Sewing	Monet/Cassat	17,500	35.00	35.00
82-P-CX-07-003	Sara in Green Bonnet	Monet/Cassat	17,500	35.00	35.00
83-P-CX-07-004	Margot in Blue	Monet/Cassat	17,500	35.00	35.00
Curator Collection		**Magical Moment**			
81-P-CX-08-001	Happy Dreams	B. Pease Gutmann	Open	29.95	70.00
81-P-CX-08-002	Harmony	B. Pease Gutmann	Open	29.95	60.00
82-P-CX-08-003	His Majesty	B. Pease Gutmann	Open	29.95	29.95
83-P-CX-08-004	The Lullaby	B. Pease Gutmann	Open	29.95	29.95
82-P-CX-08-005	Waiting for Daddy	B. Pease Gutmann	Open	29.95	29.95
82-P-CX-08-006	Thank You God	B. Pease Gutmann	Open	29.95	29.95
Curator Collection		**Masterpieces of the West**			
80-P-CX-09-001	Texas Night Herder	Johnson	17,500	35.00	35.00
80-P-CX-09-002	Indian Trapper	Remington	17,500	35.00	35.00
82-P-CX-09-003	Cowboy Style	Leigh	17,500	35.00	35.00
82-P-CX-09-004	Indian Style	Perillo	17,500	35.00	75.00
Curator Collection		**Playful Pets**			
82-P-CX-10-001	Curiosity	J. H. Dolph	7,500	45.00	45.00
82-P-CX-10-002	Master's Hat	J. H. Dolph	7,500	45.00	45.00
Curator Collection		**The Tribute Series**			
82-P-CX-11-001	I Want You	J. M. Flagg	Open	29.95	29.95
82-P-CX-11-002	Gee, I Wish	H. C. Christy	Open	29.95	29.95
83-P-CX-11-003	Soldier's Farewell	N. Rockwell	Open	29.95	29.95
Curator Collection		**The Carnival Series**			
82-P-CX-12-001	Knock em' Down	T. Newsom	19,500	35.00	35.00
82-P-CX-12-002	Carousel	T. Newsom	19,500	35.00	35.00
Curator Collection		**Nursery Pair**			
83-P-CX-13-001	In Slumberland	C. Becker	Open	25.00	25.00
Curator Collection		**Nursery Pair**			
83-P-CX-13-002	The Awakening	C. Becker	Open	25.00	25.00
Curator Collection		**Melodies of Childhood**			
83-P-CX-14-001	Twinkle, Twinkle Little Star	H. Garrido	19,500	35.00	35.00
83-P-CX-14-002	Row, Row, Row Your Boat	H. Garrido	19,500	35.00	35.00
83-P-CX-14-003	Mary had a Little Lamb	H. Garrido	19,500	35.00	35.00
Curator Collection		**Unicorn Magic**			
83-P-CX-15-001	Morning Encounter	J. Terreson	7,500	50.00	50.00
83-P-CX-15-002	Afternoon Offering	J. Terreson	7,500	50.00	50.00
Curator Collection		**Baker Street**			
83-P-CX-16-001	Sherlock Holmes	M. Hooks	9,800	55.00	55.00
83-P-CX-16-002	Watson	M. Hooks	9,800	55.00	55.00
Curator Collection		**Angler's Dream**			
83-P-CX-17-001	Brook Trout	J. Eggert	9,800	55.00	55.00
83-P-CX-17-002	Striped Bass	J. Eggert	9,800	55.00	55.00
83-P-CX-17-003	Largemouth Bass	J. Eggert	9,800	55.00	55.00
83-P-CX-17-004	Chinook Salmon	J. Eggert	9,800	55.00	55.00
Curator Collection		**On the Road Series**			
84-P-CX-18-001	Pride of Stockbridge	N. Rockwell	Open	35.00	35.00
84-P-CX-18-002	City Pride	N. Rockwell	Open	35.00	35.00
84-P-CX-18-003	Country Pride	N. Rockwell	Open	35.00	35.00
Curator Collection		**Mother's Love**			
84-P-CX-19-001	Daddy's Here	B. P. Gutmann	Open	29.95	29.95
Curator Collection		**Bessie's Best**			
84-P-CX-20-001	Oh! Oh! A Bunny	B. P. Gutmann	Open	29.95	29.95
84-P-CX-20-002	The New Love	B. P. Gutmann	Open	29.95	29.95
84-P-CX-20-003	My Baby	B. P. Gutmann	Open	29.95	29.95
84-P-CX-20-004	Looking for Trouble	B. P. Gutmann	Open	29.95	29.95
84-P-CX-20-005	Taps	B. P. Gutmann	Open	29.95	29.95
Curator Collection		**The Great Trains**			
85-P-CX-21-001	Santa Fe	J. Deneen	7,500	35.00	35.00
85-P-CX-21-002	Twentieth Century Ltd.	J. Deneen	7,500	35.00	35.00
86-P-CX-21-003	Empire Builder	J. Deneen	7,500	35.00	35.00
Curator Collection		**Becker Babies**			
83-P-CX-22-001	Snow Puff	C. Becker	Open	29.95	29.95
84-P-CX-22-002	Smiling Through	C. Becker	Open	29.95	29.95
84-P-CX-22-003	Pals	C. Becker	Open	29.95	29.95
Curator Collection		**Portrait Series**			
86-P-CX-23-001	Chantilly	J. Eggert	14 Day	24.50	24.50
86-P-CX-23-002	Dynasty	J. Eggert	14 Day	24.50	24.50
86-P-CX-23-003	Velvet	J. Eggert	14 Day	24.50	24.50
86-P-CX-23-004	Jambalaya	J. Eggert	14 Day	24.50	24.50
Curator Collection		**Sailing Through History**			
86-P-CX-24-001	Flying Cloud	K. Soldwedel	14 Day	29.50	29.50
86-P-CX-24-002	Santa Maria	K. Soldwedel	14 Day	29.50	29.50
86-P-CX-24-003	Mayflower	K. Soldwedel	14 Day	29.50	29.50
Curator Collection		**How Do I Love Thee?**			
82-P-CX-25-001	Alaina	R. Sauber	19,500	39.95	39.95
82-P-CX-25-002	Taylor	R. Sauber	19,500	39.95	39.95
83-P-CX-25-003	Rendezvouse	R. Sauber	19,500	39.95	39.95
83-P-CX-25-004	Embrace	R. Sauber	19,500	39.95	39.95
Curator Collection		**Childhood Delights**			
83-P-CX-26-001	Amanda	R. Sauber	7,500	45.00	45.00
Curator Collection		**Songs of Stephen Foster**			
84-P-CX-27-001	Oh! Susannah	R. Sauber	3,500	60.00	60.00
84-P-CX-27-002	Jeanie with the Light Brown Hair	R. Sauber	3,500	60.00	60.00
84-P-CX-27-003	Beautiful Dreamer	R. Sauber	3,500	60.00	60.00
Curator Collection		**Curator Gift Editions**			
84-P-CX-28-001	Happy Birthday	R. Sauber	Open	37.50	37.50
85-P-CX-28-002	Home Sweet Home	R. Sauber	Open	37.50	37.50
85-P-CX-28-003	The Wedding	R. Sauber	Open	37.50	37.50
86-P-CX-28-004	The Anniversary	R. Sauber	Open	37.50	37.50
86-P-CX-28-005	Sweethearts	R. Sauber	Open	37.50	37.50
86-P-CX-28-006	The Christening	R. Sauber	Open	37.50	37.50
85-P-CX-28-007	All Adore Him	R. Sauber	Open	37.50	37.50
87-P-CX-28-008	Motherhood	R. Sauber	Open	37.50	37.50
87-P-CX-28-009	Fatherhood	R. Sauber	Open	37.50	37.50
87-P-CX-28-010	Sweet Sixteen	R. Sauber	Open	37.50	37.50
Curator Collection		**Curator Christian Collection**			
87-P-CX-29-001	Bring to Me the Children	A. Tobey	Unkn.	35.00	35.00
87-P-CX-29-002	Wedding Feast at Cana	A. Tobey	Unkn.	35.00	35.00
87-P-CX-29-003	The Healer	A. Tobey	Unkn.	35.00	35.00
Curator Collection		**American Maritime Heritage**			
87-P-CX-30-001	U.S.S. Constitution	K. Soldwedel	14 Day	35.00	35.00
Curator Collection		**Special Issue**			
87-P-CX-31-001	We the People	H. C. Christy	Open	35.00	35.00
D'Arceau Limoges		**Lafayette**			
73-P-DB-01-001	The Secret Contract	A. Restieau	Unkn.	14.82	15.00
73-P-DB-01-002	North Island Landing	A. Restieau	Unkn.	19.82	20.00
74-P-DB-01-003	City Tavern Meeting	A. Restieau	Unkn.	19.82	20.00
74-P-DB-01-004	Battle of Brandywine	A. Restieau	Unkn.	19.82	20.00
75-P-DB-01-005	Messages to Franklin	A. Restieau	Unkn.	19.82	23.00
75-P-DB-01-006	Siege at Yorktown	A. Restieau	Unkn.	19.82	20.00
D'Arceau Limoges		**Christmas**			
75-P-DB-02-001	La Fruite en Egypte	A. Restieau	Unkn.	24.32	35.00
76-P-DB-02-002	Dans la Creche	A. Restieau	Unkn.	24.32	30.00
77-P-DB-02-003	Refus d' Hebergement	A. Restieau	Unkn.	24.32	30.00
78-P-DB-02-004	La Purification	A. Restieau	Yr.Iss	26.81	30.00
79-P-DB-02-005	L' Adoration des Rois	A. Restieau	Yr.Iss	26.81	35.00
80-P-DB-02-006	Joyeuse Nouvelle	A. Restieau	Yr.Iss	28.74	29.00
81-P-DB-02-007	Guides par L' Etoile	A. Restieau	Yr.Iss	28.74	30.00
82-P-DB-02-008	L' Annuciation	A. Restieau	Yr.Iss	30.74	45.00
Duncan Royale		**History of Santa Claus I**			
85-P-DR-01-001	Medieval	S. Morton	10,000	40.00	40.00
85-P-DR-01-002	Kris Kringle	S. Morton	10,000	40.00	40.00
85-P-DR-01-003	Pioneer	S. Morton	10,000	40.00	40.00
86-P-DR-01-004	Russian	S. Morton	10,000	40.00	40.00
86-P-DR-01-005	Soda Pop	S. Morton	10,000	40.00	40.00
86-P-DR-01-006	Civil War	S. Morton	10,000	40.00	40.00
86-P-DR-01-007	Nast	S. Morton	10,000	40.00	40.00
87-P-DR-01-008	St. Nicholas	S. Morton	10,000	40.00	40.00
87-P-DR-01-009	Dedt Moroz	S. Morton	10,000	40.00	40.00
87-P-DR-01-010	Black Peter	S. Morton	10,000	40.00	40.00
87-P-DR-01-011	Victorian	S. Morton	10,000	40.00	40.00
87-P-DR-01-012	Wassail	S. Morton	10,000	40.00	40.00
XX-P-DR-01-013	Collection of 12 Plates	S. Morton	10,000	480.00	480.00
Enesco Imports Corporation		**Inspired Thoughts**			
85-P-EA-01-001	Love One Another - E-5215	S. Butcher	15,000	40.00	60.00
82-P-EA-01-002	Make a Joyful Noise - E-7174	S. Butcher	15,000	40.00	60.00
83-P-EA-01-003	I Believe In Miracles - E-9257	S. Butcher	15,000	40.00	60.00
84-P-EA-01-004	Love is Kind - E-2847	S. Butcher	15,000	40.00	60.00
Enesco Imports Corporation		**Mother's Love**			
81-P-EA-02-001	Mother Sew Dear - E-5217	S. Butcher	15,000	40.00	70.00
82-P-EA-02-002	The Purr-fect Grandma - E-7173	S. Butcher	15,000	40.00	70.00
83-P-EA-02-003	The Hand that Rocks the Future - E-9256	S. Butcher	15,000	40.00	70.00
84-P-EA-02-004	Loving Thy Neighbor - E-2848	S. Butcher	15,000	40.00	70.00
Enesco Imports Corporation		**Christmas Collection**			
81-P-EA-03-001	Come Let Us Adore Him - E-5646	S. Butcher	15,000	40.00	60.00
82-P-EA-03-002	Let Heaven and Nature Sing - E-2347	S. Butcher	15,000	40.00	45.00
83-P-EA-03-003	Wee Three King's - E-0538	S. Butcher	15,000	40.00	45.00
84-P-EA-03-004	Unto Us a Child Is Born - E-5395	S. Butcher	15,000	40.00	40.00
Enesco Imports Corporation		**Joy of Christmas**			
82-P-EA-04-001	I'll Play My Drum For Him - E-2357	S. Butcher	Yr.Iss.	40.00	95.00
83-P-EA-04-002	Christmastime is for Sharing - E-0505	S. Butcher	Yr.Iss.	40.00	80.00
84-P-EA-04-003	The Wonder of Christmas - E-5396	S. Butcher	Yr.Iss.	40.00	60.00
85-P-EA-04-004	Tell Me the Story of Jesus - 15237	S. Butcher	Yr.Iss.	40.00	90.00
Enesco Imports Corporation		**The Four Seasons**			
85-P-EA-05-001	The Voice of Spring - 12106	S. Butcher	Yr.Iss.	40.00	85.00
85-P-EA-05-002	Summer's Joy - 12114	S. Butcher	Yr.Iss.	40.00	70.00
86-P-EA-05-003	Autumn's Praise - 12122	S. Butcher	Yr.Iss.	40.00	70.00
86-P-EA-05-004	Winter's Song - 12130	S. Butcher	Yr.Iss.	40.00	70.00
Enesco Imports Corporation		**Open Editions**			
82-P-EA-06-001	Our First Christmas Together - E-2378	S. Butcher	Suspd.	30.00	30.00
81-P-EA-06-002	The Lord Bless You and Keep You - E-5216	S. Butcher	Suspd.	30.00	35.00
82-P-EA-06-003	Rejoicing with You - E-7172	S. Butcher	Suspd.	30.00	35.00
83-P-EA-06-004	Jesus Loves Me - E-9275	S. Butcher	Suspd.	30.00	50.00
83-P-EA-06-005	Jesus Loves Me - E-9276	S. Butcher	Suspd.	30.00	50.00
Enesco Imports Corporation		**Christmas Love**			
86-P-EA-07-001	I'm Sending You a White Christmas - 101834	S. Butcher	Yr.Iss.	45.00	45.00
Ernst Enterprises		**Women of the West**			
79-P-EB-01-001	Expectations	D. Putnam	10,000	39.50	39.50
81-P-EB-01-002	Silver Dollar Sal	D. Putnam	10,000	39.50	39.50
82-P-EB-01-003	School Marm	D. Putnam	10,000	39.50	39.50
83-P-EB-01-004	Dolly	D. Putnam	10,000	39.50	39.50
Ernst Enterprises		**A Beautiful World**			
81-P-EB-02-001	Tahitian Dreamer	S. Morton	27,500	27.50	27.50
82-P-EB-02-002	Flirtation	S. Morton	27,500	27.50	27.50
84-P-EB-02-003	Elke of Oslo	S. Morton	27,500	27.50	27.50
Ernst Enterprises		**Seems Like Yesterday**			
81-P-EB-03-001	Stop & Smell the Roses	R. Money	10-day	24.50	35.00
82-P-EB-03-002	Home by Lunch	R. Money	10-day	24.50	30.00
82-P-EB-03-003	Lisa's Creek	R. Money	10-day	24.50	35.00
83-P-EB-03-004	It's Got My Name on It	R. Money	10-day	24.50	30.00
83-P-EB-03-005	My Magic Hat	R. Money	10-day	24.50	24.50
84-P-EB-03-006	Little Prince	R. Money	10-day	24.50	24.50
Ernst Enterprises		**Turn of The Century**			
81-P-EB-04-001	Riverboat Honeymoon	R. Money	10-day	35.00	35.00
82-P-EB-04-002	Children's Carousel	R. Money	10-day	35.00	35.00
84-P-EB-04-003	Flower Market	R. Money	10-day	35.00	35.00
85-P-EB-04-004	Balloon Race	R. Money	10-day	35.00	35.00
Ernst Enterprises		**Hollywood Greats**			
81-P-EB-05-001	John Wayne	S. Morton	27,500	29.95	50.00
81-P-EB-05-002	Gary Cooper	S. Morton	27,500	29.95	29.95
82-P-EB-05-003	Clark Gable	S. Morton	27,500	29.95	65.00
84-P-EB-05-004	Alan Ladd	S. Morton	27,500	29.95	60.00

Plates

Plates

Company / Number	Name	Series / Artist	Edition limit	Issue Price	Quote
Gorham		**A Boy and His Dog Four Seasons Plates**			
71-P-GO-02-001	Boy Meets His Dog	N. Rockwell	Annual	50.00	230.00
71-P-GO-02-002	Adventures Between Adventures	N. Rockwell	Annual	set	set
81-P-GO-02-003	The Mysterious Malady	N. Rockwell	Annual	set	set
71-P-GO-02-004	Pride of Parenthood	N. Rockwell	Annual	set	set
Gorham		**Young Love Four Seasons Plates**			
72-P-GO-03-001	Downhill Daring	N. Rockwell	Annual	60.00	150.00
72-P-GO-03-002	Beguiling Buttercup	N. Rockwell	Annual	set	set
72-P-GO-03-003	Flying High	N. Rockwell	Annual	set	set
72-P-GO-03-004	A Scholarly Pace	N. Rockwell	Annual	set	set
Gorham		**Four Ages of Love**			
73-P-GO-04-001	Gaily Sharing Vintage Time	N. Rockwell	Annual	60.00	200.00
73-P-GO-04-002	Flowers in Tender Bloom	N. Rockwell	Annual	set	set
73-P-GO-04-003	Sweet Song So Young	N. Rockwell	Annual	set	set
73-P-GO-04-004	Fondly We Do Remember	N. Rockwell	Annual	set	set
Gorham		**Grandpa and Me Four Seasons Plates**			
74-P-GO-05-001	Gay Blades	N. Rockwell	Annual	60.00	100.00
74-P-GO-05-002	Day Dreamers	N. Rockwell	Annual	set	set
74-P-GO-05-003	Goin' Fishing	N. Rockwell	Annual	set	set
74-P-GO-05-004	Pensive Pals	N. Rockwell	Annual	set	set
Gorham		**Me and My Pals Four Seasons Plates**			
75-P-GO-06-001	A Lickin' Good Bath	N. Rockwell	Annual	70.00	100.00
75-P-GO-06-002	Young Man's Fancy	N. Rockwell	Annual	set	set
75-P-GO-06-003	Fisherman's Paradise	N. Rockwell	Annual	set	set
75-P-GO-06-004	Disastrous Daring	N. Rockwell	Annual	set	set
Gorham		**Grand Pals Four Seasons Plates**			
76-P-GO-07-001	Snow Sculpturing	N. Rockwell	Annual	70.00	230.00
76-P-GO-07-002	Soaring Spirits	N. Rockwell	Annual	set	set
76-P-GO-07-003	Fish Finders	N. Rockwell	Annual	set	set
76-P-GO-07-004	Ghostly Gourds	N. Rockwell	Annual	set	set
Gorham		**Going on Sixteen Four Seasons Plates**			
77-P-GO-08-001	Chilling Chore	N. Rockwell	Annual	75.00	120.00
77-P-GO-08-002	Sweet Serenade	N. Rockwell	Annual	set	set
77-P-GO-08-003	Shear Agony	N. Rockwell	Annual	set	set
77-P-GO-08-004	Pilgrimage	N. Rockwell	Annual	set	set
Gorham		**Tender Years Four Seasons Plates**			
78-P-GO-09-001	New Year Look	N. Rockwell	Annual	100.00	100.00
78-P-GO-09-002	Spring Tonic	N. Rockwell	Annual	set	set
78-P-GO-09-003	Cool Aid	N. Rockwell	Annual	set	set
78-P-GO-09-004	Chilly Reception	N. Rockwell	Annual	set	set
Gorham		**A Helping Hand Four Seasons Plates**			
79-P-GO-10-001	Year End Count	N. Rockwell	Annual	100.00	100.00
79-P-GO-10-002	Closed for Business	N. Rockwell	Annual	set	set
79-P-GO-10-003	Swatter's Rights	N. Rockwell	Annual	set	set
79-P-GO-10-004	Coal Season's Coming	N. Rockwell	Annual	set	set
Gorham		**Dad's Boys Four Seasons Plates**			
80-P-GO-11-001	Ski Skills	N. Rockwell	Annual	135.00	135.00
80-P-GO-11-002	In His Spirits	N. Rockwell	Annual	set	set
80-P-GO-11-003	Trout Dinner	N. Rockwell	Annual	set	set
80-P-GO-11-004	Careful Aim	N. Rockwell	Annual	set	set
Gorham		**Old Timers Four Seasons Plates**			
81-P-GO-12-001	Canine Solo	N. Rockwell	Annual	100.00	100.00
81-P-GO-12-002	Sweet Surprise	N. Rockwell	Annual	set	set
81-P-GO-12-003	Lazy Days	N. Rockwell	Annual	set	set
81-P-GO-12-004	Fancy Footwork	N. Rockwell	Annual	set	set
Gorham		**Life with Father Four Seasons Plates**			
82-P-GO-13-001	Big Decision	N. Rockwell	Annual	100.00	100.00
82-P-GO-13-002	Blasting Out	N. Rockwell	Annual	set	set
82-P-GO-13-003	Cheering the Champs	N. Rockwell	Annual	set	set
82-P-GO-13-004	A Tough One	N. Rockwell	Annual	set	set
Gorham		**Old Buddies Four Seasons Plates**			
83-P-GO-14-001	Shared Success	N. Rockwell	Annual	115.00	115.00
83-P-GO-14-002	Endless Debate	N. Rockwell	Annual	set	set
83-P-GO-14-003	Hasty Retreat	N. Rockwell	Annual	set	set
83-P-GO-14-004	Final Speech	N. Rockwell	Annual	set	set
Gorham		**Bas Relief**			
81-P-GO-15-001	Sweet Song So Young	N. Rockwell	Undis.	100.00	100.00
81-P-GO-15-002	Beguiling Buttercup	N. Rockwell	Undis.	62.50	62.50
82-P-GO-15-003	Flowers in Tender Bloom	N. Rockwell	Undis.	100.00	100.00
82-P-GO-15-004	Flying High	N. Rockwell	Undis.	62.50	62.50
Gorham		**None**			
74-P-GO-16-001	Weighing In	N. Rockwell	Annual	12.50	50.00
Gorham		**None**			
74-P-GO-17-001	The Golden Rule	N. Rockwell	Annual	12.50	30.00
Gorham		**None**			
75-P-GO-18-001	Ben Franklin	N. Rockwell	Annual	19.50	40.00
Gorham		**Boy Scout Plates**			
75-P-GO-19-001	Our Heritage	N. Rockwell	18,500	19.50	60.00
76-P-GO-19-002	A Scout is Loyal	N. Rockwell	18,500	19.50	55.00
77-P-GO-19-003	The Scoutmaster	N. Rockwell	18,500	19.50	60.00
77-P-GO-19-004	A Good Sign	N. Rockwell	18,500	19.50	50.00
78-P-GO-19-005	Pointing the Way	N. Rockwell	18,500	19.50	50.00
78-P-GO-19-006	Campfire Story	N. Rockwell	18,500	19.50	50.00
80-P-GO-19-007	Beyond the Easel	N. Rockwell	18,500	45.00	45.00
Gorham		**None**			
76-P-GO-20-001	The Marriage License	N. Rockwell	Numb-rd	37.50	40.00
Gorham		**Presidential**			
76-P-GO-21-001	John F. Kennedy	N. Rockwell	9,800	30.00	55.00
76-P-GO-21-002	Dwight D. Eisenhower	N. Rockwell	9,800	30.00	35.00
Gorham		**None**			
78-P-GO-22-001	Triple Self Portrait Memorial Plate	N. Rockwell	Annual	37.50	60.00
Gorham		**Four Seasons Landscapes**			
80-P-GO-23-001	Summer Respite	N. Rockwell	Annual	45.00	45.00
81-P-GO-23-002	Autumn Reflection	N. Rockwell	Annual	45.00	45.00
82-P-GO-23-003	Winter Delight	N. Rockwell	Annual	50.00	50.00
Gorham		**None**			
80-P-GO-24-001	The Annual Visit	N. Rockwell	Annual	32.50	32.50
Gorham		**None**			
81-P-GO-25-001	Day in Life of Boy	N. Rockwell	Annual	50.00	80.00
81-P-GO-25-002	Day in Life of Girl	N. Rockwell	Annual	50.00	80.00
Gorham		**Gallery of Masters**			
71-P-GO-26-001	Man with a Gilt Helmet	Rembrandt	10,000	50.00	50.00
72-P-GO-26-002	Self Portrait with Saskia	Rembrandt	10,000	50.00	50.00
73-P-GO-26-003	The Honorable Mrs. Graham	Gainsborough	7,500	50.00	50.00
Gorham		**Barrymore**			
71-P-GO-27-001	Quiet Waters	Barrymore	15,000	25.00	25.00
72-P-GO-27-002	San Pedro Harbor	Barrymore	15,000	25.00	25.00
Gorham		**Barrymore**			
72-P-GO-28-001	Nantucket, Sterling	Barrymore	1,000	100.00	100.00
72-P-GO-28-002	Little Boatyard, Sterling	Barrymore	1,000	100.00	145.00
Gorham		**Pewter Bicentennial**			
71-P-GO-29-001	Burning of the Gaspee	N. Rockwell	5,000	35.00	35.00
72-P-GO-29-002	Boston Tea Party	N. Rockwell	5,000	35.00	35.00
Gorham		**Vermeil Bicentennial**			
72-P-GO-30-001	1776 Plate	N. Rockwell	250	750.00	800.00
Gorham		**Silver Bicentennial**			
72-P-GO-31-001	1776 Plate	N. Rockwell	750	500.00	500.00
72-P-GO-31-002	Burning of the Gaspee	N. Rockwell	750	500.00	500.00
73-P-GO-31-003	Boston Tea Party	N. Rockwell	750	550.00	575.00
Gorham		**China Bicentennial**			
72-P-GO-32-001	1776 Plate	N. Rockwell	18,500	17.50	35.00
76-P-GO-32-002	1776 Bicentennial	N. Rockwell	8,000	17.50	35.00
Gorham		**Remington Western**			
73-P-GO-33-001	A New Year on the Cimarron	F. Remington	Annual	25.00	35.00
73-P-GO-33-002	Aiding a Comrade	F. Remington	Annual	25.00	30.00
73-P-GO-33-003	The Flight	F. Remington	Annual	25.00	30.00
73-P-GO-33-004	The Fight for the Water Hole	F. Remington	Annual	25.00	30.00
75-P-GO-33-005	Old Ramond	F. Remington	Annual	20.00	35.00
75-P-GO-33-006	A Breed	F. Remington	Annual	20.00	35.00
76-P-GO-33-007	Cavalry Officer	F. Remington	5,000	37.50	40.00
76-P-GO-33-008	A Trapper	F. Remington	5,000	37.50	40.00
Gorham		**Moppet Plates - Christmas**			
73-P-GO-34-001	M. Plate Christmas	Unknown	Annual	10.00	35.00
74-P-GO-34-002	M. Plate Christmas	Unknown	Annual	12.00	22.00
75-P-GO-34-003	M. Plate Christmas	Unknown	Annual	13.00	15.00
76-P-GO-34-004	M. Plate Christmas	Unknown	Annual	13.00	15.00
77-P-GO-34-005	M. Plate Christmas	Unknown	Annual	13.00	14.00
78-P-GO-34-006	M. Plate Christmas	Unknown	Annual	10.00	10.00
79-P-GO-34-007	M. Plate Christmas	Unknown	Annual	12.00	12.00
80-P-GO-34-008	M. Plate Christmas	Unknown	Annual	12.00	12.00
81-P-GO-34-009	M. Plate Christmas	Unknown	Annual	12.00	12.00
82-P-GO-34-010	M. Plate Christmas	Unknown	Annual	12.00	12.00
83-P-GO-34-011	M. Plate Christmas	Unknown	Annual	12.00	12.00
Gorham		**Moppet Plates - Mother's Day**			
73-P-GO-35-001	M. Plate Mother's Day	Unknown	Annual	10.00	30.00
74-P-GO-35-002	M. Plate Mother's Day	Unknown	Annual	12.00	20.00
75-P-GO-35-003	M. Plate Mother's Day	Unknown	Annual	13.00	15.00
76-P-GO-35-004	M. Plate Mother's Day	Unknown	Annual	13.00	15.00
77-P-GO-35-005	M. Plate Mother's Day	Unknown	Annual	13.00	15.00
78-P-GO-35-006	M. Plate Mother's Day	Unknown	Annual	10.00	10.00
Gorham		**Moppet Plates - Anniversary**			
76-P-GO-36-001	M. Plate Anniversary	Unknown	20,000	13.00	13.00
Gorham		**Julian Ritter, Fall in Love**			
77-P-GO-37-001	Enchantment	J. Ritter	5,000	100.00	100.00
77-P-GO-37-002	Frolic	J. Ritter	5,000	set	set
77-P-GO-37-003	Gusty Gal	J. Ritter	5,000	set	set
77-P-GO-37-004	Loney Chill	J. Ritter	5,000	set	set
Gorham		**Julian Ritter**			
77-P-GO-38-001	Christmas Visit	J. Ritter	9,800	24.50	29.00
Gorham		**Julian Ritter, To Love a Clown**			
78-P-GO-39-001	Awaited Reunion	J. Ritter	5,000	120.00	120.00
78-P-GO-39-002	Twosome Time	J. Ritter	5,000	120.00	120.00
78-P-GO-39-003	Showtime Beckons	J. Ritter	5,000	120.00	120.00
78-P-GO-39-004	Together in Memories	J. Ritter	5,000	120.00	120.00
Gorham		**Julian Ritter**			
78-P-GO-40-001	Valentine, Fluttering Heart	J. Ritter	7,500	45.00	45.00
Gorham		**Christmas/Children's Television Workshop**			
81-P-GO-41-001	Sesame Street Christmas	Unknown	Annual	17.50	17.50
82-P-GO-41-002	Sesame Street Christmas	Unknown	Annual	17.50	17.50
83-P-GO-41-003	Sesame Street Christmas	Unknown	Annual	19.50	19.50
Gorham		**Pastoral Symphony**			
82-P-GO-42-001	When I Was a Child	B. Felder	7,500	42.50	50.00
82-P-GO-42-002	Gather the Children	B. Felder	7,500	42.50	50.00
84-P-GO-42-003	Sugar and Spice	B. Felder	7,500	42.50	50.00
XX-P-GO-42-004	He Loves Me	B. Felder	7,500	42.50	50.00
Gorham		**Encounters, Survival and Celebrations**			
82-P-GO-43-001	A Fine Welcome	J. Clymer	7,500	50.00	62.50
83-P-GO-43-002	Winter Trail	J. Clymer	7,500	50.00	62.50
83-P-GO-43-003	Alouette	J. Clymer	7,500	62.50	62.50
83-P-GO-43-004	The Trader	J. Clymer	7,500	62.50	62.50
83-P-GO-43-005	Winter Camp	J. Clymer	7,500	62.50	62.50
83-P-GO-43-006	The Trapper Takes a Wife	J. Clymer	7,500	62.50	62.50
Gorham		**Charles Russell**			
80-P-GO-44-001	In Without Knocking	C. Russell	9,800	38.00	50.00
81-P-GO-44-002	Bronc to Breakfast	C. Russell	9,800	38.00	38.00
82-P-GO-44-003	When Ignorance is Bliss	C. Russell	9,800	45.00	45.00
83-P-GO-44-004	Cowboy Life	C. Russell	9,800	45.00	45.00
Gorham		**Gorham Museum Doll Plates**			
84-P-GO-45-001	Lydia	Gorham	5,000	29.00	125.00
84-P-GO-45-002	Belton Bebe	Gorham	5,000	29.00	55.00
84-P-GO-45-003	Christmas Lady	Gorham	7,500	32.50	32.50
85-P-GO-45-004	Lucille	Gorham	5,000	29.00	35.00
85-P-GO-45-005	Jumeau	Gorham	5,000	29.00	29.00
Gorham		**Time Machine Teddies Plates**			
86-P-GO-46-001	Miss Emily, Bearing Up	B. Port	5,000	32.50	32.50
87-P-GO-46-002	Big Bear, The Toy Collector	B. Port	5,000	32.50	32.50
Gorham/Hamilton		**Lewis & Clark Expedition-Trailblazers of N.W.**			
81-P-GP-01-001	Lewis & Clark in the Bitterroots	J. Clymer	10-day	55.00	75.00
81-P-GP-01-002	Sacajawea at the Big Water	J. Clymer	10-day	55.00	65.00
81-P-GP-01-003	The Lewis Crossing	J. Clymer	10-day	55.00	55.00
81-P-GP-01-004	Captain Clark and the Buffalo Gangue	J. Clymer	10-day	55.00	55.00
82-P-GP-01-005	The Salt Maker	J. Clymer	10-day	55.00	55.00
82-P-GP-01-006	Up the Jefferson	J. Clymer	10-day	55.00	55.00
82-P-GP-01-007	Arrival of Sergeant Pryor	J. Clymer	10-day	55.00	55.00
82-P-GP-01-008	Visitors at Fort Clatsop	J. Clymer	10-day	55.00	55.00
Grande Copenhagen		**Christmas**			
75-P-GQ-01-001	Alone Together	Unknown	Undis.	24.50	29.50
76-P-GQ-01-002	Christmas Wreath	Unknown	Undis.	24.50	29.50
77-P-GQ-01-003	Fishwives at Gammelstrand	Unknown	Undis.	26.50	27.00
78-P-GQ-01-004	Hans Christian Andersen	Unknown	Undis.	32.50	40.00

Company		Series			
Number	**Name**	**Artist**	**Edition limit**	**Issue Price**	**Quote**
79-P-GQ-01-005	Pheasants	Unknown	Undis.	34.50	35.00
80-P-GQ-01-006	Snow Queen in the Tivoli	Unknown	Undis.	39.50	40.00
81-P-GQ-01-007	Little Match Girl in Nyhavn	Unknown	Undis.	42.50	45.00
82-P-GQ-01-008	Shepherdess/Chimney Sweep	Unknown	Undis.	45.00	60.00
83-P-GQ-01-009	Little Mermaid Near Kronborg	Unknown	Undis.	45.00	140.00
84-P-GQ-01-010	Sandman at Amalienborg	Unknown	Undis.	45.00	75.00
Hackett American		**Endangered Species**			
80-P-HA-01-001	California Sea Otters	S. Mano	7,500	35.00	75.00
81-P-HA-01-002	Asian Pandas	S. Mano	7,500	37.50	65.00
82-P-HA-01-003	Australian Koalas	S. Mano	7,500	37.50	37.50
82-P-HA-01-004	River Otters	S. Mano	7,500	39.50	39.50
Hackett American		**Playful Memories**			
81-P-HA-02-001	Renee	S. Etem	10,000	39.50	75.00
82-P-HA-02-002	Jeremy	S. Etem	10,000	42.50	50.00
82-P-HA-02-003	Jamie	S. Etem	10,000	42.50	50.00
83-P-HA-02-004	Randy	S. Etem	10,000	45.00	45.00
Hamilton/Boehm		**Award Winning Roses**			
79-P-HB-01-001	Peace Rose	Boehm	15,000	45.00	100.00
79-P-HB-01-002	White Masterpiece Rose	Boehm	15,000	45.00	75.00
79-P-HB-01-003	Tropicana Rose	Boehm	15,000	45.00	65.00
79-P-HB-01-004	Elegance Rose	Boehm	15,000	45.00	55.00
79-P-HB-01-005	Queen Elizabeth Rose	Boehm	15,000	45.00	55.00
79-P-HB-01-006	Royal Highness Rose	Boehm	15,000	45.00	55.00
79-P-HB-01-007	Angel Face Rose	Boehm	15,000	45.00	55.00
79-P-HB-01-008	Mr. Lincoln Rose	Boehm	15,000	45.00	55.00
Hamilton/Boehm		**Owl Collection**			
80-P-HB-02-001	Boreal Owl	Boehm	15,000	45.00	75.00
80-P-HB-02-002	Snowy Owl	Boehm	15,000	45.00	62.50
80-P-HB-02-003	Barn Owl	Boehm	15,000	45.00	62.50
80-P-HB-02-004	Saw Whet Owl	Boehm	15,000	45.00	62.50
80-P-HB-02-005	Great Horned Owl	Boehm	15,000	45.00	62.50
80-P-HB-02-006	Screech Owl	Boehm	15,000	45.00	62.50
80-P-HB-02-007	Short Eared Owl	Boehm	15,000	45.00	62.50
80-P-HB-02-008	Barred Owl	Boehm	15,000	45.00	62.50
Hamilton/Boehm		**Hummingbird Collection**			
80-P-HB-03-001	Calliope	Boehm	15,000	62.50	75.00
80-P-HB-03-002	Broadbilled	Boehm	15,000	62.50	62.50
80-P-HB-03-003	Rufous Flame Bearer	Boehm	15,000	62.50	62.50
80-P-HB-03-004	Broadtail	Boehm	15,000	62.50	62.50
80-P-HB-03-005	Streamertail	Boehm	15,000	62.50	62.50
80-P-HB-03-006	Blue Throated	Boehm	15,000	62.50	62.50
80-P-HB-03-007	Crimson Topaz	Boehm	15,000	62.50	62.50
80-P-HB-03-008	Brazilian Ruby	Boehm	15,000	62.50	62.50
Hamilton/Boehm		**Water Birds**			
81-P-HB-04-001	Canada Geese	Boehm	15,000	62.50	75.00
81-P-HB-04-002	Wood Ducks	Boehm	15,000	62.50	62.50
81-P-HB-04-003	Hooded Merganser	Boehm	15,000	62.50	62.50
81-P-HB-04-004	Ross's Geese	Boehm	15,000	62.50	62.50
81-P-HB-04-005	Common Mallard	Boehm	15,000	62.50	62.50
81-P-HB-04-006	Canvas Back	Boehm	15,000	62.50	62.50
81-P-HB-04-007	Green Winged Teal	Boehm	15,000	62.50	62.50
81-P-HB-04-008	American Pintail	Boehm	15,000	62.50	62.50
Hamilton/Boehm		**Roses of Excellence**			
81-P-HB-05-001	Love Rose	Boehm	Yr.Iss	62.50	85.00
82-P-HB-05-002	White Lightnin'	Boehm	Yr.Iss	62.50	72.00
83-P-HB-05-003	Brandy	Boehm	Yr.Iss	62.50	62.50
83-P-HB-05-004	Sun Flare	Boehm	Yr.Iss	62.50	62.50
Hamilton/Boehm		**Life's Best Wishes**			
82-P-HB-06-001	Longevity	Boehm	15,000	75.00	75.00
82-P-HB-06-002	Happiness	Boehm	15,000	75.00	75.00
82-P-HB-06-003	Fertility	Boehm	15,000	75.00	75.00
82-P-HB-06-004	Prosperity	Boehm	15,000	75.00	75.00
Hamilton/Boehm		**A Tribute to Award-Winning Roses**			
83-P-HB-07-001	Irish Gold	Boehm	15,000	62.50	62.50
83-P-HB-07-002	Handel	Boehm	15,000	62.50	62.50
83-P-HB-07-003	Queen Elizabeth	Boehm	15,000	62.50	62.50
83-P-HB-07-004	Elizabeth of Glamis	Boehm	15,000	62.50	62.50
83-P-HB-07-005	Iceberg	Boehm	15,000	62.50	62.50
83-P-HB-07-006	Mountbatten	Boehm	15,000	62.50	62.50
83-P-HB-07-007	Silver Jubilee	Boehm	15,000	62.50	62.50
83-P-HB-07-008	Peace	Boehm	15,000	62.50	62.50
Hamilton/Boehm		**Gamebirds of North America**			
84-P-HB-08-001	Ring-necked Pheasant	Boehm	15,000	62.50	62.50
84-P-HB-08-002	Bob White Quail	Boehm	15,000	62.50	62.50
84-P-HB-08-003	American Woodcock	Boehm	15,000	62.50	62.50
84-P-HB-08-004	California Quail	Boehm	15,000	62.50	62.50
84-P-HB-08-005	Ruffed Grouse	Boehm	15,000	62.50	62.50
84-P-HB-08-006	Wild Turkey	Boehm	15,000	62.50	62.50
84-P-HB-08-007	Willow Partridge	Boehm	15,000	62.50	62.50
84-P-HB-08-008	Prairie Grouse	Boehm	15,000	62.50	62.50
Hamilton Collection		**The Nutcracker Ballet**			
78-P-HC-01-001	Clara	S. Fisher	28-day	19.50	125.00
79-P-HC-01-002	Godfather	S. Fisher	28-day	19.50	65.00
79-P-HC-01-003	Sugar Plum Fairy	S. Fisher	28-day	19.50	55.00
79-P-HC-01-004	Snow Queen and King	S. Fisher	28-day	19.50	47.00
80-P-HC-01-005	Waltz of the Flowers	S. Fisher	28-day	19.50	47.00
80-P-HC-01-006	Clara and the Prince	S. Fisher	28-day	19.50	47.00
Hamilton Collection		**Precious Moments Plates**			
79-P-HC-02-001	Friend in the Sky	T. Utz	28-day	21.50	50.00
80-P-HC-02-002	Sand in her Shoe	T. Utz	28-day	21.50	40.00
80-P-HC-02-003	Snow Bunny	T. Utz	28-day	21.50	40.00
80-P-HC-02-004	Seashells	T. Utz	28-day	21.50	27.00
81-P-HC-02-005	Dawn	T. Utz	28-day	21.50	27.00
82-P-HC-02-006	My Kitty	T. Utz	28-day	21.50	27.00
Hamilton Collection		**Rockwell's 'Man's Best Friend' Copper**			
79-P-HC-03-001	The Hobo	N. Rockwell	9,500	40.00	60.00
79-P-HC-03-002	The Doctor	N. Rockwell	9,500	40.00	40.00
79-P-HC-03-003	Making Friends	N. Rockwell	9,500	40.00	40.00
79-P-HC-03-004	Gone Fishing	N. Rockwell	9,500	40.00	40.00
80-P-HC-03-005	Puppy Love	N. Rockwell	9,500	40.00	40.00
80-P-HC-03-006	The Thief	N. Rockwell	9,500	40.00	40.00
Hamilton Collection		**The Greatest Show on Earth**			
81-P-HC-04-001	Clowns	F. Moody	10-day	30.00	75.00
81-P-HC-04-002	Elephants	F. Moody	10-day	30.00	40.00
81-P-HC-04-003	Aerialists	F. Moody	10-day	30.00	35.00
81-P-HC-04-004	Great Parade	F. Moody	10-day	30.00	30.00
81-P-HC-04-005	Midway	F. Moody	10-day	30.00	30.00
81-P-HC-04-006	Equestrians	F. Moody	10-day	30.00	30.00
82-P-HC-04-007	Lion Tamer	F. Moody	10-day	30.00	30.00
82-P-HC-04-008	Grande Finale	F. Moody	10-day	30.00	30.00
Hamilton Collection		**Rockwell Home of the Brave**			
81-P-HC-05-001	Reminiscing	N. Rockwell	18,000	35.00	75.00
81-P-HC-05-002	Hero's Welcome	N. Rockwell	18,000	35.00	50.00
81-P-HC-05-003	Back to his Old Job	N. Rockwell	18,000	35.00	40.00
81-P-HC-05-004	War Hero	N. Rockwell	18,000	35.00	35.00
82-P-HC-05-005	Willie Gillis in Church	N. Rockwell	18,000	35.00	35.00
82-P-HC-05-006	War Bond	N. Rockwell	18,000	35.00	35.00
82-P-HC-05-007	Uncle Sam Takes Wings	N. Rockwell	18,000	35.00	35.00
82-P-HC-05-008	Taking Mother over the Top	N. Rockwell	18,000	35.00	35.00
Hamilton Collection		**Japanese Floral Calender**			
81-P-HC-06-001	New Year's Day	Shuho/kage	10-day	32.50	60.00
82-P-HC-06-002	Early Spring	Shuho/Kage	10-day	32.50	40.00
82-P-HC-06-003	Spring	Shuho/Kage	10-day	32.50	32.50
82-P-HC-06-004	Girl's Doll Day Festival	Shuho/Kage	10-day	32.50	32.50
82-P-HC-06-005	Buddha's Birthday	Shuho/Kage	10-day	32.50	32.50
82-P-HC-06-006	Early Summer	Shuho/Kage	10-day	32.50	32.50
82-P-HC-06-007	Boy's Doll Day Festival	Shuho/Kage	10-day	32.50	32.50
82-P-HC-06-008	Summer	Shuho/Kage	10-day	32.50	32.50
82-P-HC-06-009	Autumn	Shuho/Kage	10-day	32.50	32.50
83-P-HC-06-010	Fesival of the Full Moon	Shuho/Kage	10-day	32.50	32.50
83-P-HC-06-011	Late Autumn	Shuho/Kage	10-day	32.50	32.50
83-P-HC-06-012	Winter	Shuho/Kage	10-day	32.50	32.50
Hamilton Collection		**Treasures of the Chinese Mandarins**			
81-P-HC-07-001	The Bird of Paradise	Unknown	2,500	75.00	135.00
82-P-HC-07-002	The Guardians of Heaven	Unknown	2,500	75.00	105.00
82-P-HC-07-003	The Tree of Immortality	Unknown	2,500	75.00	95.00
82-P-HC-07-004	The Dragon of Eternity	Unknown	2,500	75.00	85.00
Hamilton Collection		**Portraits of Childhood**			
81-P-HC-08-001	Butterfly Magic	T. Utz	28-day	24.95	45.00
82-P-HC-08-002	Sweet Dreams	T. Utz	28-day	24.95	30.00
83-P-HC-08-003	Turtle Talk	T. Utz	28-day	24.95	24.95
84-P-HC-08-004	Friends Forever	T. Utz	28-day	24.95	24.95
Hamilton Collection		**Carefree Days**			
82-P-HC-09-001	Autumn Wanderer	T. Utz	10-day	24.50	24.50
82-P-HC-09-002	Best Friends	T. Utz	10-day	24.50	24.50
82-P-HC-09-003	Feeding Time	T. Utz	10-day	24.50	24.50
82-P-HC-09-004	Bathtime Visitor	T. Utz	10-day	24.50	24.50
82-P-HC-09-005	First Catch	T. Utz	10-day	24.50	24.50
82-P-HC-09-006	Monkey Business	T. Utz	10-day	24.50	24.50
82-P-HC-09-007	Touchdown	T. Utz	10-day	24.50	24.50
82-P-HC-09-008	Nature Hunt	T. Utz	10-day	24.50	24.50
Hamilton Collection		**Utz Mother's Day**			
83-P-HC-10-001	A Gift of Love	T. Utz	Time	27.50	45.00
83-P-HC-10-002	Mother's Helping Hand	T. Utz	Time	27.50	27.50
83-P-HC-10-003	Mother's Angel	T. Utz	Time	27.50	27.50
Hamilton Collection		**Single Issues**			
83-P-HC-11-001	Princess Grace	T. Utz	21-day	39.50	52.00
Hamilton Collection		**Summer Days of Childhood**			
83-P-HC-12-001	Mountain Friends	T. Utz	10-day	29.50	29.50
83-P-HC-12-002	Garden Magic	T. Utz	10-day	29.50	29.50
83-P-HC-12-003	Little Beachcomber	T. Utz	10-day	29.50	29.50
83-P-HC-12-004	Blowing Bubbles	T. Utz	10-day	29.50	29.50
83-P-HC-12-005	The Birthday Party	T. Utz	10-day	29.50	29.50
83-P-HC-12-006	Playing Doctor	T. Utz	10-day	29.50	29.50
83-P-HC-12-007	A Stolen Kiss	T. Utz	10-day	29.50	29.50
83-P-HC-12-008	Kitty's Bathtime	T. Utz	10-day	29.50	29.50
83-P-HC-12-009	Cooling Off	T. Utz	10-day	29.50	29.50
83-P-HC-12-010	First Customer	T. Utz	10-day	29.50	29.50
83-P-HC-12-011	A Jumping Contest	T. Utz	10-day	29.50	29.50
83-P-HC-12-012	Balloon Carnival	T. Utz	10-day	29.50	29.50
Hamilton Collection		**Birds of Prey**			
83-P-HC-13-001	Golden Eagle	C. F. Riley	12,500	55.00	65.00
83-P-HC-13-002	Coopers Hawk	C. F. Riley	12,500	55.00	65.00
83-P-HC-13-003	Great Horned Owl	C. F. Riley	12,500	55.00	65.00
83-P-HC-13-004	Bald Eagle	C. F. Riley	12,500	55.00	65.00
83-P-HC-13-005	Barred Owl	C. F. Riley	12,500	55.00	65.00
83-P-HC-13-006	Sparrow Hawk	C. F. Riley	12,500	55.00	65.00
83-P-HC-13-007	Peregrine Falcon	C. F. Riley	12,500	55.00	65.00
83-P-HC-13-008	Osprey	C. F. Riley	12,500	55.00	65.00
Hamilton Collection		**Eternal Wishes of Good Fortune**			
83-P-HC-14-001	Friendship	Shuho	10-day	34.95	37.50
83-P-HC-14-002	Purity and Perfection	Shuho	10-day	34.95	37.50
83-P-HC-14-003	Illustrious Offspring	Shuho	10-day	34.95	37.50
83-P-HC-14-004	Longevity	Shuho	10-day	34.95	37.50
83-P-HC-14-005	Youth	Shuho	10-day	34.95	37.50
83-P-HC-14-006	Immortality	Shuho	10-day	34.95	37.50
83-P-HC-14-007	Marital Bliss	Shuho	10-day	34.95	37.50
83-P-HC-14-008	Love	Shuho	10-day	34.95	37.50
83-P-HC-14-009	Peace	Shuho	10-day	34.95	37.50
83-P-HC-14-010	Beauty	Shuho	10-day	34.95	37.50
83-P-HC-14-011	Fertility	Shuho	10-day	34.95	37.50
83-P-HC-14-012	Fortitude	Shuho	10-day	34.95	37.50
Hamilton Collection		**Gardens of the Orient**			
83-P-HC-15-001	Flowering of Spring	S. Suetomi	10-day	19.50	19.50
83-P-HC-15-002	Festival of May	S. Suetomi	10-day	19.50	19.50
83-P-HC-15-003	Cherry Blossom	S. Suetomi	10-day	19.50	19.50
83-P-HC-15-004	Winter's Repose	S. Suetomi	10-day	19.50	19.50
83-P-HC-15-005	Garden Sanctuary	S. Suetomi	10-day	19.50	19.50
83-P-HC-15-006	Summer's Glory	S. Suetomi	10-day	19.50	19.50
83-P-HC-15-007	June's Creation	S. Suetomi	10-day	19.50	19.50
83-P-HC-15-008	New Year's Dawn	S. Suetomi	10-day	19.50	19.50
83-P-HC-15-009	Autumn Serenity	S. Suetomi	10-day	19.50	19.50
83-P-HC-15-010	Harvest Morning	S. Suetomi	10-day	19.50	19.50
83-P-HC-15-011	Tranquil Pond	S. Suetomi	10-day	19.50	19.50
83-P-HC-15-012	Morning Song	S. Suetomi	10-day	19.50	19.50
Hamilton Collection		**Chinese Symbols of the Universe**			
84-P-HC-16-001	The Dragon	M. Tseng	7,500	90.00	90.00
84-P-HC-16-002	The Phoenix	M. Tseng	7,500	90.00	90.00
84-P-HC-16-003	The Tiger	M. Tseng	7,500	90.00	90.00
84-P-HC-16-004	The Tortoise	M. Tseng	7,500	90.00	90.00
84-P-HC-16-005	Man	M. Tseng	7,500	90.00	90.00
Hamilton Collection		**A Garden of Verses**			
84-P-HC-17-001	Picture Books in Winter	J. W. Smith	10-day	24.50	24.50
84-P-HC-17-002	Little Drops	J. W. Smith	10-day	24.50	24.50

Plates

Company / Number	Name	Series / Artist	Edition limit	Issue Price	Quote
84-P-HC-17-003	A Child's Question	J. W. Smith	10-day	24.50	24.50
84-P-HC-17-004	Looking Glass	J. W. Smith	10-day	24.50	24.50
84-P-HC-17-005	The Little Busy Bee	J. W. Smith	10-day	24.50	24.50
84-P-HC-17-006	At the Sea-side	J. W. Smith	10-day	24.50	24.50
84-P-HC-17-007	The Tea Party	J. W. Smith	10-day	24.50	24.50
84-P-HC-17-008	Foreign Lands	J. W. Smith	10-day	24.50	24.50
84-P-HC-17-009	The Mayloft	J. W. Smith	10-day	24.50	24.50
84-P-HC-17-010	Among the Poppies	J. W. Smith	10-day	24.50	24.50
84-P-HC-17-011	Five O'Clock Tea	J. W. Smith	10-day	24.50	24.50
84-P-HC-17-012	I Love Little Kitty	J. W. Smith	10-day	24.50	24.50
Hamilton Collection		**Flower Festivals of Japan**			
85-P-HC-18-001	Chrysanthemum	N. Hara	10-day	45.00	55.00
85-P-HC-18-002	Hollyhock	N. Hara	10-day	45.00	55.00
85-P-HC-18-003	Plum Blossom	N. Hara	10-day	45.00	55.00
85-P-HC-18-004	Morning Glory	N. Hara	10-day	45.00	55.00
85-P-HC-18-005	Cherry Blossom	N. Hara	10-day	45.00	55.00
85-P-HC-18-006	Iris	N. Hara	10-day	45.00	55.00
85-P-HC-18-007	Lily	N. Hara	10-day	45.00	55.00
85-P-HC-18-008	Peach Blossom	N. Hara	10-day	45.00	55.00
Hamilton Collection		**Tale of Genji**			
85-P-HC-19-001	Serene Autumn Moon	S. Hotta	10-day	45.00	45.00
85-P-HC-19-002	Dragon and Phoenix Boats	S. Hotta	10-day	45.00	45.00
85-P-HC-19-003	Romantic Duet	S. Hotta	10-day	45.00	45.00
85-P-HC-19-004	Waves of the Blue Ocean Dance	S. Hotta	10-day	45.00	45.00
85-P-HC-19-005	Evening Faces	S. Hotta	10-day	45.00	45.00
85-P-HC-19-006	The Archery Meet	S. Hotta	10-day	45.00	45.00
85-P-HC-19-007	Moon Viewing	S. Hotta	10-day	45.00	45.00
85-P-HC-19-008	The Table Game	S. Hotta	10-day	45.00	45.00
Hamilton Collection		**Passage to China**			
83-P-HC-20-001	Empress of China	R. Massey	15,000	55.00	55.00
83-P-HC-20-002	Alliance	R. Massey	15,000	55.00	55.00
85-P-HC-20-003	Grand Turk	R. Massey	15,000	55.00	55.00
85-P-HC-20-004	Sea Witch	R. Massey	15,000	55.00	55.00
85-P-HC-20-005	Flying Cloud	R. Massey	15,000	55.00	55.00
85-P-HC-20-006	Romance of the Seas	R. Massey	15,000	55.00	55.00
85-P-HC-20-007	Sea Serpent	R. Massey	15,000	55.00	55.00
85-P-HC-20-008	Challenge	R. Massey	15,000	55.00	55.00
Hamilton Collection		**Springtime of Life**			
85-P-HC-21-001	Teddy's Bathtime	T. Utz	14-day	29.50	29.50
85-P-HC-21-002	Just Like Mommy	T. Utz	14-day	29.50	29.50
85-P-HC-21-003	Among the Daffodils	T. Utz	14-day	29.50	29.50
85-P-HC-21-004	My Favorite Dolls	T. Utz	14-day	29.50	29.50
85-P-HC-21-005	Aunt Tillie's Hats	T. Utz	14-day	29.50	29.50
85-P-HC-21-006	Little Emily	T. Utz	14-day	29.50	29.50
85-P-HC-21-007	Granny's Boots	T. Utz	14-day	29.50	29.50
85-P-HC-21-008	My Masterpiece	T. Utz	14-day	29.50	29.50
Hamilton Collection		**Chinese Blossoms of the Four Seasons**			
85-P-HC-22-001	Spring Peony Blossom	Unknown	9,800	95.00	95.00
85-P-HC-22-002	Summer Lotus Blossom	Unknown	9,800	95.00	95.00
85-P-HC-22-003	Autumn Chrysanthemum	Unknown	9,800	95.00	95.00
85-P-HC-22-004	Winter Plum Blossom	Unknown	9,800	95.00	95.00
Hamilton Collection		**A Child's Best Friend**			
85-P-HC-23-001	In Disgrace	B. P. Gutmann	14-day	24.50	40.00
85-P-HC-23-002	The Reward	B. P. Gutmann	14-day	24.50	24.50
85-P-HC-23-003	Who's Sleepy	B. P. Gutmann	14-day	24.50	24.50
85-P-HC-23-004	Good Morning	B. P. Gutmann	14-day	24.50	24.50
85-P-HC-23-005	Sympathy	B. P. Gutmann	14-day	24.50	24.50
85-P-HC-23-006	On the Up and Up	B. P. Gutmann	14-day	24.50	24.50
85-P-HC-23-007	Mine	B. P. Gutmann	14-day	24.50	24.50
85-P-HC-23-008	Going to Town	B. P. Gutmann	14-day	24.50	24.50
Hamilton Collection		**A Country Summer**			
85-P-HC-24-001	Butterfly Beauty	N. Noel	10-day	29.50	29.50
85-P-HC-24-002	The Golden Puppy	N. Noel	10-day	29.50	29.50
85-P-HC-24-003	The Rocking Chair	N. Noel	10-day	29.50	29.50
85-P-HC-24-004	My Bunny	N. Noel	10-day	29.50	29.50
87-P-HC-24-005	The Brahma Calf	N. Noel	10-day	29.50	29.50
87-P-HC-24-006	The Tricycle	N. Noel	10-day	29.50	29.50
Hamilton Collection		**The Little Rascals**			
85-P-HC-25-001	Three for the Show	Unknown	10-day	24.50	24.50
85-P-HC-25-002	My Gal	Unknown	10-day	24.50	24.50
85-P-HC-25-003	Skeleton Crew	Unknown	10-day	24.50	24.50
85-P-HC-25-004	Roughin' It	Unknown	10-day	24.50	24.50
85-P-HC-25-005	Spanky's Pranks	Unknown	10-day	24.50	24.50
85-P-HC-25-006	Butch's Challenge	Unknown	10-day	24.50	24.50
85-P-HC-25-007	Darla's Debut	Unknown	10-day	24.50	24.50
85-P-HC-25-008	Pete's Pal	Unknown	10-day	24.50	24.50
Hamilton Collection		**The Japanese Blossoms of Autumn**			
85-P-HC-26-001	Bellflower	Koseki/Ebihara	10-day	45.00	45.00
85-P-HC-26-002	Arrowroot	Koseki/Ebihara	10-day	45.00	45.00
85-P-HC-26-003	Wild Carnation	Koseki/Ebihara	10-day	45.00	45.00
85-P-HC-26-004	Maiden Flower	Koseki/Ebihara	10-day	45.00	45.00
85-P-HC-26-005	Pampas Grass	Koseki/Ebihara	10-day	45.00	45.00
85-P-HC-26-006	Bush Clover	Koseki/Ebihara	10-day	45.00	45.00
85-P-HC-26-007	Purple Trousers	Koseki/Ebihara	10-day	45.00	45.00
Hamilton Collection		**Star Wars**			
87-P-HC-27-001	Han Solo	T. Blackshear	14-day	29.50	29.50
87-P-HC-27-002	R2-D2 and Wicket	T. Blackshear	14-day	29.50	29.50
87-P-HC-27-003	Luke Skywalker and Darth Vader	T. Blackshear	14-day	29.50	29.50
87-P-HC-27-004	Princess Leia	T. Blackshear	14-day	29.50	29.50
87-P-HC-27-005	The Imperial Walkers	T. Blackshear	14-day	29.50	29.50
87-P-HC-27-006	Luke and Yoda	T. Blackshear	14-day	29.50	29.50
Hamilton Collection		**Noble Owls of America**			
86-P-HC-29-001	Morning Mist	J. Seerey-Lester	15,000	55.00	55.00
87-P-HC-29-002	Prairie Sundown	J. Seerey-Lester	15,000	55.00	55.00
87-P-HC-29-003	Winter Vigil	J. Seerey-Lester	15,000	55.00	55.00
87-P-HC-29-004	Autumn Mist	J. Seerey-Lester	15,000	55.00	55.00
87-P-HC-29-005	Dawn in the Willows	J. Seerey-Lester	15,000	55.00	55.00
Hamilton Collection		**Treasured Days**			
87-P-HC-31-001	Ashley	H. Bond	14-day	29.50	29.50
87-P-HC-31-002	Christopher	H. Bond	14-day	24.50	24.50
87-P-HC-31-003	Sara	H. Bond	14-day	24.50	24.50
Hamilton Collection		**Butterfly Garden**			
87-P-HC-32-001	Spicebush Swallowtail	P. Sweany	14-day	29.50	29.50
87-P-HC-32-002	Common Blue	P. Sweany	14-day	29.50	29.50
87-P-HC-32-003	Orange Sulphur	P. Sweany	14-day	29.50	29.50
87-P-HC-32-004	Monarch	P. Sweany	14-day	29.50	29.50
87-P-HC-32-005	Tiger Swallowtail	P. Sweany	14-day	29.50	29.50
87-P-HC-32-006	Crimson Patched Longwing	P. Sweany	14-day	29.50	29.50

Company / Number	Name	Series / Artist	Edition limit	Issue Price	Quote
Hampton House Studios		**Single Issue**			
77-P-HD-01-001	Nancy Ward Cherokee/Nation	B. Hampton	3,000	48.00	300.00
Haviland		**Twelve Days of Christmas**			
70-P-HE-01-001	Partridge	R. Hetreau	30,000	25.00	110.00
71-P-HE-01-002	Two Turtle Doves	R. Hetreau	30,000	25.00	45.00
72-P-HE-01-003	Three French Hens	R. Hetreau	30,000	27.50	40.00
73-P-HE-01-004	Four Colly Birds	R. Hetreau	30,000	28.50	40.00
74-P-HE-01-005	Five Golden Rings	R. Hetreau	30,000	30.00	35.00
75-P-HE-01-006	Six Geese a'laying	R. Hetreau	30,000	32.50	30.00
76-P-HE-01-007	Seven Swans	R. Hetreau	30,000	38.00	30.00
77-P-HE-01-008	Eight Maids	R. Hetreau	30,000	40.00	45.00
81-P-HE-01-009	Nine Ladies Dancing	R. Hetreau	30,000	45.00	45.00
79-P-HE-01-010	Ten Lord's a'leaping	R. Hetreau	30,000	50.00	50.00
80-P-HE-01-011	Eleven Pipers Piping	R. Hetreau	30,000	55.00	55.00
81-P-HE-01-012	Twelve Drummers	R. Hetreau	30,000	60.00	60.00
Haviland & Parlon		**Tapestry I**			
71-P-HF-01-001	Unicorn in Captivity	Unknown	10,000	35.00	130.00
72-P-HF-01-002	Start of the Hunt	Unknown	10,000	35.00	60.00
73-P-HF-01-003	Chase of the Unicorn	Unknown	10,000	35.00	100.00
74-P-HF-01-004	End of the Hunt	Unknown	10,000	37.50	90.00
75-P-HF-01-005	Unicorn Surrounded	Unknown	10,000	40.00	50.00
76-P-HF-01-006	Brought to the Castle	Unknown	10,000	42.50	45.00
Haviland & Parlon		**Tapestry II**			
77-P-HF-02-001	Lady and Unicorn	Unknown	20,000	45.00	60.00
78-P-HF-02-002	Sight	Unknown	20,000	45.00	55.00
79-P-HF-02-003	Sound	Unknown	20,000	47.50	55.00
80-P-HF-02-004	Touch	Unknown	15,000	52.50	60.00
81-P-HF-02-005	Scent	Unknown	10,000	59.00	60.00
82-P-HF-02-006	Taste	Unknown	10,000	59.00	50.00
Haviland & Parlon		**Christmas Madonnas**			
72-P-HF-03-001	By Raphael	Raphael	5,000	35.00	80.00
73-P-HF-03-002	By Feruzzi	Feruzzi	5,000	40.00	100.00
74-P-HF-03-003	By Raphael	Raphael	5,000	42.50	60.00
75-P-HF-03-004	By Murillo	Murillo	7,500	42.50	45.00
76-P-HF-03-005	By Botticelli	Botticelli	7,500	45.00	45.00
77-P-HF-03-006	By Bellini	Bellini	7,500	48.00	55.00
78-P-HF-03-007	By Lippi	Lippi	7,500	48.00	70.00
79-P-HF-03-008	By Botticelli	Botticelli	7,500	49.50	100.00
Edna Hibel Studios		**Arte Ovale**			
80-P-HG-01-001	Takara, Gold	E. Hibel	300	1000.00	3300.00
80-P-HG-01-002	Takara, Blanco	E. Hibel	700	450.00	950.00
80-P-HG-01-003	Takara, Cobalt Blue	E. Hibel	1,000	595.00	1750.00
84-P-HG-01-004	Tauro-kun, Gold	E. Hibel	300	1000.00	1700.00
84-P-HG-01-005	Tauro-kun, Blanco	E. Hibel	700	450.00	495.00
84-P-HG-01-006	Tauro-kun, Colbalt Blue	E. Hibel	1,000	595.00	650.00
Edna Hibel Studios		**The World I Love**			
81-P-HG-02-001	Leah's Family	E. Hibel	17,500	85.00	175.00
82-P-HG-02-002	Kaylin	E. Hibel	17,500	85.00	175.00
83-P-HG-02-003	Edna's Music	E. Hibel	17,500	85.00	175.00
83-P-HG-02-004	O, Hana	E. Hibel	17,500	85.00	175.00
Hutschenreuther		**Gunther Granget**			
72-P-HU-01-001	American Sparrows	G. Granget	5,000	50.00	175.00
72-P-HU-01-002	European Sparrows	G. Granget	5,000	30.00	70.00
73-P-HU-01-003	American Kildeer	G. Granget	2,250	75.00	100.00
73-P-HU-01-004	American Squirrel	G. Granget	2,500	75.00	85.00
73-P-HU-01-005	European Squirrel	G. Granget	2,500	35.00	55.00
74-P-HU-01-006	American Partridge	G. Granget	2,500	75.00	90.00
75-P-HU-01-007	American Rabbits	G. Granget	2,500	90.00	90.00
76-P-HU-01-008	Freedom in Flight	G. Granget	5,000	100.00	50.00
76-P-HU-01-009	Wrens	G. Granget	2,500	100.00	110.00
76-P-HU-01-010	Freedom in Flight, Gold	G. Granget	200	200.00	200.00
77-P-HU-01-011	Bears	G. Granget	2,500	100.00	100.00
78-P-HU-01-012	Foxes' Spring Journey	G. Granget	1,000	125.00	200.00
Hutschenreuther		**The Glory of Christmas**			
82-P-HU-05-001	The Nativity	W./C. Hallett	25,000	80.00	100.00
83-P-HU-05-002	The Annunciation	W./C. Hallett	25,000	80.00	90.00
84-P-HU-05-003	The Shepherds	W./C. Hallett	25,000	80.00	80.00
85-P-HU-05-004	The Wiseman	W./C. Hallett	25,000	80.00	80.00
Hutschenreuther		**Enchantment Series**			
79-P-HU-15-001	Princess Snowflake	D. Valenza	5,000	50.00	60.00
79-P-HU-15-002	Blossom Queen	D. Valenza	5,000	62.50	62.50
80-P-HU-15-003	Princess Marina	D. Valenza	5,000	87.50	87.50
81-P-HU-15-004	Princess Starbight	D. Valenza	5,000	87.50	87.50
81-P-HU-15-005	Princess Aura	D. Valenza	5,000	87.50	87.50
82-P-HU-15-006	Harvest Queen	D. Valenza	5,000	87.50	87.50
Hutschenreuther		**Arzberg**			
86-P-HU-36-001	Bodo and the Boat	K. Berger	Open	47.50	47.50
Incolay		**Romantic Poets**			
77-P-IN-01-001	She Walks in Beauty	G. Appleby	Yr.Iss	60.00	80.00
78-P-IN-01-002	A Thing of Beauty	G. Appleby	Yr.Iss	60.00	65.00
79-P-IN-01-003	Ode to a Skylark	G. Appleby	Yr.Iss	65.00	65.00
80-P-IN-01-004	Phantom of Delight	G. Appleby	Yr.Iss	65.00	65.00
81-P-IN-01-005	The Kiss	R. Akers	Yr.Iss	65.00	70.00
82-P-IN-01-006	My Heart Leaps Up	R. Akers	Yr.Iss	70.00	70.00
83-P-IN-01-007	I Stood Tiptoe	R. Akers	Yr.Iss	70.00	70.00
84-P-IN-01-008	The Dream	R. Akers	Yr.Iss	70.00	70.00
85-P-IN-01-009	The Recollection	R. Akers	Yr.Iss	70.00	70.00
International Silver		**Bicentennial**			
72-P-IT-01-001	Signing Declaration	M. Deoliveira	7,500	40.00	310.00
73-P-IT-01-002	Paul Revere	M. Deoliveira	7,500	40.00	160.00
74-P-IT-01-003	Concord Bridge	M. Deoliveira	7,500	40.00	115.00
75-P-IT-01-004	Crossing Delaware	M. Deoliveira	7,500	50.00	80.00
76-P-IT-01-005	Valley Forge	M. Deoliveira	7,500	50.00	65.00
77-P-IT-01-006	Surrender at Yorktown	M. Deoliveira	7,500	50.00	60.00
Svend Jensen		**Christmas**			
70-P-JS-01-001	H. C. Anderson House	G. Sausmark	Annual	14.50	85.00
71-P-JS-01-002	Little Match Girl	M. Stage	Annual	15.00	40.00
72-P-JS-01-003	Maid of Copenhagen	E. Eriksen	Annual	16.50	45.00
73-P-JS-01-004	The Fir Tree	S. Otto	Annual	22.00	40.00
74-P-JS-01-005	The Chimney Sweep	S. Otto	Annual	25.00	30.00
75-P-JS-01-006	The Ugly Duckling	S. Otto	Annual	27.50	27.50
76-P-JS-01-007	The Snow Queen	M. Stage	Annual	27.50	39.00
77-P-JS-01-008	Snowman	S. Otto	Annual	29.50	40.00
78-P-JS-01-009	Last Dream of the Old Oak Tree	S. Otto	Annual	32.00	45.00
79-P-JS-01-010	The Old Street Lamp	S. Otto	Annual	36.50	40.50
80-P-JS-01-011	Willie Winkie	S. Otto	Annual	42.50	42.50
81-P-JS-01-012	Uttermost Parts Of the Sea	S. Otto	Annual	49.50	49.50

Company		Series			
Number	**Name**	**Artist**	**Edition limit**	**Issue Price**	**Quote**
82-P-JS-01-013	Twelve by the Mailcoach	S. Otto	Annual	54.50	54.50
83-P-JS-01-014	The Story of the Year	S. Otto	Annual	54.50	54.50
84-P-JS-01-015	The Nightingale	S. Otto	Annual	54.50	54.50
Svend Jensen		**Mother's Day**			
70-P-JS-02-001	Bouquet for Mother	Unknown	Unkn.	14.50	75.00
71-P-JS-02-002	Mother's Love	Unknown	Unkn.	15.00	40.00
72-P-JS-02-003	Good Night	Unknown	Unkn.	16.50	35.00
73-P-JS-02-004	Flowers for Mother	Unknown	Unkn.	20.00	35.00
74-P-JS-02-005	Daisies For Mother	Unknown	Unkn.	25.00	35.00
75-P-JS-02-006	Surprise for Mother	Unknown	Unkn.	27.50	27.50
76-P-JS-02-007	The Complete Gardener	Unknown	Unkn.	27.50	27.50
77-P-JS-02-008	Little Friends	Unknown	Unkn.	29.50	29.50
78-P-JS-02-009	Dreams	Unknown	Unkn.	32.00	32.00
79-P-JS-02-010	Promenade	Unknown	Unkn.	36.50	36.50
80-P-JS-02-011	Nursery Scene	Unknown	Unkn.	42.50	42.50
81-P-JS-02-012	Daily Dutiės	Unknown	Unkn.	49.50	49.50
82-P-JS-02-013	My Best Friend	Unknown	Unkn.	54.50	54.50
83-P-JS-02-014	An Unexpected Meeting	Unknown	Unkn.	54.50	54.50
84-P-JS-02-015	Who are you?	M. Stage	Annual	54.50	54.50
Kaiser		**Oberammergau Passion Play**			
70-P-KA-01-001	Oberammergau	T. Schoener	Unkn.	25.00	30.00
70-P-KA-01-002	Oberammergau	K. Bauer	Unkn.	40.00	40.00
Kaiser		**Christmas Plates**			
70-P-KA-02-001	Waiting for Santa Claus	T. Schoener	Unkn.	12.50	50.00
71-P-KA-02-002	Silent Night	K. Bauer	Unkn.	13.50	15.00
72-P-KA-02-003	Welcome Home	K. Bauer	Unkn.	16.50	20.00
73-P-KA-02-004	Holy Night	T. Schoener	Unkn.	18.00	39.00
74-P-KA-02-005	Christmas Carolers	K. Bauer	8,000	25.00	30.00
75-P-KA-02-006	Bringing Home the Tree	J. Northcott	Unkn.	25.00	30.00
76-P-KA-02-007	Christ/Saviour Born	C. Maratti	Unkn.	25.00	36.00
77-P-KA-02-008	The Three Kings	T. Schoener	Unkn.	25.00	30.00
78-P-KA-02-009	Shepherds in The Field	T. Schoener	Unkn.	30.00	30.00
79-P-KA-02-010	Christmas Eve	H. Blum	Unkn.	32.00	32.00
80-P-KA-02-011	Joys of Winter	H. Blum	Unkn.	40.00	43.00
81-P-KA-02-012	Adoration by Three Kings	K. Bauer	Unkn.	40.00	41.00
82-P-KA-02-013	Bringing Home the Tree	K. Bauer	Unkn.	40.00	45.00
Kaiser		**Memories of Christmas**			
83-P-KA-03-001	The Wonder of Christmas	G. Neubacher	19,500	42.50	42.50
84-P-KA-03-002	A Christmas Dream	G. Neubacher	19,500	39.50	42.50
85-P-KA-03-003	Christmas Eve	G. Neubacher	19,500	39.50	39.50
86-P-KA-03-004	A Visit with Santa	G. Neubacher	19,500	39.50	39.50
Kaiser		**Mother's Day**			
71-P-KA-04-001	Mare and Foal	T. Schoener	Unkn.	13.00	50.00
72-P-KA-04-002	Flowers for Mother	T. Schoener	Unkn.	16.50	20.00
73-P-KA-04-003	Cats	T. Schoener	Unkn.	17.00	67.50
74-P-KA-04-004	Fox	T. Schoener	Unkn.	20.00	50.00
75-P-KA-04-005	German Shepherd	T. Schoener	Unkn.	25.00	75.00
76-P-KA-04-006	Swan and Cygnets	T. Schoener	Unkn.	25.00	27.50
77-P-KA-04-007	Mother Rabbit and Young	T. Schoener	Unkn.	25.00	57.50
78-P-KA-04-008	Hen and Chicks	T. Schoener	Unkn.	30.00	55.00
79-P-KA-04-009	A Mother's Devotion	N. Peterner	Unkn.	32.00	52.50
80-P-KA-04-010	Raccoon Family	J. Northcott	Unkn.	40.00	50.00
81-P-KA-04-011	Safe Near Mother	H. Blum	Unkn.	40.00	40.00
82-P-KA-04-012	Pheasant Family	K. Bauer	Unkn.	40.00	45.00
83-P-KA-04-013	Tender Care	K. Bauer	Unkn.	40.00	65.00
Kaiser		**Anniversary**			
72-P-KA-05-001	Love Birds	T. Schoener	Unkn.	16.50	30.00
73-P-KA-05-002	In the Park	T. Schoener	Unkn.	16.50	24.50
74-P-KA-05-003	Canoeing	T. Schoener	Unkn.	20.00	30.00
75-P-KA-05-004	Tender Moment	K. Bauer	Unkn.	25.00	27.50
76-P-KA-05-005	Serenade	T. Schoener	Unkn.	25.00	25.00
77-P-KA-05-006	Simple Gift	T. Schoener	Unkn.	25.00	25.00
78-P-KA-05-007	Viking Toast	T. Schoener	Unkn.	30.00	30.00
79-P-KA-05-008	Romantic Interlude	H. Blum	Unkn.	32.00	32.00
80-P-KA-05-009	Love at Play	H. Blum	Unkn.	40.00	40.00
81-P-KA-05-010	Rendezvous	H. Blum	Unkn.	40.00	40.00
82-P-KA-05-011	Betrothal	K. Bauer	Unkn.	40.00	40.00
83-P-KA-05-012	Sunday Afternoon	T. Schoener	Unkn.	40.00	40.00
Kaiser		**Great Yachts**			
72-P-KA-06-001	Cetonia	K. Bauer	1,000	50.00	50.00
72-P-KA-06-002	Westward	K. Bauer	1,000	50.00	50.00
Kaiser		**Garden and Song Birds**			
73-P-KA-07-001	Cardinals	W. Gawantka	2,000	200.00	250.00
73-P-KA-07-002	Titmouse	W. Gawantka	2,000	200.00	250.00
Kaiser		**King Tut**			
78-P-KA-08-001	King Tut	Unknown	Unkno-wn	65.00	65.00
Kaiser		**Feathered Friends**			
78-P-KA-09-001	Blue Jays	G. Loates	Unkn.	70.00	100.00
79-P-KA-09-002	Cardinals	G. Loates	Unkn.	80.00	90.00
80-P-KA-09-003	Waxwings	G. Loates	Unkn.	80.00	80.00
81-P-KA-09-004	Goldfinch	G. Loates	Unkn.	80.00	80.00
Kaiser		**Happy Days**			
79-P-KA-10-001	The Aeroplane	G. Neubacher	5,000	75.00	75.00
80-P-KA-10-002	Julie	G. Neubacher	5,000	75.00	75.00
81-P-KA-10-003	Winter Fun	G. Neubacher	5,000	75.00	75.00
82-P-KA-10-004	The Lookout	G. Neubacher	5,000	75.00	75.00
Kaiser		**Egyptian**			
80-P-KA-11-001	Nefertiti	Unknown	10,000	275.00	275.00
80-P-KA-11-002	Tutankhamen	Unknown	10,000	275.00	275.00
Kaiser		**Four Seasons**			
81-P-KA-12-001	Spring	I. Cenkovcan	Unkn.	50.00	50.00
81-P-KA-12-002	Summer	I. Cenkovcan	Unkn.	50.00	50.00
81-P-KA-12-003	Autumn	I. Cenkovcan	Unkn.	50.00	50.00
81-P-KA-12-004	Winter	I. Cenkovcan	Unkn.	50.00	50.00
Kaiser		**Romantic Portraits**			
81-P-KA-13-001	Lilie	G. Neubacher	5,000	200.00	225.00
82-P-KA-13-002	Camelia	G. Neubacher	5,000	175.00	200.00
83-P-KA-13-003	Rose	G. Neubacher	5,000	175.00	185.00
84-P-KA-13-004	Daisy	G. Neubacher	5,000	175.00	180.00
Kaiser		**On The Farm**			
81-P-KA-14-001	The Duck	A. Lohmann	Unkn.	50.00	50.00
82-P-KA-14-002	The Rooster	A. Lohmann	Unkn.	50.00	50.00
83-P-KA-14-003	The Pond	A. Lohmann	Unkn.	50.00	50.00
83-P-KA-14-004	The Horses	A. Lohmann	Unkn.	50.00	50.00
XX-P-KA-14-005	White Horse	A. Lohman	Unkn.	50.00	50.00
XX-P-KA-14-006	Ducks on the Pond	A. Lohman	Unkn.	50.00	50.00
XX-P-KA-14-007	Girl with Goats	A. Lohman	Unkn.	50.00	50.00
XX-P-KA-14-008	Girl Feeding Animals	A. Lohman	Unkn.	50.00	50.00
Kaiser		**Classic Fairy Tales Collection**			
82-P-KA-15-001	Frog King	G. Neubacher	Unkn.	39.50	48.00
83-P-KA-15-002	Puss in Boots	G. Neubacher	Unkn.	39.50	42.00
83-P-KA-15-003	Little Red Riding Hood	G. Neubacher	Unkn.	39.50	42.00
84-P-KA-15-004	Hansel and Gretel	G. Neubacher	Unkn.	39.50	40.00
84-P-KA-15-005	Cinderella	G. Neubacher	Unkn.	39.50	40.00
84-P-KA-15-006	Sleeping Beauty	G. Neubacher	Unkn.	39.50	40.00
Kaiser		**Dance, Ballerina, Dance**			
82-P-KA-16-001	First Slippers	R. Clarke	14,500	47.50	47.50
83-P-KA-16-002	At the Barre	R. Clarke	14,500	47.50	47.50
XX-P-KA-16-003	The Recital	R. Clarke	14,500	47.50	47.50
XX-P-KA-16-004	Pirouette	R. Clarke	14,500	47.50	47.50
XX-P-KA-16-005	Swan Lake	R. Clarke	14,500	47.50	47.50
XX-P-KA-16-006	Opening Night	R. Clarke	14,500	47.50	47.50
Kaiser		**Children's Prayer**			
82-P-KA-17-001	Now I Lay Me Down to Sleep	W. Freuner	5,000	29.50	29.50
82-P-KA-17-002	Saying Grace	W. Freuner	5,000	29.50	29.50
Kaiser		**Famous Horses**			
83-P-KA-18-001	Snow Knight	A. Lohmann	3,000	95.00	95.00
84-P-KA-18-002	Northern Dancer	A. Lohmann	3,000	95.00	95.00
Kaiser		**Traditional Fairy Tales**			
83-P-KA-19-001	Cinderella	D. King	Unkn.	39.50	39.50
83-P-KA-19-002	Jack and the Beanstalk	D. King	Unkn.	39.50	39.50
84-P-KA-19-003	Three Little Pigs	D. King	Unkn.	39.50	39.50
84-P-KA-19-004	Tom Thumb	D. King	Unkn.	39.50	39.50
85-P-KA-19-005	Goldilocks	D. King	Unkn.	39.50	39.50
85-P-KA-19-006	Dick Wittington	D. King	Unkn.	39.50	39.50
Kaiser		**Racing for Pride and Profit**			
84-P-KA-20-001	The Aging Victor	R. Horton	9,500	50.00	55.00
85-P-KA-20-002	Second Goes Hungry	R. Horton	9,500	50.00	50.00
86-P-KA-20-003	No Time to Boast	R. Horton	9,500	50.00	50.00
87-P-KA-20-004	First Fish to Market	R. Horton	9,500	50.00	50.00
88-P-KA-20-005	Gypsy Traders	B. Horton	9,500	50.00	50.00
Kaiser		**Bird Dog Series**			
XX-P-KA-21-001	Cocker Spaniel	J. Francis	19,500	39.50	39.50
XX-P-KA-21-002	Beagle	J. Francis	19,500	39.50	39.50
XX-P-KA-21-003	English Setter	J. Francis	19,500	39.50	39.50
XX-P-KA-21-004	Black Labrador	J. Francis	19,500	39.50	39.50
XX-P-KA-21-005	German Short Hair Pointer	J. Francis	19,500	39.50	39.50
XX-P-KA-21-006	Golden Labrador	J. Francis	19,500	39.50	39.50
XX-P-KA-21-007	English Pointer	J. Francis	19,500	39.50	39.50
XX-P-KA-21-008	Irish Setter	J. Francis	19,500	39.50	39.50
Kaiser		**Childhood Memories**			
85-P-KA-22-001	Wait a Little	A Schlesinger	9,800	29.00	29.00
Kaiser		**Harmony and Nature**			
85-P-KA-23-001	Spring Encore	J. Littlejohn	9,800	39.50	39.50
Kaiser		**Woodland Creatures**			
85-P-KA-24-001	Springtime Frolic	R. Orr	10-day	37.50	37.50
85-P-KA-24-002	Fishing Trip	R. Orr	10-day	37.50	37.50
85-P-KA-24-003	Resting in the Glen	R. Orr	10-day	37.50	37.50
85-P-KA-24-004	Meadowland Vigil	R. Orr	10-day	37.50	37.50
85-P-KA-24-005	Morning Lesson	R. Orr	10-day	37.50	37.50
85-P-KA-24-006	First Adventure	R. Orr	10-day	37.50	37.50
85-P-KA-24-007	The Hiding Place	R. Orr	10-day	37.50	37.50
85-P-KA-24-008	Startled Sentry	R. Orr	10-day	37.50	37.50
Kaiser		**Water Fowl**			
85-P-KA-25-001	Mallard Ducks	E. Bierly	19,500	55.00	55.00
85-P-KA-25-002	Canvas Back Ducks	E. Bierly	19,500	55.00	55.00
85-P-KA-25-003	Wood Ducks	E. Bierly	19,500	55.00	55.00
85-P-KA-25-004	Pintail Ducks	E. Bierly	19,500	55.00	55.00
Kaiser		**Wildflowers**			
86-P-KA-26-001	Trillium	G. Neubacher	9,500	39.50	45.00
87-P-KA-26-002	Spring Beauty	G. Neubacher	9,500	45.00	45.00
88-P-KA-26-003	Wild Asters	G. Newbacher	9,500	45.00	45.00
Kaiser		**Famous Lullabies**			
85-P-KA-27-001	Sleep Baby Sleep	G. Neubacher	Unkn.	39.50	48.00
86-P-KA-27-002	Rockabye Baby	G. Neubacher	Unkn.	39.50	39.50
86-P-KA-27-003	A Mockingbird	G. Neubacher	Unkn.	39.50	39.50
86-P-KA-27-004	Au Clair De Lune	G. Neubacher	Unkn.	39.50	39.50
87-P-KA-27-005	Welsh Lullabye	G. Neubacher	Unkn.	39.50	39.50
88-P-KA-27-006	Brahms' Lullabye	G. Newbacher	Unkn.	39.50	39.50
Kaiser		**Bicentennial Plate**			
76-P-KA-28-001	Signing Declaration	J. Trumball	1,000	75.00	150.00
Kaiser		**The Graduate**			
86-P-KA-29-001	Boy	J. McKernan	7,500	39.50	39.50
86-P-KA-29-002	Girl	J. McKernan	7,500	39.50	39.50
Edwin M. Knowles		**Wizard of Oz**			
77-P-KN-01-001	Over the Rainbow	J. Auckland	Undis.	19.00	68.00
78-P-KN-01-002	If I Only Had a Brain	J. Auckland	Undis.	19.00	30.00
78-P-KN-01-003	If I Only Had a Heart	J. Auckland	Undis.	19.00	35.00
78-P-KN-01-004	If I Were King of the Forest	J. Auckland	Undis.	19.00	30.00
79-P-KN-01-005	Wicked Witch of the West	J. Auckland	Undis.	19.00	40.00
79-P-KN-01-006	Follow the Yellow Brick Road	J. Auckland	Undis.	19.00	35.00
79-P-KN-01-007	Wonderful Wizard of Oz	J. Auckland	Undis.	19.00	50.00
80-P-KN-01-008	The Grand Finale	J. Auckland	Undis.	24.00	60.00
Edwin M. Knowles		**Gone with the Wind**			
78-P-KN-02-001	Scarlett	R. Kursar	Undis.	21.50	300.00
79-P-KN-02-002	Ashley	R. Kursar	Undis.	21.50	230.00
80-P-KN-02-003	Melanie	R. Kursar	Undis.	21.50	75.00
81-P-KN-02-004	Rhett	R. Kursar	Undis.	23.50	50.00
82-P-KN-02-005	Mammy Lacing Scarlett	R. Kursar	Undis.	23.50	64.00
83-P-KN-02-006	Melanie Gives Birth	R. Kursar	Undis.	23.50	90.00
84-P-KN-02-007	Scarlet's Green Dress	R. Kursar	Undis.	25.50	50.00
85-P-KN-02-008	Rhett and Bonnie	R. Kursar	Undis.	25.50	38.00
85-P-KN-02-009	Scarlett and Rhett: The Finale	R. Kursar	Undis.	29.50	30.00
Edwin M. Knowles		**Csatari Grandparent**			
80-P-KN-03-001	Bedtime Story	J. Csatari	Undis.	18.00	28.00
81-P-KN-03-002	The Skating Lesson	J. Csatari	Undis.	20.00	25.00
82-P-KN-03-003	The Cookie Tasting	J. Csatari	Undis.	20.00	28.00
83-P-KN-03-004	The Swinger	J. Csatari	Undis.	20.00	20.00
84-P-KN-03-005	The Skating Queen	J. Csatari	Undis.	22.00	25.00
Edwin M. Knowles		**Americana Holidays**			
78-P-KN-04-001	Fourth of July	D. Spaulding	Undis.	26.00	35.00

Number	Name	Artist	Edition limit	Issue Price	Quote
79-P-KN-04-002	Thanksgiving	D. Spaulding	Undis.	26.00	35.00
80-P-KN-04-003	Easter	D. Spaulding	Undis.	26.00	28.00
81-P-KN-04-004	Valentine's Day	D. Spaulding	Undis.	26.00	26.00
82-P-KN-04-005	Father's Day	D. Spaulding	Undis.	26.00	26.00
83-P-KN-04-006	Christmas	D. Spaulding	Undis.	26.00	26.00
84-P-KN-04-007	Mother's Day	D. Spaulding	Undis.	26.00	26.00
XX-P-KN-04-008	Complete Collection	D. Spaulding	Undis.	182.00	202.00
Edwin M. Knowles	**Annie**				
83-P-KN-05-001	Annie and Sandy	W. Chambers	Undis.	19.00	25.00
83-P-KN-05-002	Daddy Warbucks	W. Chambers	Undis.	19.00	26.00
83-P-KN-05-003	Annie and Grace	W. Chambers	Undis.	19.00	35.00
84-P-KN-05-004	Annie and the Orphans	W. Chambers	Undis.	21.00	29.00
85-P-KN-05-005	Tomorrow	W. Chambers	Undis.	21.00	30.00
86-P-KN-05-006	Annie and Miss Hannigan	W. Chambers	Undis.	21.00	24.00
86-P-KN-05-007	Annie, Lily and Rooster	W. Chambers	Undis.	24.00	25.00
86-P-KN-05-008	Grand Finale	W. Chambers	Undis.	24.00	24.00
XX-P-KN-05-009	Complete Collection	W. Chambers	Undis.	168.00	218.00
Edwin M. Knowles	**The Four Ancient Elements**				
84-P-KN-06-001	Earth	G. Lambert	Undis.	27.50	33.00
84-P-KN-06-002	Water	G. Lambert	Undis.	27.50	32.00
85-P-KN-06-003	Air	G. Lambert	Undis.	29.50	35.00
85-P-KN-06-004	Fire	G. Lambert	Undis.	29.50	38.00
XX-P-KN-06-005	Complete Collection	G. Lambert	Undis.	114.00	138.00
Edwin M. Knowles	**Biblical Mothers**				
83-P-KN-07-001	Bathsheba and Solomon	E. Licea	Undis.	39.50	100.00
84-P-KN-07-002	Judgment of Solomon	E. Licea	Undis.	39.50	75.00
84-P-KN-07-003	Pharoah's Daughter and Moses	E. Licea	Undis.	39.50	60.00
84-P-KN-07-004	Mary and Jesus	E. Licea	Undis.	39.50	50.00
85-P-KN-07-005	Sarah and Isaac	E. Licea	Undis.	44.50	55.00
86-P-KN-07-006	Rebekah, Jacob and Esau	E. Licea	Undis.	44.50	46.00
XX-P-KN-07-007	Complete Collection	E. Licea	Undis.	247.50	386.00
Edwin M. Knowles	**Hibel Mother's Day**				
84-P-KN-08-001	Abby and Lisa	E. Hibel	Undis.	29.50	50.00
85-P-KN-08-002	Erica and Jamie	E. Hibel	Undis.	29.50	33.00
86-P-KN-08-003	Emily and Jennifer	E. Hibel	Undis.	29.50	35.00
87-P-KN-08-004	Catherine and Heather	E. Hibel	Undis.	34.50	34.00
Edwin M. Knowles	**Friends I Remember**				
83-P-KN-09-001	Fish Story	J. Downs	Undis.	17.50	32.00
84-P-KN-09-002	Office Hours	J. Downs	Undis.	17.50	25.00
84-P-KN-09-003	A Coat of Paint	J. Downs	Undis.	17.50	25.00
85-P-KN-09-004	Here Comes the Bride	J. Downs	Undis.	19.50	29.00
85-P-KN-09-005	Fringe Benefits	J. Downs	Undis.	19.50	30.00
85-P-KN-09-006	High Society	J. Downs	Undis.	19.50	28.00
86-P-KN-09-007	Flower Arrangement	J. Downs	Undis.	21.50	30.00
86-P-KN-09-008	Taste Test	J. Downs	Undis.	21.50	44.00
XX-P-KN-09-009	Complete Collection	J. Downs	Undis.	134.50	243.00
Edwin M. Knowles	**Father's Love**				
84-P-KN-10-001	Open Wide	B. Bradley	Undis.	19.50	22.00
84-P-KN-10-002	Batter Up	B. Bradley	Undis.	19.50	25.00
85-P-KN-10-003	Little Shaver	B. Bradley	Undis.	19.50	26.00
85-P-KN-10-004	Swing Time	B. Bradley	Undis.	22.50	27.00
XX-P-KN-10-005	Complete Collection	B. Bradley	Undis.	81.00	100.00
Edwin M. Knowles	**The King and I**				
84-P-KN-11-001	A Puzzlement	W. Chambers	Undis.	19.50	55.00
85-P-KN-11-002	Shall We Dance?	W. Chambers	Undis.	19.50	40.00
85-P-KN-11-003	Getting to Know You	W. Chambers	Undis.	19.50	29.00
85-P-KN-11-004	We Kiss in a Shadow	W. Chambers	Undis.	19.50	19.50
XX-P-KN-11-005	Complete Collection	W. Chambers	Undis.	78.00	143.00
Edwin M. Knowles	**Ency. Brit. Birds of Your Garden**				
85-P-KN-12-001	Cardinal	K. Daniel	Undis.	19.50	33.00
85-P-KN-12-002	Blue Jay	K. Daniel	Undis.	19.50	19.50
85-P-KN-12-003	Oriole	K. Daniel	Undis.	22.50	22.50
86-P-KN-12-004	Chickadees	K. Daniel	Undis.	22.50	22.50
86-P-KN-12-005	Bluebird	K. Daniel	Undis.	22.50	22.50
86-P-KN-12-006	Robin	K. Daniel	Undis.	22.50	22.50
86-P-KN-12-007	Hummingbird	K. Daniel	Undis.	24.50	24.50
87-P-KN-12-008	Goldfinch	K. Daniel	Undis.	24.50	24.50
Edwin M. Knowles	**Frances Hook Legacy**				
85-P-KN-13-001	Fascination	F. Hook	Undis.	19.50	21.00
85-P-KN-13-002	Daydreaming	F. Hook	Undis.	19.50	25.00
86-P-KN-13-003	Discovery	F. Hook	Undis.	22.50	22.50
86-P-KN-13-004	Disappointment	F. Hook	Undis.	22.50	22.50
86-P-KN-13-005	Wonderment	F. Hook	Undis.	22.50	22.50
87-P-KN-13-006	Expectation	F. Hook	Undis.	22.50	22.50
Edwin M. Knowles	**Hibel Christmas**				
85-P-KN-14-001	The Angel's Message	E. Hibel	Undis.	45.00	46.00
86-P-KN-14-002	The Gifts of the Magi	E. Hibel	Undis.	45.00	50.00
Edwin M. Knowles	**Upland Birds of North America**				
86-P-KN-15-001	The Pheasant	W. Anderson	Undis.	24.50	24.50
86-P-KN-15-002	The Grouse	W. Anderson	Undis.	24.50	24.50
Edwin M. Knowles	**Oklahoma!**				
85-P-KN-16-001	Oh, What a Beautiful Mornin'	M. Kunstler	Undis.	19.50	19.50
86-P-KN-16-002	Surrey with the Fringe on Top	M. Kunstler	Undis.	19.50	19.50
86-P-KN-16-003	I Cain't Say No	M. Kunstler	Undis.	19.50	19.50
86-P-KN-16-004	Oklahoma	M. Kunstler	Undis.	19.50	19.50
XX-P-KN-16-005	Complete Collection	M. Kunstler	Undis.	78.00	78.00
Edwin M. Knowles	**Sound of Music**				
86-P-KN-17-001	Sound of Music	T. Crnkovich	Undis.	19.50	19.50
86-P-KN-17-002	Do-Re-Mi	T. Crnkovich	Undis.	19.50	19.50
86-P-KN-17-003	My Favorite Things	T. Crnkovich	Undis.	22.50	22.50
86-P-KN-17-004	Laendler Waltz	T. Crnkovich	Undis.	22.50	22.50
Edwin M. Knowles	**American Innocents**				
86-P-KN-18-001	Abigail in the Rose Garden	B. Marsten/V. Mandrajji	Undis.	19.50	19.50
86-P-KN-18-002	Ann by the Terrace	B. Marsten/V. Mandrajji	Undis.	19.50	19.50
Edwin M. Knowles	**J. W. Smith Holiday Series**				
86-P-KN-19-001	Easter	J. Smith	Undis.	19.50	19.50
86-P-KN-19-002	Thanksgiving	J. Smith	Undis.	19.50	19.50
86-P-KN-19-003	Christmas	J. Smith	Undis.	19.50	19.50
86-P-KN-19-004	Valentine's Day	J. Smith	Undis.	22.50	22.50
Edwin M. Knowles	**Living with Nature-Jerner's Ducks**				
86-P-KN-20-001	The Pintail	B. Jener	Undis.	19.50	19.50
86-P-KN-20-002	The Mallard	B. Jener	Undis.	19.50	19.50
Edwin M. Knowles	**Lincoln Man of America**				
86-P-KN-21-001	The Gettysburg Address	M. Kunstler	Undis.	24.50	24.50

Number	Name	Artist	Edition limit	Issue Price	Quote
Edwin M. Knowles	**Portraits of Motherhood**				
87-P-KN-22-001	Mother's Here	W. Chambers	Undis.	29.50	29.50
Konigszelt Bayern	**Hedi Keller Christmas**				
79-P-KO-01-001	The Adoration	H. Keller	Unkn.	29.50	38.00
80-P-KO-01-002	Flight into Egypt	H. Keller	Unkn.	29.50	35.00
81-P-KO-01-003	Return into Galilee	H. Keller	Unkn.	29.50	35.00
82-P-KO-01-004	Following the Star	H. Keller	Unkn.	29.50	35.00
83-P-KO-01-005	Rest on the Flight	H. Keller	Unkn.	29.50	35.00
84-P-KO-01-006	The Nativity	H. Keller	Unkn.	29.50	45.00
85-P-KO-01-007	Gift of the Magi	H. Keller	Unkn.	34.50	42.00
86-P-KO-01-008	Annunciation	H. Keller	Unkn.	34.50	50.00
KPM-Royal Berlin	**Christmas**				
69-P-KP-01-001	Christmas Star	Unknown	5,000	28.00	380.00
70-P-KP-01-002	Three Kings	Unknown	5,000	28.00	300.00
71-P-KP-01-003	Christmas Tree	Unknown	5,000	28.00	290.00
72-P-KP-01-004	Christmas Angel	Unknown	5,000	31.00	300.00
73-P-KP-01-005	Christ Child on Sled	Unknown	5,000	33.00	280.00
74-P-KP-01-006	Angel and Horn	Unknown	5,000	35.00	180.00
75-P-KP-01-007	Shepherds	Unknown	5,000	40.00	165.00
76-P-KP-01-008	Star of Bethlem	Unknown	5,000	43.00	140.00
77-P-KP-01-009	Mary at Crib	Unknown	5,000	46.00	100.00
78-P-KP-01-010	Three Wise Men	Unknown	5,000	49.00	54.00
79-P-KP-01-011	The Manger	Unknown	5,000	55.00	55.00
80-P-KP-01-012	Shepherds in Fields	Unknown	5,000	55.00	55.00
Lalique	**Annual**				
65-P-LA-01-001	Deux Oiseaux (Two Birds)	M. Lalique	2,000	25.00	1000.00
66-P-LA-01-002	Rose de Songerie (Dream Rose)	M. Lalique	5,000	25.00	200.00
67-P-LA-01-003	Ballet de Poisson (Fish Ballet)	M. Lalique	5,000	25.00	125.00
68-P-LA-01-004	Gazelle Fantaisie (Gazelle Fantasy)	M. Lalique	5,000	25.00	70.00
69-P-LA-01-005	Papillon (Butterfly)	M. Lalique	5,000	30.00	80.00
70-P-LA-01-006	Paon (Peacock)	M. Lalique	5,000	30.00	45.00
71-P-LA-01-007	Hibou (Owl)	M. Lalique	5,000	35.00	60.00
72-P-LA-01-008	Coquillage (Shell)	M. Lalique	5,000	40.00	55.00
73-P-LA-01-009	Petit Geai (Jayling)	M. Lalique	5,000	42.50	66.00
74-P-LA-01-010	Sous d'Argent (Silver Pennies)	M. Lalique	5,000	47.50	70.00
75-P-LA-01-011	Duo de Poisson (Fish Duet)	M. Lalique	5,000	50.00	75.00
76-P-LA-01-012	Aigle (Eagle)	M. Lalique	5,000	60.00	100.00
Lenox	**Boehm Birds**				
70-P-LE-01-001	Wood Thrush	E. Boehm	Yr.Iss	35.00	225.00
71-P-LE-01-002	Goldfinch	E. Boehm	Yr.Iss	35.00	65.00
72-P-LE-01-003	Mountain Bluebird	E. Boehm	Yr.Iss	37.50	60.00
73-P-LE-01-004	Meadowlark	E. Boehm	Yr.Iss	50.00	55.00
74-P-LE-01-005	Rufous Hummingbird	E. Boehm	Yr.Iss	45.00	55.00
75-P-LE-01-006	American Redstart	E. Boehm	Yr.Iss	50.00	50.00
76-P-LE-01-007	Cardinals	E. Boehm	Yr.Iss	53.00	55.00
77-P-LE-01-008	Robins	E. Boehm	Yr.Iss	55.00	55.00
78-P-LE-01-009	Mockingbirds	E. Boehm	Yr.Iss	58.00	58.00
79-P-LE-01-010	Golden-Crowned Kinglets	E. Boehm	Yr.Iss	65.00	65.00
80-P-LE-01-011	Black-Throated Blue Warblers	E. Boehm	Yr.Iss	80.00	80.00
81-P-LE-01-012	Eastern Phoebes	E. Boehm	Yr.Iss	92.50	92.50
Lenox	**Boehm Woodland Wildlife**				
73-P-LE-02-001	Racoons	E. Boehm	Yr.Iss	50.00	80.00
74-P-LE-02-002	Red Foxes	E. Boehm	Yr.Iss	52.50	52.50
75-P-LE-02-003	Cottontail Rabbits	E. Boehm	Yr.Iss	58.50	58.50
76-P-LE-02-004	Eastern Chipmunks	E. Boehm	Yr.Iss	62.50	62.50
77-P-LE-02-005	Beaver	E. Boehm	Yr.Iss	67.50	67.50
78-P-LE-02-006	Whitetail Deer	E. Boehm	Yr.Iss	70.00	70.00
79-P-LE-02-007	Squirrels	E. Boehm	Yr.Iss	76.00	76.00
80-P-LE-02-008	Bobcats	E. Boehm	Yr.Iss	82.50	82.50
81-P-LE-02-009	Martens	E. Boehm	Yr.Iss	100.00	100.00
82-P-LE-02-010	River Otters	E. Boehm	Yr.Iss	100.00	120.00
Lenox	**The Confederacy Plates**				
72-P-LE-03-001	States of the Confederacy	Unknown	Unkn.	900.00	900.00
Lenox	**Boehm Birds/Young America**				
72-P-LE-04-001	Eaglet	E. Boehm	5,000	175.00	175.00
73-P-LE-04-002	Eaglet	E. Boehm	6,000	175.00	175.00
75-P-LE-04-002	Eaglet	E. Boehm	6,000	175.00	175.00
Lenox	**Colonial Christmas Wreath**				
81-P-LE-05-001	Colonial Virginia	Unknown	Yr.Iss	65.00	100.00
82-P-LE-05-002	Massachusetts	Unknown	Yr.Iss	70.00	90.00
83-P-LE-05-003	Maryland	Unknown	Yr.Iss	70.00	80.00
84-P-LE-05-004	Rhode Island	Unknown	Yr.Iss	70.00	70.00
85-P-LE-05-005	Connecticut	Unknown	Yr.Iss	70.00	70.00
Lenox	**Butterflies and Flowers**				
82-P-LE-06-001	Question Mark/Aster	V. R. Gerischer	25,000	60.00	60.00
82-P-LE-06-002	Sonorarn Blue/Lily	V. R. Gerischer	25,000	65.00	65.00
83-P-LE-06-003	Malachite/Orchid	V. R. Gerischer	25,000	65.00	65.00
84-P-LE-06-004	Ruddy Daggerwing/Lantana	V. R. Gerischer	25,000	70.00	70.00
84-P-LE-06-005	American Painted Lady/Virginia Rose	V. R. Gerischer	25,000	70.00	70.00
Lenox	**Nature's Nursery**				
83-P-LE-07-001	Snow Leopard	L. Chase	15,000	65.00	65.00
83-P-LE-07-002	Koalas	L. Chase	15,000	65.00	65.00
83-P-LE-07-003	Llamas	L. Chase	15,000	70.00	70.00
84-P-LE-07-004	Bengal Tigers	L. Chase	15,000	70.00	70.00
85-P-LE-07-005	Emperor Penguins	L. Chase	15,000	75.00	75.00
85-P-LE-07-006	Polar Bears	L. Chase	15,000	75.00	75.00
Lenox	**Lenox Christmas Tree Series**				
76-P-LE-08-001	Douglas Fir	Unknown	Yr.Iss	50.00	50.00
77-P-LE-08-002	Scotch Pine	Unknown	Yr.Iss	55.00	55.00
78-P-LE-08-003	Blue Spruce	Unknown	Yr.Iss	65.00	65.00
79-P-LE-08-004	Balsam Fir	Unknown	Yr.Iss	65.00	65.00
80-P-LE-08-005	Brewer's Spruce	Unknown	Yr.Iss	75.00	75.00
81-P-LE-08-006	China Fir	Unknown	Yr.Iss	75.00	75.00
82-P-LE-08-007	Aleppo Pine	Unknown	Yr.Iss	80.00	80.00
Lenox	**The Confederacy Collection**				
71-P-LE-09-001	The White House of the Confederacy	W. Schiener	1,201	900.00	900.00
71-P-LE-09-002	The Great Seal of the Confederacy	W. Schiener	1,201	set	set
71-P-LE-09-003	A Call to Arms	W. Schiener	1,201	set	set
71-P-LE-09-004	The General	W. Schiener	1,201	set	set
71-P-LE-09-005	Lee and Jackson	W. Schiener	1,201	set	set
71-P-LE-09-006	The Merrimac	W. Schiener	1,201	set	set
71-P-LE-09-007	J.E.B. Stuart	W. Schiener	1,201	set	set
71-P-LE-09-008	Confederate Camp	W. Schiener	1,201	set	set
71-P-LE-09-009	Blockade Runner	W. Schiener	1,201	set	set
71-P-LE-09-010	Fort Sumter	W. Schiener	1,201	set	set
Lenox	**Lenox Boehm Single Issues**				
72-P-LE-10-001	Bird of Peace-Mute Swan	E. Boehm	5,000	150.00	150.00
73-P-LE-10-002	Young America 1776-Eaglet	E. Boehm	6,000	175.00	175.00

Number	Name	Artist	Edition limit	Issue Price	Quote
Company		**Series**			
Lenox		**American Wildlife Plates**			
83-P-LE-11-001	Red Foxes	N. Adams	9,500	65.00	65.00
83-P-LE-11-002	Ocelets	N. Adams	9,500	65.00	65.00
83-P-LE-11-003	Sea Lions	N. Adams	9,500	65.00	65.00
83-P-LE-11-004	Raccoons	N. Adams	9,500	65.00	65.00
83-P-LE-11-005	Dall Sheep	N. Adams	9,500	65.00	65.00
Lihs Linder		**Christmas**			
72-P-LI-01-001	Little Drummer Boy	J. Neubauer	6,000	25.00	50.00
73-P-LI-01-002	Carolers	J. Neubauer	6,000	25.00	25.00
74-P-LI-01-003	Peace	J. Neubauer	6,000	25.00	31.00
75-P-LI-01-004	Christmas Cheer	J. Neubauer	6,000	30.00	31.00
76-P-LI-01-005	Joy of Christmas	J. Neubauer	6,000	30.00	30.00
77-P-LI-01-006	Holly Jolly Christmas	J. Neubauer	6,000	30.00	30.00
78-P-LI-01-007	Holy Night	J. Neubauer	6,000	40.00	40.00
Maruri USA		**Eagle Plate Series**			
84-P-MC-01-001	Free Flight	W. Gaither	995	150.00	150.00
Mingolla/Home Plates		**Christmas**			
73-P-MI-01-001	Copper, Enamel	Mingolla	1,000	95.00	165.00
74-P-MI-01-002	Copper, Enamel	Mingolla	1,000	110.00	145.00
75-P-MI-01-003	Copper, Enamel	Mingolla	1,000	125.00	145.00
76-P-MI-01-004	Copper, Enamel	Mingolla	1,000	125.00	125.00
77-P-MI-01-005	Winter Wonderland (Copper Enamel)	Mingolla	2,000	200.00	200.00
Mingolla/Home Plates		**Christmas**			
74-P-MI-02-001	Porcelain	Mingolla	5,000	35.00	65.00
75-P-MI-02-002	Porcelain	Mingolla	5,000	35.00	45.00
76-P-MI-02-003	Porcelain	Mingolla	5,000	35.00	30.00
Norman Rockwell Museum		**American Family I**			
79-P-NO-01-001	Baby's First Step	N. Rockwell	9,900	28.50	135.00
79-P-NO-01-002	Happy Birthday Dear Mother	N. Rockwell	9,900	28.50	60.00
79-P-NO-01-003	Sweet Sixteen	N. Rockwell	9,900	28.50	45.00
79-P-NO-01-004	First Haircut	N. Rockwell	9,900	28.50	45.00
79-P-NO-01-005	First Prom	N. Rockwell	9,900	28.50	35.00
79-P-NO-01-006	Wrapping Christmas Presents	N. Rockwell	9,900	28.50	35.00
79-P-NO-01-007	The Student	N. Rockwell	9,900	28.50	35.00
79-P-NO-01-008	Birthday Party	N. Rockwell	9,900	28.50	35.00
79-P-NO-01-009	Little Mother	N. Rockwell	9,900	28.50	35.00
79-P-NO-01-010	Washing Dog	N. Rockwell	9,900	28.50	35.00
79-P-NO-01-011	Mother's Little Helpers	N. Rockwell	9,900	28.50	35.00
79-P-NO-01-012	Bride and Groom	N. Rockwell	9,900	28.50	35.00
Norman Rockwell Museum		**Christmas**			
79-P-NO-02-001	Day After Christmas	N. Rockwell	Yr.Iss	75.00	87.50
80-P-NO-02-002	Checking His List	N. Rockwell	Yr.Iss	75.00	85.00
81-P-NO-02-003	Ringing in Good Cheer	N. Rockwell	Yr.Iss	75.00	85.00
82-P-NO-02-004	Waiting for Santa	N. Rockwell	Yr.Iss	75.00	75.00
83-P-NO-02-005	High Hopes	N. Rockwell	Yr.Iss	75.00	75.00
84-P-NO-02-006	Space Age Santa	N. Rockwell	Yr.Iss	55.00	55.00
Norman Rockwell Museum		**American Family II**			
80-P-NO-03-001	New Arrival	N. Rockwell	22,500	35.00	55.00
80-P-NO-03-002	Sweet Dreams	N. Rockwell	22,500	35.00	37.50
80-P-NO-03-003	Little Shaver	N. Rockwell	22,500	35.00	37.50
80-P-NO-03-004	We Missed You Daddy	N. Rockwell	22,500	35.00	37.50
80-P-NO-03-005	Home Run Slugger	N. Rockwell	22,500	35.00	37.50
80-P-NO-03-006	Giving Thanks	N. Rockwell	22,500	35.00	37.50
80-P-NO-03-008	Little Salesman	N. Rockwell	22,500	35.00	37.50
80-P-NO-03-009	Almost Grown Up	N. Rockwell	22,500	35.00	37.50
80-P-NO-03-010	Courageous Hero	N. Rockwell	22,500	35.00	37.50
81-P-NO-03-011	At the Circus	N. Rockwell	22,500	35.00	37.50
81-P-NO-03-012	Good Food, Good Friends	N. Rockwell	22,500	35.00	37.50
Nostalgia Collectibles		**Shirley Temple Collectibles Series**			
82-P-NS-01-001	Baby Take a Bow	Unknown	22,500	75.00	75.00
83-P-NS-01-002	Curly Top	Unknown	22,500	75.00	75.00
83-P-NS-01-003	Stand Up and Cheer	Unknown	22,500	75.00	100.00
Nostalgia Collectibles		**Shirley Temple Collectibles Series**			
83-P-NS-02-001	Baby Take a Bow, autographed	Unknown	2,500	100.00	160.00
83-P-NS-02-002	Curly Top, autographed	Unknown	2,500	100.00	150.00
83-P-NS-02-003	Stand Up and Cheer, autographed	Unknown	2,500	100.00	100.00
Nostalgia Collectibles		**Shirley Temple Classics**			
83-P-NS-03-001	Captain January	Unknown	25,000	35.00	42.50
84-P-NS-03-002	Heidi	Unknown	25,000	35.00	35.00
84-P-NS-03-003	Little Miss Marker	Unknown	25,000	35.00	40.00
84-P-NS-03-004	Bright Eyes	Unknown	25,000	35.00	35.00
85-P-NS-03-005	The Little Colonel	Unknown	25,000	35.00	35.00
85-P-NS-03-006	Rebecca of Sunnybrook Farm	Unknown	25,000	35.00	35.00
86-P-NS-03-007	Poor Little Rich Girl	Unknown	25,000	35.00	35.00
86-P-NS-03-008	Wee Willie Winkie	Unknown	25,000	35.00	35.00
Opa's House		**Annual German Christmas (Weihnachten)**			
78-P-OH-01-001	Annual Christmas Plate	Unknown	2,500	58.00	58.00
79-P-OH-01-002	Annual Christmas Plate	Unknown	2,500	58.00	58.00
80-P-OH-01-003	Annual Christmas Plate	Unknown	2,500	58.00	58.00
81-P-OH-01-004	Annual Christmas Plate	Unknown	2,500	58.00	58.00
82-P-OH-01-005	Annual Christmas Plate	Unknown	2,500	58.00	58.00
83-P-OH-01-006	Annual Christmas Plate	Unknown	2,500	58.00	58.00
84-P-OH-01-007	Annual Christmas Plate	Unknown	2,500	58.00	58.00
Pickard		**Lockhart Wildlife**			
70-P-PI-01-001	Woodcock/Ruffled Grouse, pair	J. Lockhart	2,000	150.00	290.00
71-P-PI-01-002	Teal/Mallard, pair	J. Lockhart	2,000	150.00	198.00
72-P-PI-01-003	Mockingbird/Cardinal, pair	J. Lockhart	2,000	162.50	190.00
73-P-PI-01-004	Turkey/Pheasant, pair	J. Lockhart	2,000	162.50	162.50
74-P-PI-01-005	American Bald Eagle	J. Lockhart	2,000	150.00	850.00
75-P-PI-01-006	White Tailed Deer	J. Lockhart	2,500	100.00	100.00
76-P-PI-01-007	American Buffalo	J. Lockhart	2,500	165.00	165.00
77-P-PI-01-008	Great Horn Owl	J. Lockhart	2,500	100.00	100.00
78-P-PI-01-009	American Panther	J. Lockhart	2,000	175.00	175.00
79-P-PI-01-010	Red Foxes	J. Lockhart	2,500	120.00	120.00
80-P-PI-01-011	Trumpeter Swan	J. Lockhart	2,000	200.00	200.00
Pickard		**Annual Christmas**			
76-P-PI-03-001	Alba Madonna	Raphael	7,500	60.00	90.00
77-P-PI-03-002	The Nativity	L. Lotto	7,500	65.00	65.00
78-P-PI-03-003	Rest on Flight into Egypt	G. David	10,000	65.00	65.00
79-P-PI-03-004	Adoration of the Magi	Botticelli	10,000	70.00	70.00
80-P-PI-03-005	Madonna and Child	Sodoma	10,000	80.00	80.00
81-P-PI-03-006	Madonna and Child with Angels	Memling	10,000	90.00	90.00
Pickard		**Children of Renoir**			
78-P-PI-04-001	Girl with Watering Can	A. Renoir	5,000	50.00	125.00
u8-P-PI-04-002	Child in White	A. Renoir	5,000	50.00	125.00
79-P-PI-04-003	Girl with Hoop	A. Renoir	5,000	55.00	75.00
79-P-PI-04-004	At the Piano	A. Renoir	5,000	55.00	75.00
80-P-PI-04-005	Two Little Circus Girls	A. Renoir	5,000	60.00	70.00
80-P-PI-04-006	Artist's Son Jean	A. Renoir	5,000	60.00	65.00
Pickard		**Mother's Love**			
80-P-PI-05-001	Miracle	I. Spencer	7,500	95.00	150.00
81-P-PI-05-002	Story Time	I. Spencer	7,500	110.00	130.00
82-P-PI-05-003	First Edition	I. Spencer	7,500	115.00	125.00
83-P-PI-05-004	Precious Moment	I. Spencer	7,500	120.00	140.00
Pickard		**Children of Mexico**			
81-P-PI-06-001	Maria	J. Sanchez	5,000	85.00	190.00
81-P-PI-06-002	Miguel	J. Sanchez	5,000	85.00	110.00
82-P-PI-06-003	Regina	J. Sanchez	5,000	90.00	95.00
83-P-PI-06-004	Raphael	J. Sanchez	5,000	90.00	90.00
Pemberton & Oakes		**Wonder of Childhood**			
82-P-PO-01-001	Touching the Sky	D. Zolan	Undis.	19.00	40.00
83-P-PO-01-002	Spring Innocence	D. Zolan	Undis.	19.00	37.00
84-P-PO-01-003	Winter Angel	D. Zolan	Undis.	22.00	45.00
85-P-PO-01-004	Small Wonder	D. Zolan	Undis.	22.00	36.00
86-P-PO-01-005	Grandma's Garden	D. Zolan	Undis.	22.00	33.00
87-P-PO-01-006	Day Dreamer	D. Zolan	Undis.	22.00	22.00
Pemberton & Oakes		**Children and Pets**			
84-P-PO-02-001	Tender Moment	D. Zolan	Undis.	19.00	60.00
84-P-PO-02-002	Golden Moment	D. Zolan	Undis.	19.00	65.00
85-P-PO-02-003	Making Friends	D. Zolan	Undis.	19.00	45.00
86-P-PO-02-004	Backyard Discovery	D. Zolan	Undis.	19.00	33.00
86-P-PO-02-005	Waiting to Play	D. Zolan	Undis.	19.00	39.00
Pemberton & Oakes		**Children at Christmas**			
81-P-PO-03-001	A Gift for Laurie	D. Zolan	15,000	48.00	125.00
82-P-PO-03-002	Christmas Prayer	D. Zolan	15,000	48.00	96.00
83-P-PO-03-003	Erik's Delight	D. Zolan	15,000	48.00	60.00
84-P-PO-03-004	Christmas Secret	D. Zolan	15,000	48.00	55.00
85-P-PO-03-005	Christmas Kitten	D. Zolan	15,000	48.00	75.00
86-P-PO-03-006	Laurie and the Creche	D. Zolan	15,000	48.00	54.00
Porsgrund		**Christmas (Annual)**			
68-P-PR-01-001	Church Scene	G. Bratile	Undis.	12.00	115.00
69-P-PR-01-002	Three Kings	G. Bratile	Undis.	12.00	20.00
70-P-PR-01-003	Road to Bethlehem	G. Bratile	Undis.	12.00	13.00
71-P-PR-01-004	A Child is Born	G. Bratile	Undis.	12.00	16.00
72-P-PR-01-005	Hark the Herald Angels	G. Bratile	Undis.	12.00	24.00
73-P-PR-01-006	Promise of the Savior	G. Bratile	Undis.	12.00	32.00
74-P-PR-01-007	The Shepherds	G. Bratile	Undis.	15.00	43.00
75-P-PR-01-008	Road to Temple	G. Bratile	Undis.	19.50	22.00
76-P-PR-01-009	Jesus and the Elders	G. Bratile	Undis.	22.00	22.00
77-P-PR-01-010	Draught of the Fish	G. Bratile	Undis.	24.00	24.00
Reco International		**The World of Children**			
77-P-RA-01-001	Rainy Day Fun	J. McClelland	10,000	50.00	130.00
78-P-RA-01-002	When I Grow Up	J. McClelland	15,000	50.00	95.00
79-P-RA-01-003	You're Invited	J. McClelland	15,000	50.00	55.00
80-P-RA-01-004	Kittens for Sale	J. McClelland	15,000	50.00	60.00
Reco International		**Mother Goose**			
79-P-RA-02-001	Mary, Mary	J. McClelland	Yr.Iss	22.50	315.00
80-P-RA-02-002	Little Boy Blue	J. McClelland	Yr.Iss	22.50	130.00
81-P-RA-02-003	Little Miss Muffet	J. McClelland	Yr.Iss	24.50	45.00
82-P-RA-02-004	Little Jack Horner	J. McClelland	Yr.Iss	24.50	42.50
83-P-RA-02-005	Little Bo Peep	J. McClelland	Yr.Iss	24.50	45.00
84-P-RA-02-006	Diddle, Diddle Dumpling	J. McClelland	Yr.Iss	24.50	33.00
85-P-RA-02-007	Mary Had a Little Lamb	J. McClelland	Yr.Iss	27.50	42.00
86-P-RA-02-008	Jack and Jill	J. McClelland	Yr.Iss	27.50	27.50
Reco International		**The McClelland Children's Circus Collection**			
82-P-RA-03-001	Tommy the Clown	J. McClelland	100day	29.50	30.00
82-P-RA-03-002	Katie, the Tightrope Walker	J. McClelland	100day	29.50	35.00
83-P-RA-03-003	Johnny the Strongman	J. McClelland	100day	29.50	32.50
84-P-RA-03-004	Maggie the Animal Trainer	J. McClelland	100day	29.50	36.00
Reco International		**Becky's Day**			
85-P-RA-04-001	Awakening	J. McClelland	90-day	24.50	30.00
85-P-RA-04-002	Getting Dressed	J. McClelland	90-day	24.50	28.50
86-P-RA-04-003	Breakfast	J. McClelland	90-day	27.50	27.50
86-P-RA-04-004	Learning is Fun	J. McClelland	90-day	27.50	27.50
86-P-RA-04-005	Muffin Making	J. McClelland	90-day	27.50	27.50
86-P-RA-04-006	Tub Time	J. McClelland	90-day	27.50	27.50
86-P-RA-04-007	Evening Prayer	J. McClelland	90-day	27.50	27.50
Reco International		**Games Children Play**			
79-P-RA-08-001	Me First	S. Kuck	10,000	45.00	52.00
80-P-RA-08-002	Forever Bubbles	S. Kuck	10,000	45.00	50.00
81-P-RA-08-003	Skating Pals	S. Kuck	10,000	45.00	47.50
82-P-RA-08-004	Join Me	S. Kuck	10,000	45.00	45.00
Reco International		**The Grandparent Collector's Plates**			
81-P-RA-09-001	Grandma's Cookie Jar	S. Kuck	Yr.Iss	37.50	37.50
81-P-RA-09-002	Grandpa and the Dollhouse	S. Kuck	Yr.Iss	37.50	37.50
Reco International		**Little Professionals**			
82-P-RA-10-001	All is Well	S. Kuck	10,000	39.50	47.50
83-P-RA-10-002	Tender Loving Care	S. Kuck	10,000	39.50	55.00
84-P-RA-10-003	Lost and Found	S. Kuck	10,000	39.50	42.50
85-P-RA-10-004	Reading, Writing and...	S. Kuck	10,000	39.50	39.50
Reco International		**Days Gone By**			
83-P-RA-11-001	Sunday Best	S. Kuck	14-day	29.50	120.00
83-P-RA-11-002	Amy's Magic Horse	S. Kuck	14-day	29.50	60.00
84-P-RA-11-003	Little Anglers	S. Kuck	14-day	29.50	54.00
84-P-RA-11-004	Afternoon Recital	S. Kuck	14-day	29.50	52.00
84-P-RA-11-005	Little Tutor	S. Kuck	14-day	29.50	38.00
85-P-RA-11-006	Easter at Grandma's	S. Kuck	14-day	29.50	36.00
85-P-RA-11-007	Morning Song	S. Kuck	14-day	29.50	32.50
85-P-RA-11-008	The Surrey Ride	S. Kuck	14-day	29.50	39.00
Reco International		**A Childhood Almanac**			
85-P-RA-12-001	Fireside Dreams-January	S. Kuck	14-day	29.50	29.50
85-P-RA-12-002	Be Mine-February	S. Kuck	14-day	29.50	29.50
86-P-RA-12-003	Winds of March - March	S. Kuck	14-day	29.50	29.50
85-P-RA-12-004	Easter Morning-April	S. Kuck	14-day	29.50	35.00
85-P-RA-12-005	For Mom-May	S. Kuck	14-day	29.50	29.50
85-P-RA-12-006	Just Daydreaming-June	S. Kuck	14-day	29.50	29.50
85-P-RA-12-007	Star Spangled Sky-July	S. Kuck	14-day	29.50	29.50
85-P-RA-12-008	Summer Secrets-August	S. Kuck	14-day	29.50	29.50
85-P-RA-12-009	School Days-September	S. Kuck	14-day	29.50	35.00
86-P-RA-12-010	Indian Summer - October	S. Kuck	14-day	29.50	29.50
86-P-RA-12-011	Giving Thanks - November	S. Kuck	14-day	29.50	40.00
85-P-RA-12-012	Christmas Magic - December	S. Kuck	14-day	29.50	29.50

Number	Name	Artist	Edition limit	Issue Price	Quote
Company		**Series**			
Reco International		**Mother's Day Collection**			
85-P-RA-13-001	Once Upon a Time	S. Kuck	Yr.Iss	29.50	50.00
86-P-RA-13-002	Times Remembered	S. Kuck	Yr.Iss	29.50	36.00
87-P-RA-13-003	A Cherished Time	S. Kuck	Yr.Iss	29.50	29.50
Reco International		**A Children's Christmas Pageant**			
86-P-RA-14-001	Silent Night	S. Kuck	Yr.Iss	32.50	32.50
87-P-RA-14-002	Hark the Hearld Angels Sing	S. Kuck	Yr.Iss	32.50	32.50
Reco International		**The Barefoot Children**			
87-P-RA-15-001	Night-Time Story	S. Kuck	14 day	29.50	29.50
87-P-RA-15-002	Golden Afternoon	S. Kuck	14 day	29.50	29.50
87-P-RA-15-003	Little Sweethearts	S. Kuck	14 day	29.50	29.50
Reco International		**The Sophisticated Ladies Collection**			
85-P-RA-25-001	Felicia	A. Fazio	21-day	29.50	31.50
85-P-RA-25-002	Samantha	A. Fazio	21-day	29.50	29.50
85-P-RA-25-003	Phoebe	A. Fazio	21-day	29.50	29.50
85-P-RA-25-004	Cleo	A. Fazio	21-day	29.50	29.50
86-P-RA-25-005	Cerissa	A. Fazio	21-day	29.50	29.50
86-P-RA-25-006	Natasha	A. Fazio	21-day	29.50	29.50
86-P-RA-25-007	Bianka	A. Fazio	21-day	29.50	29.50
86-P-RA-25-008	Chelsea	A. Fazio	21-day	29.50	29.50
Reco International		**The Springtime of Life**			
85-P-RA-26-001	Teddy's Bathtime	T. Utz	14-day	29.50	29.50
86-P-RA-26-002	Just Like Mommy	T. Utz	14-day	29.50	29.50
86-P-RA-26-003	Among the Daffodils	T. Utz	14-day	29.50	29.50
86-P-RA-26-004	My Favorite Dolls	T. Utz	14-day	29.50	29.50
86-P-RA-26-005	Aunt Tillie's Hats	T. Utz	14-day	29.50	29.50
86-P-RA-26-006	Little Emily	T. Utz	14-day	29.50	29.50
86-P-RA-26-007	Granny's Boots	T. Utz	14-day	29.50	29.50
86-P-RA-26-008	My Masterpiece	T. Utz	14-day	29.50	29.50
Reco International		**Vanishing Animal Kingdoms**			
86-P-RA-27-001	Rama the Tiger	S. Barlowe	21,500	35.00	35.00
86-P-RA-27-002	Olepi the Buffalo	S. Barlowe	21,500	35.00	35.00
87-P-RA-27-003	Coolibah the Koala	S. Barlowe	21,500	35.00	35.00
87-P-RA-27-004	Ortwin the Deer	S. Barlowe	21,500	35.00	35.00
87-P-RA-27-005	Yen-Poh the Panda	S. Barlowe	21,500	35.00	35.00
Reco International		**Arabelle and Friends**			
82-P-RA-29-001	Ice Delight	C. Greunke	15,000	35.00	35.00
83-P-RA-29-002	First Love	C. Greunke	15,000	35.00	35.00
Reco International		**Arta Christmas**			
73-P-RA-30-001	Nativity	Unknown	220	50.00	70.00
Reco International		**Arta Mother's Day**			
73-P-RA-31-001	Family with Puppy	Unknown	300	50.00	70.00
Reco International		**Bohemian Annuals**			
74-P-RA-32-001	1974	Unknown	500	130.00	155.00
75-P-RA-32-002	1975	Unknown	500	140.00	160.00
76-P-RA-32-003	1976	Unknown	500	150.00	160.00
Reco International		**Americanna**			
72-P-RA-33-001	Gaspee Incident	S. Devlin	1,500	200.00	325.00
Reco International		**Dresden Christmas**			
71-P-RA-34-001	Shepherd Scene	Unknown	3,500	15.00	50.00
72-P-RA-34-002	Niklas Church	Unknown	6,000	15.00	25.00
73-P-RA-34-003	Schwanstein Church	Unknown	6,000	18.00	35.00
74-P-RA-34-004	Village Scene	Unknown	5,000	20.00	30.00
75-P-RA-34-005	Rothenburg Scene	Unknown	5,000	24.00	30.00
76-P-RA-34-006	Village Church	Unknown	5,000	26.00	35.00
77-P-RA-34-007	Old Mill (Issue Closed)	Unknown	5,000	28.00	30.00
Reco International		**Dresden Mother's Day**			
72-P-RA-35-001	Doe and Fawn	Unknown	8,000	15.00	20.00
73-P-RA-35-002	Mare and Colt	Unknown	6,000	16.00	25.00
74-P-RA-35-003	Tiger and Cub	Unknown	5,000	20.00	23.00
75-P-RA-35-004	Dachshunds	Unknown	5,000	24.00	28.00
76-P-RA-35-005	Owl and Offspring	Unknown	5,000	26.00	30.00
77-P-RA-35-006	Chamois (Issue Closed)	Unknown	5,000	28.00	30.00
Reco International		**Furstenberg Christmas**			
71-P-RA-36-001	Rabbits	Unknown	7,500	15.00	30.00
72-P-RA-36-002	Snowy Village	Unknown	6,000	15.00	20.00
73-P-RA-36-003	Christmas Eve	Unknown	4,000	18.00	35.00
74-P-RA-36-004	Sparrows	Unknown	4,000	20.00	30.00
75-P-RA-36-005	Deer Family	Unknown	4,000	22.00	30.00
76-P-RA-36-006	Winter Birds	Unknown	4,000	25.00	25.00
Reco International		**Furstenberg Deluxe Christmas**			
71-P-RA-37-001	Wise Men	E. Grossberg	1,500	45.00	45.00
72-P-RA-37-002	Holy Family	E. Grossberg	2,000	45.00	45.00
73-P-RA-37-003	Christmas Eve	E. Grossberg	2,000	60.00	65.00
Reco International		**Furstenberg Easter**			
71-P-RA-38-001	Sheep	Unknown	3,500	15.00	150.00
72-P-RA-38-002	Chicks	Unknown	6,500	15.00	60.00
73-P-RA-38-003	Bunnies	Unknown	4,000	16.00	80.00
74-P-RA-38-004	Pussywillow	Unknown	4,000	20.00	32.50
75-P-RA-38-005	Easter Window	Unknown	4,000	22.00	30.00
76-P-RA-38-006	Flower Collecting	Unknown	4,000	25.00	25.00
Reco International		**Furstenberg Mother's Day**			
72-P-RA-39-001	Hummingbirds, Fe	Unknown	6,000	15.00	45.00
73-P-RA-39-002	Hedgehogs	Unknown	5,000	16.00	40.00
74-P-RA-39-003	Doe and Fawn	Unknown	4,000	20.00	30.00
75-P-RA-39-004	Swans	Unknown	4,000	22.00	23.00
76-P-RA-39-005	Koala Bears	Unknown	4,000	25.00	30.00
Reco International		**Furstenberg Olympic**			
72-P-RA-40-001	Munich	J. Poluszynski	5,000	20.00	75.00
76-P-RA-40-002	Montreal	J. Poluszynski	5,000	37.50	37.50
Reco International		**Grafburg Christmas**			
75-P-RA-41-001	Black-Capped Chickadee	Unknown	5,000	20.00	60.00
76-P-RA-41-002	Squirrels	Unknown	5,000	22.00	22.00
Reco International		**King's Christmas**			
73-P-RA-42-001	Adoration	Merli	1,500	100.00	265.00
74-P-RA-42-002	Madonna	Merli	1,500	150.00	250.00
75-P-RA-42-003	Heavenly Choir	Merli	1,500	160.00	235.00
76-P-RA-42-004	Siblings	Merli	1,500	200.00	225.00
Reco International		**King's Flowers**			
73-P-RA-43-001	Carnation	A. Falchi	1,000	85.00	130.00
74-P-RA-43-002	Red Rose	A. Falchi	1,000	100.00	145.00
75-P-RA-43-003	Yellow Dahlia	A. Falchi	1,000	110.00	162.00
76-P-RA-43-004	Bluebells	A. Falchi	1,000	130.00	165.00
77-P-RA-43-005	Anemones	A. Falchi	1,000	130.00	175.00
Reco International		**King's Mother's Day**			
73-P-RA-44-001	Dancing Girl	Merli	1,500	100.00	225.00
74-P-RA-44-002	Dancing Boy	Merli	1,500	115.00	250.00
75-P-RA-44-003	Motherly Love	Merli	1,500	140.00	225.00
76-P-RA-44-004	Maiden	Merli	1,500	180.00	200.00
Reco International		**Four Seasons**			
73-P-RA-45-001	Spring	J. Poluszynski	2,500	50.00	75.00
73-P-RA-45-002	Summer	J. Poluszynski	2,500	50.00	75.00
73-P-RA-45-003	Fall	J. Poluszynski	2,500	50.00	75.00
73-P-RA-45-004	Winter	J. Poluszynski	2,500	50.00	75.00
Reco International		**Marmot Father's Day**			
70-P-RA-46-001	Stag	Unknown	3,500	12.00	100.00
71-P-RA-46-002	Horse	Unknown	3,500	12.50	40.00
Reco International		**Marmot Christmas**			
70-P-RA-47-001	Polar Bear, Fe	Unknown	5,000	13.00	60.00
71-P-RA-47-002	Buffalo Bill	Unknown	6,000	16.00	55.00
72-P-RA-47-003	Boy and Grandfather	Unknown	5,000	20.00	50.00
71-P-RA-47-004	American Buffalo	Unknown	6,000	14.50	35.00
73-P-RA-47-005	Snowman	Unknown	3,000	22.00	45.00
74-P-RA-47-006	Dancing	Unknown	2,000	24.00	30.00
75-P-RA-47-007	Quail	Unknown	2,000	30.00	40.00
76-P-RA-47-008	Windmill	Unknown	2,000	40.00	40.00
Reco International		**Marmot Mother's Day**			
72-P-RA-48-001	Seal	Unknown	6,000	16.00	60.00
73-P-RA-48-002	Bear with Cub	Unknown	3,000	20.00	140.00
74-P-RA-48-003	Penquins	Unknown	2,000	24.00	50.00
75-P-RA-48-004	Racoons	Unknown	2,000	30.00	45.00
76-P-RA-48-005	Ducks	Unknown	2,000	40.00	40.00
Reco International		**Moser Christmas**			
70-P-RA-49-001	Hradcany Castle	Unknown	400	75.00	170.00
71-P-RA-49-002	Karlstein Castle	Unknown	1,365	75.00	80.00
72-P-RA-49-003	Old Town Hall	Unknown	1,000	85.00	85.00
73-P-RA-49-004	Karlovy Vary Castle	Unknown	500	90.00	100.00
Reco International		**Moser Mother's Day**			
71-P-RA-50-001	Peacocks	Unknown	350	75.00	100.00
72-P-RA-50-002	Butterflies	Unknown	750	85.00	90.00
73-P-RA-50-003	Squirrels	Unknown	500	90.00	95.00
Reco International		**Royale**			
69-P-RA-51-001	Apollo Moon Landing	Unknown	2,000	30.00	80.00
Reco International		**Royale Christmas**			
69-P-RA-52-001	Christmas Fair	Unknown	6,000	12.00	125.00
70-P-RA-52-002	Vigil Mass	Unknown	10,000	13.00	110.00
71-P-RA-52-003	Christmas Night	Unknown	8,000	16.00	50.00
72-P-RA-52-004	Elks	Unknown	8,000	16.00	45.00
73-P-RA-52-005	Christmas Down	Unknown	6,000	20.00	37.50
74-P-RA-52-006	Village Christmas	Unknown	5,000	22.00	60.00
75-P-RA-52-007	Feeding Time	Unknown	5,000	26.00	35.00
76-P-RA-52-008	Seaport Christmas	Unknown	5,000	27.50	30.00
77-P-RA-52-009	Sledding	Unknown	5,000	30.00	30.00
Reco International		**Royale Mother's Day**			
70-P-RA-53-001	Swan and Young	Unknown	6,000	12.00	80.00
71-P-RA-53-002	Doe and Fawn	Unknown	9,000	13.00	55.00
72-P-RA-53-003	Rabbits	Unknown	9,000	16.00	40.00
73-P-RA-53-004	Owl Family	Unknown	6,000	18.00	40.00
74-P-RA-53-005	Duck and Young	Unknown	5,000	22.00	40.00
75-P-RA-53-006	Lynx and Cubs	Unknown	5,000	26.00	40.00
76-P-RA-53-007	Woodcock and Young	Unknown	5,000	27.50	32.50
77-P-RA-53-008	Koala Bear	Unknown	5,000	30.00	30.00
Reco International		**Royale Father's Day**			
70-P-RA-54-001	Frigate Constitution	Unknown	5,000	13.00	80.00
71-P-RA-54-002	Man Fishing	Unknown	5,000	13.00	35.00
72-P-RA-54-003	Mountaineer	Unknown	5,000	16.00	55.00
73-P-RA-54-004	Camping	Unknown	4,000	18.00	45.00
74-P-RA-54-005	Eagle	Unknown	2,500	22.00	35.00
75-P-RA-54-006	Regatta	Unknown	2,500	26.00	35.00
76-P-RA-54-007	Hunting	Unknown	2,500	27.50	32.50
77-P-RA-54-008	Fishing	Unknown	2,500	30.00	30.00
Reco International		**Royale Game Plates**			
72-P-RA-55-001	Setters	J. Poluszynski	500	180.00	200.00
73-P-RA-55-002	Fox	J. Poluszynski	500	200.00	250.00
74-P-RA-55-003	Osprey	W. Schiener	250	250.00	250.00
75-P-RA-55-004	California Quail	W. Schiener	250	265.00	265.00
Reco International		**Royale Germania Christmas Annual**			
70-P-RA-56-001	Orchid	Unknown	600	200.00	650.00
71-P-RA-56-002	Cyclamen	Unknown	1,000	200.00	325.00
72-P-RA-56-003	Silver Thistle	Unknown	1,000	250.00	290.00
73-P-RA-56-004	Tulips	Unknown	600	275.00	310.00
74-P-RA-56-005	Sunflowers	Unknown	500	300.00	320.00
75-P-RA-56-006	Snowdrops	Unknown	350	450.00	500.00
76-P-RA-56-007	Flaming Heart	Unknown	350	450.00	450.00
Reco International		**Royale Germania Crystal Mother's Day**			
71-P-RA-57-001	Roses	Unknown	250	135.00	650.00
72-P-RA-57-002	Elephant and Youngster	Unknown	750	180.00	250.00
73-P-RA-57-003	Koala Bear and Cub	Unknown	600	200.00	225.00
74-P-RA-57-004	Squirrels	Unknown	500	240.00	250.00
75-P-RA-57-005	Swan and Young	Unknown	350	350.00	360.00
Reco International		**Western**			
74-P-RA-58-001	Mountain Man	E. Berke	1,000	165.00	165.00
Reco International		**Marmot President Series**			
71-P-RA-59-001	Washington	Unknown	1,500	25.00	30.00
72-P-RA-59-002	Jefferson	Unknown	1,500	25.00	30.00
73-P-RA-59-003	John Adams	Unknown	1,500	25.00	30.00
Reco International		**Great Stories from the Bible**			
87-P-RA-60-001	Moses in the Bulrushes	G. Katz	14 day	29.50	29.50
87-P-RA-60-002	King David & Saul	G. Katz	14 day	29.50	29.50
87-P-RA-60-003	Joseph's Coat of Many Colors	G. Katz	14 day	29.50	29.50
87-P-RA-60-004	Moses and the Ten Commandments	G. Katz	14 day	29.50	29.50
88-P-RA-60-005	Rebekah at the Well	G. Katz	14 day	29.50	29.50
88-P-RA-60-006	Daniel Reads the Writing on the Wall	G. Katz	14 day	29.50	29.50
88-P-RA-60-007	King Solomon	G. Katz	14 day	29.50	29.50
88-P-RA-60-008	The Story of Ruth	G. Katz	14 day	29.50	29.50
Reece		**Waterfowl**			
73-P-RE-01-001	Mallards & Wood Ducks (Pair)	Unknown	900	250.00	375.00
74-P-RE-01-002	Canvasback & Canadian Geese (Pair)	Unknown	900	250.00	375.00
75-P-RE-01-003	Pintails & Teal (Pair)	Unknown	900	250.00	425.00
Reed and Barton		**Audubon**			
70-P-RF-01-001	Pine Siskin	Unknown	5,000	60.00	175.00
71-P-RF-01-002	Red-Shouldered Hawk	Unknown	5,000	60.00	75.00

Plates

Company / Number	Name	Series / Artist	Edition limit	Issue Price	Quote
72-P-RF-01-003	Stilt Sandpiper	Unknown	5.000	60.00	70.00
73-P-RF-01-004	Red Cardinal	Unknown	5.000	60.00	65.00
74-P-RF-01-005	Boreal Chickadee	Unknown	5.000	65.00	65.00
75-P-RF-01-006	Yellow-Breasted Chat	Unknown	5.000	65.00	65.00
76-P-RF-01-007	Bay-Breasted Warbler	Unknown	5.000	65.00	65.00
77-P-RF-01-008	Purple Finch	Unknown	5.000	65.00	65.00
River Shore		**Famous Americans**			
76-P-RG-01-001	Rockwell's Lincoln	Rockwell-Brown	9.500	40.00	250.00
77-P-RG-01-002	Rockwell's Triple Self-Portrait	Rockwell-Brown	9.500	45.00	55.00
78-P-RG-01-003	Peace Corps	Rockwell-Brown	9.500	45.00	75.00
79-P-RG-01-004	Spirit of Lindbergh	Rockwell-Brown	9.500	50.00	50.00
River Shore		**Remington's Bronze**			
77-P-RG-02-001	Bronco Buster	R. Brown	15.000	55.00	70.00
78-P-RG-02-002	Coming Through the Rye	R. Brown	15.000	60.00	60.00
79-P-RG-02-003	Cheyenne	R. Brown	15.000	60.00	60.00
81-P-RG-02-004	Mountain Man	R. Brown	15.000	60.00	60.00
River Shore		**Della Robbia**			
79-P-RG-03-001	Adoration	R. Brown	5.000	550.00	550.00
80-P-RG-03-002	Virgin and Child	R. Brown	5.000	450.00	450.00
River Shore		**Norman Rockwell Single Issue**			
79-P-RG-04-001	Spring Flowers	N. Rockwell	17.000	75.00	145.00
80-P-RG-04-002	Looking Out to Sea	N. Rockwell	17.000	75.00	130.00
82-P-RG-04-003	Grandpa's Guardian	N. Rockwell	17.000	80.00	80.00
82-P-RG-04-004	Grandpa's Treasures	N. Rockwell	17.000	80.00	80.00
River Shore		**Baby Animals**			
79-P-RG-05-001	Akiku	R. Brown	20.000	50.00	105.00
80-P-RG-05-002	Roosevelt	R. Brown	20.000	50.00	90.00
81-P-RG-05-003	Clover	R. Brown	20.000	50.00	70.00
82-P-RG-05-004	Zuela	R. Brown	20.000	50.00	65.00
River Shore		**Rockwell Four Freedoms**			
81-P-RG-06-001	Freedom of Speech	N. Rockwell	17.000	65.00	65.00
82-P-RG-06-002	Freedom of Worship	N. Rockwell	17.000	65.00	65.00
82-P-RG-06-003	Freedom from Fear	N. Rockwell	17.000	65.00	65.00
82-P-RG-06-004	Freedom from Want	N. Rockwell	17.000	65.00	65.00
River Shore		**Grant Wood Single Issue**			
81-P-RG-07-001	American Gothic	G. Wood	17.000	80.00	80.00
River Shore		**Rockwell Vignette**			
81-P-RG-08-001	Broken Window	N. Rockwell	22.500	19.50	19.50
82-P-RG-08-002	Sunday Best	N. Rockwell	22.500	19.50	19.50
River Shore		**Rockwell Cats**			
82-P-RG-09-001	Jennie and Tina	N. Rockwell	9.500	39.50	39.50
River Shore		**Rockwell/Good Old Days**			
82-P-RG-10-001	Old Oaken Bucket	N. Rockwell	Unkn.	24.50	24.50
82-P-RG-10-002	Boy Fishing	N. Rockwell	Unkn.	24.50	24.50
82-P-RG-10-003	Barefoot Boy	N. Rockwell	Unkn.	24.50	24.50
River Shore		**Timberlake 'Chrsms aftr Chrsms'**			
82-P-RG-11-001	Kay's Doll	Timberlake	9.500	75.00	75.00
River Shore		**America at Work**			
84-P-RG-12-001	The School Teacher	N. Rockwell	10-day	29.50	29.50
84-P-RG-12-002	The Piano Tuner	N. Rockwell	10-day	29.50	29.50
84-P-RG-12-003	Zoo Keeper	N. Rockwell	10-day	29.50	29.50
84-P-RG-12-004	The Cleaning Ladies	N. Rockwell	10-day	29.50	29.50
84-P-RG-12-005	The Hatcheck Girls	N. Rockwell	10-day	29.50	29.50
84-P-RG-12-006	The Artist	N. Rockwell	10-day	29.50	29.50
84-P-RG-12-007	The Cincus Taker	N. Rockwell	10-day	29.50	29.50
84-P-RG-12-008	The Store Owner	N. Rockwell	10-day	29.50	29.50
River Shore		**Favorite American Songbirds**			
85-P-RG-13-001	Western Tanager	L. Thompson	14-day	19.50	19.50
85-P-RG-13-002	Purple Finches	L. Thompson	14-day	19.50	19.50
85-P-RG-13-003	Mountain Bluebirds	L. Thompson	14-day	19.50	19.50
85-P-RG-13-004	Cardinal	L. Thompson	14-day	19.50	19.50
85-P-RG-13-005	Barn Swallow	L. Thompson	14-day	19.50	19.50
85-P-RG-13-006	Canyon Wren	L. Thompson	14-day	19.50	19.50
85-P-RG-13-007	Mockingbird	L. Thompson	14-day	19.50	19.50
85-P-RG-13-008	Wood Thrush	L. Thompson	14-day	19.50	19.50
River Shore		**Lovable Teddies**			
85-P-RG-14-001	Bedtime Blues	M. Hague	10-day	21.50	21.50
85-P-RG-14-002	Bearly Frightful	M. Hague	10-day	21.50	21.50
85-P-RG-14-003	Caught in the Act	M. Hague	10-day	21.50	21.50
85-P-RG-14-004	Fireside Friends	M. Hague	10-day	21.50	21.50
85-P-RG-14-005	Harvest Time	M. Hague	10-day	21.50	21.50
85-P-RG-14-006	Missed a Button	M. Hague	10-day	21.50	21.50
85-P-RG-14-007	Tender Loving Bear	M. Hague	10-day	21.50	21.50
85-P-RG-14-008	Sunday Stroll	M. Hague	10-day	21.50	21.50
River Shore		**Little House on the Prairie**			
85-P-RG-15-001	Founder's Day Picnic	E. Christopherson	10-day	29.50	29.50
85-P-RG-15-002	Women's Harvest	E. Christopherson	10-day	29.50	29.50
85-P-RG-15-003	Medicine Show	E. Christopherson	10-day	29.50	29.50
85-P-RG-15-004	Caroline's Eggs	E. Christopherson	10-day	29.50	29.50
85-P-RG-15-005	Mary's Gift	E. Christopherson	10-day	29.50	29.50
85-P-RG-15-006	A Bell for Walnut Grove	E. Christopherson	10-day	29.50	29.50
85-P-RG-15-007	Ingall's Family	E. Christopherson	10-day	29.50	29.50
85-P-RG-15-008	The Sweetheart Tree	E. Christopherson	10-day	29.50	29.50
River Shore		**Children of the American Frontier**			
86-P-RG-16-001	In Trouble Again	D. Crook	10-day	24.50	24.50
86-P-RG-16-002	Tubs and Suds	D. Crook	10-day	24.50	24.50
86-P-RG-16-003	A Lady Needs a Little Privacy	D. Crook	10-day	24.50	24.50
86-P-RG-16-004	The Desperadoes	D. Crook	10-day	24.50	24.50
86-P-RG-16-005	Riders Wanted	D. Crook	10-day	24.50	24.50
87-P-RG-16-006	A Cowboy's Downfall	D. Crook	10-day	24.50	24.50
87-P-RG-16-007	Runaway Blues	D. Crook	10-day	24.50	24.50
87-P-RG-16-008	A Special Patient	D. Crook	10-day	24.50	24.50
Rockwell Society		**Christmas**			
74-P-RK-01-001	Scotty Gets His Tree	N. Rockwell	Undis.	24.50	120.00
75-P-RK-01-002	Angel with Black Eye	N. Rockwell	Undis.	24.50	61.00
76-P-RK-01-003	Golden Christmas	N. Rockwell	Undis.	24.50	60.00
77-P-RK-01-004	Toy Shop Window	N. Rockwell	Undis.	24.50	40.00
78-P-RK-01-005	Christmas Dream	N. Rockwell	Undis.	24.50	40.00
79-P-RK-01-006	Somebody's Up There	N. Rockwell	Undis.	24.50	26.00
80-P-RK-01-007	Scotty Plays Santa	N. Rockwell	Undis.	24.50	26.00
81-P-RK-01-008	Wrapped Up in Christmas	N. Rockwell	Undis.	25.50	30.00
82-P-RK-01-009	Christmas Courtship	N. Rockwell	Undis.	25.50	30.00
83-P-RK-01-010	Santa in the Subway	N. Rockwell	Undis.	25.50	30.00
84-P-RK-01-011	Santa in His Workshop	N. Rockwell	Undis.	27.50	45.00
85-P-RK-01-012	Grandpa Plays Santa	N. Rockwell	Undis.	27.50	28.00
86-P-RK-01-013	Dear Santy Claus	N. Rockwell	Undis.	27.90	27.90
Rockwell Society		**Mother's Day**			
76-P-RK-02-001	A Mother's Love	N. Rockwell	Undis.	24.50	110.00
77-P-RK-02-002	Faith	N. Rockwell	Undis.	24.50	80.00
78-P-RK-02-003	Bedtime	N. Rockwell	Undis.	24.50	90.00
79-P-RK-02-004	Reflections	N. Rockwell	Undis.	24.50	35.00
80-P-RK-02-005	A Mother's Pride	N. Rockwell	Undis.	24.50	30.00
81-P-RK-02-006	After the Party	N. Rockwell	Undis.	24.50	30.00
82-P-RK-02-007	The Cooking Lesson	N. Rockwell	Undis.	25.50	30.00
83-P-RK-02-008	Add Two Cups and Love	N. Rockwell	Undis.	25.50	37.00
84-P-RK-02-009	Grandma's Courting Dress	N. Rockwell	Undis.	25.50	28.00
85-P-RK-02-010	Mending Time	N. Rockwell	Undis.	27.50	35.00
86-P-RK-02-011	Pantry Raid	N. Rockwell	Undis.	27.90	28.00
Rockwell Society		**Heritage**			
77-P-RK-03-001	Toy Maker	N. Rockwell	Undis.	14.50	160.00
78-P-RK-03-002	Cobbler	N. Rockwell	Undis.	19.50	130.00
79-P-RK-03-003	Lighthouse Keeper's Daughter	N. Rockwell	Undis.	19.50	55.00
80-P-RK-03-004	Ship Builder	N. Rockwell	Undis.	19.50	40.00
81-P-RK-03-005	Music Maker	N. Rockwell	Undis.	19.50	24.00
82-P-RK-03-006	Tycoon	N. Rockwell	Undis.	19.50	25.00
83-P-RK-03-007	Painter	N. Rockwell	Undis.	19.50	28.00
84-P-RK-03-008	Storyteller	N. Rockwell	Undis.	19.50	35.00
84-P-RK-03-009	Gourmet	N. Rockwell	Undis.	19.50	40.00
86-P-RK-03-010	Professor	N. Rockwell	Undis.	22.90	25.00
86-P-RK-03-011	Shadow Artist	N. Rockwell	Undis.	22.90	22.90
Rockwell Society		**Rockwell's Rediscovered Women**			
84-P-RK-04-001	Dreaming in the Attic	N. Rockwell	Undis.	19.50	33.00
84-P-RK-04-002	Waiting on the Shore	N. Rockwell	Undis.	22.50	27.00
84-P-RK-04-003	Pondering on the Porch	N. Rockwell	Undis.	22.50	30.00
84-P-RK-04-004	Making Believe at the Mirror	N. Rockwell	Undis.	22.50	32.00
84-P-RK-04-005	Waiting at the Dance	N. Rockwell	Undis.	22.50	35.00
84-P-RK-04-006	Gossiping in the Alcove	N. Rockwell	Undis.	22.50	29.00
84-P-RK-04-007	Standing in the Doorway	N. Rockwell	Undis.	22.50	44.00
84-P-RK-04-008	Flirting in the Parlor	N. Rockwell	Undis.	22.50	30.00
84-P-RK-04-009	Working in the Kitchen	N. Rockwell	Undis.	22.50	27.50
84-P-RK-04-010	Meeting on the Path	N. Rockwell	Undis.	22.50	25.00
84-P-RK-04-011	Confiding in the Den	N. Rockwell	Undis.	22.50	22.50
84-P-RK-04-012	Reminiscing in the Quiet	N. Rockwell	Undis.	22.50	35.00
XX-P-RK-04-013	Complete Collection	N. Rockwell	Undis.	267.00	309.50
Rockwell Society		**Rockwell on Tour**			
83-P-RK-05-001	Walking Through Merrie Englande	N. Rockwell	Undis.	16.00	35.00
83-P-RK-05-002	Promenade a Paris	N. Rockwell	Undis.	16.00	22.00
83-P-RK-05-003	When in Rome	N. Rockwell	Undis.	16.00	22.00
84-P-RK-05-004	Die Walk am Rhein	N. Rockwell	Undis.	16.00	25.00
XX-P-RK-05-005	Complete Collection	N. Rockwell	Undis.	64.00	105.00
Rockwell Society		**Rockwell's Light Campaign**			
83-P-RK-06-001	This is the Room that Light Made	N. Rockwell	Undis.	19.50	65.00
84-P-RK-06-002	Grandpa's Treasure Chest	N. Rockwell	Undis.	19.50	20.00
84-P-RK-06-003	Father's Help	N. Rockwell	Undis.	19.50	19.50
84-P-RK-06-004	Evening's Ease	N. Rockwell	Undis.	19.50	23.00
84-P-RK-06-005	Close Harmony	N. Rockwell	Undis.	21.50	22.00
84-P-RK-06-006	The Birthday Wish	N. Rockwell	Undis.	21.50	21.50
XX-P-RK-06-007	Complete Collection	N. Rockwell	Undis.	121.00	171.00
Rockwell Society		**Rockwell's American Dream**			
85-P-RK-07-001	A Young Girl's Dream	N. Rockwell	Undis.	19.90	19.90
85-P-RK-07-002	A Couple's Commitment	N. Rockwell	Undis.	19.90	19.90
85-P-RK-07-003	A Family's Full Measure	N. Rockwell	Undis.	22.90	22.90
86-P-RK-07-004	A Mother's Welcome	N. Rockwell	Undis.	22.90	22.90
86-P-RK-07-005	A Young Man's Dream	N. Rockwell	Undis.	22.90	22.90
86-P-RK-07-006	The Musician's Magic	N. Rockwell	Undis.	22.90	22.90
87-P-RK-07-007	An Orphan's Hope	N. Rockwell	Undis.	24.90	24.90
87-P-RK-07-008	Love's Reward	N. Rockwell	Undis.	24.90	24.90
XX-P-RK-07-009	Complete Collection	N. Rockwell	Undis.	181.20	181.20
Rockwell Society		**Colonials - The Rarest Rockwells**			
85-P-RK-08-001	Unexpected Proposal	N. Rockwell	Undis.	27.90	27.90
86-P-RK-08-002	Words of Comfort	N. Rockwell	Undis.	27.90	27.90
86-P-RK-08-003	Light for the Winter	N. Rockwell	Undis.	30.90	30.90
Rockwell Society		**A Mind of Her Own**			
86-P-RK-09-001	Sitting Pretty	N. Rockwell	Undis.	24.90	24.90
Royal Cornwall		**Creation**			
77-P-RN-01-001	In the Beginning	Y. Koutsis	10.000	37.50	90.00
77-P-RN-01-002	In His Image	Y. Koutsis	10.000	45.00	130.00
78-P-RN-01-003	Adam's Rib	Y. Koutsis	10.000	45.00	125.00
78-P-RN-01-004	Banished from Eden	Y. Koutsis	10.000	45.00	125.00
78-P-RN-01-005	Noah and the Ark	Y. Koutsis	10.000	45.00	120.00
80-P-RN-01-006	Tower of Babel	Y. Koutsis	10.000	45.00	75.00
80-P-RN-01-007	Sodom and Gamorrah	Y. Koutsis	10.000	45.00	75.00
80-P-RN-01-008	Jacob's Wedding	Y. Koutsis	10.000	45.00	75.00
80-P-RN-01-009	Rebekah at the Well	Y. Koutsis	10.000	45.00	75.00
80-P-RN-01-010	Jacob's Ladder	Y. Koutsis	10.000	45.00	75.00
80-P-RN-01-011	Joseph's Coat of Many Colors	Y. Koutsis	10.000	45.00	75.00
80-P-RN-01-012	Joseph Interprets Pharaoh's Dream	Y. Koutsis	10.000	45.00	75.00
Royal Cornwall		**Creation Calhoun Charter Release**			
77-P-RN-02-001	In The Beginning	Y. Koutsis	19.500	29.50	152.00
77-P-RN-02-002	In His Image	Y. Koutsis	19.500	29.50	120.00
77-P-RN-02-003	Adam's Rib	Y. Koutsis	19.500	29.50	100.00
77-P-RN-02-004	Banished from Eden	Y. Koutsis	19.500	29.50	90.00
77-P-RN-02-005	Noah and the Ark	Y. Koutsis	19.500	29.50	90.00
78-P-RN-02-006	Tower of Babel	Y. Koutsis	19.500	29.50	80.00
78-P-RN-02-007	Sodom and Gomorrah	Y. Koutsis	19.500	29.50	80.00
78-P-RN-02-008	Jacob's Wedding	Y. Koutsis	19.500	29.50	80.00
78-P-RN-02-009	Rebekah at the Well	Y. Koutsis	19.500	29.50	80.00
78-P-RN-02-010	Jacob's Ladder	Y. Koutsis	19.500	29.50	80.00
78-P-RN-02-011	Joseph's Coat of Many Colors	Y. Koutsis	19.500	29.50	80.00
78-P-RN-02-012	Joseph Interprets Pharaoh's Dream	Y. Koutsis	19.500	29.50	80.00
Roman, Inc.		**The Masterpiece Collection**			
79-P-RO-01-001	Adoration	F. Lippe	5.000	65.00	65.00
80-P-RO-01-002	Madonna with Grapes	P. Mignard	5.000	87.50	87.50
81-P-RO-01-003	The Holy Family	G. Delle Notti	5.000	95.00	95.00
82-P-RO-01-004	Madonna of the Streets	R. Ferruzzi	5.000	85.00	85.00
Roman, Inc.		**A Child's World**			
80-P-RO-02-001	Little Children, Come to Me	F. Hook	15.000	45.00	45.00
Roman, Inc.		**A Child's Play**			
82-P-RO-03-001	Breezy Day	F. Hook	30-day	29.95	45.00
82-P-RO-03-002	Kite Flying	F. Hook	30-day	29.95	45.00
84-P-RO-03-003	Bathtub Sailor	F. Hook	30-day	29.95	45.00
84-P-RO-03-004	The First Snow	F. Hook	30-day	29.95	45.00

Number	Name	Artist	Edition limit	Issue Price	Quote
Roman, Inc.		**Frances Hook Collection-Set I**			
82-P-RO-04-001	I Wish, I Wish	F. Hook	15,000	24.95	75.00
82-P-RO-04-002	Baby Blossoms	F. Hook	15,000	24.95	75.00
82-P-RO-04-003	Daisy Dreamer	F. Hook	15,000	24.95	75.00
82-P-RO-04-004	Trees So Tall	F. Hook	15,000	24.95	75.00
Roman, Inc.		**Frances Hook Collection-Set II**			
83-P-RO-05-001	Caught It Myself	F. Hook	15,000	24.95	50.00
83-P-RO-05-002	Winter Wrappings	F. Hook	15,000	24.95	50.00
83-P-RO-05-003	So Cuddly	F. Hook	15,000	24.95	50.00
83-P-RO-05-004	Can I Keep Him?	F. Hook	15,000	24.95	50.00
Roman, Inc.		**Petty Girls of the Ice Capades**			
83-P-RO-06-001	Ice Princess	G. Petty	30-day	24.50	24.50
Roman, Inc.		**The Ice Capades Clown**			
83-P-RO-07-001	Presenting Freddie Trenkler	G. Petty	30-day	24.50	24.50
Roman, Inc.		**Roman Memorial**			
84-P-RO-08-001	The Carpenter	F. Hook	Yr.Iss.	100.00	125.00
Roman, Inc.		**Roman Cats**			
84-P-RO-09-001	Grizabella	Unknown	30-day	29.50	29.50
84-P-RO-09-002	Mr. Mistoffelees	Unknown	30-day	29.50	29.50
84-P-RO-09-003	Rum Rum Tugger	Unknown	30-day	29.50	29.50
Roman, Inc.		**The Magic of Childhood**			
85-P-RO-10-001	Special Friends	A. Williams	10-day	24.50	24.50
85-P-RO-10-002	Feeding Time	A. Williams	10-day	24.50	24.50
85-P-RO-10-003	Best Buddies	A. Williams	10-day	24.50	24.50
85-P-RO-10-004	Getting Acquainted	A. Williams	10-day	24.50	24.50
86-P-RO-10-005	Last One In	A. Williams	10-day	24.50	24.50
86-P-RO-10-006	A Handful Of Love	A. Williams	10-day	24.50	24.50
86-P-RO-10-007	Look Alikes	A. Williams	10-day	24.50	24.50
86-P-RO-10-008	No Fair Peaking	A. Williams	10-day	24.50	24.50
Roman, Inc.		**Frances Hook Legacy**			
85-P-RO-11-001	Fascination	F. Hook	100day	19.50	19.50
85-P-RO-11-002	Daydreaming	F. Hook	100day	19.50	19.50
85-P-RO-11-003	Discovery	F. Hook	100day	22.50	22.50
85-P-RO-11-004	Disappointment	F. Hook	100day	22.50	22.50
86-P-RO-11-005	Wonderment	F. Hook	100day	22.50	22.50
86-P-RO-11-006	Expectation	F. Hook	100day	22.50	22.50
Roman, Inc.		**The Lord's Prayer**			
86-P-RO-12-001	Our Father	A. Williams	10-day	24.50	24.50
86-P-RO-12-002	Thy Kingdom Come	A. Williams	10-day	24.50	24.50
86-P-RO-12-003	Give Us This Day	A. Williams	10-day	24.50	24.50
86-P-RO-12-004	Forgive Our Trespasses	A. Williams	10-day	24.50	24.50
86-P-RO-12-005	As We Forgive	A. Williams	10-day	24.50	24.50
86-P-RO-12-006	Lead Us Not	A. Williams	10-day	24.50	24.50
86-P-RO-12-007	Deliver Us From Evil	A. Williams	10-day	24.50	24.50
86-P-RO-12-008	Thine Is The Kingdom	A. Williams	10-day	24.50	24.50
Roman, Inc.		**The Sweetest Songs**			
86-P-RO-13-001	A Baby's Prayer	I. Spencer	30-day	39.50	45.00
86-P-RO-13-002	This Little Piggie	I. Spencer	30-day	39.50	39.50
Roman, Inc.		**Fontanini Annual Christmas Plate**			
86-P-RO-14-001	A King Is Born	E. Simonetti	Annual	60.00	60.00
87-P-RO-14-002	O Come, Let Us Adore Him	E. Simonetti	1987	60.00	60.00
Rorstrand		**Christmas**			
68-P-RP-01-001	Bringing Home the Tree	G. Nylund	Annual	12.00	425.00
69-P-RP-01-002	Fisherman Sailing Home	G. Nylund	Annual	13.50	50.00
70-P-RP-01-003	Nils with His Geese	G. Nylund	Annual	13.50	20.00
71-P-RP-01-004	Nils in Lapland	G. Nylund	Annual	15.00	15.00
72-P-RP-01-005	Dalecarlian Fiddler	G. Nylund	Annual	15.00	28.00
73-P-RP-01-006	Farm in Smaland	G. Nylund	Annual	16.00	70.00
74-P-RP-01-007	Vadslena	G. Nylund	Annual	19.00	50.00
75-P-RP-01-008	Nils in Vastmanland	G. Nylund	Annual	20.00	25.00
76-P-RP-01-009	Nils in Uapland	G. Nylund	Annual	20.00	28.00
77-P-RP-01-010	Nils in Varmland	G. Nylund	Annual	29.50	29.50
78-P-RP-01-011	Nils in Fjallbacka	G. Nylund	Annual	32.50	32.50
79-P-RP-01-012	Nils in Vaestergoetland	G. Nylund	Annual	38.50	38.50
80-P-RP-01-013	Nils in Halland	G. Nylund	Annual	55.00	55.00
81-P-RP-01-014	Nils in Gotland	G. Nylund	Annual	55.00	55.00
82-P-RP-01-015	Nils at Skansen	G. Nylund	Annual	47.50	50.00
83-P-RP-01-016	Nils in Oland	G. Nylund	Annual	42.50	54.00
84-P-RP-01-017	Angerman land	G. Nylund	Annual	42.50	42.50
85-P-RP-01-018	Christmas	G. Nylund	Annual	42.50	43.00
86-P-RP-01-019	Nils in Karlskr	G. Nylund	Annual	42.50	45.00
Rosenthal		**Christmas**			
10-P-RQ-01-001	Winter Peace	Unknown	Annual	Unknown	550.00
11-P-RQ-01-002	Three Wise Men	Unknown	Annual	Unknown	325.00
12-P-RQ-01-003	Stardust	Unknown	Annual	Unknown	255.00
13-P-RQ-01-004	Christmas Lights	Unknown	Annual	Unknown	235.00
14-P-RQ-01-005	Christmas Song	Unknown	Annual	Unknown	350.00
15-P-RQ-01-006	Walking to Church	Unknown	Annual	Unknown	180.00
16-P-RQ-01-007	Christmas During War	Unknown	Annual	Unknown	240.00
17-P-RQ-01-008	Angel of Peace	Unknown	Annual	Unknown	200.00
18-P-RQ-01-009	Peace on Earth	Unknown	Annual	Unknown	200.00
19-P-RQ-01-010	St. Christopher with Christ Child	Unknown	Annual	Unknown	225.00
20-P-RQ-01-011	Manger in Bethlehem	Unknown	Annual	Unknown	325.00
21-P-RQ-01-012	Christmas in Mountains	Unknown	Annual	Unknown	200.00
22-P-RQ-01-013	Advent Branch	Unknown	Annual	Unknown	200.00
23-P-RQ-01-014	Children in Winter Woods	Unknown	Annual	Unknown	200.00
24-P-RQ-01-015	Deer in the Woods	Unknown	Annual	Unknown	200.00
25-P-RQ-01-016	Three Wise Men	Unknown	Annual	Unknown	200.00
26-P-RQ-01-017	Christmas in Mountains	Unknown	Annual	Unknown	195.00
27-P-RQ-01-018	Station on the Way	Unknown	Annual	Unknown	200.00
28-P-RQ-01-019	Chalet Christmas	Unknown	Annual	Unknown	185.00
24-P-RQ-01-020	Christmas in Alps	Unknown	Annual	Unknown	225.00
30-P-RQ-01-021	Group of Deer Under Pines	Unknown	Annual	Unknown	225.00
31-P-RQ-01-022	Path of the Magi	Unknown	Annual	Unknown	225.00
32-P-RQ-01-023	Christ Child	Unknown	Annual	Unknown	185.00
33-P-RQ-01-024	Thru the Night to Light	Unknown	Annual	Unknown	190.00
34-P-RQ-01-025	Christmas Peace	Unknown	Annual	Unknown	190.00
35-P-RQ-01-026	Christmas by the Sea	Unknown	Annual	Unknown	190.00
36-P-RQ-01-027	Nurnberg Angel	Unknown	Annual	Unknown	195.00
37-P-RQ-01-028	Berchtesgaden	Unknown	Annual	Unknown	195.00
38-P-RQ-01-029	Christmas in the Alps	Unknown	Annual	Unknown	195.00
39-P-RQ-01-030	Schneekoppe Mountain	Unknown	Annual	Unknown	195.00
40-P-RQ-01-031	Marien Church in Danzig	Unknown	Annual	Unknown	250.00
41-P-RQ-01-032	Strassburg Cathedral	Unknown	Annual	Unknown	250.00
42-P-RQ-01-033	Marianburg Castle	Unknown	Annual	Unknown	300.00
43-P-RQ-01-034	Winter Idyll	Unknown	Annual	Unknown	300.00
44-P-RQ-01-035	Wood Scape	Unknown	Annual	Unknown	300.00
45-P-RQ-01-036	Christmas Peace	Unknown	Annual	Unknown	400.00

Number	Name	Artist	Edition limit	Issue Price	Quote
46-P-RQ-01-037	Christmas in an Alpine Valley	Unknown	Annual	Unknown	240.00
47-P-RQ-01-038	Dillingen Madonna	Unknown	Annual	Unknown	985.00
48-P-RQ-01-039	Message to the Shepherds	Unknown	Annual	Unknown	875.00
49-P-RQ-01-040	The Holy Family	Unknown	Annual	Unknown	185.00
50-P-RQ-01-041	Christmas in the Forest	Unknown	Annual	Unknown	185.00
51-P-RQ-01-042	Star of Bethlehem	Unknown	Annual	Unknown	450.00
52-P-RQ-01-043	Christmas in the Alps	Unknown	Annual	Unknown	195.00
53-P-RQ-01-044	The Holy Light	Unknown	Annual	Unknown	195.00
54-P-RQ-01-045	Christmas Eve	Unknown	Annual	Unknown	195.00
55-P-RQ-01-046	Christmas in a Village	Unknown	Annual	Unknown	195.00
56-P-RQ-01-047	Christmas in the Alps	Unknown	Annual	Unknown	195.00
57-P-RQ-01-048	Christmas by the Sea	Unknown	Annual	Unknown	195.00
58-P-RQ-01-049	Christmas Eve	Unknown	Annual	Unknown	195.00
59-P-RQ-01-050	Midnight Mass	Unknown	Annual	Unknown	195.00
60-P-RQ-01-051	Christmas in a Small Village	Unknown	Annual	Unknown	195.00
61-P-RQ-01-052	Solitary Christmas	Unknown	Annual	Unknown	225.00
62-P-RQ-01-053	Christmas Eve	Unknown	Annual	Unknown	195.00
63-P-RQ-01-054	Silent Night	Unknown	Annual	Unknown	195.00
64-P-RQ-01-055	Christmas Market in Nurnberg	Unknown	Annual	Unknown	225.00
65-P-RQ-01-056	Christmas Munich	Unknown	Annual	Unknown	185.00
66-P-RQ-01-057	Christmas in Ulm	Unknown	Annual	Unknown	275.00
67-P-RQ-01-058	Christmas in Reginburg	Unknown	Annual	Unknown	185.00
68-P-RQ-01-059	Christmas in Bremen	Unknown	Annual	Unknown	195.00
69-P-RQ-01-060	Christmas in Rothenburg	Unknown	Annual	Unknown	220.00
70-P-RQ-01-061	Christmas in Cologne	Unknown	Annual	Unknown	175.00
71-P-RQ-01-062	Christmas in Garmisch	Unknown	Annual	42.00	100.00
72-P-RQ-01-063	Christmas in Franconia	Unknown	Annual	50.00	95.00
73-P-RQ-01-064	Lubeck-Holstein	Unknown	Annual	77.00	105.00
74-P-RQ-01-065	Christmas in Wurzburg	Unknown	Annual	85.00	100.00
Rosenthal		**Wiinblad Christmas**			
71-P-RQ-02-001	Maria & Child	B. Wiinblad	Undis.	100.00	1250.00
72-P-RQ-02-002	Caspar	B. Wiinblad	Undis.	100.00	540.00
73-P-RQ-02-003	Melchior	B. Wiinblad	Undis.	125.00	450.00
74-P-RQ-02-004	Balthazar	B. Wiinblad	Undis.	125.00	520.00
75-P-RQ-02-005	The Annunciation	B. Wiinblad	Undis.	195.00	195.00
76-P-RQ-02-006	Angel with Trumpet	B. Wiinblad	Undis.	195.00	195.00
77-P-RQ-02-007	Adoration of Shepherds	B. Wiinblad	Undis.	225.00	250.00
78-P-RQ-02-008	Angel with Harp	B. Wiinblad	Undis.	275.00	278.00
79-P-RQ-02-009	Exodus from Egypt	B. Wiinblad	Undis.	310.00	310.00
80-P-RQ-02-010	Angel with Glockenspiel	B. Wiinblad	Undis.	360.00	360.00
81-P-RQ-02-011	Christ Child Visits Temple	B. Wiinblad	Undis.	375.00	375.00
82-P-RQ-02-012	Christening of Christ	B. Wiinblad	Undis.	375.00	400.00
Rosenthal		**Nobility of Children**			
76-P-RQ-03-001	La Contessa Isabella	E. Hibel	12,750	120.00	150.00
77-P-RQ-03-002	La Marquis Maurice-Pierre	E. Hibel	12,750	120.00	120.00
78-P-RQ-03-003	Baronesse Johanna	E. Hibel	12,750	130.00	140.00
79-P-RQ-03-004	Chief Red Feather	E. Hibel	12,750	140.00	140.00
Rosenthal		**Oriental Gold**			
76-P-RQ-04-001	Yasuko	E. Hibel	2,000	275.00	850.00
77-P-RQ-04-002	Mr. Obata	E. Hibel	2,000	275.00	550.00
78-P-RQ-04-003	Sakura	E. Hibel	2,000	295.00	425.00
79-P-RQ-04-004	Michio	E. Hibel	2,000	325.00	375.00
Rosenthal		**Classic Rose Christmas**			
74-P-RQ-05-001	Memorial Church in Berlin	H. Drexel	Annual	84.00	160.00
75-P-RQ-05-002	Freiburg Cathedral	H. Drexel	Annual	75.00	80.00
76-P-RQ-05-003	Castle of Cochem	H. Drexel	Annual	95.00	85.00
77-P-RQ-05-004	Hanover Town Hall	H. Drexel	Annual	125.00	125.00
78-P-RQ-05-005	Cathedral at Aachen	H. Drexel	Annual	150.00	150.00
79-P-RQ-05-006	Cathedral in Luxenbourg	H. Drexel	Annual	165.00	165.00
80-P-RQ-05-007	Christmas in Brussels	H. Drexel	Annual	190.00	190.00
81-P-RQ-05-008	Christmas in Trier	H. Drexel	Annual	190.00	190.00
82-P-RQ-05-009	Milan Cathedral	H. Drexel	Annual	190.00	190.00
83-P-RQ-05-010	Church at Castle Wittenberg	H. Drexel	Annual	195.00	195.00
84-P-RQ-05-011	City Hall of Stockholm	H. Drexel	Annual	195.00	195.00
85-P-RQ-05-012	Christmas in Augsburg	H. Drexel	Undis.	195.00	195.00
Royal Bayreuth		**Christmas**			
72-P-RR-01-001	Carriage in the Village	Unknown	4,000	15.00	80.00
73-P-RR-01-002	Snow Scene	Unknown	4,000	16.50	20.00
74-P-RR-01-003	The Old Mill	Unknown	4,000	24.00	24.00
75-P-RR-01-004	Forest Chalet "Serenity"	Unknown	4,000	27.50	27.50
76-P-RR-01-005	Christmas in the Country	Unknown	5,000	40.00	40.00
77-P-RR-01-006	Peace on Earth	Unknown	5,000	40.00	40.00
78-P-RR-01-007	Peaceful Interlude	Unknown	5,000	45.00	45.00
79-P-RR-01-008	Homeward Bound	Unknown	5,000	50.00	50.00
Royal Copenhagen		**Christmas**			
08-P-RS-01-001	Madonna and Child	C. Thomsen	Annual	1.00	1800.00
09-P-RS-01-002	Danish Landscape	S. Ussing	Annual	1.00	144.00
10-P-RS-01-003	The Magi	C. Thomsen	Annual	1.00	120.00
11-P-RS-01-004	Danish Landscape	O. Jensen	Annual	1.00	150.00
12-P-RS-01-005	Christmas Tree	C. Thomsen	Annual	1.00	120.00
13-P-RS-01-006	Frederik Church Spire	A. Boesen	Annual	1.50	128.00
14-P-RS-01-007	Holy Spirit Church	A. Boesen	Annual	1.50	113.00
15-P-RS-01-008	Danish Landscape	A. Krog	Annual	1.50	128.00
16-P-RS-01-009	Shepherd at Christmas	R. Bocher	Annual	1.50	84.00
17-P-RS-01-010	Our Savior Church	O. Jensen	Annual	2.00	90.00
18-P-RS-01-011	Sheep and Shepherds	O. Jensen	Annual	2.00	84.00
19-P-RS-01-012	In the Park	O. Jensen	Annual	2.00	95.00
20-P-RS-01-013	Mary and Child Jesus	G. Rode	Annual	2.00	78.00
21-P-RS-01-014	Aabenraa Marketplace	O. Jensen	Annual	2.00	80.00
22-P-RS-01-015	Three Singing Angels	E. Selschau	Annual	2.00	54.00
23-P-RS-01-016	Danish Landscape	O. Jensen	Annual	2.00	68.00
24-P-RS-01-017	Sailing Ship	B. Olsen	Annual	2.00	105.00
25-P-RS-01-018	Christianshavn	O. Jensen	Annual	2.00	84.00
26-P-RS-01-019	Christianshavn Canal	R. Bocher	Annual	2.00	101.00
27-P-RS-01-020	Ship's Boy at Tiller	B. Olsen	Annual	2.00	165.00
28-P-RS-01-021	Vicar's Family	G. Rode	Annual	2.00	75.00
29-P-RS-01-022	Grundtvig Church	O. Jensen	Annual	2.00	90.00
30-P-RS-01-023	Fishing Boats	B. Olsen	Annual	2.50	96.00
31-P-RS-01-024	Mother and Child	G. Rode	Annual	2.50	96.00
32-P-RS-01-025	Frederiksberg Gardens	O. Jensen	Annual	2.50	110.00
33-P-RS-01-026	Ferry and the Great Belt	B. Olsen	Annual	2.50	113.00
34-P-RS-01-027	The Hermitage Castle	O. Jensen	Annual	2.50	95.00
35-P-RS-01-028	Kronborg Castle	B. Olsen	Annual	2.50	147.00
36-P-RS-01-029	Roskilde Cathedral	R. Bocher	Annual	2.50	138.00
37-P-RS-01-030	Main Street Copenhagen	N. Thorsson	Annual	2.50	150.00
38-P-RS-01-031	Round Church in Osterlars	H. Nielsen	Annual	3.00	195.00
39-P-RS-01-032	Greenland Pack-Ice	S. Nielsen	Annual	3.00	180.00
40-P-RS-01-033	The Good Shepherd	K. Lange	Annual	3.00	300.00
41-P-RS-01-034	Danish Village Church	T. Kjolner	Annual	3.00	315.00

Number	Name	Artist	Edition limit	Issue Price	Quote
Company		**Series**			
42-P-RS-01-035	Bell Tower	N. Thorsson	Annual	4.00	290.00
43-P-RS-01-036	Flight into Egypt	N. Thorsson	Annual	4.00	510.00
44-P-RS-01-037	Danish Village Scene	V. Olson	Annual	4.00	185.00
45-P-RS-01-038	A Peaceful Motif	R. Bocher	Annual	4.00	300.00
46-P-RS-01-039	Zealand Village Church	N. Thorsson	Annual	4.00	162.00
47-P-RS-01-040	The Good Shepherd	K. Lange	Annual	4.50	215.00
48-P-RS-01-041	Nodebo Church	T. Kjolner	Annual	4.50	150.00
49-P-RS-01-042	Our Lady's Cathedral	H. Hansen	Annual	5.00	140.00
50-P-RS-01-043	Boeslunde Church	V. Olson	Annual	5.00	195.00
51-P-RS-01-043	Christmas Angel	R. Bocher	Annual	5.00	300.00
52-P-RS-01-044	Christmas in the Forest	K. Lange	Annual	5.00	120.00
53-P-RS-01-045	Frederiksberg Castle	T. Kjolner	Annual	6.00	125.00
54-P-RS-01-046	Amalienborg Palace	K. Lange	Annual	6.00	148.00
55-P-RS-01-047	Fano Girl	K. Lange	Annual	7.00	195.00
56-P-RS-01-048	Rosenborg Castle	K. Lange	Annual	7.00	140.00
57-P-RS-01-049	The Good Shepherd	H. Hansen	Annual	8.00	90.00
58-P-RS-01-050	Sunshine over Greenland	H. Hansen	Annual	9.00	120.00
59-P-RS-01-051	Christmas Night	H. Hansen	Annual	9.00	110.00
60-P-RS-01-052	The Stag	H. Hansen	Annual	10.00	135.00
61-P-RS-01-053	Training Ship	K. Lange	Annual	10.00	140.00
62-P-RS-01-054	The Little Mermaid	Unknownown	Annual	11.00	200.00
63-P-RS-01-055	Hojsager Mill	K. Lange	Annual	11.00	63.00
64-P-RS-01-056	Fetching the Tree	K. Lange	Annual	11.00	66.00
65-P-RS-01-057	Little Skaters	K. Lange	Annual	12.00	125.00
66-P-RS-01-058	Blackbird	K. Lange	Annual	12.00	125.00
67-P-RS-01-059	The Royal Oak	K. Lange	Annual	13.00	107.50
68-P-RS-01-060	The Last Umiak	K. Lange	Annual	13.00	105.00
69-P-RS-01-061	The Old Farmyard	K. Lange	Annual	14.00	102.50
70-P-RS-01-062	Christmas Rose and Cat	K. Lange	Annual	14.00	100.00
71-P-RS-01-063	Hare In Winter	K. Lange	Annual	15.00	97.50
72-P-RS-01-064	In the Desert	K. Lange	Annual	16.00	97.50
73-P-RS-01-065	Train Homeward Bound	K. Lange	Annual	22.00	87.50
74-P-RS-01-066	Winter Twilight	K. Lange	Annual	22.00	87.50
75-P-RS-01-067	Queen's Palace	K. Lange	Annual	27.50	87.50
76-P-RS-01-068	Danish Watermill	S. Vestergaard	Annual	27.50	80.00
77-P-RS-01-069	Immervad Bridge	K. Lange	Annual	32.00	80.00
78-P-RS-01-070	Greenland Scenery	K. Lange	Annual	35.00	80.00
79-P-RS-01-071	Choosing Christmas Tree	K. Lange	Annual	42.50	77.50
80-P-RS-01-072	Bringing Home the Tree	K. Lange	Annual	49.50	75.50
81-P-RS-01-073	Admiring Christmas Tree	K. Lange	Annual	52.50	72.00
82-P-RS-01-074	Waiting for Christmas	K. Lange	Annual	54.50	70.00
83-P-RS-01-075	Merry Christmas	K. Lange	Annual	54.50	67.50
84-P-RS-01-076	Jingle Bells	K. Lange	Annual	54.50	65.00
85-P-RS-01-077	Snowman	K. Lange	Annual	54.50	54.50
86-P-RS-01-078	Wait for Me	K. Lange	Annual	54.50	54.50
Royal Copenhagen		**Mother's Day**			
71-P-RS-02-001	American Mother	K. Svennson	Annual	12.50	130.00
72-P-RS-02-002	Oriental Mother	K. Svennson	Annual	14.00	65.00
73-P-RS-02-003	Danish Mother	A. Ungermann	Annual	16.00	62.50
74-P-RS-02-004	Greenland Mother	A. Ungermann	Annual	16.50	60.00
75-P-RS-02-005	Bird in Nest	A. Ungermann	Annual	20.00	57.50
76-P-RS-02-006	Mermaids	A. Ungermann	Annual	20.00	55.00
77-P-RS-02-007	The Twins	A. Ungermann	Annual	24.00	52.50
78-P-RS-02-008	Mother and Child	S. Olsen	Annual	26.00	26.00
79-P-RS-02-009	A Loving Mother	S. Olsen	Annual	29.50	29.50
80-P-RS-02-010	An Outing with Mother	S. Olsen	Annual	37.50	47.50
81-P-RS-02-011	Reunion	S. Olsen	Annual	39.00	45.00
82-P-RS-02-012	Children's Hour	S. Olsen	Annual	39.00	42.50
Royal Copenhagen		**The Motherhood Collection**			
82-P-RS-03-001	Mother and Baby Robin	S. Vestgaard	Yr.Iss	29.50	47.50
83-P-RS-03-002	Cat and Kitten	S. Vestgaard	Yr.Iss	29.50	45.00
84-P-RS-03-003	A Mare and Foal	S. Vestgaard	Yr.Iss	29.50	42.50
85-P-RS-03-004	Mother and Baby Rabbit	S. Vestgaard	Yr.Iss	32.00	32.00
86-P-RS-03-005	Dog and Puppies	S. Vestgaard	Yr.Iss	32.50	38.00
87-P-RS-03-006	Goat and Kid	S. Vestgaard	Yr.Iss	37.50	37.50
Royal Devon		**Rockwell Christmas**			
75-P-RT-01-001	Downhill Daring	N. Rockwell	Yr.Iss	24.50	30.00
76-P-RT-01-002	The Christmas Gift	N. Rockwell	Yr.Iss	24.50	55.00
77-P-RT-01-003	The Big Moment	N. Rockwell	Yr.Iss	27.50	85.00
78-P-RT-01-004	Puppets for Christmas	N. Rockwell	Yr.Iss	27.50	27.50
79-P-RT-01-005	One Present Too Many	N. Rockwell	Yr.Iss	31.50	31.50
80-P-RT-01-006	Gramps Meets Gramps	N. Rockwell	Yr.Iss	33.00	33.00
Royal Devon		**Rockwell Mother's Day**			
75-P-RT-02-001	Doctor and Doll	N. Rockwell	Yr.Iss	23.50	60.00
76-P-RT-02-002	Puppy Love	N. Rockwell	Yr.Iss	24.50	50.00
77-P-RT-02-003	The Family	N. Rockwell	Yr.Iss	24.50	95.00
78-P-RT-02-004	Mother's Day Off	N. Rockwell	Yr.Iss	27.00	65.00
79-P-RT-02-005	Mother's Evening Out	N. Rockwell	Yr.Iss	30.00	31.00
80-P-RT-02-006	Mother's Treat	N. Rockwell	Yr.Iss	32.50	32.50
Royal Orleans		**Pink Panther Christmas Collection**			
82-P-RV-07-001	Sleigh Ride	D. DePatie	13,000	18.50	18.50
83-P-RV-07-002	Happy Landings	D. DePatie	13,000	18.50	18.50
84-P-RV-07-003	Down the Chimney	D. DePatie	13,000	18.50	18.50
85-P-RV-07-004	Pass the Blast	D. DePatie	13,000	18.50	18.50
Royal Orleans		**M*A*S*H**			
83-P-RV-08-001	The M*A*S*H Plate	J. LaBonte	Yr.Iss	25.00	37.50
Royal Orleans		**Dynasty**			
85-P-RV-09-001	Dynasty	S. Fischer	Yr.Iss	35.00	35.00
Royal Orleans/Dave Grossman		**Tom Sawyer**			
76-P-RW-01-001	Whitewashing Fence	N. Rockwell	Annual	25.00	145.00
77-P-RW-01-002	First Smoke	N. Rockwell	Annual	25.00	45.00
77-P-RW-01-003	Take Your Medicine	N. Rockwell	Annual	25.00	50.00
78-P-RW-01-004	Lost in Cave	N. Rockwell	Annual	25.00	50.00
Royal Orleans/Hoyle		**Nostalgia**			
81-P-RX-01-001	Pepsi Cola Girl	Unknown	5,000	25.00	65.00
82-P-RX-01-002	Olympia Girl	Unknown	5,000	30.00	30.00
82-P-RX-01-003	Savannah Beer Girl	Unknown	5,000	30.00	30.00
83-P-RX-01-004	Dr. Pepper Girl	Unknown	5,000	30.00	30.00
Royal Orleans/Hoyle		**Nostalgia Children**			
83-P-RX-02-001	Pear's Soap Ad	E. Munier	12,500	35.00	35.00
Royal Orleans/Hoyle		**Remember When**			
82-P-RX-03-001	A Surprise for Kitty	M. Humphrey	10,000	30.00	30.00
82-P-RX-03-002	Washday	M. Humphrey	10,000	30.00	30.00
83-P-RX-03-003	Playing Grandmother	M. Humphrey	10,000	30.00	30.00
83-P-RX-03-004	The Physician	M. Humphrey	10,000	30.00	30.00
Royal Orleans/Hoyle		**Bygone Days**			
83-P-RX-04-001	Breakfast with Teddy	J. Willcox Smith	12,500	35.00	35.00
83-P-RX-04-002	A Flower Basket	J. Willcox Smith	12,500	35.00	35.00

Number	Name	Artist	Edition limit	Issue Price	Quote
Company		**Series**			
Royal Orleans/Hoyle		**Nostalgia Magazine Covers**			
83-P-RX-05-001	Ladies' Home Journal	H. Hayden	12,500	35.00	35.00
Royal Worcester		**The American History**			
72-P-RZ-01-001	Boston Tea Party	P.W. Baston	10,000	45.00	325.00
73-P-RZ-01-002	Paul Revere	P.W. Baston	10,000	45.00	300.00
74-P-RZ-01-003	Concord Bridge	P.W. Baston	10,000	50.00	200.00
75-P-RZ-01-004	Signing Declaration	P.W. Baston	10,000	65.00	200.00
76-P-RZ-01-005	Crossing Delaware	P.W. Baston	10,000	65.00	175.00
77-P-RZ-01-006	Washington's Inauguration	P.W. Baston	1,250	65.00	300.00
Royal Worcester		**Doughty Birds**			
72-P-RZ-02-001	Redstarts & Beech	D. Doughty	2,750	150.00	150.00
73-P-RZ-02-002	Myrtle Warbler & Cherry	D. Doughty	3,000	175.00	175.00
74-P-RZ-02-003	Blue-Grey Gnatcatchers	D. Doughty	3,000	195.00	210.00
75-P-RZ-02-004	Blackburnian Warbler	D. Doughty	3,000	195.00	195.00
76-P-RZ-02-005	Blue-Winged Sivas & Bamboo	D. Doughty	3,000	195.00	195.00
77-P-RZ-02-006	Paradise Wydah	D. Doughty	3,000	195.00	200.00
78-P-RZ-02-007	Bluetits & Witch Hazel	D. Doughty	3,000	195.00	195.00
79-P-RZ-02-008	Mountain Bluebird & Pine	D. Doughty	3,000	195.00	195.00
60-P-RZ-02-009	Cerulean Warblers & Beech	D. Doughty	3,000	315.00	315.00
81-P-RZ-02-010	Willow Warbler	D. Doughty	3,000	315.00	315.00
82-P-RZ-02-011	Ruby-crowned Kinglets	D. Doughty	3,000	330.00	330.00
83-P-RZ-02-012	Wren & Jasmine	D. Doughty	3,000	330.00	330.00
Royal Worcester		**Currier and Ives Plates**			
74-P-RZ-03-001	Road in Winter	P.W. Baston	Closed	59.50	125.00
75-P-RZ-03-002	Old Grist Mill	P.W. Baston	Closed	59.50	125.00
76-P-RZ-03-003	Winter Pastime	P.W. Baston	Closed	59.50	150.00
77-P-RZ-03-004	Home to Thanksgiving	P.W. Baston	500	59.50	200.00
Royal Worcester		**Fabulous Birds Plates**			
76-P-RZ-04-001	Peacocks	Unknown	10,000	65.00	65.00
78-P-RZ-04-002	Peacocks II	Unknown	10,000	65.00	65.00
Royal Worcester		**Single Release Plates**			
75-P-RZ-05-001	The Spirit of 1776	P. W. Baston	Closed	Unknown	150.00
Royal Worcester		**Audubon Bird Plates**			
77-P-RZ-08-001	Audubon Birds	Unknown	5,000	150.00	150.00
Royal Worcester		**Christmas Plates**			
79-P-RZ-09-001	Christmas Eve	Unknown	Unkn.	60.00	60.00
80-P-RZ-09-002	Christmas Morning Ewnece	Unknown	Unkn.	65.00	65.00
80-P-RZ-09-003	Christmas Day	Unknown	Unkn.	70.00	70.00
Royal Worcester		**Spode Christmas Pastimes Plates**			
82-P-RZ-10-001	Sleigh Ride	Unknown	Unkn.	75.00	75.00
Royal Worcester		**Spode Maritime Plates**			
80-P-RZ-11-001	United States/Macedonian	Unknown	2,000	150.00	150.00
80-P-RZ-11-002	President & Little Belt	Unknown	2,000	150.00	150.00
80-P-RZ-11-003	Shannon & Chesapeake	Unknown	2,000	150.00	150.00
80-P-RZ-11-004	Constitution & Guerriere	Unknown	2,000	150.00	150.00
80-P-RZ-11-005	Constitution & Java	Unknown	2,000	150.00	150.00
80-P-RZ-11-006	Pelican & Argus	Unknown	2,000	150.00	150.00
Royal Worcester		**The American Expansion**			
76-P-RZ-12-001	American Independence	P.W. Baston	Closed	Unknown	175.00
77-P-RZ-12-002	American Expansion	P.W. Baston	Closed	Unknown	175.00
78-P-RZ-12-003	The American War Between the States	P.W. Baston	Closed	Unknown	200.00
Royal Worcester		**Water Birds of North America**			
85-P-RZ-13-001	Mallards	J. Cooke	15,000	55.00	55.00
85-P-RZ-13-002	Canvas Backs	J. Cooke	15,000	55.00	55.00
85-P-RZ-13-003	Wood Ducks	J. Cooke	15,000	55.00	55.00
85-P-RZ-13-004	Snow Geese	J. Cooke	15,000	55.00	55.00
85-P-RZ-13-005	American Pintails	J. Cooke	15,000	55.00	55.00
85-P-RZ-13-006	Green Winged Teals	J. Cooke	15,000	55.00	55.00
85-P-RZ-13-007	Hooded Mergansers	J. Cooke	15,000	55.00	55.00
85-P-RZ-13-008	Canada Geese	J. Cooke	15,000	55.00	55.00
Royal Worcester		**Kitten Encounters Plate**			
87-P-RZ-14-001	Fishful Thinking	P. Cooper	14-day	29.50	29.50
87-P-RZ-14-002	Puppy Pal	P. Cooper	14-day	29.50	29.50
87-P-RZ-14-003	Just Ducky	P. Cooper	14-day	29.50	29.50
87-P-RZ-14-004	Bunny Chase	P. Cooper	14-day	29.50	29.50
87-P-RZ-14-005	Flutter By	P. Cooper	14-day	29.50	29.50
87-P-RZ-14-006	Bedtime Buddies	P. Cooper	14-day	29.50	29.50
Royal Worcester		**Kitten Classics**			
85-P-RZ-15-001	Cat Nap	P. Cooper	14-day	29.50	29.50
85-P-RZ-15-002	Purrfect Treasure	P. Cooper	14-day	29.50	29.50
85-P-RZ-15-003	Wild Flower	P. Cooper	14-day	29.50	29.50
85-P-RZ-15-004	Birdwatcher	P. Cooper	14-day	29.50	29.50
85-P-RZ-15-005	Tiger's Fancy	P. Cooper	14-day	29.50	29.50
85-P-RZ-15-006	Country Kitty	P. Cooper	14-day	29.50	29.50
85-P-RZ-15-007	Little Rascal	P. Cooper	14-day	29.50	29.50
86-P-RZ-15-008	First Prize	P. Cooper	14-day	29.50	29.50
Schmid		**Christmas**			
71-P-SC-01-001	Angel	B. Hummel	Annual	15.00	30.00
72-P-SC-01-002	Angel With Flute	B. Hummel	Annual	15.00	27.00
73-P-SC-01-003	The Navitity	B. Hummel	Annual	15.00	210.00
74-P-SC-01-004	The Guardian Angel	B. Hummel	Annual	18.50	22.50
75-P-SC-01-005	Christmas Child	B. Hummel	Annual	25.00	25.00
76-P-SC-01-006	Sacred Journey	B. Hummel	Annual	27.50	45.00
77-P-SC-01-007	Herald Angel	B. Hummel	Annual	27.50	27.50
78-P-SC-01-008	Heavenly Trio	B. Hummel	Annual	32.50	32.50
79-P-SC-01-009	Starlight Angel	B. Hummel	Annual	38.00	38.00
80-P-SC-01-010	Parade Into Toyland	B. Hummel	Annual	45.00	57.50
81-P-SC-01-011	A Time To Remember	B. Hummel	Annual	45.00	45.00
82-P-SC-01-012	Angelic Procession	B. Hummel	Annual	45.00	50.50
83-P-SC-01-013	Angelic Messenger	B. Hummel	Annual	45.00	60.00
84-P-SC-01-014	A Gift from Heaven	B. Hummel	Annual	45.00	47.50
85-P-SC-01-015	Heavenly Light	B. Hummel	Annual	45.00	46.50
86-P-SC-01-016	Tell The Heavens	B. Hummel	Annual	45.00	45.00
87-P-SC-01-017	Angelic Gifts	B. Hummel	Annual	47.50	47.50
Schmid		**Peanuts Christmas**			
72-P-SC-02-001	Snoopy Guides the Sleigh	C. Schulz	Annual	10.00	90.00
73-P-SC-02-002	Christmas Eve at Doghouse	C. Schulz	Annual	10.00	120.00
74-P-SC-02-003	Christmas At Fireplace	C. Schulz	Annual	10.00	65.00
75-P-SC-02-004	Woodstock and Santa Claus	C. Schulz	Annual	12.50	12.50
76-P-SC-02-005	Woodstock's Christmas	C. Schulz	Annual	13.00	32.50
77-P-SC-02-006	Deck The Doghouse	C. Schulz	Annual	13.00	15.00
78-P-SC-02-007	Filling the Stocking	C. Schulz	Annual	15.00	27.50
79-P-SC-02-008	Christmas at Hand	C. Schulz	15,000	17.50	15.00
80-P-SC-02-009	Waiting for Santa	C. Schulz	15,000	17.50	52.00
81-P-SC-02-010	A Christmas Wish	C. Schulz	15,000	17.50	25.00
82-P-SC-02-011	Perfect Performance	C. Schulz	15,000	18.50	33.00

Company / Number	Name	Series / Artist	Edition limit	Issue Price	Quote
Schmid		**Mother's Day**			
72-P-SC-03-001	Playing Hooky	B. Hummel	Annual	15.00	25.00
73-P-SC-03-002	Little Fisherman	B. Hummel	Annual	15.00	54.00
74-P-SC-03-003	Bumblebee	B. Hummel	Annual	18.50	72.50
75-P-SC-03-004	Message of Love	B. Hummel	Annual	25.00	25.00
76-P-SC-03-005	Devotion For Mother	B. Hummel	Annual	27.50	30.00
77-P-SC-03-006	Moonlight Return	B. Hummel	Annual	27.50	62.50
78-P-SC-03-007	Afternoon Stroll	B. Hummel	Annual	32.50	60.00
79-P-SC-03-008	Cherub's Gift	B. Hummel	Annual	38.00	38.00
80-P-SC-03-009	Mother's Little Helpers	B. Hummel	Annual	45.00	52.00
81-P-SC-03-010	Playtime	B. Hummel	Annual	45.00	52.00
82-P-SC-03-011	The Flower Basket	B. Hummel	Annual	45.00	47.50
83-P-SC-03-012	Spring Bouquet	B. Hummel	Annual	45.00	54.00
84-P-SC-03-013	A Joy to Share	B. Hummel	Annual	45.00	45.00
85-P-SC-03-014	A Mother's Journey	B. Hummel	Annual	45.00	45.00
86-P-SC-03-015	Home From School	B. Hummel	Annual	45.00	55.00
87-P-SC-03-016	Mother's Little Learner	B. Hummel	Annual	47.50	47.50
Schmid		**Disney Christmas**			
73-P-SC-04-001	Sleigh Ride	Disney Studio	Annual	10.00	450.00
74-P-SC-04-002	Decorating The Tree	Disney Studio	Annual	10.00	200.00
75-P-SC-04-003	Caroling	Disney Studio	Annual	12.50	13.00
76-P-SC-04-004	Building A Snowman	Disney Studio	Annual	13.00	32.50
77-P-SC-04-005	Down The Chimney	Disney Studio	Annual	13.00	30.00
78-P-SC-04-006	Night Before Christmas	Disney Studio	Annual	15.00	21.00
79-P-SC-04-007	Santa's Suprise	Disney Studio	15,000	17.50	25.00
80-P-SC-04-008	Sleigh Ride	Disney Studio	15,000	17.50	22.50
81-P-SC-04-009	Happy Holidays	Disney Studio	15,000	17.50	20.00
82-P-SC-04-010	Winter Games	Disney Studio	15,000	18.50	18.50
Schmid		**Disney Mother's Day**			
74-P-SC-05-001	Flowers For Mother	Disney Studio	Annual	10.00	60.00
75-P-SC-05-002	Snow White & Dwarfs	Disney Studio	Annual	12.50	45.00
76-P-SC-05-003	Minnie Mouse	Disney Studio	Annual	13.00	15.00
77-P-SC-05-004	Pluto's Pals	Disney Studio	Annual	13.00	25.00
78-P-SC-05-005	Flowers For Bambi	Disney Studio	Annual	15.00	30.00
79-P-SC-05-006	Happy Feet	Disney Studio	10,000	17.50	30.00
80-P-SC-05-007	Minnie's Surprise	Disney Studio	10,000	17.50	25.00
81-P-SC-05-008	Playmates	Disney Studio	10,000	17.50	20.00
82-P-SC-05-009	A Dream Come True	Disney Studio	10,000	18.50	18.50
Schmid		**Davis Country Pride Plates**			
81-P-SC-08-001	Surprise in the Cellar	L. Davis	7,500	35.00	125.00
81-P-SC-08-002	Plum Tuckered Out	L. Davis	7,500	35.00	40.00
81-P-SC-08-003	Duke's Mixture	L. Davis	7,500	35.00	65.00
82-P-SC-08-004	Bustin' with Pride	L. Davis	7,500	35.00	45.00
Schmid		**Davis Cat Tales Plates**			
82-P-SC-09-001	Right Church, Wrong Pew	L. Davis	12,500	37.50	55.00
82-P-SC-09-002	Company's Coming	L. Davis	12,500	37.50	50.00
82-P-SC-09-003	On the Move	L. Davis	12,500	37.50	42.00
82-P-SC-09-004	Flew the Coop	L. Davis	12,500	37.50	40.00
Schmid		**Davis Special Edition Plates**			
83-P-SC-10-001	The Critics	L. Davis	12,500	45.00	65.00
86-P-SC-10-002	Home From Market	L. Davis	7,500	55.00	55.00
Schmid		**Davis Christmas Plates**			
83-P-SC-11-001	Country Christmas	L. Davis	7,500	45.00	50.00
84-P-SC-11-002	Country Christmas	L. Davis	7,500	45.00	50.00
85-P-SC-11-003	Christmas at Foxfire Farm	L. Davis	7,500	45.00	45.00
86-P-SC-11-004	Christmas At Red Oak	L. Davis	7,500	45.00	45.00
87-P-SC-11-005	Blossom's Gift	L. Davis	7,500	47.50	47.50
Schmid		**Ferrandiz Music Makers Porcelain Plates**			
81-P-SC-12-001	The Flutist	J. Ferrandiz	10,000	25.00	25.00
81-P-SC-12-002	The Entertainer	J. Ferrandiz	10,000	25.00	25.00
82-P-SC-12-003	Magical Medley	J. Ferrandiz	10,000	25.00	27.50
82-P-SC-12-004	Sweet Serenade	J. Ferrandiz	10,000	25.00	25.00
Schmid		**Ferrandiz Beautiful Bounty Porcelain Plates**			
82-P-SC-13-001	Summer's Golden Harvest	J. Ferrandiz	10,000	40.00	47.50
82-P-SC-13-002	Autumn's Blessing	J. Ferrandiz	10,000	40.00	45.00
82-P-SC-13-003	A Mid-Winter's Dream	J. Ferrandiz	10,000	40.00	42.50
82-P-SC-13-004	Spring Blossoms	J. Ferrandiz	10,000	40.00	40.00
Schmid		**Ferrandiz Wooden Birthday Plates**			
72-P-SC-14-001	Boy	J. Ferrandiz	Unkn.	15.00	150.00
72-P-SC-14-002	Girl	J. Ferrandiz	Unkn.	15.00	160.00
73-P-SC-14-003	Boy	J. Ferrandiz	Unkn.	20.00	200.00
73-P-SC-14-004	Girl	J. Ferrandiz	Unkn.	20.00	150.00
74-P-SC-14-005	Boy	J. Ferrandiz	Unkn.	22.00	160.00
74-P-SC-14-006	Girl	J. Ferrandiz	Unkn.	22.00	160.00
Schmid		**Juan Ferrandiz Porcelain Christmas Plates**			
72-P-SC-20-001	Christ in the Manger	J. Ferrandiz	Unkn.	30.00	179.00
73-P-SC-20-002	Christmas	J. Ferrandiz	Unkn.	30.00	229.00
Schmid		**Paddington Bear/Musician's Dream Plates**			
83-P-SC-24-001	The Beat Goes On	Unknown	10,000	17.50	22.50
83-P-SC-24-002	Knowing the Score	Unknown	10,000	17.50	20.00
83-P-SC-24-003	Perfect Harmony	Unknown	10,000	17.50	17.50
83-P-SC-24-004	Tickling The Ivory	Unknown	10,000	17.50	17.50
Schmid		**Raggedy Ann Christmas Plates**			
75-P-SC-25-001	Gifts of Love	Unknown	Unkn.	12.50	45.00
76-P-SC-25-002	Merry Blades	Unknown	Unkn.	13.00	37.50
77-P-SC-25-003	Christmas Morning	Unknown	Unkn.	13.00	22.50
78-P-SC-25-004	Checking the List	Unknown	Unkn.	15.00	20.00
79-P-SC-25-005	Little Helper	Unknown	Unkn.	17.50	19.50
Schmid		**A Year With Paddington Bear Plates**			
79-P-SC-26-001	Pyramid of Presents	Unknown	25,000	12.50	27.50
80-P-SC-26-002	Springtime	Unknown	25,000	12.50	25.00
81-P-SC-26-003	Sandcastles	Unknown	25,000	12.50	22.50
82-P-SC-26-004	School Days	Unknown	25,000	12.50	12.50
Schmid		**Peanuts Mother's Day Plates**			
72-P-SC-28-001	Linus	C. Schulz	Unkn.	10.00	55.00
73-P-SC-28-002	Mom?	C. Schulz	Unkn.	10.00	50.00
74-P-SC-28-003	Snoppy/Woodstock/Parade	C. Schulz	Unkn.	10.00	45.00
75-P-SC-28-004	A Kiss for Lucy	C. Schulz	Unkn.	12.50	40.00
76-P-SC-28-005	Linus and Snoopy	C. Schulz	Unkn.	13.00	35.00
77-P-SC-28-006	Dear Mom	C. Schulz	Unkn.	13.00	30.00
78-P-SC-28-007	Thoughts That Count	C. Schulz	Unkn.	15.00	25.00
79-P-SC-28-008	A Special Letter	C. Schulz	Unkn.	17.50	22.50
80-P-SC-28-009	A Tribute to Mom	C. Schulz	Unkn.	17.50	22.50
81-P-SC-28-010	Mission for Mom	C. Schulz	Unkn.	17.50	20.00
82-P-SC-28-011	Which Way to Mother	C. Schulz	Unkn.	18.50	18.50
Schmid		**Peanuts Valentine's Day Plates**			
77-P-SC-30-001	Home Is Where the Heart is	C. Schulz	Unkn.	13.00	32.50
78-P-SC-30-002	Heavenly Bliss	C. Schulz	Unkn.	13.00	30.00
79-P-SC-30-003	Love Match	C. Schulz	Unkn.	17.50	27.50
80-P-SC-30-004	From Snoppy, With Love	C. Schulz	Unkn.	17.50	25.00
81-P-SC-30-005	Hearts-A-Flutter	C. Schulz	Unkn.	17.50	20.00
82-P-SC-30-006	Love Patch	C. Schulz	Unkn.	17.50	17.50
Schmid		**Peanuts World's Greatest Athlete**			
82-P-SC-31-001	Go Deep	C. Schulz	10,000	17.50	25.00
82-P-SC-31-002	The Puck Stops Here	C. Schulz	10,000	17.50	22.50
82-P-SC-31-003	The Way You Play The Game	C. Schulz	10,000	17.50	20.00
82-P-SC-31-004	The Crowd Went Wild	C. Schulz	10,000	17.50	17.50
Schmid		**Peanuts Special Edition Plate**			
76-P-SC-33-002	Bi-Centennial	C. Schulz	Unkn.	13.00	30.00
Schmid		**Raggedy Ann Valentine's Day Plates**			
78-P-SC-34-001	As Time Goes By	Unknown	Unkn.	13.00	25.00
79-P-SC-34-002	Daisies Do Tell	Unknown	Unkn.	17.50	20.00
Schmid		**Raggedy Ann Annual Plates**			
80-P-SC-35-001	The Sunshine Wagon	Unknown	10,000	17.50	80.00
81-P-SC-35-002	The Raggedy Shuffle	Unknown	10,000	17.50	27.50
82-P-SC-35-003	Flying High	Unknown	10,000	18.50	18.50
83-P-SC-35-004	Winning Streak	Unknown	10,000	22.50	22.50
84-P-SC-35-005	Rocking Rodeo	Unknown	10,000	22.50	22.50
Schmid		**Raggedy Ann Bicentennial Plate**			
76-P-SC-37-001	Bicentennial Plate	Unknown	Unkn.	13.00	30.00
Schmid		**Walt Disney Special Edition Plates**			
78-P-SC-46-001	Mickey Mouse At Fifty	Disney Studio	15,000	25.00	45.00
80-P-SC-46-002	Happy Birthday Pinocchio	Disney Studio	7,500	17.50	25.00
81-P-SC-46-003	Alice in Wonderland	Disney Studio	7,500	17.50	17.50
82-P-SC-46-004	Happy Birthday Pluto	Disney Studio	7,500	17.50	17.50
82-P-SC-46-005	Goofy's Golden Jubilee	Disney Studio	7,500	18.50	18.50
Schmid		**Christmas**			
71-P-SC-56-001	St. Jakob in Groden	J. Malfertheiner	10,000	37.50	125.00
72-P-SC-56-002	Pipers at Alberobello	J. Malfertheiner	10,000	45.00	130.00
73-P-SC-56-003	Alpine Horn	J. Malfertheiner	10,000	45.00	400.00
74-P-SC-56-004	Young Man and Girl	J. Malfertheiner	10,000	50.00	100.00
75-P-SC-56-005	Christmas in Ireland	J. Malfertheiner	10,000	60.00	95.00
76-P-SC-56-006	Alpine Christmas	J. Malfertheiner	10,000	65.00	225.00
77-P-SC-56-007	Legend of Heligenblut	J. Malfertheiner	6,000	65.00	130.00
78-P-SC-56-008	Klockler Singers	J. Malfertheiner	6,000	80.00	185.00
79-P-SC-56-009	Moss Gatherers	Undis.	6,000	135.00	140.00
80-P-SC-56-010	Wintry Churchgoing	Undis.	6,000	165.00	175.00
81-P-SC-56-011	Santa Claus in Tyrol	Undis.	6,000	165.00	168.00
82-P-SC-56-012	The Star Singers	Undis.	6,000	165.00	170.00
83-P-SC-56-013	Unto Us a Child is Born	Undis.	6,000	165.00	165.00
84-P-SC-56-014	Yuletide in the Valley	Unknown	6,000	165.00	165.00
85-P-SC-56-015	Good Morning, Good Year	J. Malfertheiner	6,000	165.00	165.00
86-P-SC-56-016	A Groeden Christmas	J. Malfertheiner	6,000	80.00	80.00
87-P-SC-56-017	Down From the Alps	J. Malfertheiner	6,000	195.00	195.00
Schmid		**Ferrandiz Mother's Day Series**			
72-P-SC-57-001	Mother Sewing	J. Ferrandiz	2,500	35.00	200.00
73-P-SC-57-002	Alpine Mother & Child	J. Ferrandiz	1,500	40.00	150.00
74-P-SC-57-003	Mother Holding Child	J. Ferrandiz	1,500	50.00	150.00
75-P-SC-57-004	Dove Girl	J. Ferrandiz	1,500	60.00	150.00
76-P-SC-57-005	Mother Knitting	J. Ferrandiz	1,500	60.00	200.00
77-P-SC-57-006	Alpine Stroll	J. Ferrandiz	3,000	65.00	125.00
78-P-SC-57-007	The Beginning	J. Ferrandiz	3,000	75.00	150.00
79-P-SC-57-008	All Hearts	J. Ferrandiz	3,000	120.00	170.00
80-P-SC-57-009	Spring Arrivals	J. Ferrandiz	3,000	150.00	165.00
81-P-SC-57-010	Harmony	J. Ferrandiz	3,000	150.00	150.00
82-P-SC-57-011	With Love	J. Ferrandiz	3,000	150.00	150.00
Schmid		**Anri Mother's Day**			
72-P-SC-58-001	Alpine Mother & Children	Undis.	5,000	35.00	50.00
73-P-SC-58-002	Alpine Mother & Children	Undis.	5,000	40.00	55.00
74-P-SC-58-003	Alpine Mother & Children	Undis.	5,000	50.00	55.00
75-P-SC-58-004	Alpine Stroll	Undis.	5,000	60.00	65.00
76-P-SC-58-005	Knitting	Undis.	5,000	60.00	65.00
Schmid		**Anri Father's Day**			
72-P-SC-59-001	Alpine Father & Children	Undis.	5,000	35.00	100.00
73-P-SC-59-002	Alpine Father & Children	Undis.	5,000	40.00	95.00
74-P-SC-59-003	Cliff Gazing	Undis.	5,000	50.00	100.00
76-P-SC-59-004	Sailing	Undis.	5,000	60.00	90.00
Schmid		**Ferrandiz Wooden Wedding Plates**			
72-P-SC-60-001	Boy and Girl Embracing	J. Ferrandiz	Unkn.	40.00	150.00
73-P-SC-60-002	Wedding Scene	J. Ferrandiz	Unkn.	40.00	150.00
74-P-SC-60-003	Wedding	J. Ferrandiz	Unkn.	48.00	150.00
75-P-SC-60-004	Wedding	J. Ferrandiz	Unkn.	60.00	150.00
76-P-SC-60-005	Wedding	J. Ferrandiz	Unkn.	60.00	150.00
Seeley Ceramics		**Old French Doll Collection**			
79-P-SE-01-001	The Bru	M. Seeley	5,000	39.00	200.00
79-P-SE-01-002	The E.J.	M. Seeley	5,000	39.00	75.00
79-P-SE-01-003	The A.T.	M. Seeley	5,000	39.00	55.00
80-P-SE-01-004	Alexandre	M. Seeley	5,000	39.00	45.00
81-P-SE-01-005	The Schmitt	M. Seeley	5,000	39.00	43.00
81-P-SE-01-006	The Marque	M. Seeley	5,000	39.00	43.00
Spode		**Christmas**			
70-P-SH-01-001	Partridge	G. West	Undis.	35.00	35.00
71-P-SH-01-002	Angel's Singing	G. West	Undis.	35.00	35.00
72-P-SH-01-003	Three Ships A'Sailing	G. West	Undis.	35.00	35.00
73-P-SH-01-004	We Three Kings of Orient	G. West	Undis.	35.00	60.00
74-P-SH-01-005	Deck the Halls	G. West	Undis.	35.00	45.00
75-P-SH-01-006	Christbaum	G. West	Undis.	45.00	40.00
76-P-SH-01-007	Good King Wenceslas	G. West	Undis.	45.00	40.00
77-P-SH-01-008	Holly & Ivy	G. West	Undis.	45.00	40.00
78-P-SH-01-009	While Shepherds Watched	G. West	Undis.	45.00	45.00
79-P-SH-01-010	Away in a Manger	G. West	Undis.	50.00	45.00
80-P-SH-01-011	Bringing in the Boar's Head	P. Wood	Undis.	60.00	35.00
81-P-SH-01-012	Make We Merry	P. Wood	Undis.	65.00	55.00
Spode		**American Song Birds**			
72-P-SH-02-001	Set of Twelve	R. Harm	Undis.	350.00	765.00
U.S. Historical Society		**Young America**			
73-P-US-02-001	Young America of Winslow Homer	W. Homer	2,500	425.00	1100.00
U.S. Historical Society		**Annual Stained Glass & Pewter Christmas Plate**			
78-P-US-03-001	The Nativity- Canterbury Cathedral	Unknown	10,000	97.00	175.00
79-P-US-03-002	Flight Into Egypt- St. Johns, New York	Unknown	10,000	97.00	175.00
80-P-US-03-003	Madonna And Child- Washington Cathedral	Unknown	10,000	125.00	175.00
81-P-US-03-004	The Magi- St. Pauls San Francisco	Unknown	10,000	125.00	175.00
82-P-US-03-005	Flight Into Egypt- Los Angeles Cathedral	Unknown	10,000	135.00	175.00

Plates

Number	Name	Artist	Edition limit	Issue Price	Quote
Company		**Series**			
83-P-US-03-006	The Shepherds At Bethlehem- St. Johns,N. Orl	Unknown	10,000	135.00	150.00
84-P-US-03-007	The Nativity - St. Anthony's, St. Louis	Unknown	10,000	135.00	135.00
85-P-US-03-008	Good Tidings of Great Joy-Boston	Unknown	10,000	160.00	160.00
86-P-US-03-009	The Nativity from Old St. Mary's Church-Phila	Unknown	10,000	160.00	160.00
87-P-US-03-010	O Come, Little Children	Unknown	10,000	160.00	Unknown
U.S. Historical Society		**The Christmas Carol Plate**			
82-P-US-05-001	Deck the Halls with Boughs of Holly	J. Landis	10,000	55.00	65.00
83-P-US-05-002	O Christmas Tree	J. Woodson	10,000	55.00	65.00
84-P-US-05-003	Winter Wonderland	J. Woodson	10,000	55.00	55.00
85-P-US-05-004	Here We Come A Caroling	J. Woodson	10,000	55.00	55.00
86-P-US-05-005	The Christmas Song	J. Woodson	10,000	55.00	55.00
87-P-US-05-006	I Heard the Bells on Christmas Day	J. Landis	10,000	55.00	Unknown
U.S. Historical Society		**Great American Sailing Ships**			
83-P-US-08-001	U.S.S. Constitution (Old Ironsides)	J. Woodson	10,000	135.00	150.00
84-P-US-08-002	Charles W. Morgan	J. Woodson	10,000	135.00	135.00
85-P-US-08-003	Flying Cloud	J. Woodson	10,000	135.00	135.00
U.S. Historical Society		**Annual Spring Flowers**			
83-P-US-09-001	Flowers in a Blue Vase	J. Clark	10,000	135.00	150.00
84-P-US-09-002	Spring Flowers	M. Wampler	10,000	135.00	135.00
Vague Shadows		**The Chieftains**			
79-P-VC-01-001	Chief Sitting Bull	G. Perillo	7,500	65.00	550.00
79-P-VC-01-002	Chief Joseph	G. Perillo	7,500	65.00	100.00
80-P-VC-01-003	Chief Red Cloud	G. Perillo	7,500	65.00	140.00
80-P-VC-01-004	Chief Geronimo	G. Perillo	7,500	65.00	90.00
81-P-VC-01-005	Chief Crazy Horse	G. Perillo	7,500	65.00	150.00
Vague Shadows		**The Plainsmen**			
78-P-VC-02-001	Buffalo Hunt	G. Perillo	2,500	300.00	350.00
79-P-VC-02-002	The Proud One	G. Perillo	2,500	300.00	350.00
Vague Shadows		**The Professionals**			
79-P-VC-03-001	The Big Leaguer	G. Perillo	15,000	29.95	135.00
80-P-VC-03-002	Ballerina's Dilemna	G. Perillo	15,000	32.50	60.00
81-P-VC-03-003	Quarterback	G. Perillo	15,000	32.50	35.00
81-P-VC-03-004	Rodeo Joe	G. Perillo	15,000	35.00	35.00
82-P-VC-03-005	Major Leaguer	G. Perillo	15,000	35.00	45.00
83-P-VC-03-006	The Hockey Player	G. Perillo	15,000	35.00	35.00
Vague Shadows		**Pride of America's Indians**			
86-P-VC-04-001	Brave and Free	G. Perillo	10-day	24.50	24.50
86-P-VC-04-002	Dark-Eyes Friends	G. Perillo	10-day	24.50	24.50
86-P-VC-04-003	Noble Companions	G. Perillo	10-day	24.50	24.50
87-P-VC-04-004	Kindred Spirits	G. Perillo	10-day	24.50	24.50
87-P-VC-04-005	Loyal Alliance	G. Perillo	10-day	24.50	24.50
87-P-VC-04-006	Small and Wise	G. Perillo	10-day	24.50	24.50
87-P-VC-04-007	Winter Scouts	G. Perillo	10-day	24.50	24.50
87-P-VC-04-008	Peaceful Comrades	G. Perillo	10-day	24.50	24.50
Vague Shadows		**Legends of the West**			
82-P-VC-05-001	Daniel Boone	G. Perillo	10,000	65.00	65.00
83-P-VC-05-002	Davy Crockett	G. Perillo	10,000	65.00	65.00
83-P-VC-05-003	Kit Carson	G. Perillo	10,000	65.00	65.00
83-P-VC-05-004	Buffalo Bill	G. Perillo	10,000	65.00	65.00
Vague Shadows		**Chieftains 2**			
83-P-VC-06-001	Chief Pontiac	G. Perillo	7,500	70.00	70.00
83-P-VC-06-002	Chief Victorio	G. Perillo	7,500	70.00	70.00
84-P-VC-06-003	Chief Tecumseh	G. Perillo	7,500	70.00	70.00
84-P-VC-06-004	Chief Cochise	G. Perillo	7,500	70.00	70.00
84-P-VC-06-005	Chief Black Kettle	G. Perillo	7,500	70.00	70.00
Vague Shadows		**Child Life**			
83-P-VC-07-001	Siesta	G. Perillo	10,000	45.00	45.00
84-P-VC-07-001	Sweet Dreams	G. Perillo	10,000	45.00	45.00
Vague Shadows		**Indian Nations**			
83-P-VC-08-001	Blackfoot	G. Perillo	7,500	35.00	50.00
83-P-VC-08-002	Cheyenne	G. Perillo	7,500	35.00	50.00
83-P-VC-08-003	Apache	G. Perillo	7,500	35.00	50.00
83-P-VC-08-004	Sioux	G. Perillo	7,500	35.00	50.00
Vague Shadows		**The Storybook Collection**			
80-P-VC-09-001	Little Red Ridinghood	G. Perillo	18 day	45.00	45.00
81-P-VC-09-002	Cinderella	G. Perillo	18 day	45.00	45.00
81-P-VC-09-003	Hansel & Gretel	G. Perillo	18 day	45.00	45.00
82-P-VC-09-004	Goldilocks & 3 Bears	G. Perillo	18 day	45.00	45.00
Vague Shadows		**Perillo Santa's**			
80-P-VC-10-001	Santa's Joy	G. Perillo	Unkn.	29.95	29.95
81-P-VC-10-002	Santa's Bundle	G. Perillo	Unkn.	29.95	29.95
Vague Shadows		**The Princesses**			
82-P-VC-11-001	Lily of the Mohawks	G. Perillo	7,500	50.00	100.00
82-P-VC-11-002	Pocahontas	G. Perillo	7,500	50.00	80.00
82-P-VC-11-003	Minnehaha	G. Perillo	7,500	50.00	75.00
82-P-VC-11-004	Sacajawea	G. Perillo	7,500	50.00	75.00
Vague Shadows		**Nature's Harmony**			
82-P-VC-12-001	The Peaceable Kingdom	G. Perillo	12,500	100.00	100.00
82-P-VC-12-002	Zebra	G. Perillo	12,500	50.00	50.00
82-P-VC-12-003	Bengal Tiger	G. Perillo	12,500	50.00	50.00
83-P-VC-12-004	Black Panther	G. Perillo	12,500	50.00	50.00
83-P-VC-12-005	Elephant	G. Perillo	12,500	50.00	50.00
Vague Shadows		**Arctic Friends**			
82-P-VC-13-001	Siberian Love	G. Perillo	7,500	100.00	180.00
82-P-VC-13-002	Snow Pals	G. Perillo	7,500	Pair	Pair
Vague Shadows		**The Plainsmen Series**			
81-P-VC-14-001	Buffalo Hunt (bronze)	G. Perillo	2,500	300.00	300.00
81-P-VC-14-002	The Proud One (bronze)	G. Perillo	2,500	350.00	475.00
Vague Shadows		**Motherhood Series**			
83-P-VC-15-001	Madre	G. Perillo	10,000	50.00	100.00
84-P-VC-15-002	Madonna of the Plains	G. Perillo	3,500	50.00	75.00
85-P-VC-15-003	Abuela	G. Perillo	3,500	50.00	50.00
86-P-VC-15-004	Nap Time	G. Perillo	3,500	50.00	50.00
Vague Shadows		**The War Ponies**			
83-P-VC-16-001	Sioux War Pony	G. Perillo	7,500	60.00	120.00
83-P-VC-16-002	Nez Perce War Pony	G. Perillo	7,500	60.00	100.00
83-P-VC-16-003	Apache War Pony	G. Perillo	7,500	60.00	100.00
Vague Shadows		**The Tribal Ponies**			
84-P-VC-17-001	Arapaho Tribal Pony	G. Perillo	3,500	65.00	65.00
84-P-VC-17-002	Comanche Tribal Pony	G. Perillo	3,500	65.00	65.00
84-P-VC-17-003	Crow Tribal Pony	G. Perillo	3,500	65.00	90.00
Vague Shadows		**The Thoroughbreds**			
84-P-VC-18-001	Whirlaway	G. Perillo	9,500	50.00	90.00
84-P-VC-18-002	Secretariat	G. Perillo	9,500	50.00	80.00
84-P-VC-18-003	Man o' War	G. Perillo	9,500	50.00	50.00
84-P-VC-18-004	Seabiscuit	G. Perillo	9,500	50.00	50.00
Vague Shadows		**Special Issue**			
81-P-VC-19-001	Apache Boy	G. Perillo	5,000	95.00	175.00
Vague Shadows		**Special Issue**			
84-P-VC-20-001	The Lovers	G. Perillo	Unkn.	50.00	50.00
Vague Shadows		**Special Issue**			
84-P-VC-21-001	Navajo Girl	G. Perillo	3,500	95.00	150.00
Vague Shadows		**Special Issue**			
86-P-VC-22-001	Navajo Boy	G. Perillo	3,500	95.00	95.00
Vague Shadows		**The Arabians**			
86-P-VC-23-001	Silver Streak	G. Perillo	3,500	95.00	95.00
Vague Shadows		**The Colts**			
85-P-VC-24-001	Appaloosa	G. Perillo	5,000	40.00	40.00
85-P-VC-24-002	Pinto	G. Perillo	5,000	40.00	40.00
85-P-VC-24-003	Arabian	G. Perillo	5,000	40.00	40.00
85-P-VC-24-004	The Thoroughbred	G. Perillo	5,000	40.00	40.00
Vague Shadows		**Tender Moments**			
85-P-VC-25-001	Sunset	G. Perillo	2,000	150.00	150.00
85-P-VC-25-002	Winter Romance	G. Perillo	2,000	Pair	Pair
Vague Shadows		**Young Emotions**			
86-P-VC-26-001	Tears	G. Perillo	5,000	75.00	75.00
86-P-VC-26-002	Smiles	G. Perillo	5,000	Pair	Pair
Vague Shadows		**Special Issue**			
83-P-VC-27-001	Papoose	G. Perillo	3,000	100.00	100.00
Vague Shadows		**The Maidens**			
85-P-VC-28-001	Shimmering Waters	G. Perillo	5,000	60.00	60.00
85-P-VC-28-002	Snow Blanket	G. Perillo	5,000	60.00	60.00
85-P-VC-28-003	Song Bird	G. Perillo	5,000	60.00	60.00
Vague Shadows		**The Young Chieftains**			
85-P-VC-29-001	Young Sitting Bull	G. Perillo	5,000	50.00	50.00
85-P-VC-29-002	Young Joseph	G. Perillo	5,000	50.00	50.00
86-P-VC-29-003	Young Red Cloud	G. Perillo	5,000	50.00	50.00
86-P-VC-29-004	Young Geronimo	G. Perillo	5,000	50.00	50.00
86-P-VC-29-005	Young Crazy Horse	G. Perillo	5,000	50.00	50.00
Vague Shadows		**Perillo Christmas**			
87-P-VC-30-001	Christmas Star	G. Perillo	Yr.Iss	35.00	35.00
Veneto Flair		**Bellini**			
71-P-VE-01-001	Madonna	V. Tiziano	500	45.00	425.00
Veneto Flair		**Christmas**			
71-P-VE-02-001	Three Kings	V. Tiziano	1,500	55.00	160.00
72-P-VE-02-002	Shepherds	V. Tiziano	2,000	55.00	90.00
73-P-VE-02-003	Christ Child	V. Tiziano	2,000	55.00	55.00
74-P-VE-02-004	Angel	V. Tiziano	Pair	55.00	55.00
Veneto Flair		**Wildlife**			
71-P-VE-04-001	Deer	V. Tiziano	500	37.50	450.00
72-P-VE-04-002	Elephant	V. Tiziano	1,000	37.50	275.00
73-P-VE-04-003	Puma	V. Tiziano	2,000	37.50	65.00
74-P-VE-04-004	Tiger	V. Tiziano	2,000	40.00	50.00
Veneto Flair		**Dogs**			
72-P-VE-05-001	German Shepherd	V. Tiziano	2,000	37.50	75.00
73-P-VE-05-002	Poodle	V. Tiziano	2,000	37.50	45.00
73-P-VE-05-003	Doberman	V. Tiziano	2,000	37.50	35.00
73-P-VE-05-004	Collie	V. Tiziano	2,000	40.00	45.00
73-P-VE-05-005	Dachshund	V. Tiziano	2,000	45.00	43.00
Veneto Flair		**Birds**			
72-P-VE-06-001	Owl	Unknown	2,000	37.50	100.00
72-P-VE-06-002	Falcon	Unknown	2,000	37.50	37.50
73-P-VE-06-003	Mallard	Unknown	2,000	45.00	45.00
Veneto Flair		**Easter**			
73-P-VE-07-001	Rabbits	Unknown	2,000	50.00	90.00
74-P-VE-07-002	Chicks	Unknown	2,000	50.00	55.00
75-P-VE-07-003	Lamb	Unknown	2,000	50.00	55.00
76-P-VE-07-004	Composite	Unknown	2,000	55.00	55.00
Veneto Flair		**St. Mark's of Venice**			
84-P-VE-08-001	Noah and the Dove	Unknown	Undis.	60.00	60.00
Viletta		**Disneyland**			
76-P-VI-01-001	Signing The Declaration	Unknown	3,000	15.00	100.00
76-P-VI-01-002	Crossing The Delaware	Unknown	3,000	15.00	100.00
76-P-VI-01-003	Betsy Ross	Unknown	3,000	15.00	100.00
76-P-VI-01-004	Spirit of '76	Unknown	3,000	15.00	100.00
79-P-VI-01-005	Mickey's 50th Anniversary	Unknown	5,000	37.00	50.00
Viletta		**Zolan's Children**			
78-P-VI-02-001	Erik and the Dandelion	D. Zolan	Undis.	19.00	240.00
79-P-VI-02-002	Sabrina in the Grass	D. Zolan	Undis.	22.00	180.00
80-P-VI-02-003	By Myself	D. Zolan	Undis.	24.00	38.00
81-P-VI-02-004	For You	D. Zolan	Undis.	24.00	27.00
Villeroy & Boch		**Russian Fairytales Snow Maiden**			
81-P-VL-01-001	The Snow Maiden	B. Zvorykin	27,500	70.00	190.00
81-P-VL-01-002	Snegurochka at the Court of Tsar Berendei	B. Zvorykin	27,500	70.00	125.00
81-P-VL-01-003	Snegurochka and Lei, the Shepherd Boy	B. Zvorykin	27,500	70.00	125.00
Villeroy & Boch		**Russian Fairytales The Red Knight**			
81-P-VL-02-001	Vassilissa the Fair	B. Zvorykin	27,500	70.00	125.00
81-P-VL-02-002	Vassilissa and her Stepsisters	B. Zvorykin	27,500	70.00	85.00
81-P-VL-02-003	Vassilissa is Presented to the Tsar	B. Zvorykin	27,500	70.00	85.00
Villeroy & Boch		**Russian Fairytales The Firebird**			
81-P-VL-03-001	In Search of the Firebird	B. Zvorykin	27,500	70.00	70.00
81-P-VL-03-002	Ivan and Tsarevna on the Grey Wolf	B. Zvorykin	27,500	70.00	70.00
81-P-VL-03-003	The Wedding of Tsarevna Elena the Fair	B. Zvorykin	27,500	70.00	70.00
Villeroy & Boch		**Russian Fairytales Maria Morevna**			
82-P-VL-04-001	Maria Morevna and Tsarevich Ivan	B. Zvorykin	27,500	70.00	70.00
82-P-VL-04-002	Koshchey Carries Off Maria Morevna	B. Zvorykin	27,500	70.00	70.00
82-P-VL-04-003	Tsarevich Ivan and the Beautiful Castle	B. Zvorykin	27,500	70.00	70.00
Villeroy & Boch		**Flower Fairy**			
79-P-VL-05-001	Lavender	C. Barker	21-day	35.00	48.00
80-P-VL-05-002	Sweet Pea	C. Barker	21-day	35.00	35.00
80-P-VL-05-003	Candytuft	C. Barker	21-day	35.00	35.00
81-P-VL-05-004	Heliotrope	C. Barker	21-day	35.00	35.00
81-P-VL-05-005	Blackthorn	C. Barker	21-day	35.00	35.00
81-P-VL-05-006	Appleblossom	C. Barker	21-day	35.00	35.00
Villeroy & Boch		**Flower Fairy II**			
85-P-VL-06-001	Columbine	C. Barker	21-day	39.00	39.00
85-P-VL-06-002	Cornflower	C. Barker	21-day	39.00	39.00
85-P-VL-06-003	Mallow	C. Barker	21-day	39.00	39.00

Company		Series			
Number	**Name**	**Artist**	**Edition limit**	**Issue Price**	**Quote**
85-P-VL-06-004	Black Medick	C. Barker	21-day	39.00	39.00
85-P-VL-06-005	Canterbury Bell	C. Barker	21-day	39.00	39.00
85-P-VL-06-006	Fuchsia	C. Barker	21-day	39.00	39.00
Val St. Lambert		**Annual Old Masters**			
70-P-VS-01-003	Da Vinci and Michelangelo, pair	Unknown	5,000	50.00	90.00
71-P-VS-01-004	El Greco and Goya, pair	Unknown	5,000	50.00	85.00
72-P-VS-01-005	Reynolds, Gainsborough, pair	Unknown	5,000	50.00	70.00
Val St. Lambert		**American Heritage**			
69-P-VS-02-001	Pilgrim Fathers	Unknown	500	200.00	450.00
70-P-VS-02-002	Paul Revere's Ride	Unknown	500	200.00	225.00
71-P-VS-02-003	Washington on Delaware	Unknown	500	200.00	225.00
Wedgwood		**Christmas**			
69-P-WE-01-001	Windsor Castle	T. Harper	Annual	25.00	225.00
70-P-WE-01-002	Trafalgar Square	T. Harper	Annual	30.00	30.00
71-P-WE-01-003	Picadilly Circus	T. Harper	Annual	30.00	40.00
72-P-WE-01-004	St. Paul's Cathedral	T. Harper	Annual	35.00	40.00
73-P-WE-01-005	Tower of London	T. Harper	Annual	40.00	42.00
74-P-WE-01-006	Houses of Parliament	T. Harper	Annual	40.00	40.00
75-P-WE-01-007	Tower Bridge	T. Harper	Annual	45.00	45.00
76-P-WE-01-008	Hampton Court	T. Harper	Annual	50.00	50.00
77-P-WE-01-009	Westminister Abbey	T. Harper	Annual	55.00	55.00
78-P-WE-01-010	Horse Guards	T. Harper	Annual	60.00	60.00
79-P-WE-01-011	Buckingham Palace	Unknown	Annual	65.00	65.00
80-P-WE-01-012	St. James Palace	Unknown	Annual	70.00	70.00
81-P-WE-01-013	Marble Arch	Unknown	Annual	75.00	75.00
82-P-WE-01-014	Lambeth Palace	Unknown	Annual	80.00	80.00
83-P-WE-01-015	All Souls, Langham Palace	Unknown	Annual	80.00	80.00
84-P-WE-01-016	Constitution Hill	Unknown	Annual	80.00	80.00
85-P-WE-01-017	The Tate Gallery	Unknown	Annual	80.00	80.00
86-P-WE-01-018	The Albert Memorial	Unknown	Annual	80.00	80.00
87-P-WE-01-019	Guildhall	Unknown	Annual	80.00	80.00
Wedgwood		**Mother's Day**			
71-P-WE-02-001	Sportive Love	Unknown	Unkn.	20.00	20.00
72-P-WE-02-002	The Sewing Lesson	Unknown	Unkn.	20.00	20.00
73-P-WE-02-003	The Baptism of Achilles	Unknown	Unkn.	20.00	25.00
74-P-WE-02-004	Domestic Employment	Unknown	Unkn.	30.00	33.00
75-P-WE-02-005	Mother and Child	Unknown	Unkn.	35.00	37.00
76-P-WE-02-006	The Spinner	Unknown	Unkn.	35.00	35.00
77-P-WE-02-007	Leisure Time	Unknown	Unkn.	35.00	35.00
78-P-WE-02-008	Swan and Cygnets	Unknown	Unkn.	40.00	40.00
79-P-WE-02-009	Deer and Fawn	Unknown	Unkn.	45.00	45.00
80-P-WE-02-010	Birds	Unknown	Unkn.	47.50	47.50
81-P-WE-02-012	Mare and Foal	Unknown	Unkn.	50.00	50.00
82-P-WE-02-013	Cherubs with Swing	Unknown	Unkn.	55.00	55.00
83-P-WE-02-014	Cupid and Butterfly	Unknown	Unkn.	55.00	55.00
84-P-WE-02-015	Musical Cupids	Unknown	Unkn.	55.00	55.00
85-P-WE-02-016	Cupids and Doves	Unknown	Annual	55.00	55.00
86-P-WE-02-017	Cupids Fishing	Unknown	Annual	55.00	55.00
87-P-WE-02-018	Anemones	Unknown	Annual	55.00	55.00
88-P-WE-02-019	Tiger Lilly	Unknown	Annual	55.00	55.00
Wedgwood		**Bicentennial**			
72-P-WE-03-001	Boston Tea Party	Unknown	Unkn.	30.00	30.00
73-P-WE-03-002	Paul Revere's Ride	Unknown	Unkn.	35.00	100.00
74-P-WE-03-003	Battle of Concord	Unknown	Unkn.	40.00	40.00
75-P-WE-03-004	Across the Delaware	Unknown	Unkn.	45.00	45.00
75-P-WE-03-005	Victory at Yorktown	Unknown	Unkn.	45.00	45.00
76-P-WE-03-006	Declaration Signed	Unknown	Unkn.	45.00	45.00
Wedgwood		**Blossoming of Suzanne**			
77-P-WE-04-001	Innocence	M. Vickers	17,000	60.00	60.00
78-P-WE-04-002	Cherish	M. Vickers	17,000	60.00	60.00
79-P-WE-04-003	Daydream	M. Vickers	24,000	65.00	65.00
80-P-WE-04-004	Wistful	M. Vickers	24,000	70.00	70.00
Wedgwood		**Vickers 'My Memories'**			
81-P-WE-05-001	Be My Friend	M. Vickers	Unkn.	27.00	27.00
82-P-WE-05-002	Playtime	M. Vickers	Unkn.	27.00	27.00
83-P-WE-05-003	Our Garden	M. Vickers	Unkn.	27.00	50.00
84-P-WE-05-004	The Recital	M. Vickers	Unkn.	27.00	48.00
85-P-WE-05-005	Mother's Treasures	M. Vickers	Unkn.	27.00	35.00
85-P-WE-05-006	Riding High	M. Vickers	Unkn.	29.00	29.00
Wedgwood		**Eyes of the Child**			
XX-P-WE-06-004	Little Lady Love	Fromme-Douglas	15,000	65.00	65.00
XX-P-WE-06-005	My Best Friend	Fromme-Douglas	15,000	65.00	65.00
XX-P-WE-06-006	I Wish Upon a Star	Fromme-Douglas	15,000	65.00	65.00
XX-P-WE-06-007	In a Child's Thought	Fromme-Douglas	15,000	65.00	65.00
XX-P-WE-06-008	Puppy Love	Fromme-Douglas	15,000	65.00	65.00
Wedgwood		**Calendar Plates**			
71-P-WE-07-001	Victorian Almanac	Unknown	Annual	12.00	12.00
71-P-WE-07-001	Victorian Almanac	Unknown	Annual	12.00	12.00
72-P-WE-07-002	The Carousel	Unknown	Annual	12.95	12.95
73-P-WE-07-003	Bountiful Butterfly	Unknown	Annual	12.95	12.95
74-P-WE-07-004	Camelot	Unknown	Annual	14.00	75.00
75-P-WE-07-005	Children's Games	Unknown	Annual	15.00	15.00
76-P-WE-07-006	Robin	Unknown	Annual	25.00	25.00
77-P-WE-07-007	Tonatiuh	Unknown	Annual	30.00	30.00
78-P-WE-07-008	Samurai	Unknown	Annual	30.00	30.00
79-P-WE-07-009	Sacred Scarab	Unknown	Annual	35.00	35.00
80-P-WE-07-010	Safari	Unknown	Annual	42.50	42.50
81-P-WE-07-011	Horses	Unknown	Annual	47.50	47.50
82-P-WE-07-012	Wild West	Unknown	Annual	52.00	52.00
83-P-WE-07-013	The Age of the Reptiles	Unknown	Annual	54.00	54.00
84-P-WE-07-014	Dogs	Unknown	Annual	54.00	54.00
85-P-WE-07-015	Cats	Unknown	Annual	54.00	54.00
86-P-WE-07-016	British Birds	Unknown	Annual	54.00	54.00
87-P-WE-07-017	Water Birds	Unknown	Annual	54.00	54.00
88-P-WE-07-018	Sea Birds	Unknown	Annual	54.00	54.00
Wedgwood		**Child's Christmas**			
79-P-WE-08-001	Children and Snowman	Unknown	Annual	35.00	35.00
80-P-WE-08-002	Collecting the Christmas Tree	Unknown	Annual	37.50	37.50
81-P-WE-08-003	Children Sledding	Unknown	Annual	40.00	40.00
82-P-WE-08-004	Skaters	Unknown	Annual	40.00	40.00
83-P-WE-08-005	Carol Singing	Unknown	Annual	40.00	40.00
84-P-WE-08-006	Mixing the Christmas Pudding	Unknown	Annual	40.00	40.00
Wedgwood		**Children's Story**			
71-P-WE-09-001	The Sandman	Unknown	Annual	7.95	23.00
72-P-WE-09-002	The Tinder Box	Unknown	Annual	7.95	9.00
73-P-WE-09-003	The Emperor's New Clothes	Unknown	Annual	9.00	9.00
74-P-WE-09-004	The Ugly Duckling	Unknown	Annual	10.00	10.00
75-P-WE-09-005	The Little Mermaid	Unknown	Annual	11.00	12.00

Company		Series			
Number	**Name**	**Artist**	**Edition limit**	**Issue Price**	**Quote**
76-P-WE-09-006	Hansel and Gretel	Unknown	Annual	12.00	12.00
77-P-WE-09-007	Rumpelstiltskin	Unknown	Annual	15.00	15.00
78-P-WE-09-008	The Frog Prince	Unknown	Annual	15.00	24.00
79-P-WE-09-009	The Golden Goose	Unknown	Annual	15.00	15.00
80-P-WE-09-010	Rapunzel	Unknown	Annual	16.00	16.00
81-P-WE-09-011	Tom Thumb	Unknown	Annual	18.00	18.00
82-P-WE-09-012	The Lady and the Lion	Unknown	Annual	20.00	20.00
83-P-WE-09-013	The Elves and the Shoemaker	Unknown	Annual	20.00	20.00
84-P-WE-09-014	King Roughbeard	Unknown	Annual	20.00	20.00
85-P-WE-09-015	The Brave Little Tailor	Unknown	Annual	20.00	20.00
Wedgwood		**Queen's Christmas**			
80-P-WE-10-001	Windsor Castle	A. Price	Annual	24.95	24.95
81-P-WE-10-002	Trafalgar Square	A. Price	Annual	24.95	24.95
82-P-WE-10-003	Piccadilly Circus	A. Price	Annual	32.50	32.50
83-P-WE-10-004	St. Paul's	A. Price	Annual	32.50	32.50
84-P-WE-10-005	Tower of London	A. Price	Annual	35.00	35.00
85-P-WE-10-006	Palace of Westminster	A. Price	Annual	35.00	35.00
86-P-WE-10-007	Tower Bridge	A. Price	Annual	35.00	35.00
Wedgwood		**Child's Birthday Plate Series**			
81-P-WE-11-001	Peter Rabbit	B. Potter	Annual	24.00	24.00
82-P-WE-11-002	Mrs. Tiggy-winkle	B. Potter	Annual	27.00	27.00
83-P-WE-11-003	Peter Rabbit & Benjamin Bunny	B. Potter	Annual	29.00	29.00
84-P-WE-11-004	Peter Rabbit	B. Potter	Annual	29.00	29.00
85-P-WE-11-005	Peter Rabbit	B. Potter	Annual	29.00	29.00
86-P-WE-11-006	Peter Rabbit	B. Potter	Annual	29.00	29.00
87-P-WE-11-007	Oakapple Wood	J. Partridge	Annual	29.00	29.00
88-P-WE-11-008	Oakapple Wood	J. Partridge	Annual	29.00	29.00
Wedgwood		**Peter Rabbit Christmas**			
81-P-WE-12-001	Peter Rabbit	B. Potter	Annual	27.00	27.00
82-P-WE-12-002	Peter Rabbit	B. Potter	Annual	27.00	27.00
83-P-WE-12-003	Peter Rabbit	B. Potter	Annual	29.00	29.00
84-P-WE-12-004	Peter Rabbit	B. Potter	Annual	29.00	29.00
85-P-WE-12-005	Peter Rabbit	B. Potter	Annual	29.00	29.00
86-P-WE-12-006	Peter Rabbit	B. Potter	Annual	29.00	29.00
87-P-WE-12-007	Peter Rabbit	B. Potter	Annual	29.00	29.00
Wedgwood		**Bicentennial**			
72-P-WE-13-001	Boston Tea Party	Unknown	Annual	40.00	40.00
73-P-WE-13-002	Paul Revere's Ride	Unknown	Annual	40.00	115.00
74-P-WE-13-003	Battle of Concord	Unknown	Annual	40.00	55.00
75-P-WE-13-004	Across the Delaware	Unknown	Annual	40.00	105.00
75-P-WE-13-005	Victory at Yorktown	Unknown	Annual	45.00	53.00
76-P-WE-13-006	Declaration Signed	Unknown	Annual	45.00	45.00
Wedgwood		**Cathedrals Christmas Plate**			
86-P-WE-14-001	Canterbury Cathedral	Unknown	Annual	40.00	40.00
Wedgwood		**Portraits of First Love**			
86-P-WE-15-001	The Love Letter	M. Vickers	Undis.	27.00	27.00
Wedgwood		**Street Sellers of London**			
86-P-WE-16-001	The Baked Potato Man	J. Finnie	Undis.	25.00	25.00
Wedgwood		**The Legend of King Arthur**			
86-P-WE-17-001	Arthur Draws the Sword	R. Hook	Undis.	39.00	39.00
Wedgwood		**Christmas Traditions**			
87-P-WE-18-001	Dressing the Tree	Unknown	Annual	35.00	35.00
Wedgwood		**Valentine Plate**			
88-P-WE-19-001	The First Meeting	Unknown	Annual	55.00	55.00
Wedgewood		**Statue of Liberty**			
86-P-WF-20-001	In Celebration of Liberty	Unknown	Yr.Iss.	45.00	45.00
Wildlife Internationale		**Sporting Dog Series**			
85-P-WF-01-001	Decoy (Labrador Retriever)	J. Ruthven	5,000	55.00	110.00
85-P-WF-01-002	Rummy (English Setter)	J. Ruthven	5,000	55.00	55.00
85-P-WF-01-003	Dusty (Golden Retriever)	J. Ruthven	5,000	55.00	80.00
85-P-WF-01-004	Scarlett (Irish Setter)	J. Ruthven	5,000	55.00	110.00
Wildlife Internationale		**Owl Family Series**			
83-P-WF-02-001	Saw-Whet Owl Family	J. Ruthven	5,000	55.00	55.00
83-P-WF-02-002	Great Horned Owl Family	J. Ruthven	5,000	55.00	55.00
83-P-WF-02-003	Snowy Owl Family	J. Ruthven	5,000	55.00	55.00
83-P-WF-02-004	Barred Owl Family	J. Ruthven	5,000	55.00	55.00

Steins

Cornell Importers, Inc.		**Oldies-Old Blue**			
80-S-CL-01-001	Beer Here	Unknown	5,000	Unknown	45.00
80-S-CL-01-002	Bicycle	Unknown	5,000	Unknown	45.00
80-S-CL-01-003	Railroad	Unknown	5,000	Unknown	45.00
80-S-CL-01-004	Thewalt Commemorative	Unknown	5,000	Unknown	45.00
80-S-CL-01-005	Physician	Unknown	5,000	Unknown	49.00
80-S-CL-01-006	Pharmacist/Alchemist	Unknown	5,000	Unknown	49.00
83-S-CL-01-007	Gymnast	Unknown	5,000	Unknown	45.00
84-S-CL-01-008	Meteor	Unknown	5,000	Unknown	49.00
84-S-CL-01-009	Zeppelin	Unknown	5,000	Unknown	45.00
86-S-CL-01-010	Prosit	Unknown	10,000	Unknown	50.00
Cornell Importers, Inc.		**Oldies-Blue Multicolor**			
80-S-CL-02-001	Beer Here	Unknown	5,000	Unknown	65.00
80-S-CL-02-002	Bicycle	Unknown	5,000	Unknown	65.00
80-S-CL-02-003	Railroad 3	Unknown	5,000	Unknown	65.00
80-S-CL-02-004	Commemorative	Unknown	5,000	Unknown	65.00
80-S-CL-02-005	Physician	Unknown	5,000	Unknown	69.00
80-S-CL-02-006	Pharmacist/Alchemist	Unknown	5,000	Unknown	69.00
83-S-CL-02-007	Gymnast	Unknown	5,000	Unknown	65.00
84-S-CL-02-008	Meteor	Unknown	5,000	Unknown	69.00
84-S-CL-02-009	Zeppelin	Unknown	5,000	Unknown	65.00
86-S-CL-02-010	Prosit	Unknown	10,000	Unknown	65.00
Cornell Importers, Inc.		**Oldies-Rustica**			
80-S-CL-03-001	Beer Here	Unknown	5,000	Unknown	100.00
80-S-CL-03-002	Bicycle	Unknown	5,000	Unknown	100.00
80-S-CL-03-003	Railroad	Unknown	5,000	Unknown	100.00
80-S-CL-03-004	Commemorative	Unknown	5,000	Unknown	100.00
80-S-CL-03-005	Physician	Unknown	5,000	Unknown	110.00
80-S-CL-03-006	Pharmacist/Alchemist	Unknown	5,000	Unknown	110.00
83-S-CL-03-007	Gymnast	Unknown	5,000	Unknown	100.00
84-S-CL-03-008	Meteor	Unknown	5,000	Unknown	110.00
84-S-CL-03-009	Zeppelin	Unknown	5,000	Unknown	100.00
86-S-CL-03-010	Prosit	Unknown	10,000	Unknown	100.00
Cornell Importers, Inc.		**Authentic Reproductions**			
78-S-CL-04-001	Jausting tankard	Unknown	5,000	Unknown	300.00
78-S-CL-04-002	14.5 cm. Siegburg Wine Jug	Unknown	5,000	Unknown	45.00
78-S-CL-04-003	18 cm. Siegburg Wine Jug	Unknown	5,000	Unknown	60.00
78-S-CL-04-004	30 cm. Siegburg Wine Jug	Unknown	5,000	Unknown	80.00
78-S-CL-04-005	Fox Jug	Unknown	5,000	Unknown	100.00

Steins

Company / Number	Name	Series / Artist	Edition limit	Issue Price	Quote
78-S-CL-04-006	Rhine Pint	Unknown	5,000	Unknown	55.00
83-S-CL-04-007	Herring Stein	Unknown	5,000	Unknown	150.00
Cornell Importers, Inc.		**Commemoratives**			
83-S-CL-05-001	Harley Davidson	C. Cardinales	5,000	Unknown	120.00
Cornell Importers, Inc.		**Commemoratives**			
82-S-CL-06-001	Coors	Unknown	50	Unknown	3500.00
Cornell Importers, Inc.		**Commemorative**			
84-S-CL-07-001	1984 Summer Olympics	C. Calsbeek	25,000	70.00	70.00
Cornell Importers, Inc.		**Annual Steins**			
74-S-CL-08-001	Annual Stein	Unknown	1,725	Unknown	Unknown
75-S-CL-08-002	Annual Stein	Unknown	1,725	Unknown	Unknown
76-S-CL-08-003	Annual Stein	Unknown	1,725	Unknown	Unknown
77-S-CL-08-004	Annual Stein	Unknown	1,725	Unknown	Unknown
78-S-CL-08-005	Annual Stein	Unknown	1,725	Unknown	Unknown
79-S-CL-08-006	Annual Stein	Unknown	1,725	Unknown	Unknown
80-S-CL-08-007	Annual Stein	Unknown	1,725	Unknown	Unknown
81-S-CL-08-008	Annual Stein	Unknown	1,725	Unknown	115.00
82-S-CL-08-009	Annual Stein	Unknown	1,725	Unknown	115.00
83-S-CL-08-010	Annual Stein	Unknown	1,725	Unknown	115.00
84-S-CL-08-011	Annual Stein	Unknown	1,725	Unknown	115.00
84-S-CL-08-012	Annual Stein	Unknown	1,725	Unknown	Unknown
85-S-CL-08-013	Annual Stein	Unknown	Yr.Iss	118.00	118.00
86-S-CL-08-014	Annual Stein	Unknown	Yr.Iss	118.00	118.00
Cornell Importers, Inc.		**Masters**			
81-S-CL-09-001	Apostle	Unknown	5,000	Unknown	1060.00
83-S-CL-09-002	Fayence	Unknown	5,000	Unknown	980.00
84-S-CL-09-003	Altenburg	Unknown	5,000	Unknown	900.00
Cornell Importers, Inc.		**Various**			
83-S-CL-10-001	300 Year	Unknown	Unkn.	Unknown	196.00
83-S-CL-10-002	Boar Hunt	Unknown	12,000	Unknown	94.00
83-S-CL-10-003	Tyrol	Unknown	9,000	Unknown	85.00
83-S-CL-10-004	Club Hunt	Unknown	8,000	Unknown	75.00
83-S-CL-10-005	Old Sachsen	Unknown	3,000	Unknown	760.00
83-S-CL-10-006	Zille	Unknown	8,000	Unknown	240.00
83-S-CL-10-007	Tournament	Unknown	6,000	Unknown	84.00
85-S-CL-10-008	The Waldenburg	Unknown	12,000	Unknown	65.00
Cornell Importers, Inc.		**Peter Duemler**			
85-S-CL-11-001	Dr. Faust	P. Duemler	10,000	Unknown	90.00
85-S-CL-11-002	The Bicycle Riders	P. Duemler	10,000	Unknown	90.00
85-S-CL-11-003	Centurian	P. Duemler	10,000	Unknown	90.00
85-S-CL-11-004	Patrizier	P. Duemler	10,000	Unknown	80.00
86-S-CL-11-005	The Card Player	P. Duemler	10,000	Unknown	150.00
86-S-CL-11-006	The Bible	P. Duemler	10,000	Unknown	100.00
86-S-CL-11-007	The Cherusker Stein	P. Duemler	10,000	Unknown	200.00
Cornell Importers, Inc.		**Wildlife Series**			
85-S-CL-12-001	Rabbit	E. Breiden	4,000	Unknown	90.00
85-S-CL-12-002	Fox	E. Breiden	4,000	Unknown	90.00
85-S-CL-12-003	Mallard	E. Breiden	4,000	Unknown	90.00
85-S-CL-12-004	Quail	E. Breiden	4,000	Unknown	90.00
85-S-CL-12-005	Wild Boar	E. Breiden	4,000	Unknown	90.00
85-S-CL-12-006	Brown Bear	E. Breiden	4,000	Unknown	90.00
Cornell Importers, Inc.		**The Van Ijmeren Series**			
85-S-CL-13-001	The Stag Stein	Van Ijmeren	5,000	Unknown	250.00
85-S-CL-13-002	The Sea Battle	Van Ijmeren	5,000	Unknown	250.00
85-S-CL-13-003	The Jausting	Van Ijmeren	5,000	Unknown	250.00
Cornell Importers, Inc.		**Scheffer-Klute Pewter Annual Steins**			
85-S-CL-14-001	Annual	Unknown	Yr.Iss	180.00	180.00
86-S-CL-14-002	Annual	Unknown	Yr.Iss	180.00	180.00
Ernst Enterprises		**John Wayne**			
XX-S-EB-01-001	Here's Looking at You, Pilgrim	S. Horton	100	16.95	20.00
XX-S-EB-01-002	That Was My Drink, Partner	S. Horton	100	19.95	19.95
XX-S-EB-01-003	Fill Your Hand...	S. Horton	100	19.95	19.95
Ernst Enterprises		**Various**			
XX-S-EB-02-001	A Drink at Trout Lake	J. Hamilton	100	19.95	19.95
Ernst Enterprises		**Elvira**			
86-S-EB-03-001	Night Rose	S. Morton	90-day	19.95	19.95
Ernst Enterprises		**Star Trek**			
86-S-EB-04-001	Mr. Spock	S. Morton	90-day	19.95	19.95
86-S-EB-04-002	Captain Kirk	S. Morton	90-day	19.95	19.95
Gorham		**Various**			
76-S-GO-01-001	Pride of Parenthood	N. Rockwell	9,800	25.00	75.00
77-S-GO-01-002	Boy Meets His Dog	C. Rockwell	9,800	25.00	50.00
78-S-GO-01-003	The Mysterious Malady	N. Rockwell	9,800	27.50	50.00
79-S-GO-01-004	Adventurers Between Adventures	N. Rockwell	9,800	27.50	50.00
80-S-GO-01-005	Going Fishing	N. Rockwell	9,800	32.50	32.50
81-S-GO-01-006	Day Dreamers	N. Rockwell	9,800	35.00	35.00
82-S-GO-01-007	Pensive Pals	N. Rockwell	9,800	37.50	37.50
83-S-GO-01-008	Gay Blades	N. Rockwell	9,800	37.50	37.50
Mader's		**Christmas, King Werks**			
76-S-MA-01-001	Tannenbaum	Unknown	7,500	25.00	95.00
77-S-MA-01-002	Christmas Eve, 1902	Unknown	7,500	30.00	80.00
78-S-MA-01-003	Silent Night Chapel	Unknown	7,500	30.00	75.00
79-S-MA-01-004	Leading the Way	Unknown	7,500	30.00	70.00
80-S-MA-01-005	Christmas Eve	Unknown	7,500	30.00	65.00
81-S-MA-01-006	Angels Christmas Melody	Unknown	7,500	35.00	60.00
82-S-MA-01-007	Yuletide Glow	Unknown	7,500	35.00	55.00
83-S-MA-01-008	A Puppy for Christmas	Unknown	7,500	35.00	50.00
84-S-MA-01-009	Gnome for Christmas	Unknown	7,500	35.00	45.00
85-S-MA-01-010	Beginning a Journey	Unknown	7,500	35.00	40.00
86-S-MA-01-011	Come Let Us Adore Him	Unknown	7,500	35.00	40.00
87-S-MA-01-012	Adoration	Unknown	7,500	39.95	40.00
Mader's		**King Werks Musical Christmas Steins**			
78-S-MA-02-001	Silent Night Chapel	Unknown	7,500	40.00	95.00
79-S-MA-02-002	Leading the Way	Unknown	7,500	40.00	85.00

Company / Number	Name	Series / Artist	Edition limit	Issue Price	Quote
80-S-MA-02-003	Christmas Eve	Unknown	7.500	40.00	100.00
81-S-MA-02-004	Angels Christmas Melody	Unknown	7.500	50.00	75.00
82-S-MA-02-005	Yuletide Glow	Unknown	7.500	50.00	70.00
83-S-MA-02-006	A Puppy for Christmas	Unknown	7.500	50.00	95.00
84-S-MA-02-007	Gnome for Christmas	Unknown	7.500	50.00	60.00
85-S-MA-02-008	Beginning a Journey	Unknown	7.500	50.00	60.00
86-S-MA-02-009	Come Let Us Adore Him	Unknown	7.500	50.00	60.00
87-S-MA-02-010	Adoration	Unknown	7.500	54.95	54.95
Mader's		**Regimental - Thewalt, Stoneware**			
78-S-MA-03-001	Infantry	Unknown	5.000	60.00	100.00
79-S-MA-03-002	Artillery	Unknown	5.000	60.00	100.00
80-S-MA-03-003	Cavalry	Unknown	5.000	75.00	100.00
81-S-MA-03-004	Navy	Unknown	5.000	85.00	100.00
82-S-MA-03-005	Locomotive	Unknown	5.000	85.00	100.00
Mader's		**Regimental - Thewalt, Porcelain**			
84-S-MA-04-001	Cavalry	Unknown	Unkn.	75.00	100.00
85-S-MA-04-002	Navy	Unknown	Unkn.	75.00	100.00
Mader's		**European Great Masters - Sks Solid Pewter**			
85-S-MA-05-001	German Artists	Unknown	Annual	130.00	200.00
86-S-MA-05-002	Italian Artists	Unknown	Annual	156.00	179.00
87-S-MA-05-003	English Artists	Unknown	Annual	179.00	179.00
Mader's		**St. George and the Dragon**			
76-S-MA-06-001	St. George and the Dragon	Unknown	7.500	40.00	75.00
Mader's		**Historical Commemoratives**			
86-S-MA-07-001	Statue of Liberty	Unknown	9.800	85.00	95.00
87-S-MA-07-002	Constitution	Unknown	9.800	95.00	95.00
Mader's		**Olympic Sports Steins**			
80-S-MA-08-001	Winter, Lake Placid	Unknown	4.500	35.00	100.00
80-S-MA-08-002	Winter, Sarejevo, Pewter Lid	Unknown	7.500	39.00	55.00
80-S-MA-08-003	Winter, Sarejevo, Gold Lid	Unknown	5.000	65.00	85.00
80-S-MA-08-004	Summer, Los Angeles, Pewter Lid	Unknown	7.500	39.00	55.00
80-S-MA-08-005	Summer, Los Angeles, Gold Lid	Unknown	5.000	65.00	85.00
80-S-MA-08-006	Summer, Los Angeles, Pewter Lid, Signed	Unknown	600	75.00	95.00
80-S-MA-08-007	Summer, Los Angeles, Gold Lid, Signed	Unknown	500	95.00	150.00
Norman Rockwell Museum		**Limited Edition Collector Steins**			
80-S-NO-01-001	Looking Out to Sea	N. Rockwell	9,900	125.00	200.00
81-S-NO-01-002	For A Good Boy	N. Rockwell	9,900	125.00	150.00
82-S-NO-01-003	The Music Lesson	N. Rockwell	9,900	125.00	125.00
82-S-NO-01-004	Braving the Storm	N. Rockwell	9,900	125.00	125.00
83-S-NO-01-005	Fishin' Pals	N. Rockwell	9,900	125.00	125.00
Opa's House		**Annual Limited Edition**			
74-S-OH-01-001	Annual Stein	Unknown	Yr.Iss	Unknown	Unknown
75-S-OH-01-002	Annual Stein	Unknown	Yr.Iss	Unknown	Unknown
76-S-OH-01-003	Annual Stein	Unknown	Yr.Iss	Unknown	Unknown
77-S-OH-01-004	Annual Stein	Unknown	Yr.Iss	Unknown	Unknown
78-S-OH-01-005	Annual Stein	Unknown	Yr.Iss	Unknown	Unknown
79-S-OH-01-006	Annual Stein	Unknown	Yr.Iss	Unknown	Unknown
80-S-OH-01-007	Annual Stein	Unknown	Yr.Iss	Unknown	Unknown
81-S-OH-01-008	Annual Stein	Unknown	Yr.Iss	Unknown	118.00
82-S-OH-01-009	Annual Stein	Unknown	Yr.Iss	Unknown	118.00
83-S-OH-01-010	Annual Stein	Unknown	Yr.Iss	Unknown	118.00
84-S-OH-01-011	Annual Stein	Unknown	Yr.Iss	118.00	118.00
Opa's House		**Miscellaneous Reproductions**			
78-S-OH-02-001	The Jousting Tankard	Unknown	5,000	Unknown	290.00
82-S-OH-02-002	The Herring Stein	Unknown	5,000	Unknown	150.00
Opa's House		**Oldie**			
80-S-OH-03-001	Beer Here	Unknown	5,000	Unknown	64.00
80-S-OH-03-002	Bicycle	Unknown	5,000	Unknown	100.00
80-S-OH-03-003	Railway	Unknown	5,000	Unknown	70.00
80-S-OH-03-004	Thewalt Commemorative	Unknown	5,000	Unknown	42.50
80-S-OH-03-005	Physician	Unknown	5,000	Unknown	105.00
80-S-OH-03-006	Pharmacist	Unknown	5,000	Unknown	47.00
83-S-OH-03-007	Gymnastics	Unknown	5,000	Unknown	63.50
Opa's House		**Commissioned Reproduction**			
82-S-OH-05-001	The Festival Stein	Unknown	1,000	79.00	79.00
Opa's House		**American Wildlife - Group A**			
83-S-OH-07-001	Night Stalker	P. Ford	1,950	110.00	110.00
83-S-OH-07-002	Explosion in the Marsh	P. Ford	1,950	110.00	110.00
83-S-OH-07-003	Time to Scatter !	P. Ford	1,950	110.00	110.00
84-S-OH-07-004	Title To Be Announced	P. Ford	1,950	110.00	110.00
Opa's House		**Bavarian Art Crystal**			
83-S-OH-09-001	Ruby Panel Stein	Rimpler	150	360.00	360.00
83-S-OH-09-002	Blue Diamond Stein	Rimpler	250	220.00	220.00
83-S-OH-09-003	Barred Blue and White Stein	Rimpler	250	260.00	260.00
83-S-OH-09-004	Minstrel Amber Crystal Stein	Rimpler	150	378.00	378.00
83-S-OH-09-005	Stag and Doe Amber Crystal Stein	Rimpler	150	277.00	277.00
83-S-OH-09-006	Green Pheasants Stein	Rimpler	250	220.00	220.00
Villeroy & Boch		**Fairy Tale**			
82-S-VL-01-001	Peter Pan	R. Faure	10,000	195.00	195.00
82-S-VL-01-002	Hansel and Gretel	R. Faure	10,000	195.00	195.00
82-S-VL-01-003	Pied Piper of Hamlin	R. Faure	10,000	195.00	195.00
82-S-VL-01-004	Pinocchio	R. Faure	None	195.00	195.00
Villeroy & Boch		**Four Seasons**			
82-S-VL-02-001	Spring	J. Van Zundert	10,000	275.00	275.00
82-S-VL-02-002	Summer	J. Van Zundert	10,000	275.00	275.00
82-S-VL-02-003	Fall	J. Van Zundert	10,000	275.00	275.00
82-S-VL-02-004	Winter	J. Van Zundert	10,000	275.00	275.00
Villeroy & Boch		**Famous Sea Battles**			
82-S-VL-03-001	Battle of Trafalgar	J. Van Zundert	Yr.Iss	130.00	130.00
82-S-VL-03-002	Battle of Flamborough Head	J. Van Zundert	Yr.Iss	130.00	130.00
82-S-VL-03-003	Battle of Lepanto 1571	J. Van Zundert	Yr.Iss	130.00	130.00
XX-S-VL-03-004	Spanish Armada	J. Van Zundert	Yr.Iss	130.00	130.00

Keep Abreast of Today's Changing Collectibles Market...

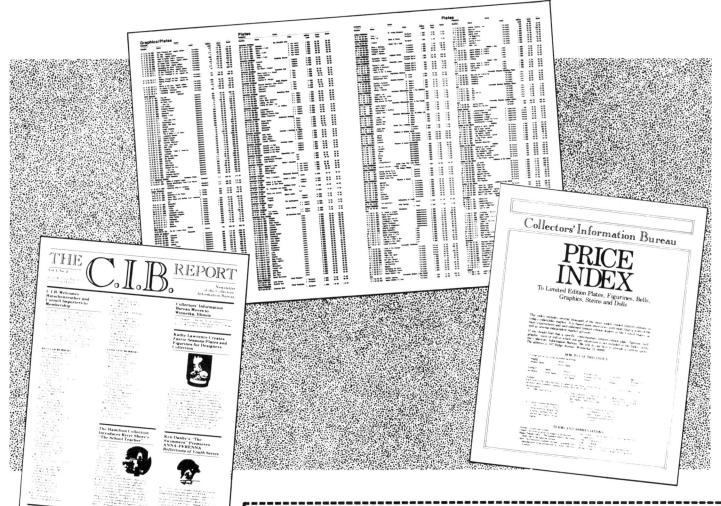

Diane Carnevale, Executive Director

COLLECTORS' INFORMATION BUREAU

2420 Burton S.E.

Grand Rapids, MI 49506